THE REVOLUTION WILL NOT BE THEORIZED

SUNY series in African American Studies
———
John R. Howard and Robert C. Smith, editors

THE REVOLUTION WILL NOT BE THEORIZED

Cultural Revolution in the Black Power Era

ERROL A. HENDERSON

This book is freely available in an open access edition thanks to TOME (Toward an Open Monograph Ecosystem)—a collaboration of the Association of American Universities, the Association of University Presses, and the Association of Research Libraries—and the generous support of The Pennsylvania State University. Learn more at the TOME website, available at: openmonographs.org. DOI: 10.26209/eh19rwnbt

The text of this book is licensed under a Creative Commons Attribution-Non Commercial 4.0 International License (CC BY-NC 4.0), available at https://creativecommons.org/licenses/by-nc/4.0

Cover art: iStock by Getty Images.

Published by State University of New York Press, Albany

© 2019 State University of New York

All rights reserved

No part of this book may be used or reproduced in any manner whatsoever without written permission. No part of this book may be stored in a retrieval system or transmitted in any form or by any means including electronic, electrostatic, magnetic tape, mechanical, photocopying, recording, or otherwise without the prior permission in writing of the publisher.

For information, contact State University of New York Press, Albany, NY www.sunypress.edu

Library of Congress Cataloging-in-Publication Data

Names: Henderson, Errol Anthony, author.
Title: The Revolution Will Not Be Theorized : Cultural Revolution in the Black Power Era / Errol A. Henderson.
Description: Albany : State University of New York Press, 2019. | Series: SUNY Series in African American Studies | Includes bibliographical references and index.
Identifiers: LCCN 2018040337 | ISBN 9781438475431 (hardcover): ISBN 9781438475424 (pbk.) | ISBN 9781438475448 (ebook) Subjects: LCSH: Black Panther Party—History—20th century | Black power—
   United States—History—20th century. | African American political activists—
   History—20th century. | African Americans—Politics and government—20th
   century. | United States—Race relations—History—20th century.
Classification: LCC E185.615 .H3625 2019 | DDC 322.4/20973—dc23
LC record available at https://lccn.loc.gov/2018040337

10 9 8 7 6 5 4 3 2 1

Contents

Acknowledgments		vii
Introduction: The Revolution Will Not Be Theorized		ix
Chapter 1	Malcolm X and the Revolutionary Turn in the Civil Rights Movement	1
Chapter 2	Black Nationalism: Civilizationism and Reverse Civilizationism	43
Chapter 3	The General Strike and the Slave Revolution of the U.S. Civil War	95
Chapter 4	Cultural Revolution and Cultural Evolution	135
Chapter 5	Theorizing Cultural Revolution in the Black Power Era	177
Chapter 6	RAM, Us, the Black Panther Party	233
Chapter 7	Republic of New Africa, League of Revolutionary Black Workers	309
Chapter 8	CAP, Shrine of the Black Madonna/Pan-African Orthodox Christian Church	373
Conclusion: Black Revolutionary Theory in the BPM		423

Notes 439

References 457

Index 473

Acknowledgments

I appreciate the people and institutions that assisted in this project. This book would not have been possible without the encouragement, support and cooperation of many of the activists and intellectuals from the Black Power Movement that I discuss in these pages—some of whom have passed on; and, most importantly, Harold Cruse, whose work, more than any other from that era motivated this study. I want to thank Bishop Nkenge Abi, Muhammad Ahmad, Chris Alston, General Baker, Amiri Baraka, David Barber, Clementine Barfield, James Boggs, Grace Lee Boggs, Teferi Brent, Scott Brown, Cruz Caridad Bueno, Safiya Bukhari, Kathleen Cleaver, Sarah Fila-Bakabadio, Keith Gilyard, Tommy (Halifu) Jacquette, Rickey Hill, "Reparations Ray" Jenkins, Mack Jones, Wesley Kabaila, Anthony Kaye, Marian Kramer, Cicero Love, Chokwe Lumumba, Haki Madhubuti, Wilson Moses, Queen Mother Audley Moore, Akua Njeri, Imari Obadele, Robert Packer, Mrs. Rosa Parks, Geronimo Ji Jaga Pratt, Bishop Frank Reid, Cedric Robinson, Clovis (Jabulani) Semmes, Robert Smith, Robert Starks, James Taylor, Ronald Walters, Hanes Walton, Alvin Williamson, Andrew Zimmerman for their comments, suggestions, and/or discussions over the years about the substantive arguments and analyses in this work. Thanks for the encouragement and example of UNIA Division 407 members Ruth Smith, Leroy Jackson, and Arthur Thomas. Thanks also to Bishop Reid and the congregants of Bethel AME Church in Baltimore, Rev. Wendell Anthony and the congregants of Fellowship Chapel in Detroit, and the Liberation Film Series at Charles Wright Museum of African American History in Detroit for providing venues to present aspects of this work and inspiration to carry it out.

Parts of this work were presented at several conferences and symposia, including the 50th Anniversary of *The Crisis of the Negro Intellectual* at the University of San Francisco; the Civil Rights Conference at University of Tennessee-Martin; the Race, Roots & Resistance: Revisiting the Legacies of Black Power conference at the University of Illinois; the Transatlantic Roundtable on Religion and Race at Howard University; The Cost of Freedom, Debt and Slavery conference at Brooklyn College; the *Millennium* Conference at the London School of Economics; the Scholar Activism in the 21st Century conference at the British Library in London; the European Conference on African Studies at Université Sorbonne Nouvelle in Paris; the National Conference of Black Political Scientists in Chicago; the National Council for Black Studies in San Diego; and the 80th Anniversary Malcolm X Commemoration conference in Harlem, New York. I appreciate the comments, critiques, and suggestions of participants at each of these programs.

Parts of chapter 2 draw on my essay "Unintended Consequences of Cosmopolitanism: Malcolm X, Africa and Revolutionary Theorizing in the Black Power Movement in the US," *African Identities* 16, no. 2 (2018): pp. 161–175, reprinted by permission of Taylor & Francis Ltd (http://www.tandfonline.com). Chapter 3 draws on my essay "Slave Religion, Slave Hiring, and the Incipient Proletarianization of Enslaved Black Labor: Developing Du Bois' Thesis on Black Participation in the Civil War as a Revolution" *Journal of African American Studies* 19, no. 2 (2015): pp. 192–213; and chapter 4 draws from "Missing the Revolution Beneath Their Feet: The Significance of the Slave Revolution in the Civil War to the Black Power Movement," *Journal of African American Studies* 22, no. 2–3 (2018): pp. 174–190. I acknowledge Nature/Springer/Palgrave for granting permission for their use. Parts of chapter 4 also draw from "The Revolution Will Not Be Theorised: The 'Howard School's Challenge to White Supremacist IR Theory," *Millennium* 45, no. 3 (June 2017): pp. 492–510. I acknowledge SAGE Publications for granting permission for their use.

Finally, I'm grateful for the encouragement of family, friends, and colleagues over the more than a decade of writing this book. I am especially thankful to my son, Errol. I also hope the work is indicative of the potential of those of us who arose from poverty and were not among those for whom many viewed an academic career as an option; thus, I am grateful for my family and friends from the Brewster Douglass Housing Projects, Detroit, Michigan, especially my big sister, Patricia Delores. I dedicate this book to one of my former professors at the University of Michigan who challenged me to develop meaningful black social theory, which, given my often-strident critiques of some of his work at the time, would probably surprise him greatly to find that the result reflected in this book heavily draws on his own: Professor Harold Cruse.

Errol Anthony Henderson
University Park, Pennsylvania

Introduction

The Revolution Will Not Be Theorized

This study critically examines some of the influential theories of black revolution in the United States devised by prominent black revolutionists and their organizations during the Black Power Movement (BPM) of the mid-1960s to mid-1970s through an engagement of their African American intellectual and activist precursors. Although their revolutionary theses informed and guided their programs, practices, and pronouncements, BPM revolutionists are typically acknowledged for their activism, but rarely for their acumen as revolutionary theorists. In fact, they put forth some of the most incisive, timely, and enduring theses of black radical change in the twentieth century; and influenced their own and subsequent generations seeking to transform U.S. society in fundamental ways. Although a wellspring of research has emerged on the BPM—especially in the last decade or so, much of it has been narrative/historical, providing detailed insights and discussions of individuals and organizations, rather than analytical, focusing on the revolutionists' actual theories, especially as they were informed by their revolutionary—as opposed to reformist—antecedents in the United States.[1] As a result, these works are often limited in their ability to assess, much less develop, the theoretical arguments of the chief protagonists of the BPM era; and delineating the African American intellectual precursors of their political, economic, and social revolutionary theses. Further, while the political and economic aspects of black revolutionists' arguments are widely discussed in the "black power" literature, less appreciated are the cultural aspects of their revolutionary theses.[2] Thus, this study focuses on the intellectual precursors of BPM revolutionists who attempted to integrate their understanding of black culture in their revolutionary theory, as well as the precepts, programs, and practices that emerged from it, while critically examining those who situated themselves in this tradition and attempted to draw from it: mainly, the black nationalist revolutionists of the era ranging from the Revolutionary Action Movement (RAM), Us, the Black Panther Party (BPP), the Republic of New Africa (RNA), the League of Revolutionary Black Workers (LRBW), the Congress of African Peoples (CAP), and the Pan-African Orthodox Christian Church (i.e., the Shrine of the Black Madonna), among others.[3] Through its focus on the cultural aspects of black revolutionary theory, this study situates the theoretical contributions of BPM revolutionists in a broader historiography of African American revolutionary theory tied to arguments from the early postbellum era; to novel theses on black revolution from the interwar era from W. E. B. Du Bois, Alain Locke, Harry Haywood, and Claudia Jones; to prominent postwar theorists such as Harold Cruse, James and Grace Lee Boggs, and Audley Moore; and epitomized in the theses that would have the greatest influence on revolutionists of the BPM, those of Malcolm X. In the next section, I lay out the main argument of the book, followed by an outline of each of the subsequent chapters.

Main Argument

This work argues that BPM revolutionists made important contributions to revolutionary theory. They posited revolutionary changes focused on the simultaneous affirmation of the human rights of individual black Americans and the promotion of the self-determination claims of the black nation in the United States. The latter viewed as consisting not only of a group differentiable by its race, but by its culture as well. Thus, the struggle for black self-determination implicated black culture, which was assumed to facilitate the mobilization of the black nation to achieve its political, economic, and social objectives. A key element of arguments of black nationalist revolutionists of the BPM was the critical role that culture played in their theories, practices, and programs. This was evident in the revolutionary theses of the most influential theorist of the BPM, Malcolm X, who argued the necessity of black cultural revolution in the political revolution he sought, making it a central objective of his major organization, the Organization of Afro-American Unity. The major BPM revolutionists took Malcolm X's revolutionary program as their point of departure; thus, it's necessary to understand Malcolm's thesis on black cultural revolution to comprehend the broader revolutionary theses of the BPM.

In this study, I critically examine black nationalists' engagement with black culture in their formulations of revolutionary theory during the BPM. I focus on activists and organizations that propounded explicit theories of black cultural revolution or put forth arguments on the contributions of black culture to revolutionary theory and practice. I take as my theoretical point of departure, Malcolm X's thesis on black revolution in the United States, which evolved with his black nationalism from a static, unidimensional, religious-based conceptualization of his Nation of Islam (NOI) years into a dynamic, multidimensional, secular framework of his post-NOI years. At its most developed, it included a thesis on black cultural revolution, which Malcolm X (1970, p. 427) argued was necessary to "unbrainwash an entire generation of black people" and served as a link between the black revolution in the United States that he envisioned and the worldwide revolution that he saw unfolding abroad. These concomitant processes, Malcolm was convinced, were radically transforming the United States.

After reviewing Malcolm's thesis, I offer a critique of it, noting among its major shortcomings Malcolm's "reverse civilizationism," which assumed that black Americans had been stripped of their culture by the depredations and travails of enslavement. Following Malcolm, prominent BPM revolutionists and organizations became convinced that black Americans had no meaningful national culture to speak of, and their theses became preoccupied with *African* rather than *African American* cultural expressions and institutions (e.g., RAM, Us, CAP, PAOCC), New African formulations of the same (e.g., the RNA), or lumpenproletarian aspects of black urban culture (e.g., the BPP). As a result, their theory, with notable exceptions (e.g., the LRBW) insufficiently appreciated the urbanized, Christian-identified, working-class black culture that both guided and comprised a pivotal segment of the black communities that they sought to mobilize. Relatedly, reverse civilizationism privileged contemporary African anticolonial struggles over historical African American revolutionism as referents; thus, BPM revolutionists often did not appreciate the significance of African American revolts in U.S. history, including the only successful black revolution in the United States—the Slave Revolution of the U.S. Civil War. Interestingly, in his major study of 1935, *Black Reconstruction*, W. E. B. Du Bois had historicized the Civil War Slave Revolution as an instance of a black cultural revolution initiating a political revolution in the United States; and a decade later Alain Locke had theorized American cultural revolution. Therefore, even as Malcolm invoked the necessity of a black cultural revolution in conjunction with a black political revolution on the cusp of the BPM, a framework for both was available from Du Bois and Locke to guide and inform the incipient BPM; however, these domestic African American sources were largely unrecognized or ignored.

Synthesizing Du Bois and Locke, it suggested the importance of black participation in the U.S. Civil War—and the "General Strike" that accompanied it—as an indigenous political revolution in the United States; and the emancipatory potential of black culture—especially black religion—to generate cultural revolution; and, thus, provided both a historic example and a contemporary model for black political and cultural revolution in the

United States. Malcolm and other BPM revolutionists didn't appreciate the extent to which it was a more meaningful referent than the contemporary anticolonial revolutions in "third world" countries that they drew on for guidance and often sought to emulate. Largely oblivious to Du Bois's and Locke's theses, BPM revolutionists deferred to Malcolm as both theorist and activist and inculcated reverse civilizationism in their often diverse theories and programmatic formulations. As a result, BPM revolutionists failed to adequately historicize their own movement; and, instead, spent an inordinate amount of time and resources attempting to import models of revolution from abroad that often did not fit the historical context or developmental trajectory of their uniquely African American experience. Without a theoretical compass oriented to the peculiar landscape of their very American oppression, they sought to coordinate a revolution across the terrain of the most powerful country in the world using strategies and tactics better suited for an African or third world country (Henderson, 2015).

Further, black power advocates, with notable exceptions (e.g., the PAOCC), failed to link their incipient revolutionary theses to the prominent cultural institution in black communities, the Black Church, which was also the institutional hub of black political mobilization throughout the United States at the time, much as it is today. The prospect of mobilizing black communities on a national scale for revolution—or almost any major political objective—without a strategy that utilized, neutralized, or mobilized the Black Church was doomed to failure. Moreover, failing to link black cultural revolution to the major black cultural institution was both a practical and theoretical nonstarter. The vacuum left by the distancing of BPM activists from the Black Church was filled by black elected officials (BEOs) who, although largely integrationist, nonetheless drew heavily on black nationalist rhetoric, practices, and initiatives to gain political power, not through an independent black political party but by binding their programs to the Democratic Party. This drew the BEOs—and the political trajectory of black communities—away from the political orientation of the BPM; and even farther away from its revolutionary thrust. As a result, by the mid-1970s the BPM on a national scale petered out, nonetheless leaving an influential set of insights, practices, and programs that would continue to inform black activism in the United States to the present.

Plan of the Book

Following the Introduction, chapter 1 introduces and critically examines Malcolm X's thesis on black revolution, which was the centerpiece of theorizing among black nationalist revolutionists during the BPM. As noted above,

Malcolm's thesis evolved from a static, unidimensional, religious-based program of his NOI years into a dynamic, multidimensional, secular framework of his post-NOI years. At its most developed, Malcolm's thesis envisioned black revolution in the United States as part of a "worldwide revolution." A key conduit linking the two was what Malcolm called a black cultural revolution. Malcolm's worldwide revolution proceeded in two stages: the first was a classic political (military) revolution against Western imperialism as evident in the anticolonial wars occurring throughout the "third world" at the time; and the second was a cultural reawakening, galvanizing black Americans to mobilize against white supremacy in a black cultural revolution, which would be associated with a political revolution in the United States. In radically transforming the most powerful country in the world, the black revolution in the United States would culminate the worldwide revolution. The breadth of his revolution reflected Malcolm X's view that political, economic, and social/cultural factors were intimately tied together—thus the broad program of his two post-NOI organizations, the Organization of Afro-American Unity (OAAU) and Muslim Mosque Inc. (MMI). Yet, Malcolm's theses suffered from reverse civilizationism, which assumes that black Americans were stripped of their African culture through enslavement and Jim Crow, thus, they had no culture apart from the detritus of white American culture. Reverse civilizationism implied that African Americans trailed Africans in their degree of cultural consciousness; and given that such a consciousness was a requisite for national consciousness, it was critical in the struggle for national self-determination. Absent such a cultural consciousness, black Americans were compelled to follow the lead of their African cousins on the continent in deriving their models, programs, and theory for black revolution in the United States. Second, and relatedly, Malcolm's reverse civilizationism contributed to his failure to both identify and appreciate the historical role of African American culture in the social transformation of blacks in the United States. Third, and most telling, it led to his failure to appreciate the revolutionary antecedents in U.S. history to inform black revolutionary praxis in the 1960s. In these ways, reverse civilizationism informed both Malcolm's black nationalism and his thesis of black revolution, which derived from it. These shortcomings, individually and in combination, confounded the major BPM revolutionists and their organizations that derived their analyses and conception of black revolution from Malcolm X.

In chapter 2, I historicize Malcolm's reverse civilizationism in the broader scholarship on black nationalism. The chapter begins with a discussion of black nationalism as a concept, and its historical evolution, in order to demonstrate its dynamic, multifaceted, and multidimensional aspects as an ideology; and to delineate how it gave rise to Malcolm's thesis of black revolution in the United States. I point out that the shortcomings in Malcolm's and subsequent

BPM activists' rendering of black nationalism were not specific to them but were evident among critics as well as advocates of black nationalism, more broadly. Some of them resulted from misunderstandings of the characteristics of black nationalism rooted in its dualities, as a concept, and a specific program for black liberation; and three of these stand out: (1) the duality of statist and nonstatist definitions of black nationalism; (2) emigrationist and non/anti-emigrationist aspects of black nationalism; and (3) Eurocentric and Afrocentric (or Anglophilic and Afrophilic) cultural orientations in black nationalism. I show how much of the theoretical synthesis of black nationalism with respect to these dualities was achieved by Du Bois (1903) at the outset of the twentieth century and are reflected in his "modernized" conception of black nationalism, which rejected the civilizationist narrative often adopted by nineteenth-century emigrationists, which appropriated the technological and cultural component of the "civilizing mission" of Western imperialist discourse for black people, in general, and Africans in particular (Moses, 1978). Du Bois, in contrast, promoted the cultural practices and cultural heritage of African people throughout the world, including those of African Americans; thus, modern black nationalism in the United States after Du Bois became synonymous with black cultural nationalism; and it insisted that African Americans possessed an African American culture. Du Boisian modernized black nationalism also promoted particular forms of black revolution emanating from its view of black culture: black cultural revolution. I show how Malcolm and subsequent BPM activists "reversed" some of the Du Boisian contributions to both black nationalist theory and black revolutionary theory that derived from it, dislodging them from their African American conceptual, cultural, and historical roots. One result was that black American revolutionaries in the BPM privileged African culture and revolutionary antecedents more than African American referents, leading them to orient their movement across the terrain of the most powerful country in the world using a theoretical compass better suited for an African or third world country. The difficulties conceptualizing black revolution in the United States were not unique to Malcolm X; but, many analysts, activists, and scholars also misunderstood the processes operative in black liberation struggles tracing back more than a century, including those that would assist the BPM in realizing its revolutionary objectives. This orientation largely precluded them from searching U.S. history for useful referents and analogues for the black revolution that they were attempting to organize in the black power era. Drawing again on Du Bois, I examine what may be the most significant revolutionary referent in the United States, which was largely ignored by BPM revolutionists—and their nonblack allies, as well—the Slave Revolution that occasioned the U.S. Civil War, and this is the subject of chapter 3.

In chapter 3, I point out that the major repercussion of reverse civilizationism was that it led revolutionists of the BPM to become preoccupied with African and third world revolutions and inattentive to the history of African American revolutionary struggle in the United States and, specifically, to ignore Du Bois's argument that black participation in the U.S. Civil War constituted a revolution. In *Black Reconstruction* (1935), Du Bois argued that enslaved blacks waged a General Strike during the war to gain their freedom in what was "the largest and most successful slave revolt." The salience of this "Slave Revolution" as a model for BPM revolutionists should not be obscured by the fact that many of its successes were aborted by the postbellum reestablishment of white supremacy in the U.S. South. The Slave Revolution had been successful in destroying the socioeconomic system of chattel slavery and overthrowing the government of the Confederate States of America (CSA). The historical analysis of the processes associated with black participation in the U.S. Civil War demonstrated a connection between slave religion and "hiring-out" slaves, and the "General Strike" that emerged from their confluence, suggesting that black cultural revolution inspired political revolution, just as Malcolm emphasized a century later, while failing to draw on this historical example. Moreover, although Du Bois historicized black revolution in *Black Reconstruction*, he did not theorize what he observed. A theory of cultural revolution was supplied by Alain Locke, who argued that cultures were intrinsically dynamic as a result of transvaluation and the transposition of values within culture groups; along with the intercultural transmission resultant from tolerance and reciprocity between them. These processes, according to Locke, are heightened in democratic societies; thus, Locke's thesis links cultural change with democracy. Cultural revolution results from the expansion of the claims for political and economic democracy to the cultural sphere in ways that implicate multiracial democracy. As applied to the Slave Revolution, Locke's thesis suggests that the transformation of slave religion and slave hiring constituted cultural changes that ramified into the political and economic spheres and motivated the General Strike and the political revolution of the Civil War. In theorizing the black cultural revolution that Du Bois historicized in *Black Reconstruction*, Locke's thesis suggested to BPM revolutionists the need to draw on Aframerican cultural initiatives and institutions—epitomized in the Black Church—to realize its revolutionary objectives; but, most revolutionists of the BPM—largely under the influence of Malcolm X's reverse civilizationism—were unaware of this revolutionary thesis "beneath their feet" (Henderson, 2018b).

Given the anteriority of the concept of cultural revolution in the academic literature—especially in Marxism—chapter 4 begins with a brief discussion of the applicability of Maoist, Leninist, and Gramscian theses of cultural revolution to black America; as well as the allusions to it in Harry Haywood's "Black Belt" thesis. I trace the roots of early formulations of black cultural *evolution* to the social development theses of black nationalists—especially black nationalist feminists—in the nineteenth century and discuss how it informed later theses of black cultural *revolution* before turning to Du Bois' formulations on black culture as a change agent during the Harlem Renaissance, which became a prominent perspective among subsequent theorists. As noted in chapter 3, cultural revolution was central to Du Bois's exegesis in *Black Reconstruction*; but, in practice, he advocated evolutionary more than revolutionary pursuits for black Americans in the twentieth century, which, for him, focused on the development of independent black institutions of civil society led by the Black Church, black economic cooperatives, and black schools and colleges. Interestingly, this cultural *evolutionary* focus on developing parallel institutions of black civil society became a mainstay of BPM revolutionists, rather than the cultural revolutionary focus in *Black Reconstruction*. In addition, as the Harlem Renaissance ensued, Du Bois became increasingly critical of the Black Church as a progressive change agent; therefore, the cultural evolution he sought became distant from the major cultural institution in the black community, which subsequent BPM revolutionists would replicate as well, and to their detriment. Projecting forward, while BPM revolutionists seemed oblivious to these major indigenous theses on political and cultural revolution and the relationship between them, they adopted evolutionary approaches to guide their revolutionary programs; and while appreciating the centrality of black culture, they distanced themselves from the major black cultural institution. Their approaches both reflected and rejected aspects of extant black American theorizing on cultural revolution and evolution, which, inter alia, left them advocating revolution while neglecting their most relevant source of revolutionary theory.

In chapter 5, I discuss Harold Cruse's thesis, which was the first explicit thesis of black cultural revolution in the United States during the BPM, and argued that the interrelationship of culture, politics, and economics necessitated that blacks focus on the weakest aspect of their domestic colonial milieu, and this was the cultural front; thus, his cultural revolution had as its objective capturing the "cultural apparatus" of U.S. society and putting it under democratic control. Since cultural issues and institutions are embedded in and reinforce the white racist political and economic institutions of the country, then an American revolution would have to address cultural dimensions of black oppression. Cruse (1968, p. 117) contends that "it is precisely the economic spheres of cultural communications in America that must be revolutionized for more humanistic social use before such changes take place in commodity production, political organization or racial democratization." Building on C. Wright Mills's conception of the "power elite," he asserted that mass media in the United States was controlled by an increasingly unified and coordinated elite, which reduced the public to media markets and U.S. citizens to individuated consumers of mass media, increasingly vulnerable to its manipulation. The development of mass media provided opportunities for the black intelligentsia to lead a black cultural revolution; but, for Cruse, "the Negro" of the black power era was "the victim of the incompetence of radical social theory" and the intellectual atrophy of "the Negro intelligentsia," who did not comprehend the salience of cultural revolution to black liberation (p. 65). The cultural apparatus seemed insufficiently salient as an objective to orient, or a theme by which to mobilize for, the black cultural revolution that Cruse sought, especially considering more relevant black cultural claims related to chattel slavery and Jim Crow, such as black reparations. In addition, Cruse's thesis insufficiently focused on the cultural apparatus of the black community itself as a precursor to this broader struggle, insofar as it ignored the major black cultural institution, the Black Church, in his theoretical arguments on cultural revolution. Cruse also largely ignored the role of sexism as a major institutional impediment to the cultural change that he sought. Nevertheless, Cruse's thesis provided a point of departure for BPM revolutionists theorizing the role of culture in black liberation, anticipating both the Black Arts Movement and the broader engagement of black cultural revolution in the BPM. Contrasting Cruse's thesis with those of Haywood and Boggs, which were rival theses of the era, I contend that these three approaches represented the major theoretical trajectories of BPM organizations that seriously considered cultural revolution in the era.

Chapter 6 provides a more detailed focus on several prominent organizations of the BPM that saw themselves as heirs of Malcolm's legacy—both theoretically and programmatically—and their attempts to develop a theory of black cultural revolution to inform their strategies, programs, and practices. Specifically, I examine the Revolutionary Action Movement (RAM), which was the first BPM organization other than Malcolm's OAAU to formally advocate black cultural revolution; and the organization Us (as opposed to "them"), which developed one of the most influential theses of black cultural revolution; and contrast those with the theoretically eclectic, but heavily Maoist-influenced theses of culture and revolution of the Black Panther Party (BPP). The differing perspectives reflected in large part the tension among Harold Cruse's, James Boggs', and Harry Haywood's perspectives on the role of culture in black revolutionary struggle, with RAM—true to its origins as a group initially organized around Cruse's theoretical precepts, but also mentored by Boggs, who served on its executive board—embracing aspects of both before moving closer to those of Haywood. Us adopted prominent aspects of Cruse's orientation—namely its open advocacy of cultural revolution and its critique of American Marxism, while the BPP rejected cultural revolution theses—at least those proffered by Us, and was at least partly in line with aspects of Haywood's and Boggs's neo-Marxist perspectives. Interestingly, RAM advocated a general strike strategy, but did not integrate it into a thesis of black cultural revolution. RAM's approach involved at different times advocacy of guerilla warfare to liberate the "Black Belt," consistent with Robert Williams's and Haywood's thesis; and later this was augmented with an electoral strategy to promote an independent black political party in order to consolidate black power in the North. RAM's dual strategy for activism in the South and North was a precursor to those strategies of both Us and the BPP. Although Us advocated black cultural revolution, embracing reverse civilizationism it insisted that African Americans did not possess a culture and should view themselves as Africans, which is a view that Cruse rejected. The BPP, consistent with Boggs, viewed black culture as minimally relevant to the political change that it sought, and largely epiphenomenal of class dynamics. The BPP saw the vanguard of their revolution as the lumpenproletariat, which was a view that Boggs wavered on and Haywood and Cruse rejected. Both Us and the BPP would change aspects of their theses over time, and RAM was even more fluid with theirs; however, while their divergent arguments contributed to the theoretical diversity and vitality of the BPM, they also reflected the difficulty of BPM activists to develop Malcolm's thesis on black cultural revolution even among major BPM organizations more closely tied to Malcolm's approach.

For example, chapter 7 begins with an examination of the organization most closely associated with the political doctrine of Malcolm X other than his own OAAU and MMI, the Republic of New Africa (RNA). The RNA focused on the liberation of the Black Belt, which it viewed as the five contiguous states of Louisiana, Mississippi, Alabama, Georgia, and South Carolina, where blacks were long settled. They made a compelling historical, political, legal and moral argument for reparations for black descendants of enslaved Africans, New Africans. Where neither was forthcoming, they advocated "people's war" against the United States to liberate New Africa. Unlike many of the national groups that advocated armed struggle, the RNA, which began in the North, moved South to press its claims. They employed a minister of culture and incorporated the concept of cultural revolution into their doctrine. Although the RNA drew on Haywood's "Black Belt Thesis," their program was not Marxist, which brought them into fraternal dispute with the BPP. Moreover, without a more expansive program rooted in the major cultural institutions of the black community, such as the Black Church, the RNA in Mississippi foundered before it could develop social networks that could strengthen its ties to the local community. Also, their intellectual distancing from important aspects of Haywood's thesis, which focused on organizing rural workers of the Black Belt, may have contributed to their insufficient coordination with black farm workers, sharecroppers, and other rural elements who were central to their plans for both revolutionary transformation of the counties of the Black Belt as well as armed resistance in the South.

Contemporaneously with the development of the RNA in Detroit was the emergence of the League of Revolutionary Black Workers (LRBW). The League incorporated in its revolutionary strategy a focus on organizing a national general strike. In this way, unlike most major organizations of the BPM, it aligned itself with the strategy that black Americans had employed successfully in the Slave Revolution. The League emphasized developing independent black unions, beginning in the automobile industry in Detroit. It also focused on community-based organizations ranging from student-based initiatives in high schools and universities, to parent-based school decentralization groups, as well as those focusing on anti–police brutality, welfare rights, and tenants' rights. Its dual strategy simultaneously centering on in-plant and out-of-plant organizing allowed it to initiate strikes against the auto industry with assistance from community supporters. Unlike the BPP, the League insisted that the black working class, the proletariat—not the lumpenproletariat–was the vanguard of the black political revolution because only the proletariat held power at "the point of production," which it could leverage for concessions from the auto companies to address the immediate demands of black workers and, ultimately, the broader objectives of revolutionary change in the United States.

Pursuant to the latter, the League embraced black reparations and the liberation of the Black Belt. However, where Haywood focused on black agricultural workers in the South as the key to liberating the Black Belt, the League's focus was on industrial workers in the North. Further, the League failed to fuse its class/race–based analyses into a coherent theory to guide its actions, consolidate its program, and coordinate its supporters; devolving into sectarianism, it imploded under its own weight. Ironically, the League probably came closest to developing a black cultural revolution as envisioned by Du Bois, Locke, and Cruse; but it hardly drew on these theoretical referents, opting instead for poorly fitted, mainly third world models to inform their project. I synthesize their sectarian orientations, wedding them to earlier theses of black cultural revolution in a theoretical and programmatic fusion, and demonstrate how the tensions within the group might have been resolved in such a way as to facilitate their revolutionary objectives. Nevertheless, even with such a composite strategy, the League was battling against time, as deindustrialization in the United States was decentralizing industry offshore while simultaneously transporting the industrial core of Northern cities to suburbs and nonunionized Southern venues, removing the most potent base of League organization from the central cities in which unionized black workers were concentrated.

Chapter 8 focuses on two of the most influential BPM organizations that espoused black cultural revolution: the Congress of African Peoples (CAP) and the Pan-African Orthodox Christian Church (PAOCC). CAP's Newark chapter was led by Amiri Baraka, and its Midwest chapter was led by Haki Madhubuti. The former harnessed black cultural revolutionary theses to urban electoral mobilization and independent political party organizing before abandoning black nationalism and adopting Haywood's Marxist political thrust. The latter rose from similar origins, however, it remained committed to independent black community institutionalization, focusing on black independent schools and black publishing, while explicitly rejecting Marxism. Baraka's organization, CFUN, initially worked closely with Us and drew on its kawaida approach in its development in Newark. CFUN integrated the emergent black elected officials under black nationalist leadership and institutions; and its successes motivated the founding of CAP in 1970. However, eventually Baraka's CAP was outflanked by those same BEOs it had assisted in gaining office for a variety of reasons, which he attributed to the shortcomings of black nationalism itself, and motivated him to abandon nationalism for Marxism. In contrast, Chicago CAP—like Brooklyn CAP led by Jitu Weusi—maintained its black nationalist orientation and developed a critical response to the neo-Marxism of Baraka's CAP and the broader ideological sectarianism in the BPM. Chicago (Midwest) CAP grew out of Madhubuti's development of Third World Press in 1967, which provided an independent publishing arm for the Black Arts Movement (BAM); and the Institute of Positive Education, which became a blueprint for independent black schools around the country. As a result, Madhubuti was key to the promotion of black culture in the BPM, laying a basis for the Afrocentrism that would become even more prominent in the 1980s. Chicago-CAP, however, retained aspects of reverse civilizationism through its embrace of kawaida; and, as a result, the Afrocentrism that emerged from it had two tracks: the activist one, focused on the development of independent black organizations; and the reverse civilizationist one that led to an overindulgence in the study of ancient African societies and practices, instead of the largely urban-based industrial working-class culture of African

Americans living in the most powerful country in the world. The former was consistent with the development of parallel institutions and was a mainstay of the BPM and essential to the continuation of its revolutionary thrust, while the latter was a departure from the revolutionary spirit and praxis of black cultural revolution as Malcolm foresaw it, and into the almost purely rhetorical and increasingly escapist fantasies of embracing ancient traditions that were often devoid of incentives toward revolutionary or even progressive political activism beyond the creation of book clubs or study groups with little if any activist component.

The final organization examined is the PAOCC (i.e., the Shrine of the Black Madonna), which was led by Albert Cleage (Jaramogi A. Agyeman), and has been among the most enduring BPM organizations espousing black cultural revolution. Cleage, an ordained minister, did not share BPM revolutionists' dismissal of the Black Church, but argued that it should be the central organization of their black revolution. The PAOCC fused political, economic, and social aspects of the BPM. It utilized the methods of the Essene order to train cadres capable of organizing churches, as well as informational and cultural centers throughout the United States and abroad. Cleage had a powerful impact on the culture and politics of Detroit, playing a prominent role in the election of Coleman Young as Detroit's first black mayor in 1973. While he emphasized the primacy of the Black Church in black cultural revolution, he did not specify which institutions should be subsequently transformed or in what order. Relatedly, it was unclear what would constitute a critical mass of counterinstitutions that would effectuate the cultural revolution that he envisioned; nor was it evident how the values associated with the church would transfer to secular domains such as in politics and economics, beyond elections. Subsumed by the need to overhaul the church and develop the PAOCC as its own denomination, Cleage did not attend adequately to the development of the other prospective counterinstitutions. Nevertheless, his focus on the Black Church and the development of counterinstitutions was one of the most influential theses of black cultural revolution in the United States. Ironically, in helping support the ascendancy of the black elected officials, the PAOCC helped bring to power the leadership group that would supplant the black power organizations of the era and end the BPM.

The Conclusion summarizes some of the major implications of the work, reminding us that on the cusp of the BPM, there was an extant thesis of black political and cultural revolution in the United States, which could have provided a theoretical point of departure for BPM revolutionists. Ignoring or oblivious to these, their formulations, nonetheless, were insightful, transformative, and in some cases groundbreaking; however, they suffered from important weaknesses, paramount among them reverse civilizationism. In the event, BPM revolutionists inadequately historicized their own movement; and did not avail themselves of the revolutionary framework that a fusion of Du Bois's and Locke's theses provided. Instead, where the importance of religiously inspired workers in the Slave Revolution and the ongoing CRM and BPM should have inspired them to focus on that group's revolutionary propensities—as well as the Black Church in which many of them were institutionally grounded or emotionally attached—BPM revolutionists often dismissed, denigrated, or denied the salience of the Black Church, promoted quasi-African cultural forms, and largely distanced themselves from the very community they sought to organize and mobilize for revolution. This theoretical enervation (along with governmental repression) contributed to their lack of cohesion and reinforced their sectarianism, which left them vulnerable to organized efforts of reformists often wedded to the Democratic Party, giving rise to the black elected officials and the decline of the BPM.

The point is not that the failure of BPM revolutionists to adopt the revolutionary framework of Du Bois and Locke was the reason for the dissensus in the BPM and its sectarianism; but only that it contributed to the lack of intellectual grounding in African American political science in their revolutionary theories, programs, and practices. Consumed by the view that black revolution in the United States would take the form of an armed struggle resembling contemporary anticolonial insurgencies or earlier Marxist revolutions, they were hesitant to draw on their own revolutionary antecedents in the United States, epitomized in the Slave Revolution in the Civil War. A better appreciation of these black American intellectual precursors to their theorizing on black revolution would have tempered their preoccupation with adopting and adapting frameworks from the third world to their first world conditions in the most powerful country in the world and encouraged a more serious engagement with the "revolution beneath their feet." Such theoretical myopia regarding black revolution in the United States persists in both black and nonblack social movements today.

Chapter 1

Malcolm X and the Revolutionary Turn in the Civil Rights Movement

During the 1960s in the United States, the salience of revolution as a strategy to achieve the objectives of freedom, justice, and equality for African Americans became a prominent consideration among participants in the Civil Rights Movement (CRM), as well as broader groups of political activists, observers, and analysts. Anticolonial struggles in Africa and Asia, such as the Mau Mau in Kenya, the FLN in Algeria, and the National Liberation Front in Vietnam became important revolutionary referents; and especially influential was the Cuban Revolution that brought Castro's regime to power and introduced many African Americans to the revolutionary theses of Che Guevara. Coupled with the independence movement in Africa, which made personages such as Nkrumah, Lumumba, Touré, Mandela, and Ben Bella as prominent in the discourse of the CRM as Gandhi had been, the expression of support for the CRM of extant revolutionary regimes such as Mao's China encouraged the view that the reformist objective of the CRM to eradicate Jim Crow was insufficient to achieve the revolutionary objective of ending white supremacism in the United States. A constant—albeit marginal—strain in black activism of the twentieth century, in the post–World War II era revolution as a political objective became a prominent focus of African American political mobilization.

Among CRM activists of the late 1950s and early 1960s, Robert Williams of the Monroe, North Carolina, NAACP was a prominent and early advocate of armed self-defense for blacks seeking an end to white racist oppression. A Korean War veteran, after his highly publicized armed resistance to white racists and his open opposition to nonviolence, his treatise on black self-defense, *Negroes with Guns*, influenced black revolutionists throughout the black power era. There were other proponents of armed self-defense such as the Deacons for Defense, which emerged in 1964 in Jonesboro and later Bogalusa, Louisiana (Hill, 2004); as well as supporters of "defensive violence," such as the Defenders, which organized in 1964 in Tuscaloosa, Alabama (Nelson, 2006). Many more groups advocating armed resistance would emerge following the Watts revolt of August 1965, which for many marked the onset of the BPM. While discussions related to the desirability of revolution, beyond armed defense, took many forms and drew from myriad sources, the most influential proponent of black revolution emerging from the CRM itself was Malcolm X. Malcolm X drew inspiration from activists such as Robert Williams, for whom he raised funds and featured as a presenter in his Harlem NOI mosque; nevertheless, by 1961 Williams was in exile in Cuba and by 1966 in China, and he would not return to the United States until 1969. Well before then, his influence as a revolutionary leader of the BPM had been eclipsed by Malcolm X, who by no later than 1963 had proposed a novel and influential conception of black revolution in the United States in what would become one of the most popular speeches of the black power era, "Message to the Grassroots." Malcolm's base in the Nation of Islam (NOI), which he helped expand dramatically given his administrative skill and restless energy, extended his influence even farther, as did his prominence in national and international media.

Malcolm X's advocacy of black revolution to overthrow white supremacist rule stood in contrast to Martin L. King Jr's contemporaneous call for nonviolent protest to end Jim Crow segregation. Malcolm X endorsed armed self-defense and rejected the nonviolence of mainstream CRM organizations; promoted black separation and rejected black integration; viewed land as the basis of independence, rather than desegregation as a political objective; linked black liberation in the United States to international politics, rather than strictly focusing on domestic politics in the United States; supported the interests of the black masses (i.e., the "grass roots") over those of black liberal and conservative elites; and promoted African more than African American culture, history, and identity. These were among Malcolm X's perspectives that provided the theoretical and programmatic latticework of the major organizations that generated and defined what became known as the black power movement (BPM). These ranged from the Revolutionary Action Movement (RAM), the Student Non-violent Coordinating Committee (SNCC)—during its black power phase, Us, the Black Panther Party (BPP), the Republic of New Africa (RNA), the League of Revolutionary Black Workers (LRBW), the Congress of African Peoples (CAP), and the Pan-African Orthodox Christian Church (PAOCC) (aka the Shrine of the Black Madonna), among others. They inspired the Black Arts Movement (BAM), and encouraged revolutionary formations such as the Black Liberation Army, as well as revolutionary groups among Latinos, Asian Americans, Native Americans, and European Americans.

As seminal as Malcolm's thesis on black revolution in the United States was to the BPM, it is important to remember that it had been developing over his last two years—mainly from November 1963 to February 1965. It was multifaceted, multidimensional, and multistaged. It also was often contradictory. In fact, by 1965 Malcolm's thesis on black revolution had modified or, in some cases, contradicted almost every one of the major orientations listed above, that he had previously promoted. For example, in his "Message to the Grassroots" speech of November 1963, he was unequivocal in his claim that revolutions were violent; but, in "The Ballot or the Bullet" speech of April 1964, he asserted that revolutions could be nonviolent; and in "The Black Revolution" of April 1964 he argued that revolutions could be violent or nonviolent. By 1965 Malcolm X had asserted that separation and integration were only methods—not philosophies—for black liberation; and advocacy of—or opposition to—either should not preclude blacks from working toward the common goal of black liberation. In 1964 he championed the mainstream CRM's efforts toward desegregation and offered support to SNCC's initiatives in the South. During that time, he also promoted black electoral participation and an independent black political party.

The modifications, contradictions, and nuances in Malcolm's framework for black liberation in the United States reflected changes in his black nationalist ideology in which it was situated. In fact, Malcolm's thesis of black revolution in the United States derived from and developed along with his black nationalist ideology, from the separatist-oriented, millenarian conception of black nationalism that he drew on as a member of the NOI to the pluralist-oriented, secular conception of black nationalism embedded in the charter of his major post-NOI organization, the Organization of Afro-American Unity (OAAU). The former viewed the black nation as a pan-Islamic, race-based entity, based on the "Asiatic black man," and was at most rhetorically fitted to revolutionary activity in the United States or abroad. The latter viewed the black nation as a pan-Africanist, culture-based entity that, while aligned to black racial identity—and identified explicitly with the American Negro—also associated "blackness" with the diverse nonwhite people of the "third world" struggling to overthrow white imperialism. Consistent with his pan-Africanist and culture-based conception of black nationalism, Malcolm viewed the black revolution as part of a "worldwide revolution." For Malcolm, the worldwide revolution proceeded in two stages: the first was a classic political (military) revolution against Western imperialism and was evident in the anticolonial wars throughout the third world; the second was a cultural reawakening, galvanizing black Americans to mobilize against white supremacy in a black cultural revolution, which would be associated with a political revolution in the United States. In radically transforming the most powerful country in the world, the black revolution in the United States would culminate the worldwide revolution.

For Malcolm, the black revolution in the United States could be violent, nonviolent, or both, depending on the leverage exerted by black revolutionists and their domestic allies inside the United States, supplemented by their international supporters and coordinated through the OAAU, and on the resistance these forces faced from white supremacists and their allies. The breadth of this revolution influenced Malcolm X's view that political, economic, and social/cultural factors were intimately tied together—thus the broad program of the OAAU. These political, economic, and social factors were linked in Malcolm's theoretical arguments, which were grounded in his black nationalism, which, likewise, focused on political, economic, and social dimensions of black liberation. Consistent with the breadth of the black nationalism in which it was embedded, Malcolm's thesis on black revolution similarly focused on liberation from political, economic, and social domination.

As influential as Malcolm X was to a generation of revolutionists, rarely was his revolutionary thesis appreciated in its fullness, as a multifaceted, multidimensional, and multistaged thesis for black liberation. Instead, many who saw themselves as heirs to Malcolm's revolutionary legacy adopted singular aspects of his thesis as representative of the whole—often with little appreciation of the challenges and contradictions that compelled Malcolm to modify elements of it in whole or in part. For example, the BPP adopted his approach to the necessity of revolutionary violence but dismissed and even denigrated his focus on bloodless revolution. Similarly, they ignored his thesis on cultural revolution, going so far as to insist that "cultural nationalism"—as opposed to "revolutionary nationalism," a term they appropriated for themselves—was inherently reactionary, making it an epitaph in the organization's lexicon. The RNA focused on the "land question" but paid less attention to Malcolm's focus on electoral politics.[1] The BPP, the LRBW, and eventually CAP accepted Malcolm's critique of capitalist-inspired consumerism but minimized his concerns regarding communism. And nearly all ignored his assertion of the importance of women's rights in black liberation struggles.

Just as apparent was the failure of those who saw themselves operating in Malcolm's tradition to reconcile his theoretical arguments with those of previous theorists of black revolution in the United States—especially those that recognized the peculiarity of American national development and the role of blacks in it, as well as the significance of black culture as a galvanizing force to orient blacks toward revolutionary objectives (e.g., Du Bois, 1935).

This is no slight to BPM revolutionists, who were more consumed with the challenges and opportunities of their active participation in revolutionary struggle than with providing an exegesis of the myriad works of their revolutionary predecessors, but recognition that these activists were often theorists as well, and in several cases developed original theses on black revolution in the United States, even as they engaged a range of forces aligned against them. For example, Woodard (1999) notes that in Detroit, Michigan, in particular, many of the leading activists were also theorists, such as Albert Cleage (aka Jaramogi Agyeman), who was not only a leader of the Group on Advanced Leadership (GOAL), the Freedom Now Party (FNP), and most notably, the Shrine of the Black Madonna, but also an important theorist of black liberation theology. Imari Obadele was not only the leader of the RNA, but an important theorist of black nationalism; James and Grace Lee Boggs were central to several black liberation organizations including RAM and the FNP, and they were theorists of dialectical humanism, as well. The confluence of activism and theory was not unique to Detroit, but was representative of black power theorists more generally: Stokely Carmichael was not only a leader of SNCC but a theoretician of black power; Maulana Karenga was both leader of Us and a progenitor of kawaida theory; Huey Newton was not only a co-founder of the BPP, but he proffered his revolutionary intercommunalism; and Frances Beal of SNCC contributed to feminism in her thesis of double jeopardy, which is a direct forerunner of intersectionality. Thus, it makes sense to focus on BPM revolutionists as theorists as well in their engagement of Malcolm's revolutionary thesis.

Yet, BPM revolutionists generally failed to capture the breadth of Malcolm's thesis on revolution, although many had interacted with Malcolm personally. They often insufficiently engaged the major shortcomings of Malcolm's thesis, as well, including (1) Malcolm's assumption that black Americans had no culture—he assumed that it was stripped from them during slavery, which led him to diminish the centrality of African American culture in his conception of black nationalism and the black revolution it was assumed to stimulate; (2) Malcolm's privileging of events in Africa over those in the United States as a focus of black revolutionary praxis, which precluded him from drawing on prior black revolutionary praxis in the United States; (3) Malcolm's assumption that the conditions facing African Americans were similar to those faced by Africans on the continent, which suggested the salience of a colonial—or in the case of African Americans, a domestic colonial—framework as the key to understanding black oppression in the United States and its amelioration; (4) Malcolm's misunderstanding of the calculus of third world leaders ostensibly willing to challenge the United States in support of black Americans, which led him to focus on a UN plebiscite as a rallying tool for black claims against the U.S. government, following a strategy that had largely failed when attempted two decades before. To better appreciate these claims, it's important to review the development of Malcolm's thesis on black revolution in the United States.

The Revolutionary Theses of Malcolm X

NOI Precursors and Revolutionizing the Civil Rights Movement

Malcolm X's conception of black revolution evolved from his earliest formulations during his tenure with the NOI under Elijah Muhammad's leadership. The NOI was a black nationalist offshoot of Garvey's UNIA & ACL and the Moorish Science Temple of Timothy Drew (aka Noble Drew Ali), which advocated black separatism in the form of emigration to Africa or the establishment of an independent black territory in the continental United States—ostensibly under Muhammad's leadership—funded by compensation from the United States as a form of reparations. The NOI's variant of black nationalism was a religious-based millenarian conceptualization, which in Muhammad's rendering was only marginally pan-Africanist internationally (its pan-Islamism made sacrilegious for most Muslims worldwide by the apostasy of the NOI's belief that Wallace Ford aka W. Fard Muhammad was Allah incarnate, or that Elijah Muhammad was the Messenger of Allah, and not Prophet Muhammad ibn Abdullah of seventh-century Arabia), while failing to engage with the institutions of American politics (e.g., NOI members did not vote or involve themselves in civil rights protests) domestically. Elijah Muhammad's aversion to organized protest against racial discrimination was as personal as it was political. He lived in perpetual fear of the federal government, which had imprisoned him in Milan, Michigan, for sedition from 1942–46, and subsequently imprisoned his son Wallace for fourteen months for refusing induction into the U.S. military in 1961.

While he was a member of the NOI, Malcolm's thesis on black revolution reflected the NOI's theology as espoused by Elijah Muhammad. For example, as an NOI minister, Malcolm contrasted the "black revolution," which was the separatist program that the NOI proposed, with the "Negro revolution" of the mainstream CRM, which he derided. Where the latter sought integration into the political, economic, and social institutions of U.S. society mainly through large-scale protest based on the principles of nonviolent noncooperation, the NOI's "black revolution" advocated separation of blacks from the United States and their reconstitution under self-rule, but eschewed sociopolitical protest while reserving for themselves the right of self-defense, mainly for fellow NOI members. For example, in June 1963, while still a member of the NOI, Malcolm gave a speech, "The Black Revolution"—a title he used many times for what often were quite different speeches—in which he argued that the "black revolution against the injustices of the white world is all part of God's divine plan" (Malcolm X, 1971, p. 71). Malcolm acknowledged that he and other followers of Elijah Muhammad "religiously believe that we are living at the end of this wicked world, the world of colonialism, the world of slavery, the end of the Western world, the white world or the Christian world, or the end of the wicked white man's Western world of Christianity."

Malcolm shared Elijah Muhammad's opposition to integration and stated that "[w]e want no part of integration with this wicked race of devils." The revolution—as envisioned by Muhammad and articulated by Malcolm—sought physical separation of blacks from whites in the United States through emigration to Africa or the establishment of a separate black territory in the United States. Malcolm echoed Muhammad's contention that blacks "should not be expected to leave America empty-handed" because "[a]fter four hundred years of slave labor, we have some back pay coming." Therefore, the NOI demanded that upon either emigration or the establishment of an independent black state, the U.S. government should provide "everything else" that repatriated or resettled blacks "need to get started again in our own country . . . in the form of machinery, material, and finance—enough to last for twenty to twenty-five years until we can become an independent people and an independent nation in our own land." He concluded:

> If the government of America truly repents of its sins against our people and atones by giving us our true share of the land and the wealth, then America can save herself. But if America waits for God to step in and force her to make a just settlement, God will take this entire continent away from the white man. (1971, p. 75)

Upon leaving the NOI, Malcolm abandoned Muhammad's religion-based, fatalistic conception of black revolution, for a more historically grounded, activist formulation, while retaining elements of the NOI's program such as its focus on land and reparations.[2] Malcolm's emergent perspective was first broadcast to a major audience in his "Message to the Grassroots" speech, delivered in Detroit in November 1963 (Breitman, 1965). It was markedly different from any of his—or Elijah Muhammad's—previous statements on black revolution and was the most influential conception of black revolution in the United States for black power activists at the time. In "Message to the Grassroots," Malcolm wholly detached his conception of black revolution from the NOI's millenarian program. Malcolm argued that unlike the *Negro* revolution, which was his characterization of the mainstream CRM that sought integration into the segregated institutions of U.S. society through nonviolent direct action, the *black* revolution was part of an international struggle against white supremacy—especially against Western imperialism—which was evident in anticolonial struggles throughout Africa, Asia, and Latin America. In Malcolm's view, the CRM remained out of touch with these revolutionary developments in world politics. He argued that this was largely a result of the failure of the CRM leadership, and African Americans more generally, to appreciate, historically, what constituted a revolution, its characteristics, and its objectives; and in "Message," Malcolm sought to remove any confusion regarding these issues.

Malcolm was unambiguous that unlike the ongoing nonviolent protests for blacks' civil rights that characterized the CRM, revolutions were violent, they were based on the desire for land, and they were aimed at overthrowing political systems. Malcolm challenged his Detroit audience:

> Sometimes I'm inclined to believe that many of our people are using this word "revolution" loosely, without taking careful consideration of what this word actually means, and what its historic characteristics are. (1990, p. 7)

He noted that the American, French, Russian, and Chinese revolutions were all based on the violent acquisition of land. Malcolm chided:

> Look at the American Revolution in 1776. That revolution was for what? For land. Why did they want land? Independence. How was it carried out? Bloodshed. . . . The French Revolution, what was it based on? The landless against the landlord. What was it for? Land. How did they get it? Bloodshed. . . . The Russian Revolution, what was it based on? Land: the landless against the landlord. How did they bring it about? Bloodshed. You haven't got a revolution that doesn't involve bloodshed. (ibid.)

Then, in his typical fashion, he levied a discomfiting charge at his primarily black audience:

> And you're afraid to bleed. I said, you're afraid to bleed.[3] As long as the white man sent you to Korea, you bled. He sent you to Germany, you bled. He sent you to the South Pacific to fight

the Japanese, you bled. You bleed for white people, but when it comes to seeing your own churches being bombed and little black girls murdered you haven't got any blood! You bleed when the white man says bleed; you bite when the white man says bite; and you bark when the white man says bark. I hate to say this about us, but it's true. How are you going to be nonviolent in Mississippi, as violent as you were in Korea? How can you justify being nonviolent in Mississippi and Alabama, when your churches are being bombed, and your little girls are being murdered, and at the same time you are going to be violent with Hitler, and Tojo, and somebody else you don't even know. (ibid., pp. 7–8)

Then Malcolm raised the key contradiction regarding the salience of the use of violence in defense of the rights of black Americans:

> If violence is wrong in America, violence is wrong abroad. If it is wrong to be violent defending black women and black children and black babies and black men, then it is wrong for America to draft us and make us violent abroad in defense of her. And if it is right for America to draft us, and teach us how to be violent in defense of her, then it is right for you and me to do whatever is necessary to defend our own people right here in this country. (ibid., p. 8)

Malcolm argued that, in contrast to the Negro revolution, "[t]here's been a revolution, a black revolution, going on in Africa." For example,

> In Kenya, the Mau Mau were revolutionary . . . they believed in scorched earth, they knocked everything aside that got in their way, and their revolution also was based on land. . . . The Algerians were revolutionists, they wanted land. France offered to let them be integrated into France. They told France, to hell with France, they wanted some land, not some France. And they engaged in a bloody battle. (ibid., pp. 8–9)

Malcolm brought home the point by contrasting these historic and contemporary revolutions with the Negro revolution, which he did not view as a revolution at all:

> There's no such thing as a nonviolent revolution. The only kind of revolution that is nonviolent is the *Negro* revolution. The only

revolution in which the goal is loving your enemy is the *Negro* revolution . . . the only revolution in which the goal is a desegregated lunch counter, a desegregated theater, a desegregated park, and a desegregated public toilet—you can sit down next to white folks on the toilet. That's no revolution. Revolution is based on land. Land is the basis of all independence. Land is the basis of freedom, justice, and equality. (ibid., p. 9)

Malcolm affirmed:

Revolution is bloody, revolution is hostile, revolution knows no compromise, revolution overturns and destroys everything that gets in its way. And you, sitting around here like a knot on the wall, saying, "I'm going to love these folks no matter how much they hate me." No, *you* need a revolution. Whoever heard of a revolution where they lock arms, as Rev. Cleage was pointing out beautifully, singing "We Shall Overcome"? You don't do that in a revolution. You don't do any singing, you're too busy swinging. (ibid.)

Malcolm was unequivocal:

It's based on land. A revolutionary wants land so he can set up his own nation, an independent nation. These Negroes aren't asking for any nation. They're trying to crawl back on the plantation. (ibid., pp. 9–10)

For Malcolm, to the extent that the ongoing CRM came close to approximating the black revolution it happened during the mobilization in local communities preceding the "March on Washington" of 1963. Malcolm distinguished between the masses of blacks, the grassroots or "field Negroes," who were imbued with a spirit of revolt and initiated the "march talk," and those blacks who, redirecting this spirit of revolt toward integration and the interests of liberal whites, came to comprise the leadership of the march, the "house Negroes"—specifically the "Big Six" (Martin L. King of SCLC, Whitney Young of the Urban League, Roy Wilkins of the NAACP, A. Philip Randolph of the AFL-CIO, James Farmer of CORE, and John Lewis of SNCC). Malcolm saw the origins of the march in the increasing number of protests, disruptions, disturbances, and acts of resistance among blacks in 1963, epitomized in the militant protests in Birmingham. Malcolm argued that

> [t]he Negroes were out there in the streets. They were talking about how they were going to march on Washington . . . march on the Senate, march on the White House, march on the Congress, and tie it up, bring it to a halt, not let the government proceed. They even said they were going out to the airport and lay down on the runway and not let any airplanes land. . . . That was the black revolution. It was the grassroots out there in the street. It scared the white man to death, scared the white power structure in Washington, D.C., to death. (ibid., p. 14)

Malcolm argued that in the event, the march was taken over by the Big Six, through manipulation by liberal whites who controlled the finances of the movement. He said, "They joined it, became a part of it, took it over. And as they took it over, it lost its militancy. It ceased to be angry, it ceased to be hot, it ceased to be uncompromising. Why, it even ceased to be a march. It became a picnic, a circus" (ibid., p. 16). Tied down by its adherence to integration, and guided by a leadership dedicated to nonviolence and financially beholden to white liberal interests, the CRM, for Malcolm, was doomed to failure insofar as it remained detached from the black revolution and the black nationalism that inspired it.

Malcolm saw nationalism as the transformative force in contemporary revolutions throughout Africa and Asia, and he maintained that the same was true for the United States. Focusing on African Americans, he asserted that "[a] revolutionary is a black nationalist"; and "[i]f you're afraid of black nationalism, you're afraid of revolution. And if you love revolution, you love black nationalism" (ibid., p. 10). Malcolm viewed black nationalism as a broad, dynamic, and evolving ideology having political, economic, and social dimensions rooted in the belief that African Americans comprised a "nation within a nation," and as such it had the right of self-determination, which meant that the black nation had the right and responsibility to determine the political entity that would govern it.

Black nationalism was then, as now, the historic theoretical and programmatic counterpoise to the integrationism that dominated the major organizations and institutions of the CRM. From just prior to his departure from the NOI, Malcolm had been consciously reworking his theoretic and programmatic conception of black nationalism from the fatalist millenarianism of the NOI to the revolutionary, culturally based nationalism of his post-NOI phase. Contrary to what some analysts have argued—including his recent biographer, Manning Marable—following his departure from the NOI, Malcolm was not loosening his ideological moorings *away* from black nationalism, but revising his black nationalism and reconciling his thesis of black revolution with it. For example, Marable alleges that during his final months Malcolm X resisted identifying himself as a black nationalist. This is incorrect. In an exchange on a New York City radio show three days before his death, Malcolm remarked: "If you think that nationalism has no influence whatsoever, the nationalists, the Organization of Afro-American Unity, are having a rally at the Audubon Ballroom" (Breitman, 1965, p. 181). These are hardly the comments of—or the context for—someone reticent to associate himself with black nationalism.

To appreciate the development of Malcolm's black nationalism it is important to understand the historical development of black nationalism in general. Although we will examine black nationalism more fully in the next chapter, at this point its sufficient to point out several key misconceptions in the literature related to it. Lost on many otherwise insightful analysts is an appreciation of black nationalism as the seminal ideology that emerged from the collective consciousness, practices, statements, institutions, and early organizations of a multinational largely enslaved diasporic African society, whose members comprised diverse African peoples captured and transported to the United States (Moses, 1996). This diaspora synthesized an amalgam of its African cultures into an African American culture manifest in folk customs and a host of African retentions that ultimately were given American institutional forms (Stuckey, 1987). These customs provided the bedrock of African American culture, which endured through slavery and both provided and reflected the commonalities that are the foundation of black national consciousness. This incipient national consciousness was reinforced by the commonality of black racial oppression in terms of white exploitation of black labor through racial slavery for the black majority in the South and racist discrimination for the black minority in the North. In addition, the galvanizing impact of the concerted effort of blacks to fight to overthrow slavery during the Civil War, the reconstitution of black families after enslavement, and the institutionalization of prominent black cultural practices ensured the enduring significance of racial identification for black Americans. These factors combined to provide a sense of national identity among African Americans and a framework for black culture (Franklin, 1984). Black nationalism, which emerged from this diasporan sense of national identity, reflected "a spirit of Pan-African unity and an emotional sense of solidarity with the political and economic struggles of African peoples throughout the world" (Moses, 1996, p. 20).

The oft-repeated critique of the "narrowness" of nationalism is hollow with respect to the scope and content of black nationalism in the United States. As any serious student of American politics realizes, black nationalism has not only focused on the domestic politics of the United States, but it has had an international dimension since its inception, rooted in its pan-Africanism. Beyond the pan-Africanist roots of its "internationalism," black nationalism has and continues to have among its programmatic objectives international goals. As early as the eighteenth century, black nationalism manifested a dual focus on territorial objectives abroad in Africa, North America, and the Caribbean, as well as in the United States; and these are evident, for example, in Cuffee's request for the establishment of a settlement both in Africa as well as on the frontiers of the young U.S. republic, while advancing a strategy to industrialize Africa and undermine U.S. slavery (he previously had petitioned for voting rights of free blacks in New England). These initiatives predate the emigrationist initiatives of other prominent black nationalists such as Martin Delany, Mary Shadd Cary, and Alexander Crummell of the nineteenth century; the anticolonialism of the Pan-Africanist Congresses led by W. E. B. Du Bois, J. E. Casely-Hayford, and later Kwame Nkrumah in the twentieth century; or similar global programs of Marcus Garvey's UNIA & ACL. Relatedly, to refute the erroneous claim that nationalists imagined a singular homogenous unified black national monolith, by the time of Malcolm's articulation of his distinction between field and house Negroes—and demonstrably, at least a half-century before—black nationalists had recognized the class stratification within black communities and the variability across black communities in different regions of the country—both North and South, urban and rural. They did not assume a singular black political entity, but simply articulated their preferences for the establishment of black nationhood. Distinctions regarding the form that such an entity should take were evident in the contrasting arguments among black nationalists for and against emigration no later than the nineteenth century.

Wilson Moses (1978) noted that classical black nationalism endorsed a form of civilizationism that advocated territorial separation but cultural assimilation. He distinguished between two eras of black nationalism: classical and modern.[4] Classical black nationalism often advocated emigration, and although supportive of the overthrow of slavery, largely viewed enslaved African Americans as uncultured displaced Africans. Moreover, it conceived the purpose of repatriation to Africa as an endeavor to not only free blacks from racial oppression—including racial slavery—in the United States, but to bring American Christianity and technology to the benighted African. The latter is what Moses refers to as the cultural assimilation of classical black nationalism, which employed a similar cultural arrogance—though without the racial supremacy—consistent with the prominent argument of Western imperialists, especially in its Anglophile version. This orientation toward territorial separation (i.e., emigration) and cultural assimilation (i.e., shared

Anglophilia) was a common view of nationalists ranging from Delaney and Crummell to Turner; and characterized much of black nationalism's "golden age" during the latter half of the nineteenth and the early twentieth century (Moses, 1978). It was Du Bois who modernized black nationalism from the Anglophilia of the classical era to a positive conception of African and African American culture. While hailing both the roots of civilization in Africa as well as the prominent contributions of African peoples and their cultures to world history, Du Bois highlighted the importance of African American culture in the United States as well. African American culture was constituted, in part, from African cultural retentions such as found in black churches, and, more directly, it derived from black folk culture, which emerged from the slave plantations and was becoming increasingly urbanized in the early twentieth century, especially in the post–World War I era.

Similarly, Malcolm was modernizing black nationalism to address the challenges of the post–World War II and Cold War era, and the incipient BPM. Malcolm's black nationalism built on many of the factors that Du Bois had highlighted. Although Malcolm demurred on the issue of African American culture—an important distinction that we will return to below—he appreciated that blacks constituted "a nation within a nation," and he advocated black autonomy within the communities in which blacks were situated in large numbers. That is, he argued that blacks should control the politics, economics, and society of their communities. Malcolm's black nationalism emphasized the relevance of black liberation theology (especially but not exclusively Sunni Islam), third world solidarity, domestic colonialism, and women's rights. In addition, it recognized that revolution in the United States should reflect the interests of the "field Negro," which was Malcolm's characterization of the black masses whom he differentiated from "house Negroes," suggesting an incipient intraracial class analysis for Malcolm. Given these multidimensional foci of Malcolm's black nationalism in which his thesis of black revolution was situated, Malcolm was convinced that just as political, economic, and social/cultural factors were intimately tied together in his black nationalism, they should be similarly linked in his thesis of black revolution. Thus, his conception of black revolution focused on liberation from racist, classist, and sexist domination.[5] The breadth of Malcolm's focus is evident in the broad program of the OAAU, which addressed issues of politics, economics, and society; and the cultural sinews binding these in black communities, which political mobilization needed to address. These multiple dimensions of black communities converged in a common conception of black cultural identity that suggested a political and economic orientation for the community toward black liberation. Attentive to its socially cohesive and liberating aspect, Malcolm advocated an anthropological conception of culture in its material as well as its aesthetic senses, to encapsulate, inculcate, and direct the revolutionary change that he sought. His resultant formulation was his thesis on black cultural revolution.

These intellectual and programmatic developments in Malcolm's black nationalism were evident in his arguments in his "The Ballot or the Bullet" speech of 1964. Free of the intellectual fetters of the NOI (he was still a member of the NOI at the time of "Message to the Grassroots"), in "The Ballot or the Bullet," Malcolm advocated centering the black liberation struggle on human rights instead of civil rights, while broadening his examination of U.S. domestic politics and the role of blacks in it, paying particular attention to the contradiction between black support for the Democratic Party nationally and the party's failure to support the CRM's agenda—epitomized in the opposition of segregationists within the party, the Dixiecrats.[6] Abandoning the NOI's refusal to participate in electoral politics, Malcolm advocated electoral engagements in his support of a national black political convention, while endorsing armed insurgency as a strategy for black liberation if electoral options were continually blocked by whites. Remarkably, in "Ballot," he no longer argued that revolution was inherently violent; proffering instead a conception of "bloodless revolution," an orientation he had disparaged in "Message to the Grassroots."

Malcolm's rationale for advocating human rights as the focus of black mobilization over civil rights was actually a continuation of the abortive strategy of the National Negro Congress (NNC), which was adopted by the NAACP and spearheaded by Du Bois in 1946–47. The NAACP sought to petition the UN to intervene on behalf of African Americans on the basis of the violation of their human rights as detailed in Du Bois's edited treatise *An Appeal to the World* (Dudziak, 2000). Cold War intrigue, including the duplicitousness of NAACP board member and UN delegate Eleanor Roosevelt, who foreswore her nominal affinity for human rights in favor of maintaining her bona fides as a liberal cold warrior, undermined Du Bois's efforts (Anderson, 2003). She threatened to resign from the board of the NAACP if it sided with Du Bois, allying herself with segregationists, assorted racists in the State Department, Congress, and the Truman administration—and eventually Walter White, the executive director of the NAACP, who previously had championed the petition—thereby ensuring that the petition would not be heard, much less voted on by the UN General Assembly (Anderson, 2003). Moreover, the support that advocates of the UN petition strategy assumed would be forthcoming from the Soviet bloc and third world nations revealed the naiveté of their assumptions in light of the serious problems these states often faced with their own subjugated minorities, which gave them little incentive to either raise the issue of human rights violations with respect to minority populations in the United States—lest attention be turned on their own repressive records (e.g., it was an issue the Soviets had no interest in seriously supporting)—or to risk the loss of U.S. economic and technical support through supporting its oppressed black minority. It was not clear how Malcolm X planned to overcome these obstacles that beset Du Bois and previous supporters of the UN petition strategy, which were no less prevalent during the BPM. Seemingly oblivious to developments roughly a decade and a half prior to the March on Washington, Malcolm viewed a focus on human rights as original and timely.[7] For example, he argued:

> When you expand the civil-rights struggle to the level of human rights, you can then take the case of the black man in this country before the nations in the UN. You can take it before the General Assembly. You can take Uncle Sam before a world court. . . . Civil rights means you're asking Uncle Sam to treat you right. Human rights are something you were born with. Human rights are your God-given rights. Human rights are the rights that are recognized by all nations of this earth. And any time anyone violates your human rights, you can take them to the world court. (Breitman, 1965, pp. 34–35)

Malcolm advised:

> Expand the civil rights struggle to the level of human rights, take it into the United Nations, where our African brothers can throw their weight on our side, where our Asian brothers can throw their weight on our side, where our Latin-American brothers can throw their weight on our side, and where 800 million Chinamen are sitting there waiting to throw their weight on our side. . . . Let the world know how bloody his hands are. Let the world know the hypocrisy that's practiced over here. Let it be the ballot or the bullet. (ibid., p. 35)[8]

Malcolm argued that blacks increasingly saw the limitations of appeals to civil rights through their alliance with the Democratic Party because they realized that their support of Democrats empowered the Dixiecrats, who formed a bloc against civil rights legislation. He argued, "A Dixiecrat is nothing but a Democrat in disguise," and, "The Northern Democrats have never put the Dixiecrats down," which is one reason why the "Dixiecrats in Washington, D.C., control the key committees that run the government." Malcolm noted that "[t]he only reason the Dixiecrats control these committees is because they have seniority. The only reason they have seniority is because they come from states where Negroes can't vote" (ibid., p. 28). He repeated this charge throughout 1964, thusly:

> If Negroes in the South could vote, the Dixiecrats would lose power. When the Dixiecrats lose power, the Democrats would lose power. A Dixiecrat lost is a Democrat lost. Therefore the two of them have to conspire with each other to stay in power. The Northern Dixiecrat puts all the blame on the Southern Dixiecrat. It's a con game, a giant political con game. The job of the Northern Democrat is to make the Negro think that he is our friend. He is always smiling and wagging his tail and telling us how much he can do for us if we vote for him. But at the same time that he's out in front telling us what he's going to do, behind the door he's in cahoots with the Southern Democrat setting up the machinery to make sure he'll never have to keep his promise. (ibid., p. 56)[9]

Although Malcolm argued that blacks should focus on human rights rather than civil rights in their broader struggle, he found resonance with blacks' increasing recognition of the "con game" being played by Democrats. Thus, unlike "Message to the Grassroots," in "The Ballot or the Bullet" Malcolm supported independent black electoral politics and even black political parties—as well as many initiatives of CRM activists—as part of a dual strategy for the attainment of black political power in the United States. In fact, Malcolm advocated working with the major CRM organizations—including those practicing nonviolence—in an array of projects such as voter registration (ibid., p. 42); and advocated a black national political convention by the end of 1964, which he insisted "will consist of delegates from all over the country who are interested in the political, economic and social philosophy of black nationalism" (ibid., p. 41). He added that "[a]fter these delegates convene, we will hold a seminar, we will hold discussions, we will listen to everyone. We want to hear new ideas and new solutions and new answers. And at that time if we see fit then to form a black nationalist party, we'll form a black nationalist party." The latter initiative, probably informed in part by the influence of the black Freedom Now Party led by associates and colleagues of Malcolm such as William Worthy, Harold Cruse, James Boggs, and Albert Cleage, among others, was indicative of Malcolm's plan to challenge the hegemony of the Democratic Party among blacks, and not simply to contribute to a slew of black elected officials, who would do the Democratic Party's bidding, instead of politically conscious black nationalist politicians who would be ideologically and practically disposed to act in the interests of black people—especially the "grassroots."

Nevertheless, in the next line of "The Ballot or the Bullet," he advises that "[i]f it's necessary to form a black nationalist army, we'll form a black nationalist army" (ibid., p. 41), which reflected the second component of Malcolm's dual strategy for black political power. Malcolm admonished that if whites foreclosed the option of blacks' use of "the ballot," then those blacks had the right to pursue their liberation through "the bullet," that is, armed insurgency. In his words: "It'll be the ballot or the bullet. It'll be liberty or it'll be death" (ibid.). Significantly, although Malcolm continued to endorse revolutionary violence; he seemed to be less tied to its historic inevitability—or to the centrality of violence as a characteristic of revolution. Malcolm continued to stress the importance and utility of guerilla warfare in the United States in order to achieve the political objectives of black Americans that could not or would not be realized through electoral means (ibid., pp. 37–38); yet, in his "Ballot" speech delivered in April 1964 in Detroit, he referred to the possibility of a "bloodless revolution" in the United States, as well.

Malcolm provided a more expansive discussion of the prospect for "bloodless revolution" in his "The Black Revolution" speech of 1964. To understand the increased prospects of a bloodless revolution, for Malcolm, it was important to appreciate the rising influence of black nationalists in black communities throughout the United States. Their rise, in turn, was reflected in the increased concerns with human rights more than civil rights among black activists and the black grassroots more generally. For example, in "The Black Revolution," Malcolm rejected both separation and integration as strategies, concentrating instead on what he saw as a more important distinction between advocacy of human rights and advocacy of civil rights, which had important implications for revolutionary struggle. For example, Malcolm argued that

> [o]ur people have made the mistake of confusing the methods with the objectives. As long as we agree on objectives, we should never fall out with each other just because we believe in different methods or tactics or strategy to reach a common objective. (ibid., p. 51)

He added that

> [i]ntegration is only a method that is used by some groups to obtain freedom, justice, equality and respect as human beings.

> Separation is only a method that is used by other groups to obtain freedom, justice, equality or human dignity. (ibid.)

Malcolm asserted that blacks

> have to keep in mind at all times that we are not fighting for integration, nor are we fighting for separation. We are fighting for recognition as human beings. We are fighting for the right to live as free humans in this society. In fact, we are actually fighting for rights that are even greater than civil rights and that is human rights. (ibid.)

Malcolm added that "so-called Negroes" in the United States who are most concerned with civil rights typically view themselves as a minority in the country, and are more concerned with compromise, while viewing the black struggle as a matter of domestic politics; and these folks, he maintained, predominated in civil rights organizations. In contrast, those most concerned with human rights saw themselves as a majority among the world's population, viewed the black struggle as a matter of international politics, and were more concerned with revolution, and these were the black nationalists, who predominated in black nationalist organizations and were emerging in civil rights organizations as well (ibid., pp. 52–53). So Malcolm differentiated between

> two different types of Afro-Americans—the type who looks upon himself as a minority and [whites] as the majority, because his scope is limited to the American scene; and . . . the type who looks upon himself as part of the majority and [whites] as part of a microscopic minority. And this one uses a different approach in trying to struggle for his rights. He doesn't beg. He doesn't thank you for what you give him, because you are only giving him what he should have had a hundred years ago. He doesn't think you are doing him any favors. (ibid., p. 52)

For Malcolm, the black nationalist was not fooled by the hollow overtures of liberal racists any more than by those of conservative racists. Nevertheless, Malcolm observed an important synthesis of these tendencies insofar as "these two different types of black people . . . are beginning to wake up and their awakening is producing a very dangerous situation" (ibid., p. 53).

In "The Black Revolution," Malcolm anticipated the volatility wrought from an expanding black nationalism among so-called Negroes in the

CRM, and reaffirmed the earlier point in "Message to the Grassroots" that "[i]n the past revolutions have been bloody. Historically you just don't have a peaceful revolution . . . revolutions are violent, revolutions cause bloodshed and death follows in their paths" (ibid., p. 56). Nevertheless, by the end of "Revolution," Malcolm appears to pivot; and he states that "America today is at a time . . . where she is the first country on this earth that can actually have a bloodless revolution" (ibid.). He repeats for emphasis: "America is the only country in history in a position to bring about a revolution without violence and bloodshed" (ibid.),[10] and he asks rhetorically, "Why is America in a position to bring about a bloodless revolution?" He answers:

> Because the Negro in this country holds the balance of power, and if the Negro in this country were given what the Constitution says he is supposed to have, the added power of the Negro in this country would sweep all of the racists and the segregationists out of office. It would change the entire political structure of the country. It would wipe out the Southern segregationism that now controls America's foreign policy, as well as America's domestic policy. *And the only way without bloodshed that this can be brought about is the black man has to be given full use of the ballot in every one of the fifty states.* (ibid., p. 57; emphasis added)

Here Malcolm was again invoking the importance of blacks garnering the right to vote and wielding their votes in pursuit of their electoral interests and not simply aligning themselves with the Democratic Party, which was increasingly seeking their support.

Malcolm's call should be wedded to his view of the necessity of a black independent party. Implicit in it was his conviction that the liberating black vote he envisioned was not manipulated by gerrymandering—a powerful tool of white supremacists, which he castigated. It stands to reason that Malcolm's electoral strategy would entail advocacy of some form of proportional representation so that black self-determination would not be undermined by the winner-take-all approach of the two-party system, which often left minorities subject to an overwhelming white and racist majority not only in Southern voting districts but throughout the United States as well. So, for Malcolm, the "ballot" aspect of "The Black Revolution" was not adequately addressed by simply observing black voting rights, but required changes in both voting procedures and the voting system to provide mechanisms to ensure that where warranted the vote would facilitate and not undermine black political representation and would make possible black community control. To be effective, Malcolm's approach would have to be extended to abolishing the U.S. Senate and the Electoral College, two of the most undemocratic institutions of U.S. governance, which undermine even the façade of representative government. Only these types of structural changes would make the "ballot" aspect of his thesis meaningful and a constructive alternative to the pursuit of revolutionary violence to achieve the ends of black liberation.

Malcolm explained this important "electoral strategy" addendum to his heretofore violence-oriented, land-based conception of revolution, in terms of the deepening insights of blacks as they contrasted the promises of democracy with the concrete reality of the practice of white supremacist Herrenvolk democracy. He noted that the "low condition" of "the black man" was "because he has had no control whatsoever over any land" and as a result "[h]e has been a beggar economically, a beggar politically, a beggar socially, a beggar even when it comes to trying to get some education" (ibid., p. 57). This was a situation Malcolm analogized to a "colonial system among our people," which was generating a "colonial mentality" among blacks (ibid.). Yet Malcolm also witnessed important challenges to this mentality as well (ibid). He noted that "as the young ones come up, they know what they want. And as they listen to your beautiful preaching about democracy and all those other flowery words, they know what they're supposed to have" (ibid.). Further, these blacks who were "awakening" were gaining insights into the contradictions of the electoral system—and other domestic institutions of the United States—through which they were ostensibly to realize their political objectives. They understood better the political "con game" represented by black allegiance to the Democratic Party, which included the Dixiecrats, and the unlikelihood of meaningful change resulting from nonviolent appeals to the political system, which was controlled by these white supremacist forces. As a result, only fundamental changes in the electoral system, such as universal black proportional representation, would facilitate the full citizenship rights of black Americans. Thus, Malcolm's allusion to the "ballot" represented a dramatic democratic restructuring of the U.S. political system targeting the institutional protections of white supremacism, transforming it from a Herrenvolk democracy to a multiracial democracy recognizing black autonomy.

At the same time as there were those committed to transforming the United States to make it live up to its promises of political democracy, Malcolm argued that there were some among them who did not hold out any hope that the political system could be changed in this way. In fact, he noted that "today we have a new generation of black people . . . who have become disenchanted with the entire system, who have become disillusioned over the system, and who are ready now and willing to do something about it" (ibid., p. 56). He was convinced that "[t]he new generation of blacks that have grown up in this country in recent years are already forming the opinion . . . that if there is to be bleeding, it should be reciprocal—bleeding on both sides" (ibid., p. 48). For this group, the "ballot" was no longer a meaningful option, the "bullet" was necessary. These orientations were both reflecting and motivating a resurgence of black nationalism, which Malcolm was seeing evinced among young people even in prominent civil rights organizations such as SNCC, CORE, and the NAACP. It was associated with the increasing tendency of so-called Negroes, in Malcolm's view, to reject nonviolence as a philosophy rather than as a tactic; and to view their fight as part of a broader struggle for freedom, justice, and equality as typified in the anticolonial struggles occurring throughout the third world—what Malcolm referred to as the "world-wide revolution."

Malcolm X and the Worldwide Revolution

Malcolm noted that

> [w]hat happens to a black man in America today happens to the black man in Africa. What happens to a black man in America and Africa happens to the black man in Asia and to the man down in Latin America. What happens to one of us today happens to all of us. And when this is realized, I think that the whites . . . will realize that when they touch this one, they are touching all of them, and this in itself will have a tendency to be a checking factor. (ibid., p. 48)

In the absence of such a "checking factor," Malcolm augured that "the racial sparks that are ignited here in America today could easily turn into a flaming fire abroad, which means it could engulf all the people of this earth into a giant race war" (ibid.). These connections formed the basis of Malcolm's conception of a "worldwide revolution."

Malcolm was convinced that

> 1964 will see the Negro revolt evolve and merge into the world-wide black revolution that has been taking place on this earth since 1945. The so-called revolt will become a real black revolution. Now the black revolution has been taking place in Africa and Asia and Latin America; when I say black, I mean non-white—black, brown, red or yellow. Our brothers and sisters in Asia . . . our brothers and sisters in Africa . . . and in Latin America . . . who were colonized by the Europeans, have been involved in a struggle since 1945 to get the colonialists, or the colonizing powers, the Europeans, off their land, out of their country. This is a real revolution. (ibid., pp. 49–50)

This revolution—especially in Africa—was influencing the consciousness of African Americans, as well. Malcolm told a New York audience less than a week before his assassination that "[y]ou and I are living at a time when there's a revolution going on. A worldwide revolution. It goes beyond Mississippi. It goes beyond Alabama. It goes beyond Harlem. There's a worldwide revolution going on" (Perry, 1989, 127). Malcolm argued that the revolutions in Africa and Asia were not only checking white imperialist power in the periphery, they were providing a model for so-called Negroes suffering under an only slightly different form of white imperialist oppression within the United States. Malcolm argued that African independence struggles had a huge impact on black America because prior to the decolonization struggles American Negroes "used to be ashamed of ourselves, used to look down upon ourselves, used to have no tendency whatsoever to stick together"; but "[a]s the African nations become independent and mold a new image—a positive image, a militant image, an upright image, the image of a man, not a boy . . . It has given pride to the Black man right here in the United States." He observed that

> as fast as the brother in Africa and Asia get their independence . . . begin to rise up, begin to change their image from negative to positive—this African image that has jumped from negative to positive affects the image that the Black man in the Western Hemisphere has of himself. . . . So that when the Black revolution begins to roll on the African continent it affects the Black man in the United States and affects the relationship between the Black man and the white man in the United States. (ibid., p. 128)

The effect of black liberation struggles brought together the disparate strands of the global African community under a common banner of struggle against white political (military) and economic power; but, as Malcolm observed, it also rejuvenated a sense of shared value in being a black person in a way that checked white cultural domination. For example, Malcolm noted that whereas blacks had been divided by a lack of positive racial identity and a lack of cultural pride,

> as the African nation got its independence and changed its image [black Americans] became proud of it. And to the same degree that [black Americans] became proud of it [black Americans] began to have something in common. . . . So, whereas formerly it was difficult to unite Black people, today it is easier to unite

> Black people . . . today you find Black people want to come together with Black people. . . . And as the brothers on the African continent lead the way, it has an effect and an impact upon the brothers here. (ibid., pp. 128–129)

Malcolm rooted the latter development in the "spirit of Bandung," referring to the 1955 conference in Bandung, Indonesia, aimed at promoting Afro-Asian economic and cultural cooperation and opposing aspects of the colonialism and neocolonialism of the Cold War blocs (Vitalis, 2013; Wright, 1956). He argued that

> it was the spirit of Bandung that fed the flames of nationalism and freedom not only in Asia, but especially on the African continent. And that same spirit . . . got into the heart and the mind and the soul of the Black man in the Western Hemisphere who supposedly had been separate from the African continent for almost 400 years. (Perry, 1989, 168)

Malcolm noted that "the same desire for freedom that moved the Black man on the African continent began to burn in the heart and the mind and the soul of the Black man here" (ibid., p. 168). He argued that "[u]p until 1959 when you and I thought of an African, we thought of someone naked, coming with the tom-toms, with bones in his nose" (ibid., p. 170). He admonished that

> [t]his was the only image you had in your mind of an African. And from [19]59 on when they begin to come into the UN and you'd see them on the television you'd get shocked. Here was an African who could speak better English than you. He made more sense than you. He had more freedom than you. Why places where you couldn't go . . . all he had to do was throw on his robes and walk right past you. . . . The Black man throughout the Western Hemisphere . . . began to identify with that emerging positive African image. . . . And when he saw the Black man on the African continent taking a stand, it made him become filled with the desire also to take a stand. (ibid., pp. 170–171)

For Malcolm, in their efforts to overthrow the system of colonial domination in their states, African revolutionists were providing African Americans a model of successful revolutionary struggle to guide their activism in the context of domestic colonialism in the United States. Simultaneously, they were generating a cultural reawakening among black Americans that was helping to transform their self-concept, self-identity, and appreciation of their self-determination, as well. These processes and developments led Malcolm to differentiate between types of revolution, in particular, distinguishing between political and cultural revolutions. Thus, in the 1964 "Statement of the Basic Aims and Objectives of the Organization of Afro-American Unity," Malcolm X (1970, p. 427) stated that "[w]e must launch a cultural revolution to unbrainwash an entire people." He insisted that "[c]ulture is an indispensable weapon in the freedom struggle" and that blacks "must take hold of it and forge the future with the past." He emphasized that "[a]rmed with the knowledge of the past, we can with confidence charter a course for our future" (ibid.). Cultural revolution would affirm a sense of black national culture, and national identity; and help establish and reinforce the drive for national self-determination that would provide the ideological support for black political revolution. Malcolm's call for cultural revolution was consistent with his recognition that the black liberation struggle in the United States was part of a larger "world-wide revolution," which consisted of both a political (military) revolution against Western imperialism, modeled on the anticolonial struggles occurring throughout the third world, and a cultural revolution galvanizing black Americans, in particular, to mobilize against white supremacy in the United States. The former suggested a politico-military mobilization against white racist rule in the United States to liberate the black domestic colony; and the latter entailed a simultaneous process of mobilizing black culture to transform the major politico-economic institutions of black communities and the broader U.S. society, as well. Through these two processes, the worldwide revolution would be brought home to the United States.

On its face, Malcolm's thesis did not necessitate that one need follow the other. Malcolm's cultural revolution may have reinforced the revolutionary processes extant among blacks, and in that way encouraged a subsequent political revolution, or it may have occasioned a simultaneous political revolution. Malcolm's thesis left room for both possibilities and he did not seem to privilege either, nor did he fuse them into a single coherent process; however, the ambiguity therein could have been addressed if not resolved by linking them to their intellectual precursors beginning in the Harlem Renaissance (which we'll expand on in chapter 3). In that era, W. E. B Du Bois and Alain Locke historicized and theorized, respectively, a relationship between black cultural and political revolution in the United States. Du Bois argued in *Black Reconstruction* (1935) that profound changes in slave religion motivated the "largest slave revolt" in U.S. history, the General Strike, in which slaves allied with the Union military to fight for their freedom in the U.S. Civil

War. This Slave Revolution compelled Lincoln to change his war aims from simply ending secession to overthrowing chattel slavery, making the Civil War a political revolution. Du Bois's historical account demonstrated how a black cultural revolution motivated a political revolution. Locke provided a theoretical formulation of the process Du Bois outlined. He insisted that African American culture, like cultures in general, is diverse, dynamic, and gravitates to expressing its latent cosmopolitanism, which he argues is facilitated by democracy. For Locke, the struggle for cultural democracy involves expanding the domain of political and economic democracy into the cultural sphere, and in such a way that facilitates racial democracy. Inferring from this relationship, the attainment of cultural democracy in the United States necessitates a black cultural revolution. As applied to Du Bois's historical depiction from *Black Reconstruction*, Locke's thesis suggests that a transformation in black culture (i.e., slave religion) ramified into the political and economic spheres in ways implicating multiracial democracy; and the resolution of this confluence compelled a political revolution for both black America (i.e., through the General Strike) and the United States (the Civil War—with the revolutionary aim of ending chattel slavery). Thus, the historical black revolution in the United States, the Slave Revolution, proceeded from a cultural revolution that stimulated a political revolution.

This exegesis makes clear that on the cusp of the CRM there was an extant thesis of black revolution in the United States that was available to BPM revolutionists who would study their African American intellectual precursors; yet, what should have been a maxim or at least a point of departure for Malcolm X and many BPM revolutionists instead remained an unresolved and exceptionally factious issue for them, and for many future activists and scholars, as well. Further, although Malcolm's Harlem contemporary—and the first BPM revolutionist to proffer an explicit thesis of black cultural revolution—Harold Cruse was aware of these precursors and their salience to the incipient black liberation struggles of the late 1950s and early 1960s, Malcolm and most BPM revolutionists seemed oblivious to them. As a result, Malcolm's thesis on black revolution—and black cultural revolution, in particular—was undertheorized, yet this aspect of Malcolm's broader revolutionary thesis was to heavily influence the BPM.

At the time of his death, Malcolm's thesis on political revolution also was in a state of flux. The trajectory of the political revolution, for Malcolm, seemed to follow the path of recently successful revolutions in China, Cuba, and Algeria and ongoing insurgencies, such as in Vietnam. He viewed it as two-pronged: aimed first at achieving political power through the expansion of the realm of democratic civil society and reform of the state through electoral means; and if and when those efforts were rebuffed, then, second, organizing militia for insurrection, targeting local police forces in urban enclaves, or centering on rural bases from which to engage the country in a protracted guerilla insurgency. The actual coordination of such an insurgency, understandably, was largely an underground affair; thus, Malcolm made reference to it but did not articulate its specifics publicly (see Ahmad, 2007). Nevertheless, his approach converged with that which was being formulated and articulated by Robert Williams (1964).

For Malcolm, the cultural revolution was as difficult to conceptualize as the politico-military revolution was to organize. This was not only because the two revolutions were related—with one possibly embedded in the other—but because of the difficulty of conceptualizing black culture, delimiting its preferred institutional forms, and outlining the way it might be employed to realize revolutionary objectives. Malcolm did not sufficiently develop these aspects of his argument, which contributed to the misunderstanding of his thesis on black revolution. This explains why, for most black activists and analysts, the Black Arts Movement (BAM) represented the cultural revolution that Malcolm sought. But this is at best debatable. For Malcolm, the concept of black culture central to his thesis and program was one that motivated the revolutionary orientation, practices, and insights of the "grassroots," epitomized in his conception of the field Negro. The dichotomy of field and house Negro was Malcolm's characterization of the prominent socioeconomic differentiation in black America, which generated divergent political interests. For Malcolm, the field Negro approximated the masses and their political perspectives, regardless of their specific class station. They were mainly black nationalist, and the house Negroes were mainly integrationist. In considering the revolutionary orientation of the black masses, Malcolm drew on his experience with the NOI and his personal transformation from pimp, drug dealer, and burglar to Muslim minister and revolutionist. Malcolm's transformation—and his seeming ability to help others transform—convinced him of the importance of culture, especially religion—in his case, Islam—in the process. For him, transforming "so-called Negroes" into committed participants in black liberation struggle required, inter alia, a radical *cultural* transformation.

Also key for Malcolm was the necessity of organizing the varied elements of the black masses, including former criminals—those whom Marx called the "lumpenproletariat"—who would have to be committed to the transformation necessary to allow them to contribute to the black liberation struggle. Malcolm was convinced that they could be organized, educated, and politicized to realize their revolutionary potential. Malcolm was convinced by his *positive experience with the NOI* that the transformation of the lumpenproletariat should include a strong cultural element—specifically, an ethical thrust—and religion was essential to this process. Malcolm was convinced by his *negative experience with the NOI* that the lumpen would have to be transformed before joining—much less given positions of responsibility in—movement organizations, and then very selectively being admitted to responsible positions after a period of training, education, participation, and supervision—especially positions associated with leadership, finances, education, or security. Malcolm had no intention of replicating in any of his subsequent organizations the NOI's Fruit of Islam, which had suborned and nurtured many of the lumpen in the NOI to continue their criminal activities—usually carried out against NOI members.

Moreover, Malcolm was convinced that a mass-based organization would be essential in facilitating either political or cultural revolution, and that it should operate on political, economic, and social fronts. Malcolm's plan to realize these objectives was a dual one: the construction of a religious-based organization, Muslim Mosque Inc. (MMI), which was essential to continuing Malcolm's work of promoting Sunni Islam in the United States and maintaining and expanding the links with Islamic states, movements, and leaders globally; and a secular political organization, the Organization of Afro-American Unity (OAAU)—patterned after the Organization of African Unity (OAU), formed in 1963 by independent African state leaders—which would facilitate the pan-Africanist links that Malcolm had fostered with African leaders and organizations, and, just as importantly, promote the panoply of domestic initiatives in the United States essential for transforming the CRM into a revolutionary struggle for black liberation. Thus, MMI would be a traditional Sunni Muslim mosque, with the OAAU as a black nationalist organization that would participate in the CRM and the incipient BPM. A key focus of both organizations, for Malcolm, was the promotion of a black cultural revolution.

Malcolm X and Black Cultural Revolution

Since Malcolm never proposed an actual theory of cultural revolution, he never completed the second component of his revolutionary thesis. This would contribute to one of the enduring fissures among black revolutionists of the BPM: the distinction between political and cultural revolution. Following his assassination, Malcolm X's views were characterized by some as "revolutionary nationalism," in contrast with ostensibly nonrevolutionary "cultural nationalism," but such a dichotomy ignores Malcolm's clear advocacy of both political and cultural revolution in the United States. For Malcolm's ideological heirs, such as the Black Panther Party, political revolution in the United States was viewed in terms of those ongoing in the third world such as in Cuba and Vietnam, and earlier ones in Russia and China, which were aimed both at overthrowing governmental authority and establishing communist rule. For the BPP, this was not only consistent with Malcolm's thesis of black revolution but was viewed as the only legitimate form of revolution that the BPM could have as an objective. The BPP and other advocates of this perspective appropriated the title *revolutionary nationalists* for themselves and viewed supporters of cultural revolution as "nonrevolutionary" and improperly focused on superficial aspects of black oppression—e.g,. black culture—that were easily compromised and accommodated to the status quo, as well as inattentive to the fundamental basis of black oppression, which they viewed mainly in terms of class and capitalism.

In contrast, advocates of cultural revolution such as RAM viewed themselves as following Malcolm's admonition that a cultural reawakening of black people was necessary to throw off the psychological yoke of white supremacism, which they saw as a prerequisite for political revolution. In their view, culture was anthropological—comprising both material and aesthetic aspects—informing and interconnecting the major institutions of black Americans, and not simply reflecting the aesthetics of black art and literature. Advocates of this view, such as Us and the RNA, asserted that without an affirming and liberating black culture and its grounding in the key political, economic, and social institutions of black communities, then blacks would not have the wherewithal to assert their rights of national self-determination. Denied their culture—including their history of resistance to white oppression—blacks required a cultural revolution to provide the basis for the political revolution such as that which the BPP and the LRBW sought. For revolutionists, such as RAM, Us, and the RNA, the key mode of domination was race more than class; therefore, they had less faith that eradicating capitalism would lead to the overthrow of white supremacism.[11]

While these competing viewpoints will be discussed more fully later, for now it's important to point out that Malcolm did not cast these perspectives in opposition to each other, but saw important aspects of each as complementary. As noted above, he did not seem to cast political and cultural revolution as sequential, but, seemed to understand that they could be coincidental. In Malcolm's view, they seemed to be parallel, potentially self-reinforcing, and dependent on the popular support, institutional development, and resistance that each generated. The view that these could be simultaneous processes seems contradictory to Malcolm's larger theoretical formulation in which his theory was embedded. This is evident given that cultural revolution presupposes, or at least strongly implies, the existence of a culture and/or cultural institutions that may serve as a basis for cultural transformation or cultural (re)construction that the term *cultural revolution* embodies. That is, to re-Africanize culturally seems to require a preexisting African culture (e.g., Wolof, Kikuyu, Zulu, Yoruba, Fon) to which one could re-Africanize after some period of cultural suppression, typically from slavery or colonialism. Revolutionzing and reconstructing African American culture, implies a preexistent African American culture to serve as a referent. But Malcolm's reverse civilizationism suggests that there is no referent African American culture—since so-called Negroes presumably were stripped of their culture during slavery; hence, such a culture would have to be developed. For Malcolm, there seemed to be only one legitimate source for this culture: Africa. Therefore, to follow the path of cultural revolution or reconstruction for African Americans required the attainment of African culture.

The latter contention is consistent with Malcolm's speech on the founding of the OAAU of June 28, 1964. When Malcolm X (1970, p. 427) turned to concerns of culture he asserted that "[o]ur history and our culture were completely destroyed when we were forcibly brought to America in chains." He insisted that black Americans had culture before slavery in the United States, that it was "as old as man himself," and that it was "a high state of culture [which] existed in Africa"; but slavery had "stripped us of all cultural knowledge," such that now "we know almost nothing about it" ibid.). This was consistent with his earlier comments in a 1963 speech in which he argued "the poor so-called Negro doesn't have his own name, doesn't have his own language, doesn't have his own culture, doesn't have his own history. He doesn't have his own country. He doesn't even have his own mind" (Perry, 1989, p. 33). As a result, black Africans were more conscious of themselves as cultural and political agents as compared to black Americans; therefore, black Americans needed to follow their lead. In light of this, Malcolm X (1970, p. 427) insisted that black Americans "must launch a cultural revolution to un-brainwash an entire people"; and that "cultural revolution must be the means of bringing us closer to our African brothers and sisters." In Malcolm's view, "[t]his cultural revolution will be the journey to our rediscovery of ourselves" (ibid.); allowing blacks to confidently "charter a course for our future" because "[c]ulture is an indispensable weapon in the freedom struggle" (ibid.).

In this rendering, Malcolm's reverse civilizationism is unambiguous: African Americans do not possess a culture because their original African culture was stripped from them in the brutal process of American slavery. Eight months later, in the version of the OAAU Charter that was to be presented on February 15, 1965, his reverse civilizationist view of African American culture is no less evident as he discusses the desire to "renew the culture that was crushed by a slave government." Malcolm emphasized that "we are determined to rediscover our true African culture, which was crushed and hidden for over four hundred years in order to enslave us and keep us enslaved up to today." He asserted that the cultural revolution that the OAAU would pursue would "provide the means for restoring our identity that we might rejoin our brothers and sisters on the African continent, culturally, psychologically, economically, and share with them the sweet fruits of freedom from oppression and independence of racist governments." He emphasized that "we are determined to rediscover our true African culture, which was crushed and hidden for over four hundred years in order to enslave us and keep us enslaved up to today." He was convinced that "[w]e must change the thinking of the Afro-American by liberating our minds through the study of philosophies and psychologies, cultures and languages that did not come from our racist oppressors"; and Malcolm maintained that this liberation of Afro-American minds should center on Africa more than black America. Pursuant to the latter, the Charter noted that "[p]rovisions are being made for the study of languages such as Swahili, Hausa, and Arabic," which, in Malcolm's view would "give our people access to ideas and history of mankind at large and thus increase our mental scope." The OAAU would "encourage the Afro-American to travel to Africa, the Caribbean, and to other places where our culture has not been completely crushed by brutality and ruthlessness." Not surprisingly, a Cultural Committee was one of the nine major committees of the OAAU (Malcolm X, 2018).

Malcolm's reverse civilizationism as reflected in both versions of the OAAU Charter asserts that black Americans were stripped of their culture, and their hope for acquiring a culture rested on reconnecting with historic and contemporary African cultures to reconstruct those that were stripped from them; yet, in the later version of the Charter there is reference to *both* "African culture and Afro-American culture," which seems to reject the view that black Americans are devoid of culture. It also suggests that these two cultures are at least distinguishable, notwithstanding that the latter might be derivative of the former. It appears, then, that Malcolm X recognized that there was an existing "Afro-American culture," one that should be "respectably" expressed and whose "survival" he was intent on ensuring.

This apparent ambiguity is the result of the fluidity of Malcolm's thesis in the last tortuous months of his life, and also in his focus on implicating white supremacism in the oppression of black America. With respect to the latter, Malcolm excoriated the trans-Atlantic slave trade and U.S. chattel slavery, often emphasizing heinous and even genocidal acts of specific aspects of the slave system. To demonstrate the magnitude of whites' depravity, Malcolm, understandably, paid less attention to the slaves' acts of resistance and retention of Africanisms, or the reconstitution of a cultural essence that became the "slave culture" that Stuckey (1987) observed in the antebellum era;

yet, he spoke of the historical significance of slave resistance—evoking Nat Turner, Denmark Vesey, and Gabriel, among others—especially the Haitian Revolution, and he situated himself and the field Negroes in this tradition. Thus, with respect to its historical significance, a black culture of resistance was clearly evident to Malcolm from the slave era. Therefore, Sales (1994, p. 80) is probably correct that "[t]he political role that Malcolm assigned to African American culture assumed that the only legitimate Black culture was that of the masses of dispossessed African Americans." For Malcolm, there was at least an aspect of African American culture that may have been dormant, but when it was expressed it supported black liberation. Therefore, Malcolm's reverse civilizationism did not appear to have been total—it allowed for the existence of some aspect of African American culture—but on the whole, it maintained that black Americans were deficient in terms of culture compared to their African brothers and sisters, and as a result they were deficient in terms of their revolutionary consciousness.

Returning to the relationship between culture and revolution, it seems that while Malcolm X's argument about the worldwide revolution posits that the cultural and political revolutions may be simultaneous or sequential, the logic of his reverse civilizationism seems to necessitate that the cultural and political revolutions are consecutive. That is, blacks seem to require a cultural revolution in order to pursue political revolution. Not surprisingly, given the influence of reverse civilizationism on subsequent BPM theorists, the first of the major BPM organizations that openly advocated cultural revolution, RAM and Us, both accepted the view that the cultural and political revolutions were sequential. This perspective would have implications for their development as organizations, their interaction with other BPM organizations, and the trajectory of the development of the BPM itself. What was unambiguous was that Malcolm did not envision the cultural revolution simply in terms of the appropriation of African aesthetics or black arts, nor did he envision the political revolution in Marxist terms. Although he understood the importance of race, class, culture, and gender, Malcolm envisioned and attempted to foster a distinctly African American process that would fuse the political and cultural in a revolutionary synthesis. Thus, not surprisingly, Harold Cruse would characterize Malcolm's thesis as "revolutionary cultural nationalist."

Although Malcolm's conception of black cultural revolution was the least developed aspect of his revolutionary thesis, he thought that the manner by which it would be constructed would require an engagement with the peculiar history and circumstances of black America that tied political, economic, and cultural forces together in novel ways. Du Bois, Locke, as well as Cruse, had made seminal contributions to such theorizing—and Malcolm may have been familiar with some of these, and Cruse's arguments in particular; nevertheless, he did not live to develop this aspect of his revolutionary theory. Instead, Malcolm analogized the construction of such a theory to the improvisation of the jazz artist. He saw black music as one of the rare areas of black autonomy that could stimulate, generate, and reinforce African American values, aesthetics, and institutions. No less creativity and insight would be required for the construction of black revolutionary social theory that would provide a template for revolutionary praxis. Where Du Bois evoked the "sorrow songs," Malcolm evoked the "soul" in black music that he found at the root of black experience and ethos. The key was to capture it, improvise, and mold it for black liberation. But theory construction is not something one simply improvises; it comes from rigorous study of the historical conditions and contemporary reality facing peoples.[12] Malcolm X did not have time to develop such a theory before five members of the NOI assassinated him in front of his wife, children, and supporters in Harlem.[13]

To be sure, Malcolm's thesis on black cultural revolution was a major theoretical focus in his last year. Although it was undeveloped, it was influential among his acolytes, while often misunderstood by both supporters and critics, which was as evident during the BPM as it is now. For example, in his recent Pulitzer Prize–winning biography of Malcolm X, Manning Marable does not mention Malcolm's thesis on black cultural revolution. Marable is hardly alone in this neglect of black nationalist theorizing given that black nationalism is often treated as inherently conservative, with progressive and revolutionary aspects only to the extent that it embraces some form of Marxism or Social Democracy. Malcolm's thesis of black revolution is likewise poorly analyzed on its theoretical merits and in its multidimensional aspects. Malcolm was a religiously inspired, black nationalist revolutionist whose thesis on black revolution developed concurrently with his understanding of the black nationalism in which it was embedded. He formulated his black nationalism into a progressive thesis on revolution eschewing the millenarianism of the NOI; but he incorporated its reverse civilizationism, which likewise informed his thesis on black revolution. The latter led him to conceive of black revolution in the United States as largely a function of the replication of methods practiced by Africans on the continent. Accordingly, his black cultural revolution would to a large extent rest on replicating the processes if not the extant forms of African cultures found on the continent. Reverse civilizationism led Malcolm away from a deeper focus on the transformative elements of African American culture in the United States—largely black urban culture, which was more relevant to, and practicable in, U.S. society.

One wonders whether if Malcolm had lived to see the Watts revolt in Los Angeles, the first of the large-scale urban rebellions of the Long Hot Summers of the 1960s, he would have reconsidered his view that black

Americans lagged behind Africans in their propensity to revolutionary social change, leading him to channel the energy of Watts into more enduring and focused revolutionary struggle? Whether such revolts might have been coordinated—much less by Malcolm's OAAU or other BPM organizations—is beside the point for the moment, but what Watts displayed was that major policy victories such as the Voting Rights Act, which had been signed a week before the uprising in August 1965, were inadequate to address the demands of blacks seeking racial justice, especially outside of the South. If, through revolt, black Americans could exercise greater leverage on the racist policies of the United States, then this would allow them to assume greater leadership in the worldwide revolution, given the strategic position of the United States.

In the event, Malcolm's reverse civilizationism drew his focus away from the revolutionary praxis of black Americans that preceded and should have informed his and others' theses on black revolution in the United States during the BPM. BPM revolutionists—including Malcolm—derived inspiration from revolutions around the world, but they ignored the theoretical significance of Du Bois's thesis in *Black Reconstruction*, published in 1935.[14] As a result, they had not drawn from the one revolution aimed at black liberation that probably had the greatest salience for their struggles: the Slave Revolution during the U.S. Civil War. Although the Civil War occurred a century prior to the CRM, its relevance to 1960s activists was fourfold: (1) it occurred in the United States; (2) it involved descendants of the same or similar protagonists; (3) it occurred in the context of a sectarian crisis, one even greater than the dissension during the Vietnam War in which the BPM was situated; and, most importantly, (4) it secured freedom for enslaved blacks, overthrew chattel slavery, and defeated the CSA. As will be fleshed out more fully in chapter 3, a key to the success of the black revolution during the Civil War was the role of religiously inspired black folk—similar to Malcolm personally and the grassroots whom he imbued with so much revolutionary potential.

Malcolm X's reverse civilizationism affected his acolytes' discernment of the salience of culture in revolutionary struggle, which led to the bifurcation between "revolutionary" nationalists and "cultural" nationalists (the latter a redundancy after Du Bois modernized black nationalism), but even where black liberation activists theorized the impact of black culture on political change they often built on one or the other of the two aspects of Malcolm X's conception of black cultural revolution. The first was evident in the Black Arts Movement's attempt to articulate and develop a Black aesthetic, to create Black cultural organizations, and through them, to institutionalize Black art—including Black theater, Black music, and especially Black literature. The second was evident in the political organizing of cultural revolution theorists, whose institutions were largely seen as vehicles to facilitate and encourage culturally based activism necessary to "unbrainwash" blacks as a precursor to their acceptance of the relevance and necessity of political revolution. The latter suggested the need to develop parallel institutions of civil society staffed by black revolutionists, which would publicize the contradictions embodied in the provision of ostensibly public services to blacks—especially the poor—by dedicated activists by making clear the absence of the same from the actions of the government agencies mandated to provide them. It raised the contradiction of the exceptionally poor quality of the provision, content, and delivery of services and resources to black people and black communities by government institutions and social service agencies as compared to those given to whites and white communities.

The promotion of black aesthetics and the development of parallel institutions were tied to a conception of culture that wedded it to promoting political objectives, which was reminiscent of Du Bois and Locke's discourse from the Harlem Renaissance. Moreover, following Harold Cruse's arguments, which incorporated aspects of Haywood's Black Belt thesis—both of which we examine more fully in later chapters, many leading BPM theorists, including Malcolm X, adopted his domestic colonialism model as both the descriptive metaphor of the black American context in the United States and the analytical framework for understanding black oppression and strategizing black liberation. In light of it, BPM revolutionists proposed a variety of theoretical formulations aimed at organizing revolution to free the black "colony" from its "colonizers" in the manner that had proven successful throughout the so-called third world. In this way, theses of black cultural revolution grafted more from third world modalities, while largely ignoring the peculiar trajectory of black political development in the United States—which did not approximate domestic colonialism—when formulating their theses of social change. The latter was exacerbated in those instances in which activists/theorists explicated domestic colonialism through neo-Marxist formulations, which further reduced the applicability of the models to the historical development of black America, as Du Bois (1935) and Cruse (1963), among others, would demonstrate (and we examine more fully in chapters 3 and 4).

The problem of the domestic colonialism analogy involved less the conception of black America as a nation within the territorial borders of the United States than the deduction that black liberation in such a context must take the form of similar anticolonial struggles in the post–World War II era. One result was that many black nationalist domestic colonialism theorists, in their attempts to mirror liberation struggles occurring throughout Africa and the broader colonized world, adopted rural and communal African precepts and practices in the name of "returning to the source" or seeking "full re-Africanization," and applied these largely communal African "traditions" to a predominately urban and increasingly industrialized working-class African American context. Such conceptions misunderstand the unique context of black America, to which the domestic colonialism analogy does not seem to apply: it comprises a subjugated, nonindigenous, racial minority nation located within the most powerful country in the world. There is simply no other colonial or domestic colonial relationship that mirrors that of African Americans in the twentieth century, and certainly not during the Cold War era. The colonial analogy simply did not fit the structural conditions of black America, nor did it pose strategies to liberate the presumed black colony given the absence of analogues in the modern era. Thus, Cruse was correct that American blacks would have to formulate their own original thesis of national liberation to overcome their oppression, arising from the unique historical conditions that gave rise to it. Unfortunately, the availability of the colonial analogy decreased the motivation of black revolutionists to articulate a theoretical argument rooted in the peculiarities of black America rather than one grafted from an often imagined, traditional colonial Africa. The colonial analogy offered a ready-made theoretical framework to graft on to a very different U.S. society.

Given the different systems of white supremacism in the de jure segregation of the South and the de facto segregation of the North, the hypothesized black political revolution in the United States was unlikely to occur simultaneously in the South and North, and it was proceeding unevenly during the second half of the twentieth century. As a result of contention among different white supremacist social systems, the black struggle in the South promoted intraracial unity across classes in black communities as they fought a largely interracial conflict, while the black struggle in the North (and West) was less racially cohesive, stratified across intraracial class interests, and aimed at specific institutions of white power, especially those implicated in the devastation in the black ghettos (e.g., police, schools, housing authorities, private real estate agencies, banks and lenders, insurance companies, retail businesses, white homeowners associations, etc.). The Southern CRM did not articulate a program for the transformation of the whole of African American society (i.e., the entire black domestic colony in the United States) because its material conditions and subsequent demands were qualitatively different from those in the North. This is not to say that Northern and Southern blacks could not find common cause, but only that, facing different institutional forms of oppression, they were not likely to develop a convergent strategy on their liberation. In fact, the convergent strategy of the CRM was for blacks throughout the United States to come South to help overthrow Jim Crow. Once the locus of the CRM moved North, major fissures developed as it attempted to address the myriad forms of Northern white racism that did not require Jim Crow signs, yet ensured Jim Crow outcomes (see Rothstein, 2017). The impact of region (e.g., South, North, West) not only shaped the institutional expressions of white supremacy, but also the type of resistance likely to form within each region.

The colonial analogy did not fit the black domestic colony in another important way: colonialism usually suggested a relationship between a relatively powerful rich Western country and a much weaker, poor non-Western country. But the situation in the United States didn't match on either front. First, the United States was not simply a powerful and rich Western country, it was the most powerful and richest country in the world; and second, the black domestic colony was not a third world backwater, but a highly technological, heavily industrialized, relatively well-educated, and politically developed society whose per capita income would have registered it well above most third world countries—and many "second world" countries, as well. Nationalists in search of an analogy were so preoccupied with the third world revolutionaries that they ignored the greater structural similarities between ostensibly domestic colonialism in the United States and that found in other advanced industrialized nations, such as Great Britain with respect to Northern Ireland.[15] This suggests that Michael Collins may have been a more useful referent than Che Guevara. Struggling if not in the "belly of the beast" then surely in its "large intestine," the revolutionary leader of the IRA devised a successful strategy of urban guerrilla warfare that relied heavily on counterintelligence and counter-counterinsurgency strategy that brought the world's most powerful empire at the time to the negotiation table. It was clear that the political revolution involving the U.S. "domestic colony" was not going to be carried out in the jungles and swamps of some third world country but in the well-paved streets, highways, buildings, parks, backyards as well as the fields, forests, and streams of the metropolitan homeland.

In sum, the problems of conceptual and historical fit of the colonial analogy to the conditions of black America redound to the fact that there was no contemporary equivalent to the black liberation struggle in the postwar era. There was no analogue among the twentieth-century revolutions from which BPM theorists drew on for guidance of a poor racial minority waging a successful revolution against a rich racial majority government of a major power in a homeland that they both shared. The national liberation struggles of the twentieth century on which BPM revolutionists drew were not remotely equivalent to those of black America. The colonial analogy was an artful metaphor, but it was unsuitable as an analytical device. BPM revolutionists would have been better served drawing on the historical case from the United States that fit better the context of black American oppression: the revolution that blacks waged during the U.S. Civil War, which, as we'll explain in the next chapter, was as relevant to the theory and program of BPM revolutionists as it was ignored by them.

The problems of the domestic colonial analogy that are evident with respect to political revolutions are even more debilitating when applied to cultural revolution. For example, cultural revolution theses needed to specify the culture that was being overthrown and the one replacing it. The most prominent of such theses in the BPM—such as Malcolm's influential one—relied too much on the analogy to African cultural processes, which largely ignored the ways differences in cultural development under settler and domestic colonialism would affect cultural revolution. African American cultural development would require much more than simply continuing extant cultural practices that had been restricted or undermined during colonialism. Instead, it would entail a process of cultural education, which would have to be far more extensive than would be necessary in Africa. Unlike in Africa, it was not simply a matter of a Somali resuming his/her precolonial cultural practices once the fetters of colonialism were removed; or even the more difficult task of an Ewe, Yoruba, Acholi, or Bakongo maintaining their ethnic identity as their postcolonial nationality became Ghanaian, Nigerian, Ugandan, or Congolese, respectively. Black Americans had an astronomically more difficult task of cultural reacquisition since they did not have a readily identifiable precolonial culture to serve as a referent for identification, much less for revolutionizing.

African Americans were a diverse pan-African amalgam of predominantly West and Central African culture groups from which there was no single, identifiable, preexisting, national culture that they practiced. Moreover, even if such a referent culture existed, the processes by which blacks would adopt it were much more profound than that which faced postcolonial Africans. Black Americans of the black power era were not going to stop speaking English or attending church to adapt to such a preexisting culture if one were uncovered. Clearly, among an influential group of BPM activists there was a promotion of Kiswahili as a lingua franca; and there were small communities in the United States focusing on Yoruba culture, as well as African-associated (or "black") forms of Islam (e.g., the Moorish Science Temple, the NOI, MMI) and Judaism (e.g., the Black Hebrew Israelites); these were minimal in comparison to the prevalence of English and the association with Christianity, respectively, among black Americans of the era—and today. What is more, most black Americans were unlikely to accept a vision of themselves as African, New African, or other arbitrarily imposed designations of their identity over their more enduring racial and/or religious identities. In fact, many blacks had come to even more strongly embrace a synthesis of their identity as a particular type of American whose ancestry was from Africa, African Americans, and on that basis were asserting their rights as American citizens who had overcome slavery and were attempting the same with respect to Jim Crow. This they were undertaking while acknowledging and reinforcing their cultural roots in their overwhelmingly black churches, which were increasingly demonstrating both their spiritual and political salience in the apogee of the CRM.

To be sure, if nothing else, the CRM under Martin L. King Jr's influence was giving new political life to the Black Church, as an institution, and as a key locus of black political mobilization, which Malcolm also was clearly recognizing. The contradictions facing black nationalists was that the Black Church, historically, was built on a black nationalist base, but its programmatic and political thrust during the CRM had been integrationist. The contradictions didn't run one way because integrationists' organizations relied on the Black Church, which even if no longer nationalist was an independent black institution, and one that was hardly intent on "integrating" itself out of existence. This inconsistency provided an opening for black nationalists if they cared to engage the Black Church as it was, and not as so many of them imagined it: an institution whose time had passed. In light of the latter, even as many of Malcolm's acolytes advocated black cultural revolution they had difficulty integrating the major black cultural institution, the Black Church, into their theoretical arguments and often were antagonistic toward it—with the exception of the PAOCC. Ambivalent, at best, on whether African Americans possessed a culture—much less a liberating one—and often rejecting the major black cultural institution, the Black Church, nevertheless they seemed to recognize the need to fill the spiritual and institutional vacuum created by this and sought to create parallel spiritual equivalents such as Us's "Temple of Kawaida" (see Brown, 2003; Woodard, 1999), or the BPP's "Son of Man Temple" (see Alkebulan, 2007). As a result, a largely metaphorical construct deriving from black nationalism, the domestic colonialism thesis, worked against one of the novel theoretical frameworks informing black revolutionary theses, black cultural revolution.

The failure to adequately engage the Black Church as an important institution in the black cultural revolution that BPM activists sought both resulted from and reflected a broader problem of BPM theorists that was exacerbated by reverse civilizationism. That is, advocates of black cultural revolution often did not adequately distinguish between aesthetic and material dimensions of black culture, nor did they synthesize their respective roles in the revolutionary change they sought. To be sure, aesthetic and material aspects of culture are imbricated; but in the event, BPM activists were more attentive to the former than the latter. Thus, this era was marked by a resurgence of African referents not seen since the Garvey era, including the adoption of African fashion in dress and names, a deference—mostly superficial and very selective—to perceived African customs, rituals, and even religion, but with much less attention paid to the development and articulation of the material aspects of the respective societies from which these largely aesthetic expressions were drawn. For example, Congolese dress or dance might be appropriated, but the Congolese institution of palaver would not be seriously considered as a mechanism for democratic decision making by BPM organizations. The musical forms of South Africans Miriam Makeba and Hugh Masekela were celebrated and copied, but much less attention paid to the strategic doctrine of Umkhonto we Sizwe. With respect to black culture, the BAM was mostly an assertion of aesthetic more than material claims. Cruse attempted to fuse the two, but with several notable exceptions that are discussed in subsequent chapters, most activists either misunderstood or failed to institutionalize his vision. Without a prominent materialist thrust, Malcolm's black cultural revolution, in particular, devolved to an assertion of aesthetic representation or even reclamation, but it did not pose a materialist corollary to its aesthetic critique.

Relatedly, reverse civilizationism dictated that where black revolutionists invoked culture it often would be either some variant of a mythologized monolithic African culture or some bricolage of "traditional African" village or communal culture, but rarely would it take as its reference the modern urbanized culture evident throughout African states in the era. Those BPM organizations advocating black cultural revolution saw themselves as following the path laid out by anticolonial revolutionists in Africa and the third world more broadly; thus, they often had little use for those cultural—as well as political and economic—institutions in the United States, and the "first world" more broadly, that were not associated in their minds with the revolutionary pursuit of black liberation. As a result, they had little use for extant African American cultural forms or, more importantly, African American cultural institutions, which would have to be made anew. This view had its most dramatic impact on the relationship between the BPM and the Black Church. By privileging developments on the African continent instead of in the United States, reverse civilizationism militated against drawing from African American culture those elements, processes, and objectives that would help generate black cultural revolution in the United States. It also would compel BPM activists to couch not only their revolutionary rhetoric but their material claims in terms that were more befitting a colony seeking redress from a metropolitan power abroad, rather than seeking a basis for asserting the cultural claims of African American citizens of the United States, and in such a way as would implicate broader economic and political demands tied to the liberation of the black nation within the United States.

In combination, reverse civilizationism and an overemphasis on aesthetic rather than material aspects of black culture (e.g., a focus on names, language, dress, and creative arts as opposed to developing independent black cultural institutions such as black churches, black labor unions, black businesses, black political parties, or black militia) would complicate and often undermine the programs and projects of black revolutionists throughout the BPM who attempted to fuse black culture with their revolutionary projects and in that way build on the revolutionary thesis of Malcolm X. Nevertheless, Malcolm X's theses on black political and cultural revolution informed the theoretical arguments, programs, and policy preferences of the major organizations of the BPM, including RAM, Us, the BPP, the RNA, the LRBW, CAP, and the PAOCC. Yet, these BPM organizations had difficulty articulating a coherent theory of black cultural revolution applicable to U.S. society. In fact, many BPM theorists seemed to pay little heed to the precursors of their theoretical, formulaic, and institutional expressions in the Harlem Renaissance and especially the complementary and contrasting revolutionary theses of Du Bois and Locke, who, as will be discussed more fully in chapter 3, historicized and theorized black political and cultural revolution in the United States prior to the BPM. Their work suggested a theory of black revolution in the United States that was as relevant as it was ignored by BPM activists and theorists.

Conclusion

Malcolm X's thesis on black revolution in the United States evolved from a static, unidimensional, religious-based conceptualization of his NOI years into a dynamic, multidimensional, secular framework of his post-NOI years; yet, those who built on his legacy rarely captured the fullness or complexity of Malcolm's thesis, and as a result, did not incorporate it into their strategy for black liberation or in their important institutions. For example, Malcolm's focus on revolutionary violence and petitioning the UN was adopted most notably by the BPP; his focus on land and statehood by the RNA; his focus on Africa and cultural revolution by Us; his focus on electoral politics by CAP; his critique of capitalism by the BPP and the LRBW; his focus on worldwide revolution and the field Negro by all of his major legacy organizations; and his challenge to sexism by almost none of them.[16] With respect to the latter, although Malcolm elevated women to leadership in the OAAU, "no clear pattern of women's leadership was established for the organizations that claimed Malcolm's legacy" (Woodard, 1999, p. 123). Just as notably, these legacy organizations adopted many of the shortcomings in Malcolm's analysis: his reverse civilizationism was adopted by Us, the RNA, CAP, and the PAOCC; and his failure to link the black revolution with previous black revolutionary initiatives in the United States was evident in all the major BPM organizations.

Malcolm's successors often did not appreciate or sufficiently capture in their revolutionary theses and programs the valences and inconsistencies in Malcolm's thesis, which modified, challenged, and in some cases even contradicted almost every one of the major orientations that they adopted. Adherents of Malcolm's thesis on black revolution insufficiently appreciated its varied dimensions and stages, as well as its major shortcomings, and as a result fell prey to its deficiencies. Three were particularly salient: (1) Malcolm's reverse civilizationism, which informed his black nationalism and his thesis of black revolution; (2) his failure to fully appreciate the role of African American culture in the social transformation of African Americans, including their revolutionary initiatives in the United States; and most importantly, (3) his failure to appreciate the revolutionary antecedents in African American history to inform revolutionary praxis in the 1960s. Each of these shortcomings would confound the major BPM organizations that derived their analyses of black revolution from Malcolm X.

The problems in Malcolm's conceptualization of black revolution in the United States were indicative of historical difficulties in articulating a cogent and coherent thesis of black revolution dating back to the nineteenth century. They reflected the challenge for theorists and activists to devise such a thesis that appreciated the peculiar political economic development of U.S. society and the role of blacks in each phase of its development as slaves, landless peasants, proletarians in a split labor market, and consistently a culturally debased racial minority population in a white supremacist society that was nominally free. These difficulties were not unique to Malcolm X, but many analysts, activists, and scholars also misunderstood the processes operative in black liberation struggles tracing back more than a century, including those that would assist the BPM in realizing its revolutionary objectives. Ironically, W. E. B. Du Bois's *Black Reconstruction*, which was published in 1935, provided a historical example of black political revolution in the United States, and one which implied a thesis of black cultural revolution as well. Thus, as Malcolm X was arguing the necessity of black cultural and political revolution while looking abroad for examples of both, there was an extant thesis of both that was as relevant as it was ignored. Du Bois's thesis is the subject of chapter 3, but before taking up that issue, it is important to examine the intellectual roots of Malcolm's revolutionary thesis that so strongly influenced the BPM, black nationalism. As noted above, black nationalism is rarely analyzed as a dynamic, multifaceted ideology, but it is important to understand it conceptually and historically in order to appreciate Malcolm's thesis of black revolution—and especially his argument on black cultural revolution in the United States, which was its centerpiece. It is to these issues that we turn in chapter 2.

Chapter 2

Black Nationalism

Civilizationism and Reverse Civilizationism

As noted in the previous chapter, Malcolm X's thesis on black revolution in the United States was rooted in his black nationalism. Malcolm saw nationalism as the major progressive force in U.S. politics as well as in contemporary revolutions throughout Africa and Asia. Post-NOI Malcolm saw black nationalism as a broad, dynamic, and evolving ideology having political, economic, and social dimensions. Malcolm had been reworking his theoretic and programmatic conceptualization of black nationalism from the millenarianism of the NOI to the revolutionism of his post-NOI conception. It was this bedrock black nationalism that was the theoretical framework of the Black Power Movement (BPM) and the impetus for its most important political objective: black revolution in the United States. While Malcolm's black nationalism provided the impetus for his revolutionary theorizing, it also transferred its shortcomings to his thesis of black revolution and those of subsequent BPM revolutionists who adopted it; and the most deleterious shortcoming was Malcolm's reverse civilizationism.

Civilizationism, in the context of black nationalism, is Moses's (1978) characterization of the tendency within classical black nationalism, which throughout the nineteenth century endorsed a sanguine view of the developmental efficacy of Western "modernization"—including proselytizing the assumedly "heathen" Africans—to provide industrial and technological development for Africans in the colonies, ostensibly under the direction of African American emigres, especially, industrialists, technicians, teachers, and missionaries. Classical black nationalism, Moses reminds us, depicted enslaved African Americans as uncultured displaced Africans and viewed indigenous Africans in similar benighted terms. Although classical black nationalists often advocated emigration for enslaved blacks, they actively supported the overthrow of slavery, as well, and fought for the extension of the civil rights of blacks in the North. Nevertheless, guided by their civilizationism, classical black nationalists, in Moses's view, endorsed repatriation to Africa not only to free blacks from racial oppression—including racial slavery—in the United States, but to bring American Christianity and technology to "backward" African "heathens." The latter goal reflects what Moses refers to as the cultural assimilationism of classical black nationalism, which employed the cultural arrogance—though without the racial supremacy—of the prominent arguments of Western imperialists. This orientation toward territorial separation (i.e., emigration) and cultural assimilation (i.e., civilizationism) was shared by black nationalists from Martin Delany to Alexander Crummell to Henry McNeal Turner, and characterized much of its "golden age" from 1850–1925 (Moses, 1978). Moses acknowledges that Du Bois (1903) modernized black nationalism from the emigrationism and Anglophilia of the classical era to incorporation of positive conceptions of African and African American culture. While hailing both the roots of civilization in Africa as well as the prominent contributions of African peoples and their culture to world history, Du Bois affirmed and highlighted the importance of African American culture in the United States, as well. African American culture was constituted, in part, from African cultural retentions such as found in the Black Church but, more directly, it derived from black folk culture, which was incubated in—and emerged from—the slave plantations and was becoming increasingly urbanized in the early twentieth century, especially during the Great Migration.

Seemingly oblivious to Du Bois's arguments more than a half-century earlier affirming African American culture, rejecting civilizationism, and establishing black *cultural* nationalism, Malcolm's reverse civilizationism denied African American culture while inverting the teleology of civilizationists: instead of Africans being "behind" African Americans developmentally, as the civilizationists had argued, the reverse was true (i.e., *reverse* civilizationism). Malcolm was convinced that African American revolutionary thought and praxis languished behind that of Africans who were engaged in revolutionary struggles on the continent and that this was in part owed to black Americans' lack of cultural identity. As a result, Malcolm's thesis on black nationalism—and the thesis of black revolution that emerged from it—was hamstrung by its reverse civilizationism, which subsequent BPM activists and theorists who followed Malcolm adopted as well. Attributing much of this "backwardness" to black Americans' lack of culture and their failure to recognize and practice their basic "African-ness," nearly all the major organizations of the BPM advocated reverse civilizationism to some degree, and its adoption explains African Americans' open advocacy of African "traditions," "customs," languages, dress, and aesthetics, during the BPM. Such tendencies led Cruse (1967, p. 557), among others, to admonish "Negroes to cease romanticizing Africa and pre-feudal tribalism," while castigating reverse civilizationists whose "readiness . . . to lean heavily on the African past and the African image" he viewed as "nothing but a convenient cover-up for an inability to come to terms with the complex demands of the American reality" (ibid., p. 554).

The shortcomings of Malcolm's and subsequent BPM activists' rendering of black nationalism were not specific to them, but were evident among analysts and advocates of black nationalism in general. Some of these shortcomings were rooted in the dualities of black nationalism itself, both as a concept and as a specific program for black liberation. There was/is a tendency of both analysts and activists to view these dualities as contradictory, requiring adoption of one aspect and the rejection of the other instead of viewing them as potentially mutually constitutive, complementary, or simply as multiple dimensions of the ideology that might be usefully synthesized. Three of these dualities with respect to black nationalism stand out. First, is the duality reflected in statist and nonstatist definitions of black nationalism. Second, and related to the first, is the distinction between emigrationist and non/anti-emigrationist aspects of black nationalism. Third, is the duality represented by the contrasting Eurocentric and Afrocentric (or, better, Anglophilic and Afrophilic) cultural orientations in black nationalism; specifically, the tension between centering the cultural orientation of black nationalism on replicated European/white cultural forms—especially European American religious conceptions, liberal democracy, and market practices—as opposed to grounding it in African/black cultural, political, and economic forms. The latter duality is represented in large part by the civilizationism of classical black nationalism and its rejection in modern black nationalism, which posits, inter alia, a distinct African American culture. Appreciating these historic and contemporary dualities in black nationalism provides a context for understanding how and why Malcolm adopted and modified his conception of black nationalism in specific ways, and how his choices informed those of subsequent BPM activists and the theses on black revolution they proposed.

For antinationalists and many other critics of black nationalism, these dualities do not reflect the richness and diversity of black nationalism as an ideology, but instead demonstrate its contradictory and even destructive tendencies, suggesting its inability to cohere at the level of political ideology, much less to serve as an organizational or mobilizing basis for black liberation. For example, one grossly misleading claim is that black nationalism is inherently sexist, a viewpoint often proffered by liberals, integrationists, Marxists, and assorted antinationalists while ignoring the sexist practices common to their own perspectives. For example, the most enduring sexist institution in black communities has been the Black Church, which, although black nationalist in its founding and early years, throughout the twentieth and early twenty-first centuries it has been a center of liberalism and integrationism. Although the Black Church has been liberal and integrationist for the last century, the implications for these ideologies of black women's toiling in every major activity in the church with little hope for advancement in its hierarchy do not typically include the charge that they are inherently sexist.

Liberal, integrationist, and Marxist sexism is often overlooked or minimized by focusing on black nationalist groups such as the NOI as prototypal, for example, or by ignoring sexism endemic in the labor movement and in Marxist organizations such as the Communist Party (Jones, 1948), or in the Black Panther Party, whose leadership included Eldridge Cleaver, a rapist and untransformed misogynist who was elevated by the White Left as the "voice" of black liberation. The prevalence of sexism in the most important White Left organization of the 1960s, SDS (Students for a Democratic Society), is rarely associated with its ideology (see Barber, 2008). In contrast, even sexist statements (as opposed to policies or practices) from black nationalists endure in a way unlike those of non-nationalists. For example, the oft-repeated reference to Stokely Carmichael's comment on the allegedly "prone" position of women in the Student Non-Violent Coordinating Committee (SNCC) are not only lifted out of its context, but it is seldom noted that it was asserted at a time when he and SNCC were integrationist or "radical democrats." It is rarely cited as evidence of the "inherent sexism" of integrationism or radical democracy as ideologies. Carmichael's appointments of black women to leadership positions is infrequently highlighted, as is the recognition that it was in its presumably black nationalist black power phase that SNCC articulated an unequivocal black feminist perspective in SNCC member Frances Beal's (1970) enunciation of her seminal thesis on "double jeopardy," which laid the basis for subsequent intersectionality perspectives (e.g., Crenshaw, 1989).

It is only with respect to black nationalism that female subordination is viewed as among the core principles of the ideology. The contributions of Mary Shadd Cary, Mary Bibb, Adelaide Casely Hayford, Henrietta Vinton Davis, Amy Ashwood, Amy Jacques Garvey, Audley Moore, Dara Abubakari, Amina Baraka, or Adjoa Aiyetoro to black nationalist feminism typically are ignored because they belie the view of the irreconcilability of black nationalism and feminism. At times, the feminism of black nationalist women is attributed to "internationalism," which is excised from black nationalism. Given that international/transnational elements and orientations have been embedded in black nationalism since its founding, then, to excise internationalism from black nationalism is to lift black nationalism out of its own history (see Henderson 2018b). Thus, antinationalist feminists are among those who contribute to silencing black nationalist feminists' voices, activism, and contributions to theory. Black nationalism is imagined as embodying patriarchy in its core precepts, presumably unlike the patriarchy in liberalism, integrationism, radical democracy, Marxism, or progressive ideologies—"progressive" being an adjective rarely applied to black nationalism.

Such unabashedly uninformed and misleading views regarding black nationalism, which are so prominent in academic discourse on black nationalism, are not limited to analyses of black nationalism and feminism but redound to a broader tendency of many scholars to dismiss black nationalism as a viable ideology of black liberation and to ignore or reduce its dynamic multidimensionality to self-negating contradictions, apparently impervious to theoretical synthesis, treating black nationalism as static and one-dimensional. Some of the apparent contradictions arise from the dualities mentioned above, but they also reflect challenges stemming from the dynamic context of the U.S. sociopolitical economy in which black nationalism has been incubated. Nevertheless, it is clear, as Hanes Walton pointed out decades ago, that black nationalism may be the most misunderstood ideology in the United States. Therefore, it's important to challenge inaccurate preconceptions of black nationalism—as well as outright misrepresentations of the ideology in the literature—in order to demonstrate both Malcolm's contribution to its development as well as the shortcomings in Malcolm's perspective, which would inform subsequent theses of BPM activists.

In the following sections, I review each of these apparent inconsistencies and explain how they represent dualities within a singular ideology, black nationalism, and discuss how black nationalism promotes black revolution, both historically and during the BPM. First, I define black nationalism and situate this definition in the broader political science literature on nationalism. Given the contrasting definitions of nationalism—some insisting that nationalism must have as its objective sovereign statehood and others that it does not have to—then by defining *black* nationalism we begin to address the dualisms outlined above, recognizing its logical coherence and multidimensionality as an ideology. I also examine the related issues of whether black nationalism is synonymous with a commitment to emigrationism, and discuss Eurocentric and Afrocentric conceptualizations of the constituent elements and orientation of black nationalism. Second, I examine Du Bois's conception of black nationalism at the outset of the twentieth century, which provided a theoretical synthesis of several of the dualities in black nationalism. Du Bois's modernized black nationalism—as opposed to the classical black nationalism of the eighteenth and nineteenth centuries—emphasized the importance of African American culture; and it proffered, inter alia, a particular form of revolution: black cultural revolution. Malcolm X and subsequent BPM activists reversed some of the Du Boisian contributions to both black nationalist theory and the black revolutionary theses that derived from it. The major result of this reversal was that while it asserted the importance of cultural factors in the black freedom struggle, it promoted a largely imagined and ahistorical African culture while failing to seriously consider liberating aspects of African American culture. As a result, it posited a theory of black cultural revolution in the United States devoid of a demonstrable and relevant black American culture to propel it. The lack of appreciation of historical and contemporary African American culture to the BPM also contributed to the failure to recognize antecedents of black political revolution in the United States—e.g., the Slave Revolution of the U.S. Civil War, which a study of black culture would reveal. At minimum, such a focus on black culture—and Du Bois's cultural thesis in particular—would provide a point of departure for BPM revolutionists attempting to theorize—much more to engage in—revolutionary struggle in the United States.

Nationalism and Black Nationalism

Black nationalism in the United States is an ideology that maintains that black Americans constitute a nation, and that this nation has the right to determine the political entity that governs it. While straightforward, this definition is hardly undisputed. For example, one of the most cited definitions of black nationalism is Essien-Udom's (1962, p. 6):

> the belief of a group that it possesses, or ought to possess, a country; that it shares, or ought to share, a common heritage of language, culture, and religion; and that its heritage, way of life, and ethnic identity are distinct from those of other groups. Nationalists believe that they ought to rule themselves and shape their own destinies and that they should therefore be in control of their social, economic, and political institutions.

Acknowledging that his definition identifies an ideal type and that no black nationalist organization "wholly conforms" to it, he adds that "although black nationalism shares some characteristics of all nationalisms, it must be considered a unique type of separatist nationalism seeking an actual physical and political withdrawal from existing society" (ibid., p. 7). Moses (1996, p. 2) agrees with this basically statist definition of black nationalism, especially that which emerged in the "classical era of black nationalism" from 1850–1925.

For him, classical black nationalism may be defined as "the effort of African Americans to create a sovereign nation-state and formulate an ideological basis for a concept of national culture." He adds that "the essential feature of classical black nationalism is its goal of creating a black nation-state or empire with absolute control over a specific territory, and sufficient economic and military power to defend it." Clearly, Moses views black nationalism—essentially its classical variant—in statist terms.

Moses also acknowledges different connotations of the concept, noting a few pages later in the same volume that "in a broader sense, it may indicate a spirit of Pan-African unity and an emotional sense of solidarity with the political and economic struggles of African peoples throughout the world" (ibid., p. 20). But, in general, Moses does not accept "nonstatist" definitions of nationalism. For example, he argues that David Walker's thesis, which viewed blacks as constituting "a nation within a nation" and called for slave insurrection on the basis of what amounts to national self-determination, was not black nationalist because Walker did not support black statehood nor emigrationism. Similarly, he notes that Maria Stewart "clearly viewed black Americans as a nation" and "possessed a religiously based black nationalism," which viewed blacks "as a modern Israel in Babylon," but, like Walker, "she opposed the idea of territorial separatism" either in the form of colonization in general or the Back to Africa movements in particular, thus failing "to carry her nationalism to its ultimate logical expression of territorial separatism" (Moses, 1990, p. 161). He concluded that Stewart's ideology "therefore lacked the geopolitical ambitions of the true nationalist" (ibid.).

Moses distinguishes classical black nationalism from "modern" black nationalism with respect to the former's advocacy of Anglophilia and territorial sovereignty, and the latter's promulgation of an affirming African American culture and nonterritorial or nonsovereign objectives. Modern black nationalism became synonymous with black cultural nationalism by asserting African American culture as its centerpiece and eschewing the Anglophilia of the classical period. It also advocated political autonomy, while demurring on the necessity of establishing a territorial state. The former closes a breach in classical black nationalism first identified by Moses, but the latter betrays the essential characteristic of black nationalism—and all nationalisms—for Moses, the objective of acquiring a territorial state. Pinkney (1976, p. 2) seems to disagree slightly with Moses; and while not eschewing statist definitions of black nationalism, he notes that such definitions "appear to be narrowly applicable to nationality in the sense of nation-states, rather than to the aspirations and actions of national minorities within already existing states." For him, "historical circumstances and the specific social conditions of a country determine the form in which nationalism manifests itself" (ibid.).

These forms range from a drive for "complete separation from the dominant group and the right to establish a nation-state of its own, either in a part of the territory of the host society or in a different area," to the demand for "some degree of control over the social institutions which are ostensibly responsive to their needs" (ibid.). Focusing mainly on black nationalism of the 1960s, he argues that it rests on unity, pride in cultural heritage, and autonomy—but not necessarily statehood.

For Carlisle (1975, p. 158), black nationalism is less an ideology than a "cluster of related ideas," which has discernible features that are comparable to European forms of nationalism, while manifesting doctrines peculiar to African American history. He argues that nationalism "presumes a black nation existing unassimilated alongside the American nation" and, borrowing from Shafer (1955), he argues that nationalists focus on "a territory, a language and culture, common institutions, sovereign government, a common history, love for fellows, devotion to the nation, common pride, hostility to opponents, and hope for the future." He notes that certain points recur regularly in nationalist discourse, including an "emphasis on African past glories, rejection of white association, rejection of miscegenation, advocacy of high personal morality, interest in pan-African unity, elevation of black womanhood, pride in standards of beauty unique to the black race, and interest in and support for the education of blacks" (Carlisle, 1975, p. 6). He insists that "beyond a shared national identity there is little which can be said to unite black nationalists" and "perhaps the most common feature of those advocating black nationalist ideas has been the ideal of overcoming black powerlessness in the American context by setting up mechanisms of self-determination." While "for some, revolution or emigration to a black state seemed the proper approach," and "[o]thers preferred the slow and careful building of separately controlled black institutions," nevertheless, "[a]ll sought control of their own destiny and liberation outside the white-dominated society" (ibid.).

Bracey et al. (1970, p. xxvi) embrace a broad conceptualization of black nationalism, which, for them, describes "a body of social thought, attitudes, and actions ranging from the simplest expressions of ethnocentrism and racial solidarity to the comprehensive and sophisticated ideologies of Pan-Negroism or Pan-Africanism." They add that "the concept of racial solidarity is essential to all forms of black nationalism," and racial solidarity is "the simplest expression of racial feeling that can be called a form of black nationalism" (ibid.). Van Deburg (1997, pp. 3–4) recognizes that "[black] nationalism can be blended with a host of related 'isms' and approaches—to better address the specific needs of individual adherents or to . . . adapt to changed social conditions." He adds that "[n]ationalists can lean either to the right or the left of their customary place on the political spectrum" and "can be 'classical' or 'modern'—sometimes even 'neo' or 'proto'"; and "[t]heir issue orientation may tend toward territorial, religious, economic, or cultural concerns" (ibid., p. 4). A "common denominator" for Van Deburg, whether "nationalism is expressed in demands for territorial cession, political empowerment, or increased cultural autonomy" is the "high value" it places "on self-definition and self-determination" (ibid., p. 2).

The diverse and even contrasting views on what constitutes black nationalism are reflective of the broader argument on nationalism in the political science literature. To be sure, a preponderance if not a majority of nationalist scholars seem to be of the opinion that nationalism seeks to reconcile the nation with a state, which is captured in Gellner's (1983) famous definition of nationalism as the doctrine that the political unit (the state) and the cultural unit (the nation) should be congruent. Thus, on the one hand, the prevalent view in the social science literature is that nationalists seek to possess a state, which ties nationalism to political sovereignty as an objective. This is evident across the political spectrum among liberals such as Woodrow Wilson, conservatives like Elie Kedourie, and socialists such as Lenin, Luxemburg, Stalin, and Hobsbawm. On the other hand, scholars such as Hutchinson (1987) argue that different types of nationalism (in this case, political and cultural nationalisms) have different orientations toward statehood. In one of the most popular political science formulations, Smith (1991, 73) defines nationalism as an "ideological movement for attaining and maintaining autonomy, unity and identity on behalf of a population deemed by some of its members to constitute an actual or potential 'nation.'" He points out that the "core doctrine" of nationalism does not include the acquisition of a sovereign state (ibid., p. 74). He insists that nationalism is "an ideology of the nation, not the state," which "places the nation at the centre of its concerns, and its description of the world and its prescriptions for collective action" (ibid.). He acknowledges that early nationalists including Rousseau, Herder, Achad Ha'am, and Aurobindo "were not particularly interested in the acquisition of a state, either in general or for the nation with whose aspirations they identified" (ibid.). He is emphatic that the "notion that every nation must have its own state is a common, but not a necessary, deduction from the core doctrine of nationalism" (ibid.). Thus, a statist conception of nationalism is "neither necessary nor universal" (ibid.).

Smith's view is echoed in the more recent work of political scientists, such as Snyder (2000), which posits that while nationalism may have a civic or ethnic orientation, neither necessitates statehood and they might seek sovereignty or autonomy within a federal framework. For Snyder, "defining the aim of nationalism as achieving a sovereign state would seem to exclude the seeking of political rights short of sovereign statehood by cultural groups"; and "these broader meanings are an integral part of the thing people call nationalism" and "common parlance links these phenomena not out of confusion, but because they have related causes, dynamics, and consequences, which a theory of nationalism . . . ought to try to capture" (2000, pp. 22–23). For Snyder, nationalism is "the doctrine that a people who see themselves as distinct in their culture, history, institutions, or principles should rule themselves in a political system that expresses and protects those distinctive characteristics. A nation is, therefore, a group of people who see themselves as distinct in these terms and who aspire to self-rule" (ibid., p. 23).

Similarly, black nationalism, conceptually, like nationalism in general, has both statist and nonstatist orientations (Price, 2012), and historically has had aspects of both as well. This doesn't reflect any internal incoherence in black nationalism as an ideology but, instead, mirrors the particular historiography of African American political development. For example, while Moses (1990, p. 36) endorses statist definitions of *pure* black nationalism, he recognizes that there are more inclusive forms of black nationalism as well:

> In its purest form, American black nationalism is concerned with territorial separatism and with the establishment of a separate government. In its more inclusive forms, it is broadly concerned with the codification and maintenance of culture and ideology to reflect realities of black American history and to serve as a guide towards a happier future.

What unites the two perspectives is the broadly accepted nationalist maxim that the social and the political should be congruent. Both statist and nonstatist conceptions of nationalism accept this maxim; however, the congruence of the social and political units can be achieved through either their reconciliation in a sovereign state or in an autonomous polity within a state. Thus, black nationalism, like nationalism in general, can seek either sovereign statehood or nonstatist/sovereign autonomy in a federal arrangement. Further, black nationalism reflects the range of political options available to blacks in the United States who sought their freedom as Africans (and their descendants) who had been captured and taken from Africa to enslavement in the Americas. These options are evident in the prominent strategies of early black nationalists, such as Paul Cuffee, who proffered a "dual colonization" program entailing African American emigration to Africa and/or their establishment of autonomous settlements in territory in North America. The statist and nonstatist aspects of black nationalism reflect the nuance and historical specificity of the form of nationalism that emerged among diasporic Africans in the United States.

The differences in the definition of black nationalism with respect to its statist and/or nonstatist dimensions are related to differences among scholars on the origins of black nationalism in the United States. This is expected given that scholars who assume a statist basis of black nationalism would likely only locate its ideological origins with those articulating an objective of acquiring statehood while scholars focusing on nonstatist black nationalism would do likewise with respect to non-state-based orientations. Thus, not surprisingly, there are clear differences among scholars on the origins of black nationalism in the United States, which are associated with disagreements on what constitutes black nationalism as an ideology in the first place. For example, Stuckey (1972, p. 2) associates black nationalism with a quest for autonomy among African Americans and suggests it was "surely as old as the 1600's," although it "crystallized" as an ideology during the 1830s and 1840s. In fact, he argues that "[i]n the period from the 1780s to the 1830s, nationalists dominated the ranks of Afro-American leaders" (ibid., p. 214). Also associating black nationalism with a quest for autonomy in either state or nonstate political formations, Pinkney (1976, p. 3) traces "black nationalist sentiment" to the first documented slave conspiracy in the United States in 1526. For Carlisle (1975, pp. 16–23), the roots of black nationalism are evident in Paul Cuffee's emigrationist and settlement efforts in the early 1800s. Miller (1975, pp. 93–94) also traces nationalism to the late eighteenth and early nineteenth century in the persons of Paul Cuffee, Newport Gardner, Richard Allen, and Samuel Cornish, but notes that Woodson was "the first to articulate a genuine nationalist-emigrationist creed and place it in a coherent ideological framework" between 1837 and 1841 (ibid., p. 94). In a co-edited volume, Meier and Rudwick disagree with Bracey on the roots of black nationalism. While they all seem to agree that "nationalist sentiment" first became prominent in "Negro thought" in the 1790s (Bracey et al., 1970, pp. xxv–xxvi), Meier and Rudwick seem to view black nationalism as emerging from the 1840s and 1850s (1971, p. xxxv), while for Bracey its developoment has been "persistent and intensifying, from 1787, if not earlier, to the present" (ibid., p. lvii). Brotz (1992) traces black nationalism to the emigrationism of the early nineteenth century.

Moses (1996, p. 6) argues that black nationalism is "one of the earliest expressions of nationalism" and insists that "while it originated in unison with the American and French Revolution, it was not an imitation of North American or European nationalism." Though often paralleled to Zionism—especially in its emigrationist variant—black nationalism preceded Herzl's articulation of the Zionist desire for a homeland for the Jewish diaspora, which at the time lacked a consensus territorial base. He acknowledges that a "dearth of contemporary writing makes it impossible to determine precisely when African Americans began to develop a nationalistic ideology"; nevertheless, "evidence of such thinking predates the American Declaration of Independence" (ibid., p. 7). Moses traces the contours of black nationalism from the proto-nationalism of the 1700s to its classical nationalist phase which "came into existence at the end of the eighteenth century" (ibid., p. 6). Acknowledging proto-nationalistic drives for self-determination in the Brazilian quilombist republic of Palmares, which existed for more than a hundred years and withstood armed aggression by Europeans as well as engaged in international diplomacy with the Portuguese and Dutch, he cites similar cases of nationalist self-determination drives among Maroon societies in Jamaica, South America, and North America, but he does not argue that slave uprisings were necessarily expressions of black nationalist ideology as much as discontent with conditions of servitude (ibid., pp. 6–7). Rather, he focuses on a 1773 emigrationist appeal of free Africans in Boston who sought to set aside one day a week in which to earn money to return to Africa. Though lacking a sense of "national destiny" or an intent to create a "nation-state" or a "distinctive national culture" (thus its designation as "proto-nationalistic") it is a clear call for self-determination in a context of racism in its allusion to Africans in Latin America whose conditions the emigrationists contrasted with their own (ibid., p. 7).

In 1787, Prince Hall led a delegation that petitioned Massachusetts with a plan for resettlement in Africa to relieve themselves of the "disagreeable and disadvantageous circumstances they faced in America as well as for "[b]oth Christianizing and 'civilizing' the indigenous peoples, setting up missionary schools, and establishing domestic and international commerce" (Moses, 1996, pp. 8–9). Moses sees the goals of the Hall delegations' petitions as an expression of pan-Africanism "in the sense that they linked the concerns of African Americans to the advancement of African peoples on the African continent" (ibid., p. 9) and acknowledges that this internationally or transnationally focused pan-Africanism has been a key element of black nationalism since its inception, which belies the view of those who attempt to excise "internationalist" thought/practice from black nationalism (Henderson, 1997). Moses traces this nascent black nationalism through the emigrationism of Cuffee as well as the messianism of Maria Stewart and David Walker, who both spoke of a national destiny of black Americans, while eschewing emigration. Notably, he characterizes the ideology of David Walker—Stuckey's prototypal nationalist—as "stateless," which for him, disqualifies Walker as a classical black nationalist. For Moses, Blyden was the most influential proponent of classical black nationalism in the nineteenth century, followed by Delany, Garnet—as well as non-African-oriented emigrationists such as Holly and Ward (Haiti), and Shadd (Canada)—and exemplified in Alexander Crummell and Henry McNeal Turner. Garvey is the last of the major classical black nationalists of the golden age, for Moses. Although Du Bois, for Moses, is disqualified as a classical black nationalist given his lack of support for emigrationism, he represents a turning point toward modern black nationalism.

In sum, although the prominent view in the political science literature is that nationalism may endorse a range of objectives related to political autonomy, rather than an exclusive focus on sovereignty, there is a prominent statist bias in much of the scholarly literature on black nationalism. The result is that nonstatist forms of black nationalism often are construed as not actually nationalist. Such a conclusion is not only myopic but ahistorical, limiting our ability to trace the actual contours of black nationalism from its origins to its present manifestations. The statist bias in analyses of black nationalism contributes to a related one that argues that black nationalism is essentially emigrationist, and we examine that flawed assumption in the next section.

Black Nationalism and Emigrationism

The statist bias in analyses of black nationalism is associated with the view that black nationalism is inseparable from black emigrationism. For example, David Walker is Stuckey's seminal black nationalist who in his *Appeal* to enslaved Africans to insurrection asserted that "enslaved children of Africa will have, in spite of all their enemies, to take their stand among the *nations* of the earth" (1830, p. 15). He also asserts that the "full glory and happiness" of black people "shall never be fully consummated, but with the entire emancipation of your enslaved brethren all over the world," and the "greatest happiness" of black people could only be derived from "working for the salvation of our whole body," such that, according to Stuckey (1987, p. 135), Walker "helped to establish the rationale for pan-Africanism." But this important black nationalist also adamantly eschewed emigration, which for some analysts is the sine qua non of black nationalism. For example, Moses (1996, p. 69) asserts that Walker's *Appeal* "despite its continuing popularity with black nationalists, cannot be said to represent classical black nationalism, because it does not call specifically for a separate nation-state." In this quote we can see how the conflict about the centrality of emigrationism to black nationalism is tied to the statist versus nonstatist dispute discussed above. Interestingly, earlier Moses (1978, p. 38) argued that Walker was a "fervent black nationalist" who, "like most black nationalists of the nineteenth century, blended radical and conservative elements in his philosophy, advocating violent means to achieve fundamental changes in the nature of American life." Walker, like Douglass after him, according to Moses, "belonged to that tradition of black nationalists who militantly asserted their right to American citizenship." He adds that this tradition "exemplifies the distinction between nationalism and emigrationism" (ibid.). Walker's nationalism, in Moses's earlier formulation, was evident even as "he opposed colonization, emigration, racial separation, and laws prohibiting intermarriage" (ibid.).

Walker is emblematic of pre–Civil War black nationalists whose ideology Moses views as "pragmatic," that is, not necessarily tied to emigration, but culturally assimilationist in its appeals to "Christianizing" and "civilizing" Africa, "and not as clearly distinct from colonizationists as the emigrationists would have liked to appear"—a recognition of Walker's civilizationism (Moses, 1978, p. 45). We can infer from Moses, then, that while Walker might have been a black nationalist, he was not a *classical* black nationalist; therefore, in Moses's statist, if not emigrationist, prerequisite for black nationalism, Walker's *Appeal* does not seem to qualify. Moses's more developed argument on the subject suggests that "in a broader sense [black nationalism] may indicate a support of Pan-African unity and an emotional sense of solidarity with the political and economic struggles of African peoples throughout the world" (1996, p. 20). Nonetheless, in evaluating Walker's nationalism he notes that Walker viewed African Americans as a "nation in bondage," but since Walker did not, in Moses's view, "advocate a separate national destiny," and—in spite of his revolutionary rhetoric—he held out the possibility that with God's Providence blacks and whites should become a "united and happy people," then Walker's *Appeal*, for Moses, is "not compatible with classical black nationalism, which always aimed at the creation of a separate nation-state" (ibid., p. 15). This argument reflects Moses's statist criterion for black nationalism; however, as argued above, like nationalism in general, black nationalism has both statist and nonstatist orientations—the latter such as those proposed by Cuffee or Woodson and arguably Walker, as well as postbellum Exodusters and twentieth-century black nationalists of the BPM who advocated separate black settlement in the United States.

Historically, black nationalism is not synonymous with black emigrationism. Moreover, the bias that reduces black nationalism to emigrationism typically misses the dual aspect of black nationalist emigrationist arguments. First, it assumes that black nationalists assert that there is little reason to pursue citizenship rights in the United States since white supremacism is so entrenched that blacks could never be fully integrated in U.S. society much less achieve full political and economic rights. Antinationalist critics often view this tendency as defeatist, justifying the abandonment of black liberation struggles in the United States or, worse, the abandonment of enslaved blacks to their lot. Second, it argues that an independent African state or states could produce goods to compete with "King Cotton" and undermine the economic basis for slavery, thereby transforming the United States as a whole. The second aspect of emigrationist strategy is usually neglected by antinationalists. In its place is either the contention that black emigrationists were simply escapists or, worse, that they were seeking to colonize Africa themselves and to set up a similar arrangement as white slavemasters in the United States but this time with émigré black Americans dominating the indigenous Africans. The historical example of Liberia shows that for some emigrationists this last charge was not without merit. For, coupled with a civilizationist discourse, some emigrationists sought in Africa the black equivalent of the "white man's burden," and they expropriated land and lives in the name of Christianizing the African "heathen." However, while the practices of some African American settlers are deserving of opprobrium, they constituted an extremely small portion of black emigrationists. Further, some of the worst policies of the Americo-Liberians, in particular, attracted the censure of black emigrationists such as Crummell—although he shared the view of the *mission civilatrice* for the black race and saw himself as an agent of a benign black imperialism of sorts.

More telling is the emigrationism of Mary Shadd Cary which was no imitation of the white man's burden. She had no intention of "civilizing" black natives or exploiting them (or other indigenous peoples). Instead, her emigrationism was focused on Canada and the opportunities that it allowed for black settlement and the development of institutions of black uplift (more below). But Shadd Cary disappears from the discourse of antinationalists because (1) to focus on her is to problematize emigrationism itself and turn it away from Africa and notions of "escapism" to absent oneself from the liberation struggle of African Americans; and (2) she is among the most important first wave feminists, which on its face challenges the view that black nationalists are inherently sexist. Shadd's emigrationism was clearly related to engagement with abolitionist struggle and her focus on Canada West was consistent with her view of the need to construct a meaningful stopping point on the Underground Railroad.[1]

Emigrationism simply cannot be reduced to an escapist desire to return to Africa or some other international destination, but it should be understood as a strategy focused on two fronts: Africa (or another region, such as Canada or the Caribbean) and the United States. The former advocates emigration out of the United States while the latter focuses on the establishment of black sovereignty or autonomy within the United States. But some view the focus on autonomy within the United States as not quite legitimate within the panoply of black nationalist objectives. To be sure, in its classical era black nationalism was strongly tied to emigration, but even at that time this dual focus was present, evident in Cuffee's request for both the establishment of a settlement in an African colony, as well as a colony on the frontiers of the emerging U.S. republic, while advancing a strategy to industrialize Africa and to undermine U.S. slavery. Cuffee's "dual colonization" sought the establishment of a black settlement in Africa as well as a separate territory in the United States (Miller, 1975, p. 47). This is evident in a letter of August 7, 1816, to Samuel Aiken wherein Cuffee makes clear that he sought to convince Southern planters that it was in their interest to "provide means to effectively abolish the Slave trade and then free their Slaves and Colonyze them either in America or Africa or in both places or free them and give them their plantation to work on . . . until such time as they are capable of managing for themselves" (Bracey et al., 1970, p. 39). In a subsequent letter of January 8, 1817, to Robert Finley, Cuffee (1970, pp. 44–45) again notes with favor the desirability of an African or American site for black settlement:

> [I]f there were a spot fixed on the coast of Africa, and another in the United States of America, would it not answer the best purpose to Draw off the coulored Citizens. I think it would be a good Plan, that Vessel and suitable Persons, to discover which Place would be most advantageous to colonize these people.

Miller (1975, p. 47) notes that Cuffee's "dual colonization scheme would also provide undefined opportunities for those free blacks bound inexorably by race and humanity to their enslaved brethren in the South," and concludes that "[m]ost likely, Cuffee thought independent black colonies would demonstrate to white Americans the capabilities of blacks. Perhaps he also held nascent free labor views—that free labor produce and goods could, if patronized, challenge the economic underpinning to the slave South" (ibid.). Miller is clear that Cuffee, who "demonstrated nationalistic tendencies which prefigured the full-blown nationalism of the 1850's" (ibid., p. 52) was "the first black of stature to connect colonization with emancipation" (ibid.). Carlisle (1975, p. 21) also acknowledges the dual colonization plan of Cuffee, and that nationalists considered alternative locations for the prospective colony for emigrating blacks including Africa, the Caribbean, Latin America, and autonomous enclaves within the United States (ibid., pp. 4–5). It is important to note that if Miller and Carlisle are correct, then the connection between emigration and emancipation is evident in the earliest forms of black nationalism in the eighteenth rather than the nineteenth century.

The black nationalist Henry Highland Garnet called for the establishment of "a grand centre of negro nationality, from which shall flow the streams of commercial, intellectual, and political power which shall make colored people respected everywhere" and argued for its establishment in either Africa or the Americas (see Moses, 1998, p. 25; Stuckey, 1987, p. 183). In 1848, Garnet (pp. 201–202), who in 1843 made an open call for insurrection among slaves in the South in order to eradicate slavery, was a serious opponent of emigration and argued emphatically that

> America is my home, my country, and I have no other. I love whatever good there may be in her institutions. I hate her sins. I loathe her slavery, and I pray Heaven that ere long she may wash away her guilt in tears of repentance. . . . I love my country's flag, and I hope that soon it will be cleansed of its stains, and be hailed by all nations as the emblem of freedom and independence.

He even favored the reopening of the slave trade if necessary, to effect his desired slave insurrection: "Let them bring in a hundred thousand a year! We do not say it is not a great crime, but we know that from the wickedness of man God brings forth good; and if they do it, before half a century shall pass over us we shall have a Negro nationality in the United States" (quoted in Stuckey, 1987, p. 183). But Moses (1978, p. 38) notes that Garnet's attitude shifted dramatically within the next few months, leading him to write in February 1849 that "I am in favor of colonization in any part of the United States, Mexico or California, or in the West Indies, or Africa, wherever it promises freedom and enfranchisement." He then became one of the most ardent supporters of emigration for the remainder of his life. Clearly then, emigrationism, when seen through the lens of those black nationalists who actually advocated it, was an emancipatory and not escapist pursuit and the duality of nationalism is evident among nineteenth-century nationalists such as Garnet, Delany, and Crummell who were both champions and detractors of emigrationism in their lifetime.

For many blacks—including some of the most prominent black nationalists—emigrationism dovetailed too comfortably with the racist views of the American Colonization Society (ACS), established in 1817, which sought to solidify slavery by deporting free blacks and in this way removing a persistent aggravant on the structure of the slave system. Racist ACS founders such as Henry Clay were vocal in their denunciation of abolition and their espousal of black inferiority. But black emigrationists preceded the ACS and usually advocated a selective—and completely voluntary—repatriation of selected blacks to Africa simultaneously with a commitment to the continuation of the liberation struggle in the United States. They simply put little faith in white America to live up to its creed, and they admonished blacks to fight on two fronts—at home and abroad. Nevertheless, the convergence of black nationalist views with racist ventures would haunt black nationalism through the Garvey movement and the NOI. Critics of black nationalism would rightfully assail such associations but, too often, attempt to project such a critique onto black nationalism as a concept or ideology, in a type of guilt by association linking selected nationalists with white supremacists, in ways such critics were not likely to treat Stalin's pre–World War II alliance with Hitler as a meaningful critique of Marxism *as an ideology*, or Carrie Chapman Catt's support for white supremacism as a meaningful critique of feminism *as an ideology*, or Mao's rapprochement with Richard Nixon as a meaningful critique of Maoism *as an ideology*, or U.S. slavery as a meaningful critique of liberal democracy *as an ideology*. What is often lost is an appreciation of black nationalism *as an ideology*; thus, the appropriate focus in considering its value as an ideology is an examination of it as a concept, rather than as a biography of individuals (or groups) that may be associated with it. Once this is realized, then it is evident that black nationalism is the original ideology of African Americans; and at its most progressive and radical it has been an emancipatory ideology in the United States.[2]

Further, as influential as black emigrationism was in the nineteenth century, several key black nationalists did not support its goals, while several integrationists—the ideological counter to nationalists—advocated emigration. For example, Delaney, who Cruse (1967) argues was the prototypal black nationalist, shifted his sites for emigration from Liberia and Nigeria, to Central and South America and even the U.S. frontier. In fact, Delany opposed emigration until roughly the passage of the Fugitive Slave Act in 1850 (the beginning of Moses's classical period), but he subsequently served in the Union Army before becoming involved in Democratic Party politics in the South where he was harangued as the "nigger Democrat." As noted above, Garnet, whom Moses views as a classical black nationalist, argued for both slave insurrection and emigration.

Black nationalists did not share the view that emigrationism was a cornerstone of their ideology, nor did they agree on the site for their colonizationist schemes. For example, Samuel Ringgold Ward and Reverend Holly sought settlement in Haiti, Mary Shadd Cary viewed Canada as a site for black emigration, while African Methodist Episcopalian (AME) Bishop Henry McNeal Turner sought colonization in Africa. Even Frederick Douglass, for most the archetypal integrationist, flirted briefly with Haitian emigration, although for most of his life he was an adamant opponent of colonization. Eventually his integrationism would lead him to eschew racially named organizations, institutions, and initiatives; and even aspects of his personal life were consistent with his integrationist views given his marriage to a white woman.

Where Douglass sometimes invoked nationalist rhetoric toward integrationist ends, Mary Shadd Cary employed emigrationism for integrationist ends, creating a conflation of perspectives that confounds analysts attempting to pigeonhole black nationalism under a simplistic monolith. For example, she advocated black emigration to Canada but often quarreled with fellow emigrationist Henry Bibb's initiatives to create independent black schools there because she supported racially integrated schools. Her emigrationism may be viewed as instrumental to her integrationist goals, in which she apparently found no contradiction. Silverman (1988, p. 99) recognizes her "long-held preference for integration" and "her lifelong goal" of achieving equality "for all black men and women," yet, "[t]o achieve this she was ready at various times during her life to endorse emigration and even separate institutions" (ibid., p. 100). Rhodes (1999, p. 87) situates Shadd's contending perspectives in her black nationalism, and argues that she

> cultivated a black nationalist ideology that was dependent on identification with a nation-state—in this case British North America. Traditionally the ideological basis of nationalism has its roots in a people's ties to a geographic region which they feel entitled to possess. Black nationalism, as it evolved in the nineteenth century, was less connected to a particular nation-state than to the unifying ties of skin color and culture. Shadd's nationalism blended these two impulses: blacks could not hope to possess and control Canada, but could claim their rightful place within a nation state that promised them equality and citizenship. At the same time, she believed that the political, social, and cultural unification of black people was essential for their survival. Shadd shared Martin Delany's advocacy of an autonomous black political force that could fight white supremacy from beyond the borders of the United States. But she was fundamentally at odds with Delany's romance with Africa as the "Fatherland," and his assertions of black hegemony.

Alexander Crummell's advocacy of emigrationism and black statehood ebbed after his nearly twenty years' service in Liberia where black American émigrés, Americo-Liberians, replicated the Southern plantation system and systematically oppressed the indigenous peoples so thoroughly that their yoke was not thrown off until 1980—and then only temporarily. Yet, Crummell's nationalism became stateless and anti-emigrationist as he laid the basis for the Talented Tenth orientation of Du Bois and the establishment of the American Negro Academy, of which Du Bois was a member. So, by the end of his life, Crummell, one of the fathers of classical black nationalism, seemed to no longer fit that designation. Moses (1989, p. 295) is clear that "Crummell eventually abandoned all activities on behalf of a black American nation-state and became downright abusive toward those who attempted to revitalize emigrationism after the end of Reconstruction." Nevertheless, he continued to employ a nationalistic rhetoric, to refer to black people as "a nation within a nation," and to speak of the "destined superiority of the Negro." Moses is clear that Crummell "obviously did not remain a black nationalist" and near the end, "he seemed uncertain whether he was advancing 'black power' ideology or a continuing accommodation and cultural assimilation" (ibid., p. 296). This type of ideological vacillation even among committed individuals resulted from the vicissitudes of their own individual biographies, which is why black nationalism—like any ideology—is not the biography of an individual but the biography of a concept.

Not only nationalists but integrationists, their ideological counterpoise, manifest apparent ambivalence in their ideologies over their lifespans. There is probably no better example than the prototypal black integrationist William Whipper, who at one time admonished against using any "complexional" markers in organizations, in general, or even those comprised of blacks or oriented toward black uplift, advocating instead a "color blind America" (Stuckey, 1987, p. 204). For example, he lobbied on behalf of the right of whites to participate in the antebellum black conventions. Although he "was willing to sign his name to, and perhaps help draft, a nationalist declaration" that "declared that the black population of America constituted something of a nation" (ibid.), within a year, Whipper "began to move toward . . . a position of calling for the dissolution of organizations with complexional features," and he put forth a declaration at the 1865 meeting of the convention movement to "abandon the use of the word 'colored' when either speaking or writing concerning themselves; and especially to remove the title African from their institutions, the marbles of churches, etc." (ibid.). Nevertheless, Stuckey observes that "at the time Delany was purging whites from the ranks of the African Civilization Society, of which he had become an important member, William Whipper joined the organization" (ibid., p. 231). The transformation of the most noted integrationist from colorblindness to nationalism is indicative of the challenges black leaders faced in an America whose basic creed promised freedom but whose basic practices enshrined, institutionalized, and celebrated white racism. Stuckey (p. 231) put it thusly:

This is a measure of the continuing strength of racism and perhaps the supreme example of how black leaders kept their options open, refusing to be frozen in ideological time when living in a world of shifting realities. Whipper's movement towards nationalism makes it clear that even his earlier stand for a color-blind America was not and could not have been a permanent one for a man of his intelligence and sincerity, which suggests precisely what occurred: his adjusting of strategies to meet perceived change or rigidity in oppressing structures, the jettisoning of a course pursued for years. Given American racial realities, a change was at least as likely to occur in the attitudes of black leaders as in the objective conditions of the times.

But it was not only the changes in the objective conditions of the times but also in the articulation of white supremacism, which is partly a response to the challenges of black organization and the reformulation of racism in response to them. Moses (1989, p. 295) appreciates this in his consideration of the transformation of Crummell away from nationalism, which he attributes to inconsistencies derived from the vagaries of a racist United States rather than intellectual shortcomings on the part of Crummell. He is emphatic that the black nationalism of Crummell—and by implication, black nationalism, in general—has been "marked by certain inconsistencies, but they derived from the inconsistencies and hypocrisy of American racism," insofar as "it was impossible to create an ideology that responded rationally to an irrational system."

In sum, it should be obvious at this point that black nationalism is not reducible to, nor synonymous with, emigrationism. Historically, black nationalism has both proposed and opposed emigration, and even when it has advocated it, destinations often varied. Further, none of the major black nationalist orientations pursued emigrationism for escapist reasons, but largely as a concomitant of a concerted strategy for black liberation in its broadest sense.

Eurocentric and Afrocentric Orientations of Black Nationalism

The third duality within black nationalism reflects the extent to which its cultural orientation is Afrocentric or Eurocentric, and bears directly on the issue of Malcolm X's—and subsequent BPM activists'—reverse civilizationism. Specifically, this tension focuses on whether black nationalism in its origins, especially, is rooted in African American or European American culture. For example, Stuckey insists on the African-centered roots of black nationalism expressed in the "slave culture" of the black masses of the antebellum South, while Moses argues that it was rooted in Anglophilic civilizationism terms of a largely Northern black clerical elite. Stuckey (1972, p. 1) argues that the originators of black nationalism "emphasized the need for black people to rely primarily on themselves in vital areas of life—economic, political, religious, and intellectual—in order to effect their liberation." He observes the "desire for autonomy" among a significant number of blacks evident as far back as the 1600s, but black nationalism in his conceptualization "crystallizes around the 1830s." Stuckey views David Walker's *Appeal* as "the most all-embracing black nationalist formulation to appear in America during the nineteenth century." The call of his *Appeal* for African peoples to overthrow their oppressors, to rule themselves, to see themselves as a nation within a nation, to transcend their ignorance born of their subjugation, to take responsibility for their own liberation, demonstrates that "there is scarcely an important aspect of Afro-America nationalist thought in the twentieth century which is not prefigured in that document" (ibid., p. 9).

He traces the evolution of black nationalism from Walker's *Appeal* and Robert Young's *Ethiopian Manifesto* (published months apart), through Lewis Woodson, who was a teacher of Martin Delany, and who argued for the moral elevation of black people, while noting their creativity and decrying the disunity among them. Woodson called for a "general convention" of black leaders to construct enduring institutions, including a national one. His most distinctive contribution, according to Stuckey, "was his exhortation to his people to move to the countryside, to form separate settlements" (1972, p. 15). The mysterious "Sidney" is next in Stuckey's pantheon of black nationalist leaders, followed by Garnet, who called for slave insurrection, the founding of black towns and settlements, as well as selective emigration to Africa—which he had earlier opposed. Delany is next for Stuckey, notable for his candid calls for black emigration, and he is followed by Crummell and other emigrationists. Interestingly, but not surprisingly, Stuckey notes the diversity among black nationalists and insists that there were no monolithic conceptions of the ideology projected by major nationalist forces in the nineteenth century (p. 28). In *Slave Culture*, Stuckey expanded the list of notable contributors to black nationalism to include Du Bois and Paul Robeson in the first half of the twentieth century, although with the glaring omission of Garvey, whom he regarded as among the "less sophisticated 'nationalist' thinkers" (1987, p. 229); nevertheless, he acknowledged that Garvey "affected the sense of African consciousness of more black people in Africa, the West

Indies, and the United States over the first forty years of the [twentieth] century" than any other (ibid., p. 350).

Stuckey is of the view that slave society synthesized an amalgam of African cultures in an African American cultural form, the remnants of which were manifest in such folk customs as the "ring shout," the "Buzzard Lope," "Pinkster festivals," trickster tales (e.g., Brer Rabbit and Red Hill Churchyard), burial practices, spiritually inspired water immersions (e.g., kalunga), and a host of other African retentions that ultimately were given American institutional forms. According to Stuckey, these customs provided the bedrock of African American culture, which endured through slavery and provided the commonalities that are the foundation of national consciousness.

Moreover, Franklin (1992) insists that the national consciousness of African Americans was reinforced by the commonality of racial oppression in terms of white exploitation of black productive and reproductive labor through racial slavery for the black majority in the South and racist discrimination of the black minority in the North, the destruction of black familial-based kin groups, the destruction of African cultural practices, and the imposition of European American cultural practices, which eventuated in a syncretic Aframerican culture. These factors combined to provide a sense of national identity among African Americans and a framework for their culture.

Stuckey's—and Franklin's—conceptualization of the Afrocentric roots of African American culture and its association with black nationalism contrasts with Moses's view that African American culture derived less from "slave culture" and more from the "high culture" espoused and practiced by free black intellectuals who were situated in prominent black cultural institutions such as the AME Church. For Moses, the black nationalism that emerged during the classical era drew less from slave culture—a notion that black nationalists such as Crummell abhorred—and more from the emigrationist arguments of free black intellectuals who were largely Anglophilic, elitist, and disparaging of both African American mass "culture" and the "barbarism" of continental Africans. This orientation, for Moses (1978), was just as evident in the nationalist and integrationist strands of black feminism as well, which informed their seminal views on black cultural transformation. In these conceptions, the ascendant culture to which blacks aspired was one that facilitated the acquisition of the technological attributes of material civilization associated with the "high culture" of white Europeans and white Americans, coupled with the "civilizing" influence of Christianity. This Anglophilic view was common to what might otherwise be viewed as the "progressive" if not "radical" tendencies of the nineteenth century. For example, it underwrote the assimilationist strains of black integrationism; but it also was not absent from Marxist views, which privileged the acquisition of Western material culture—especially Western industrial technology—as a precursor to the socialization of industrial workers into a proletarian class. Similarly, black feminist theorizing (both nationalist and integrationist) often promoted elitist Westernized conceptions of womanhood and excoriated the "peasant values" of many poor black women (Moses, 1978). Even among black nationalists of the nineteenth century, for whom "assimilation" should have been anathema, insurrectionists such as Walker (1829), restorationists such as Garnet (1843), and civilizationists such as Crummell (1898) articulated an ideology that even as it was territorially separatist was culturally assimilationist (Moses, 1978).

Such tendencies led to the primary contradiction of classical black nationalism for Moses: even as it posited itself as geopolitically separatist in advocating African emigration, it was culturally assimilationist in its advocacy of the "civilizing mission" of its emigrationist advocates exemplified in Crummell. Moses (1996, p. 1) argues that classical black nationalism "originated in the 1700s, reached its first peak in the 1850s, underwent a decline toward the end of the Civil War, and peaked again in the 1920s, as a result of the Garvey movement." While Stuckey puts great effort into delineating the process contributing to black nationalism, Moses pays closer attention to delineating its origins and distinguishing its types (e.g., classical and modern). But Moses's major contribution is his articulation of the contradictions within classical black nationalism. Among these are its focus, on the one hand, on the need for black uplift in the United States, given the depredations of slavery and racial discrimination, while, on the other hand, this uplift was assumed to require blacks' acquisition of the attributes of "civilization" associated with the very people who were oppressing them. That is, classical black nationalists enjoined blacks to acquire the "high culture" of their white—especially British—oppressors, and to promote the civilizing influence of Christianity to both enslaved African Americans and benighted Africans. Moses notes the contradiction between black nationalists' advocacy of geopolitical separation from white supremacists and their appropriation of the "civilizationist" discourse of white colonizationists.

Moreover, Moses (1990, p. 28) asserts, in contrast to Stuckey, that black nationalism was not born of African survivals and folkways among enslaved Africans in the U.S. South but from a culturally assimilationist, free black, largely clerical elite in the North with a messianic vision of black Americans' national destiny. Moses (1989, p. 9) acknowledges that "[t]here is no denying the continuity between black intellectual life and black mass culture in the United States," but he contends that it was not from "slave culture" that "the literate classes of black Americans derived their conceptions of what black culture ought, ideally, to become," but "from the English/American literary traditions." Therefore, for Moses, it was "necessary that we attempt to understand those aspects of nineteenth-century black culture that have their roots in places other than retained African folk traditions and slave culture." He insists that "[s]ome legitimacy must also be accorded to the perspectives of black men and women who not only experienced nineteenth-century black life, but who enjoyed sufficient knowledge and literacy to develop their own theories of black American culture, civilization, and destiny" (ibid.).[3] Thus, Moses rejects the argument that black nationalism emerged from African survivals and folk traditions of the slave quarters, and adds that there has been no systematic link established between black slave religion and black nationalism.[4] Instead,

> [b]lack nationalism was the creation of the Northern free-black community. Its ideology revealed no influence of an African priesthood, although it was clearly influenced by the "redeemer nationalist" rhetoric of the Northeastern clergy. Unlike their European nationalist counterparts, black nationalists were not obsessed with the search for cultural inspiration among the masses. It was more to their purposes to argue that the masses were deprived of all culture, including true religion because of the ravages of slavery. (1989, p. 28)

He cites Alexander Crummell's attitude as typical of this clerical elite's perspective toward the religion of the black masses:

> Their religion, both of preachers and people, was a religion without the Bible—a crude medley of scraps of Scripture, fervid imaginations, dreams, and superstitions. . . . The Ten Commandments were as foreign from their minds and memories as the Vedas of India. . . . Ignorance of the MORAL LAW was the main characteristic of "PLANTATION RELIGION!" (1989, p. 238)

For Moses, both black nationalism and black integrationism—as well as American nationalism—derive from a common source: American civil religion. Following Bellah (1967), Moses (1990, p. 29) notes that "[t]his was the myth of Americans as a chosen people with a message for the world and a covenantal duty to respect the enlightenment doctrines of political and economic freedom." He adds that the

> rhetoric of American messianism could be adapted to these three apparently conflicting purposes, because of the complexity

of Christian symbolism. The messiah is both a suffering servant and a King of Glory; both a protector of *chosen* peoples and a redeemer of *all* mankind. The rhetoric of American messianism could be modified by blacks to assert black militancy, to support racial harmony, and at the same time to instruct self-righteous white Americans, a chosen people, as to their covenantal responsibilities. (ibid., p. 29; original emphasis)

Bracey (1970) counters that a lack of historical documentation of a link between slave religion and black nationalism does not, in itself, demonstrate that such a link doesn't exist. Franklin (1992) challenges Moses on his own terms—primary-source documentary support—and marshals evidence from slave narratives and testimonies to support his argument that a nationalist consciousness emerged in the slave quarters in a manner similar to that which gives rise to working-class consciousness, helping to create black nationalist sentiments among slaves. The crux of the issue is what would constitute persuasive evidence of what is, in essence, public opinion among slaves where there are no published records, much less polling data: the writings of predominantly Northern black religious elites, or slave narratives and oral testimonies? Further, with regard to Moses's critique that there is no systematically established link between slave religion and black nationalism, there is no such link between civil religion and black nationalism either.

The putative relationship between civil religion and black nationalism should not be confused with that between American Christianity and black nationalism, which for Moses and many others is readily demonstrable from a review of primary sources. What is debatable is a relationship between civil religion and black nationalism. Civil religion, as a concept, is difficult to define, and even more difficult to measure as an analytical construct; and the thesis in which it is embedded doesn't appear to be falsifiable. To begin with, civil religion is not directly observable, but is inferred from documents and statements of political elites, such as the Declaration of Independence and the Gettysburg Address, as well as presidential inaugural addresses—and less so from actual practices. American civil religion, Bellah (1967, p. 8) insists, "is a collection of beliefs, symbols, and rituals with respect to sacred things and institutionalized in a collectivity" in the public sphere, which is evident "from the earliest years of the republic." It views the United States as a modern day Biblical Israel, "the promised land," in which "God has led his people to establish a new sort of social order that shall be a light unto all the nations." It presumably provides a "genuine apprehension of universal and transcendent religious reality . . . as revealed through the experience of the American people" (ibid., p. 12).

In referencing Bellah's disputed concept as "the main influence on black nationalism," Moses (1990, p. 28) does not point out that both historians and sociologists have challenged Bellah's concept and the thesis related to it. For example, Wilson (1979) views the concept as ambiguous and is skeptical of the historical support for Bellah's thesis. Fenn (1977, p. 507) raised the question of whether "religious symbols contributed an aspect or dimension of American nationalism or were in fact a separate and autonomous civil religion"? He acknowledged "some question as to whether the civil religion is essentially an elitist version of American nationalism which is more easily located in presidential speeches than in the ideas and values of the average citizen" (ibid.). He recognized that "there are serious problems of interpretation—for instance, the question of distinguishing rhetoric from serious communication, or literal usage from metaphor" (ibid., p. 508); and "formidable" analytical problems in determining "whether the civil religion is elitist or popular; whether it persists at all times or is the ideological response to times of crisis; and whether it is best located in official documents or can be found in less formal contexts" (ibid., pp. 507–508).

Bellah's civil religion is probably more accurately viewed as an aspect of U.S. political culture, specifically, an aspect of American nationalism. In fact, civil religion seems little more than a quasi-religious gloss on a race-based American nationalism that promotes itself as civic-based when it is actually part of an American ideology consistent with that which Hunt (2009) asserts has guided U.S. foreign policy since the country's founding, comprised of a myth of national greatness, white racism, and an anti-revolution bias. By invoking "civil religion," rather than "slave religion," as "the main influence on black nationalism," Moses might have unintentionally appealed not only to a nonfalsifiable construct that is unmeasurable even in its effects, but simply, as Fenn notes, to one that provides "definitions-of-the-situation" that cannot serve as causal factors generating outcomes such as American or black nationalism. Instead, to my mind, civil religion reflects descriptive elements of the American nationalism it is assumed to generate. Simply put, civil religion, to the extent that it exists, is an attribute or result of American nationalism rather than a cause of it; and given Moses's broader thesis and persuasive argument that black nationalism is not derivative of American nationalism—or any other form of nationalism—then Bellah's civil religion, which at most is an outgrowth of American nationalism, cannot be a cause of black nationalism, which is temporally prior to and logically independent of it.

Returning to Stuckey and Franklin, an important implication of their main points is that if the cultural aspect of black nationalism was imbricated in slave culture (i.e., indigenous African American mass culture), then Moses's privileging of Northern clerical elites in the genesis of black nationalism, while informed, is not dispositive of the issue. That is, given the temporal priority of slave culture over the later development of the black Northern clerical elite, the incubation of African American culture is more likely to have taken place in the slave quarters than the stained glass edifices of the North. Relatedly, the emphasis on the development of modern black nationalism as a function of the formulations of Du Bois reflects the recognition of the enduring slave culture that generated it. In addition, the centrality of black women to its development is readily apparent. In the context of the transformative capacity argument, the importance of black women in generating, articulating, and sustaining African American culture reflects the salience of black women in conceptions and practices of black culture, which is in contrast to Moses's focus on black Northern clerical elites, who overwhelmingly have been men.

The arguments of Stuckey and Moses highlight the contrasting views of black nationalism among two of the most learned scholars of the subject; however, rarely have scholars engaged the subject of black nationalism in the sophisticated, nuanced, and erudite manner of these authors, with their keen sense of synthesizing divergent views of advocates and detractors while poring through reams of primary source material in order to capture the voices of black nationalists themselves. For example, although Moses (1978) asserts that classical black nationalism can be "conservative," he is careful to qualify this point, especially as he confronts the radicalism of Walker and Garnet, who both call for wholesale slave insurrection, hardly a conservative objective. Further, the notion that blacks could effectively organize an independent state in the antebellum era, especially—the objective of emigration—coupled with a conception of black national destiny was inherently "nonconservative." Moreover, Moses (1996, p. 22) observes that classical black nationalists "were unequivocally committed to the development of Africa as an economic, industrial, and military power controlled by Africans"—again, hardly a conservative goal. Further, while Moses (1978, p. 10) asserts that black nationalism "assumes the shape of its container and undergoes transformations in accordance with changing fashions in the white world," he points out that black nationalism is "one of the earliest expressions of nationalism" and "while it originated in unison with the American and French Revolutions, it was not an imitation of North American or European nationalism" (Moses, 1996, p. 6). He is emphatic that the attempts of black nationalists to "construct a theory of history, a philosophy of religion, and an ideology of nationalism must not be misconstrued as unimaginative imitations of what white intellectuals were doing" (1989, p. 9). Such arguments and Glaude (2002), who maintain that black nationalism has a conservative bias and is a mimetic imitation of white nationalism or even white racism, typically through their antinationalist, and often ahistorical, research projects resting on myopic and ossified conceptions of black nationalism and a liberal ransacking of history.[5]

What many serious analysts fail to appreciate is that an understanding of black nationalism requires nuance that does not reflexively wed the concept to the *biography of black nationalists* as individuals, such as undertaken by Stuckey and especially Moses, but to the *biography of black nationalism*, the concept. Individuals may adopt, alter, and even reject ideologies throughout the course of their lives and with divergent contexts, which such change often precipitates, and may also transform their ideological perspective in light of different political developments. In contrast, ideologies are much more stable; open to change, to be sure, but resting less on the vicissitudes that affect individuals over their lifespan. To put it simply: nationalism is not the biography of nationalists, but the biography of a concept. In light of this, the challenge for analysts is to conceptualize nationalism as a concept but without unduly imposing on it a contrived structure predicated on what has been a dynamic intellectual, programmatic, and theoretical orientation. Both Stuckey and Moses appreciate the tendencies and trajectories in/of black nationalism, although they differ on its precise origins. At first blush, these differences appear to reflect a divergence of class focus between the scholars, with Stuckey focusing on the mass culture of mostly illiterate black slaves who formed the vast majority of black Americans for most of antebellum U.S. history and through their everyday practices of "slave culture" gave rise to black nationalism, and Moses privileging the elite culture of literate "free blacks" intent on developing a culturally based source of legitimacy, which provided the basis for their nationalist claims. Put simply, Stuckey focuses on the practical or mass origins of black nationalism and Moses on its intellectual or institutional origins. A concern with practical origins leads Stuckey to focus on black mass culture—slave culture, which he conceptualizes in Afrocentric terms—while a concern with intellectual origins seems to lead Moses to focus on black institutional elite culture, which he conceptualizes in Eurocentric terms. The resolution of these perspectives—actually a useful synthesis of the two—turns, to some degree, on the evidence of the persistence of Africanisms in the United States, which is supported by a broad literature located mainly in history, anthropology, ethnomusicology, and black studies (see Henderson, 1995). To a greater extent, it rests on which of several characterizations of African American culture are prevalent in the United States at any given time—whether it is viewed as African or European, at

States at any given time—whether it is viewed as African or European, at times irrespective of whether it was an actual African or European cultural retention; or a syncretic mix of diasporic African, European, and Amerindian cultures. Given this context, the resolution of the issue of the form of culture—Afrocentric or Eurocentric—upon which black culture is based, and modern black nationalism is situated, would be affirmed near the beginning of the twentieth century by Du Bois—a point on which both Stuckey and Moses agree.

Du Bois provided a modernized black nationalism, which asserted an African American cultural identity rooted in the commonality of African American experience epitomized and articulated in the sorrow songs and black folk culture of the U.S. South (i.e., Stuckey's slave culture). His analysis of "the souls of black folk" asserted the salience of black culture in U.S. society; and provided the basis for modern black nationalism, or black *cultural* nationalism, as opposed to classical black nationalism. The former, unlike the latter, no longer disparaged African cultures, but promoted them and those of their diasporic progeny, in particular, African American culture. Du Bois drew on these cultures as evidence of the inherent equality of black folk and to accentuate the achievements of black Americans in the cultural realm, and to recognize their possession of a culture that was in many ways superior to white American culture and one that could be a tool for black liberation. Thus, while one might usefully distinguish between classical and modern black nationalism, and accept that the former, following Moses, had important Eurocentric aspects—a view that Stuckey and Franklin reject—one may agree that modern black nationalism is more clearly Afrocentric.[6]

To be sure, for much of U.S. history, blacks were not viewed as possessing a culture—at least not in a meaningful sense. In two seminal works, "The Conservation of Races" (1897) and, more famously, *The Souls of Black Folk* (1903), Du Bois proffered initial arguments asserting the existence and persistence of an identifiable black culture rooted in black folk traditions epitomized in "slave religion" and reflected in the "sorrow songs." As discussed more fully below, he argued that this culture was not only central to black society, but central to U.S. society in general. Having established the parameters of black culture and its importance to the black community, he began formulating a thesis of black cultural change. In fact, beyond developing a thesis on black cultural change, Du Bois provided a basis for considering American national development through the impact of black culture. As a result, his work laid the basis for future conceptualizations of black nationalism, and also of black cultural revolution in the United States.

Du Bois and Modernized Black Nationalism

In "The Conservation of Races," Du Bois articulated the first major cultural nationalist statement on black political struggle in the United States and abroad. He maintained that "the history of the world is the history, not of individuals, but of groups, not of nations, but of races, and he who ignores or seeks to override the race idea in human history ignores and overrides the central thought of all history" (1897, p. 21). This thesis was tied to the prevalent view at the time that races have stable essences that are transhistorical; however, the progressive tendency in this view is Du Bois's eschewing the Anglophilic, cultural assimilationist arguments of his mentor Alexander Crummell in his argument that African culture reflected an ancient and glorious heritage of black people who had made major contributions to human history (an orientation he would develop further in *The Negro*, *Black Folk Then and Now*, and *The World and Africa*) although the "full, complete Negro message of the whole Negro race has not as yet been given to the world" (ibid., p. 23).[7] Du Bois did not espouse what Mazrui calls "African glorianna" or, for Moses, "Afrotopia"; instead, he recognized the importance that black people—and African Americans, in particular—not attempt to become pale imitations of Anglo-Saxons through the emulation of the latters' culture. In a statement prefiguring the closing words of Fanon's *The Wretched of the Earth*,[8] Du Bois admonished,

> If [Negroes] are to take their just place in the van of Pan-Negroism, then their destiny is *not* absorption by the white Americans . . . their destiny is not a servile imitation of Anglo-Saxon culture, but a stalwart originality which shall unswervingly follow Negro ideals. (1897, p. 23)

For Du Bois, it was incumbent upon blacks to assert their cultural values, carve out their cultural destiny, recognize their African cultural roots, and draw on their African American cultural practices. He was clear that only black people themselves could lead this transformation of the race and lift the banner of African people to the summit of world history. He stated that

> if the Negro is ever to be a factor in the world's history—if among the gaily-colored banners that deck the broad ramparts of civilization is to hang one uncompromising black, then it must be placed there by black hands, fashioned by black heads and hallowed by the travail of 200,000,000 black hearts beating in one glad song of jubilee. (ibid.)

He saw African Americans as an "advance guard" of this project of racial uplift and cultural transformation. But the double consciousness that he articulated so eloquently in *The Souls of Black Folk* was clearly a factor that confounded the process of black cultural transformation, since it left African Americans at a "crossroads" asking themselves the questions:

> What, after all, am I? Am I an American or am I a Negro? Can I be both? Or is it my duty to cease to be a Negro as soon as possible and be an American? If I strive as a Negro, am I not perpetuating the very cleft that threatens and separates Black and White America? Is not my only possible practical aim the subduction of all that is Negro in me to the American? Does my black blood place upon me any more obligation to assert my nationality than German, or Irish or Italian blood would? (ibid., p. 24)

The answers to these types of questions generated the vacillation and contradictions evident in black society; and to answer them he examined the race prejudice that kept the two nations—white and black—apart, with the black subjugated. He thought that, at its root, this prejudice reflected the difference "in aim, in feeling, in ideals" of two races and the friction that was common to interracial interactions. He continued:

> If . . . this difference exists touching territory, laws, language, or even religion, it is manifest that these people cannot live in the same territory without fatal collision; but if, on the other hand, there is substantial agreement in laws, language and religion; if there is a satisfactory adjustment of economic life, then there is no reason why, in the same country and on the same street, two or three great national ideals might not thrive and develop. (ibid.)

This led Du Bois to solve the "riddle" of what he would later call "double consciousness":

> We are Americans, not only by birth and by citizenship, but by our political ideals, our language, our religion. Farther than that, our Americanism does not go. At that point, we are Negroes, members of a vast historic race that from the very dawn of creation has slept, but half awakening in the dark forest of its African fatherland. We are the first fruits of the new nation. (1897, p. 24).

The culture of these "first fruits of the new nation" had yet to congeal around a distinct religious orientation in Du Bois's mind, but in a few short years he would assert the distinctiveness of black culture in religious terms, as well, and maintain that slave religion was the centerpiece of a distinct African American culture, whose institutional expression, the Black Church, was an African cultural retention in the United States, with the black preacher serving as no less than an African priest. In his exegesis of 1897, black people were African Americans, a nation within a nation that was not only identified by the range of skin color within the darker hues of humanity, but by a common culture and a shared purpose of racial uplift that would proceed from the cultural transformation of black peoples, which required recognition of the "gifts of black folk" and the special role that blacks had already played in world and U.S. history. For example, Du Bois saw blacks as

> that people whose subtle sense of song has given America its only American music, its only American fairy tales, its only touch of pathos and humor amid its mad money-getting plutocracy. As such it is our duty to conserve our physical powers, our intellectual endowments, our spiritual ideals. (ibid., pp. 24–25)

Du Bois then suggests the vehicle for the "conservation" of the black race: "[A]s a race we must strive by race organization, by race solidarity, by race unity to the realization of that broader humanity which freely recognizes differences in men, but sternly deprecates inequality in their opportunities of development" (ibid., p. 25). Specifically, "we need race organizations: Negro colleges, Negro newspapers, Negro business organizations, a Negro school of literature and art, and an intellectual clearing house, for all these products of the Negro mind, which we may call a Negro Academy" (ibid.).

Du Bois advocated both "positive advance" and "negative defense," since blacks were "hated here, despised there and pitied everywhere" (1897, p. 25). He called on African Americans as the vanguard of this struggle, and stated that "there is no power under God's high heaven that can stop the advance of eight thousand thousand honest, earnest, inspired and united people"; but, he argued, "they *must* be honest, fearlessly criticising their own faults, zealously correcting them; they must be *earnest*." He was unequivocal that "[n]o people that laughs at itself, and ridicules itself, and wishes to God it was anything but itself ever wrote its name in history." On the contrary, "it *must* be inspired with the Divine faith of our black mothers, that out of the blood and dust of battle will march a victorious host, a mighty nation, a peculiar people, to speak to the nations of earth a Divine truth that shall make them free" (ibid.).

Du Bois's call was rooted in his understanding that the battle for the human rights of the oppressed would fundamentally transform U.S. society much more comprehensively than a battle for political spoils within a fundamentally flawed and inhumane society. His was one of the earliest statements on pluralism in the cultural sphere, which today we might refer to as multiculturalism; however, the brand of multiculturalism he advocated took seriously the view that blacks comprised a nation within the nation of the United States, and it held out the possibility that the two nations could coexist if the institutions of white supremacism were destroyed. Each of these components reflected Du Bois's modernized version of black nationalism. In contrast to classical black nationalism, which, while pan-Africanist, contained a powerful emigrationist orientation, modern black nationalism rested on more pluralist assumptions; although it did not reject emigrationism or state-centeredness altogether, it started from the premise that blacks comprised a nation and as such had the right of national self-determination. However, modern black nationalism suggested that self-determination could be realized either in a separate state, a politically autonomous formation, or possibly in a federal structure. Moreover, modern black nationalism rejected Anglophilia and the civilizationist claims of classical black nationalism, emphasizing instead the centrality of African American culture in its conception of the African American nation and its articulation of the prospect for African American political development in the United States. That is, modern black nationalism was black *cultural* nationalism; and black culture was African American culture.

In addition, modern black nationalism with its pan-Africanist underpinnings challenged imperialism as epitomized in Du Bois's "The African Roots of War" in 1915, in which he argued that white workers in the metropole were not only racist toward nonwhite workers at home, but had fused their interests with those of their respective national bourgeoisies to find common cause in the exploitation of Africans (and Asians) abroad. Thus, modern black nationalism appreciated the role of class dynamics in the international and domestic spheres—and also the gradations of class in black America. It assailed the racism of white workers and rejected the assumption of both a "natural alliance" among workers across races or genders as well as the role of the white proletariat as the vanguard of a revolutionary struggle both abroad and in the United States, as most Marxists envisioned. For Du Bois, World War I was the result of disputes over imperial acquisitions in the colonial world that reflected this commitment of white labor to national imperialism, and white workers' willingness to find common cause with white commercial and political interests to subjugate nonwhites. The Red Summer of 1919, shortly following the war, saw attacks by white mobs on blacks in more than three dozen cities and towns across the United States and reflected the continued commitment of white workers to utilize terrorism, murder, rape, and mayhem against darker proletarians. Du Bois's thesis on imperialism and World War I prefigured and predated, and is usefully contrasted with Lenin's *Imperialism: The Highest Stage of Capitalism*, which was published the following year (Henderson 2017a).

In demonstrating that there was a rich African American culture, derived in part from seminal and enduring African cultures—represented by the diverse cultures of the continent—Du Bois nullified the Eurocentrism inherent in civilizationism, excising both from black nationalism. Modern black nationalism, after Du Bois, asserted the centrality of black American culture and forswore the civilizationism of classical black nationalism. It was this orientation toward black American culture, essential to modern black nationalism—indeed, its defining construct—that Malcolm X and black revolutionists of the 1960s implicitly rejected, reversing Du Bois's arguments in their claims that black Americans had no culture worthy of the name, and were fundamentally behind their African brothers and sisters in that regard (i.e., reverse civilizationism). Malcolm's reverse civilizationism owed its existence in no small part to the impact of Garveyism on Malcolm's initial conception of black nationalism, and its lingering impact on Malcolm's acolytes even as he began to embrace aspects of the modernized version.[9] Garvey's program was forward-looking in some of its pan-Africanist views, and progressive in its attacks on white supremacism in the global system, but, the Anglophilism of his "back to Africa" program was no less prevalent. The forward-looking project included fighting for the citizenship rights of black Americans—especially black workers of the industrialized northern United States where Garveyites were well represented during the Great Migration, and its backward-looking project reflected the civilizationist program of the classical black nationalist era aimed at emigration and racial uplift of benighted Africans. These contrasting aspects of Garvey's program contributed to Moses's view of Garveyism as having one foot in the twentieth century and the other in the nineteenth. Moreover, Garvey's suggestion that the fate of Africans in the diaspora was incumbent upon their development of Africa and/or repatriation to the continent reflected the reverse civilizationism that Malcolm X would embrace decades later.[10]

While the largest black nationalist organization, the Universal Negro Improvement Association & African Communities League (UNIA & ACL), failed to fully adopt the modernized version of black nationalism, in contrast, leaders of the earliest black Marxist organizations, such as the African Blood Brotherhood (ABB), seemed more accepting of it. In particular, the head of the ABB, Cyril Briggs, proclaimed that blacks constituted a "nation within a nation"—almost two decades before Du Bois's more famous essay; and, more significantly, former ABB member Harry Haywood proffered a "Black Belt Thesis" that would become a centerpiece of Communist Party theorizing in the interwar era, and the theoretical impetus for the domestic colonialism thesis that underwrote much of the political theory of the black power era. Haywood's perspective relied on an appreciation of black Americans as a nation with the right of self-determination, including secession, and marked the clearest and most compelling statement by the Communist Party in both the USSR and the United States on this issue. The Communist Party-USA's (CPUSA) abandonment of this view at the outset of the CRM—as well as repression from McCarthyism—helped relegate it as an organization into irrelevance during the CRM and the BPM. The importance of Haywood's thesis and its grounding in modern black nationalism warrants further consideration.

Haywood and a Black Marxist Perspective on Black Nationalism

Harry Haywood proffered a thesis on black nationalism in the United States situated within a broader Marxist conception. Haywood served in the all-black Eighth Regiment in World War I (and later in the Abraham Lincoln Brigade in the Spanish Civil War and the Merchant Marines in World War II). A former member of the ABB, in 1925 he joined the CPUSA and in that year became one of the few African Americans to study at Moscow's Communist University of the Toilers of the East (KUTVA). In 1927 he was the first black American student at the International Lenin School, where he met, among others, future Vietnamese leader Ho Chi Minh. From 1927 to 1938 he served on the Central Committee of the CPUSA and from 1931 to 1938 on its Politburo. Haywood helped formulate the draft of the Comintern's resolutions on "The Negro Question" of 1928 and 1930, which stated that blacks in the Deep South of the United States, the Black Belt, constituted an oppressed nation with the right of self-determination—including secession.

Haywood was convinced that African Americans in the Black Belt satisfied the criteria for nationhood enunciated in Stalin's (1913) "Marxism and the National Question": "A nation is a historically constituted, stable community of people, formed on the basis of a common language, territory, economic life, and psychological makeup manifested in a common culture." This view informed the Soviet policy of *korenizatsiya*, which as adopted in 1923 was aimed at promoting the indigenous cultures of the constituent national republics of the Soviet Union through the promotion of their local languages into the major spheres of public life, for example, encouraging their widespread use in education, publishing, cultural institutions, government affairs, and Party activities. It also entailed promoting representatives of these nationalities to positions in their administrative divisions and governing bureaucracies to reverse the forced Russification that these nations had been subjected to under czarist rule; even ethnic Russians who served in the local governments in these republics were compelled to learn the local language and culture. Typically, there was a delimitation of the national borders of the administrative and political units, following the criteria for nationality as outlined above, and *korenizatsiya* would be implemented thereafter. The demarcation of the Black Belt in the United States seemed to follow along this course, for Haywood.

In *Negro Liberation*, Haywood asserted that black nationalism was at the root of understanding the "real problem" of the Negro masses in the United States. He saw "the so-called racial persecution of the Negro in the United States [a]s a particular form and device of national oppression" (1948, p. 137). In particular, he noted that "[t]he secret to unraveling the tangled skein of America's Negro question lies in its consideration as the issue of an oppressed nation," which exists simultaneously "[w]ithin the borders of the United States, and under the jurisdiction of a single central government" (ibid., p. 140). Thus, the United States consists of "not one, but two nations: a dominant white nation, with its Anglo-Saxon hierarchy, and a subject black one"—a clear restatement of the "nation within a nation" thesis of classical black nationalists, and a slogan that Du Bois himself would adopt by the 1930s (ibid.). Further, "[u]nlike the white immigrant minorities, the Negro, wearing his badge of color, which sets the seal of permanency on his inferior status, cannot, under contemporary economic and social conditions, be absorbed into the American community as a full fledged citizen"; therefore, "the Negro remains in America a 'perpetual alien'" (ibid.). The Negro has been shaped "over the years" as "a distinct economic, historical, cultural, and, in the South, geographical entity in American life" (ibid.). Haywood is emphatic that "[t]he Negro is American" and that "[h]e is the product of every social and economic struggle that has made America"; nevertheless, he asserts that "the Negro is a special kind of American, to the extent that his oppression has set him apart from the dominant white nation" (ibid., pp. 140–141). Most importantly for our discussion here, Haywood affirms that "[u]nder the pressure of these circumstances, he has generated all the objective attributes of nationhood" (ibid., p. 141).

Given that they constituted a nation, Haywood asserted that African Americans in the South had the right of self-determination and that communists should support their claims. Specifically, blacks had a "national territory," which was the historical "Black Belt" South. Haywood's conception of black nationalism was rooted in his understanding of the prerequisites and prerogatives of black people in the peculiar context of American political, economic, and social development. Although they approached the issue from different ideological vantage points, in important ways Haywood's understanding of black nationalism converged with Du Bois's modernized version of black nationalism, in his recognition of the importance of African American culture in their formulations. For Haywood, this convergence is evident in his exegesis of "Negro" culture, which was one of the foundations of the black nation. Haywood focused on the cultural initiatives and institutions of the black nation that served as both change agents and precipitants of political mobilization. For example, Haywood (1948, p. 146) observed that "[a] common tradition and culture, native to Negro America, has been in the making since the first Negroes were landed at Jamestown." It had been forged in the "special history" of oppression of black Americans and their resistance against it, beginning with "the misery of the chattel slave sold from the holds of the slaveships into bondage where an unknown tongue prevailed," and including "more than two hundred heroic slave revolts and insurrectionary plots" (ibid., pp. 146–147). He added,

> The history of the Negro people has infused the Negro with hopes, ideals, customs, and traits which are blended in a psychology whose activities and aims move . . . toward freedom and equality. This psychology has been evidenced in slave revolts, in participation in the democratic wars of this country and in its political life, especially during Reconstruction, and in the . . . organizations which developed the liberation movement of modern times. (ibid., p. 147)

He was emphatic that

> [t]he entire development of Negro music, literature, poetry, and painting, of churches, fraternal groups, and social societies, bears the imprint of this struggle for liberation. The psychological as well as the economic need for continuous struggle to gain equal democratic status, to throw off the oppressive chains and assume the upright posture of a free people—this is and has been the dynamic of Negro culture. (ibid.)

Haywood wedded his argument to Du Bois's, which was articulated in the NAACP's 1947 "Appeal to the World" and stated:

The so-called American Negro group, therefore, while it is in no sense absolutely set off physically from its fellow Americans, has nevertheless a strong, hereditary cultural unity, born of slavery, of common suffering, prolonged proscription and curtailment of political and civil rights; and especially because of economic and social disabilities. Largely from this fact have arisen their cultural gifts to America—their rhythm, music and folk-song; their religious faith and customs; their contributions to American art and literature; their defense of their country in every war, on land, sea and in the air; and especially the hard, continuous toil upon which the prosperity and wealth of this continent has largely been built. (p. 147)

Haywood concluded that

[n]otwithstanding its many points of contact with the culture of the dominant white nation, this Negro culture has its own distinctive features. Thus there has arisen within the Negro community a socio-cultural structure corresponding to the status of fixed inequality forced upon him by the dominant white nation. There is among the Negro community a multiplicity of organizations, national and local, devoted to every field of human interest and endeavor: to education, to civil rights, to the special interest of various professional groups and of women, youth, veterans, and business enterprises. There is a Negro church which in many parts of the country is a social rallying point of the Negro community. (ibid., p. 148)

He drew on Drake and Cayton's (1945) description of Negro culture in Chicago's Bronzeville section and argued that the cultural patterns there have their "replica in Harlem, in Detroit's 'Paradise Valley,' in the Pittsburgh Hill section, in Los Angeles' Central Avenue, indeed in every Black ghetto in America, the greatest of which is the Black Belt itself" (1948, p. 149). For Haywood, "National Negro culture" was expressed "in a rich folk lore, in music, in the dance, in an expanding and virile theatre movement . . . a highly developed literature . . . in a rapidly growing press," and, importantly, "through whatever medium it manifests itself, this culture is built around themes of distinctly Negro life and Negro problems" (ibid.). This national Negro culture, for Haywood, emanated "from the heart of the masses of people welded together by like yearnings, stirred by the same causes, this culture expresses the deep-felt aspirations of the Negro people, their strivings to break through the walls of the Jim-Crow ghetto and to achieve recognized status as a free people."

Haywood also recognized the role of Negro artists, writers, dramatists, as well as Negro scientists and scholars such as Du Bois and Locke, among others, who helped give expression not only to the Negro's massive yet often hidden contributions to civilization in general but to U.S. history, in particular. Such scholars

> have done yeoman work in unearthing the Negro's pre-American past, in piecing together that broken line of Negro history and the contribution the black man has made throughout time and throughout the world. They have refuted the spurious race stereotypes depicting the Negro as a man without a past, without a history, and, therefore, unworthy of an equal place at the table of civilization. (1948, p. 150)

For Haywood, the "New Negro" of the Harlem Renaissance was evident in even greater numbers by the World War II era, and one of the factors propelling their prevalence was the development of the black industrial worker. He noted that "behind this new Negro is the emerging dynamic force of the Negro industrial working class, which is playing an increasingly important role in the councils of Negro leadership" (ibid., p. 151). While acknowledging some of the "non-progressive" features of Negro culture, which he described as "self isolationism" and "Negro particularism," he debunked notions that denied Negro nationality on the basis of its lack of a distinctive language, insisting only that the Negro practiced a common language though not necessarily an exclusive language. He was convinced that

> in the course of their three hundreds years' sojourn on the American continent, the Negroes have adopted the English language as their own in the same manner that they have adopted other institutions of the dominant American nation. They have become transformed from the enslaved descendants of various African tribes and nations . . . speaking different dialects and languages, into an ethnically homogeneous and tightly welded people. They are today a people strengthened and hardened by oppression and rapidly gaining maturity. (1948, pp. 151–152)

In fact, African Americans are "a nation within a nation," albeit "a young nation whose advance to political consciousness and strength is retarded by imperialistic oppression" of the United States in which it is situated, contributing to the "weak development of national consciousness" among blacks, which is also "characteristic of young nations" (ibid., p. 152). Yet, Haywood argued, "this very oppression is creating the basis for the rise of a fully conscious national movement among them" (ibid.).

Haywood's thesis marked a dramatic shift in Marxist conceptualizations of the African American liberation struggle. To be sure, Lenin distinguished the nationalism of oppressor nations from that of oppressed nations, and supported the former in his broader anticolonial vision; and he made positive parallels between national liberation struggles in the colonies and the black liberation struggle in the United States. In fact, in his 1920, "Preliminary Draft Theses on the National and the Colonial Questions," Lenin (1966a, 148) directed that "all Communist parties should render direct aid to the revolutionary movements among the dependent and underprivileged nations (for example, Ireland, the American Negroes, etc.) and in the colonies." Yet, this view was opposed by most American communists, including the leaders of the incipient CPUSA, who preferred to view black oppression as a problem of racial prejudice or in moral terms, and not as a result of national oppression. Further, Lenin's position regarding African Americans stood as a proposition, but it had not been fleshed out historically or developed theoretically as a black nationalist program within Marxism until Haywood's exegesis. To appreciate this more fully, it's important to trace how Haywood derived his thesis, which he first articulated in the 1920s and the CPSU adopted in 1928. According to him, it was rooted in an argument he had with his brother, Otto Hall, while they were both attending KUTVA (Haywood, 1978). Otto argued a prominent line among many CP members at the time—and most American Marxists—that "any type of nationalism among Blacks was reactionary" because it obscured the more accurate conception of blacks as a persecuted racial minority whose struggle should be viewed as one of workers within the broader class struggle that would be resolved through socialist revolution in the United States. While blacks should pursue political and social equality, theirs was a race problem, not a national problem. Thus, the struggle for equal rights for blacks outside of this framework—i.e., black nationalism—was a diversion that subverted working-class unity and could undermine the struggle for socialism in the United States. For Haywood, Otto's view—and the prominent ones among white American CP members—"saw only the 'pure proletarian' class struggle as the sole revolutionary struggle against capitalism"; but, for him, this "denial of nationalism as a legitimate trend in the Black freedom movement . . . amounted to throwing out the baby with the bathwater" (1978, p. 229). Rejecting his brother's contention—largely born of negative relations with the Garvey Movement—that black nationalism was a "foreign transplant," Haywood asserted that "[o]n the contrary, it was an indigenous product, arising from the soil of Black super-exploitation and oppression in the United States. It expressed the yearnings of millions of Blacks for a nation of their own" (ibid., p. 230). Although the Garvey movement had ended, black nationalism, in Haywood's view, persisted because it spoke to the interests and conditions of blacks in the United States, and it was likely to reemerge as a movement, "to flare up again in periods of crisis and stress" (ibid.). It was important for Marxists, then, to ensure that in the future black nationalism not be diverted by "the leadership of utopian visionaries" away from the "main enemy," U.S. imperialism; therefore, it was incumbent upon communists to present "a revolutionary alternative to Blacks" (ibid.). Thus, Haywood asserted, in contrast to Garvey's program, one that viewed "the U.S. Black rebellion" as focused on black self-determination centered in the U.S. South, "'with full equality throughout the country,' to be won through revolutionary alliance with politically conscious white workers against the common enemy—U.S. imperialism" (ibid.).

Haywood's orientation was not simply a pragmatic framework to supplant the appeal of Garveyism, but a well-formulated thesis on black nationalism that he synthesized with Marxism. In his autobiography, *Black Bolshevik*, Haywood relates the development of his synthesis and the centrality of black nationalism in the United States to it. He noted that "[t]he evolution of American Blacks as an oppressed nation was begun in slavery," but, mainly, "it was the result of the unfinished bourgeois democratic revolution of the Civil War and the betrayal of Reconstruction" in the Hayes-Tilden Compromise of 1877, which withdrew federal troops from the South, abandoned nominally free blacks to the Redeemer governments, compelled ex-slaves to return to the plantations as peonage farmers and institutionalized sharecropping, and subjugated them through the black codes and Jim Crow apartheid, as well as the terrorism of the Ku Klux Klan and other armed white supremacist groups (1978, p. 231). Following that,

> [t]he advent of imperialism, the epoch of trusts and monopolies at the turn of the century, froze the Blacks in their post-Reconstruction position: landless, semi-slaves in the South. It blocked the road to fusion of Blacks and whites into one nation on the basis of equality and put the final seal on the special oppression of Blacks. (ibid., pp. 231–232)

"These events," Haywood contended, foreclosed "[t]he path towards equality and freedom via assimilation," "and the struggle for Black equality thenceforth was ultimately bound to take a national revolutionary direction" (ibid., p.

232). Thus, "[u]nder conditions of imperialist and racist oppression, Blacks in the South were to acquire all the attributes of a subject nation" (p. 232). Nevertheless, "imperialist oppression created the conditions for the eventual rise of a national liberation movement, with its base in the South" and "[t]he content of this movement would be the completion of the agrarian democratic revolution in the South" with its important implication, "complete equality throughout the country" (ibid.).

For Haywood, African Americans

> are a people set apart by a common ethnic origin, economically interrelated in various classes, united by a common historical experience, reflected in a special culture and psychological makeup. The territory of this subject nation is the Black Belt, an area encompassing the Deep South, which despite massive outmigrations, still contained (and does to this day) the country's largest concentration of Blacks. (ibid.)

Haywood's "new analysis," which came to be known as the "Black Belt thesis," also "defined the status of Blacks in the north as an unassimilable national minority who cannot escape oppression by fleeing the South" because "[t]he shadow of the plantation falls upon them throughout the country, as the semi-slave relations in the Black Belt continually reproduce Black inequality and servitude in all walks of life" (1978, p. 232). Haywood was clear that

> [t]here are certain singular features of the submerged Afro-American nation which differentiate it from other oppressed nations and which have made the road towards national consciousness and identity difficult. . . . Afro-Americans are not only "a nation within a nation," but a captive nation, suffering a colonial-type oppression, while trapped within the geographic bounds of one of the world's most powerful imperialist countries. (ibid.)

He added that "[t]he Afro-American nation is also unique in that it is a new nation evolved from a people forcibly transplanted from their original African homeland. A people comprised of various tribal and linguistic groups, they are a product not of their native African soil, but of the conditions of their transplantation" (ibid.). These peculiarities were due, in part, to the circumstance that "Blacks were forced into the stream of U.S. history in a peculiar manner, as chattel slaves, and are victims of an excruciatingly destructive system of oppression and persecution, due not only to the economic and social survivals of slavery, but also to its ideological heritage, racism" (ibid.,

p. 233). The "race factor," as Haywood referred to it, not only perpetuated the doctrine of black inferiority and ensured that blacks would "remain permanently unabsorbed in the new world's 'melting pot,'" but it "also left its stigma on the consciousness of the Black nation, creating a powerful mystification about Black Americans which has served to obscure their objective status as an oppressed nation. It has twisted the direction of the Afro-American liberation movement and scarred it while still in its embryonic state" (ibid.).

Departing from Marxist arguments of the day, Haywood challenged its misconceptualization of racism as a concoction of the bourgeoisie to use as a wedge against a multiracial proletariat, making racism epiphenomenal of class dynamics. Haywood opposed such views and associated them with the white racism that his "new theory" rejected. He stated:

> The new theory destroys forever the white racist theory traditional among class-conscious white workers which had relegated the struggle of Blacks to a subsidiary position in the revolutionary movement. Race is defined as a device of national oppression, a smokescreen thrown up by the class enemy, to hide the underlying economic and social conditions involved in Black oppression and to maintain the division of the working class. (1978, p. 234)

Thus, race is employed not to deny class oppression but to obscure the national oppression of blacks. This mystification of race, class, and nation was even more evident when compared to the objective conditions transforming black America, the United States, and the international system. In reverse order, the mobilization and prosecution of World War I—the most destructive war in human history up to that time—which Du Bois, Lenin, and many other observers associated with imperialist rivalry; the bloody Red Summer of 1919, which saw white pogroms against blacks in more than three dozen cities and towns in the United States; and the onset of the Great Migration, which began the movement of millions of blacks from the South to the North and West, and the massive urbanization of blacks in the twentieth century. Haywood noted that "[c]onditions . . . were maturing for the rise of a mass nationalist movement," which came to fruition "with the rise of the Garvey movement" (1978, p. 233); but this "potentially revolutionary movement of Black toilers was diverted into utopian reactionary channels of a peaceful return to Africa" (ibid.). Nevertheless, he was resolute that "[t]he issue of Black freedom" remained "the most vulnerable area on the domestic front of U.S. capitalism, its 'Achilles heel'—a major focus of the contradictions in U.S. society" (ibid.). Haywood realized that

> [t]his new line established that the Black freedom struggle is a revolutionary movement in its own right, directed against the very foundations of U.S. imperialism, with its own dynamic pace and momentum, resulting from the unfinished democratic and land revolutions in the South. It places the Black liberation movement and the class struggle of U.S. workers in their proper relationship as two aspects of the fight against the common enemy—U.S. capitalism. It elevates the Black movement to a position of equality in that battle. (ibid., p. 234)

Thus, for black nationalists, anti-imperialism began "at home"—i.e., the battle for black national liberation was an anti-imperialist struggle in the United States. Haywood concluded that "Blacks, therefore, in the struggle for national liberation and the entire working class in its struggle for socialism are natural allies. The forging of this alliance is enhanced by the presence of a growing Black industrial working class with direct and historical connections with white labor" (ibid.).

Reflecting in his autobiography, Haywood argued that his "new theory was to sensitize the Party to the revolutionary significance of the Black liberation struggle," such that "[d]uring the crisis of the [1930s], a significant segment of radicalized white workers would come to see the Blacks as revolutionary allies" (1978, p. 234). While retrospection may have shone a brighter light on the extent to which the Black Belt thesis had the effect on white workers that Haywood suggests, it clearly made the most significant synthesis of Marxism and black nationalism in the United States and the basis for the domestic colonial perspective that would dominate the black nationalist arguments of the BPM. Situating this in our broader argument, what Haywood had done was to excise the civilizationism from Marxism itself. That is, the Marxist teleology was no less guided by a Eurocentric trajectory than its liberal counterpart—not only Marx's evolutionary stages, but his paternalistic view of colonialism as a modernizing force insofar as he assumed that it would lead to the creation of a proletariat in the colonial world, ultimately contributing to the overthrow of metropolitan power there. Du Bois (1935) demonstrated the fallacy of this assumption, and Robinson (1983) concurs, showing that one lesson of the U.S. Civil War and Reconstruction was that capital could extend to peripheral areas and result in underdevelopment rather than development—a view that Rodney (1974), among others, would substantiate more broadly for Africa.

Haywood's thesis became the policy of the Communist Party in the Soviet Union (CPSU) and, as a result, the CPUSA; adopted by Bolsheviks in 1928, it declined during the Popular Front era, before its lukewarm reacceptance in the immediate aftermath of World War II, and its final rejection by the CPUSA just prior to the onset of the 1960s signaled by the purging of Haywood from the Party. In its ultimate rejection of Haywood's thesis, the CPUSA was rejecting the revolutionary significance of black liberation struggles in the United States even as the CRM was demonstrating just such significance; and this—along with the devastation of McCarthyism—helped to ensure the practical and theoretical irrelevance of the CPUSA during the CRM and the BPM. But just as with black nationalism in the era, neo-Marxists would pose their own form of reverse civilizationism in their assumption that the vanguard of revolutionary struggle had passed from the white working class to the third world proletariat—or peasantariat—which "true" revolutionaries in the United States were enjoined to follow, and this undergirded the rationale of Maoists and Castroists that guided many revolutionists of the BPM. For Haywood, this orientation mandated that he wed his thesis not to the black urban masses, but to the rural blacks of the South. Thus, he opined that the organization of the black "peasantariat," consisting of sharecroppers, tenant farmers, and broader agricultural workers in the U.S. South, was essential to a successful revolution in the United States.

Constrained by the compulsion to mirror third world revolutions in the most advanced industrial country in the world, this aspect of Haywood's thesis was a throwback to nineteenth-century political economy, which was increasingly irrelevant to postwar black America. While Haywood appreciated the impact of the mechanization of agriculture, which was displacing unskilled and semi-skilled agricultural workers—and black agricultural workers in particular—he didn't modify his thesis to reflect the impact of this displacement on his assumptions about the salience of the peasantry in the revolution he envisioned. Even greater was the demographic impact of both World War II and the Second Great Migration that had further urbanized blacks in their dispersal from the South to the North and West, and their movement within the South from rural to urban areas. These would lead to such a transformation that by the middle of the BPM most black Americans were living in or adjacent to cities rather than in rural areas. The basic problem was that Haywood's thesis recognized the uniqueness of African American social development but at the same time assumed that African Americans needed to draw on the examples of successful revolutions in the third world rather than their own historical referents in the United States. Where novel creative theorizing was required to address the particularity of black America, such as Haywood had demonstrated in his Black Belt thesis, at this critical point in his theorizing, Haywood grafted from third world contexts that were not generalizable to the United States—especially the emergent black urban experience. Haywood's was not the only Marxist thesis proffering such a view within the BPM, but its implications for the BPM were immense.

Further, while Haywood's thesis rejected some aspects of Marxist civilizationism it was less attentive to other major weaknesses evident in Marxist formulations and organizations, such as those attendant to gender. Thus, while Haywood recognized his fellow Marxist Claudia Jones's inspirational support of his Black Belt thesis in a 1945 article in which she challenged the CPUSA leadership as they began to abandon it, he failed to address an important corollary of Jones's support, which was her assertion of the importance of gender in their analysis of U.S. society in general, and the prospects of the CPUSA in particular. In 1949, she argued in her seminal essay "An End to the Neglect of the Problems of the Negro Woman!," in ways that anticipated the intersectional analysis of the present period, that "Negro women—as workers, as Negroes, and as women—are the most oppressed stratum of the whole population" (Jones, 2011, p. 75). Further, she noted the rising militancy of "Negro women," which she viewed as an "outstanding feature of the present stage of the Negro liberation movement" especially in the face of the "intensified oppression of the Negro people, which has been the hallmark of the postwar reactionary offensive" (ibid., p. 74). She noted that

> [t]he bourgeoisie is fearful of the militancy of the Negro woman. . . . The capitalists know, far better than many progressives seem to know, that once Negro women begin to take action, the militancy of the whole Negro people, and thus of the anti-imperialist coalition, is greatly enhanced. (ibid.)

This relationship reflected, in part, the fact that

> [h]istorically, the Negro woman has been the guardian, the protector, of the Negro family. . . . As mother, as Negro, and as worker, the Negro woman fights against the wiping out of the Negro family, against the Jim Crow ghetto existence which destroys the health, morale, and very life of millions of her sisters, brothers, and children. (ibid.)

She continued:

> Viewed in this light, it is not accidental that the American bourgeoisie has intensified its oppression, not only of the Negro people in general, but of Negro women in particular. Nothing so exposes the drive to *fascization* in the nation as the callous

attitude which the bourgeoisie displays and cultivates toward Negro women. (ibid., pp. 74–75; original emphasis)

Nevertheless, for Jones, "the labor movement generally," "Left-progressives," and the "Communist Party" had grossly neglected this aspect of the liberation struggle.

She recognized, for example, that although "[i]n union after union, even in those unions where a large concentration of workers are Negro women, few Negro women are to be found as leaders or active workers" (2011, p. 78). This is all the more surprising given that "Negro women are among the most militant trade unionists," of which she provided examples (ibid.).

> The sharecroppers' strikes of the [19]30's were spark-plugged by Negro women. Subject to the terror of the landlord and white supremacist, they waged magnificent battles together with Negro men and white progressives in that struggle of great tradition led by the Communist Party. Negro women played a magnificent part in the pre-CIO days in strikes and other struggles, both as workers and as wives of workers, to win recognition of the principle of industrial unionism, in such industries as auto, packing, steel, etc. More recently, the militancy of Negro women unionists is shown in the strike of the packing-house workers and even more so, in the tobacco workers' strike . . . which led to the election of the first Negro in the South (in Winston-Salem, NC) since Reconstruction days. (ibid.)

She was unequivocal that "[i]t is incumbent on progressive unionists to realize that in the fight for equal rights for Negro workers, it is necessary to have a special approach to Negro women workers, who, far out of proportion to other women workers, are the main bread winners in their families" (2011, pp. 78–79); nevertheless, she criticized unionists especially for neglecting women in their organizing efforts and organizational leadership. She also assailed that the "crassest manifestations of trade-union neglect of the problems of the Negro women worker has been the failure, not only to fight against relegation of the Negro woman to domestic and similar menial work, but also to *organize* the domestic worker" (ibid., p. 79; original emphasis). In her insightful analysis she proffered:

> The lot of the domestic worker is one of unbearable misery. Usually, she has no definition of tasks in the household where she works. Domestic workers may have "thrown in," in addition to

cleaning and scrubbing, such tasks as washing windows, caring for the children, laundering, cooking, etc. and all at the lowest pay. The Negro domestic worker must suffer the additional indignity, in some areas, of having to seek work in virtual "slave markets" on the streets where bids are made, as from a slave block, for the hardiest workers. Many a domestic worker, on returning to her own household, must begin housework anew to keep her own family together. (ibid.)

Jones did not restrict her analysis to the political and economic conditions of "Negro women" and what they foretold for "Negro liberation," but addressed directly several of the major social dimensions of the "women question" as well. She admonished that

> the question of social relations with Negro men and women is above all a question of strictly adhering to social equality. This means ridding ourselves of the position which sometimes finds certain progressives and Communists fighting on the economic and political issues facing the Negro people, but "drawing the line" when it comes to social intercourse or intermarriage. To place the question as a "personal" and not a political matter, when such questions arise, is to be guilty of the worst kind of Social-Democratic, bourgeois-liberal thinking as regards the Negro question in American life. (2011, p. 81)

She counseled against

> shielding children from the knowledge of this struggle. This means ridding ourselves of the bourgeois-liberal attitudes which "permit" Negro and white children of progressives to play together at camps when young, but draw the line when the children reach teen-age and establish boy-girl relationships. (ibid.)

She highlighted crimes against black women, who often were restricted by their political and economic marginalization to exposing themselves to the "virtual slave markets" of the domestic workers who were compelled to work in the homes or businesses of often physically and sexually abusive white men and boys, and she challenged white women, especially, to rebuke

> the hypocritical alibi of the lynchers of Negro manhood who have historically hidden behind the skirts of white women when they

try to cover up their foul crimes with the "chivalry" of "protecting white womanhood." But white women, today, no less than their sisters in the abolitionist and suffrage movements, must rise to challenge this lie and the whole system of Negro oppression. (2011, p. 83)

Thus, appreciating the fullness of the political, economic, and social oppression of black women as well as their resistance on each front—even calling on "progressive cultural workers to write and sing of the Negro woman in her full courage and dignity" (ibid.), she argued that

[a] developing consciousness on the women question today, therefore, must not fail to recognize that the Negro question in the United States is prior to, and not equal to, the woman question; that only to the extent that we fight all chauvinist expressions and actions as regards the Negro people and fight and fight for the full equality of the Negro people, can women as a whole advance their struggle for equal rights. For the progressive women's movement, the Negro woman, who combines in her status the worker, the Negro and the woman, is the vital link to this heightened political consciousness. To the extent, further, that the cause of the Negro woman worker is promoted, she will be enabled to take her rightful place in the Negro-proletarian leadership of the national liberation movement, and by her active participation contribute to the entire American working class, whose historic mission is the achievement of a Socialist America—the final and full guarantee of woman's emancipation. (ibid.)

In the years following the publication of Jones's essay, Marxist analyses were delinked from a civilizationism that relegated gender to a tertiary position, at best, behind class and race, rooting it in an intersectional context focused on black women. Jones projected in the 1940s a feminist insight that wouldn't become prominent until second wave feminism was challenged by Frances Beal's analysis as put forth in "Double Jeopardy" in 1970. The Afro-Trinidadian Jones was unable to develop her thesis into a full-fledged rendering of cultural revolution in the United States before her deportation from the United States, although she developed a prominent cultural thesis on black West Indians in Britain. One unfortunate result was that the CPUSA was slow to address many of the issues raised by Jones. Nevertheless, like Lucy Parsons's view of cultural evolution/revolution (Ashbaugh, 1976), Jones's was grounded inextricably in her revolutionary thesis, which was tethered to Marx's Eurocentric teleology. Importantly, however, in asserting that a focus on women and sexism should be a centerpiece of labor organizing and communist revolutionist thought, and thereby rejecting the view that feminist organizing was simply ancillary to a focus on organizing labor in general, Jones had provided a prominent radical feminism grounded in her advocacy of the Black Belt thesis to a black nationalist identification of African American culture and cultural development. The lessons for the BPM were immense, but they were rarely appreciated as theory and even less as praxis by Marxists and the White Left (see Barber, 2008).

Conclusion

Having centered the analysis of black revolutionary theory in the Black Power era on the theoretical arguments of Malcolm X, in this chapter I discussed one of the most significant shortcomings in Malcolm's revolutionary thesis, reverse civilizationism, and situated it within a broader discussion of black nationalism as a concept, as well as its historical evolution, in order to demonstrate its dynamic, multifaceted, and multidimensional aspects as an ideology, and to delineate how it gave rise to Malcolm's thesis of black revolution in the United States. The shortcomings in Malcolm's and subsequent BPM activists' rendering of black nationalism were not specific to them, but were evident among analysts and advocates of black nationalism more broadly. Some were rooted in the dualities inherent in black nationalism, as both a concept and a specific program for black liberation, and three stand out: the contrast between statist and nonstatist definitions of black nationalism, between emigrationist and non/anti-emigrationist aspects of black nationalism, and between Eurocentric and Afrocentric (or Anglophilic and Afrophilic) cultural orientations. I showed how much of the theoretical synthesis of black nationalism with respect to these dualities was achieved by Du Bois at the outset of the twentieth century and is reflected in his modernized conception of black nationalism, which rejected civilizationism and promoted the cultural practices and cultural heritage of African people throughout the world, including African Americans'. Thus, *modern* black nationalism after Du Bois became synonymous with black *cultural* nationalism. This modernized version of black nationalism also informed the Marxist arguments of Haywood, who wedded them to his Black Belt thesis, which heavily influenced the theory of many BPM revolutionists, and Jones, who associated them with feminist arguments, and whose impact, although it would not be as great, would be profoundly influential in its implications.

I pointed out that Malcolm and subsequent BPM activists reversed important Du Boisian contributions to both black nationalism and the revolutionary theory that derived from it, dislodging the latter from its

American roots, opting instead for African or "third world" revolutionist orientations. The result was that BPM revolutionists attempted to orient their movement across the terrain of the most powerful country in the world using a theoretical compass better suited for a third world country. Reverse civilizationism contributed not only to a lack of appreciation of the liberating role of African American culture in the BPM, but also to the failure to recognize the historical antecedents of black revolution in the United States, which a study of black culture would reveal. Its impact on theorizing during the BPM was twofold: (1) convinced that African Americans trailed behind Africans in their revolutionary trajectory, reverse civilizationists failed to draw on pertinent historical examples from black America for their revolutionary models—grafting instead from models from Africa and the third world that were less applicable to their conditions in the United States; and (2) convinced that blacks had no culture worthy of the name, they were unable to draw from African American culture a matrix of norms, practices, and institutions to reinforce and guide their revolutionary initiatives. The two factors exacerbated each other, so that, to the extent that black activists and theorists were convinced they lagged behind Africa, they grafted presumed African cultural practices onto black America in an effort to appropriate an "African culture" by replicating customs and languages of the African continent, and/or they adopted African revolutionary practices in order to create a "revolutionary culture" in the United States, which they assumed would emanate from mirroring anticolonial armed struggles on the continent within what they viewed as the domestic colonial context of black America. Both types of initiatives ultimately drew black revolutionists away from the reservoir of strategies and institutions of black America that had successfully waged revolution in the United States in the past, and from the increasingly urbanized, religiously inspired black proletarians who comprised a pivotal segment of the black communities that they sought to revolutionize. Divorced from their African American historical and intellectual antecedents, few BPM activists appreciated that their model for successful revolution was not forthcoming from abroad, it was to be found in their own historical past, for some, right underfoot in the U.S. Civil War. Du Bois (1986, pp. 105–106), once again, would be the source for connecting an affirming African American culture to black participation in the Civil War, which he argued "was really the largest and most successful slave revolt" in the United States. In the next chapter, we will lay out the case for the latter contention and suggest its salience for BPM revolutionists a century later.

Chapter 3

The General Strike and the Slave Revolution of the U.S. Civil War

In the previous chapter, I argued that at the outset of the Black Power Movement (BPM), Malcolm X called for both a black political and a black cultural revolution in the United States; but while his call for political revolution is widely known, his arguments on black cultural revolution are not as widely appreciated—although they were no less central to his overall thesis. Constrained by reverse civilizationism, Malcolm X and major BPM revolutionists who followed him did not develop his theory of political revolution grounded in African American historical processes or adequately explain the relationship between it and the cultural revolution they sought. Instead, they largely analogized their struggles to revolutions from abroad—notably from Africa and the third world—which were ill-suited to the peculiar history and contemporary challenges of black America. Decades before, W. E. B. Du Bois had documented the existence of a black political revolution in the United States—the Slave Revolution of the U.S. Civil War; and Alain Locke had theorized cultural revolution in the United States. Therefore, on the cusp of the BPM an African American thesis of black political and cultural revolution was available to BPM revolutionists to inform and guide their liberation struggle; but, this black American source has been largely ignored by BPM revolutionists, scholars of the BPM, and activists and academics today.[1] In this chapter, I examine Du Bois's and Locke's theses and discuss their salience for the BPM.

W. E. B. Du Bois and Black Political Revolution

In *Black Reconstruction*, published in 1935, Du Bois challenged the prevailing myth that black Americans had not fought for their liberation. He argued that during the Civil War slaves prosecuted a "General Strike" and furnished about 200,000 troops "whose evident ability to fight decided the war." The following year, in *The Negro and Social Reconstruction*, he noted:

> What was really the largest and most successful slave revolt came at the time of the Civil War when all the slaves in the vicinity of the invading armies left the plantations and rushed to the army and eventually some 200,000 ex-slaves and Northern Negroes joined armies of the North, in addition to a much larger number of laborers and servants. It was this revolt of the slaves and the prospect of a much larger movement among the 4,000,000 other slaves, which was the real cause of the sudden cessation of the war. (Du Bois, 1986, pp. 105–106)

For Du Bois (1969, p. 67), the General Strike reflected "not merely the desire to stop work" but "was a strike on a wide basis against the conditions of work." It "involved directly in the end perhaps a half million people" who "wanted to stop the economy of the plantation system, and to do that they left the plantations" (ibid.). "The Negro," he argued, "became as the South quickly saw, the key to Southern resistance. Either these four million laborers remained quietly at work to raise food for the fighters, or the fighter starved"; and, "when the dream of the North for man-power produced riots, the only additional troops that the North could depend on were 200,000 Negroes, for without them, as Lincoln said, the North could not have won the war" (ibid., p. 80). He adds that the General Strike

> was not merely a matter of 200,000 black soldiers and perhaps 300,000 other black laborers, servants, spies and helpers. Back of this half million stood 3½ million more. Without their labor the South would starve. With arms in their hands, Negroes would form a fighting force which could replace every single Northern white soldier fighting listlessly and against his will with a black man fighting for freedom. (ibid.)

In contrast to the abolitionists, whose role in emancipation was exaggerated given their limited power, especially in the South, "slaves had enormous power in their hands," because "[s]imply by stopping work, they could threaten the Confederacy with starvation," and "[b]y walking into the Federal camps," they both convinced Union forces of the value "of using them as workers and as servants, as farmers, and as spies, and finally, as fighting soldiers," while simultaneously, and "by the same gesture, depriving their enemies of their use in just these fields" (1969, p. 121). Du Bois insisted that "[i]t was the fugitive slave who made the slaveholders face the alternative of surrendering to the North, or the Negroes" (ibid.). Du Bois was emphatic that "[i]t was this plain alternative that brought Lee's sudden surrender" (ibid.); and he noted that even Lincoln acknowledged that "[w]ithout the military help of black freedmen, the war against the South could not have been won" (ibid., p. 716).[2] In fact, approximately 186,000 black troops served in the Union Army; and about 10,000 served in the Union Navy. These troops fought in more than four hundred engagements including forty major battles, most notably at Port Hudson, Milliken's Bend, and Fort Wagner. Their gallantry was such that even in the racist context of the time sixteen blacks received the Medal of Honor, the country's highest military award.[3]

Du Bois argued that the "mutiny of the Negro slave" was followed by the "disaffection of the poor whites" as thousands deserted Confederate ranks. Du Bois conceived the efforts of slaves and poor whites as "one of the most extraordinary experiments of Marxism that the world, before the Russian Revolution had seen" (1969, p. 358). In contrast to the Marxist gloss, Du Bois situated the General Strike in the religious-based claims of slaves, belying the Marxist view of religion as an "opiate of the masses"—religion seemed to be the "stimulant of the slave."[4] For Du Bois, the General Strike was a slave revolt that transformed the Civil War from a war to "save the Union" to a political revolution to transform the United States; and while its impetus was cultural, its objectives were political and economic—a relationship consistent with Locke's theorizing on cultural revolution, as discussed below.[5] From the perspective of black Americans, it was a religiously inspired political revolution—thus, a cultural revolution motivating a political revolution.

Robinson argues that Du Bois's analysis reveals that "[t]he slaves freed themselves . . . by the dictates of religious myth," and that the "idiom of revolutionary consciousness had been historical and cultural rather than the 'mirror of production'" (1983, p. 324)—that, in fact, it had been rooted in black religion. Robinson agrees with Du Bois that the "revolutionary consciousness" of the slaves motivated the General Strike, prefiguring the pattern of successful revolutions in the twentieth century (ibid.). He also agrees with Du Bois's insistence that "no bourgeois society was the setting of this revolution," and "the ideology of the plantocracy had not been the ideology of the slaves" (ibid., p. 322), but, rather, that "[t]he slaves had produced their own culture and their own consciousness by adapting the forms of the non-Black society to the conceptualizations derived from their own historical roots and social conditions. In some instances, indeed, elements produced by the slave culture had become the dominant ones in white Southern culture," and "[t]his was the human experience from which the rebellion rose" (ibid.).

Meanwhile, the presumed vanguard of Marxist revolution, the white industrial proletariat, eschewed any revolutionary pretense. Unlike most of the Southern white workers, yeoman farmers, and peasants who made common cause with the plantocracy and supported the war, Northern white workers opposed the conflict, not in solidarity with their Southern fellow-proletarians but largely as protest against those privileged Northerners who could pay to exempt themselves from military service. While the war became viewed as one to end slavery, Northern white workers—Marx's industrial proletariat—vehemently opposed it and initiated anti-draft riots and pogroms against Northern blacks, even as Southern slaves initiated the General Strike.

Although Du Bois's thesis was largely rejected by scholars of his day, some prominent historians support it today. For example, Steven Hahn argues that characterizing the actions of slaves during the Civil War as rebellion "has been almost universally denied or rejected, despite the many thousands of slaves who, by their actions, helped turn the Civil War against slavery and secured the defeat of their owners" (2009, p. xiii). He asserts that the "case for slave rebellion . . . is neither hidden, archivally silenced, nor subtly discursive"; in fact, "it stares us in the face" (ibid., p. 58), and it shared important features of other widely recognized slave rebellions in the Americas. For example,

> It erupted at a time of bitter division and conflict among the society's white rulers. It depended on networks of communication, intelligence, and interpretation among the slaves. It imagined powerful allies coming to their aid, whose goals and objectives were thought to coincide with theirs. It involved individual and collective acts of flight, not as efforts to redress particular grievances, but as a means of . . . embracing a newly available or imagined freedom. And it ultimately saw slaves take up arms against slaveholders in an attempt to defeat (if not destroy) them and abolish the institution of slavery. (ibid. p. 86)

He concludes that "[i]n these respects, the slaves rebellion during the Civil War" resembled the Stono Rebellion of 1739 in South Carolina, the establishment of maroons in Brazil and Jamaica, Gabriel's conspiracy of 1800 in Virginia, Charles Deslondes's revolt of 1811 near New Orleans, the Demerara Rebellion of 1823, and the Baptist War of 1831–32 in Jamaica (2009, p. 86). For Hahn, "in its course and outcome" the slaves rebellion during the Civil War may most resemble what has long been considered "the greatest and only successful slave rebellion in modern history," the Haitian Revolution (ibid., p. 88). Both rebellions were "provoked by massive struggles between powerful groups within the white population and by the belief among slaves that they had allies among white rulers"; "free people of color" played "important roles in setting the direction of political conflict" and influencing the post-emancipation order; "flight from the plantations . . . was integral to the rebellions and crucial to the growth and maintenance of liberating armies"; "shifting alliances with and battles against large standing armies proved decisive to the rebellions' outcomes"; and "the rebellions became social and political revolutions, eventuating in the abolition of slavery, the crushing military defeat of the slave owners, and the effective birth of new nations" (ibid., p. 96). He adds that "it is arguable that the revolution made by slave rebellion was even more far reaching in the Civil War South than it was in Saint Dominque," especially since "it took place and helped transform a slave society that was by far the largest, most economically advanced, and most resilient in the Americas" (ibid., p. 97). For him, "[a]lone among the slaves of the Americas" slaves in the U.S. South "were outnumbered by a large, mobile, and armed population of whites who either owned slaves, did the slaveholders' bidding, or wanted little to do with either slaveholders or slaves" (ibid., p. 87). Facing arguably the most powerful landed elite in the world and primarily situated in limited numbers on smaller plantations and farms, which precluded large-scale mobilization, and with memories of the suppression of insurgencies as recent as John Brown's of 1859, slaves "waited until their imagined allies struck the first blow" (ibid.).

Hahn's conclusions are echoed by Stephanie McCurry's (2010, p. 262) that the Civil War involved a "massive rebellion of the Confederacy's slaves." She notes that just as Haitian slaves won their freedom in the context of a war that was "regionally uneven, temporally protracted, dynamic and reversible . . . in which the[ir] proximity to abolition armies was crucial to [their] prospects of freedom" (ibid., p. 261), U.S. slaves pursued a common strategy to destroy slavery "in the context of war and in alliance with enemy armies." They "moved tactically and by stages, men and women both, equal and active participants in the whole array of insurrectionary activities calculated to destroy the institution of slavery, their masters' power, and the prospects of the C.S.A. [Confederate States of America] as a pro slavery nation" (ibid., p. 262). Manumission was "regionally uneven, temporally protracted, and linked to the Union army's invasion and federal emancipation policy," but, "to planters and slaves alike, it was unmistakably, too, the consequence of a massive rebellion of the Confederacy's slaves" (ibid.). For McCurry, this slave rebellion in the United States followed a pattern evident from the American Revolution "to the last surrender of slavery in Brazil in the aftermath of the Paraguayan war," including "Saint-Domingue, the Spanish-American Wars of Independence, the U.S. Civil War, [and] the Ten-Years War in Cuba" (ibid.,

p. 311). In each of these cases, "slaves fought for and won their freedom in the context of war" (ibid.) because "[i]t was in the context of war that slave men became the objects of state interest and the focus of intense competition between warring states for political loyalty and military service. In this respect, the American Civil War was hardly unique" (ibid.). For McCurry, the view of the Civil War occasioning a massive slave rebellion in the U.S. South was evident to "Union and Confederate officials with responsibility for administering the region" who "all called it what it was: a slave rebellion" (ibid., p. 258). She argues that "[e]vidence that the Civil War became a massive slave rebellion is to be found in every Confederate state where slaves seized the opportunity of war to rise against their masters, destroy slavery where they lived, and claim allegiance to a nation that had never really been theirs'"; but, "[i]t was not the existence of slave rebellion that makes the difference between say, South Carolina and Virginia, on the one hand, and Louisiana, on the other. It was only that in Mississippi and southern Louisiana, people were more likely to admit it and to make the searing historical analogy to Saint-Domingue" (ibid., pp. 260–261). She adds:

> Historians have been loath to notice the analogy deployed during the war itself and shied away from any description of the Civil War as a slave rebellion. But that owes to the explosive politics of the analogy for slaves themselves during the war, for their leaders in the postwar period, for Union officials . . . and for Confederates and their lost-cause descendants bent on denying it, far more than it does to historical conditions in the Confederate South during the Civil War. (2010, p. 261)

Hahn's, McCurry's, and McPherson's (1991) conclusions are similar to Du Bois's (1935, p. 91) from decades earlier.[6]

Du Bois did not link the causative agents of black participation in the war to its precedents in the earlier major slave revolts in the antebellum United States, epitomized in the Gabriel (Prosser), Denmark Vesey, and Nat Turner revolts. I've argued elsewhere that two overlapping and mutually reinforcing factors contributed to those revolts: (1) slave religion, which provided justifications for overthrowing the slave system and mobile slave preachers to articulate it; and (2) the system of hiring out slaves—especially slave artisans, which expanded networks across plantations and rural and urban slave and free black communities, and in some industries—began to proletarianize slave labor (Henderson, 2015). Though the revolts were brutally suppressed, the networks they emanated from persisted, broadening the scope of slave communities, which they continued to do during wartime.

The latter facilitated the provision of information and coordination for the movement of slaves to Union lines to fight their former masters. Utilizing these networks, slaves joined and transformed a war to preserve the Union into a revolution to overthrow U.S. slavery.

Du Bois demonstrated that under certain conditions black religion compelled activism over fatalism, change over stasis, resistance over submission, revolution over accommodation. More than three decades prior to the publication of *Black Reconstruction*, in *The Souls of Black Folk* (1903), Du Bois had argued that while in the antebellum era the slave's religion had been marked by a fatalism resulting from a "long system of repression and degradation of the Negro," in the decades preceding the Civil War "[h]is religion had become darker and more intense, and into his ethics crept a note of revenge, into his songs a day of reckoning close at hand. The 'Coming of the Lord' swept this side of Death, and came to be a thing hoped for in this day" (1903, p. 147). The conduit for this transformation of slave religion, according to Du Bois, was the influence of freed blacks on their enslaved brethren. He maintained that "[t]hrough fugitive slaves and irrepressible discussion this desire for freedom seized the black millions still in bondage, and became their one ideal of life" (ibid., pp. 147–148).[7] Du Bois was convinced that

> [f]or fifty years Negro religion thus transformed itself and identified itself with the dream of Abolition, until that which was a radical fad in the white North and an anarchistic plot in the white South had become a religion in the black world. Thus, when Emancipation finally came, it seemed to the freeman a literal Coming of the Lord. (ibid., p. 148)

Even as he took the reference of the "Coming of the Lord" from *Souls* (1903) as the title of his chapter on the coming of the Civil War in *Black Reconstruction*, he did not make the connection between black religion and black revolution implied by a synthesis of the two works. Consider the further discussion regarding the "Coming of the Lord" from *Souls* (p. 148):

> His fervid imagination was stirred as never before, by the tramp of armies, the blood and dust of battle, and the wail and whirl of social upheaval. *He stood dumb and motionless before the whirlwind: what had he to do with it?* Was it not the Lord's doing . . . ? Joyed and *bewildered with what came*, he stood awaiting new wonders. (emphasis added)

In contrast to the astonished bewilderment of the enslaved in *Souls*, Du Bois's view of their conception of the "Coming of the Lord" in *Black Reconstruction* evokes their agency in their emancipation, as the key actor in the Civil War through purposeful action epitomized in the General Strike. While there was religious frenzy with emancipation, *Black Reconstruction* tells a different story of the role of blacks in securing their freedom, one that focuses on and even celebrates their agency in their liberation, their attempt to restore and build families, to secure land, to found schools and educate themselves, to build the incipient institutions of black civil society in the South, and to build a multiracial democracy in the United States. Yet, Du Bois did not integrate the dominant black cultural institution, the invisible institution of slave religion, into a theoretical synthesis of his hypothesized Slave Revolution. That is, he didn't flesh out the implications of his observation that the dramatic changes in slave religion that motivated the General Strike and transformed the Civil War into a political revolution constituted a cultural revolution.

Du Bois's reticence probably was due to his ambivalence toward black religion as a progressive change agent.[8] His failure to pursue the theoretical development of the role of slave religion in motivating the General Strike left the clearest symbol of the slaves' agency in the Civil War untethered to its historical antecedents in the religiously inspired slave revolts of the first decades of the nineteenth century. Du Bois attributed the transformation of slave religion mainly to the impact of Northern abolitionism on the invisible institution, but such a focus ignores more influential developments in the slave quarters, evident in earlier slave revolts, epitomized in those led by Gabriel, Denmark Vesey, and Nat Turner.[9] Key aspects of the Slave Revolution during the Civil War were prefigured in these major slave revolts insofar as all of their leaders drew on slave religion to justify their revolts, utilizing religious arguments and invoking biblical rationales to motivate and coordinate their followers (Sidbury, 2003, p. 120). The revolts reveal that a dialectic of sorts operated, as the white Christianity that the slavemasters had intended to use as a mental chain to reinforce the physical chains of slavery had become the hammer used to break them. In these cases, far from being the opiate of the masses, religion was the stimulant of the slave (Henderson, 2015).

Moreover, hired-out slaves—especially slave artisans—were influential in each of these revolts as they would be in the General Strike, as well. The practice of slave hiring placed them into wage labor contexts and contributed to their acquisition of aspects of working-class consciousness. At the same time, it generated networks cross-circuiting slave neighborhoods (Kaye, 2007ab). Focusing on these networks allows us to appreciate more dynamic aspects of slave society that contributed to the radicalization and mobilization of slaves that Du Bois's broader thesis of the General Strike affirms. For example, an incipient industrialization of some aspects of slave labor was evident in the antebellum era, and it was taking place at the nexus of slave and free society, between cotton fields and cotton mills, throughout the South. Slave labor was not only central to agricultural production, but was increasingly employed in Southern industries (Barnes et al., 2011). By the last decade of the antebellum era, the industrial capacity of the South had doubled. Slaves worked in textile mills, iron works, brickworks, tobacco factories, hemp factories, shoe factories, tanneries, coal mines, iron mines, gold mines, salt mines, sugar refineries, rice mills, and gristmills (Starobin, 1970, p. 11).

In industry as in agriculture, slaves could be utilized directly by their owners or "hired out." The system of hiring out slaves expanded the networks of slaves across plantations and often linked rural and urban slave and free black communities. The vast majority of slaves in industrial settings were directly owned; but, among those hired out, slave artisans were particularly important and, given their skills, could earn greater profits for their owners, who only returned a small portion of their hired-out slaves' earnings while pocketing the rest. Although profitable for slaveholders, the practice of hiring out slaves was potentially dangerous, as well (Martin, 2004). It presented a problem to have slaves working in a manner similar to that of free wage laborers. Working for hire allowed the slave to directly experience how the wages they earned from the same work as their free laboring counterparts was valued differently only because they were not free—a sort of "slave wagery." For slave artisans, this slave wagery was probably even more apparent psychologically, insofar as they typically had the same level of training and craftsmanship as free laborers. Hired-out slave artisans came to realize directly the wage burden imposed on them as a condition of their servitude—evoking Marx's thesis of surplus value—while slave hire also gave them the opportunity to work in settings with increased numbers of slave artisans with similar grievances, as well as wage laborers, providing an environment for conspiratorial activity. The potential danger to the maintenance of the slave system presented by hiring out slaves was articulated by the most famous hired-out slave, Frederick Douglass (1855, p. 325), the future abolitionist leader, who said that "the practice, from week to week, of openly robbing me of all my earnings, kept the nature and character of slavery constantly before me."

For these reasons, it is not surprising that we observe hired-out slave artisans—such a small minority of slave society—as prominent among the participants in the major U.S. slave revolts of the nineteenth century. Starobin (1970, p. 90) argues that "[t]he involvement of Negro artisans and industrial slaves in conspiracies and rebellions indicates that they were greatly disaffected," and "[s]ince their work provided both a large measure of self-esteem and independence, the leadership of slave rebellions naturally gravitated to them" (1988, p. 123). Slavery appeared to be creating a consciousness among this class of hired-out slaves and artisans and some of these quasi-proletarians were intent on overthrowing the slave system.

Although Du Bois (1935, p. 14) put the black worker at the center of the Civil War as "its underlying cause" and as decisive in its outcome, he insufficiently examined the role of slave artisans in his General Strike. While he appreciated work-based distinctions among slaves, recognizing that "artisans, who had a certain modicum of freedom in their work, were often hired out, and worked practically as free laborers," he did not reflect on the role of such slaves in previous revolts and project forward to their role in the General Strike. He noted that the slaves involved in the General Strike were utilizing "the same methods that [they] had used during the period of the fugitive slave" (ibid., p. 57)—namely, they would "strike" in order "to stop the economy of the plantation system, and to do that they left the plantations" (ibid., p. 67); but, he did not seem to appreciate that among these "same methods" were organized revolt. Concerned less with antebellum slave revolts, and more with juxtaposing the repressive conditions of the antebellum South with the emancipatory opportunities that Reconstruction promised, Du Bois didn't examine how these revolts foreshadowed the General Strike and demonstrated the type of coordinated action that could be achieved even within the "armed and commissioned camp of the South."

Besides the major slave revolts, Du Bois ignored several conspiracies of the 1850s involving industrial slaves, which might have helped him to appreciate the continuity between antebellum slave revolts and the General Strike.[10] Without such a focus, the General Strike was reduced to a *spontaneous* outgrowth of religious fervor rather than the culmination of processes evident in previous revolts (1935, p. 122). The view that the General Strike was the result of *spontaneous*, religiously inspired, concerted action is only partly correct; it was actually a continuation of initiatives among religiously inspired slaves evident in the major slave revolts of the nineteenth century. What Du Bois implied—but did not examine—was that the slavemaster's religion that instilled contentment with slavery was being transformed in the slave quarters to one that opposed injustice. Syncretized with African traditions that continued to influence the enslaved, the gospels of the free blacks that counseled resistance, and the material reality of the brutality of the slave experience, slave religion generated a consciousness that justified seizing freedom more than simply a personal desire to be free—just as Du Bois maintained. Slave religion was becoming an institution of the incipient slave culture that did not necessitate revolt but encouraged it, and in this case inspired the General Strike.

Given that slave religion was the key factor motivating the General Strike, then, Du Bois was demonstrating how a cultural impetus generated politico-military revolution, and in this way he provided an incipient construction of black cultural revolution in the United States. Seen in this light, Du Bois's thesis in *Black Reconstruction* was less a Marxist exegesis of political revolution in the United States than his own original formulation: a black cultural revolution (reflected in the change of emphasis of slave religion toward emancipation, which motivated the General Strike) that generated a political revolution (the Slave Revolution that changed Lincoln's war aims from restoring the status quo ante to the revolutionary objective of ending slavery). Du Bois was positing that the emerging, highly syncretic religion of black Christianity was becoming a prominent change agent in Aframerican society. The religious faith of the slave could be put in the service of an insurgent struggle for freedom, liberty, and justice. Thus, far from being the opiate of the masses, religion had been the adrenaline of the slaves. A brief review of each of these major revolts reveals as much.

Slave Religion, Slave Hiring, and Slave Revolts

Gabriel's Rebellion

Gabriel, a slave artisan, led a slave conspiracy near Richmond, Virginia, in 1800. Religion not only provided a rationale for this attempted revolt, but "religious meetings" also served "as occasions for the recruitment of slaves and for plotting and organizing the insurrection" (Raboteau, 1980, p. 147). The influence of slave artisans in this planned revolt was so great that some scholars argue that it superseded religion as the prime motivation for the revolt (Egerton, 1993; Mullin, 1972),[11] but such claims are challenged by Levine (1977, p. 75), who notes that although "[i]n other revolts sacred elements were more prominent," nevertheless, "the Old Testament message played a role" in Gabriel's revolt. Sidbury (2003, p. 121) argues that the central role of religion in the revolt is evident in the importance of Hungary Baptist Meeting House, which Gabriel and his two brothers appear to have attended, and which was the site of many recruiting meetings, in the assertions of white commentators at the time that religion was central to the conspiracy, and in the "substantial evidence of growing black allegiance to the Baptist Church in the region around Richmond during the late 1790s." Moses (1993,

p. 36) agrees, and notes the importance of religion in the exchange between Gabriel's brother Martin and Ben Woolfolk, two of the chief conspirators, during one planning meeting, which was reported by Ben in his confession during his conspiracy trial:

> Martin said there was this expression in the Bible, delays breed danger . . . I told them that I had heard in the days of old, when the Israelites were in service to King Pharaoh, they were taken from him by the power of God, and were carried away by Moses. God had blessed him with an angel to go with him, but that I could see nothing of that kind in these days. Martin said in reply: I read in my Bible where God says if we will worship Him we should have peace in all our land, five of you shall conquer an hundred, and a hundred a thousand of our enemies. After this they went on consultation upon the time they should execute the plan. (Flournoy, 1890, p. 151)

Sidbury notes that although the exchange above constitutes "the only direct appeal to the Bible in all of the recorded testimony produced during the trials and investigations" of Gabriel's plot, nevertheless there are "reasons to believe that religion did play a central role in the conspiracy" (2003, pp. 120–121). First, although the exchange is the only recorded reference to the Bible in the planning, "that does not mean that it was the only conversation in which the Bible played a role." Second, the exchange took place during a "pivotal moment" in the planning when one conspirator, George Smith, was cautioning patience—to which Ben agreed and provided Biblical support for his position—while Gabriel, who was intent on commencing the revolt sooner, turned the floor over to Martin, who provided a Biblical counterpoint, which seemed to decide the issue. "Martin, in short, laid claim to greater interpretive authority than Woolfolk, and the other leaders of the conspiracy appear to have accepted his claim," since after Martin's speech the group went into consultation and Martin set the date for the revolt (ibid., p. 122; also see Raboteau, 1980, p. 147). That the interpretation of Biblical texts could be dispositive of an issue of such import as the timing of the revolt suggests the significance of religion to the leaders.

Gabriel's plan focused on urban slaves, primarily skilled artisans like himself, who hired out their time. Sidbury (1997, p. 61) acknowledges that "many, perhaps most, of the slaves convicted of participating in the conspiracy . . . had artisanal skills." In Gabriel's Virginia, planters faced a depressed tobacco market; thus, they reduced the cultivation of tobacco as a crop and with less demand for slave labor in the tobacco fields hired out many of their slaves in order to earn money. Slave artisans, in particular, could be hired out as skilled workers for Richmond's various industries. Egerton notes that "[e]ven the largest and most efficient plantations could not keep their bond artisans fully occupied year-round, and so many owners occasionally hired their craftsmen out to neighboring farms or town dwellers" (1993, pp. 23–24). In Henrico County, not only were slave artisans hired out, but female domestics, butlers, and coachmen were leased to elites for their large gatherings, just as unskilled farm laborers were leased to small landholders needing extra hands during planting and harvesting. In fact, "the largest slaveholder in the state, hired out more than two-thirds of his 509 slaves" (ibid., p. 21). The hire could be for a few days or leased for fifty weeks. There were designated areas, such as the steps of the County Courthouse in Richmond, from which prospective employers could choose from among the "crowds of servants, men, women, boys and girls, for hire" (ibid., p. 24).

Hiring out also gave the slave artisan the opportunity to work in industrial settings in which there were concentrations of similarly situated artisans with similar disaffection with the slave system, providing breeding grounds for conspiratorial activity. Slave artisans, and hired-out slaves more generally, were crucial to Gabriel's conspiracy, and "most of those contacted early on" to join it "were skilled men who hired their own time" (Egerton, 1993, p. 52). Gabriel was one of those slave artisans who either hired out some of his time and/or worked after hours for pay, which would afford him the time and mobility to organize others who were similarly disposed to the slave system.[12] He was one of the three blacksmiths among the five or six most important leaders of the conspiracy (Sidbury, 1997, p. 83). In Gabriel's Virginia, blacksmiths "were highly skilled and valued artisans who enjoyed a high level of autonomy while at work, and their shops were often placed on busy thoroughfares" (ibid.). For example, "the shop of Gabriel, Solomon, and Prosser's Ben bordered the road that carried wagon traffic into Richmond from western counties—so these shops could serve as communicative nodal points for slaves' communities" (ibid.). Further, "their relative autonomy on the job, their ability to sell work done 'after hours' and thus gain access to the market, and their position in Black communication networks contributed to their status within slave communities," which "along with blacksmiths' very practical ability to make and repair weapons, helps to explain their prominence within the conspiracy" (ibid.).

Thus, slave religion provided the ideological justification for the revolt, while its coordination was facilitated by a network of hired-out slaves who fashioned a conspiratorial web across plantations, and both rural and urban areas. To be sure, "[t]he slaves' Christianity was not inherently revolutionary," but it could be fashioned for that purpose; and Gabriel's "use of scriptural arguments to convince other skilled and acculturated slaves to attack their masters shows that at least in 1800 Black Virginians could use their religion for purposes that were in fact revolutionary" (Sidbury, 1997, p. 79).[13]

Denmark Vesey's Rebellion

Denmark Vesey's planned rebellion in Charleston, South Carolina, in 1822 followed a similar pattern.[14] It was no less religiously inspired than Gabriel's—in fact, even more so. Vesey was a former slave, a carpenter, and an influential member of the AME Church; and his slave revolt relied heavily on hired-out slave artisans and his fellow church members. Vesey used nightly "class meetings" to promote a radical Christianity rooted in the Old Testament and Jehovah's evocations of vengeance and retribution for his enslaved chosen people. Particularly instructive for Vesey were Old Testament passages that spoke of retribution sanctioned by God and carried out by divinely inspired leaders, such as the stories of Joshua and the Exodus (Robertson, 1999, p. 138; Stuckey, 1987, pp. 48–49). Not surprisingly, "[a]ll but one of Vesey's closest fellow conspirators were A.M.E. members" (Robertson, 1999, p. 9). One of the prominent leaders of the conspiracy, "Gullah Jack" Pritchard, was both a member of the AME Church and a conjurer; thus, Vesey's conspiracy was based in both "the doctrinal sanction of Scripture" as well as "the practical protection of conjure" (Raboteau, 1980, p. 163). Egerton (2003, p. 120) rejects the view that Vesey "consciously used Jack Pritchard to reach the African plantation constituency, while he himself used the AME Church to reach the more assimilated urban creole population," because, in his view "no such dichotomy existed" (also see Creel, 1988). After all, Gullah Jack was a member of Vesey's church, as was Monday Gell, an Ibo, and "[n]either man appeared to find any contradiction between the religious teachings of their childhood, and what they heard in Cow Alley" at the AME Church. He concludes that "[i]t was not that the old carpenter cynically used his church to recruit revolutionaries, but rather that this fusion of Old Testament law and African ritual transformed his timid disciples into revolutionaries."[15] For Starobin (1970, p. 5), "the Vesey Plot embodied an extraordinarily rich ideology," which "combined the Old Testament's harsh morality and the story of the Israelites with African religious customs, knowledge of the Haitian Revolution, and readings of antislavery speeches from the Missouri [Compromise] controversy." Creel (1988, p. 10) viewed Vesey's conspiracy as emanating from a "resistance culture" among African Carolinians, and described it as "a supreme effort to break the chains of bondage in a spirit of nationalism, unity, and religious self-determination" (ibid., p. 160).

If the influence of religion on the revolt was apparent, so was the impact of artisans—especially hired-out slaves, just as in Gabriel's revolt. Vesey was a free black carpenter, which afforded him opportunities to meet and work with other artisans—both free and slave—in urban Charleston, as well as plantation slaves in the rural areas around Charleston (Lofton, 1983, p. 78). Among his closest co-conspirators, both Gullah Jack and Monday Gell (a harness maker), apparently were hired-out slaves (Greene & Hutchins, 2004, 41), and probably Peter Poyas (a ship carpenter), as well. Other important conspirators such as Lot Forrestor, who had secured "slow match"—a length of fuse—to facilitate the fires that were to be set throughout the city, was a hired-out slave, as was William Garner, a drayman, who during his trial tried unsuccessfully to convince his triers that the privileges he enjoyed as a hired-out slave militated against his involvement in the conspiracy (Robertson, 1999). Jesse Blackwood, who was tasked with bringing slaves from the countryside into the city just prior to the uprising, was ostensibly hired-out, but actually other conspirators had raised money to pay his slave master so that he could more effectively recruit for the planned revolt (Greene & Hutchins, 2004, pp. 40–41; Pearson, 1999, p. 71).

As in Gabriel's Richmond, the system of hiring out slaves was widespread in Vesey's Charleston. In Charleston, "[n]either owners nor municipal officials could effectively monitor the enslaved bricklayers, carpenters, painters, and other craft workers who traveled freely around the city and surrounding countryside between jobs," although, "[f]rom the late seventeenth century until the Civil War, a series of provincial and municipal laws unsuccessfully sought to regulate these workers." The rebel leadership came mainly from this discontented group of urban skilled slave artisans and religious leaders (Starobin, 1970, p. 3) and, given that "recruits came mainly from the urban, industrial slaves of Charleston," this

> casts great doubt on the assertion . . . that urban bondsmen and slave hirelings were more content and less rebellious than rural, plantation bondsmen. Indeed the evidence suggests that urban slaves were, despite their supposedly greater privileges and higher standard of living, at least as discontented as rural slaves. No wonder whites were mystified and horrified when even their most trusted servants and apparently contented bondsmen were implicated in the plot. (ibid., p. 3)

As in Gabriel's Revolt, the framework for Vesey's insurgency was the fusion of leadership grounded in religious justifications coupled with the centrality of artisanal slaves—especially hired-out slaves—which facilitated a clandestine network across plantations. Also like Gabriel's strategy, Vesey's employed diversion, camouflage, concentration of forces, land and river coordination, and, uniquely, international diplomacy—through correspondence with President Boyer of Haiti; but for all its sophistication, as in Gabriel's conspiracy, betrayal of the plot—and deployment of militia—doomed it before it could be executed.[16]

Nat Turner's Rebellion

No slave revolt prior to the Civil War had the impact of Nat Turner's in Virginia in 1831. The role of religious ideology in Turner's revolt is unequivocal. Although Du Bois (1902, p. 12) characterized Turner as a slave artisan and Aptheker (1966, p. 35) describes Turner as "gifted mechanically," Turner was primarily a field hand (Oates, 1975, p. 161).[17] What's not in dispute is Aptheker's assessment that "the supreme influence" in Turner's life "undoubtedly was religion" (1966, p. 36); and that Turner "discover[ed] his rationalization for his rebellious feelings in religion" (ibid., p. 35). Turner was a slave preacher who was heavily influenced by passages in the Bible that advocated retributive justice (e.g., Luke 12:40, 49–51). Turner "perceived a close relationship between Jesus of Nazareth and the great prophets who had called down the wrath of God upon his disobedient people and their enemies" (Wilmore, 1983, p. 65). Such an exegesis of Scripture is markedly different from that found typically in the slaves' catechism from the missionaries who spoke of Jesus as the meek and humble Lamb of God, obedient to his Master, God the Father. Thus, while Gabriel and Vesey drew their religious motivations from Old Testaments texts, Turner drew his from the messianic vision of the New Testament and the Gospel of Jesus.

As Turner relates in *The Confessions*, upon seeing what he took as a sign in the heavens—a solar eclipse in February 1831, he said, "[T]he seal was removed from my lips, and I communicated the great work laid out for me to do to four in whom I had the greatest confidence." In contrast to Gabriel and Vesey, he initially confided in only four men "in whom [he] had the greatest confidence," who either lived on his farm or were from nearby plantations (Breen, 2003, p. 111). The level of secrecy he maintained appears to have been a deliberate policy, because it was not for want of an audience from which he might draw supporters, if he had so desired, that he restricted his recruitment, because as a slave preacher he had considerable freedom of movement for religious gatherings.

Although few would dispute the centrality of religion to Turner himself, and the role that it played in establishing his leadership, some maintain that it was less salient for many of Turner's followers than their own more specific grievances (ibid., p. 118). Notwithstanding the motivations of the dozens of slaves and free blacks who supported and subsequently joined the revolt, it was Nat Turner, "[i]nspired by his religious visions," who "tapped into the latent hope and discontent of slaves and free blacks in Southampton," and in this way, "[t]he prophet became a general and led his men in a desperate battle against slavery" (ibid.).

Turner's objective appears to have been to take the county seat of Jerusalem (now Courtland), and from there secure weapons and ammunition, presumably hoping to capture the entire county with the aid of supporters joining from surrounding areas. Although historians are unclear of Turner's objectives beyond Jerusalem, the strategy he employed—contrary to the opinion of many later commentators—was not poorly conceived. Egerton (2003, p. 142) is correct that "[h]indsight is often the enemy of understanding" and

> [s]ecure in the knowledge that Turner failed in his mission, scholars are tempted to assume that no other outcome was possible. But once Jerusalem was within the grasp of his army, Turner could either have fortified the village and waited for word of the rising to spread across the countryside or, if white counterassaults became too potent, could have galloped the 25 miles east into the Dismal Swamp. Here then lay the basis, not of a fanatical plan doomed to failure, but of a maroon island of black liberty deep within the slaveholding South.

Turner's plan was to move stealthily to avoid raising alarms, and to use hatchets and axes as weapons to conceal their attacks from neighboring plantations. In the event, after killing slaveholding families, they confiscated their arms, horses, powder, shot, food, spirits, and money, and recruited other slaves to join them. Turner drilled and outfitted his rebels with red bandanas—all acts to inspire esprit de corps and to instill military discipline under his military authority. Subsequently, he altered tactics and "concentrated his forces and ordered them to charge at full gallop and in full cry to exaggerate the size of their ranks and paralyze the enemy in fear, to 'carry terror and devastation wherever we went'"; and, "[f]or a time, the stratagem seemed to work, drawing ten to twenty more slaves into the uprising" (Kaye, 2007b, p. 717). Their increased numbers, however, "pulled the rebellion in different directions" (ibid.), and three miles outside of Jerusalem, Turner was compelled to split his forces, just as slaveholders and local militia had marshaled to suppress the revolt. In the decisive battle at Parker's field, Turner reconsolidated his forces after a remnant had been dispersed by a patrol's fire, and led them in a spirited attack that repulsed the patrol; however, the arrival of reinforcements forced Turner's retreat (Parramore, 2003, p. 66).

The tactical loss concealed a strategic defeat because Turner's access to the bridges to Jerusalem was cut off by militia and patrolling whites. Fighting would continue into the next day, but Nat Turner's forces were mostly scattered, captured, or killed, although he would elude militia and mobs for two months before his capture.

In total, Turner's forces, which at their largest constituted between sixty and eighty men, had killed fifty-seven whites. Slaveholders were reinforced by militia with greater manpower and more arms—eventually including several artillery companies and a detachment of sailors. Turner was among the fifty-six slaves executed for the insurrection, although between one hundred and two hundred slaves and free blacks were killed by whites in a frenzied campaign of torture, rape, and murder following the revolt. In the aftermath, the Virginia legislature made it illegal to teach slaves, free blacks, or mulattoes to read or write, and restricted all blacks from holding religious meetings outside the presence of a licensed white minister.[18]

Slave Revolts and Du Bois's Thesis

The revolts of Gabriel, Denmark Vesey, and Nat Turner were dramatic but not unique events and religious factors and slave hiring are implicated heavily in each of them. It is reasonable to conclude that the factors that motivated and supported the development of sophisticated clandestine plans for revolt, entailing the coordination and movement of people and material across plantations and even across rural and urban communities, also could motivate and support the major slave revolt of the Civil War. In the prewar revolts, slave religion provided the language of revolt, a justification for it, and a promise of its fulfillment. The capacity of slave religion to motivate revolt belies the view that it simply bred docility. Moses (1993, p. 246) is correct that it is "impossible to conceive" that "uprooted Africans learning their Christianity in North America" would do so while "remaining blind to such concepts as 'righteous wrath' and the idea of a God who expects his faithful to behave as instruments of his wrath." It's not that slave religion mandated rebellion or even counseled it over submission to the slave's lot; what is important is that slave religion *could* be reconciled with slave revolt. Relatedly, the practice of slave hiring increased the mobility of slaves and gave them opportunities to extend their social and occupational networks. For slave artisans, it increased their ability to develop a collective consciousness based on their shared exploitation as both slave and wage laborer resulting in an incipient working-class consciousness (i.e. a kind of proletarianization) of these liminal slaves/workers. Although this awareness may have been greatest for slave artisans, it likely affected hired-out unskilled laborers as well, given that their wages were subject to the same expropriations by their slave masters.[19]

In combination, slave religion and slave hiring contributed to the development of expansive, complex, and coordinated networks extending across plantations and rural and urban slave and free black communities. Such networks became characteristic of slave communities, and could be utilized to coordinate even sophisticated plans for rebellion. Although these revolts could be—and typically were—brutally suppressed, given that the factors that generated them, slave religion and slave hiring, also served the interests of the slave masters (i.e., the slave masters' desire for the profits from slave hiring, and the promise of religiously inspired slave docility), these practices persisted in some form right up to and throughout the Civil War. Given their persistent impact on slave society, it's surprising that Du Bois would not consider them in what he acknowledges as the religiously inspired and slave labor–based General Strike of the Civil War. It was Du Bois's desire to juxtapose the stultifying, repressive slave system of the antebellum era to the awesome opportunities for black autonomy and development provided by postbellum radical Reconstruction, which colored his conceptual lens. The major slave revolts were both rare and distant from what he viewed as the major precipitants of the war and its aftermath.

Clearly, Du Bois appreciated the significance of the black laborer of the South; but he did not draw the explicit link between hired-out slaves—especially slave artisans, motivated by an incipient working-class consciousness born of working in Southern industry—and the religious ideology he acknowledged as central to slave insurgency. As both slaves and wage laborers, they were both religionists and incipient proletarians, and as hired-out slaves mobile and able to establish networks that linked slave communities. Coupled with the institutional structure of the incipient Black Church, such networks provided the latticework for communities of support extending across plantations, linking rural and urban communities. They developed further in the decades leading up to the war, ultimately facilitating the movement of slaves to Union lines during the Civil War. Following these major slave revolts, and right up to the war, it was evident that slave networks were being utilized and extended to facilitate what would eventuate in the Slave Revolution of the U.S. Civil War.[20]

Slave Neighborhoods, Grapevine Telegraphs, and Networks for War

Slaves continued to utilize the social networks of the antebellum era during wartime.[21] These networks were conduits within slave society that facilitated communication, transportation, and organization within and across plantations and expanded the scope of the slave neighborhood, which comprised both the physical geography and the social terrain of the individual slave (Kaye, 2007a, p. 4). It was a nexus of social relations based in "labor, kinship, struggle, worship, and socializing of every variety" (ibid., p. 153). Slave neighborhoods were the "unintended consequences" of slave interaction in a context defined by the plantation system and the will of individual slave owners, who, often unwittingly, helped produce and reproduce them. They often included adjacent plantations and the areas around them as well (ibid., p. 4). Bonds *within* neighborhoods were stronger than those *between* them (ibid., p. 153), which posed problems for slaves planning escape—much less revolt—because in order "[t]o muster a force of any consequence, rebels had to unite across neighborhood lines" (ibid., p. 124). Given these "inextricable constraints and obstructions," the geography of neighborhoods "all but doomed slave revolts"—making the development and execution of major slave revolts all the more remarkable (ibid.).

Slaves whose labor required mobility, such as artisans, teamsters, and carriage drivers, provided a nexus between plantations, and slave preachers were especially influential. "Preachers, who were mediators in a neighborhood's relationship to God as well as literate and mobile, brought unique attainments to the task of forging ties between neighborhoods and had a special importance among the conduits" (Kaye, 2007a, p. 181). The networks within and across slave neighborhoods included formal institutions associated with slave religion and less formal ones, such as the "grapevine telegraph," both of which could facilitate revolt by serving as relatively independent conduits of information. On the latter, in his autobiography, Booker T. Washington recalled that during the Civil War he had been perplexed at how "slaves throughout the South, completely ignorant as were the masses so far as books or newspapers were concerned, were able to keep themselves so accurately and completely informed about the great National questions that were agitating the country," to the extent that "slaves often got knowledge of the events of the war before the whites did" ([1995 (1901)], p. 4). He remembered that when he was a child slaves "kept themselves informed of events by what was termed the 'grape-vine' telegraph" (ibid.). For example, he explained that when a slave "was sent to the post office for the mail," they "would linger about the place long enough to get the drift of the conversation from the group of white people who naturally congregated there, after receiving their mail, to discuss the latest news" (ibid., pp. 4–5). This news would then be reported back to the slaves upon the courier's return, "and in this way they often heard of important events before the white people at the 'big house'" (ibid., p. 5).

The grapevine telegraph was the slaves' network of communication by which "[h]ouse servants, coachmen, artisans and hired slaves, some of whom had gained the rudiments of literacy, carried news from the big house, the courthouse, the tavern and the market-place back into the quarters" (Hahn, 1997, p. 128). Once there, the information "was discussed, interpreted and then further disseminated, when slaves visited kinfolk on other plantations and farms, met each other on the back roads, or held brush-arbour religious meetings." For Hahn, "[i]n these ways the slaves, in many different locales, learned of the antislavery movement in the North, the sectional conflict and other 'great events.'" Moreover, "[t]he Civil War and early Reconstruction not only brought the slaves' communication networks to more public light, but also helped to extend, deepen and institutionalize them."

Although the neighborhood "was the main field of the grapevine telegraph," in which "slaves rapidly and extensively collected and exchanged information," the grapevine telegraph was also one of several mechanisms that could be used to circumvent some of the constraints of neighborhood boundaries on slaves and facilitated interplantation communication (Kaye, 2007a, p. 24). Litwack (1980, p. 23) agrees that "[e]xtensive black communication networks, feeding on a variety of sources, sped information from plantation to plantation, county to county, often with remarkable secrecy and accuracy." Litwack (p. 23) acknowledges that "[f]ew plantation whites were fully aware of the inventiveness with which their slaves transmitted information to other blacks," and one result was that "[m]uch of the information circulating in slave neighborhoods originated with owners" (Kaye, 2007a, p. 180), as "[a]ttentive slaves made unwitting owners serve as especially revealing informants" (ibid., p. 179). As "[p]lanters read newspapers, corresponded with sons, husbands, kin, and friends," and "men and women of discretion talked over what they knew in the garden or the yard, on the porch, and at table," often "house servants picked it up and passed it along" (ibid., p. 180).

McCurry (2010, pp. 227–228) agrees that "[e]xtensive black communication networks had existed in the slave period," and slaves demonstrated "the ability to get and relay information of personal and political significance by assembling the required elements into one human network." As war loomed, slaves "watched and pooled their intelligence on the aims and prospects of civil war" and "[t]hey fashioned lines of communication, connecting circles of men and women, drawn together in relations of kinship and work, sociability and worship in every neighborhood" (ibid., p. 179). Mobile slaves, such as preachers, teamsters, and artisans, "made themselves into homespun military experts by their ability to reconnoiter over a broad terrain, canvassing informants, sifting opinion and fancy, separating rumor from fact. Slaves in transit, gathering and dispensing information from neighborhood to neighborhood, connected them along the way" (ibid.). In this context, "a preacher's calling lent his reckonings of the war a unique authority. His exegesis of the causes of the war, its turns on the battlefield, and its likely outcome could take on the import of revelation, allegory, prophesy" (ibid., p. 181).

In the context of the war, the slave preacher's mobility—unlike that of other mobile slaves—took on added salience since it facilitated the spread of the "invisible institution" itself, further forging the links of communication, information, and religious fidelity of slave neighborhoods. These networks—along with those supplied by hired-out slaves—facilitated, inter alia, slave runaways during the antebellum era and, once the war commenced, the movement of slaves to Union lines. For example, Du Bois refers to the "mysterious spiritual telegraph" that slaves appear to have utilized to coordinate their movement to General Butler's Union forces at Fortress Monroe in Virginia (1969, p. 63). During the war, the grapevine telegraph continued to operate as it had during the antebellum era, but now its techniques of communication and information gathering and dissemination could be applied to slave revolution and Union victory in myriad forms (see, e.g., McPherson, 1993, pp. 60–64, 149–154).

Such was the case with the networks developed by the former slave William Webb, who reportedly helped coordinate a secret network of slaves in anticipation of a possible rebellion of the slave states with the coming to power of a Republican regime (Hahn, 2004). Susan O'Donovan (2011) credits Webb with "real genius . . . in mobilization," which she attributes to his experience as a hired-out slave, which "made it easier for him to create and sustain a growing network of slaves"—just as was evident in the major slave conspiracies of the antebellum era. Webb's network was a protean, decentralized, "loose assembly of disparate groups," which he began to organize among slaves as early as 1856, and which by Lincoln's election could move news across three states (Webb, 1873, p. 13). His plan sought to establish a representative in every state, who would "appoint a man to travel twelve miles, and then hand the news to another man, and so on, till the news reached from Louisiana to Mississippi." This would allow for a simultaneous rebellion, as Webb argued, "in all the States at one time, so the white people would not have a chance" (ibid.).

O'Donovan (2011, p. 2) insists that "Webb and his nebulous network was no anomaly," and that "it traveled along with marching columns of chained slaves, the infamous coffle lines that remain the iconic face of the domestic slave trade" and "the squalid confines of the South's county jails" (ibid.). For Hahn, the accounts of slaves and former slaves, confessions of slave conspirators, diaries of slaveholders, and reports in local newspapers support the claim that slaves had developed "networks of communication and forums of organization that could extend over long distances," which "could reverberate with political discussions, narratives, and discourses of expectation" (ibid., p.

74).²² The broadening of these networks was facilitated by, inter alia, work projects in the South that drew primarily from hired-out slave labor and in so doing "contained enormous subversive potential." The salience of hired-out slaves, so obvious in the major slave revolts, was no less so right up to the Civil War.²³ The resulting networks assisted the escape of an estimated five hundred to seven hundred thousand slaves to Union lines (Glatthaar, 1992, p. 142), transforming a civil war intended to maintain slavery (the Union's and the CSA's original war aim) into a revolution to overthrow it.

This revolution was a war for the national liberation of enslaved black America, situated wholly within the United States. The U.S. Civil War was a political revolution and an economic revolution—both resulting from a *black* cultural revolution, although it was not an *American* cultural revolution. It radically transformed the polity of the United States by advancing the citizenship rights of former chattel slaves—the CSA leaders were right that their politico-military project was consistent with that of the Founders and Lincoln's policies with respect to the manumission of slaves and the rights of secession were a revolutionary abandonment of that vision.²⁴ It was an economic revolution that overthrew the economic system of chattel slavery, but the failure of the war to provide to blacks reparations in the form of land, material compensation, and broader legal and socioeconomic redress for their centuries of bondage was the major issue of social justice left unresolved by the war, which persists to this day. The war did not overthrow the U.S. cultural system of white supremacism; although the Slave Revolution emerged largely from a cultural impetus within black communities that wedded political and economic factors in a larger thrust for racial democracy, it left unabated the cultural system of white supremacism. It was a *black* cultural revolution, but it did not generate an *American* cultural revolution, and this spoke to the resilience and persistence of white supremacism among white Americans, individually, and their institutions of power, generally.

With white supremacism intact, the political and economic gains that blacks secured through war would be short-lived, and white racism provided justification for the political repression of blacks in the postbellum era and the seizure of the few economic rights and limited resources they had secured. Future efforts to address these problems and to ameliorate these conditions would require strategies that wed politics, economics, and culture in novel ways that replicated the best lessons of the Slave Revolution while not repeating its shortcomings. Given the persistence of white supremacism in the cultural system of the United States, and the linkage between the cultural system and the political and economic systems, then white cultural transformation would be a salient factor in future liberation strategies, as well. However, in future formulations, culture would need to be viewed as more than a mechanism to organize the black liberation struggle internally, but also a focus of the liberation struggle externally. Black liberation would require another, broader cultural revolution, one that both utilized and transformed the American culture system in such a way as to generate political, economic, and cultural democracy, which would establish racial democracy in the United States.

Complicating this further, the white supremacism of the postbellum era had further undermined the cultural institutions of black communities, and called into question for many whether African Americans even possessed a culture at all (related to this view was whether African people, in general, possessed a culture, which European colonialism, following Hegel, among many other Enlightenment thinkers, famously denied). Thus, revolutionary programs and theses would have an uphill battle on the cultural front *within* black communities before—or simultaneous with—overturning the white supremacist cultural system of the United States in which these communities were embedded. The challenge for black intellectuals, activists, and revolutionists was to formulate such theses, which would build on these lessons and address these challenges. That is, they would need to plan for concerted action within black communities and between black and white communities.

Considering the theory and practice of revolution that emerges from the actions of enslaved blacks during the Civil War, we observe a relationship between slave religion and slave hiring, and the religiously inspired "slave-wagery" that resulted from their confluence.[25] Their actions demonstrated, inter alia, that black revolution could be fueled by cultural change. Thus, just as Du Bois situated an affirming African American culture as the centerpiece of black nationalism, evolving classical black nationalism into modern black nationalism—i.e., black *cultural* nationalism—he demonstrated that a centerpiece of this affirming African American culture, slave religion, could provide the impetus for political and economic revolution in the United States. From Du Bois onward, it would be necessary for analysts, activists, and theorists attempting to conceptualize—much less, organize—black revolution in the United States, to appreciate the historic and contemporary importance of black culture in such a revolution. That is, it was necessary to appreciate the importance of black cultural revolution. Unfortunately, the significance of this revolution—and, for most, its existence as a revolution—was rarely appreciated by scholars, analysts, activists of any race in the United States during the BPM or even decades after it. As the only successful revolution in the constituted United States (the American Revolution having taken place before its establishment as an independent, sovereign nation), it demanded consideration for anyone planning future insurgency in the country.

Both Du Bois and Haywood agreed that Reconstruction did not complete the economic revolution wrought by the overthrow of chattel slavery, insofar as it did not result in the agrarian transformation that manumission augured to undergird black political freedom with grants of land to support a multiracial proletariat in the South. For Haywood (1958), although the Civil War "destroyed chattel slavery," it "did not bring real freedom to the Negro freedman"; instead, "Left without the land—cheated out of his chief means of livelihood, he was forced back upon the plantations into a position of semi-slave servitude but slightly removed from that of his former chattel bondage." It is also important to remember that the Slave Revolution did not transform the cultural system of the United States and its white supremacism, which persisted both de jure and de facto through the Jim Crow era and during both the CRM and BPM of the twentieth century, and continued to contextualize, constrain, and confound black liberation struggles in the United States. One implication is that BPM activists could usefully draw on strategies from a century before (with some modifications) to confront this cultural system anew. Key for BPM activists was to recognize and harness their black culture, coordinating and utilizing it as a basis for mobilizing black Americans into purposive agents of cultural and political revolution.

The U.S. Slave Revolution suggested other referents for BPM revolutionists. For example, the analogues of the religiously inspired, hired-out, incipient-working-class-conscious slaves a century later were the increasingly urban, religiously inspired, working-class blacks who constituted the humanpower of the CRM. Another potentially useful analogue was the mechanism that slave rebels employed, a general strike, which enervated the South and propelled their revolutionary engagement as troops of their Union allies. The general strike strategy that had proved successful during the Civil War might be just as useful for the BPM. Du Bois's thesis implied as much in arguing that the General Strike anticipated subsequent Marxist revolutions including the Bolshevik Revolution, from which important leaders and analysts of the BPM would draw inspiration. In one of the few major admitted expansions on Du Bois's thesis, Roediger (2014) goes farthest and points out the seminal influence of the General Strike on the women's suffrage movement, the movement to recognize the civil rights of the disabled, the movement for an eight-hour work day, and the prospects for a multicultural national labor party.

The General Strike prefigured other multiracial general strikes in the United States, such as the 1892 New Orleans general strike of more than forty unions that included an alliance of black and white workers, but, as Du Bois noted, it foreshadowed major revolutions of the twentieth century as well. For example, it paralleled the Russian general strike of 1905, which, as Harcave (1970) argued, fused the respective "agrarian," "nationality," "labour," and "educated class" problems in the country to create the conditions for the revolution that ensued. Such a fusion is not unrelated to that which was evident in the boycott strategy of the CRM in the Jim Crow South. To be sure, the liberation of blacks, as a whole, North and South, would require a broader program and one geared toward a more critical politico-socio-economic institution than a municipal bus service of a single Southern city like Montgomery, Alabama, or even the broader objective of organizing black urban and rural communities in the South with respect to their voting rights.

In order not to replicate other shortcomings in the aftermath of the Civil War, the BPM would need to attend to *cultural* objectives, as well, for instance, to overthrow the cultural system of white supremacism. The latter was especially difficult given that the cultural system was the main axis of contention between blacks and their white allies—even more so their white opposition—and this fissure spelled the doom of Reconstruction inasmuch as it provided the nexus uniting Northern and Southern whites in what Du Bois labeled the "counterrevolution of property." Thus, updating and applying a general strike strategy would entail devising an approach to alliances with potential white allies especially. During the General Strike, these included Northern white abolitionists who supported the cause of black freedom, thousands of disaffected poor Southern whites who deserted the CSA, and, most decisively, whites in the Union Army. BPM revolutionists would need to leverage their position in the politico-economy in order to maximize the impact of their minority organization. Thus, the specific focus of organizing would suggest the requisite approach to alliance making. Whether the focus was on claims related to their status/condition as a subjugated race, an exploited class, an ethnic group that was discriminated against, a colonized nation or a mixture of all of them would determine whether race-based, class-based, interest group, or national organization was the preferred strategy. Such determinations would have implications for the selection of potential allies, as well. For example, if they focused on race, then organizing would be race-based regardless of class (or ethnicity or nationality), and alliances sought with other oppressed racial groups regardless of class, etc., in opposition to whites of all classes; and if the strategy focused on class, then organizing would privilege classes (e.g., the proletariat or lumpenproletariat) regardless of race, etc., and alliances would be sought with oppressed classes regardless of race, in opposition to class adversaries of any race. Likewise, if the strategy focused on ethnicity, then organizing would privilege the ethnic group, and alliances would supersede other axes of identity, in opposition to rival ethnics irrespective of race, class, or nation,[26] and similarly, if the strategy focused on nationality, then organizing would be national, and alliances sought mainly with other oppressed nations, in opposition to white colonial domination.

The focus of claims would determine the strategy for organizing and alliance making, and go far in predicting movement success.

A difficulty for BPM revolutionists drawing from the Slave Revolution a revolutionary thesis to orient their movement was that Du Bois did not explicitly theorize the cultural revolution he historicized in *Black Reconstruction*. Nevertheless, a decade after publishing *Black Reconstruction*, and well before the onset of the BPM, his contemporary Alain Locke provided such theorizing.

Alain Locke and Black Cultural Revolution

Although noted primarily for his role as an intellectual leader of the Harlem Renaissance through his editorship of the seminal volume *The New Negro*, Alain Locke's contributions to our understanding of black cultural revolution are as massive as they are ignored by both academics and activists. He studied culture as few had up to his time, in Oxford and Berlin as the first African American Rhodes Scholar. He developed his perspective from pragmatist philosophy and wed it to the cultural pluralist approaches in the emerging field of anthropology. An early proponent of cultural pluralism in the Boasian school, nonetheless he asserted the salience of "Aframerican" culture rooted in a mixture of African and American cultural tendencies. Although similar to Du Bois's view of black culture rooted in the sorrow songs and folkways of the black South, Locke's drew a clearer distinction between African and Aframerican aesthetics in a broader project linking black culture to his sociological view of race. Locke's approach provided a theoretical explanation of black cultural revolution in the United States.

To appreciate Locke's contribution to theses of black cultural revolution it is important to consider his analysis of race, culture, and cultural change. The justification for white racism progressed through several distinct, overlapping, and often mutually reinforcing rationalizations rooted initially in theology, then biology, and subsequently anthropology. The religious and biological justifications of white supremacy are well known; and Boas (1911) is credited with undermining biologically based white supremacism, ushering in the anthropological discourse of cultural relativism. Locke embraced Boas's arguments that physical, mental, and cultural traits associated with race were mutable and adaptable to different environments; but, he argued against the anthropological view of race, as well, insisting that race was sociological. In the first of five lectures at Howard University in 1916, he argued that anthropology had not isolated any permanent or static features of race (Stewart, 1992,

p. xxiv). He noted that "as applied to social and ethnic groups," race "has no meaning at all beyond that sense of kind, that sense of kith and kin"; it is "an ethnic fiction" (Locke, 1992, p. 12). For Locke (ibid., p. 11), modern conceptions of race are not "about the anthropological or biological idea at all," but the relative fortunes of "an ethnic group," which in anthropological terms are "ethnic fictions" that are the result of "countless interminglings" and "infinite crossings of types," which "maintain in name only this fetish of biological [purity]" (ibid.). The extent that a person has a race, "he has inherited either a favorable or an unfavorable social heredity, which unfortunately is [typically] ascribed to factors which have not produced [it,] factors which will in no way determine either the period of those inequalities or their eradication" (ibid., p. 12). Locke "was standing racialist theories of culture on their heads: rather than particular races creating Culture, it was culture—social, political, and economic processes—that produced racial character" (Stewart, 1992, p. xxv). For Locke, race was sociological—or in today's verbiage, a "social construct." "Consequently," he concludes "any true history of race must be a sociological theory of race" (1992, p. 11). Locke was among the first scholars to explain race this way. His contributions were as prescient and profound as they are ignored in contemporary scholarship on racism.

Locke viewed peoples of different races, including white and black Americans, as highly assimilative beings within societies whose arbitrary policies and practices were based on the assumed physical incompatibility of races, which he viewed as baseless, since "[t]he factors which really determine race inequalities," in his view, "are not at all commensurable with these physical factors," but "are factors of language, customs, habits, social adaptability, [and] social survival" (1992, p. 10). Further, although Locke demystified race as a social construct, he did not jettison the concept. In fact, he asserted the usefulness of race as a point of reference and prominent signifier that was unlikely to be "superceded except by some revised version of itself"; therefore, he sought to revise it in such a way as to serve as an ameliorative (ibid., p. 85). Locke asserted the value of race consciousness, while rejecting that race was either a "permanent biological entity or nothing at all" and insisting instead on the relevance of "social race" (Stewart, 1992, p. xxv). He argued that "[t]he only kind of race that is left to believe in and to be applied to modern problems is what we call the idea of social race, defining it more narrowly as a conception of civilization or civilization kind" (1992, p. 88). For him, "a basic law in human society" is that "[e]very civilization produces its type" and "it should be judged in terms of that civilization type, and should come to know itself in proportion as it recognizes the type" (ibid., pp. 88–89). Civilization type evokes for Locke a "sense of shared practices and modes of life consistent with participation in a competitive economy and other common core institutions" of modern society (Fraser, 1999, p. 12). "Consequently," Fraser notes, "modern societies," for Locke, "tend to produce a single 'civilization type,' an ideal-typical sort of person, which members come roughly to approximate by virtue of participating in a common social structure and institutional framework." In light of this, "[c]ivilization type, according to Locke, is the proper overarching unit of solidarity in modern societies" (ibid., pp. 12–13).

Although civilization type generates conformity, it is not so much homogenizing as generating common frames of reference for its constituent social cultures, which provide a sense of belonging and solidarity. People articulate social cultures within the context of their civilization type and the diversity within the civilization type is reflected in the diverse social cultures that participate in it. Since social culture, like all culture, is dynamic, civilization type is subject to change from within—as a result of changes among its constituent social cultures and from without—through its contacts with social cultures of other civilization types. For Locke, social cultures are highly interdependent, and he emphasized that "[t]here is no part of the universe today which is not in some way, economic[,] or political[,] or social, bound up with the other parts," such that "no social culture in the present day world will be ignorant of other types or object to [some kind of] contact with other types," and this relationship obtains "no matter how much a line is drawn theoretically between races," because "the practical demands of present day life necessitate the contact of races, and an increasing contact of races" (Locke, 1992, pp. 13–14). In addition, the social races that social cultures generate are also dynamic, and this dynamism is accentuated through contacts with other social races.

It followed for Locke that social races should be "conserved" to the extent that they promote solidarity and a sense of belonging—especially for marginalized groups such as racial minorities (and, presumably, other marginalized groups)—and therefore assist in the articulation of their cultural expression. By articulating a "consciousness of kind," which he viewed as "healthy for human societies" and "a fundamental social instinct," albeit one that has had "a very abnormal expression from time to time," he was convinced that under certain conditions, "race types and race kind can be transformed . . . into social kind" such that "essentially a man must become one of the same race [or civilization type] when he lives or [learns] to live in the same civilization and [has] conformed to a civilization type. [This] is the only essential kind of race that exists in the world today" (1992, p. 79). Therefore:

> [I]f you have the same manners and customs and have allegiance to the same social system, you belong to the same race . . . even though ethnically you many not; so that really when you conform or belong to a civilization type . . . you are of the same race in any vital or rational sense of race . . . to exclude you from that kind of race is simply arbitrary and [a] very perverse practice which comes from an abnormal conception on the part of the society of what consciousness of kind is and of what the social or civilization type consists. (ibid.)

He notes that race prejudice "falsely attributes to certain arbitrary ethnological and biological factors, sociological and social standards which do not pertain to them at all" (ibid.).

Locke was convinced that "American society is hastening the process of social assimilation by the very restrictive measures that [it is] imposing," in part because, "[w]hile social assimilation is in progress there seems to be necessary some counter-theory, or rather some counter-doctrine. This counter-doctrine one finds in racial solidarity and culture" (1992, p. 96). For Locke, "secondary race consciousness" is the race consciousness of a minority group in a society. He argued that the "stimulation of a secondary race consciousness within a group" was necessary "for several practical reasons" (ibid.). Foremost among them was the group's need "to get a right conception of itself," and "it can only do that through the stimulation of pride in itself," which secondary race consciousness provides to groups in the way self-respect does for the individual. For Locke, "Race pride seems a rather different loyalty from the larger loyalty to the joint or common civilization type." While "apparently paradoxical" in the abstract, it is not so in practice because

> the very stimulation to collective activity which race pride or racial self-respect may give will issue into the qualification test and the aim to meet that qualification test, which, of course, must be in terms of the common standard. So that through a doctrine of race solidarity and culture you really accelerate and stimulate the alien group to a rather more rapid assimilation of the social culture, the general social culture, than would be otherwise possible. (1992, p. 97)

Secondary race consciousness facilitates the recreation of the race type and its ultimate merging with the civilization type. Locke asserts that "we can only get recognition for our [contribution] collectively [and only] through a recognition . . . given a re-created race type that expresses itself in terms of a representative class or representative products," which secondary race consciousness stimulates and facilitates (ibid., p. 98). Locke's thesis insists that race consciousness "prevents the representative classes, as they develop, [from] being merged into the larger group, from being dissipated and lost in the larger group," while, coincidentally, "harnessing" the larger group to the "submerged group," stimulating "the general progress [of the group]" (ibid.).

Given its functionality for minority groups seeking a basis for cultural identity, belonging, and solidarity, social race should be "conserved" through the promotion of secondary race consciousness. But Locke is clear that "this is not a doctrine of race isolation," but, "It is really a theory of social conservation which in practice conserves the best in each group, and promotes the development of social solidarity out of heterogeneous elements" (1992, p. 98). His was not a "doctrine of race conservation" but a "doctrine of social conservation" (ibid., p. 99). As Harris and Molesworth (2008, p. 126) point out, "Locke shifts the category to one of 'social' rather than 'racial' conservation and invokes his own emergent ideas of multiculturalism to complete his thought" while "avoid[ing] any suggestion of chauvinism or separatism." The objective of "race progress and race adjustment" for Locke was the promotion of "culture-citizenship," which would result from the "group contribution to what becomes a joint civilization," and be "acquired through social assimilation" that facilitates incorporation of the "group contribution to what becomes a joint civilization" (Locke, 1992, p. 99). The achievement of that goal would be evident to the extent that "we can jointly accept whatever [of value] there is in the civilization's conception of itself" (ibid.).

Locke argued that "[u]ntil alien [group talents and] certain representative products are developed (which products for their sheer intrinsic worth are worthy of incorporation into the joint culture), I fancy no really final and satisfactory race recognition will be accorded" (p. 99). The essential "talents" and "representative products" that are candidates for incorporation and facilitate "race recognition" are artistic expressions in music, the arts, and letters. Analogizing from developments in Europe, Locke argues that

> movements by which the submerged classes are coming to their expression in art—seem to be the forerunners of that kind of recognition which they are ultimately striving for, namely, recognition [of an] economic, [a] civic, and [a] social sort; and these [movements] are the gateways through which culture-citizenship can be finally reached" (1992, p. 100)

Locke encouraged Negroes to cultivate the art derived from their syncretic Aframerican social culture characteristic of the race. Further, "[t]hrough art blacks could build social solidarity and race consciousness, without overly threatening the white power structure. Moreover, by developing their cultural productivity, blacks would contradict the notion that African Americans were a people without culture, whose only choice was complete assimilation" (Stewart, 1992, p. xxxii). He thought the "thinking Negro" would be the more effective purveyor of those elements of Aframerican culture, to articulate the representative aspects of the social culture that would "blend" with the civilization-type: "a case of putting the premium upon the capably few, and thus of accelerating the 'levelling up' processes in American society" (Locke, 1927, p. 557). The reciprocal recognition of social cultures within the civilization-type facilitated "culture-citizenship," which reflected the ideal of cultural development: the attainment of cultural cosmopolitanism, which for Locke would be realized in a multiracial democracy (Locke, 1992, p. 100).

Locke's conceptualization of social culture, inter alia, allows us to theorize the Slave Revolution that Du Bois historicized in *Black Reconstruction*. Specifically, it suggests that the change in slave religion that Du Bois delineated, from countenancing docility to promoting revolt, resulted from reciprocity, as Du Bois implied, and the transvaluation and transposition of religious values to divinely sanctioning revolt (Moses, 1993, p. 246). Further, the interaction of hired-out slaves—especially slave artisans—with their free counterparts heightened their understanding of the differences in the value of their labor and that of free persons, magnifying the extent of their exploitation. Thus, reciprocity between bond and free artisans contributed to an incipient working-class consciousness among the former. These mutually reinforcing factors of reciprocity, transvaluation, and transposition helped compel the slave revolts of the antebellum era, culminating in the Slave Revolution.

Just as Locke's framework helps explain what Du Bois observed in *Black Reconstruction*, it is also applicable to the BPM. It suggested that by tapping into the cultural institutions of black communities, the network of religiously inspired black workers, and by utilizing a general strike as a precipitant of broader struggle, BPM revolutionists might formulate a cultural revolution that would compel a political revolution in the United States.

Although in the Howard University lectures Locke did not appear to view cultures as progressing through stages, subsequently he began to imply as much (Locke, 1989 [1924]). Given the greater freedom for interaction of individuals, groups, and cultural practices and institutions in more open political systems, Locke was convinced that cultural cosmopolitanism was most likely to be actualized in a multiracial democracy; thus, his framework implies a relationship between culture and democracy. Locke viewed multiracial democracy as a stage that no state had achieved, and one that the United States with its inveterate white racism was not close to realizing. Considering this, it cannot be said that Locke's framework inevitably evolves to a white ideal; nevertheless, his model of democratic development—and the relationship of culture to that development—follows closely the development of democracy in the United States. Buck (2005) notes that Locke viewed democracy as proceeding through nine stages: (1) local democracy, (2) moral democracy, (3) political democracy, (4) economic democracy, (5) cultural democracy, (6) racial democracy, (7) social democracy, (8) spiritual democracy, and (9) world democracy. At the time, Locke saw some states proceeding through each of the first five stages, but in his view no state had achieved racial democracy. The problems of achieving racial democracy were partly embedded in one of the obstacles to states attaining its precursor phase, cultural democracy, which is that political and economic rights did not guarantee the rights of cultural minorities, and cultural democracy, "rests on . . . the guarantee of the rights of minorities" (Buck, 2005, p. 251). Moreover, Locke contends that "the race question is at the very heart of this struggle for cultural democracy" and "[i]ts solution lies beyond even the realization of political and economic democracy, although of course that solution can only be reached when we no longer have extreme political inequality and extreme economic inequality" (ibid.). Cultural democracy extends political and economic democracy to the cultural sphere, and, in so doing, facilitates racial democracy—Locke's sixth phase. Challenges on the cultural front demonstrate the need to alter the dominant cultural paradigm of the society to reflect the values, views, and interests of marginalized cultural groups; and—anticipating Cruse (1967)—in so doing implicate racial democracy as well.

The analysis at this point goes to the heart of the significance of black cultural revolution in the United States: it not only challenges the cultural hegemony of white supremacism but it does so through raising and reinforcing the political and economic demands of African Americans to the cultural sphere in such a way as to facilitate racial democracy. Considering the range of cultural issues that motivate such profound changes, we are not simply talking about culture in the aesthetic, but in the material sense as well, nor are we focusing simply on cultural representation (e.g., artistic production, its institutionalization, or even its distribution and commodification) but, broader, fundamental issues that arise from the political and economic claims of marginalized culture groups that implicate racial democracy. The eradication of racial slavery was such an issue. By raising the claim of the human rights of slaves to freedom, black revolutionaries of the Civil War were asserting a cultural claim of a people (their right to freedom) and simultaneously a political claim to civil rights (related to equal pay and provisions in the Union Army, initially, extended to citizenship rights in the United States) and economic rights (to their own labor, and to land ownership, among others); the implication of these was to create—at least on paper—a racial democracy. In this way, Locke's framework theorizes Du Bois's Slave Revolution. It explains how a black cultural revolution generated a political revolution in the United States, and this could serve as an example for theorizing in the BPM.

The success of the Slave Revolution should not be diminished because of the ultimate failure of Reconstruction, which demonstrated the extent to which the counterrevolutionaries were committed to ending it. In the event, the cultural system of white supremacism, which had not transformed but receded only briefly into the far-ranging social institutions of the predominantly white society, quickly reasserted itself in the major political and economic institutions of the former CSA, making the transformation of U.S. and Southern society short-lived. Nonetheless, a major implication of the successes of the Slave Revolution for BPM revolutionists a century later was the utility of similarly situated, religiously inspired proletarians to put forth cultural claims that could be politicized in such a way as to transform the economic structure of the United States and so to augur racial democracy. A key challenge was to focus on an issue as profound in its implications for political, economic, and racial democracy as chattel slavery had been in the 1860s and to devise a mobilizational strategy centered on it. In Locke's era, the obvious issue was Jim Crow, which was only overturned by a massive and monumental Civil Rights Movement (CRM) of 1955–65. The BPM faced the remaining major unresolved politico-economic-cultural claim of black people in the United States, directly associated with both slavery and Jim Crow: black reparations. The failure of the United States to provide an economic floor to support its newly manumitted slaves, through provisions of land and an effective franchise to ensure their political rights, made reparations for chattel slavery, Jim Crow, and state-sanctioned white racism the major unresolved culture-based claim of African Americans, having political and economic ramifications that implicate racial democracy in the United States.

The cultural claim for reparations has been both an issue of social justice and one seeking an economic/material basis for black political freedom. It has had the potential to unite blacks across classes to make real political and economic democracy in the United States, and in this way to provide for multiracial democracy in America or justify a revolution to create it. Although Locke did not focus on reparations or outline the means to achieve racial democracy, he did advocate the overthrow of Jim Crow. Relatedly, Locke appreciated the awesome struggle for cultural democracy that was a prerequisite for racial democracy—foreshadowing, at least in philosophical terms, the necessity of something approximating a black cultural revolution to overthrow the cultural system of white supremacism to achieve multiracial democracy.

In his 1943 monograph, *World View on Race and Democracy*, Locke noted that "[o]f all the barriers limiting democracy, color is the greatest, whether viewed from a standpoint of national or world democracy" (p. 1); and in 1949, he argued that the "race question" was the "number one problem of the world." Locke linked the "race problem" in the United States to the "race problem" in the world, with the former requiring a "heroic challenge and criticism" to universalize the African American struggle "into a purging and inspiring plea for justice and a fuller democracy" (cited in Buck, 2005, p. 252). For Locke, white supremacism in the United States was "the acid test of the whole problem"; and one that "will be crucial in its outcome for the rest of the world," making the United States "the world's laboratory" for the progressive solution to the challenge of racial democracy (ibid.).

Implications of Fusing Locke's and Du Bois's Views

In their shared orientation to black culture, both Du Bois and Locke rejected reverse civilizationism and its contention that African Americans did not possess a culture, which may suggest why their theses were ignored by Malcolm X and BPM activists who drew uncritically from the Muslim minister's mistaken formulation. In combination, their theses (1) established the relevance of the Slave Revolution as a historic political revolution in the United States; and (2) demonstrated how a black cultural revolution could generate a political revolution. The key components of the success of the Slave Revolution were both slave religion and the incipient working-class consciousness of the hired-out slaves who coordinated webs of networks to facilitate their insurgency. Their analogue a century later was the increasingly urban, religiously inspired working-class blacks who provided the humanpower of the CRM and the BPM. Following Du Bois and Locke, key for BPM activists was to recognize and harness the African American culture, to coordinate it, and utilize it as a basis for the mobilization of African Americans into purposive agents of revolution.

A major implication of Du Bois's analysis of the General Strike was that the success of future black liberation struggles was dependent on the ability of revolutionists to overthrow not only the political and economic systems, but the cultural system of white America. The black revolution of the Civil War did not transform the cultural system of the United States and its white supremacism, which continued to influence the major institutions of the postbellum state. This cultural system persisted both de jure and de facto through the Jim Crow era and both the CRM and BPM of the twentieth century, and continued to constrain and confound black liberation struggles in the United States. Thus, given the persistence of the white supremacist cultural system, black liberation activists might usefully draw on strategies that were effective a century earlier to address the conditions they faced during the black power era. In the context of a future general strike strategy, the cultural system would need to be both a source of inspiration internally (i.e., the cultural system within African American communities), as well as a target of mobilization externally (i.e., the cultural system of the United States).

In sum, black revolutionists would need to utilize black culture—embedded in its major cultural institutions—toward political and economic ends in order to overthrow white supremacy in the United States. Unfortunately, most BPM revolutionists did not appreciate the significance of the General Strike and the homegrown black revolution in the United States during the Civil War. The reverse civilizationism that they often uncritically accepted from Malcolm X compelled them to draw their models, programs, and theories of revolution from Africa and other "third world" cases, while discouraging the study of the revolutionary antecedents in U.S. history to inform their theorizing and praxis. Further, convinced that African Americans had been stripped of their culture, even where they appreciated the relevance of culture to revolutionary struggle, they did not recognize the centrality of the religiously inspired incipient black proletarian culture to the previous black revolution in the United States, or to the one they hoped to fashion during the BPM.

The logic of reverse civilizationism required that a black American culture would have to be created or constructed, requiring a political project to which it could be wedded. The specific project would suggest the form that this newly created black culture would take. For example, the Nation of Islam promoted a form of black culture that they defined as "Asiatic"; Us, Congress of African People (CAP), the Republic of New Africa (RNA), and the Shrine of the Black Madonna promoted forms of black culture rooted in their conception of "traditional African" culture; and the Black Panther Party (BPP) and League of Revolutionary Black Workers (LRBW) promoted a form of black culture reflected in the practices of "brothers on the block." These organizations sought commonalities between their interests and those of Africans involved in anticolonial struggles. Thus, while Africans were struggling against settler colonialism and neocolonialism, African American revolutionists construed their struggle in a context of domestic colonialism. Likewise, they viewed African American culture as African and put in the service of assisting to overthrow domestic colonialism in the United States. This perspective viewed black culture's value strictly as propaganda and encouraged its exclusive performance of that role.

However, most BPM activists had only a superficial understanding of the diverse cultures of African societies, so they appropriated or in some cases manufactured aspects of one or more of the thousands of African cultures—and hundreds of major African cultures—that seemed to fit their specific projects, their leaders' personal proclivities, their organizational programs, and/or their immediate political objectives. For the most part, they settled on hierarchical aspects of selected customs, often exclusively communal, associated with one or a few specific culture groups, in what were more than forty states of sub-Saharan Africa during the BPM, ranging from the sliver of a country that is Gambia or minute Rio Muni to the massive Saharan Desert straddling Sudan and the immense Congo. The culture groups of these African states range from the more than two hundred ethnic groups of Congo (formerly Zaire) to the almost culturally homogeneous Lesotho and Botswana. Most prominent BPM revolutionists ignored the urban, working class, egalitarian, or cosmopolitan features of the diverse cultures of Africa. Markedly absent was an adoption of African democratic forms of organization and governance such as palaver or kgotla. They constructed these extremely limited conceptions of the diverse cultures of Africa as synonymous with an almost timeless, unchanging, singular, monolithic "African" culture—as opposed to one aspect of one of hundreds if not thousands of African cultures such as Yoruba, Asante, Chokwe, Kongo, Zulu, Xhosa, Swahili, Kikuyu, Amhara, Wolof, Mende, or Fon, among many others.

Locke's conception of black cultural change and, by implication, black cultural revolution, countenanced no such limitations or boundaries on cultural expression as it gravitated toward its own cosmopolitanism. Locke wed cultural change only to democracy, which was necessary to ensure that individuals and groups within and across cultures could express and share their cultures in myriad interactions. It advocated democracy within and between culture groups—unencumbered by noncultural (i.e., political, economic, demographic) hierarchies and impositions. The fate of the BPM was that its major revolutionists—with the exception of Harold Cruse—were largely oblivious to Locke's thesis, and their programs, practices, and objectives reflected as much.

Locke did not explain how the cultural change he theorized could be implemented programmatically to assist blacks to navigate American society through the stages of democratic development he outlined. In the event, it was Du Bois's more evolutionary approach from *Social Reconstruction* (examined further in chapter 4), which focused on the development of parallel institutions of civil society in black communities to provide for national development, that BPM revolutionists practiced and programmed for—even those publicly advocating armed struggle, rather than the revolutionary approach that Du Bois's *Black Reconstruction* historicized and Locke's approach theorized. That is, BPM revolutionists instituted an evolutionary strategy to achieve ostensibly revolutionary ends—a point not lost on Harold Cruse

(1967). Locke's thesis focusing on the internal dynamism of black culture can account for the emancipatory transformations within slave religion that compelled the General Strike; and, for Locke, given the dynamism of black culture itself, cultural revolution does not require a change agent external to the black community. In the historical example of the Slave Revolution, the revolutionary capacity of black culture was actualized in the most powerful cultural institution in the black community at the time, the invisible institution or slave religion. It follows that black cultural revolution during the BPM—like the slave revolts of the antebellum era, and the Slave Revolution of the U.S. Civil War—would more likely succeed if it was grounded in the Black Church. This did not preclude the salience of other black institutions, such as black political parties, civil rights organizations, black unions, media (e.g., black newspapers, radio, and, later, television), or some yet to be developed institution (e.g., social media); but given its unambiguous grounding in African American culture, as well as a greater share of black participants, black economic resources, and black political leverage, the Black Church was the clear candidate.

Although a synthesis of their theses suggested as much, Du Bois was ambivalent on whether the Black Church might lead the social transformation of black America, while Locke saw the Black Church as a facilitator of the "self-segregation" that his broader integrationist orientation would not countenance. This ambivalence toward and/or denial of the role of the Black Church in the cultural revolution that their theses implied would morph into outright opposition to—and even denunciation of—the Black Church by many leaders of the BPM. That revolutionists of the BPM would attempt a black cultural revolution while ignoring the most powerful cultural institution in black communities was a major oversight in their theorizing even as many of the groups associated with the BPM drew on the institutional support of church leaders for their programs, while casting their appeal to a largely church-going black working class—both urban and rural, and an emerging middle class. The denial and dismissal of the Black Church among those who proposed a black cultural revolution—and a black political revolution, as well—was a fatal flaw in their theorizing and activism; and it seriously undermined their movement.[27]

While reparations for chattel slavery and Jim Crow was the most important cultural claim directed at the U.S. state, there were important cultural claims implicating political and economic democracy to be directed at institutions inside black communities, as well. The major such cultural claim was that related to the emancipation of black women and girls. The persistence of sexism in black communities was the major unresolved issue of social justice within them. Therefore, black feminism with respect to both political and cultural revolution was as salient as it was to the broader social change that blacks pursued, as black feminists had argued since no later than the nineteenth century.

A focus on culture beyond the major cultural institutions of black communities remained necessary because the enduring racist cultural system would have to be fractured again a century later during the CRM and BPM, setting Dixiecrats and their conservative Democrats and Republican allies against liberal Democrats and moderate Republicans, and conservative whites against liberal and radical ones. The heightened U.S. involvement in the Vietnam War might provide another opportunity for blacks to promote division among whites regarding war to take advantage of a sectarian crisis; however, this time it seemed that it would not be enough to generate, exacerbate, or simply exploit divisions among white Americans (e.g., as between white abolitionists and their white pro-slavery opponents), but it needed to promote a cultural transformation among white folks as well, to assist in the overthrow of a system of white cultural domination that benefited them, just as some Northern whites had assisted in the overthrow of the CSA a century earlier. Black revolutionists would have to fuse their political, economic, and social interests into a cohesive and coordinated movement that appreciated the cultural, racial, class, and gender based impetus for their activism—and to do it in such a way as to encourage divisions among whites and to institutionalize challenges to white cultural supremacism from within their own populations. That is, the black cultural revolution might have to generate a corresponding white cultural revolution, as well. The latter was necessary because although the Slave Revolution emerged largely from a cultural impetus that wedded political and economic factors in a larger thrust for racial democracy, it left unabated the cultural system of white supremacism. It was a *black* cultural revolution; but it did not generate an *American* cultural revolution, and this spoke to the resilience and persistence of white supremacism among white Americans individually and their institutions of power generally, which would make black freedom a caricature of what blacks had fought for and thought they had obtained. White supremacism undermined black claims through the maintenance of its racist cultural system throughout the United States—especially its education, criminal justice, and governance systems. Therefore, white cultural transformation would be a salient factor in future black liberation strategies, and culture would need to be viewed as more than a mechanism to organize struggles for meaningful black freedom internally, but also a focus of the liberation struggle externally.

In sum, it was clear that revolutionary change could emanate from cultural processes within the black community but they were more likely to be successful when there were not only cultural transformations toward more emancipatory programs and institutions in white communities but also major fissures in the white community itself. Splits in the white community would denude white power and potentially generate white allies for black insurgents targeting the institutional apparatus of the white supremacist cultural system in the United States. This not only suggested a strategic focus for prospective revolutionists, but it meant that extending black cultural revolution to a broader political *and* cultural revolution in the postbellum United States relied on the presence of major disruptions in U.S. society that divide white communities and correspondingly unify black communities.

Conclusion

In conclusion, at the outset of the BPM, Malcolm X called for both a black political and a cultural revolution; however, he never developed his thesis on the latter and did not adequately explain the relationship between the two. Instead, like many BPM revolutionists he privileged cases of revolutions from abroad which were often ill-fitted to the peculiar history and contemporary challenges of African American politics and culture. Ironically, W. E. B. Du Bois had historicized a black political revolution in 1935 and Alain Locke had theorized a cultural revolution in the United States a decade later. A synthesis of Du Bois and Locke suggested the importance of the Slave Revolution in the U.S. Civil War as an exemplar of black revolution in the United States, and the relationship between black cultural and political revolution, historically and in the black power era.

Largely oblivious to Du Bois's and Locke's theses, BPM revolutionists took as their theoretical point of departure the arguments of Malcolm X. While their formulations were often insightful, transformative, and in some cases groundbreaking, they suffered from several important weaknesses as well. The main one was Malcolm X's reverse civilizationism, which led them to import models of revolution from abroad that did not fit the historical context or developmental trajectory of their uniquely African American experience. As a result, BPM revolutionists failed to adequately historicize their own movement, and without a theoretical compass oriented to the peculiar landscape of their American oppression, they planned a revolution across the terrain of the most powerful country in the world using strategies and tactics better suited for an African or third world country. At the core of their difficulty was an apprehension of the centrality of cultural revolution in the black American context. Given its particular salience, it was important to appreciate it as both concept and practice. In the next chapter, I examine cultural revolution as a concept, and discuss its intellectual precursors and practitioners among African Americans.

Chapter 4

Cultural Revolution and Cultural Evolution

The last chapter discussed how W. E. B. Du Bois and Alain Locke historicized and theorized, respectively, a relationship between black cultural and political revolution. First, Du Bois argued in *Black Reconstruction* that changes in "slave religion" motivated the "largest slave revolt" in U.S. history, the General Strike, which compelled Lincoln to change his war aims to overthrow chattel slavery, making the Civil War a political revolution.[1] In this way, Du Bois observed that a black cultural revolution motivated a political revolution. Second, Locke provided a theoretical formulation of the processes outlined by Du Bois. For Locke, cultural democracy involves expanding the domain of political and economic democracy into the cultural sphere in a way that facilitates racial democracy—describing a process that approximates a cultural revolution. As applied to Du Bois's historical analysis in *Black Reconstruction*, Locke's thesis suggests that the transformation in black culture (i.e., slave religion) ramified into the political and economic spheres (the General Strike), implicating multiracial democracy; the resolution of this confluence compelled a political revolution for both black America (i.e., the Slave Revolution) and the United States (overthrowing chattel slavery, defeating the CSA). Thus, the historical black revolution in the United States resulted from a cultural revolution that stimulated a political revolution. This was an extant thesis of black revolution in the United States that was available to Black Power Movement (BPM) revolutionists prior to the Civil Rights Movement (CRM).

Given the centrality of cultural revolution to these processes, in this chapter I examine the theoretical development of the concept. First, I briefly review the component concepts of cultural revolution, that is, culture and revolution. Second, recognizing the anteriority of the concept of cultural revolution in the academic literature, especially among Marxists, I discuss the applicability of Maoist, Leninist, and Gramscian theses of cultural revolution to black America. Third, I trace the roots of early formulations of black cultural *evolution* to the social development theses of black American activists and intellectuals—including black nationalist feminists—in the nineteenth century, and discuss how it informed later theses of black cultural *revolution*. Fourth, I review Du Bois's cultural evolutionary thesis from *The Negro and Social Reconstruction*, which focused on the development of parallel institutions of black civil society. I also discuss Du Bois's arguments during the Harlem Renaissance on the use of black culture as a propaganda tool and its implications for black cultural evolution. The analysis extends the conclusion of the last chapter that prior to the BPM there was an extant thesis of black cultural revolution that BPM revolutionists could have drawn on for theoretical direction, but also available was a thesis on black cultural evolution. The latter is not only an academic point, but contextualizes the irony that it was the latter cultural evolutionary approach that BPM revolutionists drew on in their programs to inform the cultural revolution they sought. In this way, their putatively revolutionary theorizing was guided by an evolutionary orientation.

Conceptualizing Black Cultural Revolution

Cultural Revolution: Defining the Terms

Cultural development, if not cultural revolution, has been central to major ideological arguments on African American politics for at least two centuries, and it reflects, in large part, the attempt by black Americans to fashion a humanity-affirming black culture in the context of white supremacy and its deculturalization of captured Africans and their progeny over more than two centuries of enslavement and more than a century of post-slavery Jim Crow. It has been espoused by black Americans of diverse ideological bents; among its earliest and most prominent advocates were black nationalists of the eighteenth and nineteenth centuries in the AME Church, in prominent black voluntary associations such as the Prince Hall Masons and Odd Fellows, as well as in black mutual aid societies. In contrast, many contemporary integrationists argued that blacks should assimilate the culture of white Americans in order to facilitate their entry into U.S. society. For example, William Whipper advocated the removal of "complexional" terms in the names of black organizations in the nineteenth century, such as the AME Church.

For the most part, arguments for black cultural revolution have emerged from black nationalists asserting the importance of black cultural identity in challenging white supremacist notions of black inferiority. They viewed such an assertion as necessary to begin the process of recovering and reconstructing the history of black peoples and the heritage that was denied them, the rights that were due them, and the reparations that were owed them. But given that black leadership at the national level "swings" between the two prominent ideologies of nationalism and integrationism, with the greater stress on cultural revolution usually emanating from the former, the development of the concept of cultural revolution as well as a theory of cultural revolution proceeded in fits and starts, gaining steam during nationalist ascendance, dying down under integrationist hegemony, and reemerging with the next phase of nationalist prominence.[2]

Cultural revolution rests on two often less than precise concepts: culture and revolution. There may be about as many definitions of culture as authors studying the concept. For example, Kroeber and Kluckhohn (1952) provided a list of more than 150 different definitions of culture. Definitions of the concept range from Matthew Arnold's (1869) focus on culture as "the best which has been thought and said in the world" to Raymond Williams's (1952) association of it with the qualities evident in the "everyday life of the common man." Edward Tylor (1920 [1871], p. 1) viewed culture as socially patterned thought and behavior. He saw it as "that complex whole which includes knowledge, belief, art, morals, law, custom, and other capabilities and habits acquired by man as a member of society." This conception echoes anthropological definitions of the concept, such as Murphy's (1986, p. 14), which views culture as "the total body of tradition borne by a society and transmitted from generation to generation," consisting of "the norms, values, and standards by which people act," including "the ways distinctive in each society of ordering the world and rendering it intelligible." In this view, culture provides both a "mechanism of survival" as well as a "definition of reality." It is "the matrix into which we are born"; it is "the anvil upon which our persons and destinies are forged." For Bodley (1994), culture has various dimensions, including: historical (i.e., social heritage, or tradition), behavioral (shared learned behavior, or a way of life), normative (ideals, values, or rules for living), functional (the way humans solve problems of living together and adapting to their environment), structural (patterned ideas, symbols, and behaviors), and symbolic (arbitrarily arranged meanings that are shared by a society). It consists of and reflects "what people think, what they do, and the material products they produce." In sum, it is a system of shared beliefs, traditions, customs, practices, techniques, values, symbols, and the artifacts and material products of society transmitted across generations. It is the conceptual and material reservoir of a society, learned through socialization, that encompasses the institutionalized perspectives, practices, and production associated with a particular group, organization, or people. Cultures are identifiable across time with many features that are stable, some varying, and others dynamic. One of the dynamic aspects of culture is its capacity, at times, to generate revolution.

Culture also serves as an analytical tool to explain political phenomena such as decision making, collective action, and revolution, and, as such, it is distinct from the behavior it is assumed to generate. That is, in order to explain behavior, culture cannot simply be defined as the behavior itself, since there would be nothing left to explain; culture would be both cause and effect and would have no analytical value. In his study of strategic culture, Johnston (1995, p. 21) provides a useful definition of culture that avoids this logical contradiction and enhances its usefulness as an analytical tool. He suggests that culture "consists of shared decision rules, recipes, standard operating procedures, and decision routines that impose a degree of order on individual and group conceptions of their relationship to their environment, be it social, organizational, or political." Given that "cultural patterns and behavioral patterns are not the same thing," it follows that "insofar as culture affects behavior, it does so by presenting limited options and by affecting how members of these cultures learn from interaction with the environment." In this view, culture is "learned, evolutionary and dynamic," and, although "[m]ultiple cultures can exist within one social entity" such as an organization, institution, community, or state, there is usually one dominant culture whose interest is "in preserving the status quo"; "[h]ence cultures can be an instrument of control, consciously cultivated and manipulated." Culture, then, may affect the propensity of individuals and groups to make political choices for a range of individual and collective actions, including revolution.

Revolution, as discussed in the previous chapter, should be understood as the overthrow of a governing system with the aim of establishing a substantially different one. While there is a substantial amount of overlap, we can usefully distinguish among three types of revolution: political revolution, which involves the transformation of the system of government—the polity (e.g., the French, American, Russian, Chinese, and/or Cuban Revolutions); economic revolution, which involves the transformation of the economic system—the economy (e.g., the market revolution that transformed European feudalism to capitalism;[3] the overthrow of chattel slavery as an economic system in the United States); and social revolution, which involves the transformation of the social system—the society (e.g., Mao's Cultural Revolution, Pol Pot's "Year Zero" plan). We can further disaggregate social revolutions into their two principal forms: demographic and cultural. Demographic revolutions are dramatic transformations in the distribution of groups in society that result from major demographic events such as immigration, emigration, diasporazation, urbanization, suburbanization, ruralization, demographic transitions, youth bulges, or the aging of the population, which prominently change the composition of a society or revise conceptions of the identity of the society.

Cultural revolution entails the overthrow of one cultural system and its replacement with another. It may also be viewed as a dramatic transformation in the expression, representation, and prominence of a group's culture in the broader cultural system of the society (e.g., its cultural hegemony), resulting from changes in the racial, religious, ethnic, linguistic, aesthetic, and educational institutions and/or in the familial structures, voluntary associations, and gender relations of the group or the society. This process historically has involved the overthrow or radical transformation of the major cultural institutions of a state and a reordering or renunciation of their hierarchy, such as occurred in the overthrow of the secular regime of the Shah of Iran and its replacement with the theocracy of the Khomeini regime (Sobhe, 1982). Cultural revolutions may encompass an entire state or a group within it (e.g., a racial, ethnic, linguistic, or religious group); or they may occur across states.

For many BPM revolutionists, Mao's "Talks at the Yenan Forum on Literature and Art" of 1942 evoked the cultural revolution that they sought. There, the future leader of the Peoples' Republic of China (PRC) argued that culture should promote the interests of the proletariat against the bourgeoisie. He argued that

> [o]ur literary and art workers must accomplish this task and shift their stand; they must gradually move their feet over to the side of the workers, peasants and soldiers, to the side of the proletariat, through the process of going into their very midst and into the thick of practical struggles and through the process of studying Marxism and society. Only in this way can we have a literature and art that are truly for the workers, peasants and soldiers, a truly proletarian literature and art.

Such a perspective was consistent with an earlier argument of Du Bois as he contemplated the role of black culture during the Harlem Renaissance. He, like Mao, was convinced that culture should perform the function of propaganda; and this orientation would resonate with BPM activists and serve as the point of departure for the Black Arts Movement (BAM)—the "sister" of the BPM, as Larry Neal referred to it—as well. In the next section we turn to some of the influential precursors of the black cultural revolution theses proposed by many of the leading revolutionists of the BPM.

Cultural Revolution: Reviewing Some Prominent Examples

Cultural revolution may not entail the overthrow of the political or economic system of the state in which it occurs but might strengthen or weaken them.

For example, it might be undertaken by leaders attempting to solidify their political control, as in what is probably the most famous cultural revolution, the Great Proletarian Cultural Revolution of the PRC. Beginning no later than 1966, Mao Zedong attempted to purge the party, military, schools, media, and the broader society of suspected "bourgeois reactionary thinking" among those who allegedly were attempting to take the country "along the capitalist road." Mao (and his supporters) initiated the Great Proletarian Cultural Revolution (GPCR) to rally support for himself and promote a cult of personality to solidify his authority against opponents of his failed economic policies. The context that generated the GPCR was the critique of Mao's disastrous economic policies of the Great Leap Forward, which resulted in the deaths of between twenty and thirty million people from starvation and disease related to malnutrition, the collapse of the commune programs, and the withdrawal of Soviet technicians from the country. This critique among longtime and high-ranking party members and Chinese intellectuals evolved into a general crisis of confidence with Mao's leadership such that de facto control of the Chinese state was turned over to Liu Shaoqi (Mao's heir apparent for many years) and Deng Xiaopeng. Under Liu's guidance—which included reversing Mao's failed policies of the Great Leap Forward—by 1962 China's economy had begun to recover the productivity gains of the 1950s.

The original critique of Mao's policies was put forth by Defense Minister Peng Dehuai in 1959. Peng was purged—although developments in the next three years would prove him correct—and he was replaced by Lin Baio, who became one of the main protagonists of the GPCR. Following Peng's sacking, other prominent officials critiqued Mao's policies along similar lines. Mao targeted the arts and literature in order to justify attacking intellectuals and universities, which in his view were providing a source for the most potent critiques of his domestic and foreign policies, allowing him to attack both concrete policies and more abstract thought. By associating his targets with capitalist, bourgeois, reactionary, or revisionist thought he could implicate both intellectuals as well as party officials—including veteran comrades in arms, most notably Liu Shaoqi and Deng Xiaopeng.

The GPCR was less a cultural revolution than a wholesale program to ferret out opposition to Mao in all major institutions of Chinese society, from the family to the Chinese Communist Party (CCP). The GPCR elevated a notion of proletarian culture that privileged rural society and was violently anti-urban and anti-intellectual, utilizing children and teens (i.e., the Red Guards) to prosecute some of its worst excesses. A far cry from Mao's idealistic pronouncements at Yenan, the GPCR was a deadly, disruptive and disastrous period in post-revolution China, which destabilized the country and entrenched Mao's power. Agents of the GPCR burned books, destroyed museums, closed universities and schools, while targeting intellectuals, scientists, teachers, administrators, and their families. They imposed compulsory migration to rural areas (later replicated to genocidal effect by a Cambodian visitor to China at the time, Saloth Sar, aka Pol Pot); and set back China's economic, technological, and educational development for at least a decade (Pye, 1986; Thurston, 1985; Tsang, 1967). They tortured, terrorized, and humiliated those who could be labeled as going "along the capitalist road," using indiscriminate killings, political imprisonments, purges, "re-education," and relocation to rural areas. The resulting chaos, repression, and bloodletting almost led to civil war by 1968.[4] The GPCR resulted in the deaths of untold numbers of Chinese, with estimates ranging from tens of thousands to one million people. The economy floundered, the authority of the CCP was undermined, the educational system atrophied, and arts and literature were reduced to sycophantic propaganda lauding Maoist thought. Yet, the political system remained relatively intact even upon Mao's death in 1976—to no small degree as a function of the loyalty of the military—but there were dramatic transformations afterward. Power ultimately remained with the CCP but it swung away from those who had prominently supported the GPCR, the Gang of Four, to those who had been its targets, such as Deng Xiaopeng.[5]

In contrast to Mao's promotion of the GPCR, Lenin initially opposed cultural revolution in Russia, but subsequently advocated it to strengthen his regime. Major Bolsheviks encouraged proletarian culture shortly after the Russian Revolution and during the Russian Civil War.[6] For example, Alexander Bogdanov was an early proponent of the promotion of proletarian culture, *prolekult*, as was Bukharin. The initial conference of proletarian culture organizations was held in 1917, prior to the October Revolution, and "by 1920 the proletarian culture organisations had some four hundred thousand members, and published fifteen journals" (Birchall, 2000, p. 83). Bogdanov's resolution, adopted by the All-Russian Conference of Proletarian Cultural and Educational Organisations in September 1918, proclaimed:

> The proletariat must take over the treasures of past art with its own critical illumination, in a new interpretation, revealing their hidden collective principles and their organisational thought. They will then become a precious heritage for the proletariat, a tool in its struggle against the old world which created them, an instrument for organising a new world. (ibid., pp. 95–96)

Prolekult promoted, inter alia, Prolekult Theatre, which emphasized industrial motifs and the subculture of the factory floor, as well as folk songs and avant-garde art.[7] It sought, inter alia, to "defamiliarize the familiar" and make the audience reflect on the material condition of their lives.[8] Conflicts between proletarian culture organizations and the Party leadership were evident by 1921 (ibid., p. 82). For example, Leon Trotsky and Aleksandr Voronsky viewed the proletarian culture movement as contradictory and antithetical to the Marxist position on bourgeois art and science. Trotsky argued that it was impossible for the proletariat to develop its own art forms given that by the time it had fulfilled its historic mission of overthrowing the bourgeoisie it would cease to exist as a class. More importantly, Lenin subordinated the promotion of a revolutionary proletariat culture to the Party and the "Marxist world outlook" (Biggart, 1987, p. 233). For example, in his "On Proletarian Culture" of 1920, Lenin insisted "that the Marxist world outlook is the only true expression of the interests, the viewpoint, and the culture of the revolutionary proletariat" (1966b, pp. 316–317).[9] He added that since Marxism has "assimilated and refashioned everything of value in the more than two thousand years of the development of human thought and culture," (p. 317) then

> [a]ll educational work in the Soviet Republic of workers and peasants, in the field of political education in general and in the field of art in particular, should be imbued with the spirit of the class struggle being waged by the proletariat for the successful achievement of the aims of its dictatorship, i.e., the overthrow of the bourgeoisie, the abolition of classes, and the elimination of all forms of exploitation of man by man. (p. 316)

Lenin (ibid., p. 317) was convinced that this could only be realized through the efforts of the Communist Party, and concluded that "[o]nly further work on this basis and in this direction, inspired by the practical experience of the proletarian dictatorship as the final stage in the struggle against every form of exploitation, can be recognised as the development of a genuine proletarian culture."

In time, the Bolsheviks came to appreciate a role for proletarian culture in solidifying the postrevolutionary regime in the Soviet Union, to the extent that it might challenge "the problem of bourgeois cultural restoration," and Mao drew on a similar rationale decades later. As the Bolsheviks consolidated their power following their victory in the Civil War, Lenin changed suit and called for a cultural revolution. In his "On Cooperation" of 1923, Lenin (1973a, p. 474) acknowledged "a radical modification in our whole outlook on socialism," which had formerly emphasized "the political struggle, on revolution, on winning political power," but "[n]ow the emphasis

[was] changing and shifting to peaceful, organizational, 'cultural' work." He advocated a cultural revolution that would establish a cooperatives-based economic system in the Soviet Union. He thought that "the organisation of the entire peasantry in co-operative societies presupposes a standard of culture among the peasants . . . that cannot, in fact be achieved without a cultural revolution" (ibid. p. 474). For Lenin, organizing the peasantry into cooperatives was essential to organizing cooperatives throughout the entire Soviet population.

Lenin viewed a cultural revolution as necessary to further develop the communist leadership as well. Given the "deplorable" status of the state apparatus whose "defects [were] rooted in the past," which, nonetheless, in various aspects persisted beyond the Revolution, he saw a particular role for trade unions—in tight coordination with the government, the CPSU, and the masses—in this educational and practical project. Thus, in "The Role and Functions of the Trade Unions under the New Economic Policy," in 1922 Lenin stated that "[b]eing a school of communism in general, the trade unions must, in particular, be a school for training the whole mass of workers, and eventually all working people, in the art of managing socialist industry (and gradually also agriculture)" (1973b, p. 190). By 1923, in his last essay, "Better Fewer, But Better," he argued:

> Our state apparatus is so deplorable . . . that we must first think very carefully how to combat its defects, bearing in mind that these defects are rooted in the past, which, although it has been overthrown, has not yet been overcome, has not yet reached the stage of a culture . . . I say culture deliberately, because in these matters we can only regard as achieved what has become part and parcel of our culture, of our social life, our habits. (Lenin, 1973c, pp. 487–488)

Lenin argued that "the workers who are absorbed in the struggle of socialism . . . are not sufficiently educated" and are unable to build a viable state apparatus because, inter alia, "they do not know how. They have not yet developed the culture required for this; and it is culture that is required." (ibid., p. 488).

Lenin (1973a, p. 475) recognized that "in our country [Russia] the political and social revolution preceded the cultural revolution, that very cultural revolution which nevertheless now confronts us." He was hopeful that "[t]his cultural revolution would now suffice to make our country a completely socialist country"; nevertheless, he warned that "it presents immense difficulties of a purely cultural (for we are illiterate) and material character (for to be cultured we must achieve a certain development of the material means of production, we must have a certain material base)" (ibid.).

All told, neither the cultural revolution of Mao's PRC nor of Lenin's Soviet Union was the type of cultural revolution envisioned by those applying the concept to black America. Both of those cultural revolutions were prosecuted shortly after successful political revolutions. Most BPM revolutionists did not view themselves in a post-revolutionary context in the United States, notwithstanding the arguments in the previous chapter on the Slave Revolution in the U.S. Civil War. In addition, the cultural revolutions in the PRC and USSR were cultural revolutions "from above," initiated by the centralized political leadership; however, black cultural revolution was to be initiated by black Americans, who were among the most politically marginalized groups in the United States. Therefore, they were compelled to make cultural revolution "from below" to achieve their liberation.

The latter orientation seems akin to Gramsci's thesis on the need for the proletariat to challenge the cultural hegemony of the bourgeoisie prior to organizing the political revolution that would usher the ascendance of the socialist state. Gramsci was concerned with explaining why proletariat revolutions had not ensued in the West as Marx had predicted. He argued that the cultural apparatuses of advanced industrial states indoctrinated workers into a false consciousness that led them to identify with the interests of the ruling classes through socialization by mass media, compulsory public education, and popular culture that ingrained the norms and practices of the ruling class into the populace, often through appeals to overt nationalism, religious affiliation, and consumerism, or more subtly through the institutions of civil society. In such a context, Marxist revolutionists were obliged to organize a counter-hegemonic thrust on the cultural front in order to combat the hegemonic culture of the ruling class. Overthrowing this cultural hegemony was necessary before a political revolution could ensue. Therefore, Gramsci proposed a twofold strategy consisting of a war of position, which was a struggle on the cultural front, followed by a war of maneuver, which was the struggle on the political front—the classic Marxist revolution.

Gramsci's thesis did not augur political revolution in the United States, because he insisted that the countries that were least likely to achieve a cultural revolution were those with highly developed institutions of civil society, such as the United States.[10] Further, Gramsci's thesis seemed to presume that the cultural reservoir from which challenges to the cultural hegemony of the bourgeoisie could be derived were readily available to revolutionists to draw upon and employ in a war of position. This approach does not appreciate the extent of white American destruction and/or appropriation of black American culture, such that blacks were not only conditioned by the views and values of white racist cultural hegemony, but by as late as the twentieth century there were still prominent debates *inside* the black community on whether blacks possessed a culture at all. If cultural revolution was going to be salient to black Americans, a case had to be made that they had a culture in the first place, from which to construct the counter-institutions necessary to promote the counter-hegemony that Gramsci theorized. Black cultural revolution, in modified Gramscian terms, would involve blacks fighting a war of reconstruction—or what Du Bois called reformation—prior to either a war of position or maneuver.

Gramsci's negative orientation toward religious institutions as effective counter-institutions further distanced his approach from black American experiences given the centrality of the Black Church to social change historically as well as the reality that it was the most powerful cultural institution in the black community and the backbone of its civil society.[11] It was inconceivable that black cultural revolution could bypass the major cultural institution of black people. Moreover, given the role of the Black Church as a social change agent, it was clear that its potential contribution to black cultural revolution was much different than what Gramsci proposed given his experiences with the Catholic Church in Europe.

Actually, the most compelling application of Marxism to black America was Harry Haywood's Black Belt thesis, which recognized the salience of black culture to black liberation, and engaged the Black Church seriously, which, given his original articulation of his thesis in the 1920s—an era when the Church's role in social movements was at a low point compared to organizations such as the UNIA or NAACP—was particularly insightful; however, Haywood viewed it playing a tertiary role, at best, to the CPUSA and trade unions as agents of revolutionary change. Unfortunately, neither of the latter institutions was committed to a meaningful engagement with black culture—or, often, black workers—and those among the CPUSA membership that were derided as nationalistic, ultimately including Haywood and his supporters, were purged for their alleged "racial/nationalist chauvinism," while black unionization was subordinated to the white racist labor aristocracy—and general white membership—of the major unions. In the event, Haywood did not develop a thesis on cultural revolution per se. Potentially closer to such a development was Claudia Jones' Marxist feminism, which incorporated the Black Belt thesis while raising the fundamental cultural contradiction within black communities, namely, sexism, although she didn't develop a specific cultural revolution thesis either.

To be sure, black Americans did not await the insights of European and American Marxists to delineate the elements and processes of cultural change in black communities and proffer theses on black cultural revolution. Black activist/intellectual theses on the need for cultural transformation and the development of black social consciousness as a precursor to—or concomitant of—political and economic transformation had begun to be expressed by no later than the nineteenth century. These early pronouncements on the role of cultural change in black liberation were more evolutionary than revolutionary, yet, they laid the basis for later theorizing in both veins.

African American Cultural Revolution: Precursors

Broad arguments situating black cultural development at the center of black liberation struggles were prominent in the nineteenth-century discourse of black nationalists such as the emigrationist Mary Shadd Cary, who argued against both racism and sexism and advocated abolition of slavery, the advancement of black institutional development, black resettlement in Canada, and the political rights of black women in some of the earliest statements of black feminism. Shadd Cary was the first black woman in North America to establish and edit a weekly newspaper, *Provincial Freeman*, in Chatham, Ontario, in which, inter alia, she promoted black social uplift, tied to black educational and industrial development, and stressed the importance of black women in facilitating that development. Pursuant to this, she highlighted the need to establish free black communities and develop independent schools, voluntary organizations, and businesses—what we would call institutions of civil society today. Central to the development of strong black communities was the recognition of the rights of women and the cultivation of their talents in the major political, economic, and cultural institutions of black society. This was among the earliest assessments of the need for black cultural evolution in terms of the attainment of gender equality (along with those of Maria Stewart, Sojourner Truth, Frances Ellen Watkins Harper, Harriet Tubman, among others).

Shadd Cary's approach is mirrored in Ida B. Wells Barnett's practice as a newspaper editor, political organizer, and social reformer. Before she helped found the National Association of Colored Women (NACW) and the National Association for the Advancement of Colored People (NAACP), Wells Barnett wrote, rallied, and organized against white racism in the South. In Memphis, Tennessee, she wrote newspaper articles and published pamphlets and broadsides excoriating the lynchings that were occurring regularly in the final decades of the nineteenth century. She drew from her own surveys and interviews of lynchers, their supporters, and advocates, as well as victims and survivors, and heroically published her findings and conclusions—facing threats of murder, rape, and torture from her white racist detractors—in her *Southern Horrors: Lynch Law in All Its Phases* (1892), and *The Red Record* (1895). She railed against the racist propaganda of the time, such as the oft-repeated lie that the main motivation for white lynchers was the protection of white women's "virtue," and instead demonstrated through her interviews that their motivations were mainly economic, as they attempted to suppress black economic competition. Her orientation toward ending lynching is clear in her instruction that

> [t]he lesson this teaches and which every Afro-American should ponder well, is that a Winchester rifle should have a place of honor in every black home, and it should be used for that protection which the law refuses to give. When the white man who is always the aggressor knows he runs as great a risk of biting the dust every time his Afro-American victim does, he will have greater respect for Afro-American life. The more the Afro-American yields and cringes and begs, the more he has to do so, the more he is insulted, outraged and lynched. (Wells Barnett, 1892a, p. 36)

Convinced of the unwillingness of whites to support social justice for blacks, even when blacks had achieved some economic success, she advocated black migration from the South to the West and North and the establishment of black towns in areas more hospitable to an independent black presence. Wells Barnett not only demonstrated the importance of independent black institutions, but she asserted the centrality of women in the development of black society.[12] Like Shadd Cary, Wells Barnett sought change through both intraracial and interracial organizations.

Assertions such as those expressed by Shadd Cary and Wells Barnett (among others) implicate cultural *evolution* to the extent that they suggested that the attainment of black women's equality was essential to the development of black communities, of women in general, and of the United States as a whole. Only by recognizing black women as equally representative of black society could one comprehend the black community as it actually existed. The recognition of that fact and the struggle to ensure that the black community's political, economic, and social institutions reflected that reality was necessary as a first order of cultural development or cultural evolution, and thus central to cultural revolution, as well. Further, such recognition, as black feminists argued, necessitated recognizing the juridical equality of black women. Sojourner Truth expressed this equality of black women to black men (and women to men, in general) in terms of shared abilities, and Anna Julia Cooper expressed it in terms of the complementarity of women and men. In fact, it is Cooper's explication of this relationship and its centrality to black social development that epitomizes both the basic orientation and insight of nineteenth-century black nationalist feminism as well as the point of departure for conceptualizing black cultural evolution.

In her 1892 *A Voice from the South by A Black Woman of the South*, Cooper stated that "[a]ll I claim is that there is a feminine as well as a masculine side to truth; that these are related not as inferior and superior, not as better and worse, not as weaker and stronger, but as complements—complements in one necessary and symmetric whole" (p. 60). Recognizing this complementarity, the black community should facilitate the entry of the black woman into the social, economic, and political spheres with rights and opportunities equal to those of men. But the black women's entry into civil society (and attainment of equality) had an added value unique to black women, which rested upon their exclusive social position and the duality of their oppression. Cooper noted that black women occupied "a unique position in this country. . . . She is confronted by both a woman question and a race problem, and is as yet an unknown or an unacknowledged factor in both" (1892, p. 134). Cooper's thesis on multiple oppressions of black working-class women prefigured those of Claudia Jones (1949), the double/triple jeopardy perspective of Francis Beal (1970), and the intersectionality of Kimberle Crenshaw (1989); also, it suggested a double consciousness that preceded and transcended that articulated by Du Bois, and with implications that were even more profound. Black women's emancipation was not only important for their betterment, but was necessary for the advancement of the entire race because "[o]nly the BLACK WOMAN can say 'when and where I enter, in the quiet, undisputed dignity of my womanhood, without violence and without suing or special patronage, then and there the whole *Negro race enters with me'*" (ibid., p. 31). Along with its political and economic implications, with respect to black culture, Cooper was clear that if black cultural development was to proceed in earnest, the amelioration of the condition of black women would have to be its centerpiece and would facilitate the fundamental transformation of black society, as well.

Black cultural development, for Cooper, was rooted in the main institutions of nineteenth-century black communities: black labor and industry, black schools, and the Black Church. She lauded the ingenuity and creativity of blacks in both their labor and commerce. At first blush, it may appear that Cooper's views on black labor were less forward-looking than those on gender. For example, she expressed "little enthusiasm" for what she characterized as "the labor riots," which were "epidemic" in the North. She chastised and vilified Northern white workers for striking and protesting wages that were several times those found in the South (1892, p. 252). Her target was not labor per se, but *white* labor, which she viewed as unremittingly racist, including "the amalgamated associations and labor unions of immigrant laborers, who cannot even speak English" (ibid., pp. 255–256), yet, "will threaten to cut the nerve and paralyze the progress of an industry that gives work to an American-born [Negro] citizen" (ibid., p. 266). She excoriated white immigrant workers who "complain[ed] of wrong and oppression, of low wages and long hours" but "would boycott an employer if he hired a colored workman" (ibid., p. 255). She assailed the hypocrisy in the treatment of white and black women workers, remarking:

> One often hears in the North an earnest plea from some lecturer for "our working girls" (of course this means white working girls). . . . I listened to one who went into pious agonies at the thought of the future mothers of Americans having to stand all day at shop counters; and then advertised with applause a philanthropic firm who were giving their girls a trip to Europe for rest and recreation! . . . But how many have ever given a thought to the pinched and downtrodden colored women bending over wash-tubs and ironing boards—with children to feed and house rent to pay, wood to buy, soap and starch to furnish—lugging home weekly great baskets of clothes for families who pay them for a month's laundrying barely enough to purchase a substantial pair of shoes!

Thus, she found it "impossible to catch the fire of sympathy and enthusiasm for most of these labor movements at the North" (1892, pp. 254–255).

A tireless advocate of education for freepersons and their descendants, Cooper championed female literacy, higher education, and the importance of the Black Church in black society, but she was also critical of the Church for "not developing Negro womanhood as an essential fundamental for the elevation of the race, and utilizing this agency in extending the work of the Church" (1892, p. 37). Cooper asserted the "vital agency of womanhood in the regeneration and progress of a race" (ibid., pp. 23–24), and insisted that women and girls should be educated more fully. Cooper praised the AME Church's efforts in educating blacks, while challenging depictions of blacks in prominent literature—expressing her "hope to see . . . a blackman honestly and appreciatively portraying both the Negro as he is, and the white man occasionally, as seen from the Negro's standpoint" (ibid., p. 225).

Theses on black cultural evolution such as Cooper's often were embedded in broader concepts of culture and civilization that did not view black culture as an independent source of revolutionary change, viewing it instead in civilizationist terms, seeking a sort of black uplift defined often as attainment to a white ideal. Other contemporary black feminists tied black women's liberation to working-class liberation in theses that privileged a multiracial revolutionary proletariat. The latter was evident, for example, in the thesis of the anarcho-Marxist Lucy Parsons who, reportedly, was once described by the Chicago Police Department as "more dangerous than a thousand rioters."[13]

In contrast to some of the bourgeois aspects of nineteenth-century feminism, Lucy Parsons' feminism was grounded in black working-class values and her revolutionary advocacy of social change to end human oppression. She supported prominent women's rights issues of the time, such as a woman's right to divorce, remarry, and birth control; however, she viewed these issues as well below the importance of directly organizing workers against capitalist oppression, viewing issues of gender as well as race as intertwined within the larger struggle of labor against capital. Parsons' feminism brought her into ideological conflict with even her anarchist contemporaries such as Emma Goldman, whom she castigated for privileging "free love" advocacy over working-class interests. In fact, as Parsons rallied workers as a highly effective anarchist organizer, a founding member of the Industrial Workers of the World (IWW, aka the Wobblies), advocating and organizing on behalf of black and brown laborers, women, political prisoners, and "tramps," she chided Goldman for "addressing large middle-class audiences." In an 1896 essay, she castigated Goldman and her "free love" supporters for their attempts to "bind . . . labor's emancipation from wage-slavery" to "free love" advocacy and to "call them one and the same." Parsons asserted that "[v]ariety in sex relations and economic freedom have nothing in common." Her debate with Goldman also reflected Parsons' view that marriage and family were natural conditions of human existence, so she rejected the arguments of elitist white anarchist feminists such as Goldman, which criticized these institutions. Ashbaugh (1976, p. 202) explained the disagreements between Parsons and Goldman in this way: "Lucy Parsons' feminism, which analyzed women's oppression as a function of capitalism, was founded on working class values. Emma Goldman's feminism took on an abstract character of freedom for women in all things, in all times, and in all places; her feminism became separate from its working class origins." Lucy Parsons was committed to the view that the social revolution that she sought would only result from a movement focused on the working class that seized the means of production and that racial and gender equality would be achieved with the overthrow of capitalism.

In an article published in 1884, "To Tramps," she called to revolution "The Unemployed, the Disinherited, and Miserable," those who were "tramping the streets . . . with hands in pockets, gazing listlessly about you at the evidence of wealth and pleasure of which you own no part, not sufficient even to purchase yourself a bit of food with which to appease the pangs of hunger now knawing at your vitals" (Parsons, 1884, p. 144). She admonished that each of them had been "execrated and denounced as a 'worthless tramp and a vagrant' by that very class" which had been "robbing" them (ibid.). It was immaterial whether there was a "good boss" or "bad boss" because "it is the INDUSTRIAL SYSTEM and not the 'boss' which must be changed" (ibid.). She argued that they should reject religious admonitions that it is their lot to be poor; and instead "[s]end forth [their] petition" to be read "by the red glare of destruction," which is "the only language" that "these robbers . . . have ever been able to understand" (ibid.). She emphasized to the "hungry tramps who read [her] lines" to

> avail yourselves of those little methods of warfare which Science has placed in the hands of the poor man, and you will become a power in this or any other land. *Learn the use of explosives!* (ibid.; original emphasis)

At the IWW's founding convention, Parsons advocated the use of the general strike as a tactic for workers and argued that her "conception of the strike of the future is not to strike and go out and starve, but to strike and remain in and take possession of the necessary property of production"; and, in this way, her approach anticipated the sitdown strikes and factory takeovers of future labor organizations. Her view of cultural evolution/revolution was grounded in her revolutionary thesis, which was embedded in Marxist (and anarchist) conceptions and the Eurocentric teleology to which they both were tethered. Such approaches are bound by their own corresponding civilizationist vision, and it would be another half-century before Marxists such as Claudia Jones asserted a radical feminism grounded in a modernized black nationalist understanding of black culture.

The development of a thesis on black cultural evolution/revolution was central because the equality of black women challenges the two most fundamental systems of domination in the United States: racism and sexism. Moreover, within black communities women's equality not only is a recognition of human rights—monumental in that regard alone, but also given the historic role(s) women have played in black institutions, ending the oppression of women and encouraging their independent course of action also unleashes the awesome potential of these institutions since it is commonly understood that black women do the lion's share of the organizational work in major black institutions, even as they are typically denied leadership in them. The liberation of black women would redound to black institutional power. Such an orientation toward black women's liberation was largely absent among black nationalists—as well as integrationists, Marxists, and white feminists—until well into the twentieth century. Although feminist perspectives informed the earliest conceptions of black cultural evolution, they were often ignored by theorists of black cultural revolution—and black revolution in the United States more generally—well into the BPM era.

In the nineteenth century, U.S. culture (and Western culture, in general) was wedded to civilization, civilization to race, and race to biology, and whites alone were viewed as having a culture, which was a reflection of their presumably exclusive attainment of civilization, which in this view was a reflection of their racial superiority. Following Franz Boas, by the turn of the century, culture theorists were turning away from biological perspectives of culture to anthropological ones, the latter providing a basis for a less hierarchical rendering of culture in the form of cultural pluralism. Du Bois and especially Alain Locke, who authored a novel thesis on race as a sociological construct as well as a dynamic thesis of culture (as discussed in chapter 3), were central to the development of this work and its application to African American culture and ultimately to theses of black cultural revolution in the United States. Related to, if not directly building on, these culturalist precepts, Du Bois provided two theoretical frameworks on black political development that inform subsequent theses of black cultural and political change in the United States. The first he proffered in *Black Reconstruction* and juxtaposed to Marxism, and the second he articulated in *The Negro and Social Reconstruction* and contrasted with integrationism. Two transitional periods in U.S. history—the Civil War, and the Great Migration/Harlem Renaissance—witnessed dramatic black cultural change stimulating significant political change. For the nineteenth-century slave community, the fulcrum was slave religion (and slave hiring), which led to the Slave Revolution in the U.S. Civil War, and for the twentieth-century black community it was the Great Migration and resultant urbanized black institutions (e.g., black churches, schools, and businesses) that augured dramatic political change. In these two important works, completed within a year of each other, Du Bois provided frameworks for conceptualizing the former in terms of cultural revolution and the latter in terms of cultural evolution. Ironically, BPM revolutionists were seemingly unaware of the former revolutionary thesis, and they oriented their ostensibly revolutionary initiatives in the latter evolutionary program and its focus on developing parallel black institutions of civil society.

W. E. B. Du Bois and Black Cultural Evolution

Although Du Bois laid the groundwork for an understanding of black cultural revolution in *Black Reconstruction*, as we discussed in the previous chapter, his arguments on the significance of black culture to social change were not singular; they alternated between revolutionary and evolutionary perspectives. The source of this variability was Du Bois' wavering views on the role of the Black Church in progressive social change. Du Bois' ambivalence toward the Black Church—even as he lauded "slave religion"—was an impediment to his development of a thesis on black cultural revolution, and it seems to have prevented him from realizing the insurgent potential of religion in the earlier slave rebellions even as he recognized it as a catalyst of the General Strike. Du Bois's ambivalence toward the Black Church is evident in his earliest ruminations on the subject in 1897 (Evans, 2007, pp. 281–282; Green & Driver, 1978, p. 234). He argued that the Black Church should restrict its activities to spiritual matters, putting greater faith in voluntary and civil rights groups as agents of social change, as he began in earnest to develop the "race organizations" he had outlined in "Conservation of Races." Two years later, in *The Philadelphia Negro* (1899, pp. 469–470), he observed that

> [t]he Negro church is not simply an organism for the propagation of religion; it is the centre of the social, intellectual, and religious life of an organized group of people ... it serves as a newspaper and intelligence bureau, it supplants the theater, it directs the picnic and excursion, it furnishes the music ... it serves as a lyceum, library, and lecture bureau—it is, in fine, the central organ of the organized life of the American Negro.

Four years later, in *The Negro Church*, Du Bois (1903b, p. 5) argued that it was "the first distinctively Negro American social institution." Also, in that year, in *Souls*, he referred to "[t]he Negro Church" as "the social centre of Negro life in the United States," which "as a social institution ... antedated by many decades the monogamic Negro home" (1903a, pp. 117, 119). It was also "the most characteristic expression of African character" (ibid., p. 117); and the black preacher was "the most unique personality developed by the Negro on American soil" (ibid., p. 116). The Negro preacher was "[a] leader, a politician, an orator, a 'boss,' an intriguer, an idealist ... and ever, too, the centre of a group of men" (ibid.). He viewed the music of the Negro Church as "the most original and beautiful expression of human life and longing yet born on American soil" (ibid.). He called the AME Church "the greatest Negro organization in the world" (ibid., p. 120) and saw the "great city churches" such as Philadelphia's Bethel AME as "really governments of men" whose activities are "immense and far-reaching" and whose presiding bishops are "among the most powerful Negro rulers in the world" (ibid., p. 118). Regardless of its propensity to reform or stasis, Du Bois viewed the Black Church as an important progenitor and incubator of African American cultural traditions in the aesthetic, material, and institutional sense. Therefore, the cultural evolution of black society would to a large extent rest on the cultural transformation of the Black Church.

Yet, Du Bois's ambivalence toward the Black Church as a progressive change agent persisted throughout the remainder of his life. Although he praised some of its leaders and congregants, he admonished its otherworldliness, the pretentiousness and licentiousness of some black preachers, the absence of sociopolitical activism, and its failure to mobilize the economic power of the black community. He was joined in these criticisms by leaders such as Ida B. Wells Barnett, who admonished church leaders for their political timidity, for example, with respect to the antilynching activity that she spearheaded.[14] Carter G. Woodson criticized the church as the central divisive force splitting the black community between conservative religionists and progressives oriented toward reform in worship, theology, and political engagement. Du Bois had criticized how socially stratified congregations reflected and reinforced black intraracial class divisions, yet, like most black critics, he saved his harshest rebuke of organized religion for the white church and its vehement racism.

Du Bois's ambivalence toward the Black Church was recognized by his biographer, David Lewis, who acknowledged that

> [n]otwithstanding those soaring passages in *Souls [of Black Folk]* and *Gift of Black Folk*, or, later, in *Black Reconstruction*, celebrating Negroes' "peculiar spiritual quality" and the "Negro Church today . . . [as] sole surviving social institution of the African fatherland," an informed reading of Du Bois's *oeuvre* discloses virtually no modern role assigned to the Negro church. (Lewis, 2000, p. 306)

Moses (1993, p. 246) agrees that "Du Bois was clearly ambivalent about the black church," noting "its importance as the central institution of black political life" while also suggesting "that it represented only a primitive level of struggle towards full political consciousness." He could at once be both "sympathetic to the church, tracing its traditions of cultural and political resistance" while in other writing—especially his fiction—expressing "hostility" toward it.

On the other hand, Blum (2007, pp. 117–118) maintains that "a host of evidence contradicts this assessment." He notes that as late as 1950, in an article in the *Pittsburgh Courier*, Du Bois recognized that the black church of the twentieth century had "lost ground"; yet it was "still a powerful institution in the lives of a numerical majority of American Negroes if not upon the dominant intellectual classes." Du Bois had not been sanguine about the prospects of a Gandhian approach to overthrowing Jim Crow and thought that blacks "are not ready for systematic lawbreaking" (Lewis, 1995, p. 410). In contrast, in his 1948 "The Talented Tenth: Memorial Address," he argued that "[o]ur religion with all of its dogma, demagoguery and showmanship, can be a center to teach character, right conduct and sacrifice," and therein lies "a career for a Negro Gandhi and a host of earnest followers" (ibid., p. 352). Nevertheless, in his 1957 "Will the Great Gandhi Live Again?" reflecting on the Montgomery Bus Boycott, he asks, "Did this doctrine and practice of non-violence bring solution to the race problem in Alabama? It did not" (ibid., p. 359). It appeared that just as in his analyses in *Black Reconstruction*, where he could not seem to flesh out the connections between black religion and social change, he did not seem to grasp the role that black religion was playing in the CRM that was unfolding in front of him. Yet, later in that year Du Bois admitted that the issue of the applicability of Gandhi's program to black America had "long puzzled" him, but concluded that "[i]t may well be that . . . real human equality and brotherhood in the United States will come only under the leadership of another Gandhi" (ibid., pp. 91–92). Therefore, to his credit, he came to appreciate the benefits of a "Gandhian" approach—if not the Black Church as the agent of the change that the approach might facilitate—even though he did not live to see the fruition of the nonviolent direct action program of the CRM, which mainly followed his death in August 1963.[15]

The arguments on both sides of this debate have merit. That is, Lewis is correct that Du Bois's corpus of work suggests that there is "*virtually* no modern role assigned to the Negro church," the operative term being "virtually" because Du Bois remained convinced that the Church *should* perform a progressive function in the black community; but he was unconvinced that it *would* accomplish this mission. Du Bois continued to insist that if transformed, it could be the key institution for the kind of change he advocated, thus supporting Blum's more optimistic view. Therefore, convinced of the need for black institutions to articulate a vision and practice of positive social change but lacking faith in the Black Church to carry out such a mission, Du Bois promoted other black institutions in taking up this burden.

Du Bois also sought to draw on the key constituency in the Black Church, the black women who predominated in the pews, though not in the pulpit. In *Darkwater*, he argued that "strong women . . . laid the foundations of the great Negro church of today," emphasizing the importance of black women and the struggle against sexist domination in ways that prefigured more notable feminist analyses decades later (Du Bois 1920, 174). In challenging his friend Kelly Miller's rejection of women's suffrage, he argued that "[t]he meaning of the twentieth century is the freeing of the individual soul; the soul longest in slavery and still in the most disgusting and indefensible slavery is the soul of womanhood" (Lewis, 1995, p. 298). In several works, he excoriated the oppression of black women, assailed sexist renderings of black women, and asserted the centrality of women's struggles to the transformation of black society.[16] He shared Cooper's dictum that "[o]nly the black woman can say 'when and where I enter' . . . the whole race enters with me," and stated that "[t]o no modern race does its women mean so much as to the Negro" (ibid., p. 304). Du Bois concurred that if black cultural development was to proceed, the amelioration of the condition of black womanhood would have to be a centerpiece of that transformation. Du Bois viewed the importance of the liberation of black women in this way: "The uplift of women is, next to the problem of the color line and the peace movement, our greatest modern cause. When, now, two of these movements—woman and color—combine in one, the combination has deep meaning" (ibid., p. 309). Nevertheless, Du Bois' feminism—like most feminism of the day—was limited in ways that would not be addressed until the era of second wave feminism, for instance, the recognition that "peace" considerations should extend to the domestic/interpersonal/familial sphere and the sexist violence to which men subjected women and girls.

With respect to cultural evolution, it was not clear if the uplift of black women would be facilitated or circumscribed by the Black Church, which was a pressing issue given its importance in the black community and the reality of black women toiling in every major activity of the church with little hope of advancement in its hierarchy. Increasingly, for Du Bois, the Black Church was an ancillary change agent, at best, to help guide the increasingly working-class American Negro of the first few decades of the twentieth century. Du Bois had come to more fully appreciate what he had only broached in *Black Reconstruction*: the defeat of radical Reconstruction and the reconstitution of the slavocracy in all but name in the U.S. South—as a complicit act of the Negro's Northern "allies"—had so thoroughly destroyed the institutions of black civil society for the majority of black Americans that no single institution—even one as potentially powerful as the Black Church— could provide the political, economic, and social correctives to address black underdevelopment. Du Bois sought to develop parallel political, economic, and social institutions of black civil society to provide those absent from or enervated in black communities. These would focus on the Negro's access to the ballot, land ownership/property rights, access to schools, striking down discriminatory laws, anti-imperialism, pan-Africanism, and freedom from lynch law and arbitrary arrest.[17]

Pursuant to this, Du Bois turned to the black intellectual and organizational elite epitomized in the talented tenth, or the "guiding 100th"—from the institutions of black civil society such as black colleges, black churches, black lodges, black newspapers, black businesses—to civil rights organizations, such as the NAACP, as the key change agents for black America. However, the NAACP was not organically rooted in the black community (although it found a greater home there than in probably any other ethnic community in the United States), it was lacking in black leadership (Du Bois was the only black member to serve on its original governing board), and its major policies—seeking legal redress for discrimination and lobbying and organizing for antilynching legislation—were only indirectly committed to the broader political, economic, and social development of black America that Du Bois envisioned and championed.[18] The Urban League was similarly hamstrung among the major voluntary associations of increasingly urban black America because although it was more oriented to black economic and social uplift it was not as politically focused but arguably was organically rooted in the black community. The Negro women's clubs that would amalgamate in the NACW were more organically situated in the black community and more representative in their leadership and general membership, although their general orientation was no less elitist than the NAACP's.[19] Garvey's Universal Negro Improvement Association (UNIA) demonstrated the potential of a mass-based black organization rooted in black communities, representative, with predominantly black leadership and general membership, and committed to political, economic, as well as social development, but its program for black repatriation to Africa was politically myopic and civilizationist, as well as a needless drain on the organization's resources.

With the Great Migration, Du Bois saw the promise of the political, economic, and social transformation of black America in the "New Negro" phenomenon epitomized in the Harlem Renaissance, and he proposed the talented tenth (and later the "guiding 100th") as the vanguard of their cultural evolutionary project. Given his view of the shortcomings of the Black Church, he did not project on his notion of the talented tenth Kelly Miller's (1914) argument that it should assume the leadership of the Black Church and flood the ministry in order to provide guidance to it and hence the race. Even less heed was given to Woodson's more radical contention that the diverse black Christian denominations should unify under a single "United Negro Church" that would serve as a major national black mass organization that would wield substantial political power—in fact, AME Bishops Reverdy Ransom and R. R. Wright Jr. advocated linking black churches across denominational lines in a program of social service delivery and public policy engagement. For Du Bois, the Black Church was ill-suited to respond meaningfully to the depredations blacks suffered in the post-Reconstruction era or the challenges and opportunities afforded by the Great Migration. Even influential black church newspapers were being supplanted by black newspapers such as Abbott's *Chicago Defender* and Vann's *Pittsburgh Courier*, and Du Bois's editorship of *Crisis* gave him an important media stage from which to project the kind of radical change he envisioned outside the Black Church and the educational institutions it controlled.

Du Bois' ambivalence toward the Black Church contributed to the view of subsequent theorists of black politics that black cultural change could largely bypass the major cultural institution in the black community. Nevertheless, in the interwar era, Du Bois continued to insist that if transformed the Black Church could be one of three key institutions in black communities to effectuate the kind of change he advocated. This is most evident in what is probably Du Bois's most important unpublished work in his lifetime: his 1936 monograph *The Negro and Social Reconstruction*.

W. E. B. Du Bois, *The Negro and Social Reconstruction*

In *The Negro and Social Reconstruction*, Du Bois promulgated his "self-segregation" thesis.[20] For him, black social reconstruction entailed a turn inward, relying on the institutions of the black community in the context of the segregation of blacks to develop the economic basis for black politico-economic power in the United States. Convinced that the Great Depression signaled the death knell of capitalism in its present form, he was intent on saving the black nation through a transition to a national economic program of consumer and producer cooperatives, a cooperative commonwealth, rooted in the separate politico-economies of the segregated black community. He argued that given that segregation was a reality—and an irrational one at that—it was necessary to add a measure of rationality to it by using the separate conditions in which blacks found themselves to construct and wield institutions to facilitate black liberation. He argued that blacks constituted

> a separate nation within a nation. Most of us are in separate churches and separate schools; we live largely in separate parts of the city and country districts; we marry almost entirely within our own group and have our own social activities; we get at least a part of our news from our own newspapers and attend our

own theaters and entertainments, even if white men run them. (Du Bois, 1985, p. 144)

He observed that "through voluntary and increased segregation, by careful autonomy and planned economic organization, we can build so strong and efficient a group of 12 million men that no hostile group can continue to refuse them fellowship and equality" (ibid., p. 150).[21] He maintained that "[n]ever before since the abolition of slavery have the Negroes of the United States had such motives for uniting in a desperate effort to save themselves" (ibid., p. 151).

Du Bois proposed to organize black power through a "nationwide collective system" of consumer and producer cooperatives to coordinate black economic activity "on a nonprofit basis with the ideal that the consumer is the center and the beginning of the organization; and that to him all profits over the cost of production shall be returned" (1985, p. 151). The immediate aim was to develop "a body of economic leadership in the United States that can undertake the organization of the consumers' power among American Negroes and lead them to success" (ibid., p. 152). He proposed that

> the Negroes who eat food can arrange to buy a large part of it from those Negroes who raise food on their farms; the Negroes who use towels and sheets can buy them off Negroes who raise cotton and spin and weave it on machines which can be bought at public sale; the Negroes who wear clothes can have those clothes made . . . by Negro members of the various clothing unions which have welcomed them and this effective demand can supply the necessary sewing and cutting machines; the Negroes who wear shoes can make those shoes on machines of the United Shoe Machinery . . . the homes that Negroes live in can be built by Negro carpenters and masons; and so on . . . but the chief difficulty, now, is that the work has not been systematized . . . and the whole arrangement has been accidental and spasmodic rather than a carefully thought out and planned racial economy. (ibid., p. 151)

He argued that there were three institutions that should guide this program: black churches, black businesses, and black schools. He argued that it was necessary to "begin with the Negro church, which is the most complete and oldest and in some respects the most effective Negro institution" (1985, p. 153). Reflecting the ambivalence discussed above, Du Bois was emphatic that the Black Church's involvement would entail a drastic transformation of the institution, which "would involve the elimination from the present church organization just as far as possible, of theology and supernaturalism," while "prayer would become earnest and purposeful effort" (ibid., pp. 153–154). Either the Church would become "a great social organ with ethical ideals based on a reorganized economics," or simply be "a futile and mouthy excrescence on society which will always be a refuge for reaction and superstition" (ibid., p. 154). He notes that "this change need be nothing revolutionary or sudden. The co-operative enterprise could be grafted on the church in the same way that organized charity and the visiting of the sick are a part of its present program. It could gradually be incorporated into the church organization" (ibid.). Du Bois asserted that

> if the Negro church cannot do this, co-operatives can and must be set up as organizations entirely distinct from it, which means that they would have to compete in a way that would eat into the church organization even more than the fraternal lodges have, since the program of the co-operatives would be more vital and the results more satisfactory.

Moreover, he maintained that "[w]hile we are organizing for our own industrial development largely along segregated lines, there is no reason for giving up our fight for equality. On the contrary, the fight against discrimination must be emphasized, but at the same time nationalized" (1985, p. 156). He maintained that "if we move back to increased segregation it is for the sake of added strength to abolish race discrimination; if we move back to racial pride and loyalty, it is that eventually we may move forward to a great ideal of humanity and a patriotism that spans the world" (ibid.). In effect, Du Bois's program was aimed at developing parallel institutions of black civil society to facilitate black economic self-sufficiency that would then be leveraged politically.

Beyond cooperatives and churches, Du Bois also asserted the centrality of Negro colleges in his program of social reconstruction. In his 1933 "The Negro College," Du Bois averred:

> Unless the American Negro today, led by trained university men of broad vision, sits down to work out by economics and mathematics, by physics and chemistry, by history and sociology, exactly how and where he is to earn a living and how he is to establish a reasonable Life in the United States or elsewhere— unless this is done, the university has missed its field and func-

tion and the American Negro is doomed to be a suppressed and inferior caste in the United States for incalculable time. (1995b, p. 73)

Du Bois's advocacy of Negro colleges included a strong critique of not only the substandard quality but the feigned universalism of the liberal arts curriculum being taught at black universities. The chimera of universality—to use David L. Lewis's apt phrase—in college curricula obscured an underlying parochialism. Du Bois rejected such universalist mystification and insisted that

> there can be no college for Negroes which is not a Negro college and . . . while an American Negro university, just like a German or Swiss university may rightly aspire to a universal culture unhampered by limitations of race and culture, yet it must start on the earth where we sit and not in the skies whither we aspire. (1995b, p. 68)

He maintained that "the Spanish university is founded and grounded in Spain, just as surely as a French university is French" (ibid., p. 69); yet, "[t]here are some people who have difficulty in apprehending this very clear truth" (ibid.). Instead, they assume

> that the French university is in a singular sense universal, and is based on a comprehension and inclusion of all mankind and of their problems. But it is not so, and the assumption that it is arises simply because so much of French culture has been built into universal civilization. A French university is founded in France; it uses the French language and assumes a knowledge of French history. The present problems of the French people are its major problems and it becomes universal only so far as other peoples of the world comprehend and are at one with France in its mighty and beautiful history. (ibid., pp. 69–70)

He continued:

> In the same way, a Negro university in the United States of America begins with Negroes. It uses that variety of the English idiom which they understand; and above all, it is founded or it should be founded on a knowledge of the history of their people in Africa and in the United States, and their present condition. (ibid., p. 70)

Their education should begin with the particular and extend to the universal.

For Du Bois, the American Negro college "cannot begin with history and lead to Negro history. It cannot start with sociology and lead to Negro sociology" (1995b, p. 71). He argued that "[t]he American Negro problem is and must be the center of the Negro American university. It has got to be. You are teaching Negroes. There is no use pretending that you are teaching Chinese or that you are teaching white Americans or that you are teaching citizens of the world" (ibid., p. 69). He notes that "this is a different program than a similar function would be in a white university or in a Russian university or in an English university because it starts from a different point." He argues that

> starting with present conditions and using the facts and the knowledge of the present situation of American Negroes, the Negro university expands toward the possession and the conquest of all knowledge. It seeks from a beginning of the history of the Negro in America and in Africa to interpret all history; from a beginning of social development among Negro slaves and freedmen in America and Negro tribes and kingdoms in Africa, to interpret and understand the social development of all mankind in all ages. It seeks to teach modern science of matter and life from the surroundings and habits and aptitudes of American Negroes and thus lead up to understanding of life and matter in the universe. (ibid., p. 71)

As Lewis (1993, p. 313) correctly observes, Du Bois's centering of black interests at the heart of university education "was truly remarkable for its anticipation and commendation of the Afrocentric and diasporic agendas that were to contend for pride of place half a century later in America."[22]

Du Bois's tripartite focus on consumer and producer cooperatives, transformed black churches, and Afrocentric schools as the major mechanisms of black national development was also a program of black cultural evolution rather than revolution. Du Bois was unequivocal that

> [i]n any real social revolution, every step that saves violence is to the glory of the great end. We should not forget that revolution is not the objective of socialism or communism rightly conceived; the real objective is social justice, and if haply the world can find that justice without blood, the world is the infinite gainer. (Du Bois, 1985, p. 142)

Four years later, Du Bois (1991, p. 286) argued in *Dusk of Dawn* that "no revolution in America could be started by Negroes and succeed, and even if that were possible, that after what I had seen of the effects of war, I could never regard violence as an effective, much less necessary, step to reform the American state." *Social Reconstruction* was aimed at developing parallel institutions of black civil society to provide the segregated and economically depressed black community the political, economic, and social wherewithal to develop as a "nation within a nation." This was an evolutionary rather than revolutionary program, advocating peaceful change over armed conflict, and it was this peaceful program of developing parallel black institutions that would be adopted by BPM revolutionists, even as many of them attempted to wed it to paramilitary approaches—linking an evolutionary program to a revolutionary objective.

While Du Bois appreciated the role of revolution in black American liberation in the nineteenth century, he reasoned that black liberation in the twentieth century was more likely to be realized through a less militarized process; and he rejected the call of those who encouraged black Americans to "storm the barricades." In fact, Du Bois (1985, p. 143) asserted that "[t]he present radical and revolutionary program" envisioned by Moscow and the CPUSA "lack[ed] both the logic and power to emancipate the Negro." He noted that "Radical communists will learn that the Negro has too much sense to become the shock troops of its revolution" (ibid.). He recognized that

> [i]ncreased concentration of capital has not brought universal poverty and despair among laborers, but higher wages and better standards of life. Universal suffrage, including that of women, is widely exercised. While these great changes do not essentially alter the basic conflict they do make it possible to believe fundamental reform may be brought about by methods of peace and reason, if the masses interested work for this end. (ibid., p. 142)

He was just as emphatic that "[w]hat we need today is not fighting, but that basis of economic security which will permit us to fight" and to achieve "such victory over threatened starvation as will give us stamina to back our future complaints with power" (ibid., p. 156). Du Bois' orientation toward Marxist revolution in the United States reflected his view toward organized labor in general. For him, white labor—as much as, and in some ways more than, white capital—was an implacable foe of black liberation. In fact, both white labor and white capital were implicated in the domestic oppression of nonwhite people in the United States—especially blacks, as well as the international oppression of nonwhite people in the colonies.

To be sure, Du Bois celebrated black labor and *Black Reconstruction* was a homage to its revolutionary potential, yet he cautioned that black labor, which was the broad class in which most blacks were situated, should make common cause with the emerging classes that were becoming evident within black communities, rather than with the invidious and racist forces of white labor. For Du Bois, the black worker in the United States had a historic role to play and it was not as shock troops of Herrenvolk white proletarians in a Marxist scheme. Black workers would continue to play prominent roles in the transformation of America, but along a trajectory that was their own, reflecting their agency and history. Du Bois was unequivocal in his assertion of both the centrality and uniqueness of black labor in this context:

> [T]he black worker was the ultimate exploited; that he formed that mass of labor which had neither wish nor power to escape from the labor status, in order to directly exploit other laborers, or indirectly, by alliance with capital, to share in their exploitation. (Du Bois, 1969, p. 15)

Black workers had to contend not only with class enemies but with race enemies, and what emerged were race class enemies of which the white proletariat was no less significant than the white bourgeoisie. In fact, it was the fusion of the interests of white capital and white labor in the counterrevolution of property following the Civil War that subjugated newly emancipated black labor to "re-enslave" it and promoted similar processes abroad. Du Bois notes that, following the Civil War:

> The slave went free; stood a brief moment in the sun; then moved back again toward slavery. The whole weight of America was thrown to color caste. . . . A new slavery arose. The upward moving of white labor was betrayed into wars for profit based on color caste. . . . The resulting color caste founded and retained by capitalism was adopted, forwarded and approved by white labor, and resulted in subordination of colored labor to white profits the world over. Thus the majority of the world's laborers, by the insistence of white labor, became the basis of a system of industry which ruined democracy and showed its perfect fruit in World War and Depression. (1969, p. 30)

The framework for national oppression represented in a fusion of the interests of white capital and labor, which had been formalized and developed in the counterrevolution of property that destroyed Reconstruction, was cast abroad in the form of national imperialism with similar deleterious effects for the predominantly nonwhite people of the colonial world. This fusion was evocative of the process of national imperialism that would refashion the landscape of world politics a half-century later and give rise to the most destructive war in human history up to that time, World War I. Twenty years before *Black Reconstruction*, in "The African Roots of War" Du Bois (1915) examined the international implications of national imperialism; and situated black-white labor relations in the United States within its context. Du Bois argued that World War I was largely the result of disputes over imperial acquisitions that fused the interests of bourgeoisie and proletariat in European states in a mutually reinforcing pursuit of racist and economic domination of African and Asian nations,[23] which was transforming the landscape of international relations (Henderson, 2017ab).

Black Americans contended with the fusion of white capital and white labor interests in the United States that was not only economic and political but also cultural, and the cultural system of white supremacism proscribed the limits of black freedom and rationalized it. In the context of the United States, Du Bois argued, black solidarity with Herrenvolk white labor was as nonsensical as it was anathema. Instead, he saw within black communities a nation within a nation, comprised of a preponderant black peasantry, an expanding black proletariat, a nominal black petite bourgeoisie, and a largely nonexistent black haute bourgeoisie, which had not been developed as much on class lines but existed mainly as economic stratifications of a black sociopolitical outcaste. Given their much different origins in the United States politico-economy and social history, the divisions of class among black Americans did not generate the animosity that Marxism assumed would characterize class relations in Europe. This was especially evident in the relations between the black petite bourgeoisie and the black proletariat. This is one reason why the Garvey movement was not only supported by the black petite bourgeoisie, which Marxists assumed would flock to its black nationalist program, but dominated by working-class blacks, who Marxists had not expected would support it so extensively.

Du Bois understood these relationships well. For example, writing on the "Negro bourgeoisie" in his 1931 essay "The Negro and Communism," he noted that "[t]he charge of the Communists that the present set-up of Negro America is that of the petit bourgeois minority dominating a helpless black proletariat, and surrendering to white profiteers is simply a fantastic falsehood. The attempt to dominate Negro Americans by purely capitalistic ideas died with Booker T. Washington," in his view, and since Washington "there has never been a moment when the dominating leadership of the American Negro has been mainly or even largely dominated by wealth or capital or by capitalistic ideals" (Du Bois, 1995c, p. 587). Expanding on this argument, he stated:

> There are naturally some Negro capitalists . . . but the great mass of Negro capital is not owned or controlled by this group. Negro capital consists mainly of small individual savings invested in homes, and in insurance, in lands for direct cultivation and individually used tools and machines. Even the automobiles owned by Negroes represent to a considerable extent personal investments, designed to counteract the insult of the "Jim Crow" car. The Insurance business, which represents a large amount of Negro capital is for mutual co-operation rather than exploitation. Its profit is limited and its methods directed by the State. Much of the retail business is done in small stores with small stocks of goods, where the owner works side by side with one or two helpers, and makes a personal profit less than a normal American wage. Negro professional men—lawyers, physicians, nurses and teachers—represent capital invested in their education and in their office equipment, and not in commercial exploitation. There are few colored manufacturers of material who speculate on the products of hired labor. Nine-tenths of the hired Negro labor is under the control of white capitalists. (ibid.)

According to Du Bois,

> There is probably no group of 12 million persons in the modern world which exhibit smaller contrasts in personal income than the American Negro group. Their emancipation will not come . . . from an internal readjustment and ousting of exploiters; rather it will come from a wholesale emancipation from the grip of the white exploiters without. (ibid.)

He argued that it was possible that sometime in the future such a "full fledged capitalistic system may develop" (ibid.) among black Americans, but was emphatic that

> [f]or two generations the social leaders of the American Negro with very few exceptions have been poor men . . . owning little or no real property; few have been business men, none have been exploiters, and while there have been wide differences of ultimate ideal these leaders on the whole, have worked unselfishly for the uplift of the masses of Negro folk. (ibid., pp. 587–588)

Du Bois argued that "[t]here is no group of leaders on earth who have so largely made common cause with the lowest of their race as educated American Negroes, and it is their foresight and sacrifice and theirs alone that has saved the American freedman from annihilation and degradation" (1995c, p. 588). And while Du Bois recognized the "shortcomings and mistakes," some of which he argued were "legion," of this group, nonetheless, he argued that "their one great proof of success is the survival of the American Negro as the most intelligent and effective group of colored people fighting white civilization face to face and on its own ground, on the face of the earth," and "[f]or twenty years," Du Bois notes, this group "has fought a battle more desperate than any other race conflict of modern times and it has fought with honesty and courage" (ibid.).

Du Bois was recognizing that the black bourgeoisie was not functioning as a national bourgeoisie in a Marxist sense, since it possessed little capital and, more importantly, it wasn't the primary exploiter of black labor. In fact, it hardly employed even a preponderance of black workers, which were overwhelmingly in the employ of the white national bourgeoisie and white labor as well. Whatever black bourgeoisie can be said to have existed at the time was not even a managerial class—much less a class of owners of capital, a position it could hardly aspire to, much less acquire until the overthrow of Jim Crow in the South, when blacks in larger numbers obtained positions in the public sphere as salaried workers for local, state, and federal agencies. Without a black bourgeoisie in a Marxist sense, it followed that its class differences with the black working class did not constitute the class antagonisms that Marxism anticipates. That is, the class differences in black communities didn't generate the class contradictions that Marxism predicts because neither the black bourgeoisie nor petite bourgeoisie were the primary exploiters of black labor—this was the class position of white capitalists, and as Du Bois insisted, of white labor as well. It followed that the challenge for black political leaders was to organize intraracially across classes in black communities instead of organizing interracially among proletarians since class differences were not the primary mode of their oppression; it was race. Even during the Great Depression, Du Bois rejected the claim that the future of black labor lay in an alliance with white labor, arguing instead that

> [t]hroughout the history of the Negro in America, white labor has been the black man's enemy, his oppressor, his red murderer. Mobs, riots and the discrimination of trade unions have been used to kill, harass and starve black men. White labor disfranchised Negro labor in the South, is keeping them out of jobs and decent living quarters in the North, and is curtailing their education and civil and social privileges throughout the nation.

White laborers have formed the backbone of the Ku Klux Klan and have furnished hands and ropes to lynch 3,560 Negroes since 1882. (1995c, p. 589)

He assailed socialists as well:

The American Socialist party is out to emancipate the white worker and if this does not automatically free the colored man, he can continue in slavery. The only time that so fine a man and so logical a reasoner as Norman Thomas becomes vague and incoherent is when he touches the black man, and consequently he touches him as seldom as possible. (ibid., p. 590)

The absence of white espousal of "the cause of justice to black workers" is explained by socialists and communists, according to Du Bois, by their argument that in their "poverty and ignorance" white labor "has been misled by the propaganda of white capital, whose policy is to divide labor into classes, races and unions and pit one against the other" (ibid., p. 589). Du Bois concedes that "[t]here is an immense amount of truth in the explanation," as evidenced by the impact of "[n]ewspapers, social standards, race pride, competition for jobs," which, in his view, "all work to set white against black"; however, he asserts that "white American Laborers are not fools. And with few exceptions the more intelligent they are, the higher they rise, the more efficient they become, the more determined they are to keep Negroes under their heels" (ibid.). In fact, "[i]t is intelligent white labor that today keeps Negroes out of the trades, refuses them decent homes to live in and helps nullify their vote. Whatever ideals white labor today strives for in America, it would surrender nearly every one before it would recognize a Negro as a man" (ibid.). While noting that some "American Communists have made a courageous fight against the color line among the workers," though only by going "dead against the thought and desire of the overwhelming mass of white workers," yet, in the face of white labor's intransigence, "instead of acknowledging defeat in their effort to make white labor abolish the color line, they run and accuse Negroes of not sympathizing with the ideals of Labor!" (ibid., p. 590).

In light of the miscarriage of justice in the Scottsboro Boys case in Alabama, while recognizing the assistance of communists to their defense, he admonishes that while asserting their grounding with workers, they cannot speak for the white workers given that the "vast majority of these whites belong to the laboring class and they formed the white proletarian mob which is determined to kill the eight Negro boys" (1995c, pp. 590–591). He insisted that

[t]he persons who are killing blacks in Northern Alabama and demanding blood sacrifice are the white workers—sharecroppers, trade unionists and artisans. The capitalists are against mob-law and violence and would listen to reason and justice in the long run because industrial peace increases their profits. On the other hand, the white workers want to kill the competition of "Niggers." Thereupon, the Communists, seizing leadership of the poorest and most ignorant blacks head them toward inevitable slaughter and jail-slavery, while they hide in safety in Chattanooga and Harlem. (ibid., p. 591)

Du Bois emphasized that "American Negroes . . . are picking no chestnuts from the fire, neither for capital nor white labor" (ibid.). He was convinced that "Negroes know perfectly well that whenever they try to lead revolution in America, the nation will unite as one fist to crush them and them alone. There is no conceivable idea that seems to the present overwhelming majority of Americans higher than keeping Negroes 'in their place'" (ibid.). In this context, "Negroes perceive clearly that the real interests of the white worker are identical with the interests of the black worker, but until the white worker recognizes this, the black worker is compelled in sheer self-defense to refuse to be made the sacrificial goat" (ibid.). Although socialists and communists sneer at capital's support of Negro education, enfranchisement, and employment, Du Bois argued, they have offered little by comparison, and where they have secured higher wages it was for themselves and only included black labor in their benefits when they were compelled to (ibid., p. 592). Thus, Du Bois advocated the necessity of the emancipation of labor, but noted that "the first step toward the emancipation of colored labor must come from white labor" (ibid., p. 606), and central to this was the eradication of white racism in labor, which was not simply epiphenomenal of white capital's manipulation. Absent that development, black labor's future lay in its organization within the race institutions of black communities (ibid., p. 593).

For African Americans, a coalition with racist white labor was not in the offing, nor desirable to achieve black liberation; instead, a concerted intraracial effort was necessary

for the Negroes to organize a cooperative State within their own group. By letting Negro farmers feed Negro artisans, and Negro technicians guide Negro home industries, and Negro thinkers plan this integration of cooperation, while Negro artists dramatize and beautify the struggle, economic interdependence can be achieved. (1995c, p. 569)

He asserted that "any planning for the benefit of American Negroes on the part of a Negro intelligentsia is going to involve organized and deliberate self-segregation"—and in so doing he embraced the nationalist project that he so condemned Garvey for, as well as the "nation in a nation" thesis that the CPSU had recently adopted from Haywood. Anticipating his critics in the NAACP, he argued: "No sooner is this proposed than a great fear sweeps over older Negroes. They cry 'No segregation'—no further yielding to prejudice and race separation." But Du Bois distinguished his plan to utilize the segregation extant in the United States to further the development of black America, from one that would simply acquiesce to such segregation, by refusing to concede the civil rights struggle. He argued for a concomitant struggle that recognized the "peculiar position of Negroes in America," which "offer[red] an opportunity" to utilize the ballot at "critical times" when the black vote offered "a chance to hold a very considerable balance of power" (ibid., p. 568) and, more importantly, to utilize the "consuming power of 2,800,000 Negro families . . . a tremendous power when intelligently directed" (ibid.). Du Bois was recognizing that

> with the use of their political power, their power as consumers, and their brain power . . . Negroes can develop in the United States an economic nation within a nation, able to work through inner cooperation, to found its own institutions, to educate its genius, and at the same time, without mob violence or extremes of race hatred, to keep in helpful touch and cooperate with the mass of the nation. (1995c, p. 568)

Du Bois recognized that "it may be said that this matter of a nation within a nation has already been partially accomplished in the organization of the Negro church, the Negro school and the Negro retail business, and, despite all the justly due criticism, the result has been astonishing" (ibid., p. 569). He argued that "[t]he great majority of American Negroes are divided not only for religious but for a large number of social purposes into self-supporting economic units, self-governed, self-directed," and the "greatest difficulty is that these organizations have no logical and reasonable standards and do not attract the finest, most vigorous and best educated Negroes." Nevertheless,

> [w]hen all these things are taken into consideration it becomes clearer to more and more American Negroes that, through voluntary and increased segregation, by careful autonomy and planned economic organization, they may build so strong and efficient a

unit that 12,000,000 men can no longer be refused fellowship and equality in the United States. (ibid., pp. 569–570)

In sum, Du Bois was proposing a plan for black socio-politico-economic development as a nationalist project that focused on the Black Church, black business, and black schools as key institutions because these were the ones that had, at that time, the greatest potential to effectuate the change that he sought.[24] Lacking faith in the Black Church, in particular, to carry out such a transformative mission, Du Bois sought to create and promote other black institutions (i.e., black "counter-institutions" as Albert Cleage would label them in the BPM) to take up this burden. Although less sanguine of the Black Church as a progressive change agent, he remained convinced that black culture itself could serve that purpose. For Du Bois, culture was more akin to civilization, blacks were architects of an ancient civilization whose historical trajectory was truncated only by the recent depredations of the trans-Atlantic slave trade, European colonialism, and Western imperialism. Further, African American culture had given to the United States its only legitimate American culture. The challenge was to promote, popularize, and institutionalize this culture in such a way as to provide a mechanism for black entrée into the United States as full-scale citizens whose political and economic rights were recognized both de jure and de facto. Du Bois saw this progressive function as one to propagandize in favor of black culture, to provide legal redress to secure the political and economic rights of blacks, and to promote the institutions that would allow for both.

Du Bois's analysis projected a form of black culture that needed to be recognized, promoted, institutionalized, and propelled by external factors rather than by its own internal dynamism—which makes his argument on the revolutionary potential of slave religion in *Black Reconstruction* so exceptional, given this broader context of his work. For the most part, in Du Bois's view, the African American culture that provided the social resin of the black community apparently was motivated to progressive social change only by appeals to race consciousness, which could be undermined by either racist cultural hegemony or the appeal to exoticism (which was a critique he leveled at many Harlem Renaissance authors, artists, and performers). It was not enough that black culture be practiced as Locke argued (see chapter 3), it had to be propagandized, in order to have the impact that Du Bois sought. This constraint on Du Bois's conception of cultural transformation was less a problem where the main institution of change was a cultural institution itself; however, in light of his ambivalence toward the Black Church, he began to look to alternatives such as voluntary organizations, elite groups, and social classes to serve as change agents. As a result, his conception of black cultural change relied on race organizations, the talented tenth, the guiding hundredth, or the black peasant/working class to facilitate the cultural transformation he envisioned.

As Du Bois began to look toward institutions that did not necessarily embrace black culture to serve as change agents for the black culturalist project that he did so much to establish (e.g., the NAACP), he began to deemphasize black organized religion, and to focus more on the aesthetics of black folk culture expressed in its distinctive music, arts, literature, drama, and recreation. Du Bois understood that black aesthetic and material culture could provide the impetus that black religious organizations lacked; specifically, they could provide propaganda to support politico-economic change, economic development through patronage of black arts and black artistic institutions, and sociodemographic solidarity through the promotion of shared cultural norms and nonreligious cultural institutions. Such objectives seemed achievable during the Harlem Renaissance and, during its height, Du Bois argued in "Criteria of Negro Art" that "[i]t is the bounden duty of black America to begin this great work of the creation of beauty, of the preservation of beauty, of the realization of beauty, and we must use in this work all the methods that men have used before" (1995d, p. 510). He argued that among "the tools of the artist . . . he has used the truth—not for the sake of truth, not as a scientist seeking truth, but as one upon whom truth eternally thrusts itself as the highest handmaid of imagination, as the one great vehicle of universal understanding" (ibid.). He asserted the critical role of artists as advocates, chroniclers, and representatives of truth through art (ibid., p. 514); and emphasized that "[w]e [blacks] could afford the truth. White folk today cannot" (ibid., p. 515).[25] For Du Bois,

> all art is propaganda and ever must be, despite the wailing of the purists. I stand in utter shamelessness and say that whatever art I have for writing has been used always for propaganda for gaining the right of black folk to love and enjoy. I do not care a damn for any art that is not used for propaganda. (ibid., p. 514)

This quest to articulate a culture of truth was wedded to the broader political and economic aspirations of black Americans.

In this conception, Du Bois was prefiguring a thesis of cultural change that augured not only the promotion of a black cultural aesthetic or even a black culture industry but a transformation of the broader society through the integration of African American art, standards of beauty, and the truth that challenged white supremacy and its representations of whiteness, its practices of domination, and its denial of black culture that supported both.

He envisioned that the dominant society would be compelled to accommodate itself to the cultural demands of its Negro community, in part because "[w]e who are dark can see America in a way that white Americans cannot" (1995d, p. 509).

During the Harlem Renaissance, Du Bois was losing faith that the talented tenth would produce and promote this unique vision in black art and literature that would help radically transform U.S. society, because so many of them seemed to be parasitical on white patrons, and this era marked his open embrace of socialism.[26] Beyond—or as a consequence of—their dependence on white patronage, Du Bois was repulsed by black intellectuals', artists', playwrights', poets', novelists', and dramatists' "art for art's sake" disposition toward black cultural production, which led too many of them, in his view, to forgo pursuits comporting with his maxim of the propagandistic role of black creative production and opt instead for aesthetic themes, projects, and practices devoid of the culturally transformative racially emancipatory orientation that he thought should be manifest in any black art worthy of the name. In the latter vein, he targeted Alain Locke's (1928) assertions regarding the "non-propagandist" role of art in particular, which Du Bois largely dismissed. But, as we've seen in the previous chapter, Locke had a more complex view of the role of race, culture, and social change than Du Bois appreciated (Harris, 2004), and he proposed a dynamic thesis on intracultural, intercultural, and interracial contacts, which related black cultural revolution to political revolution in the United States. In fact, Locke's thesis of black culture provides a theoretical template for Du Bois's most revolutionary work on black America, *Black Reconstruction*. In so doing, it also allows us to generalize from the Slave Revolution of the Civil War era to the conditions of black America during the Civil Rights era and, as a result, provided black revolutionists with a theoretical guidepost from black culture to political revolution that only awaited their synthesis into a coherent program of action. Nevertheless, it was Du Bois's view of the propagandistic role of black art that was adopted by BPM revolutionists, especially in the Black Arts Movement (BAM), rather than Locke's more dynamic thesis, with major implications for subsequent theses of black cultural revolution, including that of the first theorist of black cultural revolution in the CRM, Harold Cruse, which we examine in the next chapter.

Conclusion

In this chapter, I examined the theoretical development of the concept of black cultural revolution in the United States. Recognizing the anteriority of the concept of cultural revolution in the academic literature, I briefly discussed the applicability of Marxist theses of cultural revolution to black America. After tracing the roots of early formulations of black cultural evolution to the social development theses of black nationalists—including black nationalist feminists—in the nineteenth century, I discussed how it informed later theses of black cultural revolution in the United States, exemplified in Du Bois's exegesis in *Black Reconstruction*. In contrast, in *The Negro and Social Reconstruction*, completed only a year later, Du Bois eschewed the revolutionary aspects of his cultural thesis in favor of a more evolutionary approach, which proposed that changes resulting in the development of separate black institutions within "self-segregated" black communities (i.e., cultural evolution) would facilitate the national development of black Americans and ultimately their integration into the political, economic, and social systems of the country as full-fledged citizens (i.e., political evolution). The analogue of the General Strike in the latter conception was the development of black consumer (and producer) power—and by implication the withholding of black consumption from white enterprises and institutions (i.e., a nationwide boycott)—and independent black institutions in a program that was primarily evolutionary rather than revolutionary.

Given Du Bois's ambivalence toward the Black Church as a change agent, he increasingly emphasized other factors. As a result, the program Du Bois devised was distant from the major cultural institution in the black community. Interestingly, the cultural revolutionary approach articulated in *Black Reconstruction* was largely ignored by BPM revolutionists, while the cultural evolutionary approach of developing parallel black institutions of civil society outlined in *Social Reconstruction* was adopted by many of them—often unwittingly. The distancing of black nationalist initiatives from the Black Church would be replicated by BPM revolutionists, as well. In addition, Du Bois advocated a propagandistic role for black art in opposition to the view of intellectuals such as Alain Locke. Yet, Locke had a more complex view of the role of race, culture, and social change than Du Bois appreciated; and Locke's dynamic thesis of black cultural change dovetailed with Du Bois's revolutionary thesis in *Black Reconstruction*, providing a framework to explain black cultural revolution in general and in this way offering a point of departure for BPM revolutionists seeking a thesis on black cultural revolution rooted in African American social dynamics. Nonetheless, it was Du Bois's orientation toward black art as propaganda that would be adopted by BPM revolutionists, rather than Locke's, and this would further enervate their cultural analyses.

Although Du Bois and Locke provided frameworks for understanding black cultural change, the theorist who provided the first explicit thesis of black cultural revolution, Harold Cruse, did not build on their specific arguments explicity, instead relying more on those of V. F. Calverton and C. Wright Mills. Cruse's thesis was novel and influential, likely informing Malcolm X's views on black cultural revolution, leading to the Revolutionary Action Movement's (RAM) advocacy of the concept, encouraging Us's promotion of it and the Congress of African Peoples' (CAP) adoption of it, influencing both the Republic of New Africa's (RNA) and the Shrine of the Black Madonna's discourse on the subject. Each of these groups would take quite different approaches to the role of culture in black liberation, and this, in part, was due to the eclectic aspects of Cruse's arguments on the subject. In the next chapter, we turn to an analysis of Cruse's thesis.

Chapter 5

Theorizing Cultural Revolution in the Black Power Era

Harold Cruse was the first to proffer an explicit thesis of black cultural revolution during the Civil Rights Movement (CRM). It drew on Du Bois's modernized black nationalism and Haywood's Black Belt thesis, the latter recast as domestic colonialism, while excising its Marxism. Cruse castigated the myopia of American Marxists in formulating theory applicable to U.S. society, which he associated with their failure to appreciate the revolutionary role of black nationalism and to sufficiently engage the white racism of the U.S. proletariat, which they continued to insist would comprise a revolutionary vanguard. He excoriated the union of white labor and white capital in its support of racism at home and racist imperialism abroad, which made the orthodox Marxist view of the white proletariat inapplicable to American realities. Instead, blacks would have to pose novel theory to transform the ongoing CRM into a revolutionary movement. Cruse's thesis was designed to serve that purpose.

Cruse's thesis informed the ideology of the Revolutionary Action Movement (RAM), which openly advocated the study of his writings, and adopted his concept of cultural revolution. Given their common residence in Harlem at the time, and Malcolm's affinity for *Studies on the Left*, which published Cruse's works, it's hard to believe that Cruse's thesis would have been foreign to Malcolm (Goose, 2004, pp. 25–27); it likely informed his discourse on cultural revolution. In the event, Malcolm's Organization of Afro-American Unity (OAAU) and RAM were the first major Black Power Movement (BPM) organizations to publicly advocate cultural revolution, and their advocacy encouraged Us's promotion of the concept; all three informed the Republic of New Africa's (RNA) and the Shrine of the Black Madonna's endorsements of it, as well. Support for cultural revolution during the BPM gained its widest acceptance from Amiri Baraka's Congress of African Peoples

(CAP), which built, in part, on his earlier cultural institutions such as the Black Arts Repertory Theater and School in Harlem (BARTS)—where Cruse lectured on history—which is widely viewed as the seminal organization of the Black Arts Movement (BAM). Thus, Cruse's thesis was foundational for revolutionists of the BPM and influential in BAM.

Harold Cruse, Black Cultural Revolution, and the Civil Rights Movement

Cruse was a cultural critic, World War II veteran, black nationalist, and former member of the CPUSA. During the late 1950s, after leaving the CPUSA, he sought to develop a revolutionary theory to address the "peculiar condition of Negroes" in the United States, which he thought orthodox Marxists, in particular, had failed to do, just as integrationists leading the CRM and black nationalists such as the Nation of Islam (NOI) had also. An aspiring but failed playwright, he struggled with the reality that black oppression was not only political and economic, but cultural as well. In a 1957 publication in *Presence Africaine*, "An Afro-American's Cultural Views," Cruse drew parallels between the revival of indigenous cultures as an aspect of anticolonial struggles and similar undercurrents among black Americans. He argued that "when one thinks of the liberation of oppressed peoples, one assumes a rebirth and flowering of that people's native 'culture' as a corollary of the rise to independence"; thus, he conjectured that

> in keeping with what is happening to colored peoples elsewhere, one might expect that in the United States the increased activity on the part of Negroes to achieve full citizenship, equality, and civil rights under the law would be accompanied by an increase in the quantity and quality of their "cultural" activities. (Cruse, 1968, p. 48)

Cruse lamented that this was not happening in the CRM.

Like Du Bois and Locke, Cruse was convinced that while the cultural roots of black America were found in Africa, "[i]t must be clearly understood that our racial and cultural experience as a group is distinctly American"—mainly as a result of the "de-Africanization process began at the point of landing of slaves on American shores" (ibid., pp. 50–51). He was not a reverse civilizationist. He asserted that in the United States "[d]uring slavery and for several decades after emancipation it was possible for one to say that Afro-Americans had a distinct culture," albeit "of the 'folk quality,'" consisting of "a distinct body of social art embodied in music, song, dance, folklore, poetry, formal literature, craftsmanship, mores, and even their own variant of Christian religious expression and experience" (ibid., p. 51). Black culture took on "more sophisticated expressions" in parallel with "our rise in social status after emancipation" (ibid.), such that "[i]t can be seen that despite our separation from the ways of Africa, Afro-Americans produced a culture that is distinctly our own and, for the most part, American in general milieu" (ibid., p. 52). Thus, like Du Bois and Locke, Cruse rejected reverse civilizationism, and like them, he was convinced that blacks were oppressed culturally as well as politically and economically, and that a focus on the cultural aspects of black oppression could ramify into the political and economic spheres.

Unlike Du Bois and Locke, Cruse was an outspoken black nationalist who viewed black Americans as a colonized nation within the United States, which he characterized as domestic colonialism. Cruse argued that the peculiar position of blacks as a colonized people in the United States made the black nationalist struggle analogous to the nationalist anticolonial struggles throughout the third world, but it also meant that black liberation would have to take place within and not apart from the colonizing power, which happened to be the most industrialized and militarily powerful country in the world. In such a context, it was necessary, Cruse argued, to target the "weakest front" in the political, economic, and social systems of the United States in order to expand the CRM in ways that would facilitate revolutionary change, and for him, this was the "cultural front."

Cruse argued the necessity of targeting the "cultural apparatus" of the United States—both in artistic production and administrative control—and democratizing it and utilizing it to transform the CRM by promoting both the development and distribution of black aesthetic production and the institutions associated with it, which would provide, among other things, an independent source of economic resources to fund the CRM. More importantly, it would raise the contradictions between black aesthetic production and its commodification, expropriation, and control by whites to advance broader legal and economic claims. In these ways, demands originating in the cultural sphere would ramify into the economic and political domains, in a manner resonating with Locke's framework. Cruse did not explicitly incorporate Locke's theoretical insights into his cultural revolutionary project, yet his thesis dovetailed with important aspects of it.[1] Cruse went farther and argued that the extension of political and economic democracy into the cultural sphere necessitated the democratization of the cultural apparatus of U.S. society (more below). Cruse was convinced that most theoreticians—especially Marxists—failed to appreciate the importance of culture in revolution, and black culture specifically, because they ignored progressive aspects of black nationalism. Therefore, they had little appreciation for the self-determination claims of black Americans, or their espousal of black nationalism, historically or contemporaneously, even as this thrust was transforming the CRM and giving rise to the BPM.

In 1962, Cruse published an article in *Studies on the Left* entitled "Revolutionary Nationalism and the Afro-American," which would become one of the most influential essays among black power activists. The essay provided an analysis of black nationalism, black power, and, subsequently, black cultural revolution in the 1960s. He asserted the revolutionary aspects of black nationalism, while lambasting the anti–black nationalist arguments of reformists of the CRM, and especially American Marxists. Unlike the theorists of cultural revolution we've examined up to this point, Cruse was purposely attempting to revolutionize an ongoing national movement of black Americans that was centered on the U.S. South. For Cruse, the reformists leading the CRM were insufficiently focused on the cultural elements of black liberation, which, he argued, when properly understood, theorized, and utilized would fuse with the political objectives of the CRM and extend them into the economic domain. Such a fusion would raise such fundamental contradictions that it would transform the CRM into a social revolution. The missing element in this process, for Cruse, was a cultural revolution, which he would continue to flesh out over the decade. Cruse saw greater promise in the black nationalist arguments that were increasingly popular inside and outside of the CRM; and argued that from them would emerge a revolutionary thesis more attuned to the realities on the ground in black America. For a former Marxist to assert the greater salience of black nationalism to Marxism in the black liberation struggle in the United States was not uncommon; it evoked Du Bois' earlier arguments, ironic now since he joined the Communist Party shortly before his death in 1963 but seemingly counterintuitive, in Cruse's case, in an era in which so many revolutionary struggles were cast in often explicitly Marxist terms, or at least drew on Marxist rhetoric. Moreover, the success of the Cuban Revolution seemed to vindicate Marxist revolutionary theory in overthrowing a comprador regime of the United States just ninety miles off the Florida coast.

Cruse characterized the success of the Cuban Revolution as a failure of the revolutionary theory of the CPUSA. He argued that for most black activists, Marxism suffered from its insistence that white workers were the revolutionary vanguard and that the revolution of the proletariat in the industrialized West would lead to liberation in the colonies. Black Americans, more than any other group, were painfully aware of the entrenched racism of the white American working class, and generally saw their racial oppression not as epiphenomenal of their class position, but as a product of a white supremacist system that may have originated from an economic system of slavery but had assumed a life of its own in the politico-legal, social, as well as economic institutions of the broader society irrespective of its provenance; just as importantly, it was perpetuated by the efforts of whites irrespective of their class. The view that working-class whites, Marx's proletariat, who were some of the most virulent racists in the United States, were going to be the vanguard of a social revolution in the country that would result in, among other things, overthrowing the system of white supremacism was ridiculous on its face to most black Americans. Further, the white American proletariat, which was not even organized as a labor party, or even gravitating to a revolutionary party, was typical of Western proletariats, more generally, which were not revolutionary in their own countries; yet, Marxism-Leninism taught that the proletariat in the industrialized West would provide revolutionary leadership for the colonies. Antirevolutionism was even more evident among the U.S. working class, which racially segregated its unions, for decades adamantly opposed organizing black workers, and was intent on achieving a modus vivendi with its white racist bourgeoisie rather than proffering a progressive challenge—much less a revolutionary one—to the racist status quo of the United States. As Du Bois had long before observed, white proletarians in the Western metropoles largely endorsed, deferred to, and/or cooperated with their respective national bourgeoisies in their imperialism in the colonies, fighting mainly for a larger share of the spoils from the extraction of surplus value from the exploited labor of the periphery as well as its raw materials and mineral resources. White labor forged an alliance with white capital to support national imperialism and its wars—including the two world wars—and it was these collaborators with capital to whom orthodox Marxists looked for emancipating humanity?

Cruse noted that the Cuban Revolution was less a vindication of American Marxism than a demonstration that third world revolutionists were not waiting for white proletarians of advanced industrialized states to serve as a vanguard for revolutions to liberate their homelands from Western imperialism—not even when they were only ninety miles away from the United States. What the Cuban Revolution—and many revolutions occurring throughout the third world—had demonstrated was that the oppressed in the colonies were not waiting for the Western proletariat to discover its "revolutionary mission" and overthrow imperialism. In fact, "the revolutionary initiative [had] passed to the colonial world," while Western Marxists continued to "theorize, temporize, and debate" (1968, p. 75). It followed, Cruse argued, that it was from the underdeveloped world that "schools of theory and practice for achieving independence have emerged" (ibid.). A similar process was at work in the United States where the revolutionary initiative was passing from Marxist proletarians to African Americans, the group that Cruse observed was "the leading revolutionary force" in the United States. Yet, U.S. Marxists enjoined black Americans to submerge their ongoing mobilizing for self-determination beneath a white worker-led, class-based, racially integrated political struggle that didn't exist in any predominantly white community in the United States. This orientation was being rejected wholesale in the ongoing CRM as well as in the incipient BPM.

Given that it had become the leading revolutionary force in the United States, Cruse maintained that "from the Negro himself must come the revolutionary social theories of an economic, cultural, and political nature that will be his guides for social action—the new philosophies of social change" (1968, p. 96). Cruse was adamant that "the Negro in the United States can no more look to American Marxist schema than the colonials and semi-dependents could conform to the Western Marxist timetable for revolutionary advances." Further, he challenged "[t]hose on the American left who support revolutionary nationalism in Asia, Africa, and Latin America" that they "must also accept the validity of Negro nationalism in the United States." For him, it was just as valid "for Negro nationalists to want to separate from American whites as it is for Cuban nationalists to want to separate economically and politically from the United States" (ibid., p. 94). He railed against arguments that opposed this view in the name of "pragmatic practicalities" (ibid.). In fact, Cruse (ibid., p. 74) argued that "the Negro has a relationship to the dominant culture of the United States similar to that of colonies and semi-dependents to their particular foreign overseers"—thus, domestic colonialism.

Cruse viewed black nationalism as emanating from the initiatives of blacks in response to the domestic colonialism they experienced, and the black nationalism of the 1960s was reflecting the interests of mainly working-class blacks who were less inclined to integrationism in its avowedly reformist guise in the CRM or its putatively radical form in orthodox Marxism. For Cruse, both international and domestic colonialism generated revolutionary forms of nationalism in the colonized world and in black America, respectively. Moreover, "[t]he failure of American Marxists to understand the bond between the Negro and the colonial peoples of the world has led to their failure to develop theories that would be of value to Negroes in the United States" (1968, p. 75) because they ignore the domestic colonial context in which black Americans are situated. As a result, the policies Marxism promotes are out of touch with the concrete conditions of black society, and particularly with respect to the revolutionary potential of black nationalism. In this essay, which became required reading for RAM members, Cruse historicized the emerging revolutionary black nationalism of the BPM.

Cruse viewed slavery in the United States, which coincided with the colonial expansion of European powers, as the specific form that U.S. colonialism took: domestic colonialism. That is, "Instead of the United States establishing a colonial empire in Africa, it brought the colonial system home and installed it in the Southern states" (1968, p. 76). In this argument, Cruse was expropriating much of Haywood's (1948) thesis on black nationalism, which the CPSU had adopted in 1928 as the Black Belt thesis, and for which he had shown affinities when he was a member of the CPUSA; however, once the CPUSA abandoned it and purged Haywood in 1959, it reverted to viewing the "Negro problem" as one of racial discrimination and not national liberation. Not surprisingly, Cruse's historical analysis up to this point mirrors Haywood's insofar as he argues that following emancipation, the Negro was only partially free, not provided an economic basis for his/her freedom, so that "[e]xcept for a very small percentage of the Negro intelligentsia, the Negro function[ed] in a subcultural world made up, usually of necessity, of his own race only" (ibid.). Importantly, Cruse adds—and Haywood would agree—that "[t]his is much more than a problem of racial discrimination, it is a problem of political, economic, cultural, and administrative underdevelopment" (ibid.).

Cruse insists that the persistence of domestic colonialism to the present contributes to U.S. Marxists' misunderstanding of black nationalism—or more accurately, their position in 1962 since they had abandoned Haywood's thesis, which Cruse was largely repeating. He argued that U.S. Marxists "have never been able to understand the implications of the Negro's position in the social structure of the United States" and, just "[a]s Western Marxism had no adequate revolutionary theory for the colonies, American Marxists have no adequate theory for the Negro" (1968, pp. 76–77). For Cruse,

> The only factor which differentiates the Negro's status from that of a pure colonial status is that his position is maintained in the "home" country in close proximity to the dominant racial group. It is not at all remarkable then that the semi-colonial status of the Negro has given rise to nationalist movements. It would be surprising if it had not. (ibid., p. 77)

Cruse asserts that "American Marxism has neither understood the nature of Negro nationalism, nor dealt with its roots in American society," and "[w]hen the Communists first promulgated the Negro question as a 'national question' in 1928, they wanted a *national question without nationalism*" (ibid., p. 78; emphasis added).

Cruse attempts to differentiate his perspective from Haywood's, which he clearly is drawing on, noting that Marxists "relegated" the Negro nationality to the Black Belt South although the Garvey movement was largely a northern black phenomenon stimulated in large part by the black migration from the South. Cruse delinks the Marxist conception of black nationalism in the United States in 1928 from Haywood's (1948) more nuanced argument, which, while recognizing the Black Belt as the national homeland of black America, included blacks outside the South as members of the black nation, as well. Thus, Haywood (1948) was closer to Cruse's view that "the national character of the Negro has little to do with what part of the country he lives in" (1968, p. 78). Nevertheless, Cruse argued that American Marxists in 1962 failed to appreciate the dimensions within black nationalism—another view that converges with Haywood's, although, unlike Haywood, Cruse roots this failure in Marxists' misunderstanding of the controversy between Washington and Du Bois at the turn of the century which he views as a debate "over the correct tactics for the emerging Negro bourgeoisie" (ibid., p. 82). He maintains that since Reconstruction,

> the would-be Negro bourgeoisie in the United States confronted unique difficulties quite unlike those experienced by the young bourgeoisie in colonial situations. As a class, the Negro bourgeoisie wanted liberty and equality, but also money, prestige, and political power. How to achieve all this within the American framework was a difficult problem, since the whites had a monopoly on these benefits. . . . The Negro bourgeoisie was trapped and stymied by the entrenched and expanding power of American capitalism. Unlike the situation in the colonial area, the Negro could not seize the power he wanted nor oust "foreigners." Hence he turned inward toward organizations of fraternal, religious, nationalistic, educational and political natures. There was much frustrated bickering and internal conflict within this new class over strategy and tactics. Finally the issues boiled down to that of politics vs. economics, and emerged in the Washington Du Bois controversy. (ibid.)

Their contestation resulted from the apparent incompatibility of Washington's attempt to develop a separate black economy in the South with Du Bois's cosmopolitan project aimed at political rights.

For Cruse, Marxists' adoption of Du Bois's argument and vilification of Washington's was tantamount to "saying that the Negro bourgeoisie had no right to try to become capitalists—an idea that makes no historical sense whatever" (1968, p. 83). Cruse offered this analogy: "If a small proprietor, native to an underdeveloped country, should want to oust foreign capitalists and take over the internal markets, why should not the Negro proprietor have the same desire?" (ibid., pp. 83–84). Although a Negro bourgeoisie did not develop in any meaningful sense—only a black petite bourgeoisie emerged—Cruse asserts that this obscures the larger point that "Washington's role in developing an economic program to counteract the Negro's social position is central to the emergence of Negro nationalism, and accounts for much of his popularity among Negroes" (ibid., p. 84). With this view in mind, Cruse chastises Marxist historians, typified by Aptheker, for failing to appreciate the salience of Washington's economic program for Negroes and insisting on only assessing him in political terms, and on that basis finding Washington "not 'revolutionary' or 'militant' in the fashion that befits a Negro leader"—at least not one that Marxists would commend; but in so doing, "rejects the historic-economic-class basis of Washington's philosophy, although these are essential in analyzing social movements, personalities, or historical situations" (ibid.). Marxists, then, according to Cruse, tend to view Negroes as an undifferentiated mass that more properly should have been wedded to protest movements and trade unionism in the South, to which Cruse admonishes:

> It is naïve to believe that any aspiring member of the bourgeoisie [in the nineteenth century U.S. South] would have been interested in trade-unionism and the political action of farmers. But American Marxists cannot "see" the Negro at all unless he is storming the barricades, either in the present or in history. Does it make any sense to look back into history and expect to find Negroes involved in trade unionism and political action in the most lynch-ridden decade the South has ever known? Anyone reading about the South at the turn of the century must wonder how Negroes managed to survive at all, let alone become involved in political activity when politics was dominated by the Ku Klux Klan. (ibid., p. 85)

Cruse continues that, according to Marxists such as Aptheker, "the Negroes who supported Washington were wrong"; instead,

> It was the handful of Negro militants from above the Mason-Dixon line who had never known slavery, who had never known Southern poverty and illiteracy, the whip of the lynch-mad KKK, or the peasant's agony of landlessness, who were correct in their high-sounding idealistic criticism of Washington. These were, Aptheker tells us, within a politically revolutionary tradition—a tradition which in fact had not even emerged when Washington died! (ibid.)

This controversy continued into the ideological conflict between Garvey and the NAACP, largely as a result of the former's building on Washington's politico-economic perspective and the latter's building on Du Bois's. Cruse notes that

> [a]dopting what he wanted from Washington's ideas, Garvey carried them further—advocating Negro self-sufficiency in the United States linked, this time, with the idea of regaining access to the African homeland as a basis for constructing a viable black economy. Whereas Washington had earlier chosen an accommodationist position in the South to achieve his objectives, Garvey added the racial ingredient of black nationalism to Washington's ideas with potent effect. This development paralleled the bourgeois origins of the colonial revolutions then in their initial stages in Africa and Asia. Coming from a British colony, Garvey had the psychology of a colonial revolutionary and acted as such. (1968, pp. 85–86)

Cruse notes that

> [w]ith the rise of nationalism, Du Bois and the NAACP took a strong stand against the Garvey movement and against revolutionary nationalism. The issues were much deeper than mere rivalry between different factions for the leadership of Negro politics. The rise of Garvey nationalism meant that the NAACP became the accommodationists and the nationalists became the militants. (ibid., p. 86)

In discussing Garvey, Cruse notes the split among Marxists in their view of black nationalism, citing favorably Haywood's more perceptive views of sanguine aspects of Garvey's black nationalism, but observing that by 1959, "the Communists withdrew the concept of 'self-determination' in the black belt, and sidestepped the question of the Negro's 'national character.' Instead, they adopted a position essentially the same as that of the NAACP" with respect to the American Negro (ibid., p. 87).

Cruse argues that by the time of the CRM, Marxists found "it convenient from a theoretical standpoint to see Negroes in history as black proletarian 'prototypes' and forerunners of the 'black workers' who will participate in the proletarian revolution" (ibid., p. 88). Such "mythology" according to Cruse, relies on "a patronizing deification of Negro slave heroes," which "results in abstracting them from their proper historical context and making it appear that they are relevant to modern reality" (ibid.). For Cruse,

> To the extent that the myth of a uniform "Negro People" has endured, a clear understanding of the causes of Negro nationalism has been prevented. In reality, no such uniformity exists. There are class divisions among Negroes, and it is misleading to maintain that the interests of the Negro working and middle classes are identical. To be sure, a middle class NAACP leader and an illiterate farmhand in Mississippi or a porter who lives in Harlem all want civil rights. However, it would be enlightening to examine why the NAACP is not composed of Negro porters and farmhands, but only of Negroes of a certain type. (1968, pp. 88–89)

It's doubly ironic that Cruse, the black nationalist, is charging Marxists with treating black Americans as an "undifferentiated mass"—a monolithic whole, whose intraracial stratification was either nonexistent or immaterial to their prophesied fate as an analogue to the movement toward Marxist-led interracial proletarian revolution. Even today, many of these same radical critics of Cruse and black nationalists in general make the ahistorical and wholly inaccurate charge that black nationalists view black Americans as an undifferentiated mass, seemingly oblivious to this orientation in their own ideological formulations. Moreover, Cruse was concerned with why these classes among blacks seemed to be striving toward different objectives with different degrees of intensity—toward, away from, or indifferent to integration—and embracing different ideologies, as well. For example, among the most pressing issues for Cruse was why the emerging nationalist tendency was more strongly embraced by the black working class, while "Marxists of all groups, are at this late date tail-ending organizations such as the NAACP (King, CORE, etc.), which do not have the broad support of Negro workers and farmers" (1968, p. 89).

For Cruse, it's important to appreciate why the black bourgeoisie's interests have been separate from those of the black working class and what this portends for the CRM and the illusion of black racial unity. Drawing from the sociologist E. Franklin Frazier, Cruse notes that the divergent interests of the Negro bourgeoisie and working class reflect the reality that the former doesn't "control the Negro 'market'" in the United States,

> and since it derived its income from whatever "integrated" occupational advantages it has achieved, it has neither developed a

sense of association of its status with that of the Negro working class, nor a "community" of economic, political, or cultural interests conducive to cultivating "nationalistic sentiments." Today, except for the issue of civil rights, no unity of interests exists between the Negro middle class and the Negro working class. (1968, p. 90)

Cruse continues:

> Furthermore, large segments of the modern Negro bourgeoisie have played a continually regressive "non-national" role in Negro affairs. Thriving off the crumbs of integration, these bourgeois elements have become de-racialized and decultured, leaving the Negro working class without voice or leadership, while serving the negative role of class buffer between the deprived working class and the white ruling elites. In this respect, such groups have become a social millstone around the necks of the Negro working class.

Thus, the black bourgeoisie—more of a petite bourgeoisie—has within it "large segments" that may be better characterized as a "lumpenbourgeoisie." The duality of their position contributes to the dilemma of the black intellectual who is "[d]etached from the Negro working class," and seeking integration but "failing to gain entry to the status quo, he resorts to talking like a revolutionary, championing revolutionary nationalism and its social dynamism in the underdeveloped world" (1968, pp. 90–91). Such a "gesture" amounts to little more than "flirting with the revolutionary nationalism of the non-West," which "does not mask the fact that the American Negro intellectual is floating in ideological space . . . caught up in the world contradiction" (ibid., p. 91). In this context,

> Forced to face up to the colonial revolution and to make shallow propaganda out of it for himself, the American Negro intellectual is unable to cement his ties with the more racial-minded segments of the Negro working class. For this would require him to take a nationalistic stand in American politics—which he is loath to do. Nevertheless, the impact of revolutionary nationalism in the non-Western world is forcing certain Negro intellectuals to take a nationalist position in regard to their American situation. (ibid.)

It is the failure of the Negro bourgeoisie to develop an "economic basis" for its position, to develop an "economic self-sufficiency," that helps explain "the persistence of nationalist groupings in Negro life," because the "Negro nationalist ideology regards all the social ills from which the Negroes suffer as being caused by the lack of economic control over the segregated Negro community," which accounts for organizational attempts to "agitate for Negro ascendancy in and control of the Negro market" such as "Buy Black" programs (ibid.). He adds that since nationalists "do not envision a time when whites will voluntarily end segregation," they find it "necessary to gain control of the economic welfare of the segregated community," while others "such as the Black Muslims, actually believe that racial separation is in the best interests of both races" (ibid.). Thus, Cruse maintains that

> [w]hen Communists and other Marxists imply that racial integration represents an all-class movement for liberation, it indicates that they have lost touch with the realities of Negro life. They fail to concern themselves with the mind of the working-class Negro in the depths of the ghetto, or the nationalistic yearnings of those hundreds of thousands of ghetto Negroes whose every aspiration has been negated by white society. (1968, p. 92)

Cruse notes that

> [i]nstead, the Marxists gear their position to Negro middle-class aspirations and ideology. Such Marxists support the position of the Negro bourgeoisie in denying, condemning, or ignoring the existence of Negro nationalism in the United States—while regarding the reality of nationalism in the colonial world as something peculiar to "exotic" peoples. The measure of the lack of appeal to the working classes of the Marxist movement is indicated by the fact that Negro nationalist movements are basically working-class in character while the new Negroes attracted to the Marxist movement are of bourgeois outlook and sympathies. (ibid.)

He further castigates Marxists for not even practicing in their own organizations the "inter-racialism" they espouse in their "Negro Liberation" advocacy and programs:

> Ironically, even within Marxist organizations Negroes . . . have been subordinated to the will of a white majority on all crucial matters of racial policy. What the Marxists called "Negro-white unity" within their organization was, in reality, white domination. Thus the Marxist movement took a position of favoring a racial

equality that did not even exist within the organization of the movement itself. (ibid.)

In sum "The failure to deal adequately with the Negro question is the chief cause of American Marxism's ultimate alienation from the vital stream of American life" (ibid., p. 93).

Cruse concludes that black Americans "can no more look to American Marxist schema than the colonials and semi-dependents could conform to the Western Marxist timetable for revolutionary advances" (ibid., p. 94). For Cruse,

> It is up to the Negro to take the organizational, political, and economic steps necessary to raise and defend his status. The present situation . . . will inevitably force nationalist movements to make demands which should be supported by people who are not Negro nationalists. The nationalists may be forced to demand the right of political separation. This too must be upheld because it is the surest means of achieving Federal action on all Negro demands of an economic or political nature. It will be the most direct means of publicizing the fact that the American government's policy on underdeveloped areas must be complemented by the same approach to Negro underdevelopment in the United States. (1968, pp. 94–95)

Cruse maintains that "[i]t's pointless to argue, as many do, that Negro nationalism is an invalid ideology for Negroes to have in American life, or that the nationalist ideas of economic self-sufficiency or the 'separate Negro economy' are unrealistic or utopian" (ibid., p. 95). For Cruse, it is no more utopian than "the idea of the eventual acceptance of the Negro as a full-fledged American without regard to race, creed, or color." He notes that although "[t]here is no organized force in the United States at present capable of altering the structural form of American society . . . [d]ue to his semi-dependent status in society, the American Negro is the only potentially revolutionary force in the United States today" (ibid., pp. 95–96). Therefore, he insisted that

> [f]rom the Negro himself must come the revolutionary social theories of an economic, cultural, and political nature that will be his guides for social action—the new philosophies of social change. If the white working class is ever to move in the direction of demanding structural changes in society, it will be the Negro who will furnish the initial force. (ibid., pp. 96)

Auguring the onset of the BPM, Cruse was convinced that

> [t]he coming coalition of Negro organizations will contain nationalist elements in roles of conspicuous leadership. It cannot and will not be subordinate to any white groups with which it is allied. There is no longer room for the revolutionary paternalism that has been the hallmark of organizations such as the Communist Party. This is what the New Left must clearly understand in its future relations with Negro movements that are indigenous to the Negro community. (1968, p. 96)

Cruse's argument in "Revolutionary Nationalism and the Afro-American" in 1962 captured the imagination of black activists throughout the country—especially students—becoming a frame of reference for the Revolutionary Action Movement (RAM), which would provide a core of activists including those who would emerge at the forefront of the BPM in the Student Non-Violent Coordinating Committee (SNCC), Us, the Black Panther Party (BPP), the Republic of New Africa (RNA), CAP, and the League of Revolutionary Black Workers (LRBW), among others. It also affected many black and white leftists in Students for a Democratic Society (SDS) and Marxist organizations. It was from the latter group that critics such as Haywood would contest aspects of Cruse's thesis.

For example, in a series of articles in *Soul Book*, a publication associated with RAM, Haywood and Gwendolyn Hall asserted that it reflected a bourgeois orientation toward what they admitted was a potentially revolutionary development: the rise of black nationalism in the 1960s. They noted that "Negro nationalism is not alien or new to the American scene" but "a basic and continuing theme in Negro protest" and "a steady undercurrent in the national Negro community, existing side by side with the dominant integrationist-assimilationist trend," gaining prominence in times of "stress and crisis" (Haywood & Hall, 1965/66, p. 259). They viewed the "growth of Negro nationalist sentiment [a]s a positive development in itself" and "an essential precondition for the emergence of a national revolutionary movement" (ibid.). Nevertheless, they argued that like integrationism, nationalism had bourgeois and revolutionary elements and that Cruse's thesis was tied too closely to the former, the "ghetto-nationalists." While arguing that the integrationist program was "entirely unrealistic" for the masses of black Americans, they viewed "ghetto-nationalists" as "economically based on the northern urban Black community, indulg[ing] in fantasies of building up a separate Black 'Free Enterprise' economy as the solution," which was similarly quixotic, reflecting the fact that the Black bourgeoisie was incapable of "leading the type of struggle necessary to win Black freedom." For them, "The basic masses must . . . forge their own instrument and fight for a program of liberation that will not subordinate their interests to those of either sector of the black bourgeoisie" (Haywood & Hall, 1966, p. 71).

They acknowledge the "considerable influence in left circles" of Cruse's "Revolutionary Nationalism and the Afro-American," before caricaturing Cruse as "involv[ing] himself in the toils of the ghetto nationalists, elaborat[ing] a theory for them, and then call[ing] upon white progressives to fall in behind this 'revolutionary' leadership." They make three main criticisms: (1) Cruse assumes that the black bourgeoisie is the revolutionary element in black communities and "writes off the possibility for the basic masses to fight independently and forge their own revolutionary movement" (ibid., p. 72); (2) Cruse's critique of the Communist Party conception of black nationalism is dated and does not reflect its present views; (3) Cruse's focus on the importance of the "ghetto market" as a site of revolutionary contention is mistaken (ibid., p. 73). Taking each in turn, a cursory review of the passages quoted above from Cruse's article shows that he was not arguing that the bourgeoisie was the vanguard of the black revolution, nor did he fail to realize that there were valences in nationalism. He acknowledged the class differences among blacks, and that the black nationalism that was emerging at the time reflected the interests of working-class blacks more than that of the bourgeois blacks who held sway over the movement, whom Cruse characterized as "a social millstone around the necks of the Negro working class." Cruse also acknowledged that this same working class was largely opposed or indifferent to Marxism as well. Thus, given Cruse's argument that the revolutionary vanguard had passed from white proletarians in the metropole to third world peoples in the periphery, and that black nationalists in the United States were representative of this emerging revolutionary trend, and that black nationalism largely reflected the interests of the black working class and was largely opposed by the black bourgeoisie, then it follows that Cruse did not view the black bourgeoisie as the revolutionary vanguard nor did he propose that the black working class follow it, but quite the opposite.

Regarding the second critique, Haywood and Hall may be technically correct but they are substantively incorrect. That is, the claim that Cruse's argument is based on Old Left conceptions of black nationalism and not those of the New Left rests on the assumption that Haywood and Hall's theses represent the latter. In the first place, Cruse's analysis is consistent with Haywood's (1948) earlier claims regarding black nationalism, which, given their earlier adoption by the CPSU in 1928, seem to represent the Old Left; however, the CPUSA, the most prominent "Old Left" organization in the United States, had shied away from the Black Belt thesis during the Popular Front era in the late 1930s and ultimately rejected it wholesale by the late 1950s—and, in fact, had purged Haywood from the party for his alleged nationalist leanings. Therefore, it is difficult for Haywood and Hall to associate Haywood's earlier formulations of the Black Belt thesis with the CPUSA position post-1959, which by the time of Cruse's writing in 1962 the CPUSA had wholly rejected. The position of the CPUSA in 1962 and throughout the CRM and BPM was that the struggle for black civil rights was an issue of racial discrimination and not national self-determination and as such it was a distraction from the "legitimate" revolutionary struggle of organizing black and white (as well as brown, yellow, and red) workers as a racially integrated proletariat for class struggle to overthrow the bourgeoisie in the United States. It is this latter position of the CPUSA—the main organizational representation of the Old Left—which Cruse castigated. In fact, Haywood makes some of the same critiques of the CPUSA that Cruse did with respect to its McCarthy Era views of black nationalism and its rationale for rejecting his Black Belt thesis. Thus, while Haywood and Hall may take issue with Cruse's thesis for ignoring or minimizing some aspects of Haywood's Black Belt thesis, they are incorrect that in so doing Cruse was ignoring important aspects of the CPUSA's contemporaneous position on black nationalism.

More telling, the third critique focuses on the assumption that the crux of Cruse's thesis is the revolutionary tension in the struggle for the "ghetto market." This criticism reflects the failure of orthodox U.S. Marxists, in particular, to provide a cogent thesis for black economic development prior to the prophesied revolution. Ironically, even as purists recognized the importance of Lenin's NEP as a transitional phase between wartime communism and Stalin's collectivist Five Year Plans, they did not envision any realistic program to alleviate the gross privations among blacks in their communities that utilized free enterprise practices, nor did they seem to appreciate the importance of developing independent black economic institutions beyond white-dominated trade unionism or what were largely imagined transracial cooperative or collectivist schemes. This was part of Cruse's criticism of the myopia of doctrinaire Marxist arguments against Garvey in the 1920s and their failure to appreciate the significance of the Black Muslims in the 1960s, which were both viewed as bourgeois, utopic, and ultimately advocating "escapist fantasies." While both the UNIA and the NOI articulated what may be considered "escapist" programs, reflected in their advocacy of some form of twentieth-century black emigration, their black nationalism challenged imperialism as well. For the UNIA, this was a conscious attempt to politically confront the Western imperial powers regarding their colonial oppression of Africa—a point that Haywood drew on in posing his original thesis on black nationalism in the 1920s (i.e., the Black Belt thesis); and for the NOI—although it was less oriented toward the open protest of the UNIA—it was evident in its challenge to the white supremacy of the leading imperialist power, the United States—a fact that Haywood also acknowledged. For example, he noted that

> [t]he Black Muslims identify with the most-radical sections of the international struggle against colonialism. Their publication, Muhammed Speaks, has given favourable and extensive coverage to the Cuban Revolution, the successes in eliminating racism from the island. The newspaper featured the message of support from Mao TseTung to the Afroamerican struggle under the heading, "First Big Power to Assail Racist Doctrine in America." It reports the activism of the most militant sections of the liberation movement, such as SNCC, and exposes the hypocrisy of the Federal Government. (1967, p. 137)

Although associating them with the "ghetto bourgeoisie" and decrying their "drive" for a "Black controlled economy," Haywood noted that the NOI drew its main support from "Black workers and youth, who make up the overwhelming majority of its membership" (ibid., pp. 137–138), in no small part because the Black Muslims "articulate the bitterness and resentment of the vast majority of Black Americans, placing the onus of moral depravity where it belongs; on the white man's culture" (ibid., p. 137). Thus, Haywood noted cogently that "[w]hile it is true that the ghetto bourgeoisie, including the Muslims, are incapable of leading a revolutionary struggle for Black Power, it would be a mistake to equate them with the top assimilationist stratum," which, "as a stratum, has no revolutionary potential; whereas the ghetto bourgeoisie, when it sees a strong national revolutionary movement with a realistic program, is perfectly capable of throwing its weight as a stratum behind such a movement," which "is confirmed by the experiences of the 1930's" (ibid., p. 141). Thus, according to Haywood and Hall, the influence of at least a sector, or selected elements, of the "ghetto bourgeoisie" cannot simply be relegated to that of an aspiring bourgeoisie aimed at exploiting its "ghetto market," much less its proletariat, and it's on this sector that Cruse was casting whatever hope he had for black intellectuals, students, activists, specifically, to assume their obligation as social theorists and activists to provide a thematic frame for black revolution in the United States.

The development of black economic autonomy has been a handmaiden of black nationalism since its development in the late eighteenth century, and it is a concomitant of black nationalist consciousness—rather than simply a product of bourgeois tendencies—that reflects an assertion of self-determination in the economic sphere. It is commonly recognized—and was even more so in the Cold War era—as an appropriate focus by/for other colonized people pursuing their national liberation against imperialist domination, and no less importantly as an area of struggle to check neocolonial initiatives that often strike at the postindependence economic systems of newly liberated former colonies. Ironically, for all of Haywood and Hall's admonition of Cruse that he focuses too readily on the "Old Left," their main argument against Cruse's alleged focus on the "ghetto market" relies on an assessment of the salience of competition over the semicolonial market made by Josef Stalin, the epitome of the "Old Left," based on an analysis from nearly a half-century earlier.

All told, it is evident that Haywood's claims regarding the revolutionary potential of a sector of the black bourgeoisie were little different than Cruse's—and potentially no less insightful; however, this suggests that Haywood was guilty of the same charge that he leveled at Cruse. The difference is one of emphasis and objective: Cruse was seeking to provide a theoretical and programmatic compass to direct elements of the black petite bourgeoisie (especially intellectuals, students, artists, and activists) toward a revolutionary objective in concert with a black nationalist–oriented, largely urban, working class in a national liberation struggle for the black domestic colony and, specifically, to develop a framework to guide the CRM along a more revolutionary black nationalist trajectory, one not beholden to either integrationism or what Cruse viewed as a myopic and insufficiently theorized U.S. Marxism promoted by the CPUSA, the Trotskyist Socialist Workers' Party (SWP), and a variety of "Old Left" formations. In contrast, Haywood's objective was to tie his favored sector of the ghetto bourgeoisie to a Marxist revolution concentrated in the agricultural South

> based upon the most disprivileged sections of the Black population, the vast majority; the workers and the depressed and land hungry agricultural population in the South, the small bourgeoisie and semi proletarian elements of the urban ghettoes: a trend reflecting the basic interests of those masses, their life needs, aspirations, their fighting determination to achieve freedom and human dignity. (p. 143)

In fact, Haywood was prescient in his view that

> [a]lready the nucleus of its potential leading cadre is forming among Black industrial workers in the trade unions, the radical

section of the petty-bourgeoisie intelligentsia, the youth on the campuses and in the urban ghettoes, and among the left forces in the existing bourgeoisie led organizations and the socialist-oriented left. (ibid.)

Less than a year after this statement, the Dodge Revolutionary Union Movement (DRUM) would emerge in Detroit, consisting largely of the groups that Haywood had identified and heralding a short-lived but very influential movement among black industrial workers in the United States, which we'll examine more fully in chapter 7. But no less prescient was Cruse's thesis which not only captured the changing orientation toward revolutionary activism among blacks in general, but began to motivate those activists within the CRM and the emergent BPM toward a program of action reflecting those factors and processes he highlighted. As a result, it may be said that Cruse's thesis, more than that of any single author other than Malcolm, provided the theoretical impetus for the BPM.

Although he appropriated important aspects of Haywood's Black Belt thesis, Cruse focused less on the rural South and organization among sharecroppers and more on the urban North, and anticipated the rising BPM in the North and West. In fact, Cruse's framework became the theoretical touchstone for groups such as RAM, which organized throughout the United States taking his thesis as their point of departure. Part of the challenge of these black nationalist initiatives was reflected in Cruse's emphasis that "the peculiar position of Negro nationalists in the United States require[d] them to set themselves against the dominance of whites and still manage to live in the same country" (p. 95). In this way, Cruse's assessment evoked Cyril Briggs's, Haywood's, and Du Bois's assertions of the duality of blacks as both Negro and American—a nation within a nation—while it challenged black nationalists to devise social theory and practice that would facilitate their national liberation from a form of domestic colonialism that had no analogy with respect to the historic combination of its form of domination (racial), the demography of domination (imposed by a racial majority on a racial minority), the extent of domination (across the major political, economic, and social institutions of the country), and the setting of the domination (in the most industrialized, economically advanced, and militarily powerful country in the world, in which the racial minority was in diaspora). This peculiar position of African Americans called for a peculiar approach to revolutionary struggle, which Cruse addressed in a subsequent essay of 1963, "Rebellion or Revolution," in which he put forth the first explicit thesis of black cultural revolution in the United States.

Cruse's Thesis on Cultural Revolution

The context for Cruse's thesis of black cultural revolution was his view that what he observed in the 1960s was a continuation of the "crisis" that first became evident in the 1920s and was ushered in by, inter alia, the transformation of the United States into a mass media society. Building on C. Wright Mills's conception of the "power elite," Cruse asserted that mass media in the United States was dominated by an increasingly unified and coordinated elite, which controlled it and reduced the public to media markets and U.S. citizens to individuated consumers of mass media, increasingly vulnerable to its manipulation. The development of the United States as a mass society was traceable to the advent of the mass communications media of the post–World War 1 era. For Cruse, it was not surprising that a black cultural renaissance—i.e., the Harlem Renaissance—occurred during this time. It was the development of these mass media that provided the challenges and opportunities for the black intelligentsia to lead a black cultural revolution, which they failed to comprehend, with tragic consequences, which, according to Cruse, reverberated in the CRM and BPM. This development also contributed to the uniqueness of U.S. society, which was the society which had the most extensive mass media, further undermining the relevance of Marxism to U.S. social processes.

Although critical of applications of mechanistic Marxist arguments to the black liberation struggle in the United States, at times Cruse couched his conception of black cultural revolution in a Marxist analogy:

> During the 1920's, the development in America of mass cultural communications media—radio, films, recording industry, and ultimately, television—drastically altered the classic character of capitalism as described by Karl Marx. This new feature very obviously presented new problems (as well as opportunities) for all the anti-capitalistic radicals; problems which they apparently have never appreciated. The capitalist class, according to the Marxists, have the political and economic power through class ownership of all the industrial and technological means of production, to exploit the working class and control opinions through the press. If that be so, then consider the added range and persuasiveness, the augmented class power, the enhanced political control and prerogatives of decision making that result from the new mass communications industry. What happens to the scope of popular democracy when this new technological-electronic apparatus

spreads throughout the land, bombarding the collective mind with controlled images? (1967, p. 64)

It was "historically inevitable," in his view, "that the appearance of the mass communications media would coincide with the era of the American cultural renaissance" (ibid.). He asserted that "if the growth of capitalism creates its opposite—the working class (the Marxian source of class-struggle revolution)—then it is possible to say that the growth of the mass communications media coincided with the appearance of an opposing class-force of radical creative intellectuals" (ibid.).[2] Cruse notes that "the radical intellectuals of the 1920s did not complete—or better, follow through on—the revolution they instinctively started out to make: an American cultural revolution for which all the necessary conditions either existed or were coming into existence" (ibid.). Instead of building on African American political, economic, and social trajectories, black intellectuals "imported Russian politics" and Bolshevism to orient their struggle in ways that ultimately confounded both their programs and their relevance. For Cruse,

> The Negro intellectuals of the Harlem Renaissance could not see the implications of cultural revolution as a *political demand* growing out of the advent of mass communication media. Having no cultural philosophy of their own, they remained under the tutelage of irrelevant white radical ideas. Thus they failed to grasp the radical potential of their own movement. (1967, p. 65)

Similarly, "the Negro" of the BPM was "the victim of the incompetence of radical social theory and the forty year default of the Negro intelligentsia," who could neither comprehend the salience of cultural revolution to black liberation, nor devise meaningful strategies for its execution (ibid.).

While Cruse levied a blistering challenge to black intellectuals and activists, his most scathing critique was of white radicals—including Marxists of the Old Left and the New Left—and black Marxists, as well, and of Marxism as a social theory to inform radical change in the United States, especially with its failure to consider the impact of culture on black liberation. At the heart of this dispute was Cruse's (1967, p. 474) observation that nineteenth-century capitalism was bereft of a key element of its development in the twentieth century: "mass cultural communications," which he viewed as "a new and unprecedented capitalistic refinement of unheard of social ramifications." He was emphatic that

Marx never had to deal with this monster of capitalist accumulation. Mass cultural communications is a basic industry, as basic as oil, steel, and transportation, in its own way. Developing along with it, supporting it, and subservient to it, is an organized network of functions that are creative, administrative, propagandistic, educational, recreational, political, artistic, ecnomic and cultural. Taken as a whole this enterprise involves what Mills called the *cultural apparatus*. Only the blind cannot see that whoever controls the cultural apparatus—whatever class, power group, faction, or political combine—also controls the destiny of the United States and everything in it. (1967, p. 374)

He admonished even those among the "Black Powerites" who would subsequently—and, in this respect, following Cruse—stress the cultural front to focus on the increasingly urban African American culture and "to cease romanticizing Africa and pre-feudal tribalism" (ibid., p. 557), castigating the reverse civilizationists among them whose "readiness . . . to lean heavily on the African past and the African image" he viewed as "nothing but a convenient cover-up for an inability to come to terms with the complex demands of the American reality" (ibid., p. 554).

In "Rebellion or Revolution," Cruse (1968, p. 101) argued that "the Negro movement at this moment is not a revolutionary movement because it has no present means or program to alter the structural forms of American institutions." Thus, it was "pure political romanticism" to refer to the CRM as a "revolution" instead of what it was: a "rebellion" against the racial status quo in the United States. He argued that "to transform the Negro rebellion into a movement with revolutionary approaches, ideas, and appeals is an immense intellectual and organizational problem" (1968, p. 107). Revolution in the United States would not follow that which was proposed by Marx through the leadership of the white proletariat, as Cruse made clear in "Revolutionary Nationalism and the Afro-American," but from the unique historical trajectory of the United States and especially the role of black Americans in it, specifically the experience of blacks in a context of domestic colonialism.

Cruse recognized that black domestic colonialism was not only political and economic, but cultural. While the CRM was challenging the sociopolitical framework of black oppression, namely Jim Crow, it had little direct economic thrust and largely ignored cultural aspects of black oppression. For Cruse, the progression of the CRM from rebellion to revolution required an economic program beyond integration and a cultural thrust that linked the economic program to the political one. Like Du Bois and Locke, Cruse recognized the relationship among political, economic, and cultural democracy, and he wedded them to a strategy to revolutionize the CRM through a program of cultural revolution. He observed that

> when other semi-colonials of the colored world rebel against the political and economic subjugation of Western capitalism, it is for the aim of having the freedom to build up their own native industrial bases for themselves. Our American Negro rebellion derives from the fact that we exist side by side with the greatest industrial complex the world has ever seen, which we are not allowed to use democratically for ourselves. Hence, while the Negro rebellion emerges out of the same semi-colonial social conditions of others, it must have different objectives in order to be considered revolutionary. In other words, we must locate the weakest sector of the American capitalist "free enterprise" front and strike there. (1968, p. 110)

Cruse argued that the "weak front in the free-enterprise armor" was "the cultural front":

> Or better, it is that part of the American economic system that has to do with the ownership and administration of cultural communication in America, i.e., film, theater, radio and television, music, performing and publishing, popular entertainment booking, management, etc. In short, it is that part of the system devoted to the economics and aesthetic ideology involved in the cultural arts of America. (ibid., pp. 110–111)

What is critical about this sector is not only that it is a core area from which new ideas, practices, and conceptions of society are projected and distributed, but it is a site where culture and economics mesh in such a way that a focus on the former has the potential to transform the latter. This provides strategic leverage for blacks whose presence as a cultural force is potentially powerful but whose economic capacity is severely atrophied. The cultural revolution Cruse envisioned was

> concerned not only with the aesthetics of the form and content of artistic creation in America but also with transforming the economic, institutional, business and administrative organizational apparatus that buys and sells, limits or permits, hires and disposes of, distributes or retains, determines or negates, and profits from

the creation and distribution of cultural production in America. (ibid., p. 117)

Cruse is emphatic that "without such a revolution the Negro movement has no point of departure from which to compel the necessary social impact to effect structural changes within the American social system" (ibid.). Moreover,

> [s]ince the alliance of white capital and labor obviates any challenge to the economic status quo where the production of basic commodities takes place, the Negro movement must challenge free enterprise at its weakest link in the production chain, where no tangible commodities are produced. This becomes the "economic" aspect of the Negro movement. However, it is the cultural aspect of this problem that is most important in terms of form and content in new revolutionary ideas. (1968, pp. 112–113)

Cruse was implicitly following Locke's model in focusing on cultural democracy in such a way as to facilitate both economic and political democracy with the aim of realizing racial democracy. Not sanguine about the potential of black labor to effectuate this change—and even less toward the white Herrenvolk proletariat, he sought a cultural factor whose transformation would have immediate economic repercussions because the two were already fused. He borrowed from C. Wright Mills in describing this factor: the cultural apparatus.

In light of the forgoing, Cruse argued that black liberation required, inter alia, "that both the American national psychology and the organization of American cultural institutions be altered to fit the facts of what America really is. Culturally speaking, America is a European-African-Indian racial amalgam—an imperfect and incompletely realized amalgam," but, "[t]he American national psychology prefers to be regarded as an all-white nation, and the American cultural arts are, therefore, cultivated to preserve and reflect this all-white ideal," while "[a]ny other artistic expression is regarded as an exotic curiosity" (1968, p. 113). For Cruse, "the American racial problem is a problem of many aspects, but it is essentially a cultural problem of a type that is new in modern history" (ibid.). Crucially, he maintained that "[u]ntil this is intellectually admitted and sociologically practiced, chaotic and retrograde racial practices and conflicts will continue in American society" (ibid.). But, he notes that the centrality of culture in the problem of American race relations "has been overlooked, dismissed, and neglected" by most black intellectuals, who have been "beguiled to think of culture solely in terms of the white Anglo-Saxon ideal, which is the cultural image that

America attempts to project to the world" (ibid.). For Cruse, this myopia with respect to the centrality of culture in "the Negro question in America" extends to "the so-called theoreticians and practitioners of sociology and political and social theory" (ibid.). He was emphatic that "[i]f the Negro rebellion is limited by a lack of original social, political and economic ideas to 'fit the world into a theoretic frame,' then it is only in the cultural areas of American life that such new ideas can have any social meaning" (ibid., p. 111); therefore, "the only observable way in which the Negro rebellion can become revolutionary in terms of American conditions is for the Negro movement to project the concept of Cultural Revolution in America" (ibid.). According to Cruse, cultural revolution focuses on "revolutionizing the administration, the organization, the functioning, and the social purpose of the entire American apparatus of cultural communication and placing it under public ownership" (ibid., p. 112). Cruse argued that the concept of cultural revolution would afford "the intellectual means, the conceptual framework, the theoretical link that ties together all the disparate, conflicting and contending trends within the Negro movement" and "transform the movement from a mere rebellion into a revolutionary movement" (ibid., p. 112).

For Cruse, the democratic transformations of the political and economic systems "must be preceded by" and were dependent on the democratic transformation of the cultural systems, and the key instrument of the latter was "a thorough democratization (change of ownership) of the mass media and communications systems." He insisted that "[t]he cultural results will mark the first stages towards a complete democratization of American culture in terms of groups. As the most culturally deprived and retarded ethnic group, the Negro must be educated to raise the level of his mass politics to the point of demanding cultural revolution." Cruse admitted, however, that there was "much more analysis and research involved in this question" (1968, p. 248). In fact, in his 1957 "An Afro-American's Cultural Views," Cruse had argued that "Afro-Americans have sunk to a dismal low point in creative productivity, rapport, and inspiration in every creative field but jazz music" (p. 52), but by 1968's "Rebellion or Revolution" he expressed a more positive view of the state of black culture—though not of black intellectuals—to such an extent that, for him, black culture could serve as a fulcrum of black revolutionary change in the United States.

Cruse noted that

> if we examine the cultural side of the race question in America very closely, we will find that, historically and culturally speaking, the white American Anglo-Saxon cultural ideal of artistic and aesthetic practices is false, predicated as it is on the myth of

Western superiority in cultural tradition, and conceals the true facts of native American cultural development. (1968, pp. 113–114)

But this "white American Anglo-Saxon ideal" is primarily European and not American. Expanding on Du Bois' and Locke's theses on Aframerican culture, Cruse contends that what is American, in fact, are those prominent aspects of black culture. Cruse is unequivocal on this point, which deserves to be quoted at length:

> The historical truth is that it was the Afro-American cultural ingredient in music, dance and theatrical forms (the three forms of art in which America has innovated) that has been the basis for whatever culturally new and unique that has come out of America. Take away the Afro-American tradition of folk-songs, plantation minstrel, spirituals, blues, ragtime, jazz styles, dance forms, and the first Negro theatrical pioneers in musical comedy of the 1890's down to Sissle and Blake of the 1920's, and there would be no jazz industry involving publishing, entertainment, recording; there would have been no Gershwins, Rodgers and Hammersteins, Cole Porters or Carmichaels or popular song tradition—which is based on the Negro blues idiom; there would have been no American musical comedy form—which is America's only original contribution to theater; there would have been no foxtrot—which has formed the basis for American ballroom dancing. . . . In other words, the Afro-American ingredients formed the bases of all "popular culture." . . . Moreover, since all of these popular art forms comprise those cultural commodities involved in multimillion dollar industries (which exclude or exploit Negroes as much as possible), there is an organic connection in American capitalism between race, culture, and economics. (1968, pp. 114–115)

He adds that there is an authentic American cultural expression, jazz, but since its origins are also in the black community, white America does not promote it as a classical art form because

> this would also mean that the Afro-American ethnic minority which originally created the music would have to be culturally glorified and elevated socially, economically and politically. It would mean that the black composer would have to be accepted on this social, cultural, economic, and political level. But this the white American cultural ego would never permit. (ibid., p. 116)

According to Cruse, since the cultural standards and institutions are embedded in the white racist mythology of the United States, then the transformation of U.S. society would have to address these aesthetic and economic dimensions of black oppression. For Cruse (1967, p. 188), the path to "ethnic democratization" in U.S. society was "through its culture," that is, its "cultural apparatus, which comprises the eyes, the ears and the 'mind' of capitalism" in its twentieth-century manifestation. "Thus to democratize the cultural apparatus is to deal fundamentally with the unsolved American question of nationality—Which group speaks for America and for the glorification of which ethnic image?" He was convinced that "[e]ither all group images speak for themselves and for the nation, or American nationality will never be determined" (ibid.). This is because "[i]n America, the materio-economic conditions relate to a societal, multi-group existence in a way never before known in world history" (ibid., pp. 188–189). In this way the condition of the American Negro was sui generis; and it called for a unique form of theorizing for social revolution in such a context. As a point of departure, "Negro intellectuals" had to challenge the "cultural imperialism practiced in all of its manifold ramifications on the Negro within American culture" because "this kind of revolution would have to be predicated on the recognition that the cultural and artistic originality of the American nation is founded, historically, on the ingredients of a black aesthetic and artistic base" (ibid., p. 189). Therefore, targeting the cultural apparatus was essential to the revolutionary change that black Americans sought. Moreover, Cruse contends that "it is precisely the economic spheres of cultural communications in America that must be revolutionized for more humanistic social use before such changes take place in commodity production, political organization or racial democratization" (ibid., p. 117). Such a "peculiar" approach is necessitated for Cruse because capitalism cultivated a new class alliance between white capital and white labor; therefore, the "old Marxian formula of the revolutionary class struggle between capital and labor is passé and obsolescent." Du Bois (1915) suggested as much in "The African Roots of War" nearly a half-century earlier. For Cruse (1968, p. 117), it follows that "any theory of social revolution must be modernized with a new set of ideas, coming not from the whites . . . but from the colored races."

Cruse fleshed out the relationship between culture and politics, as well as between culture and economics, the latter evident in the economic aspects of cultural exploitation. He notes that

> in America the entire industry of popular music writing, publishing, and selling was established by white appropriation of the whole body of Afro-American folk music—the only original

music in America with a broad human appeal. This music has been cheapened, debased and commercialized for popular appeal.

He adds that

> the American music industry has been exploiting, cheating, stealing from, browbeating, excluding, plagiarizing Negro singers, jazz musicians, composers, etc., for decades and getting away with it. The cultural exploitation established by white America in the early years of the twentieth century by the white appropriation of Afro-American folk-music was the first great manifestation of the racist development in the economics of American culture. This racist cultural doctrine, once established in music, spread through the entire field of cultural expression in America. (1968, p. 119)

This led Cruse to conclude that "the Negro revolution can be economic, social, political, administrative, or racial in form, but it must be cultural in content." He is emphatic that

> if it is not cultural in content it is not revolutionary, but a mere rebellion without ideas "to fit the world in a theoretic frame." It is only the cultural needs of the Negro that coincide with or are complementary to the main humanistic need that goes unfulfilled in America despite this country's economic and administrative achievements—the need for a thriving, creative, humanistically progressive national culture. (ibid., p. 121)

Many critics of Cruse's thesis—especially Marxist and neo-Marxist critics—failed to appreciate, or were out of touch with, the prospects of independent African American cultural development or the increasing salience of black culture in black liberation strategies at home. American Marxists, in particular, having eschewed the use of free enterprise processes in black liberation, misunderstood the salience of Cruse's thesis aimed at providing blacks the economic wherewithal to finance their independent CRM initiatives and provide a supportive context for their theorizing on liberation as well as their practical attempts to achieve it.[3] With respect to the latter, following Du Bois, Cruse saw it necessary to complete the bourgeois democratic revolution that had been aborted by the "counter-revolution of property" that ended Reconstruction. He thought that this should not be surprising to American Marxists, drawing from Lenin's admonitions after the 1905 Russian Revolt in "Two Tactics of Social Democracy in the Democratic Revolution" that in colonial and semicolonial countries "the working class suffers not so much from capitalism as from the lack of capitalist development." Cruse agreed that the Negro working class suffering under domestic colonialism in the United States "is therefore interested in the widest, freest and the speediest development of capitalism" (p. 236). Thus, "[t]he removal of all the remnants of the old order which are hampering the wide, free, and speedy development of capitalism is of *absolute advantage* to the working class" (ibid.). Further quoting from Lenin, he notes:

> The bourgeois revolution is precisely such a revolution. . . . Therefore, the *bourgeois* revolution is in the *highest degree* advantageous to the proletariat. . . . The more complete, determined and consistent the bourgeois revolution is, the more secure will the proletarian struggle against the bourgeoisie and for socialism become. Such a conclusion may appear new, or strange, or even paradoxical only to those who are ignorant of the rudiments of scientific socialism. (ibid.)

This goes to the heart of the black freedom struggle in the United States and especially the call for black power, because "[w]hen we speak of Negro social disability under capitalism . . . we refer to the fact that he does not own anything—*even what is ownable in his own community*" (ibid., p. 238). Cruse adds,

> Thus to fight for black liberation *is to fight for the right to own*. The Negro is politically compromised today because he owns nothing. He can exert little political power because he owns nothing. He has little voice in the affairs of state because he owns nothing. The fundamental reason why the Negro bourgeois-democratic revolution has been aborted is because American capitalism has prevented the development of a black class of capitalist owners of institutions and economic tools. (ibid., pp. 238–239)

For example,

> Negro radicals today are severely hampered in their tasks of educating the black masses on political issues because Negroes do not own any of the necessary means of propaganda and communications. The Negro owns no printing presses, he has no stake in the networks of the means of communication. Inside his own communities he does not own the houses he lives in, the

property he lives on, nor the wholesale and retail sources from which he buys his commodities. He does not own the edifices in which he enjoys culture and entertainment, or in which he socializes. In capitalist society, an individual or group that does not own anything is powerless. In capitalist society, a group that has not experienced the many sides of capitalistic development, that has not learned the techniques of business ownership, or the intricacies of profit and loss, or the responsibilities of managing even small or medium enterprise, has not been prepared in the social disciplines required to transcend the functional limitations of the capitalist order. Thus, to paraphrase Lenin, it is not that the Negro suffers so much from capitalism in America, but from *a lack of capitalist development*. (ibid., p. 239)

Thus, Cruse was confronting an important aspect of the lived concreteness of the black experience of economic privation, which black revolutionaries similarly had to contend with while simultaneously challenging the political and social basis of their oppression; and this required both the development of the politico-economic capabilities of black communities through extant structures and institutions of the broader society—i.e., community control or "black power"—as well as, and pursuant to, the development of black politico-economic power to overturn the broader systems of their oppression. The key linking these processes in the domestic colonial context was the cultural system, which blacks could exhibit greater influence on and leverage against their relative political and economic weakness—in terms of the broader society. In Cruse's rendering, the attack on the cultural front entails *both* an aesthetic and material thrust through the development and extension of the cultural apparatus of the black community against the institutions of white culture-economic power within both black America and U.S. society more broadly. Thus, like Du Bois, Cruse cast black intellectuals and the black bourgeoisie in their "historic roles" on the cultural front—but mainly as conduits or purveyors of black mass interests in conjunction with the black proletariat in pursuit of black national development. There was no vanguardism in Cruse's analysis privileging either black intellectuals or the black bourgeoisie, but only a recognition of the atrophy of the former with respect to their responsibility to articulate a theory of black liberation, and the failure of the latter to assume the historic role of national bourgeoisies in capitalist development.

The black bourgeoisie, for Cruse, was not a national bourgeoisie but a "lumpenbourgeoisie," "with no political consciousness whatsoever as being a bourgeoisie" (Cobb, 2002, p. 292). By implication, the relationships between this black bourgeoisie and its proletariat—and peasantry, for that matter—do not reflect the class antagonisms that Marxism suggests because they are not classes in the Marxist sense. With respect to the black lumpenbourgeoisie, given that it's not a class either in itself or for itself—in Marxist terms, then, sectors within it may be brought within an amalgamation with black proletarians, and even lumpenproletarians—toward revolutionary objectives. In this context, the broad black working class, including a prominent peasantry in the South, advocated and pursued black nationalist practices to confront domestic colonialism—often in alignment with sectors of the black petite bourgeoisie (e.g., some intellectuals, religious leaders, college students, leaders of voluntary organizations, and small shop owners and businesspersons),[4] but this path, which was self-evident to black nationalists such as Cruse, was poorly understood or theorized by many Marxist, liberal, and integrationist analysts of the CRM and BPM.

So, while important aspects of Cruse's thesis converged with those of Du Bois, Locke, and Haywood, it transcended them as well, and many analysts have failed to appreciate its profundity. First, Cruse's call for democratizing the cultural apparatus should be seen in the context of his attempt to expand the CRM to include economic and cultural initiatives aimed at achieving black power. Thus, one might envision an initiative of CRM organizations such as the NAACP Legal Defense Fund and/or the predominantly black National Lawyers' Guild to support class action lawsuits undertaken by black artists—former jazz composers, blues singers, soul artists, rock and roll performers, songwriters, background vocalists, session musicians—cheated out of their cultural production by white managers, club owners, record company executives, publishing companies, and radio station managers organized with the aim of recouping the rights, royalties, residuals, earnings, and profits stolen from them through usurious contracts and unfair labor practices across decades. This initiative would be accompanied by targeted and coordinated protests of these institutions, industries and their events by movement activists, organizations and their allies. The use of a portion of the monetary awards to underwrite the budget of civil rights organizations from black funders, who would be partially beholden to them—since the latter would have provided the legal assistance to secure the funds—would have compensated for the defunding of major CRM organizations, such as SNCC and CORE, which resulted in large part from their clearing their membership rolls of whites as they were transitioning from civil rights to black power. Thus, a strategy grounded in Cruse's thesis—which he proffered prior to the onset of the BPM in 1965 and the proclamation of "black power" by SNCC in 1966—was timely.

Second, pursuit of Cruse's program would have imparted to the black community an independent institutional capacity to project a black aesthetic, such as espoused by BAM. One result was that such institutions might have emerged much earlier during the CRM, encouraging its cultural phase that helped usher in the more revolutionary BPM, as well as supporting incipient BPM organizations and institutions. In so doing, it would also raise the contradictions between those white liberals and radicals who previously positioned themselves as allies, and those more determined to support black liberation on its own terms. These contradictions would be unavoidable given the reality that black contribution to American popular culture was unassailable and the role of blacks in creating this cultural product self-evident, making challenges to white supremacism on this front both popular and profound, as well as immensely remunerative.

These "cultural compulsives" as Cruse framed them (borrowing from V. F. Calverton) were even more imperative given the demands of black power. Cruse (1968, p. 246) was emphatic that "without a cultural philosophy (or methodology) suitable for radical politics within the interracial context of American realities," then "[i]t is impossible to organize the Negro masses around the political or economic reforms of black power." Therefore, he adds,

> In the same way that the Nation of Islam used religion to bind Negroes together into a social and economic movement (without politics), the secular black radical movement must use the cultural ingredient in black reality to bind Negroes into a mass movement *with economics and politics*. This has to be done through a cultural program that makes demands for cultural equality on American society. Without cultural equality there can be no economic and political equality. (1968, p. 247)

Given that the Anglo-Saxon Protestant group in its "aesthetics, content, and forms of cultural expression, and its ideology dominates the philosophy of its cultural institutions" and through this "sets the cultural standards for all other groups"—even while its "levels of creative originality sinks lower and lower"—then, "the deepening racial crisis in America exerts a profound stress on established value-systems involved in group *cultural identity*" (ibid.). In light of this, Cruse observed that "[f]rom within the black movement arises a renewed thrust toward cultural identity as expressed through the art forms." Thus, "For the Negro, social revolution is impossible without a cultural revolution." Cruse asserts that "a cultural revolution in America cannot come as an after-product of a political and economic revolution," which Cruse viewed as "a foreign historical scheme of social progress" (ibid.); instead, in the United States, cultural revolution was required to "open . . . up the path to radical social change by removing certain roadblocks within the system which are barriers against political and economic transformations," and "[t]his require[d] a special analysis of the political and economic role of mass media and communication systems within the American industrial complex" (ibid., pp. 247–248).

The failure to appreciate the salience of Cruse's thesis was especially evident in the controversy surrounding the draft platform of the Freedom Now Party (FNP). It was not fully fleshed out and its import was largely lost on some of the leadership of the FNP. The platform included a section devoted to cultural revolution, written by Cruse, which suggested the need to inculcate a cultural program into the civil rights struggle to provide a nexus between integrationist and nationalist tendencies in the CRM. It sought to bring "cultural affairs into politics for the first time" and to include "the Negro creative artists and performer—the singer, dancer, writer, dramatist, poet, musician (jazz and classical), actor, composer" as full participants in the liberation struggle (pp. 4–5). It argued for the nationalization (i.e., "placing under public administration") of "all major systems of cultural and mass communication in America." It supported boycotts of cultural outlets such as theaters; and the promotion of Negro creative arts through "theater groups, writing groups, dance groups, acting groups, Negro and African historical and cultural groups, etc." (ibid., p. 5). Even as a draft platform it anticipated BAM, which would emerge a year later, and Malcolm X's and RAM's advocacy of cultural revolution in 1964, the creation of Baraka's Black Arts Repertory Theater and School (BARTS) in Harlem (which is often viewed as ushering in BAM) in 1965; and the founding of Us in Los Angeles in 1965, which was the group most closely associated with a program of cultural revolution, though one quite different from that which Cruse proposed.

Third, and on a theoretical level, Cruse's thesis dovetailed with Du Bois's and Locke's insofar as it focused on how cultural democracy—democratizing the cultural apparatus of U.S. society—by making demands on the state for cultural resources would be politicized and generate economic resources from cultural production, distribution, and consumption as well. These efforts would be consonant with the specific trajectory of development of blacks in different urban areas emerging from their particular migratory traditions and embedded in the political economies of their distinctive urban contexts (Cruse, 1971abc). Just as importantly, Cruse promoted a vision of black America—and black Americans—as the central revolutionary change agent in U.S. society, rejecting Marxists' reliance on a Herrenvolk proletariat to transcend its white supremacism and assume its "rightful place" and its "historic mission" as the vanguard of revolutionary change in the United States.

Ironically, given Cruse's trenchant critique of Marxism, aspects of his argument that black liberation necessitated a cultural revolution in the United States dovetailed with James Boggs's contemporaneous neoMarxist thesis of dialectical humanism. In the next section, we explore some of the contributions of Boggs's thesis to our understanding of black cultural revolution.

Boggs's Dialectical Humanism and Black Cultural Revolution in the CRM

James and Grace Lee Boggs made important contributions to black revolutionary theory dating back to the 1940s. James was an African American auto worker and Grace was a Chinese American philosophy PhD who were linked initially through their association with C. L. R. James to Trotskyism, but abandoned their alliance with him over many of the issues Cruse had been struggling with in his interaction with the CPUSA, namely, the implications of third world revolutions, and the black revolt in the United States in particular, for the Marxist view of the vanguard role of white workers. Like Cruse, the Boggses agreed that the white Western proletariat had abrogated its assumed alliance with revolutionary forces in the periphery, just as the white proletariat opposed black workers—and much of the CRM—in the United States. Like Cruse and Haywood, the Boggses viewed the CRM and the incipient BPM as analogous to revolts in the third world and acknowledged that these movements generated a similar recalcitrance if not outright hostility on the part of both white American workers as well as capitalists. They were concerned, however, that to the extent that the black freedom movement was the locus of political struggle in the United States, then its revolutionary potential was hamstrung by the lack of proletarian consciousness among movement leaders, as well as white workers. That is, as black workers—along with students, and even members of the black petite bourgeoisie—manned the ramparts of the black freedom movement, white workers in the United States had abrogated their class interests in favor of their racist interests and aligned with their management through their conciliatory labor unions, as well as their white bourgeoisie, to maintain the systems of white supremacism.

At the core of James Boggs's (1963) thesis was that advanced industrial capitalism was increasingly making traditional workers in heavy industry—and its ancillary sectors—obsolete. This was occurring in a broader context in which capitalists were utilizing automation and cybernation, which allowed them to exact enormous profits through increased efficiency while depleting the ranks of workers and making them "unemployable"—and many of these were black. Boggs saw this phase of capitalist development as a "cybercultural revolution," which by eliminating workers was removing the factory floor as a site for developing proletarian consciousness—a key to the revolutionary process that Marxists theorized. This required a rethinking of Marxism for

Boggs; thus, in his 1963 essay, "The Meaning of the Black Revolt in the USA," published in *Revolution* and circulated widely among young activists, Boggs introduced his dialectical humanism thesis.

Boggs, like Cruse, sought a theory and program of social change to synthesize the strains in the CRM and incipient BPM and send them on a more revolutionary trajectory. Boggs agreed that there was little hope of a multiracial proletarian revolution given the persistent and virulent racism of white workers, and he also focused on structural factors that precluded a Marxist revolution in the United States. They both argued that the unique context of the United States necessitated a novel theory of social change, and Boggs proposed his dialectical humanism as such a framework. Importantly for our analysis, Boggs's thesis converged with aspects of Cruse's cultural revolution thesis that they were proposing around the same time and, briefly, in the same organization, the FNP.

Boggs published his thesis in a slim volume, *The American Revolution* (1963), which heavily influenced RAM. He argued that automation and cybernation had so transformed the U.S. economy and altered the social relations that devolved from them that the basis of working-class solidarity had been undermined. This development outpaced any mechanical application of Marxism to the condition of U.S. workers, the U.S. bourgeoisie, and especially black Americans, placing the developing black revolt—and our understanding of social revolution in the United States—within a unique history that required a unique revolutionary strategy. Given that, at minimum, the vanguard role in socialist revolution in the United States had passed to black Americans engaged in the "Negro revolt," then, their praxis should provide guideposts for the nascent theory—a position that converged with Cruse's, but diverged slightly from Haywood's. It is important to remember that Haywood viewed race as a misleading category employed to obscure the national oppression of blacks—both black workers and the black bourgeoisie—and draw attention away from its other class elements, while Boggs adopted the more prominent Marxist view at the time of blacks as "workers," albeit objecting that "American Marxists have always thought of the working class as white and have themselves discriminated against Negroes by hesitating to recognize them as workers" (1963, p. 85). Moreover, even as he acknowledged this more "traditional" view, Boggs extracted from it a novel theoretical exposition.

In his view, "American Marxists have tended to fall into the trap of thinking of the Negroes as Negroes, i.e. in race terms, when in fact the Negroes have been and are today the most oppressed and submerged sections of the workers, on whom has fallen most sharply the burden of unemployment due to automation" (ibid., p. 85). Up to this point, Boggs's contention was not inconsistent with that of mainstream U.S. Marxists of the time and their main point that "[t]he Negroes have more economic grievances than any other section of American society" (ibid.). From there, Boggs drew the important inference:

> But in a country with the material abundance of the United States, economic grievances alone could not impart to their struggles all their revolutionary impact. The strength of the Negro cause and its power to shake up the social structure of the nation comes from the fact that in the Negro struggle all the questions of human rights and human relationships are posed. (1963, p. 85)

For Boggs, "It is the Negroes who represent the revolutionary struggle for a classless society," one much different from "the classless society of American folklore," which entails individuals and groups advancing socially by exploiting "newcomers at the bottom"—a process from which Negroes had been excluded (ibid., pp. 85–86). According to Boggs,

> It is this exclusion which has given the Negro struggle for a classless society its distinctive revolutionary character. For when the Negroes struggle for a classless society, they struggle that all men may be equal, in production, in consumption, in the community, in the courts, in the schools, in the universities, in transportation, in social activity, in government, and indeed in every sphere of American life. (ibid., p. 86)

Boggs is emphatic that "the crisis in the United States today and the corresponding momentum of the Negro struggle are such that it is obvious that Negroes are not going to consult whites, workers or not workers, before taking action" (ibid.), and he concludes that "[t]he chief need for all Americans is to recognize these facts and to be ready to take bold action along with Negroes, recognizing that the Negroes are the growing revolutionary force in the country, and that just as capitalist production has created new methods of production and new layers of workers, it has also produced *new Negroes*" (ibid.; emphasis added).

Boggs saw the CRM and the incipient BPM as struggling to develop a clear strategy and a theory to guide them. Drawing on a range of methods from "non-violent resistance, violent resistance, moral suasion, economic boycotts, sit-ins, stand-ins, etc." (1963, p. 87), activists were realizing that the "major lesson that these struggles had taught" them "was that they lacked 'political power'" (ibid.). He noted that "[u]p to now it has been unnatural for the Negroes to think in terms of black political power," but this has changed "and nobody knows this better than the whites" (ibid.). Thus, in 1963, well before the more famous articulation of "black power" by Stokely Carmichael on a road in Greenwood, Mississippi, in 1966 and the publication of *Black Power* a year later, James Boggs made a theoretical argument on the importance of "black political power" in the United States. He asserted that "[t]he struggle for black political power is a revolutionary struggle because, unlike the struggle for white power, it is the climax of a ceaseless struggle on the part of Negroes for human rights" (ibid.).

This analysis was only the point of departure for Boggs's broader theoretical argument on revolutionary change in the United States, which for him needed to appreciate the unique context of the U.S. political economy and the military-industrial complex that reinforced it and through which it projected its power abroad. A key transformation in the U.S. political economy, which Boggs focused on, was the increasing obsolescence of much labor-intensive work—especially in heavy industry (e.g., automotive, steel, mining). Boggs viewed automation as "the greatest revolution that has taken place in human society since men stopped hunting and fishing and started to grow their own food" (1963, p. 38). He noted that automation was "capable of displacing as many productive workers from the work force as have been brought into the work force since the invention of the automobile at the beginning of this century" (ibid.). Boggs emphasized that although there is nothing new about the capacity of automation to replace workers, "[w]hat *is* new is that now, unlike most earlier periods, the displaced men have nowhere to go" (ibid., p. 36). That is, unlike "farmers displaced by mechanization of the farms in the [19]20's," who "could go to the cities and man the assembly lines," the automation generating what would become known as the postindustrial era was occurring "when industry has already reached the point that it can supply consumer demand" (ibid.). Boggs went so far as to argue that "[w]ithin a few years, man as a productive force will be as obsolete as the mule" (ibid., p. 47).Boggs was acknowledging in 1963 what analysts such as Bluestone (1984) would later refer to as "deindustrialization," which was part of the transformation of the U.S. political economy from an industrial to a service economy and the subsequent displacement of workers, as had occurred earlier in the transformation of the U.S. economy from a largely agricultural to a more industrial society. Labor surpluses resulted from the "creative destruction" of capitalism as workers in jobs and sectors outmoded by innovations in technology, transportation, and communication, especially, were displaced by the advances and investments—and the efficiencies and dislocations related to them—that characterized the new era. For Boggs, the issue of "what to do with the surplus people who are the expendables of automation" was increasingly critical, because "[t]hese millions have never been and never can be absorbed into this society at all" (1963, p. 36) and New Deal programs to provide employment for them through labor-intensive projects were no longer practicable (ibid., p. 50). With only a few remaining workers from the earlier era of industrial production "whom capitalism can continue to employ in production at a pace killing enough to be profitable," the rest were tantamount to "refugees or displaced persons" for whom "there is no way for capitalism to employ them profitably" (ibid., p. 36). Instead, capitalists would be compelled to "feed them rather than be fed by them," which would put an additional strain on the *welfare* state—even as the *warfare* state was expanding (ibid.). He saw growing hordes of unemployable workers "becoming a tremendous drain on the whole working population, and creating a growing antagonism between those who have jobs and those who do not" (ibid.). The resulting "antagonism in the population between those who have to be supported and those who have to support them is one of the inevitable antagonisms of capitalism," which ultimately "will create one of the deepest crises for capitalism in our age" (ibid.).

For Boggs, the crisis would pit "not only the employed against the unemployed but those who propose that the unemployed be allowed to starve to death rather than continue as such a drain on the public against those who cannot stand by and see society degenerate into such barbarism," which is not a crisis in strictly class terms (ibid., p. 37). Seen in this light, according to Boggs,

> automation is that stage of production which carries the contradictions of capitalism to their furthest extreme . . . [b]ecause when you add to those who are daily being displaced from the plant the millions who have never even had a chance to work inside a plant, what you have is no longer just the unemployed and the castaways, but a revolutionary force or army of outsiders and rejects who are totally alienated from this society. (1963, pp. 38, 50)

Blacks were the most prominent of these outsiders, disproportionately among the unemployed, typically the last hired, first fired, constituting a core of the unskilled labor easily displaced by automation, lacking the relative job security of seniority even in the salaried trades soon to lose out from cybernation; in fact, they were a national racial underclass. Boggs viewed these "outsiders" as representing a "new generation" of "workless people," who "owe no allegiance to any system but only to themselves," and "[b]eing workless, they are also stateless. They have grown up like a colonial people who no longer feel any allegiance to the old imperial power and are each day searching for new means to overthrow it" (ibid., p. 52). The "outsiders" would need to be organized—either by themselves or by others—much as Fanon had argued for the lumpenproletariat previously, and the Black Panther Party (BPP) would three years later. Boggs added that "the revolution which is within these people will have to be a revolution of their minds and hearts, directed not toward increasing production but toward the management and distribution of things and toward the control of relations among people, tasks which up to now have been left to chance or in the hands of an elite" (ibid.). This insight provided the point of departure for Boggs's dialectical humanism.

Dialectical humanism was a response to the necessities of the era of the "cybercultural revolution," in which revolutionists could not rely on the further economic immiseration of workers to compel social revolution—as dialectical materialism assumed—because capitalism in the United States had progressed to a level of production and coordination of the economic sphere such that even the poor could have most of their material needs met. The welfare state had expanded and capitalists learned to both facilitate a modicum of economic progress for the broader society while coopting organized labor interests, and through the media promoting an ideologically rooted message of the obtainability of the American Dream in terms of superficial democracy and the accumulation of material goods (e.g., a job, a house, and a car). Even for blacks, the welfare state was a marked advance over previous conditions of privation—and this was before the Great Society programs of President Lyndon B. Johnson. Thus, for Boggs, the necessity of "dialectical humanism reflects the fact that in this era of capitalist development the burning question is how to create the kind of human responsibility in the distribution of material abundance that will allow everyone to enjoy and create the values of humanity" (1970, p. 18). That is, revolution in the United States would have to be political, economic, and—given the centrality of transformative values—cultural.

Grace Boggs reflected in her autobiography that by the early 1960s James Boggs had worked through the contradictions of a strict application of Marxist analyses to the issues of revolution in the United States, and he had concluded that "[i]n order to make an American revolution . . . all Americans, including workers and blacks or the most victimized" would have to "transform themselves," since "[b]eing a victim of oppression in the United States . . . is not enough to make you revolutionary" (1998, pp. 151–152) because "the oppressed internalize the values of the oppressor"; thus, "any group that achieves power, no matter how oppressed, is not going to act differently from their oppressors as long as they have not confronted the values that they have internalized and consciously adopted different values" (ibid., p. 152). It followed that "[i]f those victimized by capitalist exploitation are not necessarily revolutionary . . . then the role of revolutionists is profoundly different from that which radicals have played." That is, the role of revolutionists "cannot just be to rub raw the sores of discontent in order to get oppressed masses to rebel"; instead, "revolutionists have a responsibility to create strategies to transform ourselves as well as the victims of oppression into human beings who are more advanced in the qualities that distinguish human beings; creativity, consciousness, self-consciousness, and a sense of political and social responsibility" (ibid.). In language consonant with conceptions of cultural revolution, Grace Boggs continued that if

> those who need to make a revolution also need to transform themselves into more socially responsible, more self critical human beings, then our role as revolutionists is to involve them in activities that are self-transforming and structure-transforming, exploring and trying to resolve in theory and practice fundamental questions of human life more complex than anything Marx could possibly have dreamed of. (1998, p. 156)

These fundamental questions include:

> "What kind of an economy, what kind of technology would serve both human and economic needs? What kind of transformation do we need in our values, institutions, and behavior to reconnect us with the rhythms and processes of nature? . . . What is the difference between needs and wants? How do we meet people's psychic hungers? What does it mean to care? What is the purpose of education? How do we create community? . . . Why is community a revolutionary idea? How do communities start?" . . . For a revolutionary organization to talk about revolution and call for revolution without grappling with these questions would be the height of irresponsibility. (ibid., p. 156)

These are issues as much of cultural transformation as political or economic transformation, however, the Boggses had difficulty articulating a thesis that projected a clear mechanism for the transformation they envisioned, nor did they seem to appreciate a developmental role for black culture in the revolution they sought. For example, contrary to Grace Lee Boggs's assertion that the role of revolutionists "cannot just be to rub raw the sores of discontent in order to get oppressed masses to rebel," at the end of the 1960s James Boggs's focus was still on "organizing the struggles around the concrete grievances of the masses" (1969, p. 32) and "the constant worsening of the conditions of the masses" (ibid., p. 33). By the mid-1970s, the Boggses replaced their assertion of the need for a *black* vanguard party with a similar assertion of the need for an *American* vanguard party. Only in the 1980s would they abandon the notion that a particular group was inherently predisposed toward revolution (though they did not abandon their faith in the vanguard party, or an impending revolution), but during the BPM they restlessly sought this revolutionary vanguard.[5]

Along with Cruse's thesis, dialectical humanism contributed to the theoretical orientation of the earliest organizations explicitly focused on cultural revolution in the 1960s, particularly RAM. Where Cruse targeted the cultural apparatus of United States society, the Boggses conceived a black revolution oriented more to the organization of the cities, as the factories had been decades earlier in order to seize their productive capacity and utilize their resources to project their broader revolutionary struggle. Further, where Cruse emphasized black cultural revolution, the Boggses tended to dismiss black culture as a meaningful change agent, although they were convinced of the importance of cultural values in political revolution. Without a clear theoretical compass by which to orient their thesis on black revolution, the Boggses argued that revolutionary activity itself would generate the requisite culture that would help transform black society. James Boggs asserted this functionalist approach by no later than 1967 in his "Black Power a Scientific Concept," in which he argued that "[e]very revolution creates a new culture out of the process of revolutionary struggle against the old values and culture which an oppressing society has sought to impose upon the oppressed" (1970, p. 58). He claimed that "no past culture ever created a revolution," and emphasized that "[t]he uniqueness of Black Power stems from the specific historical development of the United States," which "has nothing to do with any special moral virtue in being black" nor any "special cultural virtues of the African heritage" (ibid.).

Boggs's view of "spontaneous cultural generation" was ahistorical and it ignored the need to ground black revolutionary activity in a cultural thrust to ensure a humanistic process toward and following revolutionary victory.[6] By the mid-1960s, he had replaced the "outsiders" with the "street force" as the revolutionary vanguard. Not surprisingly, by the mid-1970s, in his *Manifesto for a Black Revolutionary Party*, Boggs abandoned the view that the street force was "the vanguard," arguing instead that it had "degenerated into a mob of individualists, preying on one another and on other members of the community" (1969, pp. iii–iv)—succumbing, Boggs alleges, to a "slave" or "victim mentality." Nevertheless, Boggs didn't abandon vanguardism, arguing, "Blacks are potentially the most revolutionary social force in the United States" (ibid., p. vii). What is surprising is not that the "street force" remained "lumpen" but that theorists such as Boggs privileged them in their analysis, especially given his proximity to Malcolm and appreciating Malcolm's contention that without cultural transformation and disciplined training, the lumpenproletariat were not even prepared to participate in—much less lead—political struggle for black liberation. Cruse (1967) took a much less sanguine view of the street force as a transformative agent and relied less on Marxist notions of an impending, almost inevitable black revolution to guide his theorizing on the black liberation struggle, but, beholden to a Marxist teleology and a preoccupation with designating a "vanguard" for a revolution that Marxists sought with almost millenarian earnest, Boggs infused disparate elements of the black unemployed, underemployed, and lumpenproletariat with an orientation toward systemic transformation that was as detached from their actual circumstances and the progressive change taking place within black communities as the orthodox Marxism that he had recently chastised for the same.[7]

Beyond the historical or theoretical merits of his position on the "street force," Boggs seemed to ignore the cultural—not simply the political or economic—context in which such a force would emerge and its "revolutionary" objectives would become formulated and pursued. Boggs provided little insight into the process by which this revolutionary culture would develop, either through reasoned supposition or historical allusion. Even as he asserted the importance of *blacks* in this process, he failed to appreciate the relevance of *black culture* to the liberation struggle he envisioned. Instead, he often appealed to stereotypical notions of black culture and viewed cultural theorists and activists as preoccupied with kings and queens of African antiquity with little relevance to an urbanized community in the most powerful country in the world (e.g., his 1967 "Culture and Black Power"), which applied at best to some marginal elements in the black liberation struggle, but certainly not to the major theorists and activists of black cultural revolution. Such a myopic view ignored more mature theses on the relevance of cultural transformation as a change agent in black communities dating back to Du Bois and Locke or as recent as Robeson's arguments that wedded African culture to socialism, or Malcolm X's explicit advocacy of black cultural revolution in 1964, and of course, Cruse's, which he had been aware of since they worked together in the FNP in 1964.[8] This shortcoming with respect to appreciating the salience of black culture left Boggs's thesis largely untethered to the black community for which he was attempting to fashion a *black* revolution. In fact, black urban working-class (i.e., "proletarian") culture provided the only meaningful "countercultural" logic to which a black "street force" could ground itself and project a coherent image of social transformation. The caricature of black culture in Boggs's thesis, in light of his view of the political bankruptcy of many of the established political, economic, and social institutions in black America and the upper and middle classes that they benefited, meant that the only indigenous institutions in the black community from which the street force could cull its revolutionary culture were those of the lumpenproletariat, which is at odds with Boggs's (1970, pp. 180–190) subsequent critique of the Black Panther Party in "The American Revolution: Putting Politics in Command."

It is with respect to this issue of culture that Boggs's thesis would have profited from engagement with Cruse's because Boggs didn't seem to realize that the source of the humanism in his dialectical humanism was largely cultural; and the only meaningful source of it was the transformative black culture that was motivating much of the radical political change unfolding around him in the CRM and BPM.

This should not be viewed as a broader dismissal of black culture on the part of the Boggses since both were friends with many activist black artists and performers throughout the CRM and BPM and for decades after, including Ossie Davis and Ruby Dee, among many others, hosting them in their home on the east side of Detroit. It's all the more surprising that they didn't integrate black culture into their broader analyses. Its difficult to determine whether the public conflict between Boggs and Cruse on the latter's proposed cultural revolution resolution for the FNP platform in 1964 might have been symptomatic of—or simply contributed to—the Boggses distancing themselves from black cultural theses.[9] Ironically, while marginalizing just about any progressive role for black culture, Boggs lauded Chinese culture, which he saw wedded to power even as Mao's disastrous Great Proletarian Cultural Revolution was wreaking havoc in China, and the Han Chinese continued to dominate non-Han Chinese in the "people's" republic (e.g. Uighurs, Tibetans, and Mongols). Boggs continued to praise Mao's Cultural Revolution even as the repression and excesses of Mao's "Red Guards" became apparent in the West. In fact, as late as their *Revolution and Evolution in the Twentieth Century*, which was published in 1974 after Mao's rapprochement with Richard Nixon, James and Grace Lee Boggs lavished praise on Mao's regime while ignoring or rationalizing the brutal excesses of the Cultural Revolution that Mao unleashed on Chinese society from 1966 to his death in 1976. Totally incongruous with the Boggses' conception of this period as an expression of "boldness without parallel in human history" (1974, p. 76), it was a needless bloodletting and disruption of Chinese society intended to rally support to a politically weakened Mao after his disastrous socioeconomic policies of the Great Leap Forward. It promoted a cult of personality around Mao to reestablish his governmental authority against potential opposition. Mao used children and teenagers (i.e., the Red Guards) to prosecute some of the worst crimes and excesses of the Great Proletarian Cultural Revolution. The Cultural Revolution encouraged the same type of revolutionary utopianism, internecine violence, ideological purity, and blind allegiance to cultish leadership that the Boggses excoriated—and appropriately so—when espoused and practiced by black activists in the United States such as the BPP or white activists such as the Weather Underground. Nevertheless, they asserted the usefulness of this tragic episode in Mao's China to inform the BPM, but somehow found little worthwhile in African American culture to project a more germane, humane, and instructive program of action, especially given the stated objective of their dialectical humanism: to create a *more human human being*. In fact, it is hard to imagine a worse contemporary model to draw on with respect to African American political struggle in the era.

While praising China's cultural revolution, Boggs dismissed black culture as a source of revolutionary change, instead offering a counterthesis in his "The City Is the Black Man's Land," which modified Malcolm's emphasis on land as the basis of independence by discarding the RNA's conception of separate black statehood and rejecting Haywood's stress on black rural communities of the black South, which Boggs viewed as arcane given black urbanization in the South, focusing instead on urban blacks in the industrial centers in the North and West. He argued that black activists focusing on the land aspect of Malcolm's thesis should instead attempt to gain control of the major agencies of city government to utilize the resources these institutions command to promote the political, economic, and social development of black communities. Thus, Boggs suggested the importance of the development of parallel institutions to serve black urban communities in the interim as they sought to capture city and county agencies, but, unlike Cruse's thesis, Boggs's relied less on the role of black cultural institutions and instead on a coalition of black workers, students, youths, and political leaders jointly pursuing this strategy. Although he was an auto worker, Boggs did not take a sanguine view, initially, of black radical organization of auto workers in the plants, such as was emerging among those who would create the League of Revolutionary Black Workers (LRBW). Convinced as he was that the days of in-plant organization were gone, given the influence of automation and cybernation, he encouraged workers to organize the cities as the plants had been organized in the 1930s.

Like Boggs—and Du Bois and Locke before him—Cruse (1971b, p. 30) understood the importance of the cities in the BPM and acknowledged this in part toward a critique of theses such as Boggs's "The City Is the Black Man's Land," which, he viewed, "commit one fundamental error . . . common to all Black analysts of Black city problems—*they treat these different Black cities as if they were all alike simply because they are all black.*" The latter point seemed to open Cruse (1967) to criticism given that his expanded thesis on cultural revolution in *Crisis of the Negro Intellectual* privileged Harlem but ignored black cultural development in other cities, which Harlem did not typify, especially those with more powerful industrial working classes. This critique has some merit, but less than at first appears because Cruse focused on Harlem as the black cultural capital much as someone studying the U.S. cultural capital might focus on Hollywood—not as exhaustive but as an exemplar. Further, it ignores Cruse's (1971abc) engagement of this specific issue just four years later in three serialized essays in *Negro Digest/Black World*, one of which contained his critique noted above, in which he not only responded to initial critiques of his privileging of Harlem but extended his broader thesis to cities across the United States.[10] He noted that "what is lacking in the contemporary approach to Black cities is a *historical methodology* that will reveal that each *major* Black city population has a different character, has its own peculiar evolutionary history, and played a special role in the overall Black migratory developments" (1967, p. 30). He viewed the different patterns of migration and urbanization that created the concentrations of blacks throughout the Mid-Atlantic, Midwest, and West as generating different socioeconomic relations that would require specific theorizing, and viewed what he articulated in *The Crisis* as a contribution to Harlem's role in black American cultural production and the Renaissance and BAM, given the cultural imperatives brought about by the development of mass media, which presented particular opportunities for black intellectuals in Harlem—the Black "cultural capital"—to theorize and execute a cultural revolution. He acknowledged the potential impact of similar analyses of blacks in cities such as Chicago, Detroit, Pittsburgh, and Cleveland with respect to industrial production and the labor movement, and drew from distinctions in black westward migration and urbanization to help explain conflicts between the BPP that emerged in Oakland and that which emerged in New York. Thus, he was not surprised by the initiatives of militant black labor organizing in Detroit, which he encouraged, as reflected in the specific socialization trajectory of blacks in the "Motor City," even as he called for analysts to differentiate Detroit's from Chicago's role at the forefront of post-Reconstruction black politics in the North, given that it was the first to send a black congressman to Washington following the Nadir.[11] Cruse was convinced that the different contexts would require specific historicizing in an inductive process of theorizing the impact of migration and urbanization, which for Cruse was the defining aspect of black socialization since Reconstruction (see Semmes, 1992).

There were broader patterns of black urbanization, which Cruse acknowledged, that were structuring the contexts of black America in ways only superficially appreciated and insufficiently theorized by BPM revolutionists—and many scholars, as well—that were constraining the prospects of both black cultural revolution and even the more evolutionary strategy of developing black parallel institutions in the cities. African Americans were in a critical position to take advantage of the transformation of the urban landscape in the United States that they had played no small role in shaping during the post–World War I era. Just as the first migration of blacks to the cities had witnessed the rise of entrepots of black urban development, black resistance to urban white racism, and the phenomenon of the "first ghetto," the aftermath of World War II had created the conditions for the "second ghetto" as racist policies of the federal government through the GI Bill and the Federal Housing Authority, real estate firms, speculators, banks and other loan agencies, and white homeowners associations had collaborated to underwrite segregation through the promotion of white suburbanization and the urban "removal" programs that targeted black communities in what would eventually become "inner cities" (Hirsch, 1983; Sugrue, 1996). In this context, the presence of blacks in prominent positions in American cities seemed to promise "ethnic succession" that would bring them to power and facilitate the betterment of their lot in urban America. Historically, black cultural change, and American cultural change more generally, had been tied to urban development, as Du Bois and Locke and many others had recognized during and before the Harlem Renaissance (see Moses, 1990, pp. 201–222). However, the policies of the second ghetto had already begun to lay the basis for the maintenance of white control of the cities, out of proportion to their residency, and irrespective of black political control downtown (Katznelson, 1981).

The CRM in the North had been a grassroots and electoral challenge to white administrative control of the city as blacks projected out from the "central city" to assert their power beyond the second ghetto. But even as blacks challenged municipalities in order to take their turn in the ethnic succession, they came up against the "city trenches" (Katznelson, 1981) associated with the third ghetto, which ghettoized the city itself (Nightingale, 2003). The third ghetto was characterized by the accession of black municipal leadership over economically devastated cities with increasingly ineffective administrative structures. The cities' ghettoes were less dense and more spatially dispersed, and segregated black enclaves grew in the suburbs while prisons became extensions of ghettos. During this era, cities were marked by industrial flight, attacks on labor, wage decreases, persistent poverty, large tracts of vacant land and increased inequality and dilapidated infrastructures. Thus, as blacks came to power through their emergent electoral clout, the black urban regimes were compromised by corporate interests that "employed new communications technologies, plant closings, 'post-Fordist' production systems, and the capacity to move capital, facilities, and assembly lines across the globe as critical assets." They were also compromised by the black elected officials, who often acted as willing clients of corporate interests while abandoning the interests of the black masses that had been essential to their ascension to political power and the maintenance of their regimes (ibid., p. 266).

Subsequent theses of black cultural revolution would need to confront many if not most (or all) of these major developments in black urban America. Boggs, an auto worker and intellectual, integrated an appreciation of the political economy of black working classes but not their culture into his neo-Marxist conception of revolution intended to guide the peculiarly American black freedom struggle that he devoted most of his life helping to organize, guide, and build. This was consistent with his dismissive view of the revolutionary potential of black culture and his assumption that a black American revolution would develop its own revolutionary culture out of the political struggle itself—a process opposite to both what Du Bois had documented historically in the Slave Revolution and what Locke had theorized as well. Such was not the case for Cruse, who viewed black culture as potentially motivating revolution if black intellectuals and artists, especially, would utilize it in emancipatory ways. In practical terms, he viewed the opportunity for black cultural revolution during the CRM lost because movement leaders didn't understand its necessity (Cruse, 1971c), while, for him, the BPM declined due to its failure to develop a viable independent black political party (Cruse, 1974ab).

In theoretical terms, Cruse recognized the capacity of black culture to facilitate social change beyond the cultural sphere specifically, implicating political and economic factors in ways to challenge the white racial hierarchy of the United States. Cruse's conception of cultural revolution focused on democratizing and nationalizing mass media is novel. His chosen cultural strategy to revolutionize the CRM assumed that specific claims regarding the rights of black authors, writers, performers, entertainers, artists—as well as laborers and institutional supporters of black artistic production—to ownership of their cultural production; as well as the overturning of Jim Crow so that blacks could enjoy the right to public access through radio/TV, public space for performance, public investment streams in the arts and sciences (e.g., in public schools, museums, monuments, festivals), public education (administration, admissions, funding, curricula, etc.), would transform those spheres toward greater democracy and ramify to the economic sphere as well. Given that the realm of African American cultural production was demonstrably *black*, then the issue of ownership of that cultural product seemed straightforward, as were the historic and ongoing violations of the rights of blacks to their own cultural production. Cruse understood that these cultural and economic factors were connected such that by raising the cultural issues, the issues of economic inequality in both the public sphere and the private market would be implicated and the CRM's agenda could be extended into the economic domain. Once the economic boundary was breached, the broader issues of economic racism could take their place among the political, legal, and social issues that the CRM challenged.

With the CRM's turn to issues of economic democracy signaling the onset of Cruse's cultural revolution, white supremacist counterrevolutionary opposition would likely intensify, and at that point, blacks and their allies (nonwhites and whites) would need as much room as possible to maneuver within the political system to not only reinforce their legal, cultural, and economic claims but to provide political support for their emerging revolution. The U.S. political system's winner-take-all electoral systems are designed to prevent minority claims from being represented above the city or county level; therefore, a concomitant strategy to institute proportionally representative voting systems might have been necessary not only to promote greater democracy in the electoral system (a demand already asserted in the CRM) but to provide political cover for the minority constituencies advocating the initial claims and perspectives of the incipient revolutionists. Promoted as a cultural claim, proportional representation advocacy is an important avenue to draw political democracy into the cultural sphere. Resources from the struggle for economic democracy would provide support for the proportional representation initiative; and in securing those political gains, revolutionists would be able to use the resources of their control of public offices and agencies to increase their economic capacity to support and expand their political, cultural, and economic claims.

For Cruse, cultural claims provided the glue to bind civil rights to economic rights in novel ways, especially in the era of mass media. Further, Cruse's focus on bringing the cultural apparatus under public control, given that blacks are only a minority of the public, implies that blacks would not be alone in attempting to democratize the cultural apparatus, as other racial minorities and non-Anglo white American groups (and some white Anglos as well) might ally or make common cause with black Americans against the Anglo-American cultural oligarchy. Although Cruse didn't flesh out these implications, it seems clear that his conception of black cultural revolution is attentive to the need for supportive actions by nonblacks to achieve its objectives. What is less clear is the form that this struggle would take, that is, would it be violent, nonviolent, or both? Further, Cruse did not offer prescriptions on the preferred strategy that CRM activists should undertake once their movement became revolutionary in order to incorporate his cultural strategy into its program and institutions. As a result, Cruse's thesis of cultural revolution is seaworthy as a concept, but, as a program for revolution, it is rudderless.

Implicit in Cruse's thesis is that the focal issues of the cultural revolution should dovetail with those central to the CRM, linking them to the direct action focus of the CRM. It is not clear how capturing the cultural apparatus would provide the impetus for such a mobilization beyond what the CRM had already generated, in a movement that Cruse argued was not revolutionary. Although cultural factors could be linked to economic issues to add another dimension of struggle to the politico-legal focus of the CRM, capturing the cultural apparatus did not seem sufficiently salient as an objective to galvanize the kind of grassroots mobilization that revolution seemed to require. Further, once the CRM abated, it was not clear what institution would carry the black cultural revolution forward during the BPM, although for Cruse the clear candidate was an independent black political party, such as the National Black Political Assembly (NBPA), and he lamented its failure to ground itself more thoroughly in black American domestic issues.[12]

While the importance of democratizing the cultural apparatus seemed straightforward and progressive for the CRM, it seemed more appropriate as a tactic to extend the CRM, rather than a strategic objective of revolutionary struggle in general, a process to cast off the veil of centuries of miseducation among blacks insofar as "American capitalism's technological advances in mass cultural media—films, radio, and music records, etc.—was a new capitalistic feature to replace Marx's 'religion' as the real modern opium of the people" (Cruse,1968, p. 136). This is not to say that utilizing such a tactic could not evolve the CRM into a revolutionary struggle somehow, but it seems more apparent that cultural revolution required a cultural thrust centered on an issue/factor that raised more fundamental contradictions in the U.S. socio-politico-economy. As noted in chapter 3, such a cultural issue was African American reparations; but Cruse was largely silent on this issue.

The moral argument for reparations was apparent: the enslavement of millions of blacks by the United States for almost 250 years was clearly immoral. The expropriation of their labor provided for the industrialization of the United States—and the Industrial Revolution, itself—and its economic development; ironically, former slavemasters were given reparations for their treason in the form of the return of their confiscated land by the white supremacist president Andrew Johnson (as well as benefits they accrued from their renewal of black oppression in the South), but not the newly manumitted slaves. The imposition of a century of Jim Crow and its systematic repression of nominally free black people, who were taxed as full citizens without enjoying the rights of white citizens also demanded redress. The legal argument for reparations was self-evident domestically, even prior to the success of the Japanese American World War II internment reparations case, and internationally in the recognition of the human rights of national minorities in the UN Charter and the Universal Declaration of Human Rights. Establishing a legal argument for reparations might be the domain of the NAACP-LDF just as were the legal cases that culminated in the *Brown* decisions. Reparations would focus on the main unresolved issue of Reconstruction: providing an economic basis for black freedom. Thus, at minimum, compensation would take the form of allotments of land to descendants of slaves. Land redistribution would have to be protected by the establishment of special rights of recipients, akin to customary land rights employed in colonial/postcolonial arrangements, so that blacks could not be cheated out of their newly acquired capital. There would be broader economic, political, and social compensation, the latter in the form of educational and industrial training as well as permanent endowments to black universities, as well as pre-K-12 schools.

A successful black reparations case would require a major redistribution of wealth in the United States, probably the greatest since the Civil War, when most of the wealth of the CSA—in the form of human chattel—initially walked away from the servitude of slave plantations as free people; however, in little more than a decade these nominally free "ex-slaves" would be plunged back into conditions often described as "slavery by another name" (Blackmon, 2008). A successful reparations case required an unequivocal assertion of the human rights of African Americans and a commitment to the recognition of such rights—in material ways—by the United States, the richest and most powerful country in the world, which promoted itself as the leader of the "free world" during the CRM. The assertion of black culture could only reinforce the recognition of the cultural contributions of black people to U.S. society and put in bolder relief the contradictions of historic and ongoing white supremacist domination in the United States. This could not only be a movement of blacks, but given the resources at issue, it would demand a response by white Americans (among others), and in this way compel white allies of black self-determination to raise the issue of *cultural revolution for white Americans*, not simply as a counterculture, but in tangible ways that transformed those political, economic, and social institutions of the United States that were organized around white supremacy. Splits among whites—possibly along regional, class, ethnic, or even religious lines—would need to be exploited by white (and nonwhite) supporters of freedom, justice, and equality in ways not seen since the U.S. Civil War. During the CRM, such splits might generate a sectarian crisis among whites, exacerbating the intraracial frictions among them that became evident in the protests against the Vietnam War.

A reparations strategy also challenged the façade of the interest group/melting pot conceptualization of Americans instead of what is actually the Herrenvolk democracy in the United States. The assumed horizontal competition among ethnic groups contained and concealed the vertical hierarchy among racial groups, and bred interethnic competition and assimilation for non-Anglo whites but interracial subordination and repression for nonwhite racial groups. Blacks knew the problems of interest group politics from their experiences with political machines in cities in which they were concentrated—the same urban regimes that created and maintained the ghettoes that housed them—and only a decade after passage of the Voting Rights Act of 1965 allowed them to elect thousands of blacks to political offices across the country; yet, many blacks realized the hollowness of ethnic succession as a project to relieve their national underdevelopment. Reparations for the black nation could not be accommodated like other interest group claims, just as the claim of African Americans for freedom a century earlier was not simply an "interest group" claim nor was it reconcilable with a war aim to simply preserve the Union, but required that the Civil War become a part of the Slave Revolution, which ended chattel slavery as an economic, political, and social system in the United States permanently. Reparations were a cultural claim for which blacks had exclusive standing, and in addressing such a major unresolved issue of social-economic-political injustice, it was likely to create a systemic crisis. It would necessitate a major redistribution of resources unseen since Reconstruction.

Nonetheless, Cruse did not focus his thesis of black cultural revolution on a reparations strategy, although such a program of action was consistent with it. This is somewhat surprising, given that the issue of black reparations for slavery had a long history, with which Cruse was not unfamiliar, and proponents of black reparations—especially in New York and Detroit—were also familiar to Cruse. It would be surprising if Cruse was unfamiliar with Callie House, who was one of the most important leaders of the major black reparations organization following the Civil War, the *National Ex-Slave Mutual Relief, Bounty and Pension Association* (Berry, 2005). In fact, in Cruse's Harlem of the 1950s, Audley Moore had been the most prominent advocate of reparations for black Americans. Queen Mother Moore, as she is more famously known, was a life member of the UNIA, a stock owner in the Black Star Line, who had attended Garvey's first international convention in New York City. She had become a member of the CPUSA following its support of the Scottsboro Boys case, but she left it once it abandoned the Black Belt thesis and opposed the Double V campaign. She was the founder and president of the Universal Association of Ethiopian Women, the founder of the Committee for Reparations for Descendants of U.S. Slaves, bishop of the

Apostolic Orthodox Church of Judea, and during the height of the BPM she was a founding member of the RNA, influencing its support for reparations. Beginning in 1957, Moore attempted to petition the UN for reparations for African Americans for slavery and Jim Crow. She sought compensation for those blacks who desired to return to Africa and an indemnification of 200 billion dollars to those blacks choosing to remain in the United States. In 1960, Malcolm X invited Moore to his Harlem Mosque to speak on black reparations. Nonetheless, Cruse ignored black nationalists' support for reparations, and did not incorporate it into his thesis.

An even greater omission for Cruse's thesis was that it "scarcely recognize[d] the existence of religion in the [black] community" (Wilmore, 1983, p. 191). That is, his thesis of black *cultural* revolution ignored the most powerful black *cultural* institution in the United States, the Black Church. Put another way, while Cruse focused on the cultural apparatus of the United States as a target for revolutionary activity; he ignored the key institution of the cultural apparatus of the black community itself. This neglect is doubly troubling given that unlike Du Bois who died in 1963 and Locke who died in 1954, Cruse published *The Crisis* in 1967 after witnessing the major successes of the CRM, whose institutional locus was the Black Church. In addition, Cruse's thesis ignores the issue of gender relations in black institutions, and in U.S. society as a whole, and the need to address sexism in order to realize the substantive transformation he sought through cultural revolution. These are not small oversights. They represented two institutional factors within black communities that were critical aspects of black culture and among the most powerful change agents in black communities; thus, they were essential to projecting a meaningful program of cultural revolution. At minimum, Cruse might have proposed substantive changes in the Black Church and black gender relations that might have moved the black liberation struggle much farther forward in the early 1960s, but in the event Cruse paid little attention to either.[13] These problems would plague subsequent theses of BPM revolutionists as they attempted to organize around many of the principles and objectives originally put forth by Cruse.

As noted above, Cruse was directly associated with several BPM organizations such as the FNP, BARTS, and the NBPA; but his ideas had a much broader and more sustained impact on the BPM.[14] With the FNP failing to adopt his strategy of black cultural revolution in its program, this left black nationalists bereft of an electorally oriented approach that was inculcated with a cultural program. Although the FNP would run candidates for local and state offices, particularly in Michigan, in which black nationalists Milton Henry and Albert Cleage were included, given the still relatively small numbers of blacks and the failure of the FNP to tie its electoral program to a concurrent strategy to transform the winner-take-all and single member district format of the elections—replacing it with a proportional representation or single transferable voting scheme as was being undertaken in some areas of the U.S. South—the FNP candidates did not win office in these still predominantly white areas of Michigan. This signaled a missed opportunity for black nationalists to build on Malcolm X's "ballot or the bullet" approach, which also emboldened the Democratic Party in its belief that its base of Northern black support could be shored up with little concessions made to the surging black nationalists, a lesson that would become bitterly evident in the Gary and Little Rock conventions of 1972 and 1974. This breach would be temporarily addressed by the successful electioneering of Baraka's Committee for a Unified Newark (CFUN) following that city's bloody 1967 rebellion, but the latter's impact on Democratic Party hegemony in black electoral politics in the North would also be short-lived, as discussed in chapter 8. Without his own organization in which to situate his cultural revolution thesis, leadership on the issue gravitated to more prominent spokespersons, such as Malcolm X, and organizationally to RAM, Us, and the BPP. In the next chapter, we begin our discussion of how these organizations addressed the role of black culture in the revolutions they sought during the BPM.

Conclusion

In this chapter, I discussed the first explicit thesis of black cultural revolution, proffered by Harold Cruse, which was influential among BPM revolutionists. Cruse argued the necessity of advancing a cultural strategy to revolutionize the CRM. Recognizing that American political, economic, and cultural institutions were linked in a matrix of white supremacist domination that imposed domestic colonialism on black Americans, he argued that by attacking "the economic spheres of cultural communications in America" the CRM could extend its efforts into the economic and political domains, culminating in capturing and nationalizing the cultural apparatus (i.e., the mass communications media) of U.S. society in a cultural revolution (Cruse, 1968, p. 117). For Cruse, the relationship of culture, politics, and economics necessitated that blacks focus on the weakest aspect of the domestic colonial system, the cultural front. Attacks on the cultural front might include class action legal claims of black artists against white expropriators of their cultural product to both provide redress for black artists and fund independent black organizations—especially CRM organizations defunded by whites as they transitioned to black power (e.g., SNCC and CORE). Cruse's focus on the cultural apparatus was a conceptual advance that prefigured BAM and contributed to the onset of the BPM. It also suggested the institutional objective absent from Locke's thesis. One might say that while Du Bois historicized black cultural revolution, Locke theorized it and Cruse gave it its institutional focus: the mass communications media.

This novel focus on capturing the cultural apparatus was also a major shortcoming of Cruse's thesis, since it seemed insufficiently salient as an objective to orient, or a theme by which to mobilize for the black cultural revolution that he sought. Such a focus detracted from considerations of historical and contemporary black cultural claims with respect to unresolved issues of social justice related to chattel slavery and Jim Crow, epitomized in the cause of black reparations. Ironically, Cruse's thesis seemed less attuned to the challenge of capturing the cultural apparatus of the black community itself as a precursor to this broader struggle, insofar as Cruse had difficulty integrating the major black cultural institution, the Black Church, into his theoretical arguments on cultural revolution. Cruse also largely ignored the role of sexism as a major institutional impediment to the cultural change that he sought. Further, in privileging Harlem initially, it ignored an important aspect of black cultural development in urban areas with large black concentrations that Harlem did not typify, namely, cities with more powerful industrial working classes, although he addressed this issue in his 1971 follow-on essays. In general, his lack of consideration of Du Bois's cultural framework in *Black Reconstruction* and Locke's cultural thesis may have contributed to Cruse's dependence on the ongoing CRM to provide the practical momentum for his cultural revolution, which was less of an issue to the extent that his intention was to revolutionize the CRM. However, on a theoretical level, it led Cruse to appropriate aspects of Haywood's Black Belt thesis in order to provide the dynamism that his thesis lacked. Consequently, Cruse's thesis of cultural revolution did not clearly articulate a program of cultural revolution beyond the CRM because cultural claims, values, and institutions within black communities provided less of the dynamism in his general thesis than a political revolution to overthrow the system of domestic colonialism. Thus, without the motor of the CRM to propel it, Cruse's cultural thesis became static.

Cruse's conception of African American revolution is usefully contrasted with those of Haywood and Boggs, given that Cruse's thesis emphasized the role of black culture like Haywood's, while Boggs's proffered no significant role for black culture as a revolution-generating force. The latter's focus minimized considerations of the indigenous historical referents of African American revolutionary change to inform his revolutionary thesis. While Cruse, like Haywood, was more attentive to African Amerian revolutionary history, neither fleshed out its implications toward Du Bois's thesis in *Black Reconstruction*, so neither appreciated the Slave Revolution during the U.S.

Civil War as a black political revolution that was motivated by a black cultural revolution, or integrated this understanding into their respective frameworks. In addition, Cruse's thesis did not specify the institutional vehicle for organizing and mobilizing blacks to capture the cultural apparatus once the CRM had abated. With little faith in the Black Church as a change agent, his thesis relied on the development of an independent black political party to push the demands forward, but Cruse did not flesh out this aspect of his thesis either—and the short-lived NBPA did not consider it seriously (as will be discussed in chapter 8); thus, his focus on democratizing the cultural apparatus as an objective of black cultural revolution did not seem to transcend the CRM, at least not on a practical level. Nevertheless, it influenced several major BPM organizations.

In sum, the novel insights and shortcomings of Cruse's—as well as Haywood's and the Boggses'—revolutionary theses resonated among BPM revolutionists and both guided and hamstrung their programs for black liberation in the subsequent decades. Cruse seems to have influenced Malcolm X's discourse on black cultural revolution, which encouraged RAM's and Us's promotion of the concept. Both Cruse's and Boggs's broader thesis on revolution informed the ideology of RAM, while Haywood's thesis influenced it indirectly. Boggs's view that revolutions would generate the requisite revolutionary culture was consistent with the BPP's perspective as well. Thus, early in the BPM, issues related to cultural revolution were highly salient to the struggle that major BPM organizations sought to wage.

Chapter 6

RAM, Us, the Black Panther Party

In the previous chapter, we examined the first explicit thesis on black cultural revolution in the United States, proffered by Harold Cruse to revolutionize the Civil Rights Movement (CRM) by targeting the cultural apparatus of U.S. society. Cruse's cultural focus was an important theoretical contribution to the onset of the Black Power Movement (BPM), and the Black Arts Movement (BAM) as well. Cruse's thesis, along with those of Boggs and Haywood, provided contending perspectives on the role of culture in revolution for BPM revolutionists whose programs would reflect both their insights and shortcomings. In this chapter, I examine how several major BPM organizations engaged theses of black cultural revolution. I examine the Revolutionary Action Movement (RAM), which was the first major BPM organization to formally advocate black cultural revolution following Malcolm's Organization of Afro-American Unity (OAAU), and Us, which developed one of the most influential theses of black cultural revolution in the BPM, and the Marxist-influenced theses of culture and revolution of the Black Panther Party (BPP).

RAM and the Second Organizational Adoption of Black Cultural Revolution

Although Cruse initially proposed his thesis on black cultural revolution as an element of a proposed platform of the Freedom Now Party (FNP), it was never formally adopted; in fact, James Boggs was among the FNP leadership who openly opposed it. As a result, the first major organization of the BPM to advocate black cultural revolution in its public program and strategy for black liberation following Malcolm X's OAAU was RAM. Cruse's theses on the revolutionary capacity of black nationalism, domestic colonialism, and black cultural revolution were central to RAM, which was formally organized in 1962 from the efforts of students at Wilberforce College. Emerging from a campus-based group of black members and associates of Students for a Democratic Society (SDS), "Challenge," the group that would become RAM, devoted serious study to Cruse's "Revolutionary Nationalism and the Afro-American," which the group circulated among its members, and began to engage in radical politics. The early leadership centered on Donald Freeman of Cleveland, who had suggested that the group study Cruse's thesis, and included Max Stanford and Wanda Marshall in Philadelphia, who had met with Malcolm X and shared their interests in forming a radical black nationalist organization with a direct action focus, such as the Student Non-Violent Coordinating Committee (SNCC), within the Nation of Islam (NOI). Malcolm dissuaded them from joining the NOI and, instead, encouraged them to pursue independent organizing, and the formation of RAM was the major result of that advice (Stanford, 1986, p. 79). Stanford and Marshall were joined by Stan Daniels and Playthell Benjamin, among others (ibid., p. 80). The group had been tutored in Philadelphia by both Queen Mother Moore, who had already made appeals to the UN regarding black reparations, and Ethel Johnson, who had previously worked with Robert Williams in North Carolina. Max Stanford met with the Boggses in Detroit and described RAM to them (ibid., p. 90). RAM drew on the "militant internationalism" of Robert Williams, the "world-wide revolution" thesis of Malcolm X, Cruse's domestic colonialism and black cultural revolution theses, and James and Grace Lee Boggs's emergent "dialectical humanism," to promote a vision and program of black liberation that would fuse aspects of each of these perspectives.

RAM's founders intended "to start a mass black nationalist movement," which would employ "mass direct action combined with the tactics of self-defense" in order "to change the civil rights movement into a black revolution" (Stanford, 1986, p. 80). RAM created a bimonthly publication, *Black America*, which began to communicate with "other new nationalist formations," for example, in San Francisco, members of Don Warden's Afro-American Association, Huey Newton and Bobby Seale, the eventual cofounders of the BPP; in its Los Angeles affiliate, Maulana Karenga, who would later help found Us; in Detroit, UHURU members Luke Tripp, John Williams, Charles (Mao) Johnson, General Baker, and Gwen Kemp, who would become important members of the League of Revolutionary Black Workers (LRBW); in Cleveland, members of the Afro-American Institute, including Don Freeman; and in Chicago, National Afro-American Organization members Sterling Stuckey, Thomas Higgenbottom, and John Bracey. RAM expanded to both coasts as a network of organizers committed to a program to link the Northern and Southern CRM in a black nationalist initiative similar to Malcolm's OAAU. The general program was modified by local approaches that emphasized student, labor, or broader community organizing. RAM constructed itself as a cadre organization, operating openly mainly in Philadelphia and New York but otherwise as a self-proclaimed underground organization.[1] Only in Philadelphia did it operate openly as a direct action group, and by the mid-1960s its primary leader and theorist was Max Stanford (aka Muhammad Ahmad).

During the organization's brief lifetime (1962–68/69), RAM's black nationalism was eclectic, tracing the broad contours that subsequent BPM organizations would traverse. Unlike some of these organizations, RAM's leadership was diffuse and decentralized, and not surprisingly its program could be as varied as its theoretical thrust. For example, originally RAM emphasized pan-Africanism and openly advocated armed struggle in the United States, and although it was anti-imperialist it was not explicitly Marxist in the sense of centering its analysis on the class struggle. In fact, "As early as 1962, RAM declared that nationalism was the 'natural doctrine' of the black working class and through revolutionary black nationalism their anger would be aroused and would lead to the destruction of the ruling class" (Stanford, 1986, p. 152). In the Fall 1964 edition of *Black America*, Stanford (1964, p. 1) differentiated between the integrationists of the CRM and the emergent black nationalists, and situated RAM squarely within the latter, articulating and advocating a perspective that built on the revolutionary theses of Malcolm, Cruse, and Boggs. In arguments that would come to characterize the prominent revolutionary theory of the BPM, Stanford asserted the centrality of Malcolm's black nationalism, acknowledging that blacks constituted "a nation within the boundaries of another nation; a nation in captivity striving to obtain independence, self-determination, or national liberation," to be achieved through revolution (ibid., p. 1). Stanford posited that

> [t]he failure to realize our power and position in this country has been the failure of Afroamericans to see themselves as revolutionary nationalists. In doing this, they don't see our struggles as a national liberation struggle. Instead, our struggle has previously been defined along class lines only. This led to confusion and failure to make a clear analysis . . . because there are more factors involved than class. . . . We must become familiar with our revolutionary history as an oppressed nation. (1964, p. 2)

RAM emphasized the domestic colonial status of the black nation, reflecting Cruse's influence, and wedded this position to Malcolm X's argument on black self-determination and the view that land was the basis of independence. Thus, RAM viewed black Americans not as citizens of the United States, but as a domestic colony seeking national independence by overthrowing U.S. imperialism at home in coordination with anticolonial struggles abroad. As a colonized nation, African Americans were little different from other colonized nations who were aligned in their anti-imperialist cause; thus, RAM came to advocate "Bandung Humanism," which explicitly related the black struggle in the United States to the anti-imperialist and nonaligned movement that many in the BPM associated with the Bandung Conference.[2] This required that black Americans further develop an international perspective allied with, supported, and drawing lessons from anti-imperialist struggles throughout the world. The latter reflected the influence of Boggs's thesis of dialectical humanism (thus, the "humanism" of "Bandung Humanism"), which Stanford viewed as "the method of analyzing, planning and developing the sociological and cultural motivations as related to the material factors which affect man's psyche for the raising of his revolutionary humanness towards man" (Stanford, 1986, p. 151). They also characterized their perspective as "revolutionary black internationalism," focusing on an international black underclass understood as an amalgam of international "have nots," whether they were phenotypically black or not (i.e., third world peoples), opposed to a white overclass that consisted mainly of European and their offshoot settler states, including the Soviet Union, which was viewed as more white nationalist than socialist internationalist (Castro's Cuba was characterized similarly).[3] It assumed "an inevitable confrontation between Western imperialism and Bandung anti-imperialism" (ibid., p. 147). In fact, in what is probably its most developed theoretical statement on political revolution as an organization, the essay "World Black Revolution," written by Stanford in 1966, RAM proposed a "worldwide revolution"—evoking Malcolm's reference—that amounted to a global war that, if not an explicit "race war," aimed at overthrowing the white "overclass" and establishing a dictatorship of the black "underclass."

In "World Black Revolution," RAM contended that "[t]he principle contradiction in the world is between imperialism, particularly U.S. imperialism and the colonies, between the haves and the have nots" (Stanford, 1966, p. 3). Given the context of the times and the developing rival interpretations of black American oppression in terms of race and increasingly in terms of class, RAM's thesis in 1966 saw the two forces as complementary and reinforcing, instead of contradictory and mutually exclusive, manifesting on both a class and caste basis (ibid.). Nevertheless, recognizing this complementarity did not preclude RAM from acknowledging the greater salience of race:

> In the present situation, caste predominates the question of class in that the exploitation of the have nots though initially perpetrated

on class lines as of the present, maintains itself on caste (racial lines). Class thus becomes the secondary and not the primary manifestation of the principle contradiction. (ibid.)

RAM asserted that "[i]n order for this contradiction to be resolved, imperialism, capitalism and all that maintains the systems of exploitation must be destroyed by the have nots," and it understood that "[t]he destruction of these systems will mean the end of class exploitation and will also mean the end of caste (racial) exploitation" (ibid.). For RAM, since "[t]he European forces have consolidated along caste lines, and maintain their exploitation on the basis of racial lines (caste)," then "the world revolution will be a racial (caste) war between the haves, imperialists[,] and the have nots[,] majority of the world[,] while at the same time being a class war between the Black Underclass and the White Overclass to eliminate the class system, capitalism" (ibid.).

RAM, as "revolutionary black internationalists," asserted that "the Black Underclass is the vanguard of the world revolution, leadership and rulers of the 'New World'" (Stanford, 1966, p. 3). They contended that "[i]n world society, the Black Underclass being the lowest stratum, cannot achieve national liberation, self-determination, Black Power without the whole of U.S.-European bourgeois society being completely destroyed"; therefore, "[t]he first stage of the struggle for liberation of the Black Underclass against the white overclass is a national struggle" (ibid., p. 10). RAM admonished that "[t]he Black Underclass must struggle against the particular imperialist power that is directly oppressing it nationally," and thus the significance of both the CRM and the BPM in the United States as well as national liberation struggles in specific countries abroad. "But," RAM maintained, "it must be remembered that the backer of all imperialism today is U.S. imperialism" (ibid.). Therefore, following the dualism in Malcolm's thesis on black revolution, RAM asserted that "while waging a war against its immediate oppressor it must also wage war against U. S. imperialism internationally" (ibid.). Thus, while expressing solidarity with contemporary third world revolutionaries in Africa, Asia, and Latin America, RAM argued that black revolutionists in the United States needed to organize their own revolution to overthrow the domestic colonial regime of U.S. imperialism.

A contributing factor to the development of RAM was a small conference in May 1964 at Fisk University, the Afro-American Student Conference on Black Nationalism. Critiquing both what it viewed as the bourgeois reformism of mainstream civil rights organizations and bourgeois nationalism's uncritical acceptance of capitalism, the conferees "asserted that the young nationalists are the vanguard of a Black Revolution in the United States" (Freeman, 1964, p.

16). The conference's theoretical and programmatic orientations anticipated those that would dominate the BPM, including the assertion "that black radicals were the vanguard of revolution" in the United States, support for Malcolm X's "efforts to take the case of Afro-Americans to the U.N.," positive engagement with pan-Africanism, and a call "for a black cultural revolution" (Stanford 1986, 92). Many of the conference's main points would be reflected in RAM's twelve-point program put forth the following month in Detroit (Stanford, 1986, 99; Stanford, 2007, 120–123).[4] RAM endorsed Cruse's domestic colonialism thesis and asserted that "the Afro-American is not a citizen of the U.S.A., denied his rights, but rather he is a colonial subject enslaved"; thus, "black people in the U.S.A. are a captive nation suppressed," and therefore, "their fight is not for integration into the white community but one of national liberation." RAM stated its objective as "the overthrow of white rule, capitalist rule," or more simply, "the black man taking over this country" (Stanford, 1986, 206). In accordance with Malcolm's "ballot or the bullet" thesis, four years before the founding of the RNA, RAM envisioned a provisional government in exile headed by Robert Williams, and advocated an electoral strategy centered on supporting "Robert Williams for President in '68 in the black community" (ibid.). At the same time, RAM endorsed armed struggle as a means for the colonized black nation to free itself from the bonds of imperial rule, just like anticolonial struggles throughout the colonized world.

Appreciating that its revolutionary approach would necessitate both above-ground and underground initiatives, RAM promoted the former through its support of black workers' "liberation" unions, whose purpose was "to fight for better conditions on jobs, to organize Afro-American[s] to spy, etc., for the purpose of a national strike" (ibid., 205)—the latter resonating with Du Bois's General Strike and anticipating the LRBW, in which RAM members would play instrumental roles (see chapter 7). The proposed unions would also include "Women's leagues," which RAM's subsequent 12 Point Program insisted "will also play an important role in the national strike," and their purpose was to organize black women domestic workers who toiled "in whitie's homes" (ibid.). In addition, RAM sought to organize and develop the "army of black unemployed" to pressure "the Federal government by demonstrating North and South against racial discrimination on Federal backed industry," and also to "struggle against union discrimination" (ibid., p. 206). RAM also supported the development of black farmer cooperatives "[i]n the delta area (black belt) in the South, especially Mississippi," presumably to not only provide food and resources to the communities there, but also to support "community and guerrilla forces" as necessary (ibid.).

By far, RAM's major aboveground organizational focus was on students. Viewing youth as the key to the revolutionary struggle it envisioned, RAM sought to develop an "Afro-American Student Movement" (ASM) to "fight against injustices, against Afro-American students and black people in general," to educate black Americans "to the economic, political, and cultural basis of the racial situation" in the United States and the world, to develop unity among blacks nationally and globally, and to organize black students to "become active in the Afro-American Liberation Struggle" (ibid., p. 204). Pursuant to these objectives, RAM sought to "develop revolutionary cadres in the high schools, junior high and colleges," with an objective of executing "a nationwide black student school strike which would repudiate the educational system" and "show black students that the only way to succeed in life is to cause a revolution in this country." RAM argued that the ASM "would develop groups around black history, students' rights, and also over conditions under which Afro-American students must operate," eventually taking over student government and seizing power (ibid., p. 204). This "all-black national student organization" would help generate "social dislocation" and provide a "guerilla force" operating independently of them, with "a base for mass support." Black youth would also "rally young black workers and the unemployed," which would help "politicize the black student community" and also "serve as the vanguard in the struggle." Importantly, the student strike would be augmented by strikes among "other segments of the black community," which the broader RAM would coordinate (ibid., p. 204).

RAM supported the establishment of "freedom schools," to "develop cadres" tutored in its "revolutionary theory and doctrine of RAM" that would "teach the history of the movement, current events, political theory[,] methods of social action, methods of self-defense, basic principles of guerrilla warfare, techniques of social dislocation, propaganda techniques and indoctrination, black history, etc" (ibid., pp. 204–205). Following Williams, it advocated the development of "rifle clubs" comprised "of local veterans" and community members organized as a black militia capable of protecting the black community" and serving "as a base for the establishment of a community government," and ultimately a black liberation army "to carry out [the] political, economic, physical overthrow of this system" (ibid., p. 205).

RAM rejected the contention that blacks were relatively powerless against the overwhelming political, economic, and especially military capabilities of the U.S. government. Following Williams's view that U.S. cities in which blacks were increasingly concentrated were the analogue of the third world guerillas' countryside (i.e., "Our countryside is the cities all over the country"), RAM argued that "the major part of guerrilla warfare in the U.S.A. will take place in the cities," which they viewed as "the pockets of power and heart of the economy." RAM's black liberation army would be tasked "to take over cities, cause complete social dislocation of communications, etc." as part of a broader guerilla warfare strategy. This approach was consistent with Stanford's (1964, p. 1) emphasis on the three aspects of power that African Americans possess: (1) "the power to stop the machinery of government—that is, the power to cause chaos" so "that nothing runs"; (2) "the power to hurt the economy" by causing chaos in "the major urban areas in the North" and disruption of the "agricultural setup in the South" such that "the economy of the oppressor would come to almost a standstill"; and (3) "the power of unleashing violence . . . to tear up 'Charlie's [the white man's] house" (ibid., p. 1). RAM advocated the development of cadres skilled "in techniques and methods of propaganda" and proposed instruction in intelligence methods (Stanford, 1986, p. 205). Toward these ends, RAM supported establishing "a press and a publishing company" and established its "national organ," *Black America*, "a journal of ideas and direction," to help coordinate the movement (ibid., p. 205). In their twelve points, RAM laid out many of the major theoretical and programmatic thrusts that would characterize the BPM.

Although it was not stated explicitly among RAM's twelve points, black cultural revolution was a central precept of RAM's program and practice (Stanford, 1986, 2007). RAM members were among those at the black nationalism conference at Fisk in 1964 who "agreed that a fundamental cultural revolution or re-Africanization of black people in America was a prerequisite for a genuine Black Revolution" (Freeman, 1964, p. 18). For RAM, "black people needed to engage in a black cultural revolution to prepare them for a black political revolution" (Stanford, 1986, 124). Although RAM related cultural revolution to political revolution in the United States temporally, and to some degree programmatically, it had more difficulty linking them theoretically, mainly because it ignored the cultural aspects of the revolutionary antecedents in African American history, leading them to focus more on the military aspects of the political revolution. For example, RAM advocated, following Malcolm, the creation of a nationwide united front among black revolutionists, noting that "[i]n order to unite the Black community, revolutionary Afro-American organizations would have to be united into a Black Liberation Front" (Stanford, 1966, p. 21). One of the most important functions of this united front was to organize a Black General Strike involving workers, students, and gangs, among others. RAM asserted that "[a] Black General Strike to stop the oppressor's system would have to be called in order to throw chaos into the oppressor's economy and disturb his social system" (ibid.). They noted that "[t]he Black General Strike will cause complete social dislocation with the American racist system," which the black revolutionists would exploit to pursue a people's war strategy to overthrow the U.S. government (ibid.). RAM argued that

[w]hen all the Black servants are no longer there or cannot be trusted for fear they may poison, maim or murder, the enemy will be faced with a social crisis. . . . Youth, especially those in gangs would have to be organized into a political Black Liberation Army [that] . . . would become Black America's regular guerrilla army. . . . A revolutionary Afro-American government would be established to govern the liberated areas. . . . Organization would have to be structured on the cadre level. . . . Within such a cadre there must be units able to match every type of unit that the counter-revolution has at its disposal . . . to defeat them. (Stanford, 1966, p. 21)

Clearly aware of aspects of *Black Reconstruction*, which Queen Mother Moore had encouraged Philadelphia RAM members to study, in these early statements RAM invoked the sine qua non of Du Bois's revolutionary thesis on the Slave Revolution in the United States, the general strike.[5] At the point where they would have benefited from grounding their analysis further in Du Bois's thesis and in that way fleshing out the historical connection between black cultural and political revolution in the United States, RAM grounded its version of a general strike to third world anticolonial "people's war." In so doing, RAM delinked it from its historical antecedent in the United States, the Slave Revolution it spawned, and the cultural processes that stimulated it. For RAM, the general strike was mainly a means to foment a people's war such as was occurring throughout the third world; rather than examining its precursors in a black cultural revolution that would motivate it, RAM focused on its unfolding as a practical matter rather than a key aspect of its theorizing an actual political revolution in the United States. Thus, even when RAM insightfully drew on the slave revolts and promoted Nat Turner as an exemplar of revolutionary struggle, these were evoked in almost purely political and military terms. The cultural aspect of the slave revolts and the association of slave religion and slave hiring to their organization were not examined by BPM revolutionists and, thus, did not become a focus or basis of their theorizing on these important historical events and processes. Therefore, even as they evoked the necessity of black cultural revolution as a precursor to black political revolution they failed to recognize the cultural revolution underneath their feet in their own history in the United States—not in the third world.

The General Strike of the U.S. Civil War was initiated by transformations in the cultural institutions that blacks controlled (i.e., slave religion) to provide institutional justification and coordination for concerted efforts toward social justice, and from there the serpentine networks that slave hiring facilitated, clandestine stations and depots of the Underground Railroad that later became linked to armed elements of the white host country in a context in which white hegemony was already fractured to generate the Slave Revolution and the Civil War. Analogous initial conditions were evident in the CRM which had magnified the Black Church's impact and expanded its role as a key institution of social change as it effectively challenged Jim Crow white supremacism in the South (and as it was becoming a center of black electoral organization in the North and West as well). Focused more on emulating "people's war," RAM's general strike approach failed to appreciate, much less coordinate with the progressive Black Church. This was indicative of RAM's—and so many BPM organizations'—marginalization of the Black Church and, often, religion, in general, especially as they attempted to parrot contemporary anticolonial revolutions abroad. Moreover, RAM, like later BPM organizations, prematurely militarized what should have begun as a cultural approach under the misapprehension that the U.S. struggle would approximate those in third world countries. Therefore, even as RAM insightfully invoked a general strike approach to black liberation in the United States, it did not flesh out or follow Du Bois's formulation or its synthesis with Locke's cultural thesis discussed in chapter 3.

Instead, RAM emphasized the politico-military rather than the cultural factors operative in the slave revolts; therefore, they turned their focus too quickly to the militarized aspects of black resistance, in large part to replicate the processes evident in the anticolonial wars occurring throughout the third world in order to legitimate their own. As a result, they borrowed heavily from Malcolm X, and even more from Robert Williams's "Revolution Without Violence," arguing that blacks could bring the United States to a standstill by engaging in rebellions utilizing a strategy of urban guerrilla warfare (Stanford, 1986, p. 90). Stanford argued in *Black America* that "our struggle is part of a world black revolution," and, therefore "we must unite with the 'Bandung' forces" (Stanford, 1964, p. 1), but, in the meantime, "we (AfroAmericans) must make our own revolution" (ibid., p. 2). His point of departure was Williams's suggestion that black revolutionists adopt guerilla strategies to create chaos in the United States, cause division among whites, and adopt the tactics of leaders of slave revolts such as Nat Turner, to "strike at night and spare none" (ibid.). RAM drew on the history of black revolt in the United States in a manner that was both rare and common among its cohort of young BPM revolutionists. It was rare inasmuch as it drew on the slave revolts and networks associated with them in the United States, thus privileging African American history, rather than "third world" history, in developing a theory of African American revolution, and it was common, unfortunately, in failing to engage the cultural aspects of the revolutionary antecedents in black American history, as well as in its quixotic notion that a revolution could be victorious against the most powerful country in the world in short order, problems evident among almost all of the major BPM organizations in this study.

Stanford was insightful in his admonition that "[w]hat most young black intellectuals fail to do is thoroughly study the slave system, the development of slavery from the sixteenth century on to the twentieth century, how our nation was taken into bondage, and the psychology of White America during this period" (1964, p. 2). In particular, he drew on the example of the U.S. slave revolts to inform revolutionary activity in the 1960s. Stanford challenged that "[c]ontrary to the oppressor's statistics, the slave revolts were well organized, involved thousands of slaves, and sometimes had international implications." He argued that "[t]hese revolts occurred on the average of every three weeks for a three hundred year period." He acknowledged the "international perspective of the Denmark Vesey revolt" and Vesey's "attempted coordination with Toussaint L'Ouverture (military leader of the Haitian revolt which had defeated both the French and British armies in liberating Haiti) shook White America to its roots."[6] He added that the "fear of having a Haitian revolution on United States soil played a major role in the official abolishment of the slave trade." In fact, he maintains, the "Nat Turner revolt shook White America so much that the idea of abolishment of the slave system *entirely* became a feasible and practical concept" (ibid.; original emphasis). Here, Stanford was not simply noting a historical reference, but drew on the Nat Turner revolt as a historical resource to help guide black revolutionary theory and praxis in the United States more than a century later—much as I've argued in the previous chapters. For him,

> Contrary to what most white historians would have us to believe, the Turner revolt was so well coordinated and planned, that it involved hundreds of slaves. Turner struck fear into all of White America by his tactic of "strike by night and spare none." Though the revolt was short-lived, many persons in positions of power realized that they would have to cope with a black revolution if the slave system wasn't destroyed . . . if they didn't do something quick, the slaves would develop national organization and they feared that the "blacks" would take over the country. The horror of thinking of what the "blacks" would do to the whites if they were in power was the nightmare of America. The slave system would have to go in order to to [*sic*] "save the Union" (White America). This was the situation that led to the Civil War. White

power had to fight White power in order to keep control over the "blacks." (1964, p. 2)[7]

In centering on the Turner Revolt, RAM provided a revolutionary template that was historically grounded in black American political development. Stanford asserted that "Turner's philosophy of 'strike by night and spare none'" was "very important" and reflected that Turner embodied "the guerilla instinct" and "knew the psychology of White America" (1964, p. 2). Specifically, "Turner knew what black terrorism meant to the whites, and struck, even though the odds were against him." Stanford maintained that Turner's "sense of annihilation of the enemy is very important for our struggle even today, because unlike Asia, Africa, and Latin America, the AfroAmerican has a great bulk of the mass against him," and he argued that "[w]hite America can be neutralized only by fear of high stakes. That is, if they know that whole families, communities, etc. of their loved ones will be wiped off the face of the earth if they attack AfroAmercians, they won't be too eager to go to war against us" (ibid., p. 22). Stanford conjectured that

> [t]his will be especially true if the AfroAmerican revolutionary forces make it clear that they are fighting the capitalist ruling class oligarchy—but if White Americans fight on the side of the white racist oppressor's government, they will be wiped out with no questions asked. . . . With the terms of the revolution spelled out, this will divide White America. So we can do that just by observing Nat Turner, we can gain something for our coming revolution. (1964, p. 22)

While invoking Nat Turner's revolt as a template for RAM's revolutionary theorizing, Stanford did not flesh out the connections among the slave revolts, the General Strike, and the Slave Revolution of the Civil War and, in that way, devise a strategy appropriate for the scale and magnitude of the "Second Civil War" he envisioned. This left the impression that the revolution RAM sought would be conducted on the scale of an insurrection, such as the Turner revolt, instead of a full-scale war, such as the Civil War. This conceptual failure was partly tied to the practical focus of RAM's initial proposal, which was intended more as a program to revolutionize the ongoing CRM, focused on linking it to the broader movements against imperialism throughout the third world and drawing on many of the methods utilized therein to seize state power. Analogizing the black liberation struggle in the United States to those developments, RAM would be only the first of several major BPM organizations to endorse guerilla warfare strategy throughout the United States—as had Williams and Malcolm X—to free the black nation from domestic colonialism.[8] Toward this end, RAM viewed the sophistication of the U.S. politico-economy as both a strength and a weakness, and analogized its operations to that of an "IBM machine" (i.e., an early computer), whose complexity could be exploited because if one "[p]ut[s] something in the wrong place in an IBM machine . . . it's finished for a long time." Continuing the analogy, Stanford noted:

> And so it is with this racist, imperialist system. Without mass communications and rapid transportation, this system is through. . . . When war breaks out in this country, if the action is directed toward taking over institutions of power and "complete annihilation" of the racist capitalist oligarchy, then the black revolution will be successful. Guns, tanks, and police will mean nothing. The Armed Forces will be in chaos. . . . It will be a war between two governments: the revolutionary Afro-American government in exile against the racist, imperialist White American government. It will be a war of the forces of the black liberation front against the ultra-right coalition. (1964, p. 2)

At this point, drawing lessons from black participation in the Civil War may have pushed RAM into a coherent theory of black revolution based on the strategic antecedents from the major slave revolts, epitomized in the Slave Revolution during the U.S. Civil War; but Stanford's discourse doesn't return to substantive aspects of Turner's revolt and their relationship to the Civil War, and instead focuses on prospective developments of a hypothetical Second Civil War, seemingly oblivious to the actual challenges, hardships, and destructiveness that accompanied the original Civil War as it was prosecuted by the eleven states of the Confederacy, even less what its repetition portended for a racial minority of roughly 10 percent of the U.S. population. Nonetheless, he envisioned that

> black men and women in the Armed Forces will defect and come over to join the black liberation forces. Whites who claim they want to help the revolution will be sent into the white communities to divide them, fight the fascists, and frustrate the efforts of the counter-revolutionary forces. Chaos will be everywhere and with the breakdown of mass communications, mutiny will occur in great numbers in all facets of the oppressor's government. The stock market will fall; Wall Street will stop functioning; Washington, D.C. will be torn apart by riots. Officials everywhere will

run for their lives.... Mass riots will occur in the day with the AfroAmericans blocking traffic, burning buildings, etc. Thousands of AfroAmericans will be in the street fighting.... This will be the AfroAmericans battle for human survival. Thousands of our people will get shot down, but thousands more will be there to fight on. The black revolution will use sabotage in the cities—knocking out the electrical power first, then transportation, and guerilla warfare in the countryside in the South. With the cities powerless, the oppressor will be helpless. (1964, pp. 2, 22)

Stanford argues that these actions will have important international implications:

With the White American ruling class wiped off the face of this planet, and the remaining reactionary forces suffering eventual defeat, the revolutionary AfroAmerican government will call on the help of other revolutionaries and revolutionary governments to help restore order and to fulfill the ultimate objectives of the world black revolution. (ibid., p. 22)

RAM's conceptualization of this Second Civil War and the prospects of success of black revolutionaries was not uncommon among black revolutionists of the BPM, and, arguably, it was a dominant view among black militants of the era—popularized by Malcolm X and most famously articulated by Robert Williams in three essays from 1964–67 in *Crusader* on the prospects for a "minority revolution"—but, this conceptualization was as quixotic as it was ahistorical. The basic problem was that in drawing from the history of the antebellum period it focused on the scale of armed conflict tantamount to the slave revolts instead of the U.S. Civil War. The failure to project their proposed revolution to the full-scale modern warfare ushered in by the Civil War is one reason why BPM revolutionists did not appreciate the magnitude of the enterprise they had set for themselves, nor were they prepared for the protracted nature of the revolution they envisioned. As a result, many of the BPM revolutionists imagined a revolution that would take less than a year to overthrow the U.S. government, and in the case of RAM, one that could be completed in ninety days.[9]

As their revolutionary thesis matured, RAM came to appreciate the importance of what they called a "Black General Strike" (Stanford, 1970); however, even this national undertaking was wedded to a vision of a politico-military struggle with the forces of the U.S. government that was quixotic. That is, instead of coordinating the diverse interests of black workers in industrial, agricultural, and service sectors who would need to be organized for a general strike and then proposing methods to consolidate their interests around a common core of demands that would be a source of galvanizing the broader community institutions and organizations necessary to provide support for a protracted general strike that would weaken those sectors and likewise the U.S. economy, RAM, like so many black power organizations, displayed a *fetish for militarization* in an attempt to demonstrate its capacity to wage armed struggle like their contemporaries in the colonized world. Instead of drawing on the historical arguments in Du Bois's *Black Reconstruction* and integrating the insights from the organization of the General Strike, RAM sought to import and emulate strategies from abroad that were not applicable to U.S. conditions. Even their more covert operations did not seem to draw on the insurgent strategy of black Americans who coordinated the major clandestine liberation struggle in U.S. history, which freed tens of thousands of human chattel (constituting the major store of Southern wealth), from bondage, namely, the Underground Railroad; rather, they sought what they hoped would be quicker, militarized initiatives from international contexts that were not grounded in the indigenous institutions of black communities much less recognizing the staying power of the major U.S. institutions of civil society that acted as a brake on protest or channeled them into extant political, economic, and social structures. Their preferred military approach was doctrinally disjointed, strategically myopic, and tactically unsound, displaying little knowledge of, or preparation for, military intelligence and counterintelligence, and as a result the major BPM organizations were often ill-equipped to engage even municipal—much less county and state—police forces or the National Guard.

RAM's advocacy of a guerilla strategy aimed at ambush, sabotage, and raids ignored the reality that the United States was especially equipped to respond to just these types of engagements with militant elements of its domestic populations. In fact, a major error in Malcolm X's assessment of U.S. military power was his view that the United States could not defeat an adversary employing a guerrilla warfare strategy. This derived from an oft-repeated but mistaken assessment of early U.S. operations in Vietnam, which encouraged a quixotic calculation among many BPM activists on the likelihood of relative quick success for black revolutionists employing a guerrilla insurgency in the United States. In fact, even in Vietnam, where ally and adversary were not racially distinguishable, the United States and its South Vietnamese (and other) allies were effectively engaging the North Vietnamese Army (NVA) and National Liberation Front (NLF, aka Viet Cong). Moreover, during the Tet Offensive of 1968 the United States had decimated NLF guerilla forces in the South.[10] The U.S. military had learned, from the

British suppression of indigenous uprisings in Malaya and the French failures in Algeria, techniques for effective counter-guerrilla, and counterinsurgency operations. In Vietnam, this included the deployment of special operations forces, and the systematic use of terrorism, as in the Phoenix program. The application of either to a racially distinguishable black American population would likely be even more successful than they were in Vietnam. It was highly unlikely that blacks could replicate NVA successes, achieved only after massive bloodletting on the part of the Vietnamese, including combat-hardened veterans, many of whom had been fighting since World War II, first against the Japanese and then the French, before engaging U.S. forces, and after receiving massive amounts of military and economic aid from the USSR and the People's Republic of China, and after losing every major military engagement with U.S. armed forces. Ultimately, NVA victory was owed to its greater conventional military power once the United States abandoned the field. Its greatest ally against the United States was time and an almost unending supply of military support from abroad, and neither of these was likely to be forthcoming for black American revolutionists in the BPM. Probably the most critical variable in the war—the fact that U.S. forces were fighting thousands of miles from home—clearly was not applicable to the BPM in the United States.[11]

At the root of the problem was that even BPM leaders who were war veterans, such as the NAACP's Robert Williams, Us's Ngao Damu, the RNA's Gaidi Obadele, and the BPP's Geronimo Pratt, were generally lower-ranking enlisted men, with the exception of Obadele, who was a junior (company-level) officer, and as a result they were mainly familiar with squad and/or platoon-level tactics, but rarely with company or battalion, much less brigade or division-level military operations. Therefore, their analyses were often tactical but rarely strategic, because they had little experience devising or conceptualizing higher-level operations. Moreover, they had very little sense of military doctrine, which is the fundamental orientation and guide to the actions of military forces in support of national objectives. At minimum, doctrine establishes whether a military is oriented toward the offense or the defense in achieving its national security objectives. The basic contradiction at the level of doctrine for BPM revolutionists is that they sought to organize an offensive operation, that is, a politico-military revolution, based on a defensive doctrine, namely, armed self-defense. For example, in his seminal essay asserting that a minority revolution in the United States could be successful, from which RAM derived its *offensive* strategy, Robert Williams characterized the proposed operations for this revolution as *defensive*, that is, as "defense," "effective self-defense," and "massive self-defense" (1964, pp. 6–7). Williams's defensive doctrine is evident in his stated objective that "advocate[d] self-defense for brutalized Afroamericans" but "d[id] not advocate the violent overthrow of the U.S. Government." He appreciated that "[i]f in the process of executing our Constitutional and God-given right of self-defense, the racist U.S. Government, which refuses to protect our people, is destroyed," then "the end result stems from certain historical factors of social relativity" (ibid., p. 7). He also recognized that even such defensive operations required much greater military organization and coordination than his example of Monroe, North Carolina, could provide. He stated:

> The lesson of Monroe teaches that effective self-defense, on the part of our brutally oppressed and terrorized people, requires massive organization with central coordination. External oppressive forces must not be allowed to relieve the besieged racist terrorists. The forces of the state must be kept under pressure in many places simultaneously. The white supremacy masses must be forced to retreat to their homes in order to give security to their individual families. (1964, p. 6)

Williams appreciated that such a coordinated and massive undertaking would need to appeal to black troops in the U.S. armed forces, but many of these potential assets were often derided by other BPM activists as Uncle Toms or tools of racist imperialists rather than as critical actors in the envisioned revolution that black power activists were contemplating.[12]

In addition, RAM's proposed "guerilla operations" were only a small part of an actual people's war strategy, which for Mao Zedong included a mix of guerrilla warfare and mobile warfare, the latter executed with conventional military forces (which black revolutionists did not possess).[10] Peoples' war in both Mao's and North Vietnam's conception and practice ended with a conventional military operation—which is also how the North Vietnamese attacked Saigon in the failed Easter Offensive of 1972 and the successful Spring Offensive of 1975. Largely inattentive to military doctrine, what BPM revolutionists proposed was basically a "holding action," which they imagined that a racially distinct semimilitary/paramilitary/civilian force comprising less than 5 percent of the U.S. population (a very generous estimate of adult black men and women who could actually provide manpower and logistical support for black revolutionists in the United States) would be able to effectively execute against U.S. regular and special operations armed forces fighting on their home territory for their survival against a racial outcaste whose human rights they had little compunction or hesitation about violating, and motivated to do so in short order. RAM's strategy was not only quixotic, it was hallucinogenic.

Unfortunately, such views were not uncommon among BPM theorists. In addition, the persistence of such views militated against the development of the protracted strategy that a study of the Slave Revolution during the U.S. Civil War suggested—one for which the United States was actually vulnerable in the black power era and remains so today. The fixation on militarization undermined the necessity to actually leverage black social-economic-political power in the sectors in which it was manifest, that is, those sectors of the U.S. polity and economy that were vulnerable to black collective action, and during the black power era such vulnerabilities were not manifest in the military sector—at least, not initially. As it had been during the U.S. Civil War, the white community would need to be set against itself and black insurgency such as a general strike or the more expansive Slave Revolution covered by, or entangled within, a broader division of the society, from which it could draw allies, support, or neutrality.

Notwithstanding these serious problems in their conceptions of the warfare that would occasion the revolution they envisioned, the failure to flesh out the connections between the slave revolts and the Civil War—and the social networks required to facilitate both—left RAM's analysis of political revolution divorced from an appreciation of the need for a cultural revolution, although the latter was historically implicated in the former. That is, the nexus between the slave revolts and the Civil War insurgency was the development of the social networks facilitated by the cultural institutions of black communities such as the "invisible institution," the Black Church, and the nascent socioeconomic networks of hired out-slaves, the incipient working-class consciousness (i.e., proletarianization) of slave labor, and the broader clandestine networks epitomized by the Underground Railroad. Without a parallel explication of these social forces in the black power era, RAM's thesis on cultural revolution was divorced from its strateagy for political revolution. Moreover, its conception of cultural revolution remained largely tied to a program focused on black aesthetics, black ethics, and aspects of black culture largely related to psychological orientations to extirpate (ironically, in RAM's lingo) the "slave mentality" of black Americans, and sartorial expressions representative of the same, more than on material aspects of black culture and the reorientation of black cultural institutions such as the Black Church.

RAM's thesis on black cultural revolution did not have as its focus a cultural thrust that directly implicated the U.S. politico-economy as it aimed to overthrow the cultural system of white supremacism in such a way as to facilitate political, economic, and racial democracy in the United States. This would have required a thesis of cultural revolution that associated it with political revolution, such as Locke had theorized and Du Bois historicized in *Black Reconstruction*. Although RAM argued that black political revolution would emanate from a cultural revolution, RAM didn't draw on these sources for its revolutionary theory. What was lost was not only the intellectual synthesis of these African American referents in a coherent theory of black cultural revolution in the United States during the BPM as an academic issue, but, given the influence of RAM and its members, associates, and supporters on so many BPM organizations, if RAM had been able to advance such a synthesis early in the BPM, then the point of departure for later BPM organizations might have been substantially different, not only in theory but in practice as well. In the event, RAM became the first major BPM organization after Malcolm X's OAAU to call for a black cultural revolution.

RAM's Thesis on Cultural Revolution

Stanford notes that since publication of the organization's internal document *Orientation to a Black Mass Movement* in 1962, RAM maintained that "the captive nation status of black America had bred a colonial mentality which must be wiped away through a cultural or social revolution" (Stanford, 1986, p. 154) whose purpose was "to destroy the conditioned white oppressive mores, attitudes, ways, customs, philosophies, habits, etc., which the oppressor has taught and trained us to have" and to replace them "on a mass scale" with "a new revolutionary culture" (ibid., p. 124). In 1964, RAM's position was consistent with those articulated at the Fisk conference in Nashville, which viewed black cultural revolution in terms of "re-Africanization," as a "repudiation of decadent materialist values and pathological egoism inherent in American society" and a concomitant embrace of "a humanism derived from the African heritage which exalts aesthetic, intellectual and spiritual development and communalism or cooperation rather than the exploitation of humanity" (Freeman, 1964, p. 18). They asserted that "Afro-Americans must know their authentic history in Africa and America in order to demolish the psychological rape of white American indoctrination." Further, they maintained that "[t]he Afro-American self-image must be revolutionized to foster a sense of collective ethnic identity as a unique Black People before Black Nationalism can emerge triumphant" (ibid., p. 18). These conceptualizations seem consistent with Malcolm's reverse civilizationism and all the theoretical and practical problems this foretold, but actually, under the simultaneous influence of Cruse, Moore, and Boggs, RAM did not conflate African American and African culture in a way that some later BPM revolutionists would (e.g., Us, the RNA, and initially CAP). While they consistently asserted the African origins of black American culture and history, they simultaneously argued the necessity of considering black American history, culture, politics, and economics on their own terms and in their unique American context. As a result, the process by which RAM's proposed black cultural revolution was to take place was not identical to that presumed to obtain in the African or broader third world colonial context but would be tailored to the demands of the black colony in the United States. Unfortunately, RAM's elucidation of the process of this revolution was not clear.

Stanford agrees that "the specifics of this cultural revolution were never adequately described," yet, "generally it would involve the destruction of the slave mentality and those classes and institutions which supported it" (1986, p. 154). "The slave culture," according to RAM, had created "a generation of 'freaks' who identified with a hip life style," which "transcended all classes and acted as a release valve for the sense of powerlessness that black people experienced. This hip society destroyed the cultural identity of blacks and distorted the roles of men and women" (ibid.). Thus, "as part of the black cultural revolution," RAM "worked with other groups to set up black cultural committees to spread 'revolutionary black culture' in the black community" (ibid., p. 125). By and large, RAM's initiatives were aimed at developing a popular movement among some of the more alienated segments of black society including students, gangs, intellectuals, and workers. On the whole, RAM considered black youth "as the most revolutionary sector of the black community because they had the most sustained resentment against the system and the highest level of frustration" (ibid., p. 156). RAM viewed youth "as the key to the revolution" and "part of the worldwide revolutionary forces, such as, those in Angola and the Congo, where the youth made up the majority of the troops" (ibid.). The militancy of black youth was attributed to their alienation within a capitalist political economy and their social isolation borne of the hegemony of white supremacist culture. RAM argued that

> the system has displaced them and exposed its contradictions to them. They have not yet been brain-washed. They are open [sic] to attack from all sectors of white society. They are victims of a contradiction between the black reality and the lies of white America. They recognize that the education they received is meaningless and that the system does not have enough jobs for them . . . black youth realize that they have no alternative "but to go to the streets." (ibid., p. 157)

The combination of bitterness and disappointment among black youth as well as their "freedom from the slave mentality" endows them with the greatest revolutionary potential. RAM divided youth between students and ghetto youths. The former group is potentially the black intelligentsia. The latter group, which they referred to as the "street force," figured prominently in Boggs's thesis on black political power. For RAM, "[T]he task of black revolutionaries is to give this purposeless army direction and to transform it into a 'blood brotherhood' which is committed to liberation by any means necessary" (1986, p. 158). Cultural revolution played an important role in this transformation.

Increasingly, the political revolution was viewed in Maoist terms, but RAM's conception of cultural revolution evolved independently of the cultural revolution that wreaked havoc throughout China beginning in 1966 (i.e., the Great Proletarian Cultural Revolution [GPCR]). 1966 was important in RAM's thesis not because of developments in China, but because, as RAM argued, the popularization of "black power" in 1966 initiated a cultural revolution among African Americans, which "reached mass proportions" by the following year. For Stanford (1971, p. 27), "The concept of black power challenged the whole value structure of the Negro community," forcing black people to confront their need for power to realize their objectives, while "challeng[ing] the pseudo-class structure of the middle class Negro society as black became the new and fashionable thing; it was now hip to be black." Black power also challenged the escapism of the hip society and "[b]y making 'black' popular, the values of black students," in particular, "began to slowly change and so did the values of all black America. This value, cultural revolution, is still in process."

Reflecting on these earlier developments in 1971, Stanford (1971, p. 29) observed that this "cultural revolution" had by then "affected the vast majority of Black America." Coupled with the "contradictions of the Vietnam War and the rise of unemployment among black youth," these developments were "rapidly affecting the African-American student" in particular, and as these "contradictions polarize[d]" them the student community was being transformed, generating broader changes in black communities as well (ibid.). Thus, for Stanford, black students were critical to this process, which was viewed as a harbinger of the democratic or bourgeois revolution in the United States. The latter view was buttressed by Mao's public endorsement of the black liberation struggle in the United States in 1963 and his association of it with democratic revolutions and national liberation struggles against imperialism occurring throughout the colonized world. Stanford went further and theorized that, as

> [i]n most nationalist revolutions the beginnings have come from student movements; students who are the potential petty national bourgeoisie of the colonialized nation who no longer

> seek integration with the mother [colonial] country, but begin to demand independence, national autonomy, and formation of a nation-state. (ibid., pp. 28–29)

He noted that "[t]his has not happened yet with the black student movement because [it] is still in the transitional stage. But as the cultural revolution and students become more politically sophisticated, the question of an independent black nation-state will become a popular demand" (1971, p. 29).

Black college students, Stanford argued, were critical given that they represented "the more educated class of an oppressed nation" and therefore, "sociologically" they constituted "the potential colonial bourgeoisie" and, "like colonial bourgeoisies of all oppressed nations," realized that "their class interests cannot be fulfilled under the colonial regime." Similarly, given that "America is a racist capitalistic society," then "it cannot absorb all black students as a class into its economic system because its system is built on racial and economic exploitation" (1971, p. 27). Furthermore, unlike black workers, whom RAM viewed as more of a "captive" or "a super-exploited, wage slave," while "still a slave," with the conditions of servitude "remain[ing] almost the same" and "[o]nly the name of slavery" changed (ibid.), black students were "an educated class" that "have traditionally had 'higher expectations' from the system than most black captives" (ibid., p. 28). Nevertheless,

> as the struggle intensifies and more and more black students become alienated from the system . . . black students will transform as a class; from being a bourgeois assimilationist, alienated elite to becoming a revolutionary nationalist intelligentsia for the movement, developing a vanguard on the road to independent nationhood. (ibid.)

The "upsurge of black awareness" was transforming black students in what approximated "a cultural revolution that [was] first affecting the colonial alienated elite or petty bourgeoisie who, through a process of re-orientation and re-organization, will develop into a revolutionary nationalist intelligentsia which will play a significant role in the road to independent nationhood in our democratic revolution" (ibid.). In this way, the black cultural revolution was stimulating an emergent black politico-military revolution whose roots RAM had argued were evident in the revolts of the "Long Hot Summers" that had begun in earnest in Watts in 1965. RAM's view that a black cultural revolution was a precursor rather than a concomitant of a black political revolution would be the dominant pattern adopted by most black nationalist revolutionists of the era—and one that supported Malcolm X's and Cruse's rather than Boggs's or Haywood's theses on this relationship.

While lauding the revolutionary developments of black college students, Stanford saw the cultural revolution among black high school and junior high school students as having "more far reaching ramifications than in the black college community," because the younger students were "directly tied to the community" and "[n]inety per cent of them will be the future black workers, fathers, and mothers of Black America; the generation yet to come" (1971, p. 29). Revolutionists were enjoined to train these black youths in "revolutionary-nationalist theory, practice, and organization" if the revolution RAM foresaw was to "grow and continue" (ibid.). Only then would the "black revolution . . . become an inter-generational revolution" with "its new cultural dynamic producing the cultural values of the next generation." (ibid.). He insisted that *"[t]he cultural revolution is a revolution of values that can be transmitted from this youth generation to the adult generation, closing 'the generation gap,'"* but, he admonished, *"Black youth must begin to structure themselves as a nation; be active in forming black community government,* parties, and functioning as part of the black liberation army" (ibid., p. 30; original emphasis). In such a context, for example, RAM argued that "[t]he struggle for community control of schools is therefore a struggle to nationalize schools in the black community" (ibid., p. 29). Moreover, "[i]n order to make education relevant to black folks, schools must become black nationalist training centers. Education for black children must be black nationalist education, a black nationalization of the educational system. This is what black studies mean to black students" (ibid.). He continued:

> The role of black youth in the cultural revolution is to serve as agitators, re-educators, organizers, and unifiers in the struggle for independent black nationhood. The black college student can play a very constructive role in the cultural revolution. In his struggle for black studies, he should strive to make the college or university (if on a black campus) into a community center, with all the facilities of the college open to the community free of charge. He must encourage local community groups to come on campus and participate in school programs. (ibid., p. 30)

Given their centrality as the locus upon which the black petit bourgeoisie would transform its revolutionary objectives—committing "class suicide," in Amilcar Cabral's (1972) terms—black students were key to the cultural revolution that Stanford foresaw. Cabral (1972, p. 110) argued that the challenge of petit bourgeois leaders in the national liberation struggle was "committing suicide as a class in order to be reborn as revolutionary workers, completely identified with the deepest aspirations of the people to which they belong." Thus, it was important to wed these newly committed revolutionists to the main source of potential revolutionary power in black communities: black workers. As participation in the CRM was convincing some integrationists that the transformation they sought would be achieved through "black power," RAM was emphasizing that "Black people have more power than we realize, but what hinders us from having power is our lack of organization." Black workers especially, but not only the black industrial proletariat, were among the most disciplined and organized elements in black communities—and possibly the most aggrieved. Stanford was clear that "black workers," constituting "90 per cent of our people, are the base of our people's movement." "Therefore," he insisted, "the key question for black youth, students, and revolutionaries is the organization, coordination, and unity of black workers." Thus, for Stanford, black students were obligated to align with black workers to facilitate their organization into a unified, coordinated, and central constituency in the black liberation struggle. He stated that "one of the organizational goals of black youth" is to support and help coordinate the organized efforts of black workers, such that "[i]f black workers should go on a national strike, all of America would be dislocated." That is, black students should assist in a "National Black Strike" (1971, p. 31). In this analysis Stanford linked the transformation of one of the most important elements of the cultural apparatus, schools (from high school to college level), through the advancing of cultural claims of black students (e.g., Black Studies, independent black schools, black representation in school administration, black teachers/workers), to the politico-economic claims of black workers in a coordinated national general strike. In this conception, Stanford had come closest to capturing the magnitude of Du Bois's General Strike and, in so doing, appreciating the importance of asserting cultural claims that ramify to political and economic domains, as suggested by the Du Boisian-Lockean synthesis of the relationship between black cultural and political revolution in the United States. Stanford's insight was accomplished in part by focusing on an important element of the cultural apparatus (i.e., the public education system), as Cruse suggested, and by focusing less on the military aspects of revolutionary change in the United States. Unfortunately, Stanford did not flesh out the implications of this insight; and within a year he proffered a ten-point program for an "African Peoples Party" among black Americans that did not mention "cultural revolution" (Stanford, 1972).

Although these formulations reflect significant aspects of Stanford's intellectual development with respect to black cultural revolution in the decade from 1962–1971, clearly, they emerged in conversation with other revolutionists of the era; thus, it is not, technically, an assessment of RAM's views/positions on the subject as an organization, given that under the repression of U.S. government and local police agencies in the COINTELPRO, RAM had become defunct as an organization by 1969. By that year, most of RAM's leadership and broader membership had joined other BPM organizations, including Stanford who had become Minister without Portfolio/ Special Ambassador in the RNA and a key supporter of the LRBW. In fact, it probably was owing more to his experiences with the Dodge Revolutionary Union Movement (DRUM, the precursor of the LRBW) and the LRBW that he developed his arguments linking black cultural revolution among students to the initiatives of black workers. This speculation is informed by the absence of such a linkage in RAM's arguments on black cultural revolution prior to the establishment of DRUM (e.g., they are absent from RAM's *World Black Revolution*).

In addition, although it had been among the first BPM organizations to consider black cultural revolution as an objective (in 1962 in its internal documents, and publicly by 1964), throughout the 1960s RAM did not have a program for cultural revolution as such, nor a theory of how to effectuate it. For example, although Cruse saw the educational system as part of the cultural apparatus, RAM did not explicitly link its focus on students—or even the supposed cultural revolution among blacks on college campuses that Stanford asserted in 1971—to the seizure of the cultural apparatus, or flesh out how such a seizure could be related to the overthrow of the cultural system of the United States in accordance with Cruse's thesis. Further, although it recognized the significance of a general strike strategy, it didn't wed it sufficiently to its antecedents in Du Bois, nor did it associate it with the demand for reparations, opting instead to find its value only in the disruption of U.S. society to facilitate an ill-advised and poorly conceived "people's war." Thus, although RAM, as an organization, realized the importance of black cultural revolution in its broader thesis—and its view of culture, ultimately, did not suffer from the reverse civilizationism of Malcolm's framework, it failed to synthesize a coherent theory or program for black cultural revolution in the United States. Unlike what it offered in its analysis of political revolution, with respect to cultural revolution, RAM's perspective was prescriptive or descriptive, but insufficiently analytical. As the first major organization of the BPM to attempt to develop Malcolm's incomplete thesis of black cultural revolution, or Cruse's, it is not surprising that RAM encountered difficulties in working out a theory of same.

For both political and cultural revolutions, many revolutionists of the BPM provided analyses that were not well grounded historically even in U.S.

history but often amounted to revolutionary "wish lists" and theses rooted in accumulated non sequiturs that proposed some anodyne outcomes resulting from often oversimplified processes or imagined concerted actions on the part of black Americans. Nonetheless, these non sequiturs often were treated as axiomatic, making revolution as inevitable to BPM revolutionists as the Book of Revelations makes the Apocalypse for Christians. RAM suffered from this in its view that a revolutionary insurgency could be successful in the United States after ninety days, but it also was more attentive to the contributions of black American forerunners to its revolutionary practices than many of its BPM successors, even as it remained vigilant to developments among revolutionary movements abroad. But the challenge of synthesizing a thesis and practice of black cultural revolution was something that RAM did not accomplish in its short existence, and this problem of synthesis was not limited to that issue alone. For example, given the tutelage of Queen Mother Moore to RAM's core leadership, the organization did not incorporate a reparations strategy into its initial 12 Point platform; it was only added in 1967, just a year before the organization ended (Stanford, 1986, p. 165).

RAM's approach to black cultural revolution in the 1960s was geared to removing what it saw as the psychological dysfunctions that white supremacism had imposed on black political thought and practice. Black culture would eventually be seen as an instrument to facilitate power more directly through its ability to unify the "black nation," in a pan-Africanism that linked it to liberation struggles in Africa and the remaining "Bandung world." But more often, an appreciation of black culture was tied to the militarization of the BPM in the United States and less to the coordination of the major indigenous cultural institutions in black communities, chief among them—even more so after the major legal victories of the CRM—the Black Church. Although RAM was amenable to working with revolutionary, progressive, and even some liberal church leaders (and church members), its association with the Black Church was more incidental than intentional.

RAM's engagement with sexism, the other major cultural phenomenon in black communities undermining its transformational capacity, was also poor and peripheral. According to Stanford, "as part of the black cultural revolution, RAM attempted to organize a revolutionary black women's movement . . . in the black community"; however, for the most part, to the extent that it engaged issues of sexism and gender, RAM's approach was at best ambivalent, and more accurately dismissive. On a theoretical level, RAM subsumed black women as a group within the "subproletariat," a large and theoretically unwieldy agglomeration that conflated the proletariat and lumpenproletariat in one class distinguishable from the bourgeoisie. At another point, Stanford notes that RAM was inattentive to "differences in patterns of employment and/or alienation among black women" (Stanford, 1986, p. 159). This left RAM unprepared to address sexism in its organization and in the cultural revolution it sought to develop, much less in the "new society" that it hoped to construct.

While RAM's failure to develop a coherent theory or program of black cultural revolution undermined its political development, despite its avowed Maoist outlook, by not subsuming its own cultural revolution under that of Mao's GPCR it may have spared itself the purges, excommunications, and paroxysms of violence that attended the GPCR and which a closer proximity to Mao's theory and practice might have encouraged within RAM. Such intellectual distancing may have helped RAM to avoid the internecine conflicts that disrupted the other major Maoist national organization in the United States, the BPP, as well as a range of White Left organizations that fought and harassed each other on the basis of their allegiance to the varying positions adopted by the Chinese leader some seven thousand miles away. Nevertheless, RAM laid out the broad parameters of subsequent black cultural revolutionary theses of the black power era. Further, its trajectory from black nationalism to Maoism would not only anticipate the ideological trajectory of the much more famous BPP, but its debate regarding underground and aboveground activism anticipated similar debates in the BPP as well, with the latter taking a much different direction. In addition, although the BPP is much better known, it was RAM that was the first major black nationalist organization of the BPM that converted its ideology from black nationalism to Maoism. One major difference is that where RAM emphasized culture in the revolutionary process, the BPP largely downplayed, ignored, or, at times, even denigrated the role of culture in black liberation.

Ironically, the BPP's aversion to cultural revolution and cultural nationalism, as a whole, derived largely from the negative experiences of its co-founders, Bobby Seale and Huey Newton, with the RAM members they encountered in Oakland, notwithstanding that they had been associated with the RAM-affiliated Afro-American Association (AAA) in the Bay Area. Bobby Seale, more than Huey Newton, had an almost visceral disdain for the RAM members he had organized with in the AAA and later the Soul Students Advisory Council. Newton similarly denigrated RAM members as political opportunists who were not interested in "laying it on the line" and engaging in confrontational struggles with police officers in Oakland. The BPP's disdain for cultural revolution, as we'll discuss below, was reinforced by its feud with the Us organization in Los Angeles—ironically, Newton and Maulana Karenga were both members of the AAA in California, one in the Bay Area and the other in L.A. Interestingly, even within the BPP, a fissure emerged between Oakland and New York BPP chapters, which although rooted in several prominent internecine disputes between Newton and Eldridge Cleaver, was also influenced by the fact that many of the prominent members of the New York chapter had been tutored by former RAM and OAAU member, and associate of Malcolm X, Herman Ferguson, with whom they shared a considerable affinity. In fact, the antagonism between the chapters was expressed in part in Oakland's disdain for what it viewed as elements of "cultural nationalism," a term and orientation that was anathema to the BPP, among New York chapter members evident in the latters' adoption of African names, on one level, and some of their programmatic initiatives, on another, including New York chapter collaboration with RAM, which was headquartered in nearby Philadelphia.

RAM members and affiliates played important roles in almost all of the major BPM organizations including Us, the BPP, the RNA, CAP, the LBRW, and the PAOCC (as well as SNCC and CORE in their black power phases). Building on Malcolm's, Cruse's, and the Boggses' theoretical work, RAM confronted some of the most important issues related to black revolution in the BPM. Although RAM did not survive the 1960s as an organization, its chief ideologue, Max Stanford (Muhammad Ahmad), remained influential through his involvement in several BPM organizations. Ahmad built on RAM's earlier arguments and developed them throughout the BPM, including its thesis on black cultural revolution. Although it came first, RAM's thesis would not be the most popular treatment of black cultural revolution in the United States during the BPM; instead, that distinction fell to a Los Angeles organization that had come to prominence following the Watts revolt of 1965, whose members had worked with RAM affiliates in California: Us.

The Kawaida Organizations I: Us

Among organizations that advocated black cultural revolution in the BPM, none promoted it more assiduously than Us (as opposed to "them"), which arose from the Watts revolt in Los Angeles in 1965. As noted above, Us's co-founder and chairman, Maulana Karenga, had been affiliated with the AAA of Donald Warden, heading its chapter in Los Angeles. According to Brown (2003), Us was organized by several black men and women who called themselves the Circle of Seven and met regularly at a black owned bookstore in Los Angeles, including Maulana Karenga, Hakim Jamal, Dorothy Jamal, Tommy Jacquette (Halifu), Karl Key (Hekima), Ken Seaton (Msemaji), Samuel Carr (Ngao Damu), Sanamu Nyeusi, and Brenda Haiba Karenga. While Hakim Jamal, who had been a close associate of Malcolm X through both his pre- and post-NOI days (and was related to him by marriage), was originally listed as the founder of the organization, the leadership eventually fell on its chairman and chief ideologue Maulana Karenga (ibid., p. 38). Karenga helped formulate and popularize kawaida, the theoretical framework of Us, which emphasized the importance of culture in African American liberation and, most importantly for our analysis, from the organization's inception it argued the necessity of black cultural revolution in the United States.

Most were introduced to kawaida through a collection of Karenga's statements edited by two Us members, Clyde Halisi and James Mtume, in a pamphlet, *The Quotable Karenga*. In it, the editors shared Karenga's ideas on black nationalism and black cultural revolution. He argued that black society "may be American, but our values must be Afro-American," and "Black values can only come through a black culture" (Halisi & Mtume, 1967, p. 6). He noted that culture provides "identity, purpose and direction" (ibid.). He viewed it as "the basis of all ideas, images and actions," such that "to move is to move culturally, i.e., by a set of values given to you by your culture" (ibid., p. 7). Karenga outlined seven major components of culture: mythology; history; social, political, and economic organization; creative motif; and ethos (ibid.). An emphasis on culture, for Karenga, was rooted in his view that "Black people don't have a culture" (ibid.). He was emphatic that "the 'Negroes' main problem in America is that he suffers from a lack of culture." Given that culture "tells you who you are, what you must do, and how you can do it" (ibid., p. 6), then, since blacks had only "elements of a culture," it followed for Karenga that "[w]e must free ourselves culturally before we succeed politically" (ibid., p. 7).

According to Karenga, "culture provides the bases for revolution and recovery" (Halisi & Mtume, 1967, p. 7), and he saw Us as "a cultural organization dedicated to the creation, recreation and circulation of Afro-American culture" (ibid.). Like RAM, but unlike many of the major BPM organizations, Us was not a mass-based group but a cadre organization, whose objective was to "organize the organizers" around the principles, practices, and priorities of kawaida. Membership in Us required a period of catechism, apprenticeship, and lifestyle change whose analogue in the BPM with respect to the extent of indoctrination and training (or transformation) required of prospective members was probably closest of that of the NOI or the Pan-African Orthodox Christian Church (PAOCC). Like Malcolm, Us saw the need for personal transformation as a precursor and then co-evolving concomitant of social transformation and, ultimately, cultural revolution.

Karenga saw "the revolution" being fought in the United States in the mid-'60s as "a revolution to win the minds of our people," to which he noted, "If we fail to win this we cannot wage the violent one" (ibid., p. 9).

It followed, for him, that "you must have a cultural revolution before the violent revolution" because "the cultural revolution gives identity, purpose and direction" (ibid., p. 11). Thus, in this aspect Karenga's thesis was consistent with Cruse's, Malcolm X's, and RAM's argument that the cultural and political revolutions were consecutive, rather than Boggs's view that they were coincidental, or a view that they could be either. Significantly, it was consistent with the association between cultural and political revolution in the United States as historicized by Du Bois and theorized by Locke; however, it was dramatically different from the Du Bois-Locke theses, as well, given its reverse civilizationist assumptions of black American cultural inferiority relative to Africa. Further, convinced that black Americans had no culture, Karenga encouraged them to assume a communal, rural African culture to guide the twentieth-century revolution of a cosmopolitan, urban African American population in the most technologically advanced and militarily powerful country in the world. This was more than reverse civilizationism; it was cultural atavism.

This perspective led Us to create and promote a panoply of precepts, practices, and programs given an African cultural gloss, drawing superficially from Zulu, Swahili, and Gikuyu and fused into an original synthesis called kawaida, which formed the philosophical core of Us, and a range of rituals epitomized in Us's widely celebrated alternative to Christmas, Kwanzaa. With respect to Kwanzaa, Karenga stated: "If we ask people not to celebrate Christmas . . . we must be prepared to give them an alternative . . . [s]o . . . we . . . found a Zulu custom [the Zulu harvest festival, *Umkosi*] where people came together to celebrate for about a week around the first of the year" (Brown, 2003, pp. 69–70). The linchpin of kawaida is the *nguzo saba* (i.e., the seven principles of Blackness, and later the seven principles of kawaida), which Karenga conceived as core values of the aspirational national character of black Americans he envisioned. These were typically presented in English next to their Kiswahili equivalents, as Us attempted to promote the East African language as a lingua franca for the BPM: *umoja*/unity, *kujichagulia*/self-determination, *ujima*/collective work and responsibility, *ujamaa*/cooperative economics, *nia*/purpose, *kuumba*/creativity, *imani*/faith—these seven principles comprise the seven days of Kwanzaa, which has become the most widely celebrated holiday from the black power era and the most enduring cultural festival, observed regularly by millions of African Americans (and diasporic Africans, more broadly). The *nguzo saba* also became the key cultural framework of a range of BPM organizations and was even adopted by integrationist groups. In the BPM, it was "the basis for the cultural grounding and value orientation of many independent schools, rites of passage programs, cooperatives, and various other community and professional organizations and programs" ranging from

Black United Fronts like the Black Congress in Los Angeles; the Black Federation in San Diego; Committee for a Unified Newark; the Congress of African Peoples and the National Black [Political] Assembly and provided the theoretical framework which shaped the three national Black Power Conferences in the 60's. (Karenga, 2002, p. 195)

Brown (2003, p. 132) notes that "the arts were a most effective outlet for the introduction of [Us's] alternative Black culture to African American audiences." This was evident in its aesthetic contributions in fashion, dance, music, woodcarving, and literature; one of the major conduits for this cultural transmission was its celebrated Taifa Dance Troupe, which was tutored by South African singer Letta Mbulu and musician-composer Caiphus Semanya, who were political exiles from the apartheid regime. The Taifa Troupe learned some South African traditional music and dance, predominantly Zulu, including a rain dance and the miners' boot dance. Us members modified these traditional dances in their performances, and other members, James Mtume, Charles Sigidi and George Subira among them, provided musical accompaniment. Brown maintains that the Taifa troupe "was one of the most effective recruiting mechanisms for US, performing at festivals, high schools, conferences, and rallies throughout Southern California and beyond" (ibid., p. 135).[13] In fact, "A large portion of US members' initial fascination with the organization came from watching the colorful movements and chanting voices of Taifa," which contributed to Karenga's claim that Us represented "the first time that Blacks have gotten together to create a new culture based on revolution and recovery" (ibid., p. 136).

The latter point reflected Karenga's detachment from African American history and especially that of the antebellum era in which blacks drew from "slave culture" to organize and execute resistance, revolt, and finally, revolution. "Slave culture" was the "new culture" that blacks created in the United States and from it compelled their revolutionary initiatives (Stuckey, 1987). Karenga's erroneous claims derive from his reverse civilizationism, which viewed black Americans as cultureless people and suggested to him that Us's projections of "traditional" African culture during the BPM were the first genuine cultural expressions that black Americans had produced. This was a historical and theoretical deficiency in Karenga's kawaida that had repercussions for the application of Us's program, as well.

Nevertheless, it was a testament to the organizational acumen of Us's leadership, the dedicated work of its membership, and the intellectual acuity of Karenga himself that even with their dubious provenance as *African* traditions and practices, the thirst of African Americans for a renewed cultural thrust led to the adoption of many of Us's cultural expressions, such as Swahili as a sort of lingua franca, the adoption of Swahili names, and the prominence of the *nguzo saba* and Kwanzaa as enduring elements of the BPM that remain influential more than a half-century later. During the BPM, Us wedded these cultural factors to institutional structures that provided an organizational basis for both black protest and black political development. Us was central to most of the major black power initiatives in post–Watts revolt Los Angeles, ranging from the "community alert patrol" (CAP) of police (these began in 1965, before the BPP in Oakland was founded in 1966, and CAP's executive director was founding Us member Tommy (Halifu) Jacquette)[14], to an abortive attempt to separate Watts as an independent municipality from Los Angeles (i.e., Freedom City), to the struggle to develop united front efforts among various black power and civil rights groups on sundry issues affecting black communities. The latter efforts would catapult Karenga and Us into the center of organizing for the black power conferences of the late 1960s; and just as significantly, the electoral strategies that would be adopted by the Us-affiliated group Committee for a Unified Newark (CFUN), headed by Imamu Amiri Baraka, whose title "Imamu" was a rank in the Us organization that Karenga had bestowed on him (as will be seen in the next chapter, Us played an important role in Baraka's successful electoral strategies in Newark, New Jersey). To be sure, Karenga's orientation may have been cast on a distant African past, but his program was as current and even future-oriented as any of the major BPM organizations, and he saw both Us and the various united front initiatives as both a continuation of Malcolm's programs in the OAAU and a contribution to the realization of Malcolm's proposed black cultural revolution.

Karenga's hypothesized cultural revolution both converged with and diverged from Cruse's. Although Karenga's focus on the importance of culture in social change resonated with Cruse's thesis, his perspective was also symptomatic of those Cruse rejected. For example, Cruse, like Du Bois and Locke, was convinced that African American national culture was rooted in black folk culture, expressed through the sorrow songs, spirituals, and the music, art, and literature they inspired, which endured in the working-class urban culture of the black masses in the cities and was the only unambiguously American aesthetic culture. Their perspective was diametrically opposed to Karenga's conceptualization of black American culture as grounded in a communal, seemingly feudal African culture. Relatedly, Karenga's perspective on cultural revolution was less advanced than that proffered by RAM insofar as it was not only reverse civilizationist, it asserted that black Americans did not possess a culture. As a result, it maintained that black Americans needed to adopt African cultural practices and it appropriated an amalgam of feudalistic customs derived from myriad real and imagined African sources that Karenga constructed as "traditional" African culture, or what he would later claim as the "best" of African culture, which is bombast for Karenga in that even the major African culture groups number in the hundreds and one would need to study all of them to conclude which was the "best," which he clearly had not. In fact, Karenga's construction of African culture was only slightly less backwards than his conception of black American culture.

Karenga argued that black American culture would have to be created through the development of parallel cultural practices and institutions in black communities to replace white supremacist ones and imbue them with a revolutionary orientation, represented by kawaida; thus, it was essential to train cadres committed to this purpose. An important aspect of this orientation was the creation and promotion of alternative/competing cultural rituals and practices such as Kwanzaa, which led him to promote the view that culture—and black art in particular—had to perform a revolutionary function in order to be "valid." The latter reflected Karenga's view that art should serve as propaganda. He opined that "[a]rt for art's sake is an invalid concept," because "all art reflects the value system from which it comes" (Halisi & Mtume, 1967, p. 22). The "art as propaganda" frame wedded Karenga's thesis of cultural change to a static teleology, ultimately requiring that the motive force in Karenga's cultural revolutionary thesis derive from factors extrinsic to black culture itself (i.e., from outside of black cultural institutions), rather than intrinsic to it (i.e., from within black cultural institutions). Further, that Karenga and many other BAM participants took this position while seemingly oblivious to the earlier debate between Du Bois and Locke along similar lines was testament to their failure to adequately address the historical and theoretical roots of BAM in the Harlem Renaissance around such a central issue of black cultural change even as they were attempting to effect such change in their movement. The latter not only constituted a problem of the reverse civilizationism of Karenga's thesis, which was replicated among other prominent BAM figures, but also revealed that Karenga extended Malcolm's reverse civilizationism even farther backward in time. Where Malcolm argued that contemporary African revolutionaries had outpaced their black American brothers and sisters with respect to both their adherence to their cultures and their practical application of them in pursuit of their liberation, Karenga drew less from current African cultural forms and practices and, instead, constructed from an almost feudalistic precolonial imaginary a monolithic "traditional" African culture that he then attempted to retrofit to black America. Such a view retrograded Malcolm's reverse civilizationism into cultural atavism.

Convinced that blacks had no real culture, Karenga insisted that art serve as propaganda for revolutionary change. He asserted that "Black Art must be for the people, by the people and from the people . . . it must be functional, collective and committing" (Halisi & Mtume, 1967, p. 22). He emphasized that "all art must reflect and support the Black Revolution and concluded that any art that does not discuss and contribute to the revolution is invalid" (Karenga 1968, p. 5). For Karenga, "Black art must expose the enemy, praise the people, and support the revolution," because "the real function of art is to make revolution, using its own medium" (ibid., p. 6). He held out blues music as one example of "invalid" art (ibid., p. 9). The blues were "invalid," according to Karenga, because "they teach resignation, in a word, acceptance of reality—and we have come to change reality" (ibid.). For him, the blues "were locked into a discourse of suffering and oppression, rendering it incapable of inspiring revolutionary change" (Brown, 2003, p. 145). Karenga acknowledged the blues as "a very beautiful, musical and psychological achievement of our people," nevertheless, he insisted that "today they are not functional because they do not commit us to the struggle of today and tomorrow, but keep us in the past" (1968., p. 9). He argued that the present generation refused to "submit to the resignation of our fathers who lost their money, their women, and their lives and sat around wondering, 'what did they do to be so black and blue?'" (ibid.).

While some influential artists of BAM such as Nikki Giovanni (1969, p. 30) agreed with Karenga that the blues were "counterrevolutionary," others, including Larry Neal and Amiri Baraka, rejected their view. Neal had conceptualized the BAM as "the aesthetic and spiritual sister of the Black Power concept," which was "radically opposed to any concept of the artist that alienates him from his community," instead "envision[ing] an art that speaks directly to the needs and aspirations of black America," and one that "proposes a radical reordering of the Western cultural aesthetic" (Neal, 1989). He appreciated the propagandistic role of black art; however, he did not accept "protest" art, sensing as he did that it aspired to a white standard that presumably necessitated critique (1989, pp. 63–64).[15] He recognized the contribution of Baraka's BARTS, as well as groups on the West Coast, Detroit, Philadelphia, Jersey City, New Orleans, Washington D.C., and various college campuses, and he acknowledged Karenga's contribution to BAM, noting that "Karenga welded the Black Arts Movement into a cohesive cultural ideology," and one in which culture is "the most important element in the struggle for self-determination" (ibid., pp. 67–68). Yet, he challenged Karenga's dismissal of the blues, arguing that "the blues represent the ex-slave's confrontation with a more secular evaluation of the world," and he was emphatic that "[t]hey were shaped in the context of social and political oppression, but they do *not*, as Maulana Karenga said, *collectively* 'teach resignation'" (ibid., pp. 107–108). He adds, "[t]o hear the blues in this manner is to totally misunderstand the essential function of the blues, because the blues are basically defiant in their attitude toward life" (ibid., p. 108). Baraka's (1963) *Blues People* had earlier demonstrated the vitality and multidimensionality of blues music and its contribution to black aesthetics.

Karenga (1993, p. 407) would later admit that he had been wrong in his denunciation of the transformative capacity of the blues, stating that "[i]n an earlier article on Black art, I criticized blues as being essentially focused on resignation, but as my critics have rightly observed, blues is much more multidimensional than that"; however, his rejection of the blues was symptomatic of his misunderstanding of black culture in the United States—especially the culture of the black industrial working class, which was in evidence no later than the Harlem Renaissance. Karenga, like Baraka and many others in BAM, had, as Harold Cruse (1967) would remind them, only a rudimentary appreciation of the rootedness of BAM in the theoretic, artistic, and formulaic expressions of the Harlem Renaissance. To be sure, many BAM artists seemed to view the Harlem Renaissance as a localized episode of black cultural "flowering" that was too beholden to the aesthetic ideals and aspirations of their white patrons. For example, Baraka (1963, pp. 133–137) viewed the Harlem Renaissance primarily in terms of the motivations of the respective "cultural stratum" of the black community. No less troubling, after recognizing that "there is already in existence the basis for . . . a [black] aesthetic" that "[e]ssentially, consists of an African-American cultural tradition"—presumably manifest in works including those of the Harlem Renaissance—Larry Neal (1989, p. 64) then argues that "[t]he new aesthetic is mostly predicated on an ethics which asks the question: Whose vision of the world is finally meaningful, ours or the white oppressors? What is truth? . . . [W]hose truth shall we express, that of the oppressed or of the oppressors?" He then asserts—in utter disregard of previous black intellectual engagement of these issues—that "Black intellectuals of previous decades *failed to ask them*" (emphasis added).

That Neal was one of the more talented, reasoned, and historically grounded of BAM participants suggests the level of unfamiliarity of many in the movement with fundamental issues and arguments raised by Du Bois and Locke, among others, regarding black culture and black cultural revolution that they were attempting to engage. Dismissing the relevance of the Harlem Renaissance to their understanding of cultural transformation, instead they drew on later tendencies associated with Robeson, Negritude, and culminating in the reverse civilizationist arguments of the postwar era. Seen in this context, Karenga fails to appreciate the "validity" of the blues because he is largely at odds with black folk culture and its twentieth-century urban working-class expression in music—concepts that both Du Bois and Locke (among many others) readily acknowledged more than a half-century before. What is more, even as Karenga focused on African cultures, he seemed inclined in theory and practice to view the diverse cultures of the African continent—comprising more than forty different independent states at the time—as a single homogenized "African" culture ossified in a "traditional" construct of his own imagining. For some reason, his thesis rejected the urbanized culture of postcolonial Africa, which was already in evidence at the time in cities from Nairobi to Accra. Karenga opted instead for an idealized, ritualized version of precolonial "traditional" African culture of the "village" to serve as a frame for the new black culture that would lead mid-twentieth-century black Americans to cultural revolution in the most urbanized, industrialized, and technologically advanced country in the world.

Karenga's thesis on cultural revolution focused on his conception of national culture, which he later described in *Kawaida Theory* (1980, pp. 18–19) as "the self-conscious, collective thought and practice thru [*sic*] which a people creates itself, celebrates itself and introduces itself to history and humanity." In this later formulation he attempted a further differentiation between national culture, which had been his primary focus in his BPM theses, and popular culture, which he suggests was the "unconscious, fluid reaction to everyday life and environment." Karenga maintained that the imposition of European American culture—especially its white supremacist aspects—serves to legitimize the oppression of African Americans. Further, he insisted that white American cultural imposition denigrates black Americans, who, in this post-BPM version of kawaida, have only the "elements" of a national culture, and primarily a faddish popular culture that does not serve black interests (Karenga, 1988, p. 211). So, altering Cruse's thesis of cultural revolution, which for Cruse was rooted in African American culture, national and popular, derived from African American folk traditions and later cosmopolitan expressions, as it had been for Du Bois and Locke, even decades after the BPM, Karenga insisted that African Americans do not have a national culture to speak of. Karenga had even less use for African American popular culture, which he largely denigrated—in another contrast with Cruse, Du Bois, and Locke—and instead relied on his "tradition"-based African culture, retrofitted to black Americans.

Not surprisingly, during the BPM, when he even more emphatically insisted that black Americans did not possess a culture, he set out to create one from disparate practices he labeled "African tradition." From this tradition, Karenga sought to create an African American national culture to serve as a change agent for black America—including a new religion, which was how he characterized kawaida during the BPM. For example, Brown (2003, p. 35) reports an interview with Karenga at KTLA in January 1971 in which the Us leader stated: "I'm the founder of a religion called *Kawaida* . . . it's based on seven principles." Later, as Karenga and Us turned their focus on African culture to Ancient Egypt, he secularized kawaida (1994, pp. 129, 163) and then promoted Maat as a religion (see Karenga, 1994). During the BPM, Karenga joined other BPM revolutionists in dismissing Christianity as a "white man's religion" (Halisi & Mtume, 1967, p. 32).

Us attempted to develop a new black national culture utilizing appeals to black popular culture especially in music, dance, literature, and crafts. One of the most successful expressions of this cultural fusion was the aforementioned Taifa Dance Troupe, but its "ability to function as a platform for the cultural revolution depended on a receptive African American community and access to public space, both of which were in abundance at the peak of the troupe's prominence from late 1967 until early 1969" (Brown, 2003, 136). This receptivity and access to public space would end with the Us-Panther shootout at UCLA and the resultant militarization of Us, its preoccupation with security for Karenga and other members, and increased government repression, all of which ended most of Us's broader community-oriented cultural activities. Complicating this further, given that Us was unpersuaded, at best, by the revolutionary relevance of black working-class urban culture, Us missed the practical opportunities provided by its base in Los Angeles to expand its access to public space through the arts—in particular, its established forte in black dance—and link to local programs in the L.A. media hub that drew on black popular culture. One such local program with national appeal was Don Cornelius's *Soul Train* dance show, which was syndicated to L.A. from Chicago in 1971 and had its operations there. The potential influence of a black nationalist organization that focused on cultural revolution, linked with an emergent influential major media show focused on black youth, should have been obvious to black nationalists in L.A., especially given the huge success of *WattStax*, the record album and documentary film celebrating the Watts revolt, and the annual Watts Summer Festival founded in 1966 by Us charter member Tommy Jacquette (Halifu). Karenga's reverse civilizationism and the promotion of kawaida made such links between Us and major media in this way largely unthinkable; in fact, while promoting African dance among African Americans, Karenga disparaged the "Negro" who "has more records than books and is dancing his life away" (Halisi & Mtume, 1967, 3). So, as Us members did the boot dance in the Taifa troupe and recruited heavily based on its appeal to African culture, blacks from throughout L.A. were doing the "push and pull," the "breakdown," and the "penguin"—popular dances circulating throughout black America at the time—a few miles away in the L.A. studios of the nationally televised popular black dance show. It is ironic that Us, which was so focused on black culture, did not utilize—and in fact distanced itself from—actual expressions and institutions focused on black popular culture evident in most black communities in the major cities during the BPM. That Us encouraged dancing as an artistic and individual expression for its members makes its failure to connect to popular media such as *Soul Train* in Los Angeles so glaring. By the time that Us began to undertake such a popular focus, largely on James Mtume's initiatives the opportunity had been lost, because the BPM and Us were in precipitous decline. The latter point reminds us of the importance of putting the contributions of other Us members in context and not to simply view the organization as synonymous with Karenga, and one of the best examples of the necessity of this is Us member James Mtume, one of the editors of *The Quotable Karenga*. Mtume's contributions to Us's aesthetic production were massive in the BPM, and his artistic renown transcended the BPM and continues long afterward (Brown, 2003). For example, as a percussionist he performed and toured with Miles Davis, and during the BPM his eponymously named group recorded two kawaida-inspired albums. Later, the title song from their 1982 album *Juicy Fruit* went gold and became #1 on the U.S. R&B charts, and subsequently it has been sampled widely by rap artists, most notably by the Notorious B.I.G. in his 1994 hit song "Juicy." Mtume won a Grammy Award for penning Roberta Flack and Donny Hathaway's, "The Closer I Get to You." Mtume is an exemplary representation of the talented and insightful people who were found in Us.

Like other BPM revolutionists, while Karenga and Us proposed a program and thesis on cultural revolution, they rejected the dominant cultural institution in the United States, the Black Church. Karenga argued that "Christianity is a white religion" and "any 'Negro' who believes in it is a sick 'Negro'" (Brown, 2003, 69). He established kawaida as an alternative religion for black Americans—referring explicitly to it as a religion—to such an extent that the name of Us's meeting place, hekalu, is Swahili for "temple." Us's antagonistic relationship to the Black Church was shared by many BPM organizations, but for those pursuing cultural revolution their failure to engage the major cultural institution in black communities assured their failure. Larry Neal was insightful about those

> who speak of black people as "spiritually dead." Such thinkers, in their urge to develop new values for the Nation, are rejecting those aspects of the black culture experience that would truly constitute the stuff of Nationhood. . . . Christianity comes under vicious attack. . . . The church is viewed as the great brainwasher of the black people and the tool of the oppressors. We accept negative aspects of the folklore surrounding the black church, but we fail to probe the origins of this folklore. . . . Meanwhile, millions

of black people continue to support their local churches. . . . In other words, a life-style exists among black folk that is totally at odds with the attitudes of nationalist intellectuals who instead of denigrating the religion of much of the national black body should be trying to understand the influence—past and present—of the black church . . . these intellectuals often look down on their mothers and fathers whose spiritual legacy gave birth to the very struggle we all claim to support. I believe nationalism is the central model of black liberation. But nationalism can also fail if it doesn't unite all of the relevant parts of our entire experience. (Neal, 1989, p. 119)

Neal concluded that black nationalists "are going to have to reassess their attitudes toward the church . . . to understand precisely why this institution continues to serve as a wellspring of energy and truth, in spite of the rapid changes in our community" (ibid., p. 124).

With respect to the broader framework, there also is very little in kawaida that explains how the cultural revolution it espouses will ensue, much less how the political revolution will emerge from it. The kawaida thesis does not build on Cruse's focus on capturing the cultural apparatus of the United States, nor does it demonstrate how such a cultural focus would extend to the political and economic dimensions of black oppression and provide a basis for black liberation. Presumably, since the kawaida-based national culture that he proposes would be Afrocentric, it should augur conflict between its advocates and those practicing the Eurocentric national culture of white America. What results is a conflict at the cultural borders of the society, which, when heightened, engenders revolution and a basic reorientation of the society. The instrument for this revolutionary project, for Karenga, seems to be a black intelligentsia evocative of Du Bois's early theorizing of the talented tenth and/or the guiding one-hundredth. Actually, this later development of Karenga's thesis derives from his exposure, in the early 1970s, to the writings of the African revolutionary Amilcar Cabral (1972), who asserted the need for indigenous intellectuals, among other members of the colonized petite bourgeoisie, to commit "class suicide" and make common cause with revolutionary forces in colonial Guinea-Bissau and Cape Verde, among the peasants especially (also see Cabral, 1973; Nzongola-Ntalaja, 1984). Borrowing from Cabral, Karenga (1982, pp. 207–208) advocated the development of a black intellectual vanguard that would commit class suicide and subsequently "create an Afro-centric ideology or social theory which negates the ruling race/class ideology and provides the basis for a critical Afro-centric conception of reality and the possibilities and methods of changing it." Armed with this Afrocentric focus, the vanguard would then lead a cultural revolution, which would precede, and make possible, a political revolution. Within this proposed cultural revolution, Karenga suggested, there is a reaffirmation, revitalization, and reclamation of the national culture of black Americans denied by the dominant white supremacist culture. The mechanisms for this cultural revolution vary from independent black institutions (e.g., schools, businesses—especially publishing houses—and cultural centers) to Black Studies programs in universities and to black political parties, both local and national, such as Karenga had helped Baraka's CFUN to build in Newark.

What Karenga was proposing, though he didn't seem to realize it at the time, or at minimum didn't attribute it to its source, was Du Boisian cultural *evolution*, which the pan-Africanist sage had outlined in the 1930s and '40s, focusing on the development of independent black economic, social, and political institutions. Viewed only slightly differently, as Karenga began to openly advocate socialism in the 1970s, kawaida began to mirror aspects of Gramsci's perspective that since advanced industrialized capitalist states exercised control over the revolutionary elements in their society through cultural hegemony, then the politico-military revolution (i.e., the war of maneuver) would be preceded by a challenge to the cultural hegemony of the ruling class (i.e., the war of position). What Karenga was proposing at that point may have been misconstrued as a more class conscious albeit non-Marxist extrapolation from Gramsci to the BPM; but what is closer to the truth is that Karenga's kawaida was still following much of Malcolm's focus from the OAAU wedded to aspects of RAM's and Cruse's thesis and updated with elements of anticolonial socialist theses of cultural revolution from Cabral.

Karenga also altered the kawaida thesis over time to address some of its contradictory elements—such as its feudal glorification of the subjugation of women, its rejection of the notion of class struggle, its replacement of the notion that blacks have no culture with the view that blacks have no national culture but only a popular culture. Karenga, often dramatically, changed position on each of these issues while incorporating his updated views into a revised kawaida thesis. But even with revisions, kawaida's basic contradictions persist. There are three major contradictions in Karenga's formulation—logical, theoretical, and empirical. The logical contradictions should be obvious: First, if all people possess a culture, as Karenga contends, then how do African Americans exist without one, which he also contends? Second, if culture encompasses the seven dimensions outlined above, which includes politics, then how does one separate the cultural from the political and by implication the cultural revolution from the political revolution? Since culture subsumes politics, then how does one differentiate the political from the cultural? Relatedly, why is it necessary in Karenga's view to fight a cultural revolution before a political one, since culture subsumes politics in his framework? A better appreciation of the holistic context of culture may have been useful in lessening the impact of the more apparent than real contradictions between Us's putatively anthropologically based "cultural nationalism" and the Black Panther Party's ostensibly more politically focused "revolutionary nationalism," the latter a rhetorical distinction at best, which substantively (i.e., as a mutually exclusive categorical distinction) is both ahistorical and atheoretical but nonetheless has led to often-deadly disputes between the two groups and internecine conflicts throughout the BPM, which persist today. In a strange compulsion to create consistency for his kawaida thesis that it does not warrant, which is evident in his writings over the decades, recently Karenga (2015, p. A6) asserted that "Kawaida *continues to maintain* that the struggle we must wage is a *dual one of cultural revolution within and political revolution without*, resulting in the radical transformation of ourselves, society and ultimately the world" (emphasis added). Throughout the BPM and well into the twenty-first century, Karenga has argued that a cultural revolution must precede a political revolution, so this claim is false.

The second major contradiction in Karenga's formulation is that it is not clear why one should draw on *African* experiences and examples to devise a theory of revolution for blacks in *America* in such a different political, economic, social, and historical context. Karenga had argued that "the reason Blacks are failing today is because they try to gather from everybody except themselves" (Halisi & Mtume, 1967, p. 13), and that "Black people must understand history and from historical knowledge we can evolve our own theory of revolution" (ibid., p. 11). But his basic formulation conflates *African* with *African American*, and in so doing ignores remarkable differences in their contexts. With respect to culture, this perspective reverses nineteenth-century civilizationism in arguing that the acquisition of African culture was necessary to acculturate black Americans, but Karenga's kawaida during the BPM went one step farther: it argued that since black Americans do not have a culture, they must adopt a "traditional African" one. The latter is not simply reverse civilizationism but, as noted above, cultural atavism. Implicit in both is the view that black Americans are less evolved culturally than indigenous Africans. Not surprisingly, given such a position, Karenga derived many of his empirical referents, and most of his theoretical arguments, from either Africans or Africanists such as Touré, Kenyatta, Nkrumah, Nyerere, and to some degree Fanon and Cabral. This tied his analysis not only to African, rather than African American, exigencies and developmental modalities, which were hardly similar, much less identical, but also to the inconsistencies of the theoretical arguments of the proponents themselves.

For example, Touré provided Karenga's most prominent contemporary thesis on cultural revolution in his *Toward Full Re-Africanization*; however, although he had called for cultural revolution in Guinea, by 1968 Touré (1974) had argued that it was subordinate to the class struggle; but through most of the BPM, Karenga rejected class analysis as an approach to explicating black politics in the United States—much less black liberation. Similarly, Karenga accepted Nkrumah's pan-Africanism but not his socialism during the 1960s. Further, aspects of Fanon's (1961) argument in *Wretched of the Earth* supported Karenga's thesis on culture with respect to the conceptualization of national culture and assertions of its relevance (e.g., p. 233) and the importance of culture in liberation struggles (e.g., ibid., pp. 244–246); however, Fanon rejected the relevance of traditional culture over that which is born of anticolonial struggle, which diverges from Karenga's kawaida—which not only rests on a view of African traditional culture, but actually means "tradition" in Swahili (also ibid., pp. 244–246). In addition, Fanon's differentiation of the anticolonial struggle of "African Negroes" from that of "American Negroes" (ibid., p. 216), his arguments about the shortcomings of national consciousness, as well as his focus on the lumpenproletariat as a positive change agent (ibid., pp. 129–130, 137) are diametrically opposed to Karenga's kawaida.[1] Karenga—like most U.S. activists—was unfamiliar with Cabral's thesis until the early 1970s (his writings were mainly available in the West only in Portuguese); nevertheless, his focus on culture largely mirrors the African revolutionary leader's, and in the mid-1970s Karenga explicitly adapted/updated kawaida's precepts to include aspects of Cabral's cultural theses—often prominently so—and also adopted the socialism of each of these theorists, having already incorporated aspects of Nyerere's African socialism in the ujamaa of the nguzo saba.

Nevertheless, the political, military, economic, and social contexts of Guinea, Ghana, Algeria, and Guinea-Bissau (as well as Tanzania)—some of the politically, militarily, and economically weakest states in the 1960s—were so diametrically different from those of black America in the 1960s (and later), situated in the most powerful country in the world. While the differences in the political, military, and economic dimensions are apparent, it's important to appreciate that even in the social dimension, where there may appear to be some superficial similarities between African and African American societies (almost exclusively as they are related to white racism), the actual role of culture in these societies is starkly different as well. For example, the role of ethnicity in sub-Saharan African states allowed for customary law, which enshrined both actual and imagined traditional forms and often maintained traditional institutions, languages, and customs; therefore, the "full reAfricanization" that Touré sought was largely a phenomenon that called for the reestablishment of indigenous African forms that had been interrupted by a colonial interlude of relatively short duration as compared to the centuries of the trans-Atlantic slave trade that occluded the transmission of African culture to its diaspora—not to mention its further suppression upon arrival.[17] This was different across Francophone, Anglophone, and Lusophone Africa given variations in their colonial policies and different degrees of cultural assimilation in each, but throughout Africa, where assimilation occurred it was for a relatively few elites; therefore, "reAfricanization" would not entail wholesale cultural "de-assimilation." This was nothing like what would be required for black Americans, for whom both their elites as well as their masses were detached from the original culture of their African ancestors by not only thousands of miles of physical space but more importantly by several centuries of "deculturalization" from their African cultural homes, and systematic cultural erasures. Moreover, since culture is linked to politics and economics, the culture of the predominantly agrarian-based economies of sub-Saharan African countries was hardly applicable to the industrial-based economy of postwar America—even rural black America was mechanized when compared to rural Africa. A focus on such agrarian societies contributed to the heavy focus on communalism in kawaida, and also its often feudalistic conception of womanhood.

The third major contradiction in Karenga's formulation was that it did not adequately explain what constituted cultural revolution or what factors contributed to it (Henderson, 1995, pp. 125–128). It appears that cultural revolution emerges, in Karenga's view, from the contrasts between the national cultures of white and black Americans, but since blacks do not have a national culture, according to Karenga, then cultural difference itself does not seem to serve as the revolutionary change agent. Further, it seems that the process of building a cultural revolution will occasion attacks by whites and white institutions on the incipient institutions of the black nation, but this seems inconsistent with Karenga's view that the cultural revolution precedes and makes possible the political revolution (the violent one), because in this conceptualization the cultural revolution would also be violent. So the qualitative difference between the two is not clear. Beyond the difference between the cultural and political revolutions, it is still not clear how the cultural revolution emerges, according to the kawaida thesis. It does not seem to emerge from cultural difference alone, and given that such difference has been relatively constant in U.S. history one would expect that the cultural revolution that Karenga's thesis foretold would have already occurred—such a conclusion may have led Karenga to consider the Civil War era as a potential source of such a conflict, but his theoretical lens was focused more on black Africa than on black America as a historical referent.

It may have been that it was attenuated by the presumed absence of a national culture among blacks; thus, one might assume that it would emerge from the conflict associated with the persistence of Eurocentric culture and the development of the black national culture that Karenga's thesis sought to create. Relatedly, kawaida does not demonstrate how the different cultural backgrounds of the racial groups have remained distinct and antithetical even as the groups remain in such close proximity in the United States. The assumption of cultural difference is important because it is this cleavage, presumably, that represents the fault line between the two groups and fuels the anticipated intercultural conflict between them. Moreover, Karenga fails to explain how cultures sustain their impact on their adherents in the face of material, environmental, and technological change and in the face of repression by a distinct, imposing, and opposing culture.

Further, it is not clear just what kind of struggle Karenga's cultural revolution entails. Given that its major function seems to be that it "makes possible" a political revolution, then one might assume that it is not a full-fledged revolution itself. Ignoring for the moment what the political revolution entails and what processes define its origins and execution, we are left to ponder the actual processes at work in the cultural revolution and just what makes it revolutionary. Karenga is silent on these questions; instead, he assumes that once people "know themselves" then a common purpose will derive from that knowledge, which ignores the range of perspectives—across political, economic, and social dimensions—within groups of people sharing a common culture. One need only reflect on the incidence of civil wars within societies of culturally similar peoples to appreciate the limitations of the view that cultural similarity leads to similarity in political objectives.

Not only does Karenga's thesis fail to address the issues of how cultural revolution emerges and what form it takes, it also does not address basic collective action issues with respect to the political revolution thought to emerge after the cultural revolution. If there is a commonality of purpose, then what leads persons to act when the action is likely to occur without them, since the costs are borne disproportionately by those who take action, while the benefits will accrue to all in the group? That is, there is clearly a "free rider" problem within the proposed revolution. One may argue that the presence of a vanguard will overcome this problem, given that this vanguard largely consists of black intellectuals who commit "class suicide" and coordinate political struggle with the masses. But in Karenga's formulation this is more slogan and cliché than coherent social theory. It appears as a sort of "revolutionary rehash" of Du Bois's talented tenth argument, but, as noted above, Du Bois's thesis was more one of cultural "evolution" than cultural "revolution." At its best, this aspect of Karenga's thesis may be evocative of those focusing on the role of critical communities in social movements (e.g., Rochon, 1998), but such approaches recognize the salience of broader, often cross-cutting elements of communities as change agents, while Karenga's thesis during the BPM seems to have little or no focus on, or apparent role for, other potential revolutionary elements, classes, and/or sectors of black society, as is most evident in his denunciation of the Black Church.

Interestingly, it is just that element of black culture that Karenga's kawaida thesis rejects, black religion, that provides a mechanism to overcome such collective action problems. Gill (2011) is among those who emphasize the ability of religious mobilization to overcome collective action problems. More than social identity based on class, ethnicity, language, race, gender, or sexuality, religion may mobilize adherents in response to religious discrimination between religious groups within a society, and even more so when discrimination is at the hands of the state and its agents and targets the intersection of religion and race, such as in the case of the Black Church in the United States (Koubi & Bohmelt, 2014). Esteban and Ray's (2008) findings demonstrate how religious groups overcome collective action problems. They show that in the presence of economic inequality, ethnoreligious groups (e.g., the overwhelemingly Christian black Americans), more than class-based groups, are more likely to rebel as a result of the synergy generated by race and religion that induces the economically better-off within the group to supply resources for rebellion while the poor members of the group supply labor. Such synergy is rare in class-based conflict, where the rich have little incentive to materially support redistribution and the poor face very high opportunity costs. The potency of the fusion of racial and religious identity as a force for collective action is evident in the antebellum slave revolts of Gabriel, Denmark Vesey, and Nat Turner, and the Slave Revolution (see chapter 3), and this theoretical understanding and practical potency was absent from kawaida. Eventually, Karenga seemed to recognize as much; thus, he promoted his "Temple of Maat" but, like the Black Panthers' "Son of Man Temple," it did not have sufficient appeal to the black audience to which it was intended, which remained entrenched in the Black Church.

Simply put, kawaida in its original (and present) form failed to answer central questions regarding the primary mechanism of cultural change, much less provide a theory of black cultural revolution. While limited as theory, kawaida as a program provided a powerful basis for organizing and institutional development, ranging from Us's educational and self-defense programs to precinct work guiding electoral strategies in Los Angeles and Newark, to united-front efforts throughout black America, including playing crucial roles in the development of the Black Power conferences during the BPM. Us's expertise in political organizing was also reflected in its influence on other BPM organizations, serving important roles in the development of CFUN and CAP in Newark and in Karenga's appointment as one of the original Ministers of Culture in the RNA. But a critical shortcoming in the programmatic efforts of Us, as noted above, was that like its eventual nemesis the BPP, Us rejected the Black Church as a meaningful change agent in black society. Also, Karenga did not address the issue of sexism in cultural revolution in any substantive way, although women such as Haiba Karenga, Dorothy Jamal, and Sanamu Nyeusi had been prominent in the early phases of Us (Brown, 2003, pp. 40–41). Karenga promoted a feudal subjugation of women in Us, which he rationalized as "African tradition." This was among the worst examples of Karenga's myopic reading of African cultures, and it resulted in some of the most egregious practices of Us. Kawaida, and Karenga personally, encouraged black women to be submissive to black men in Us, which was evident from an initial greeting custom between members and Karenga, in which women crossed their forearms across their breasts and bowed in supplication, in contrast to the men's greeting of a hand grip and brief erect embrace, and extended to Us's doctrine, which without making polygamy a formal policy, permitted male members to have second wives, the latter often little more than mistresses (ibid., pp. 62–65).

The appeal to "African" tradition in Us perpetuated sexism by giving it a gloss of legitimacy or authenticity, constructing it as representative of an ancestral African culture that black Americans had lost; yet, Karenga's arguments on African cultures reflected a superficial appreciation of them and insufficient understanding of their diversity in even a single African country. His penchant seems to have been to study works on a particular nation's cultures and draw selectively and self-servingly from them, as he did in drawing on Kenyatta's analysis of Gikuyu culture in his 1938 *Facing Mount Kenya* to inform Us's organizational structure and his own personal transformation (Brown, 2003, pp. 11–12, 57). The latter is evident in the derivation of his last name from the Gikuyu term *kareng'a*, which describes the independent Gikuyu schools reportedly free of any missionary influence and, for Kenyatta, refers also to a "pure-blooded Gikuyu, a nationalist" (Kenyatta, 1978, p. 309). Such an orientation might have some merit, but it is more likely to promote conceptions of a people's culture limited by the author's biases. For example, the diversity of informed opinion regarding Gikuyu traditions suggests the difficulty of drawing from a single author's viewpoint, even one as informed as Kenyatta's.

For example, in a 1941 essay in the *Journal of Negro History*, the African American political scientist Ralph Bunche reported on his fieldwork among the Kikuyu (Gikuyu) of Kiambu District in Kenya, in which he observed the *irua* (circumcision) ceremony. Bunche (1941, p. 64) noted the disagreement of a Gikuyu chief, whom he describes as "one of the wisest philosophers I have ever met," with the *irua* custom. He reports that "Senior Chief Koinange of the Kiambu Kikuyu, who remembers when the first white man visited Kikuyu country" stated that "I do not approve of the circumcision of girls, since I do not believe that it does the girl any good to be circumcised." He added that "if the girls are properly educated; the more education they will get the more they will find that circumcision has no bearing on their lives, and they will stop it voluntarily" (ibid.). The chief observed that girls of other Kenyan ethnic groups were not circumcised, and admonished that "[m]ost people accept circumcision blindly as an old custom" (ibid.). In his own family, he noted that "[t]hree of my own daughters are circumcised, but the two younger ones are not," and he concluded: "I believe that it should be left to the girls themselves to decide. I do not want any of my daughters forced into either circumcision or marriage or forced to forego them, against their desires" (ibid., p. 65). Pearl Robinson (2008, p. 12) contrasts the Senior Chief's description of the ceremony, as reported by Bunche, with Kenyatta's more sanguine view of it. For her, Bunche "uses the device of quoting a Kikuyu chief to trump Kenyatta's claim of authenticity for his data, of the benign consequences of this practice for the girls who undergo the operation, and, ultimately, of the importance of the ceremony to the maintenance of Kikuyu cultural identity." It is not the accuracy of either Kenyatta's or Koinange's depiction of *irua*, but the presence of a diversity of views among the Gikuyu themselves regarding an important tradition within Gikuyu culture that matters here.[18] Gikuyu culture does not manifest a singular orientation toward even its prominent cultural practices, in this case, whether ascension to adulthood should be recognized through *irua* (there is diversity regarding *irua* among adjacent African culture groups as well).[19] At issue is not Karenga's view of *irua*, but recognizing that his bricolage from Gikuyu is probably not representative of the diversity of practices and perspectives within that single culture, and even less so was the pastiche of cultures he amalgamated as "African."

Such myopic, ahistorical conceptions of African cultures were similar to those of Eurocentric anthropologists, from social Darwinists to cultural relativists such as Malinowski, Kenyatta's mentor at the London School of Economics (LSE),[20] which are typically racist and consistently sexist. Their ahistorical image of African cultures has less to do with tradition than it emerges from the more recent history of colonialism, which constructed arbitrary practices as traditional, associated every African with a tribe and every tribe with a chief, and then institutionalized these fictions in a body of customary law to more effectively manage colonial subjects. Ranger (1983, p. 250) notes that "customary law, customary land-rights, customary political structure . . . were in fact all invented by colonial codification," and "once the 'traditions' relating to community identity and land right were written down in court records and exposed to the criteria of the invented customary model, a new and unchanging body of tradition had been created" (ibid., p. 251).[21] Berman (1998, p. 321) notes that

> relying on its local allies as sources of information on what was expected to be a fixed and consistent body of rules, the colonial state allowed chiefs, headmen and elders to define a customary law that asserted and legitimated their power and control over the allocation of resources against the interests of junior women and migrants.

For the most part, "codified custom concealed the new colonial balances of wealth and power." Mamdani (1996, p. 122) agrees that customary law "consolidated the non-customary power of colonial chiefs," such that it "came to enforce as custom rules and regulations that were hardly customary." Many such "customs" were intended to extend the power of men over women, girls, and boys for their productive and reproductive labor, and the institutionalization of these regimes of subordination by the colonial state included granting them a provenance in the precolonial era, while Western anthropologists collaborated in mythifying their historicity in the society (Henderson, 2017).

This is not to say that there were not enduring traditions and customs in Africa, but only to point out that many of those adopted by Us were caricatures of diverse and often competing African forms. Among the most common were those that justified male domination and female subordination. Karenga rationalized this sexism as "tradition"; but Us members such as Joann Kicheko opposed the group's sexism and Karenga's conception of African traditions and "was suspended from the group for arguing with the leadership over matters associated with its sexist philosophy and conduct," including the notion that black women had to be submissive (Brown, 2003, p. 57). Kicheko drew different conclusions from her interpretation of African traditions: "I had read things like Jomo Kenyatta's Mount Kenya and the Kikuyu [Gikuyu] way of setting up social structure, and when I read it I didn't read it as a male-dominated society. I read it as there were things men did and women did, and things that men and women did together, but each had their power and sources" (ibid.). South African singer Letta Mbulu, who worked closely with Us during the late 1960s, thought that the men of the organization "had a naïve or distorted view of gender relations in Africa." She remarked that what she saw in Us "was that the men wanted to be in total control—in Africa it isn't like this . . . we always give men their role but women have just as strong power as men have and that's not what I saw happening" (ibid.). Such "staunchly patriarchical" views, Brown maintains, resulted in Us "lagging behind" SNCC, the BPP, and other BPM organizations "already influenced" by second wave feminism (ibid., p. 58). He adds that the "explicitness with which the US doctrine opposed women's equality would make the organization a lasting symbol of sixties-era Black nationalist sexism," but "[i]n practice" he recognized that "the predominantly male leadership of many other political organizations that spanned the ideological gamut accepted this division" (ibid., p. 65).

The position of women in Us declined further as the organization became a cult of personality under Karenga (Brown, 2003, p. 66), and women did not regain prominent positions until Us became heavily militarized after the shootout with the Panthers at UCLA, when more women took up positions in the paramilitary formations as many in the male leadership were targeted by police and rivals (ibid., p. 123). It was only during and shortly after his imprisonment for assault with intent to do great bodily harm and false imprisonment, arising from incidents related to his torturing two Us members, Gail Idili-Davis and Brenda Jones, that Karenga appended a womanist dimension to kawaida, but it was too late to influence the BPM. Us members Luz Maria Tiamoyo (now Tiamoyo Karenga) and Fred Sefu-Glover were also convicted of assault with intent to do great bodily harm and false imprisonment related to these incidents, and Louis-Sedu Smith was convicted of false imprisonment (ibid., pp. 120–121). The latter incidents remind us that for all the myriad borrowings from African revolutionists, Karenga and Us missed one of the major lessons of Amilcar Cabral: "that in the general framework of the daily struggle this battle against ourselves—no matter what difficulties the enemy may create—remains the most difficult of all." Cabral was "convinced that any national or social revolution which is not based on the knowledge of this reality runs great risk of failure" (Davidson, 1971, p. 74). Cabral insisted that culture was key in resolving these contradictions; but under Karenga's leadership, Us became a cult of personality that militarized in the face of government repression, until its rivalry with the BPP, exacerbated by COINTELPRO, led to a shootout on the UCLA campus in which two BPP members were killed and an Us member wounded, and the organization imploded.[22]

The implosion of Us as a result of issues related to its militarization was ironic, given that, unlike many of the other militant organizations of the BPM, Us eschewed overt armed confrontations with police and other law enforcement agencies, although it maintained a paramilitary unit, the

Simba (Young Lions), which was trained by military veteran Ngao Damu. Brown agrees:

> Resisting the 1960s trend among militant radicals of embracing Che Guevera's guerrilla warfare theories as a model for revolution in the United States, Karenga was skeptical of the idea that a small insurgency could instigate a revolution. He was convinced, however, that successful and protracted armed struggle necessitated a preexisting, broad-based African American consensus and will to make great sacrifices in support of the revolution. (2003, p. 89)

Karenga asserted: "It is not a question of how can we kill the enemy, for the people must decide that that is necessary themselves, or the vanguard will vanish and the revolutionary party which has placed itself in a front position will fall flat on its face and history will hide all of them" (p. 89).[23] De-emphasizing armed confrontations allowed Us the space to develop its parallel institutions that were the hallmark of the BPM, but its militarization following the UCLA shootout led it to redirect its resources toward security, and under such conditions, it's not surprising that Us was unable to modify kawaida into a coherent thesis of black cultural revolution. In contrast, the utility of aspects of kawaida allowed groups such as Baraka's CFUN to draw on it for its programs in Newark.

Even with its limitations as black nationalist *theory*, during the BPM, Us fashioned a cogent black nationalist *program* building on Malcolm X's revolutionary theses and both its electoral and revolutionary foci. Us's *nguzo saba* became a centerpiece for organizers throughout the BPM, and it is one of the most enduring aesthetic and institutional elements originating in the 1960s that is still relevant in black communities today. Intellectual opposition and academic censoring has contributed to the lack of recognition Us has received for its major positive contributions to the BPM in comparison to other organizations—as well as its enduring impact today, but academic and movement bias toward the Panthers in the Us-BPP dispute is an important factor, as well. For example, contributing to the willful obfuscations of Us is the continued slurring of its name as an abbreviation for "United Slaves," which was never the group's name but a slur that the BPP created. Leading scholars such as Dawson (2001, p. 102) refer to Us by this slur in a major study of black ideologies. So common is it that it compelled Hayes and Jeffries's (2006) "Us Does Not Stand For United Slaves!" Such slanders are most evident in recriminations of Us by members and supporters—as well as notable scholars—of the group that became its most notable rival within the BPM, the Black Panther Party (BPP).

The Black Panther Party

It may appear strange to include the Black Panther Party in an analysis of the contributions of major theorists on black cultural revolution in the BPM, given its leadership's vehement opposition to what it described as cultural nationalism and its representation in groups such as RAM, the RNA, and especially Us. The BPP took a notable—and quite popular—position on "revolutionary culture" in opposition to "cultural revolution." Their conception was consistent with James Boggs's argument that "[e]very revolution creates a new culture out of the process of revolutionary struggle against the old values and culture which an oppressing society has sought to impose upon the oppressed" (1970, p. 58). It is unlikely that the founders of the BPP, Huey Newton and Bobby Seale, were unaware of Cruse's and Boggs's theses on both domestic colonialism and the role of culture in black revolution in the United States, given that Newton had participated in Don Warden's AAA, which was affiliated with RAM (its Los Angeles representative was Karenga) and Seale worked directly with RAM in the Soul Students Advisory Council led by Kenny Freeman. Further, both Cruse's and Boggs's theses were widely discussed in RAM-affiliated groups. At its founding, the BPP accepted the domestic colonial view of black America; however, they rejected other arguments associated with black nationalism such as cultural revolution mainly because they associated it, not with Malcolm, but with RAM in Oakland, with which they had tactical disagreements (Seale, 1970; Newton, 1973). According to Newton (1995, ch. 9–11, 15), among the disagreements that he and Seale had with members of Oakland's RAM was that he was convinced that RAM's approach was not relevant to "the brothers on the block." The main tactical dispute was RAM members' unwillingness to pursue Newton's suggestion of patrolling the police. Different experiences with RAM in Oakland as compared to New York would exacerbate what was later called the "Newton-Cleaver split" between BPP chapters in the two cities because RAM member Herman Ferguson, having been a founding member of the OAAU and the RNA, also played a seminal role in the establishment of the New York chapter of the BPP. Ferguson and RAM (as well as the RNA) were both viewed positively by members of the New York chapter of the BPP. The New York BPP adopted African names and dress, which Oakland disparaged, and many were prominent in the RNA, which at times was in conflict with the Oakland BPP.

Although the BPP openly rejected cultural revolution theses—except those that were associated with Mao's GPCR—the BPP Central Committee included a minister of culture, Emory Douglas, and promoted a musical group, The Lumpen, "whose primary purpose was . . . political education through music and song" (Newton, 1995, pp. 300–301).[24] Among the few positive references Newton makes to "black cultural revolution" is its relationship to aspects of black popular culture such as "natural" hairstyles (ibid., p. 60). Ignoring Malcolm's thesis on black cultural revolution, Newton and Seale selectively drew on Fanon's arguments on the role and relevance of culture in revolution. Fanon maintained that "the conscious and organized undertaking by a colonized people to re-establish the sovereignty of that nation constitutes the most complete and obvious cultural manifestation that exists" (1963, p. 245). For Fanon, "It is the fight for national existence which sets culture moving and opens to it the doors of creation" (ibid., p. 244), noting that this fight

> sends culture along different paths and traces out entirely new ones for it. The struggle for freedom does not give back to the national culture its former value and shapes; this struggle which aims at a fundamentally different set of relations between men cannot leave intact either the form or the content of the people's culture. After the conflict there is not only the disappearance of colonialism but also the disappearance of the colonized man. (ibid., pp. 245–246)

The BPP inferred from Fanon's claims that revolutionary activity itself, that is, political revolution, would generate the requisite culture that would help transform black society—a view similar to Boggs's contention but neither to Cruse's nor Haywood's. As late as 1970, Newton (1999, p. 153) was convinced that "we have not established a revolutionary value system; we are only in the process of establishing it."

The BPP accepted Fanon's thesis on the necessity of violence in the overthrow of colonialism, the cathartic value of the use of violence in anticolonial struggle, and the centrality of the lumpenproletariat to anticolonial revolution. Fanon viewed the lumpenproletariat as "one of the most spontaneous and the most radically revolutionary forces of a colonized people" (1963, p. 128) and its "urban spearhead" (ibid.). Former BPP leader Elaine Brown (1992, p. 136), reflecting on her catechism in the BPP, learned that

> the black *lumpen proletariat*, unlike Marx's working class, had absolutely no stake in industrial America. They existed at the bottom level of society in America, outside the capitalist system that was the basis for the oppression of black people. They were the millions of black domestics and porters, nurses' aides and maintenance men, laundresses and cooks, sharecroppers, unprop-

ertied ghetto dwellers, welfare mothers, and street hustlers. At their lowest level, at the core, they were the gang members and the gangsters, the pimps and the prostitutes, the drug users and dealers, the common thieves and murderers.

Brown's rendering of the lumpenproletariat is telling given that few orthodox Marxists—or non-Marxists—would include "porters, nurses' aides, maintenance men, cooks, and sharecroppers," who were clearly wage and agricultural workers, in the class with "pimps, common thieves and murderers," who were simply criminals mainly preying on the working class and poor. For Marx (1969 [1852], pp. 76–77), only Brown's "lowest level" comprised his lumpenproletariat, which for him were "scum," "the refuse of all classes," consisting of vagabonds, ex-convicts, ex-slaves, swindlers, pickpockets, and beggars, who he was convinced were reactionary. Brown's mischaracterization of the lumpenproletariat reflects an enduring ignorance of Marxism that was not restricted to her, but was emblematic of some of the problems of political education among the Panthers (even more so, given that Brown would eventually become a member of the Central Committee, and later the leader of the BPP in Newton's absence). Rejecting Marx's (1969 [1852], pp. 76–77) disposition toward the "lumpen," but not necessarily his description of it, Newton, in what he viewed as a Marxist methodological deduction (i.e., a dialectical materialist deduction), asserted the revolutionary potential of this group.

Although Newton's assessment of the lumpenproletariat derived from his reading of Fanon, he credited Eldridge Cleaver with articulating the Marxist formulation for the BPP, in his "On the Ideology of the Black Panther Party" in 1970. This view prevailed in the BPP, following its original nationalist phase, when it embraced Cleaver's "Yankee Doodle Socialism." Echoing Boggs, Newton asserted that since "technology is developing at such a rapid rate that automation will progress to cybernation, and cybernation probably to technocracy," then "if the ruling circle remains in power the proletarian working class will definitely be on the decline because they will be unemployables and therefore swell the ranks of the lumpens, who are the present unemployables" (Newton, 1995, pp. 27–28). He insisted that "soon the ruling circle will not need the workers" (ibid., p. 28); thus, for him, "[e]very worker is in jeopardy . . . which is why we say that the lumpenproletarians have the potential for revolution, will probably carry out the revolution, and in the near future will be the popular majority" (ibid.).

Newton's reliance on Fanon's view of the revolutionary potential of the lumpenproletariat is subject to the same critique as that levied at Karenga's selective adoption of Fanon's arguments on the centrality of national culture in anticolonial struggles. Both revolutionists ignored Fanon's arguments regarding the lack of comparability of African and African American revolutionary contexts. While Fanon recognized similarities between the two, he acknowledged that "the essential problems confronting [American Negroes] were not the same as those that confronted the African Negroes." He explained:

> The Negroes of Chicago only resemble the Nigerians or the Tanganyikans in so far as they were all defined in relation to the whites. But once the first comparisons had been made and subjective feelings were assuaged, the American Negroes realized that the objective problems were fundamentally heterogeneous. (p. 216)

He added that the struggles against racial discrimination in the United States "have very little in common in their principles and objectives with the heroic fight," for example, "of the Angolan people against the detestable Portuguese colonialism" (ibid.). Fanon insisted that "every culture is first and foremost national, and . . . the problems which kept Richard Wright or Langston Hughes on the alert were fundamentally different from those which might confront Leopold Senghor or Jomo Kenyatta" (ibid.). In fact, rather than the distillations of Newton and Karenga, Fanon's discussion converges with Cruse's (1968, p. 252) arguments, which both Newton and Karenga might have reflected on before drafting Fanon's arguments to support their contrasting programs for black Americans:

> If the American Negro is a victim of domestic colonialism (which he is), it does not follow that his war against oppression can be conducted solely along the lines of resistance established in *pure* colonial or semi-colonial countries. It means, rather, that the exigencies of struggle grow out of *both* Western social conditions and a unique kind of colonialism not experienced in Cuba, China, Asia, Africa, or Latin America generally.

Karenga's kawaida thesis was much less beholden to Fanon's thesis, given the Us leader's rejection of the revolutionary potential of the lumpenproletariat; however, Newton's thesis adopted Fanon's sanguine assertions about this class wholesale. Interestingly, Newton's view of the revolutionary potential of the lumpenproletariat was more dependent on Karenga's assertion of the relevance of culture in black liberation than either seemed to realize. For example, Newton placed greater emphasis on the *position* of the lumpenproletariat in the social relations of production in the United States, rather than on their *disposition* toward the social relations of production. Newton accepted that the lumpenproletariat were among those who were most detached from the capitalist structure; they operated at the bottom of the class structure with no meaningful relation to industrial production and in such a position they had "nothing to lose" if the capitalist system was overturned. The BPP saw the rebellions of the 1960s as precursors of future organized violence and emblematic of the readiness of the lumpenproletariat to undertake concerted action against the "power structure." What was left was to organize, educate, and mobilize them to fulfill their revolutionary potential. This plan was at least partially dependent—metaphorically—on the ability of the BPP to effectuate a program to turn lumpens into "Malcolm Xs"—a lumpen who became a principled and dedicated revolutionary. The likelihood of transforming lumpens into Malcolm Xs was dependent on the disposition of lumpens to transform themselves; however, this was as much an issue of the BPP's organizational and political acumen as it was the cultural orientation of the lumpens. That is, the success of the BPP's programs rested in large part on the extent to which the lumpen was compelled by domestic colonialism to orient itself as a class in opposition to the social relations of production that Marx argued made them a reactionary element and in accordance with that which Fanon argued made them revolutionary. Taking seriously the BPP's claim that in a context of domestic colonialism *black* lumpenproletarians were positioned largely outside of the class structure, then their propensity toward revolutionary struggle would be determined *less* by their class orientation and *more* by their relationship as a race to the broader race/class (i.e., domestic colonial) structure of the United States.

Marx had argued that the process of capitalist production disciplined, united, and organized the proletariat; therefore, the proletariat did not need to transform itself to bring about a socialist revolution. Operating outside of the system of industrial production, the lumpen—in particular, the black lumpen—was not socialized in this way; instead, the defining characteristic of its socialization was domestic colonialism, which socialized not only by class but by race. Transformation of this group into a revolutionary class required socialization outside of industrial production and within the other socializing structures that domestic colonialism created in which the lumpen participated. In the United States, this social system was defined by white supremacism—thus, white racial domination—and racial domination was national; thus, in the social system, black nationalism was revolutionary. Therefore, the transformation necessary for black lumpens was to orient themselves to a black nationalist project. Further, modern black nationalism since Du Bois had asserted the centrality of black American culture; thus, the revolutionary project of the lumpen, of necessity, would need to orient itself to that cultural project and, following the BPP's logic, possibly take the lead of it. In this context, the orientation of the lumpen to transform itself into a revolutionary class would depend not simply on its position in the class structure but in its *dis*position toward this broader nationalist project, and the socialization aspect of this project would be predominantly cultural. Given that the lumpen's socialization was a function of racist factors outside of industrial production, it followed that cultural factors would be more salient in their politicization than they would be otherwise. The BPP did not seem to appreciate these implications of their thesis, which called for a richer analysis of the subculture of the black lumpenproletariat in order to facilitate its transformation into the vanguard of the black revolution, and thus they should've taken seriously Malcolm's call for cultural revolution and the salient arguments that Us made regarding it. The BPP was correct that the motivating culture of these putatively revolutionary lumpens was unlikely to be that of precapitalist Africa, as Karenga's kawaida implied; however, the BPP's revolutionary program required an analysis of the subculture of the lumpenproletariat, since it would play a much more prominent role (as compared to the industrial proletariat) in the revolution the BPP envisioned for the "black colony."

In the event, the BPP failed to adequately theorize how the differences in the structure of colonialism affected the class orientations of the subject nations under domestic colonialism. That is, if in the context of the *territorial* (i.e., the *colonizing*) *state*, the metropole, the lumpenproletariat was a counterrevolutionary class, as Marx argued, and in the context of the *traditional colonial state* the lumpenproletariat was a revolutionary class, as Fanon argued, then in the context of the *domestic colonial state* it was not clear what orientation the lumpen would have toward revolution (following this logic, the same could be said for the other classes under domestic colonialism as well, i.e., the domestic colonial bourgeoisie, petty bourgeoise, and proletariat). Instead of appreciating that the different types of colonialism were likely to generate different relations of production, thus, different orientations of classes toward revolution in a Marxist sense, the BPP adopted wholesale Fanon's thesis on the revolutionary orientation of the lumpen to the domestic colony of black America, which was markedly different from that of (traditional) colonial Algeria. The BPP's aversion to analyses of culture left it bereft of a theory to link the black lumpenproletariat in the United States to a revolution to address the challenges of the domestic colonial context that they sought to radically transform.

At its founding, the BPP accepted the domestic colonialism explanation of black oppression and, given the peculiar position of blacks within the United States, they advocated in their 10-Point-Program a plebiscite "to be held throughout the Black colony" to determine the "national destiny" of black people.[25] After 1968—and under the influence of Eldridge Cleaver—they became distant from nationalism except in an instrumental sense as they began to advocate Marxist-Leninist-Maoist ideology, and eventually they came to view oppressed people in general, including poor whites, as "colonial subjects" to be liberated, ostensibly through the efforts of the BPP and its allies.[26] They espoused the view that *national liberation* was necessary in the black (and third world) "colonies" in America and *revolution* was necessary in the "mother country." Throughout each phase of their development, they viewed the lumpenproletariat as essential to successful revolution in the United States, they saw the BPP as the vanguard of this revolution, they viewed culture as ancillary to these processes, and they viewed cultural revolution as almost a contradiction in terms. In 1968, Huey Newton explained:

> There are two kinds of nationalism: revolutionary nationalism and reactionary nationalism. Revolutionary nationalism is a people's revolution with the people in power as its goal. Therefore, to be a revolutionary nationalist you of necessity have to be a socialist. If you are a reactionary nationalist you are not a socialist. . . . Cultural nationalism, or pork-chop nationalism . . . is basically a problem of having the wrong political perspective. . . . [C]ultural nationalists are concerned with returning to the old African culture and thereby regaining their identity and freedom . . . they feel that assuming the African culture is enough to bring political freedom. Many cultural nationalists fall into line as reactionary nationalists. (Newton, 1995, p. 92)

He added that

> [t]he Black Panther Party . . . realizes that we have to have an identity. We have to realize our Black heritage in order to give us strength to move on and progress. But as far as returning to the old African culture, it's unnecessary and in many respects unadvantageous. We believe that culture alone will not liberate us. We're going to need some stronger stuff. (ibid., p. 93)

Newton (1970, p. 539) insisted that "it's important for us to recognize our origins and to identify with the revolutionary black people of Africa and people of color throughout the world," but as far as the BPP was concerned, "the only culture that is worth holding on to is revolutionary culture." For Newton, the revolution the BPP sought would by necessity generate a revolutionary culture. Cultural revolution was at best a contradiction in terms, or at minimum a rhetorical ploy to rationalize absence from legitimate struggle, which the BPP at its inception and in its early conflicts with RAM defined in terms of armed engagements with police. Scot Brown (2003, p. 114) points out that the BPP's conception of "cultural nationalism" neglected Us's "anthropological view of culture, which contained the politics of self-defense and socialism as constituent components of culture. As a result, Panther denunciations of cultural nationalism tended to distort Us's ideology, defining it as a nonpolitical aesthetic preoccupation."[27] Newton would later modify this orientation somewhat—although he did not modify his understanding (or lack thereof) of the role of culture in revolutionary struggle—through his support of the BPP "survival programs" (e.g., the free hot breakfast for children program, the free medical clinics and ambulance services, etc.) and, eventually, electoral politics. In the interim, the BPP's perspective regarding "revolutionary culture" granted it wide latitude in determining what was revolutionary and what constituted the requisite culture it should support. Increasingly, what the BPP viewed as revolutionary were some of the worst aspects of lumpenism, and with Eldridge Cleaver's ascension in the BPP, the worst impact of lumpenism became apparent.

The Panthers' negative view of the role of culture in revolutionary struggle is ironic given the influence of Cleaver as the party developed. His reputation was earned by his literary talent, honed in California prisons, where he served time for rape and assault with intent to murder, and brought to national attention through his widely read *Soul on Ice*. With the assistance of Beverly Axelrod, he garnered a position at *Ramparts* magazine, and he established Black House in San Francisco, which became a cultural center for Bay Area artists and BAM stalwarts such as Amiri Baraka, Sonia Sanchez, Askia Touré, Ed Bullins, and Marvin X, who performed there. But as important as Cleaver's literary talent might have been, his appreciation of revolutionary struggle—and what attracted him to the BPP itself—was its association with lumpenism and violence, essential aspects of the prison subculture in which he developed his literary skills. Cleaver fused these elements into rhetorical and literary flashes of incendiary malapropisms, neologisms, streams of consciousness (and lack of consciousness), and turns of phrases of superficial depth and relevance that he and others passed off as informed theses on revolutionary struggle in the United States. Among his worst was his construction of the white man as the "omnipotent administrator," the black man as the "supermasculine menial," the white woman as the "ultrafeminine freak," and the black woman as the "self-reliant Amazon" in order to, inter alia, rationalize his rape of both black and white women—and, by implication, girls, men, and boys. Cleaver's was little more than a serial rapist's rationalization for rape, given a pseudo-intellectual, quasi-revolutionary gloss. During an era of "radical chic," it became "all the rage," and he proudly articulated it in his best-selling book, *Soul on Ice*, published with the assistance of white leftist lawyer Beverly Axelrod.

As Cleaver developed his "Yankee Doodle Socialist"—more of a revolutionary bohemian anarchist—argument, he purged from Black House many of those whom he considered cultural nationalists. With his ascension to the position of minister of information in the BPP, his personal animus with Maulana Karenga anticipated—in some ways, generated—the explosive fissure between the two former allies, the BPP and Us. For Cleaver, like Newton and Seale before him, the dispute with Us turned on the broader issue of the relevance of culture to black liberation; however, the relatively nonantagonistic relationship between the two groups exploded once Cleaver entered the fray. Beyond the broader ideological differences between the two men, the dispute between Cleaver and Karenga derived from their disagreement during the Free Huey Rally of February 1968 in Los Angeles, in which Us and the BPP (under the auspices of the Black Congress) participated. Cleaver charged that Us had brought "pigs" to perform security, which was a dishonor to Newton, and Karenga responded that the security whom Cleaver disparaged as "pigs" were not police but "bloods just doing their 8" (i.e., eight-hour work day). Recriminations followed, including Cleaver's baseless accusation of collusion between Us and the "pigs" and Karenga's assertion that the BPP's security was ill-trained and ill-prepared to perform security, much less conduct armed insurgency. While the disagreement did not negatively affect the Free Huey Rally, the die between the two had been cast.

Both in his own writings and in the art of BPP Minister of Culture Emory Douglas, Cleaver had not only recognized but celebrated the importance of culture in revolutionary struggle. Cleaver claimed that "the ideology of the Black Panther Party and the teachings of Huey P. Newton are contained in their purest form in Emory's art" (Doss, 2001, p. 184). Douglas viewed "revolutionary art" as a "tool for liberation." According to him, "revolutionary art" was for everybody and the ghetto was "the gallery" for the revolutionary artist. He maintained that "image making and consumption were, in and of themselves, revolutionary praxis" (ibid.). He promoted the view plastered on the November 21, 1970, edition of the *Black Panther* that "We Have To Begin To Draw Pictures That Will Make People Go Out And Kill Pigs."[28] Following Newton and Seale, Eldridge Cleaver promoted an amorphous and self-serving view of revolutionary culture, which legitimized their preferred lumpen activities as "revolutionary" while labeling those who opposed their lumpenism "counterrevolutionary." For example, Cleaver proclaimed that his rape of women was an "insurrectionary act"; specifically, his rape of white women was "insurrectionary" and his rape of black women was "practice." He wedded his misogyny to the "revolutionary lumpenism" of the BPP, especially—but not exclusively—among the West Coast leadership, creating a "revolutionary misogyny" epitomized in their articulation of the importance of "pussy power."

Cleaver wasn't alone in the promotion of "revolutionary misogyny" in the BPP. For example, publicly, leaders such as Bobby Seale (1970, p. 403) lauded the BPP's antisexism:

> You'll find some women's organizations that are working strictly in the capitalist system, and talking about equality under the capitalist system. But the very nature of the capitalistic system is to exploit and enslave people. . . . So we have to progress to a level of socialism to solve these problems. We have to *live* socialism. So where there's a Panther house, we try to live it. When there's cooking to be done, both brothers and sisters cook. Both wash the dishes. The sisters don't just serve and wait on the brothers. A lot of black nationalist organizations have the idea of regulating women to the role of serving their men, and they relate this to black manhood. But a real manhood is based on humanism, and it's not based on *any* form of oppression. (original emphasis)

In fact, few, if any, of the major BPP chapters adequately addressed the sexism and gendered division of labor in their chapters. Thus, in contrast to Seale's pronouncements, Elaine Brown reports an incident in 1969 at BPP headquarters in Oakland, where Panther women cooked, washed dishes, and prepared food in the kitchen. Bobby Seale "snapped his fingers" summoning a fifteen-year-old girl into the room and introduced her to Brown. Seale commanded the child to "tell the Sister here what a Brother has to do to get some from you." Her answer:

> Can't no motherfucker get no pussy from me unless he can get down with the party. . . . A Sister has to give up the pussy when the Brother is on his job and hold it back when he's not. Cause Sisters got pussy power. (Seale, 1970, p. 189)

It would be a mistake to associate such dehumanizing sexist conceptions—and the practices related to them—to only the male leadership of the BPP and adolescent girls, or to take Brown's depiction of Seale in such a context as dispositive, given her visceral hatred of him; however, her recollections are not inconsistent with those of more reliable observers regarding the sexism of the BPP, as well. New York Panther (and Black Liberation Army member) Safiya Bukhari (1993, 4), acknowledged that "there were problems with men who brought their sexist attitudes into the organization," including "[m]en who refused to take direction (orders) from women" while noting that the BPP "had a framework established to deal with that"; however, "because of liberalism and cowardice, as well as fear, a lot of times the framework was not utilized." At the same time, she insisted:

> The simple fact that the Black Panther Party had the courage to address the question of women's liberation in the first place was a monumental step forward. In a time when the other nationalist organizations were defining women as barefoot, pregnant, and in the kitchen, women in the Black Panther Party were working right alongside men, being assigned sections to organize just like the men, and receiving the same training as the men. Further, the decisions about what a person did within the ranks of the Party were determined not by gender but by ability. (Bukhari, 2010, p. 56)

She recognized that "[i]n its brief seven year history women had been involved on every level in the Party," such as

> Audrea Jones, who founded the Boston Chapter of the Black Panther Party, women like Brenda Hyson, who was the OD (officer of the day) in the Brooklyn office of the Party . . . women like Peaches, who fought side by side with Geronimo Pratt in the Southern California Chapter of the Party; and Kathleen Cleaver who was on the Central Committee. (ibid., pp. 56–57)

Insightfully, Bukhari also acknowleged that

> The other side of the coin was women who sought to circumvent the principled method of work by using their femininity as a way to achieve rank and stature within the Party. They also used their sexuality to get out of work and avoid certain responsibilities. This unprincipled behavior within the Party (just as on the streets) undermined the work of other sisters who struggled to deal in a principled manner. (ibid., p. 57)[29]

Bukhari grounds the BPP's sexism in the broader society and in the black lumpen elements it drew on for its primary membership, and these practices—and tacit or explicit endorsement of them—typically varied from chapter to chapter (e.g., see Njeri's [1991] discussion of the Illinois chapter and Rahman's [2009] of Detroit's), therefore, the reality for most BPP members was probably somewhere between hers and Elaine Brown's characterizations—and often chapter specific. To be sure, even as BPP Central Committee member Kathleen Cleaver responded in February 1970 to a *Washington Post* reporter's question regarding a woman's role in the revolution with her famous and trenchant remark, "No one ever asks what a man's place in Revolution is" (Foner, 1970, p. 145), Party members throughout the country—including prominent men and women—articulated the importance of "pussy power." Under the leadership of Elaine Brown, the party would continue some of the worst practices related to lumpen precepts, even as women were placed in more prominent positions and some of the worst verbiage associated with "Cleaverism" was expunged.[30] Nevertheless, it was the male leadership under the influence of Cleaver, Newton, Seale, and Hilliard that made "revolutionary misogyny" prominent practice if not explicit policy of the BPP.[31] It was an easily anticipated result of the glorification of lumpenism and the "man as pimp and woman as whore" mentality that it promoted. This orientation was not only used to sexually exploit women, but to character assassinate rivals, to rationalize the misuse of BPP funds by the national leadership, to justify internecine violence, or to excoriate rival BPM groups (such as the NOI, SNCC, RNA, and Us). Glorified lumpenism was so expansive that former chief of staff David Hilliard (1993, pp. 338–339) reports that Newton required that BPP members watch the film *The Godfather*, as he argued for a "progressive capitalism" (Newton, 1971). The Panther nightclub "The Lamp Post" allegedly became a front for prostitution and a funding source for Newton and the Central Committee's indulgences. Doubly ironic, it was at this point that Newton voiced support for both the womens' movement and gay liberation struggles.

The BPP's struggles on issues of sexism were clearly exacerbated by—though not created by—its privileging of lumpenism in its broader revolutionary thesis, which assumed that participation in revolution would generate the requisite revolutionary culture. However, the notion of the spontaneous generation of a revolutionary culture, like the notion of spontaneous revolution in general, is both ahistorical and fallacious. Moreover, the fact that people are engaged in revolution does not suggest that they possess a revolutionary culture—at least not in a progressive sense. Pol Pot led a revolution in Kampuchea and the product was killing fields and millions of deaths but not the creation of a revolutionary culture in any emancipatory sense. None of the successful revolutions that the BPP lauded and suggested as exemplars were explicable unless one appreciated the role by which leaders utilized their indigenous culture as a means of mobilization and transformation. Such revolutionaries did not await a revolutionary culture, instead they grounded themselves in their national heritage and evoked that which supported liberation and was in opposition to the status quo of their (neo) colonial oppressors, which denied their right of national self-determination and often cast them as barbarians or worse. In these cases, revolutionary leaders seemed to appreciate that insofar as an important aspect of struggle is to capture the hearts and minds of the people, then a revolution that attacked the cultural hegemony of their oppressors formed the basis of the larger political-military struggle for national self-determination. Without it, the masses, suffering under the cultural domination of their colonizers, would be unconvinced of their capacity to realize the objective of liberation. In this light, one may argue that the wars of national liberation that the BPP exalted were oriented by an ideology of "revolutionary nationalism" in which the cultural issue was already resolved for the insurgents; however, the cultural issue for black Americans had not been resolved, according to Cruse, necessitating a "revolutionary cultural nationalism."

The BPP's condemnation of cultural nationalism actually reflected its antipathy toward RAM and, later, Us (exacerbated by COINTELPRO as well as the intergang conflict of Los Angeles). The BPP, owing to disjointed Marxist borrowings, the influence of white leftists, and the personal battles with Us, largely ignored the challenge of cultural transformation in the BPM. This owed, in part, to its dismissal of the salience of black culture in political revolution. Further, the negation of the transformative power of cultural practice with respect to male Party members' relationship with female members and their engagement with broader movement actors, including allies and enemies and especially in the area of ethics and social conduct, exposed the BPP's vulnerability to outside manipulation and control, as warned by Cabral. The cultural transformation the party envisioned—as Seale's quote above reflects—was assumed to derive mainly from the implementation of socialism following or contemporaneous with a political revolution conceived mainly in Marxist terms. Ironically, they did not appreciate that the transformation they were intending from their survival programs was a cultural transformation rooted less in Marx and more in Malcolm. Such a misunderstanding allowed Newton (1995, pp. 92–93) to evoke Papa Doc Duvalier as a prime example of the vacuity and inappropriateness of cultural or, as he called it, "pork chop" nationalism.

The Oakland BPP, unlike the New York chapters, which Hilliard (1993, p. 168) labeled cultural nationalist, misunderstood the basic pan-African (in an anthropological, more than a political sense) and American nature of African American culture and was ultimately unable to successfully channel this rich increasingly black urban working-class culture for the party's own ends. In fact, Newton (1999, p. 192) denigrated pan-Africanism as the highest expression of cultural nationalism. This lack of appreciation of the cultural grounding of black America and the relationship of black culture to American political development led the BPP, especially on the West Coast, to become distant from the black communities they sought to transform. This both encouraged and was exacerbated by the BPP's extremely poor relations with the Black Church. Newton noted that when the BPP distanced itself from the Black Church it distanced itself from the black community. He acknowledged as much in his "On the Relevance of the Church," which he published on Malcolm X's and Ho Chi Minh's birthday in 1971. Newton (1995, pp. 63–64) acknowledged that the BPP "said the Church is only ritual, it is irrelevant and therefore we will have nothing to do with it. We said this in the context of the whole community being involved with the church on one level or another. That is one way of defecting from the community, and that is exactly what we did." Former BPP member Paul Alkebulan (2007, p. 123) notes that the Panthers came to appreciate that "the church was intertwined with the survival and well-being of black people" and that, as a result, in 1973 they "took the ultimate step" and established a church, the Son of Man Temple, "in an attempt to reconnect with a community institution that had the respect of large numbers of people" and in recognition that "ideology did not necessarily prohibit spirituality and politics from mutually beneficial cooperation."[32] Nevertheless, with decreasing support from black communities they came to rely more on white leftist support that became increasingly ambivalent as the Vietnam War wound down.

In its large-scale rejection of the revolutionary role of cultural transformation, the BPP was not only distancing itself from revolutionary practice, but from the core of the black nationalist movement itself (Van Deburg 1992, p. 176), including the arguments of the father of the "revolutionary black nationalism" that the BPP extolled, Malcolm X (as noted in chapter 1). While clearly aware of these precursors, too often the BPP operated as if they were oblivious to them. Later, Cleaver (1974, pp. 75–79), a chief antagonist of "cultural nationalists," acknowledged as much. In addition, as noted above, Fanon (1968, pp. 245–248), one of the patron saints of the BPP, also noted the significance of culture in revolution, and Cabral (1973) made pointed arguments on the subject, arguing that within culture is found the seed of opposition that leads to the fashioning of the liberation movement. The heavy rhetoric of the times made a meaningful discussion of these issues difficult at best and "counterrevolutionary" at worst. A superficial reading of Mao and the influence of the White Left (many of whom would later become some of the most truculent and self-serving critics of the BPP and the broader BPM) led the formerly nationalist BPP to embrace an almost "cultureless leftism" that even led some prominent members, such as Chief of Staff David Hilliard and Masai Hewitt, to reject, at one time, the teaching of Black Studies (Draper, 1970, pp. 105–106).

The transformative power of the BPP was not in taking up the gun—blacks had a long history of armed resistance up to that time, including fighting a revolution for their freedom during the U.S. Civil War. The transformative power on the individual level was to be found in the fusion of activism and political education, that is, not only in providing the community with patrols, but just as much in the provision of the survival programs, which served as incipient parallel institutions showing the community what revolutionists could provide for them even when the state would not. Through the survival programs, the BPP was actually "returning to the fold" of black nationalist organizing, which followed Malcolm's OAAU in focusing on the development of parallel institutions that would raise the contradictions of the provision of services by dedicated black revolutionists who staffed these institutions and the absence of such service delivery by the government agencies mandated to provide them. For the BPP, Newton (1995, p. 104) saw the survival programs also as a key organizing tool whose impact would help revolutionize the mostly poor black recipients of the services. In 1971, he noted that the BPP

> recognized that in order to bring the people to the level of consciousness where they would seize the time, it would be necessary to serve their interests in survival by developing programs which would help them to meet their daily needs. For a long time we have had such programs not only for survival but for organizational purposes. . . . All these programs satisfy the deep needs of the community but they are not solutions to our problems. That is why we call them survival programs, meaning survival pending revolution. . . . So the survival programs are not answers or solutions, but they will help us to organize the community around a true analysis and understanding of their situation. When consciousness and understanding is raised to a high level then the community will seize the time and deliver themselves from the boot of their oppressors. (ibid., p. 104)

Importantly, the survival programs were also intended to develop the revolutionary consciousness among some of the petit bourgeois owners of local businesses who would be encouraged and/or coerced to help support them. Newton recognized that the need for money to finance the survival programs led the BPP to initially seek support from "wealthy White philanthropists, humanitarians, and heirs to the corporate monopolies," which he came to view as contradictory since the BPP blanketly condemned the "small victimized Black capitalists in our communities" (ibid., p. 105). To address this error, the BPP began to differentiate the petit bourgeois black owners of local businesses who might serve the community from the corporate bourgeoisie that maintained the "capitalist empire," following the logic and published work of both Cruse and Haywood, though acknowledging neither.[33] He pointed out that

> we recognize that the small Black capitalist in our communities has the potential to contribute to the building of the machine which will serve the true interests of the people and end all exploitation. By increasing the positive qualities of the Black capitalist we may be able to bring about a non-antagonistic solution of his contradiction with the community, while at the same time heightening the oppressed community's contradiction with the large corporate capitalist empire. This will intensify the antagonistic contradiction between the oppressed community and the empire; and by heightening that contradiction there will subsequently be a violent transformation of the corporate empire. We will do this through our survival programs which have the interest of the community at heart. (Newton, 1995, p. 105)

In Newton's view, the survival programs could help revolutionize both those who were recipients of the services of the survival programs and the black businesses that helped support them. He was also convinced that the success of these programs would enable the BPP to influence local elections by mobilizing those served by, and associated with, the survival programs to support or withdraw support from candidates for local office. In this electoral capacity, the BPP could function as a political machine and acquire control of Oakland's municipal government. This would be attempted in 1973, following a successful voter registration drive in 1972 in which the BPP added thousands of new voters to the rolls, as the BPP ran Chairman Bobby Seale and Central Committee member Elaine Brown for the offices of mayor and city councilperson of Oakland, respectively. Seale surprised many observers by coming in second place, forcing a runoff election in which he lost to the incumbent. Four years later, the BPP, under the leadership of Brown, played a major role in electing Lionel Wilson as the first African American mayor of Oakland.

Instead of leveraging their electoral success, the return of Newton from exile in Cuba to face murder and assault charges disoriented the BPP and undermined its ability to build on its remarkable electoral victory in Oakland. Newton's return was marked by his descent into drug abuse and his often megalomaniacal, murderous mismanagement of the BPP, which led to internecine conflicts and the departure of Brown, which, following Seale's exit in 1974, left the BPP without the two main architects of its successful electoral strategy. Moreover, Newton's preoccupation with controling the "illegal capitalist" trade in Oakland (i.e., drugs, prostitution, and gambling) took whatever was left of his once considerable talents in a direction that could not be reconciled with successfully lobbying a sitting mayor, or even the maintenance of the BPP as a working organization, much less a revolutionary one. With Newton's return, the BPP imploded and could not exercise influence over the mayor whose election the Party, in Newton's absence, had contributed to significantly.

As for the survival programs, for BPP members and participants the service to the community that they provided had the potential to transform people of all classes from poor children to college students to gang members, and no less importantly, BPP members' participation in the survival programs was often transformative for them as well. The Oakland leadership, security elements, exiles, and many members of the underground, largely out of touch with the day to day operation of these programs, lacked the opportunity to be transformed by this reorienting of values that the survival programs were providing. Moreover, as these programs, in Oakland at least, came to be extortionist plans and strongarming attempts they lost their capacity to transform folk; instead, they simply legitimized the latent lumpenism within the BPP and reduced the organization's capacity to substantively transform itself or the larger black community (Henderson, 1997).

To their credit, notable Panther leaders—prominently, those in Chicago, New York, and Detroit—resisted some of the worst of Oakland's practices and oriented their chapters in ways more consistent with the ideals outlined in the ten-point platform, often undertaking important initiatives either more fully or well before they became the focus of the Oakland leadership. For example, Fred Hampton, Illinois BPP Deputy Chairman, resisted the adoption of some of the worst aspects of lumpenism, and instead worked to organize truces and political alliances among gangs in Chicago, including the Blackstone Rangers and the Black Disciples. The impact of Hampton, Yvonne King, Lynn French, Akua Njeri (aka Deborah Johnson), among others, challenged important aspects of sexism in the Illinois chapter, and chapter members, led by Deputy Minister of Health "Doc" Satchell and dedicated members such as Wanda Ross, promoted the survival programs often in more consistent ways than those operating on the West Coast (Henderson, 2013a). Similarly, the New York BPP chapter challenged some of the most egregious policies emanating from the West Coast leadership, and often took African names and maintained supportive relationships with RAM. The Detroit BPP was closely associated with the LRBW, the RNA, and RAM-affiliated groups such as UHURU, and with these influences focused more on community-building initiatives, landlord-tenant struggles, Black Studies programs, as well as survival programs.

In fact, probably more than any of the Panther initiatives it was the survival programs that had the capacity to generate the transformative change the BPP sought, and to that extent, Newton was right in his assessment in 1971. The contradictions raised by the provision of these "poor people's programs" by black revolutionists to communities that the state largely ignored, except for the provision of police that acted more like an occupying army than public servants (or even professional peace officers), provided a liminal space in which the outward demonstration of respect for the human decency of vulnerable black people by servicing their material needs simultaneously encouraged a cultural reorientation for participants, which when facilitated by political education allowed for the political transformation envisioned by the BPP. Given the prevalence of women in the survival programs where much of the transformative capacity of the Party was actualized, by suppressing women's leadership the BPP undermined the effectiveness of those within the Party who probably were best equipped to formulate and execute the transformative agenda that the BPP sought to create and institutionalize. In this way, sexism undermined the Party's ability to realize its programmatic objectives; thus, it was not only morally odious; it was politically debilitating. The BPP was hardly alone among BPM organizations—or those of the White Left or the CRM—in failing to appreciate the latter.

The BPP's difficult task of organizing the lumpenproletariat for revolution in the United States was complicated further by its attempt to draw on myriad models of revolution from abroad when black Americans required an example consistent with their experiences at home. Newton (1967) seemed to understand this as early as his "The Correct Handling of a Revolution," and expanded on it in his intercommunalism, but the foreign nature of Marxism to many BPP members, and its strained applicability to the conditions of black America, was exacerbated by Party members' unfamiliarity with black American revolutionary history. Former BPP/BLA member Assata Shakur concurred that the "basic problem" was that the BPP "had no systematic approach to political education."

> They were reading the Red Book but didn't know who Harriet Tubman, Marcus Garvey, and Nat Turner were. They talked about intercommunalism. . . . A whole lot of them barely understood

any kind of history, Black, African or otherwise. . . . That was the main reason many Party members . . . underestimated the need to unite with other Black organizations and to struggle around various community issues. (Shakur, 1987, p. 221)

This failure to unite with progressive elements in the black community was underscored by the BPP's alliances with nonblack groups outside of the black community—primarily SDS and other white leftists in the antiwar movement.[34] However, the white antiwar movement had no coherent ideology, nor much stomach for revolution, either cultural or political. The White Left seemed less intent on revolt and more on keeping its followers out of Vietnam, as well as keeping its antiracist activism outside of white communities where it was as needed as it was neglected by them.[35] Not surprisingly, BPP alliances with these leftists dried up as the war wound down. Further, the antagonistic language of Marxism-Leninism, vanguardism, and the cult of personality allowed for purges and the excommunication of individuals and families in a manner unforeseen in the black liberation movement community. BPP practices such as the use of the bullwhip for punishment—in arrogant indifference to its resonance with the lash of slavery—and the wholesale attack on spirituality were so far removed from black American cultural preferences that it was sure to engender disenchantment with the BPP in black communities that might otherwise have provided sanctuary and support.

Meanwhile, a prime locus of antagonism for the Panthers and others in the BPM between "revolutionary" nationalists and "cultural" nationalists was more apparent than real. There is considerable convergence between these two perspectives for black Americans, in practice if not philosophically. For example, Assata Shakur (1987, p. 242) summarizes the shortfalls of the BPP in that "[o]n the whole, we were weak, inexperienced, disorganized, and seriously lacking in training." She is clear that armed struggle could never be successful in itself unless it was wedded to an overall strategy for winning that appreciated political and military dimensions. It was apparent to Shakur (ibid.) that the "most important battle was to help politically mobilize, educate, and organize the masses of Black people and to win their minds and hearts." This converges with Karenga's assertion that "[t]he revolution being fought now is a revolution to win the minds of our people. If we fail to win this we cannot wage the violent one" (Halisi & Mtume, 1967, p. 18). A basic problem for Shakur (1987, p. 242) was lack of political education, "an overall ideology and strategy that stem from a scientific analysis of history and present conditions." Again, her "revolutionary" nationalist critique dovetails with Karenga's "cultural" nationalist admonition that blacks "must develop a new plan of revolution for Black people here in America."[36] For

Karenga this was kawaida, for Newton it was revolutionary intercommunalism, and there is more confluence between their approaches than either of them was likely to admit. Even Cleaver (1974) eventually argued that a synthesis of revolutionary nationalist and cultural nationalist orientations was possible and had been achieved in the Republic of Congo, which showed how culture and class struggle were dialectically related. Although his familiarity with Congo's politics was superficial at best (Fila-Bakabadio, 2018), his recognition of the possibility of a synthesis was revelatory given his central role in the Us-BPP dispute.[37]

Nevertheless, the BPP's assertion that revolutionary struggle would generate the requisite culture for black Americans was seriously undermined by the persistence of the worst aspects of lumpenism in the organization, which was to be expected absent an immersion in culturally transformative programs and practices. Absent this transformative context, the lumpenproletarians that the BPP exalted as the vanguard of the black revolution resorted to the historic role that Marx, Cruse, and Malcolm, among others, envisioned for them: they became agents of reaction that willfully joined the oppressive apparatus of the state to support counterrevolution. Without a transformation that preceded their involvement in political struggle, the lumpen were as likely to pursue revolution as just another criminal enterprise or another "game" to be "run" on the masses, whom they viewed primarily as "suckers," "tricks," or "chumps" to be exploited. Contrary to the BPP's view that the black lumpenproletariat was detached from the capitalist system and somehow free of its fetters, the lumpen is intimately connected to capitalism through the social welfare and criminal justice systems, and large swaths of it as parasites on the proletariat and the poor, and in its organized form, as territorial, commercial, or corporate gangs (e.g., mafia), parasitical on the petite bourgeoisie as well.[38] The source of lumpen work, income, and livelihood is not only the informal sectors such as illegal drugs/alcohol, gambling, prostitution, and loan sharking, but those formal sectors of the capitalist politico-economy that facilitate racketeering, fraud, and extortion. Viewed in this light, the lumpen is not only implicated in capitalism, it is utterly dependent on it.

Some of the worst aspects of lumpenism were implicated in the degree to which members of the BPP killed, tortured, battered, and beat their fellow members in blind deference to their "Supreme Servant" Huey Newton, in a cult of personality several magnitudes larger than that of Karenga. The internal bloodletting was barely exhausted in the mutual destruction of the internecine conflict between supporters of Newton and those of Eldridge Cleaver after their split, and it continued unabated under the "administrative lumpenism" of Elaine Brown's regime, which occassioned, condoned, and employed physical attacks and even murder against BPP members, affiliates, and community members in order to prepare a pathway for the return of Newton to Oakland after his exile to escape separate murder and assault charges. The policies of each of these BPP leaders were rooted in a blind, often fanatical, belief in the exactness and infallibility of their assessment of the requirements for revolutionary change and their willingness to employ terrorism against black people, including members of their own organization, to achieve them. A list including Robert Webb, Sam Napier, Fred Bennett, James Carr, Alex Rackley, and Michael Baynham would comprise only some of the BPP members who fell victim to internecine murder, while the victims of internecine violence are too numerous to list.[39] Panther murder victims such as seventeen-year-old Kathleen Smith are marginalized by Newton apologists such as Elaine Brown (1992, p. 356), who rarely acknowledges Smith's murder by Newton without reference to her, who was a child, as a "prostitute," as if this justifies her killing (a crime for which Newton was acquitted after witnesses failed to appear in court).[40] If Smith was involved in prostitution, she was among the lumpen that the BPP cast as the vanguard and took pride in claiming they were transforming into revolutionaries.

Just as telling is the selective moral outrage of apologists for BPP lumpenism, who will at once rightfully—and self-righteously—condemn Karenga for his torture conviction, while praising BPP members such as Ericka Huggins, who boiled the water used to torture teenager Alex Rackley over a period of two days before her fellow Panthers Lonnie McLucas and Warren Kimbro killed him and, along with George Sams, dumped his body in a river near New Haven. Yet, Huggins is celebrated among many Panther supporters not only as the widow of John Huggins but as a revolutionary feminist in her own right. New York BPP member Jamal Joseph, convicted with three other Panthers in a case related to the torture and killing of Sam Napier, circulation manager of the BPP newspaper and a Newton supporter, is a full professor and former chair of Columbia University's Graduate Film Division, an Academy Award nominee, and the artistic director of Harlem's New Heritage Theatre Group. BPP leaders such as Elaine Brown and David Hilliard, implicated in their own words in an array of crimes, or self-confessed murderers such as Florestan Forbes, seem to escape censure from many Marxist leftists who are indefatigable in their critique of non-Marxist black nationalists but are remarkably unaffected by their implication in crimes against fellow BPP members, other activists, or random black citizens, and have even published books about their crimes as BPP members (e.g., Brown, 1992; Forbes, 2006; Hilliard, 1993; Joseph, 2012). None of this approaches the extent to which crimes committed by white activists are ignored, dismissed, or minimized and to which they become exculpated, in some cases attaining very public and privileged positions. This is evident especially among members of SDS and the Weathermen, including Bill Ayers, Bernadine Dohrn, Mark Rudd, Kathy Boudin, Susan Rosenberg, and Eleanor Raskin, who all became professors at universities or colleges years after the BPM, while former members of the BPP and BLA, whom they once promoted as the "vanguard of the revolution," have languished in captivity for decades as political prisoners. For example, Ruchell Magee has been in prison almost a half a century since his 1970 capture during the Marin County Courthouse shootout in California involving the attempt to free BPP Field Marshall George Jackson, and the Soledad Brothers—the case that brought Angela Davis to national attention; and New York BPP member Jalil Muntaquin for nearly as long since his capture in 1971 at age 19 in the police shooting that became known as the "New York 3"case. Former Philadelphia BPP member, Russell "Maroon" Shoatz has been imprisoned since 1972. New York BPP member Sundiata Acoli has been in captivity since 1973. Philadelphia Black Panther Mumia Abu Jamal has been imprisoned since 1981—much of it on death row. New York BPP and BLA member Assata Shakur has been in exile in Cuba for more than 30 years since her escape from prison in 1979. Nehanda Abiodun, former RNA and BLA, died in Cuba after several decades in exile. Former BPP (and RAM and RNA) member Mutulu Shakur, godfather of rapper Tupac Shakur, has been imprisoned for more than three decades as well. Nevertheless, the BPP's elevation of lumpenism swiftly became a celebration of it, which in some quarters among African American activists and commentators still persists today.

With respect to black cultural revolution, it is fair to say that beyond an instrumentalist orientation toward culture, the BPP did not appreciate the necessity for cultural transformation in the movement; therefore, they did not pose a specific thesis on cultural revolution. Nonetheless, it would be inaccurate to say that they denigrated black culture itself; instead, they denigrated non-Marxist versions of what they considered cultural nationalism and the cultural nationalists they associated with it, even within the BPP itself. At the same time, they elevated the subculture of the lumpenproletariat, and as detrimental as that turned out to be for their specific organization, its value was in challenging the class hegemony of the black petite bourgeoisie while simultaneously challenging the vanguard status of the black proletariat. In so doing, their thesis recognized the diversity and fluidity of black revolutionary theory. Moreover, even with respect to culture, given the BPP's embrace of elements of lumpen culture—both in its aesthetic and institutional forms—their activism was at least consistent with, if not consciously reflective of, Locke's thesis, which argued against placing hegemonic strictures on the expressions of black culture, even those that might promote what appear as unflattering aspects of the black experience, because what might be viewed as retrograde in one context or aspect might be progressive in another.[41] Notwithstanding that theoretical confluence with Locke, on the whole, the BPP's approach to culture was more consistent with that espoused by Boggs than by Locke's. Unfortunately, this view that a revolutionary culture would be generated by revolution itself remains a prominent perspective among revolutionists in the United States.

Conclusion

The analyses of RAM, Us, and the BPP highlight the challenges and opportunities of key organizations in the BPM to devise revolutionary theory to guide their programs and priorities. They drew theoretical and programmatic inspiration from Malcolm X's black nationalism and his thesis on black revolution, but they each had difficulty articulating a coherent theory of black revolution applicable to U.S. society. These problems emanated in part from failures to address shortcomings of Malcolm's thesis, especially its reverse civilizationism. As a result, the major activists/theorists of these influential BPM organizations seemed to misunderstand important aspects of the development of African American culture and its relationship to revolutionary change. This was rooted in a broader misunderstanding of the relationship between black national development in contrast to that of other nationalities, and its unique role in American development. Black national development took the form of internal imperialism, according to Haywood, and domestic colonialism, according to Cruse. A key aspect of social change in such a context, as Locke highlighted it, was the wedding of black culture to the self-determination claims of blacks in the political and economic spheres to create racial democracy, thus liberating blacks from racial oppression, fundamentally transforming the white supremacist United States, and in this way completing the bourgeois revolution of the U.S. Civil War as Haywood and Cruse characterized it by extending it fully into the political, economic, cultural, and racial dimensions. Influenced by Malcolm's reverse civilizationism, BPM organizations, often inadvertently, were led to incorporate unworkable "third world" models of revolution (e.g., RAM) or devise dubious traditional African forms (e.g., Us), both cultural dead ends in terms of the likelihood of their adoption by large numbers of blacks, especially in the critical movement areas of the U.S. South and even more so in highly urbanized areas of black concentration throughout the North and West; or they rejected cultural revolution arguments wholesale, adopting the view that their revolutionary activism itself would generate the requisite culture (e.g., the BPP). Each seemed to misunderstand the evolution of the black culture that they sought to revolutionize. Among the central disagreements were those related to the *role* of culture in revolution, the *type* of culture that would facilitate revolution, and the *relationship* between cultural and political revolution in the United States. Although seemingly aware of Cruse's argument on the centrality of cultural revolution to African American national development, they often operated as if they were not.

Reverse civilizationism drew their focus away from the revolutionary praxis of African Americans that preceded and should have informed their theses on black revolution in the United States during the BPM. These problems were largely attributable to a failure to appreciate the centrality of the one revolution that probably had the greatest salience for their own: the Slave Revolution of the Civil War. Although the Civil War occurred a century prior to the CRM, its relevance to 1960s activists was fourfold: (1) it occurred in the United States; (2) it involved the same or similar protagonists; (3) it occurred in the context of a sectarian crisis, one even greater than the dissension regarding the ongoing Vietnam War; and most importantly, (4) it succeeded in overthrowing chattel slavery and the CSA and in so doing beginning the transformation of the United States into a multiracial democracy, albeit it a very short-lived one. One of the important lessons from the Slave Revolution was the role of religiously inspired black workers—similar to Malcolm personally, and to the grassroots to whom he ascribed so much revolutionary potential—who were essential to its success. In contrast, the major BPM revolutionists associated with RAM, Us, and the BPP rejected black Christianity.

Reverse civilizationism also affected their discernment of the salience of culture in revolutionary struggle in other ways. In particular, it contributed to the logically confused, ahistorical, misleading, and often self-serving bifurcation of "revolutionary" nationalists and "cultural" nationalists. To refer to the black nationalism of this era—or to black nationalists—as "cultural nationalists" is redundant at best. Since Du Bois, black nationalism in the United States, which both sides of this false dichotomy supported, was black *cultural* nationalism, that is, a nationalism rooted in identification with an affirming African American culture. In their public pronouncements, documents, and programs, both the revolutionary and the cultural nationalists of the BPM examined in this work advocated political revolution. Therefore, the adjective *revolutionary* was as redundant as cultural with respect to much of the activist black nationalism of the BPM.[42] A more meaningful distinction could be drawn between those black activists who wedded their political support of nationalism to an advocacy of Marxism and its privileging of class struggle as the key axis for understanding the black liberation struggle in the United States and those whose advocacy of nationalism reflected their privileging of the liberation struggle of African Americans conceived primarily as a black nation comprised of several classes battling a white imperial nation that dominated the United States and subjugated the black nation as a domestic colony. Such distinctions led to dramatic differences in interpretations of elements of Malcolm's thesis, especially the role of culture in revolution, as well as the relationship between black cultural and political revolution in the United States.

But even when black revolutionists theorized the salience of black culture in political revolution in the United States during the BPM, they often drew on the domestic colonialism model as the dominant descriptive metaphor of the black American context—even Martin Luther King articulated it at times—and wedded it to a variety of theoretical formulations aimed at organizing revolution to free the black "colony" from its "colonizers" in the manner that had been successful throughout the third world. In this way, theses of black cultural revolution grafted more from African, Asian, Caribbean, and even Latin American modalities, while largely ignoring the peculiar trajectory of black political development in the United States when formulating theses of social change. This was exacerbated in those prominent instances in which activists/theorists explicated domestic colonialism through neo-Marxist formulations, which further reduced the applicability of the models to the historical development of black America. One result was that many domestic colonialism theorists adopted rural, agricultural, and communal African precepts and practices to a predominately urban, industrial, and cosmopolitan African American context, in a process exacerbated by reverse civilizationism. Not surprisingly, even as they advocated black cultural revolution they had difficulty integrating the major black cultural institution, the Black Church, into their theoretical arguments, and often simply remained in confrontation with it. This was doubly ironic given the black nationalist origins of the Black Church as well as the reality that it was becoming increasingly an urban metropolitan and cosmopolitan institution whose activist bona fides had been buttressed by the CRM and whose members' political efficacy had been heightened, making them much more open to further activist mobilization that appealed to them as congregants. Moreover, theorists of cultural revolution failed to confront adequately—if at all—the major contradiction within black communities between black cultural practice and the sociopolitical transformation that they sought, namely, sexism.

For RAM, Us, and the BPP, although their common theoretical core was shaped by their understanding of Malcolm's revolutionary thesis and each accepted, to varying degrees, Haywood's Black Belt thesis in their conception of a black nation in a quasi-colonial relationship with the white supremacist

American state—although Us rejected Marxism but eventually adopted socialism—their differing perspectives reflected in large part the tension among Cruse's, Haywood's, and Boggs's perspectives on the role of culture in black revolutionary struggle. For example, RAM, true to its institutional origins as a group initially drawn to Cruse's theoretical arguments but also one whose leadership and membership were mentored by Boggs, who once served on its executive board, embraced aspects of both Cruse's and Boggs's theses. Us's kawaida was nominally sympathetic to Cruse's orientation given its centering on cultural revolution, sans its reverse civilizationist focus on "traditional African" rather than African American culture, and its lack of emphasis on capturing the cultural apparatus of the United States as a focus of black cultural change. The BPP's orientation was more consistent with Boggs's disposition toward black culture, and later Haywood's Leninist approaches, at least rhetorically, but practically, it was opposed to the latter's focus on the proletariat as the vanguard, opting for a Maoist orientation for the American revolution it envisaged. Nonetheless, the divergent arguments of these revolutionary groups continued to influence the BPM as subsequent organizations drew on them to help guide the revolution they sought. This is evident among influential organizations such as the RNA, the LRBW, CAP, and the Shrine of the Black Madonna. In the next chapter, we turn to an analysis of the revolutionary theses of the RNA and the League, before discussing CAP and the Shrine in chapter 8.

Chapter 7

Republic of New Africa, League of Revolutionary Black Workers

In the last chapter, we examined the theoretical development of the concept of black cultural revolution in the programs, practices and perspectives of the Revolutionary Action Movement (RAM), Us, and the Black Panther Party (BPP). Both RAM and Us grounded their theoretical orientations and organizational activities in a conception of black cultural revolution as articulated by Malcolm X, while directly or indirectly following aspects of Cruse thesis. These groups were challenged on theoretical grounds by the BPP, which viewed revolutionary culture emerging from revolutionary struggle itself, contradicting Malcolm X's thesis on the importance of black cultural revolution while comporting with Boggs's orientation. All of them accepted to some degree Haywood's Black Belt and/or Cruse's domestic colonialism thesis in their conception of the black nation's relationship with the white supremacist American state. The relationship between the black and white nations was viewed as a sort of imperialist relationship, which allowed a more theoretically accommodating association between the black American freedom struggle and anticolonial struggles abroad, and at the outset of the BPM, this was more reflective of Cruse's thesis, which, in that respect, was a non-Marxist variant of Haywood's. As the BPM progressed, a Marxist— although not explicitly "Haywoodian"—perspective on domestic colonialism became ascendant among BPM revolutionists, epitomized in RAM, the BPP, the League of Revolutionary Black Workers (LRBW), and the Congress of African Peoples (CAP). Each of these organizations faced difficulties promoting a plausible and identifiably *cultural* agent for black liberation, and specifically one that could fuse the economic and political interests of black people to mobilize collective protest and organize rebellion. Instead, they undertook initiatives and created some modest institutions to channel black grievances, but these were often ad hoc, following more emphatically political, economic, or cultural paths that rarely merged in a politico-economic-cultural synthesis to guide the revolution that they sought. Although these groups advocated black political revolution, and began to appreciate the importance of culture in the revolution(s) they envisioned, they integrated cultural factors poorly in their revolutionary theses.

In fact, even advocates of black cultural revolution often did not appreciate the revolutionary potential of black culture manifest in the religiously inspired working-class character of many black Americans who were mobilizing in the Civil Rights Movement (CRM) and the incipient Black Power Movement (BPM). Too often, they argued that individuals had to abandon the church or repudiate their religious advocacy in order to engage in revolutionary struggle, which, ironically, had emerged largely from initiatives rooted in the Black Church. The exemplar and main progenitor of the BPM, Malcolm X, also advocated and projected such a spiritually infused grassroots orientation. One result or reflection of this theoretical and empirical lacuna was that BPM revolutionists generally failed to confront the centrality of the Black Church to the black liberation struggle and the reality that the CRM had demonstrated that blacks could build and sustain a viable movement for social change while remaining in the church. The exception to this myopia in the BPM was the Shrine of the Black Madonna.

The denigration of the Black Church and important aspects of black spirituality reflected the deeper problem of prominent BPM groups, which, while evoking Malcolm X as their chief protagonist and architect, often didn't ground their socio-politico-economic analyses, practices, and programs in Malcolm's more developed reflections on revolution that he proffered during his last months, opting instead to privilege his more familiar, and flawed, earlier conceptions of revolution, which he had either dramatically modified or wholly abandoned. For example, Malcolm's focus on revolutionary violence was adopted most notably by the BPP, but the BPP didn't seem to appreciate his corresponding arguments about "bloodless revolution" and disparaged his thesis on cultural revolution, almost wholesale. Malcolm's focus on black cultural revolution was adopted most notably by Us, but Us exacerbated Malcolm's reverse civilizationism in its promotion of an African cultural atavism. Malcolm's critique of capitalist exploitation was adopted by the BPP, but the BPP largely ignored Malcolm's challenge to movement sexism, as did almost all of the BPM organizations. In another sense, though, these groups took aspects of Malcolm's theses farther than he had. For example, RAM integrated a Northern strategy to complement the Southern strategy of the Student Non-violent Coordinating Committee (SNCC) and other prominent CRM organizations, which Malcolm only began during his final months; Us formulated a regime of African culture to institutionalize an African American culture that Malcolm agreed was largely absent in black America; and the BPP supported a UN plebiscite, armed patrols to monitor the police, and the organization of "the grassroots"—in this case, lumpenproletarians—such as Malcolm had begun in earnest in the Nation of Islam (NOI). Two aspects of Malcolm's thesis in particular were developed by his followers beyond what Malcolm had accomplished or, in some cases, even envisioned: (1) his focus on land as the basis of independence; and (2) his insistence on black reparations. No black power organization developed these two aspects of Malcolm's thesis into its theoretical and programmatic approach more than the Republic of New Africa (RNA).

The RNA premised its organization, and its revolutionary thesis and program of action, explicitly on what it referred to as the "Malcolm X Doctrine." They largely derived this "doctrine from Malcolm's "Message to the Grassroots" speech, which argued, inter alia, that land was the basis of independence, revolution was based on land, and revolution involved bloodshed; and his "Ballot or the Bullet" speech, which emphasized the usefulness of an electoral strategy to achieve black self-determination politically, balanced with a guerrilla warfare strategy to seize power in the case of white racist repression and intransigence. The common thread in this phase of Malcolm's theoretical development was his call for UN intervention in the human rights struggle of African Americans; and his view that the black revolt in the United States was part of a worldwide revolution linked closely to the freedom struggles against Western colonialism occurring throughout the third world. The RNA stitched these threads into a novel tapestry of black revolution in the United States during the black power era.

The (Provisional Government of the) Republic of New Africa

The RNA emerged from the Black Government Conference in March 1968, which was held at several sites in Detroit, including Rev. Albert Cleage's Central Congregational Church, which would become the Shrine of the Black Madonna. The conference was convened by the Malcolm X Society, which was formed shortly after Malcolm's assassination by former members of the Group on Advanced Leadership (GOAL), which had sponsored Malcolm's famous "Message to the Grassroots" presentation in November 1963, his "Ballot or the Bullet" speech of April 1964, and his "Last Message" of February 1965, all in Detroit. Comprised of Malcolm's supporters and acolytes, the RNA was largely the brainchild of two noted black nationalists in Detroit, who were biological brothers originally from Philadelphia.

At the time of the RNA's founding, Milton Henry was an Army veteran, a friend of Malcolm X who had accompanied him on one of his trips to Africa, and a lawyer in the Detroit suburb of Pontiac, Michigan; and his younger brother Richard was a journalist who at the time was a technical writer with the Army's Tank-Automotive and Armaments Command, just outside of Detroit. The brothers took the names Gaidi and Imari Obadele, respectively, and were instrumental in the organization of both GOAL and the Malcolm X Society.[1]

GOAL was a broad-based organization centered on issues of black self-determination, while the Malcolm X Society overlapped in membership with GOAL and consisted mainly of those black nationalists intent on putting their vision of Malcolm's political program into practice. GOAL included Rev. Cleage, James and Grace Lee Boggs, the Henrys, activists, students, and workers affiliated with UHURU, RAM, and SNCC, and those who would become instrumental in the LRBW, the Detroit chapter of the BPP, and subsequently the RNA. While GOAL represented a variety of radical, reformist, and progressive tendencies in Detroit from its founding in 1961, including the motive force for the Freedom Now Party (FNP), the Malcolm X Society was organized shortly after his assassination to put into place what its members saw as Malcolm's revolutionary vision. It was the Henrys' brainchild, and it provided the main theoretical thrust of the Black Government Conference aimed at establishing a sovereign presence of black Americans in the United States: a black territorial state. To that end, conference attendees in Detroit produced a Declaration of Independence, which Queen Mother Moore was the first to sign, a Constitution, and the framework for a provisional government that included Robert F. Williams (who was exiled in China at the time), as First President, Milton Henry (Gaidi), First Vice President, Betty Shabazz, Malcolm X's widow, Second Vice President, Richard Henry (Imari), Minister of Information, Queen Mother Moore, Minister of Health and Welfare, Herman Ferguson, Minister of Education, William Grant, Minister of State and Foreign Affairs, H. Rap Brown (Jamil Al Amin), Minister of Defense, Imamu Amiri Baraka, Maulana Karenga and Nana Oserjiman Adefunmi, Co-Ministers of Culture, Joan Franklin, Minister of Justice, Raymond Willis, Minister of Finance, Oboboa Awolo (Ed Bradley), Treasurer, Muhammad Ahmad, Minister without Portfolio or Special Ambassador.

Although major figures of the BPM were associated with the RNA, its chief theorist was Imari Obadele. The RNA's theoretical framework for black revolution in the United States reflected its broader ideological program of self-determination, which was self-consciously rooted in what the group referred to as "the Malcolm X Doctrine." The doctrine had been outlined in Obadele's *War in America: The Malcolm X Doctrine* (1968) and was the centerpiece of the "New African Creed," which "citizens" of the Republic recited, and which read in part:

> i believe in the Malcolm X Doctrine: that We must organize upon this land, and hold a plebiscite, to tell the world by a vote that We are free and our land independent, and that, after the vote, We must stand ready to defend ourselves, establishing the nation beyond contradiction.[2]

The three initial objectives of the RNA were for reparations, land, and the holding of referenda among blacks to resolve their citizenship. These included: (1) a $300 billion initial payment from the U.S. government to descendants of enslaved blacks; (2) the establishment of a sovereign, independent, black majority country comprised of five states of the historic Black Belt, Louisiana, Mississippi, Alabama, Georgia, and South Carolina (and adjacent black majority counties in Texas, Arkansas, Tennessee, North Carolina, and Florida); and (3) a UN-supervised plebiscite among blacks to determine their preferences either for citizenship in the New African republic, full citizenship in a multiracial democratic United States, or emigration to Africa or some other territory.

As an organization, RNA members were advocates of African socialism reflected in the Tanzanian leader Julius Nyerere's *ujamaa,* but they did not embrace Marxism explicitly; rather, the RNA adopted Haywood's conception of the Black Belt as articulated by Malcolm. The support for the Black Belt thesis emanated from previous groups that influenced the Malcolm X Society (the precursor to the RNA), including several led by Adefunmi, Moore, and Williams that focused on the Black Belt territory as well as reparations. Queen Mother Audley Moore was especially influential; as a Garveyite and member of the CPUSA, she advocated Haywood's Black Belt thesis before leaving the Party when it abandoned this position by the 1950s. Her black nationalism fused Garvey's territorial claims with the Black Belt thesis in a framework centered on the domestic and international aspects of black self-determination—evoking Cuffee's eighteenth-century dual colonization scheme. Throughout the 1950s and 1960s, Moore, the Harlem-based head of the Universal Association of Ethiopian Women, was the most prominent advocate of African American reparations. In 1957 and 1959, she attempted to present a petition to the UN, arguing for both land and reparations for black Americans, including $200 billion to monetarily compensate for four hundred years of slavery. Before Elijah Muhammad had put his initial demand for land in his national newspaper in 1960, it was Moore who had directly influenced Malcolm X concerning reparations (see chapter 1). The Malcolm X Society adopted her focus on reparations and, following suit, so did the RNA.

For the RNA, reparations took the form of both a monetary allotment of several hundred billion dollars as well as a dispensation of what they considered the national territory of black Americans, the Black Belt states noted above, as the land upon which to establish their sovereign nation. Unlike many of the BPM organizations advocating armed struggle, the RNA, which began in the North, moved South in order to press its claims. When neither money nor land was forthcoming, they advocated an electoral strategy in districts in the South where blacks were concentrated, to use the ballot to elect officials sympathetic to "New Africanism" until these locales could declare their independence and incorporate into the New African state. Where the electoral strategy was met with repression, the RNA advocated "people's war" in order to liberate the "national territory." Obadele (1972, p. 26) emphasized that the RNA's "objective is not to overthrow the United States but to create our own nation," consisting not of "fifty states, or twenty-five states, or even ten states—though by a rule of independence for unjust enrichment we are entitled to all the wealth of the American nation," but only "five states, taken together, the poorest states in the nation, the states with the most black people in them, a mere one-tenth of the states in the Union," which he seemed convinced was an "area which the white American—with some 170 million of his number living outside of the area—is most likely to give up when he is forced to the point where giving up something will be a necessity."

Seemingly absent from his consideration was that this was the land for which the United States had fought its bloodiest war, the Civil War. The point was not lost on Obadele who saw as a compromise exchange for the cession of the "national territory" the RNA's willingness to concede the cities of the North and West in which blacks were concentrated (i.e., the "subjugated territory") although they were, technically, part of his conception of the Black Belt (as they were for Haywood). He argued that the RNA was not "naive enough to believe that in this violent, racist United States" its allies such as Detroit congressman John Conyers "will be successful in achieving laws which effect a peaceful plebiscite and the peaceful ceding of the land to New Africa"; therefore, the RNA needed to use the peaceful interregnum to "prepare for war," including "the creation of an over-ground army, properly motivated, properly equipped, and able to meet and succeed at the kind of combat which may be forced upon us" (Obadele, 1972, p. 31). Operationally, the RNA's overground armed force, the Black Legion, was tasked to engage U.S. armed forces mobilized against it in the national territory and an underground force, associated with insurrectionists such as those who had participated in the Newark and Detroit rebellions of 1967, would be tasked to launch guerilla reprisals in the North in support of the Black Legion's efforts in the South. The RNA referred to these irregulars in the North as a "second strike capability," and the effectiveness of their strategy relied on the capacity of blacks in U.S. cities (the "subjugated territory") to come to the aid of RNA armed forces. These efforts in the national and subjugated territories would not lead to the overthrow of the U.S. government but would be sufficiently taxing to compel the United States to sue for peace and grant the secession of lands to the RNA. The peoples' war strategy was reminiscent of Haywood's support for black self-determination in the Black Belt, including secession, but in its formulation the RNA's plan was more evocative of Robert Williams's (1964) abortive guerilla warfare strategy for black liberation.

In addition, the RNA—more than any other organization in the BPM—promoted the issue of reparations, which they viewed as central to the development of New Africa and a basic premise of its political platform. It rested its claims for black reparations in both constitutional and international law. Through their leading theoreticians and jurists, Gaidi Obadele, Imari Obadele, Audley Moore, and, later, Chokwe Lumumba, Adjoa Aeyitoro, and Nkechi Taifa they provided political, legal, and moral justifications for their claims. The RNA argued that when originally freed from their enslavement by the Thirteenth Amendment to the U.S. Constitution, which eradicated chattel slavery, African Americans' status in the law was as descendants of kidnapped Africans, and thereupon they should have been granted the choice of returning to Africa, establishing a new independent nation among themselves in the United States (or elsewhere), or becoming full and unfettered U.S. citizens in a multiracial democracy. Instead, in the RNA's view, the Fourteenth Amendment *imposed* U.S. citizenship on them, in what should have been a grant or offer of citizenship that, by definition, could be accepted or rejected; but newly manumitted slaves were not given this fundamental choice. Further, what was imposed was not full and unfettered citizenship in any meaningful sense, but instead a tenuous and nominal citizenship without any compensation in land or the granting of meaningful political, economic, or social rights. Not surprisingly, even this ephemeral citizenship would be set aside within nine years with the overthrow of Reconstruction in the Hayes-Tilden Compromise of 1877. Obadele explains it this way:

> Following the Thirteenth Amendment, four natural options were the basic right of the African. First, he did, of course, have a right, if he wished it, to be an American citizen. Second, he had

a right to return to Africa or go to another country—if he could arrange his acceptance. Finally, he had a right (based on a claim to land superior to the European's, subordinate to the Indian's) to set up an independent nation of his own. (1972, p. 28)

These "four fundamental consequences of freedom" would be the centerpiece of RNA theorizing on black liberation and its practical programs toward that end. The RNA pressed its right to establish an independent nation in the five contiguous Black Belt states of the former Confederacy that, for them, comprised the Republic of New Africa. They argued that this land not only constituted the national homeland of the descendants of enslaved African Americans—and as such was their inheritance, but its dispensation to the progeny of the former slaves served as an initial form of reparations to African Americans. Added to it were reparations that included a monetary allotment and technical assistance to allow the newly created Republic to become self-sustaining.

The RNA advocated the rights of blacks to support any of these options, which was evident in its call for a plebiscite among them to determine their preferred course of action. The RNA plebiscite was not the one that Malcolm called for, which was a petition for the UN to vote to have oversight of the failure of the U.S. government to ensure the human rights of African Americans given the persistence of de jure white supremacism in Jim Crow and de facto white supremacist repression and terrorism of black Americans, and Malcolm's plebiscite wasn't focused on secession, as such. The RNA plebiscite was also different from the call by the BPP; although Huey Newton (1995, 98) recognized the RNA's right to its claims, including secession, he opposed the timing of the RNA's plebiscite rather than its substance. The BPP argued that the plebiscite should only be undertaken after the liberation of the black domestic colony—thus, after the black politico-military revolution they envisioned. In contrast, the RNA favored—at least theoretically—a plebiscite prior to such a revolution.

In practice, it wasn't clear whether the plebiscite should precede or follow the establishment of a presence in the "national homeland," because part of the RNA's later claim upon its movement south was the need to establish its sovereignty in the "Kush District" (a 15,000 square mile contiguous heavily black populated territory predominantly in western Mississippi, but stretching from Memphis to Louisiana) by a plebiscite to be conducted there, which presupposes a presence in the South, which it did not begin to create in earnest until 1970. On the other hand, the logic at the founding of the RNA and in its Declaration of Independence was that those "New Africans" who had assembled in Detroit in March 1968 were affirming through a plebiscite that they were choosing for themselves the option denied their ancestors and rejecting the Fourteenth Amendment offer of citizenship and accepting their rights to separate statehood in the yet to be established Republic of New Africa. Further, before moving its national headquarters to the South, the RNA attempted in Ocean Hill-Brownsville to conduct a plebiscite among Brooklyn's black community, who were already engaged in efforts for community control (as well as similar undertakings in Detroit and other cities), which suggests that the RNA recognized that a plebiscite could be conducted prior to establishing a presence in the South. It appears that, at least theoretically if not in practice, given that the plebiscite would establish the raison d'être for either the establishment of a separate state and/or the necessity of armed struggle to secure such a state, it had to occur prior to the establishment of sovereignty or the granting of reparations. This view was supported by Obadele's (1970, p. 74) argument in *Revolution and Nation Building*, in which he stated that the RNA's approach "entails campaigns for consent, followed by plebiscites, followed by defense of our land."

Thus, the sequence that the RNA was undertaking was: the declaration of a government of New Africa; proselytizing among blacks regarding the virtues of New African citizenship; conducting a plebiscite among black Americans to determine their citizenship in New Africa, the United States, or another option; the physical independence of the "national homeland" through either an electoral strategy to insinuate New African political power at the local level and "expanding sovereignty" throughout the national territory or an armed struggle for this territory if the ceding of land was not forthcoming; and the granting of monetary reparations. The timing of the plebiscite, in particular, had huge implications for the RNA's theory of black revolution in the United States, as we'll show below.

Obadele invoked black Americans' right of jus soli (the right of the soil), the right of anyone born on the territory of a country to claim citizenship in that country, in contrast to the right of jus sanguinus (the right of the blood), in which citizenship is a function of one's parentage rather than one's place of birth, to provide the legal justifications for the citizenship and subsequent reparations claims of black Americans. Obadele noted that, at manumission,

> the African, whose freedom was now acknowledged by his former slave-masters through the Thirteenth Amendment, was not on this soil because he or his parents had come here of their own free will. . . . Rather the African—standing forth now as a free man because the Thirteenth Amendment forbade whites (who had the power, not the right), to continue slavery—was on

> American soil as a result of having been kidnapped and brought here AGAINST his will. (1970, p. 27; original emphasis)

For Obadele, with the passage of the Thirteenth Amendment the rule of jus soli "demanded" that the United States "not deny to this African, born on American soil, American citizenship—IF THE AFRICAN WANTED IT" (ibid., p. 29; original emphasis). Obadele emphasized that

> [t]his last condition is crucial: the African, his freedom now acknowledged by persons who heretofore had wrongfully and illegally (under international law) held him in slavery by force, was entitled, as a free man to decide for himself what he wanted to do—whether he wished to be an American citizen or follow some other course. (ibid.)

Obadele viewed the rule of jus soli as "protecting the kidnapped African from being left without any citizenship" while simultaneously imposing "upon America the obligation to offer the African (born on American soil) American citizenship"; but, importantly "it could not impose upon the African—a victim of kidnapping and wrongful transportation—an obligation to accept such citizenship." With respect to the latter, Obadele averred that "[s]uch an imposition would affront justice, by conspiring with the kidnappers and illegal transporters, and wipe out the free man's newly acquired freedom" (1970, p. 28). For Obadele, and members of the RNA, the Fourteenth Amendment is not legally a "grant" of citizenship, but only an "offer" of citizenship. Further, as a sincere offer, the United States had the obligation and "the power to create the mechanism—a plebiscite—whereby the African could make an informed decision, an informed acceptance or rejection of the offer of American citizenship" (ibid.). In such a context, and under such an obligation, "Congress could pass whatever law was necessary to make real the offer" (ibid.), and "[t]he first 'appropriate legislation' required at that moment—and still required—was that which would make possible for the now-free African an informed, free choice, an informed acceptance or rejection of the citizenship offer" (ibid.).[3]

Obadele deduced that following passage of the Thirteenth Amendment, which outlawed chattel slavery, "four natural options were the basic right of the African," and here he outlined the "four fundamental consequences of freedom" for Africans enslaved in the United States, as noted above. For him, "TOWERING above all the other juridical requirements" that confronted both newly manumitted Africans in the United States and U.S. citizens in general, "was the requirement to make real the opportunity for choice, for self-determination" (1970, p. 28; original emphasis). Pursuant to making such a monumental choice, "the African was entitled to full and accurate information as to his status and the principles of international law appropriate to his situation," a requirement all the more pressing given that "the African had been victim of a long-term, intense slavery policy aimed at assuring his illiteracy, dehumanizing him as a group, and de-personalizing him as an individual" (ibid.). Nevertheless, "[t]he education offered him after the Thirteenth Amendment confirmed the policy of dehumanization," and "[i]t was continued in American educational institutions" such that even up to the present "the education of the African in America seeks to base African self-esteem on how well the African assimilates white American folkways and values—a hardly more palatable de-personalization than that which occurred during slavery" (ibid.).

Following manumission, the African was not advised of "his rights under international law," which suggested "that there was no option open to him other than American citizenship," and as a result "he was co-opted into spending his political energies in organizing and participating in constitutional conventions and then voting for the legislatures which subsequently approved the Fourteenth Amendment" (Obadele, 1970, pp. 28–29). Notwithstanding many Africans for whom "[t]he pull of nationalism was strong" and who resisted "resubordination," in the event, "the presentation of the Fourteenth Amendment to state legislatures for whose members the African had voted, and the Amendment's subsequent approval by these legislatures, could in no sense be considered a plebiscite" (ibid., p. 29). According to Obadele, given that "adequate and accurate information for the advice given the freedman was so bad it amounts to fraud," what ensued amounted to "a second stealing of our birthright," as Africans were not afforded "a chance to choose among the four options: (1) U.S. citizenship, (2) return to Africa, (3) emigration to another country, and (4) the creation of a new African nation on American soil" (ibid.). The existence of the RNA, Obadele asserted, "means, among other things, that a large body of Africans in America now has accurate information as to our status and our rights under international law," and they were intent on acting on the information and exercising their rights fully (ibid.).

Just as apparent, in Obadele's reasoning the U.S. government "still has the obligation under Section Five of the Fourteenth Amendment to 'enforce' Section One (the offer of citizenship) in the only way it could be rightfully 'enforced'—by authorizing U.S. participation in a plebiscite" facilitating black Americans' "self-determined acceptance or rejection of the offer of citizenship" (1970, p. 29). He noted that "[t]here are important ramifications" of this requirement given that "[a]dequate and accurate information" is "fundamental to an informed decision," therefore, it's incumbent upon the [United States], which heretofore used its great resources to misinform Africans in America about our status, options, and rights under international law, to make available to the Republic (and to those representing the other neglected options, emigration to Africa or some other place) the airways and other media for dissemination of information. (ibid.)

He acknowledged that "[t]he terms must be worked out on a mutual basis" in order "to remove the severe technical handicap which U.S. power (flowing out of a white racist theft of and subsequent monopoly of wealth) imposes on those competing for the attention of the African mind in an atmosphere essentially controlled by white American nationalists" (ibid., p. 29). For Obadele, "[a] genuine plebiscite implies that if people vote against U.S. citizenship, the means must be provided to facilitate whatever decision they do make. Thus, persons who vote to return to Africa or to emigrate elsewhere must have the means to do so" (ibid.). For those who might misconstrue the motivations for the RNA's demands, Obadele concluded:

We are the descendants of Africans wrongfully kidnapped and brought here by whites with the explicit complicity of the U.S. government and every arm of the United States law-making and law-enforcing machinery. The kidnapping was a wrongful act for which our ancestors and we as their heirs are entitled to damages. The enslavement was a wrongful act, for which our ancestors and we as their heirs are entitled to damages. The stealing of our labor was a wrongful act, as was the cultural genocide we suffered. We are entitled to damages—to reparations. The compensations we speak of are owed to us. (ibid.)

Notwithstanding the legal merits of the RNA's reparations claim, for the moment, what is telling about the RNA's theoretical justification for black revolution in the United States is that their main argument assumes that such a revolution is necessitated by U.S. resistance to nonviolent—in this sense, electoral—strategies to achieve their independence goals. Further, the argument appreciates the contingent role of revolution as a means to achieve their political objective. It also seems to take little notice of several major implications of the logic of its revolutionary thesis that undermine its effectiveness as a strategy. For example, according to Obadele, the dissemination of information regarding the "four fundamental consequences of freedom" such that African Americans could make informed choices on their political relationship to the United States—the sine qua non of the RNA's program, practice, and social theory—was incumbent upon the provision of media and the airways for such purposes. This was a huge undertaking, which ramified beyond what Obadele and the RNA leadership seemed to appreciate. In fact, the magnitude of the effort required to accomplish it entailed what Cruse characterized as capturing and democratizing the cultural apparatus of the United States. That is, this single aspect of the RNA's thesis seemed to require a black cultural revolution. The RNA seemed oblivious to this implication of their program. In fact, although the RNA maintained a Minister of Culture—three of them originally, Adefunmi, Karenga, and Baraka—and the group appropriated aspects of what they considered "traditional" African dress and practices (e.g., the dashiki, African names, polygamy), their appreciation of the concept and necessity of cultural revolution in their doctrine was superficial and limited to broad though insufficiently theorized initiatives to "unbrainwash" black Americans from what was viewed as a "slave mentality."

The salience of cultural revolution to the RNA's thesis is even more evident when we consider that in *Revolution and Nation-Building*, Obadele (1970, p. 13) argued that blacks shared a common culture rooted in shared experiences, lifestyles, language (one distinct from American English), and common suffering. He added that "out of our attempt to build a good life in this land, we have made a distinct literature, created distinct songs, developed common habits of living." Given white supremacist repression over centuries, Obadele recognized the importation of self-defeating and pathological tendencies among far too many blacks; thus, he saw the need for "reconstructing" the "black personality" and black Americans "as a people" (ibid., pp. 70, 71). Later, Obadele (1975, p. ix–x) asserted that the black American is "a de-culturized minority in the midst of a land-possessive, racist, white majority who brook for us no ideal except assimilation (and who steadfastly make the realization of this ideal impossible)." Fleshing out the implications of this cultural stasis on the acceptability of the RNA program to the black masses, he argued that like other "oppressed people who have been de-culturized by their oppressor," blacks "tend to seek the path of least resistance in their struggle against oppression," which, among other things, makes it "difficult to gauge the actual appeal of the concept of land and independence to the black masses" (ibid., p. ix). This "deculturizing" was such that Obadele railed against the "'nigger' life-style," which he argued blacks had "created in reaction to slave status, oppression, and cultural deprivation . . . all over America" (ibid., p. 27).

It was this vortex of cultural imperialism that the RNA confronted in its attempt to appeal to blacks to support its program. Given the "mis-education of the Negro," to borrow Woodson's apt characterization, the RNA would rely on the provision of the mass media to the service of "re-educating" blacks regarding their rights born of their peculiar history in the United States. What the RNA did not seem to adequately appreciate was that this provision they sought in order to facilitate their plebiscite would entail a revolution itself. Thus, Newton and the BPP were correct in their opposition to the timing of the plebiscite—but for the wrong reason: a revolution would have to precede the plebiscite, but instead of a politico-military revolution, a cultural one. In the context of what the RNA proposed—to this extent, at least—RAM and Us were correct that a cultural revolution would have to precede a politico-military revolution, but Us focused on the wrong culture, a contrived atavistic African culture that Karenga and Us largely constructed, instead of a historically enduring contemporary African American culture that black Americans actually practiced.

It was clear that the provision of media and the airways to the RNA in order to disseminate information on blacks' rights and responsibilities with respect to their citizenship claims was a massive undertaking of "re-education." As noted above, it was commensurate with Cruse's call for the "democratization of the cultural apparatus," whose seizure he viewed necessitated a revolution itself, while Obadele seemed to assume that it would be attained by mutual consent with little attention paid to the type of leverage blacks would have to wield in order to achieve it (1975, p. 239). In essence, Obadele's thesis seemed to require a cultural revolution to facilitate its primary mechanism (i.e., the plebiscite) to establish its raison d'être (its representation as a provisional government in its national territory), but the RNA leadership did not appreciate the gravity or extent of its implications for their broader program and revolutionary thesis. Among the reasons that the magnitude and centrality of black cultural revolution were poorly envisaged by the RNA was that, following Malcolm, it adopted a reverse civilizationist orientation toward black American culture, which left it ill-equipped on a theoretical level to address the increasingly urbanized and working-class culture that was prominent among black Americans in both Northern and Southern black communities, especially those whom the RNA was attempting to mobilize. The contradictions regarding black culture were becoming apparent at a time when the RNA's two most informed and articulate theorists on the subject—two of its initial three Ministers of Culture, Baraka and Karenga—were only distantly involved with the organization. Baraka was consumed with CFUN in Newark and Karenga with the Us-Panther conflict in L.A.; nevertheless, it's not likely that either could have turned the RNA toward a more constructive or Crusian analysis of black culture and cultural revolution, given that both Baraka and Karenga were devoted to the cultural atavism of kawaida at the time. The remaining Minister of Culture, Adefunmi, was also entrenched in reverse civilizationism in his promotion of "traditional" Yoruba culture. Black cultural revolution for each of them was associated with a "return" to a traditional communal—often myopic and reactionary—conception of African culture rather than a modern, cosmopolitan African American culture, which was the focus of Du Bois, Locke, Haywood, (Claudia) Jones, and Cruse, among others.

As it was, the RNA's position raised the question of what form of struggle would that "provision" of "media and airwaves" to "unbrainwash a whole generation" of black people entail, as Malcolm remarked. Given that it seemed to require, at minimum, what Cruse viewed as a cultural revolution, then the organization should have emphasized this aspect of its nation building along with the importance of the land, reparations, and armed struggle aspects of its program. To be sure, the RNA inculcated issues of black culture in its political education courses, but much of this was oriented to kawaida precepts with its reverse civilizationist focus (e.g., through incorporation of the *nguzo saba*), which formed the bedrock of its identification with a "New African" personality. This was wedded to a collectivist orientation drawing from Julius Nyerere's *ujamaa* (socialism), which was better suited to a third world agrarian context. Absent was a consideration of the magnitude of the preparation necessary prior to the plebiscite to undo centuries of conditioning among blacks, exacerbated by the fact that "American capitalism's technological advances in mass cultural media—films, radio, and music records, etc.—was a new capitalistic feature to replace Marx's 'religion' as the real modern opium of the people" (Cruse, 1968, p. 136). What should have been evident and better theorized was that the processes of black cultural revolution would affect this crucial phase of development toward the black plebiscite that the RNA envisioned. Ironically, it was a central thesis of Karenga's kawaida thesis that the RNA nominally subscribed to which argued that cultural revolution had to precede political revolution because, inter alia, without the former, blacks would be unable as a people to make self-determined choices regarding their political objectives. Among such political choices, it's hard to imagine a more exacting and significant one than to determine the political destiny of black America. In light of this, the necessary work to prepare the populace for the plebiscite would have to be a massive national educational undertaking. But the RNA did not seem to appreciate the magnitude of the mobilization required for an informed vote by the black masses who they hoped would participate in the plebiscite, nor did they seem to recognize the need to theorize the requisites for such a mobilization in their broader thesis on revolution. This lacuna was not only a problem of theory but of program, and it severely undermined the RNA's organization building and its popular appeal.

Had the parameters of black cultural revolution been better understood, it is likely that the RNA would not have had such a sanguine view of the likelihood that the provision by the U.S. government of what amounted to the "cultural apparatus" of the United States to black America—in effect, democratizing or nationalizing its mass media—could be worked out on a "mutual basis," or quickly. Given that the subsequent choice of the "unbrainwashed" black masses would provide the raison d'être for the establishment of the Republic of New Africa, then it was essential that the democratization of the cultural apparatus, that is, the process that would facilitate the "unbrainwashing," take place *before* the plebiscite; however, the plebiscite was necessary to establish the viability of the Republic, given that without it, it's not clear whether the idea of an independent republic would actually be supported by blacks to the extent that they would choose citizenship in the Republic over the other options. Given the demands of waging a successful black cultural revolution prior to undertaking the plebiscite, which would ostensibly bring the Republic into being, it is apparent that the RNA did not take adequate account of the time and effort necessary to do the "unbrainwashing" that a successful plebiscite would require. Further, considering the requisites for the plebiscite with respect to putting the cultural apparatus of the United States in the service of a revolutionary black American project, then it doesn't take much to appreciate that if nonviolent direct action to desegregate public institutions and facilities had led to the white racist violence that had accompanied the CRM, the demands to capture, democratize, and nationalize the mass media and communications systems of the United States would unleash white violence on an even greater scale. Thus, the RNA's "people's war" may not have been required only in the *aftermath* of the establishment of the Republic or upon the initial occupation of the "national territory" in the South; it would most likely be necessary *prior* to the plebiscite. In sum, the absence of a theory of black cultural revolution exposed contradictions in the strategy and logic of the RNA program.

The engagement—or lack of engagement—with the issues attendant to the necessity of black cultural revolution left the RNA's broader argument untethered to its constituent claims. The reparations claim was not only tied to the residence of blacks on U.S. soil (jus soli), but also their claims "of the blood" (jus sanguinus) as progeny of kidnapped and enslaved people made chattel. But the land and blood claims had been torn asunder not only by the horrific trans-Atlantic slave trade, roughly 250 years in bondage, and another century of lynch law and Jim Crow, but also by the cultural imperialism that white supremacism imposed on black America. In such a context, "choice" was as meaningless as "consent" in the coercive, asymmetrical power relationships that defined black America's relationship to the white-dominated U.S. state, market, and society. At minimum, the cultural domination of white supremacism on blacks' minds had to be lifted before they could vote with their feet regarding their sovereign interests. So, at that point, what was needed was a mechanism and/or process to facilitate such cultural liberation, but the RNA took much too seriously the façade of their own state, or "provisional government," which existed in name only. That is, Obadele proposed to use his nominal "state" to create a "New African" national identity among black Americans where it largely did not exist—even among many, if not most, black nationalists. New Africans would then perform as a vanguard, comprising those who already understood the four fundamental consequences of freedom. Failing to effectively theorize black cultural revolution beyond the acquisition of African names, language, dress, religion, hairstyles, etc., the RNA plunged headlong into the creation of the Republic ahead of the masses who were much too rooted in their African American culture to identify with the superficial Africanisms that the RNA endorsed, or, in the absence of a successful cultural transformation, which the RNA supported, insufficiently "unbrainwashed" to follow the RNA vanguard.

At the heart of the problem was the RNA's reverse civilizationism, which was evident most regrettably in its adoption of polygamy in July 1971.[4] The latter rested on a rationale that not only enshrined sexist practices rooted in "traditionalism." but promoted them to an ideal (i.e., New Marriage). It rested on a rationale that was internally illogical, presuming that because census data supposedly revealed roughly 1.5 million more women than men in the United States between the ages of fifteen and fifty-four, then men should be allowed to have more than one wife in order to absorb this "surplus of women." Failing to make the case why a woman has to exist only as a wife or mother, the RNA's "New Marriage" was a "solution" to a "problem" that didn't exist. Further, such practices would clearly distance the RNA from the black communities of the U.S. South that they were trying to rally to their cause, given that they were often politically progressive but socially conservative and not likely to countenance polygamy as a policy or practice. It was also illegal.

Relatedly, the agricultural collectivism that was the hallmark of *ujamaa* socialism that the RNA borrowed from Nyerere's Tanzania may have evoked unwittingly the long-loathed sharecropping land tenure practices among the Southern residents of Kush District. In fact, the reference to the territory as Kush seemed misdirected insofar as it evoked an ancient African kingdom (although mentioned in the Bible as "Cush") instead of an obvious black American referent that might have engendered a sympathetic response from black Mississippians, such as the Harriet Tubman District, Hiram Revels District, or even the Nat Turner District. Moreover, although the RNA's leaders were not antireligion—some, such as Milton Henry, were quite religious (years later, he would become a Christian minister), and others were religiously eclectic; nevertheless, their spirituality did not appear as "Christian-friendly" as it evolved, especially given the influence of its culture ministers' respective foci on kawaida, which was adamantly anti-Christian, or traditional Yoruba religion. The upshot of such policies and practices was that the RNA, led by many seasoned veterans of a range of civil rights, human rights, grassroots, electoral, and black power organizations, arrived in what should have been the sociopolitically fertile climate of post–Voting Rights Act black Mississippi, by their names, dress, conception of marriage, religious advocacy, and economic program unnecessarily distanced themselves from many potential local allies. As a result of reverse civilizationism, the cultural bonds that should have tied these Northern blacks to their Southern kin separated them.

With such a disconnect between New African culture and local black Mississippi customs, it surely didn't help that by the time of their arrival the RNA already had been implicated—through no fault of their own—with violent resistance, if not open revolution; but what was clearly detrimental to their cause was that the RNA couched this violent resistance in terms that sounded to a Southern ear eerily reminiscent of secessionism. Centering their legitimate reparations claim on the acquisition of five separate Southern states, the RNA's "free the land" argument nestled as perilously close to the language of Southern secession as it did to black reclamation. While it could not be confused with a form of neo-Confederacy rhetoric in blackface, it was not beyond the odious aspect of such an association for most Americans; nevertheless, at minimum, it probably exacerbated what should have been a clear alliance among many Southern black veterans of the U.S. military who might have been responsive to the presence of fellow veterans such as Robert Williams and Milton Henry in the group—especially given the concentration of U.S. military bases in the South—but were less likely to identify with efforts that connoted secession in almost any respect, given the negative aspects of what it evoked for many Southern blacks.

At the core of these problems was the RNA's neglect of the uniquely American aspects of black oppression. Ignoring black American cultural orientations and trends, it borrowed too heavily from a largely imagined, constructed "traditional" African aesthetic and material culture that needlessly distanced it from the lifestyles, customs, and practices of their local communities. In so doing the RNA undermined its most potent argument for reparations, which rested on an unequivocal black American cultural claim for which the RNA provided important legal support. Without a practicable mechanism/institution through which it could leverage its reparations claims, however, it was reduced to making moral/legal/ethical appeals that relied on either concessions to black protest from a U.S. government that the RNA admitted was white supremacist, politically repressive, warmongering, and bloodthirsty or concessions to black victory in a prolonged "people's war" waged by the RNA and its allies. Given that the latter was highly unlikely—the RNA was having difficulty even resisting local police forces—what was left was the normative appeal for reparations, which, while meaningful, was little more than a petition for redress rather than a path for revolution. In effect, the RNA had a powerful reparations claim without a meaningful strategy to acquire it.

Moreover, without a more expansive cultural program rooted in the major cultural institution of the black community, the Black Church, the RNA's initiatives in Mississippi floundered before they were able to develop social networks that might have strengthened their ties to the political machinery of the local community, which could have provided cover for its broader initiatives. Its often antagonistic opposition to the ideology of the increasingly influential integrationist civil rights organizations of the Deep South, even as the CRM was yielding to an emerging BPM, limited the RNA's influence among those sectors of the black community that might otherwise have provided support. This distance between the RNA and the broader black community was further widened by the RNA's open advocacy of both armed self-defense and "peoples' war." In addition, its failure to develop an electoral strategy along the lines of Malcolm's implicit call for proportional representation in the Kush District limited its ability to utilize electoral advantages in black-dominated electoral districts. As noted above, although the RNA drew on Haywood's Black Belt thesis, its program was not Marxist, and was even anti-Marxist at times, which brought it into fraternal dispute with Marxist groups such as the BPP, and in general conflict with the Marxist White Left. Relatedly, the RNA's intellectual distancing from analyses such as Haywood's that focused on organizing the peasantariat of the Black Belt may have contributed to its lack of coordination and development of the political interests of black sharecroppers and other rural and urban elements who were central to its plans for political transformation of the counties of the Black Belt as well as for armed resistance in the South.

Notwithstanding the foregoing, the RNA's biggest challenge was the presence of federal, state, and local police forces who utilized COINTELPRO to illegally disrupt, discredit, incarcerate, and kill members of the RNA and other BPM groups (and CRM groups as well). Such illegal actions against the RNA began in earnest on the first anniversary of the group's founding when local police forces attacked members of the group congregating at Revered C. L. Franklin's (Aretha Franklin's father) New Bethel Baptist Church in Detroit. In the shootout that resulted, one policeman was killed and two others were wounded. The police raided the church and rounded up, beat, and jailed some two hundred attendees on charges related to open warrants of murder. The intervention of African American judge (and future U.S. Congressman) George Crockett, who convened court in the police precinct where the congregation of the church was being held, resulted in the dismissal of charges against nearly all of them. The subsequent trial of the alleged shooters resulted in their acquittal, but no police were charged for their attack on the church sanctuary.

Several years later, FBI raids on two RNA locations in Mississippi resulted in the arrest and imprisonment of what became known as the RNA-11, which included Obadele. An internal dispute emerged over the feasibility of the RNA functioning with its president serving a multiyear prison term, and the group split between those continuing to follow Obadele and another group under the leadership of one of Obadele's heretofore most trusted and dedicated lieutenants, RNA Second Vice President, attorney Chokwe Lumumba, called the New African Peoples Organization (NAPO). Lumumba would be involved in several high-profile legal cases, ranging from those of musician and RNA member Bilal Sunni Ali, alleged BLA members involved in a shootout with police arising from the robbery of a Brink's truck in Nyack, New York, and rap artist, and son of BPP member Afeni Shakur, Tupac Shakur. He also was a co-founder of the National Coalition of Blacks for Reparations in America (NCOBRA). Obadele served five years of a twelve-year prison term that resulted from trumped-up charges of conspiracy to assault a federal agent (in fact, it was the RNA members who had been attacked by federal, state, and local agents and police forces). Upon his release, he was reelected as leader of the RNA, becoming co-president with Dara Abubakari, and led efforts to free political prisoners while continuing to advocate for black reparations. He and Lumumba had reconciled their differences years before and continued to work together in their organizations. In 2013, Lumumba won election as mayor of Jackson, Mississippi, as a "Fannie Lou Hamer Democrat" but died in office less than a year into his term.[5] The RNA and NAPO continue as organizations, and they have an influential offshoot, the Malcolm X Grassroots Movement (MXGM).[6]

The primary theoretical shortcoming of the RNA was that it treated Malcolm X's revolutionary thesis as a completed intellectual project that only needed to be implemented as a program. As a result, the RNA did not challenge either Malcolm's reverse civilizationism or his undeveloped cultural revolution thesis. In effect, the RNA's program faltered where its thesis faltered: it misunderstood the need for a black cultural revolution to realize its objectives. And while it developed a compelling legal argument for black reparations, it did not wed this claim to an established institution rooted in black communities (e.g., the Black Church, a black political party, a black labor union, etc.) that could serve as a mechanism through which the RNA might leverage its claims under threat of meaningful repercussions on U.S. society. A contemporaneous Detroit-based group would organize around black labor unions in the automotive plants, which could be leveraged to realize the objectives of the BPM, and from Chrysler's Dodge Main Assembly plant a group of black workers emerged making claims centered on the liberation of black labor. They called themselves the Dodge Revolutionary Union Movement (DRUM), and they would become one of the most important organizations of the BPM, the League of Revolutionary Black Workers (LRBW).

The League of Revolutionary Black Workers

While groups such as RAM, Us, and the BPP incorporated some form of socialism into their black nationalist theses—and both RAM and the BPP became explicitly Marxist—the LRBW originated as a self-proclaimed black Marxist organization. The League's program fused the two main foci of Malcolm's revolutionary thesis: the black revolution in the United States and the worldwide revolution abroad. The former drew on Malcolm's black nationalism, which included an incipient class analysis, though one not explicitly Marxist, and a thesis on black cultural revolution, and the latter focused on emulating anticolonial liberation struggles throughout the world. Where RAM, Us, and the BPP attempted to build expressly on Malcolm's black nationalist thrust, the LRBW from its origins focused equally on Malcolm's differentiation between field Negroes and house Negroes. Malcolm's field Negroes were the "grassroots," the masses of blacks "catching hell," who were increasingly orienting themselves toward revolution. The League attempted to subsume Malcolm's black nationalism in a Marxist formulation, and what resulted was an organization, although short-lived, that had a profound impact on both the BPM and on Marxist Leninist organizing in the United States. In fact, although the Black Panther Party was the most popular organization of the BPM that was guided by Marxist precepts, the LRBW might have been the most promising.

What made the LRBW promising was that its strategy for black revolution focused on the need to organize a national general strike spearheaded by black industrial workers and their community allies. In this respect, the LRBW, unlike most other major organizations of the BPM, was aligning itself with the strategy that black Americans had employed in the Slave Revolution that overthrew chattel slavery. Considering the uniqueness of the LRBW's approach and its importance to the overall thesis of this work, we'll more fully examine its broader program and how its general strike strategy functioned in it, and then situate it in the broader discussion of black cultural revolution.

The League's Genesis and Program

Although both were Marxist, one of the most important distinctions between the BPP and the League is that while the BPP promoted the lumpenproletariat as the vanguard of the revolution, the LRBW saw the proletariat as the vanguard. The LRBW focused on organizing black industrial workers at "the point of production"—primarily, the auto plants that dominated the politico-economic landscape of Detroit and formed the manufacturing core of U.S. industrial production, which was central to U.S. international economic hegemony. The LRBW viewed U.S. society as "racist, capitalist, and imperialist by nature" and "aggressively expansive, exploitative, and oppressive." The LRBW argued that with its power of "financial penetration, backed up by a worldwide military regime," the United States exercised "control of the resources, wealth and labor of the capitalist world" and "use[d] the most barbarous methods of warfare and subversion to maintain its billions of dollars in profit" (LRBW, 1997 [1970], pp. 189–190). The LRBW dedicated itself "to waging a relentless struggle against racism, capitalism, and imperialism" to liberate "black people in the confines of the United States," while contributing to "the liberation of all oppressed people in the world" (ibid., p. 189). Its short range objective was "to secure state power with the control of the means of production in the hands of the workers under the leadership of the most advanced section of the working class, the black working class vanguard" (ibid., p. 191), while its "long range objective [wa]s to create a society free of race, sex, class, and national oppression, founded on the humanitarian principle of from each according to his ability, to each according to his needs" (ibid.).

The League was established in 1969, in Highland Park, Michigan, which, along with Hamtramck, is one of two independent municipalities enclaved within the boundaries of Detroit. From its inception, the League viewed itself as an umbrella group of workers' organizations, and as "a black Marxist-Leninist party, designed to liberate black people, dedicated to leading the workers' struggle" in the United States "and resolved to wage a relentless struggle against imperialism" (1997 [1970], p. 191). League members were not doctrinaire Marxists—most were not Marxists at all—and membership was comprised of workers, students, community activists, intellectuals, and professionals from an array of protest and organizational backgrounds and tendencies in Detroit at the time. Nevertheless, in its "General Program" the League defined itself as a group "guided by the principles of Marxism-Leninism" (ibid.), which it arrived at from analyses of the "concrete realities" of the condition of black people, especially black workers, in the United States (ibid.).

The League argued that, given their location in the heart of industrial production in the United States, black workers had the greatest potential to bring the U.S. economy—the most powerful economy in the world and the hub of global capitalist imperialist power—to a standstill. Given this unmatched power as a class, black workers were the most promising base from which to organize and develop the BPM toward a successful political revolution. Although the League developed and coordinated ties with the broader community beyond industrial workers and including lumpenproletarians, it rejected the contention, most popularly advocated by the BPP, that successful black liberation in the United States was contingent on mobilizing the lumpen, so in this respect the League, at its founding, advocated more orthodox Marxism. Further, the socialization of the industrial workplace, including the routinization of production procedures, the rationalization of work schedules, the privileging of coordination and teamwork, and the general discipline of the shop floor, imparted to industrial workers a sense of discipline and coordination that could be effectively applied to the organization of social movements as well. This had been demonstrated in the previous labor movements that were such a rich part of Detroit's history in the twentieth century, and especially the history of black Detroiters, whose Great Migration from the economically devastated, white racist terrorist–infested, agricultural South was compelled, in part, by automobile manufacturer Henry Ford's offer of a five dollars a day wage in 1914.

The LRBW "emerged specifically, out of the failure of the white labor movement to address itself to the racist work conditions and to the general inhumane conditions of black people" (LRBW, 1997 [1970], p. 190) and it situated this failure within a broader domestic and global system of race and class oppression. The League noted that the historic and ongoing oppression of black peoples and black workers creates "a privileged status for white people and white workers," while "the imperialist oppression and exploitation of the world creates a privileged status for the people and workers of the U.S." The LRBW acknowledged that "systems of privilege" gave "white labor a huge stake in the imperialist system," rendering "white labor unable and unfit to lead the working class in the U.S" (ibid., p. 189). The League noted that "the white labor movement has failed to deal with the worsening conditions of black workers and the key role of black workers in the economy and the working class" (ibid.).

Conceptually, the League argued that the "black community is virtually a black working class," which "comprise[s] the backbone of the productive process in this country" and which has "produced goods under the most inhumane conditions." In its view, the "black community is comprised of industrial workers, social service workers, our gallant youth, and many ad hoc community groups" (ibid.). Thus, although focusing on black industrial workers as the vanguard of a socialist revolution, the League was emphatic that it "relate[d] to the total black community," and it asserted that "[o]ur duty is to plan the most feasible means to insure freedom and justice for the liberation of black people based on the concrete conditions" they faced. The LRBW undertook "the task of training [black] people for leadership and other special capacities that make a viable organization," but it was not interested in focusing solely on "a single issue" or "talking about reforms in the system"; its primary concern was with "the seizure of state power" (ibid., pp. 190–191).

The General Program of the League included six objectives: (1) organizing black workers "on the broadest possible scale" into the League; (2) "politicizing and educating" blacks on the "nature of racism, capitalism, and imperialism" through League programs, media, and publications; (3) supporting the construction of a "broad economic base" within black communities to support revolutionary struggle; (4) developing a broad-based self-defense organization within the black community; (5) waging "unceasing struggles" in support of black workers and the broader black community; and, (6) "[f]orming principled alliances and coalitions, on the broadest possible base, with other oppressed minorities, organizations, movements, and forces, black or white, which struggle against the evils of racism, capitalism, and imperialism" (LRBW, 1997 [1970], p. 191). As expressed in its foundational documents, the League's programs, practices, and political thrust differentiated it noticeably from most groups of the BPM. For example, Ernie Mkalimoto Allen (1997, p. 75), who had been in RAM before joining the League, points out that "[t]he LRBW's approach differed in several ways from those of other black organizations seeking civil and social rights." Instead of addressing the diverse aspects of black oppression, it focused on the "specific sector" that had "the greatest potential for effecting ultimate political and social change"; instead of focusing on "the local police as the principle enemy of the black community," which often resulted in deadly and futile encounters, it viewed it "as only one important aspect of *class rule*," although it took "concrete steps to combat police oppression"; and instead of a piecemeal approach to resolving "the social problems of blacks," it "envisioned the creation of a socialist society in the United States in which all forms of exploitation ... would be eliminated forever" (ibid.; original emphasis).

The League's program initially emerged from efforts to organize black workers in various revolutionary union movements (RUMs), of which the most significant were the Dodge Revolutionary Union Movement (DRUM), the Eldon Revolutionary Union Movement (ELRUM), and the Ford Revolutionary Union Movement (FRUM). LRBW executive board member John Watson (1969, p. 3) noted in *To the Point of Production* that "[o]ur analysis tells us that the basic power of black people lies at the point of production, that the basic power we have is our power as workers," and "[a]s workers, as black workers, we have historically been, and are now, essential elements in the American economic sense." He acknowledged that this approach was different from those that focus on "organiz[ing] the so-called 'brother on the street,'" and that although the League was not opposed to such approaches "without a more solid base such as that which the working class represents," they viewed this type of organizing as "generally a pretty long, stretched-out, and futile development" (ibid., p. 4). For the League, "the best way to organize black people into a powerful unit is to organize them in the factories in which they are working," because, they were convinced, black workers "have the power to completely close down the American economic system" (ibid.). Watson notes that an additional strength in organizing industrial workers is that in a single factory there might be ten thousand people facing "the same brutal conditions under the same system from the same bastards every day, eight hours a day, ten hours a day, six or seven days a week"; however, "[w]hen you go out into the community, the interests of the people . . . more than likely are going to be much more greatly dispersed than the interests of the workers are," so that "[j]ust in terms of expediency there are greater possibilities in the organization of the plant" (ibid.).

Although the League's primary focus was on organizing the workers in the auto plants, Watson was emphatic that "it is absolutely essential that the workers have some sort of support from outside of the factory" (1969, pp. 2–3). This emphasis was evident in the League's (1970, p. 554) constitution, which stated:

> We must act swiftly to help organize DRUM type organizations wherever there are Black workers, be it in Lynn Townsend's kitchen, the White House, White Castle, Ford Rouge, the Mississippi Delta, the plains of Wyoming, the mines of Bolivia, the rubber plantations of Indonesia, the oil fields of Biafra, or the Chrysler plant in South Africa.

Watson (1969, p. 4) acknowledged that the "kinds of actions that can be taken (in the community) are not as effectively damaging to the ruling class as the kinds of actions that can be taken in the plant." For example, "when you close down Hamtramck Assembly Plant, you do a number of things automatically. If you close it down for a day you cost Chrysler corporation 1,000 cars," which "means the loss of a sizeable sum of money" (ibid.). In addition, "when you close down a large automobile plant, you automatically can mobilize the people in the streets, 5,000 or 10,000 at a single blow" (ibid.). This is considerably more people than organizers could garner going "house to house" (ibid.). Moreover, he adds, given that "workers are not people who live in factories 24 hours a day"—"[t]hey all go home and live somewhere in the community"—then, "[i]t's almost an inevitable and simultaneous development that as factory workers begin to get organized, support elements within the community are also organized" (ibid.).

Thus, the League viewed "the point of production as the major and primary sector of the society which ha[d] to be organized" and, secondarily, "the community [which] should be organized in conjunction with that development" (1969, p. 4). Therefore, in concert with its initiatives among industrial workers in the plants, the League "quickly embarked on a program of expansion into community organizing, film production, and legal defense, as well as the establishment of a small printing plant and a bookstore" (Allen, 1997, p. 75). The importance of these "support elements within the community" was emphasized by executive board member, Kenneth Cockrel:

> [W]hen you talk about the league expanding into what is called community work . . . it simply recognized . . . a broader political definition of . . . workers. And it was also an objective understanding of the fact that workers leave the plant and have to go somewhere. They live where we live so it become[s] eminently sensible, as well as objectively desirable, to have organizations that relate to workers within a context outside of the plant . . . so that we can generate the kind of support that we need in order to support the struggles inside the plant. (Geshwender & Jeffries, 2006, p. 145)

League members in their daily experience as workers in Detroit's automotive plants and its associated industries knew firsthand their oppressive conditions, including backbreaking work and arbitrary discipline that blacks were routinely subjected to by both white management and the white unions to which they paid dues. The auto industry offered relatively high wages for its workers, and to some degree may be said to have exploited all of its workers; however, Georgakas and Surkin (1975, p. 35) note that black workers in Detroit's auto plants "invariably got the worst and most dangerous jobs: the foundry, the body shop, and engine assembly, jobs requiring the greatest physical exertion and jobs which were the noisiest, dirtiest, and most dangerous in the plant." Thus,

> The exploitation experienced by all workers was compounded for black workers by the institutional racism which pervaded every aspect of factory life. Dodge Main [the Chrysler plant in Hamtramck] was typical: 99 percent of all skilled tradesmen were white, and 90 percent of all skilled apprentices were white. All the better jobs were overwhelmingly dominated by whites, and when whites did have difficult jobs, there were often two workers assigned to a task that a black worker was expected to do alone. (ibid.)

These problems were exacerbated by the arbitrary speedup of the assembly line, and this exploitation was not only evident in hiring, job placement, and work assignments, but in the strategic racist firing process employed by the auto companies. For example,

> Blacks were further abused by the 90-day rule, under which workers could be dismissed at will before coming under full contract protection. The companies made it a practice to fire hundreds of workers per week, creating a rotating and permanent pool of insecure job seekers. The UAW . . . received a $20 initial fee and $21 in dues for each 89-day worker. The companies also received poverty program fees for the purpose of "training" parolees and welfare recipients. These individuals were often blacks and they were usually put on the least desirable jobs. Any protest could mean an end to government aid and possibly a return to prison. (Georgakas & Surkin, 1975, p. 35)

Yet black workers were increasingly participating in protest, and often in novel ways. For example, General Baker, a worker at Chrysler's Dodge Main assembly plant, located in predominantly Polish American Hamtramck who, along with other future members of the League, Luke Tripp, John Williams, John Watson, Gwen Kemp, and Charles Johnson were among a cohort of young black activists in the city who were members of the group UHURU, a RAM-affiliated, student-led organization at Wayne State University in the heart of the city that had formed in 1963 and had gained attention when they organized against police brutality in the police murder of Cynthia Scott and the use of public funds in Detroit's attempt to secure the summer Olympic Games of 1968. In 1966, Baker, along with Glanton Dowdell and Rufus Griffin, was charged with carrying concealed weapons during a disturbance on the east side of Detroit—the so-called Kercheval Riot (Georgakas & Surkin, 1975, p. 23). General Baker gained national attention when he penned a scathing letter to his draft board refusing to appear to be considered for service in the Vietnam War on the basis of the racism and imperialism of the United States and the illegality of the war. Baker ([1965] 1970, p. 506) was proud, adamant, and direct in responding to his draft letter:

> You stand before me . . . With all of this blood . . . dripping from your fangs . . . White man, listen to me. . . . You ask me if I am qualified to join an army of FOOLS, ASSASSINS and MORAL DELINQUENTS who are not worthy of being called men! . . . My fight is for Freedom: UHURU, LIBERTAD, HALAUGA, and HARAMBEE! Therefore, when the call is made to free South Africa; when the call is made to liberate Latin America . . . when the call is made to free the black delta areas of Mississippi, Alabama, South Carolina, when the call is made to FREE 12TH STREET HERE IN DETROIT!: when these calls are made, send for me for these shall be Historical Struggles in which it shall be an honor to serve! (ibid., pp. 506–507; original emphasis)

Baker's activism was reflective of the depth of political consciousness among many young black Detroiters during the apex of the BPM, and, notably, the race and class consciousness of these activists seemed to be intensifying even more, especially following the Detroit rebellion of 1967. Like most Detroiters, many of Detroit's black workers were deeply affected by the rebellion and many of them participated in it as well. Arrested during the rebellion, General Baker noted that in the police lockup he saw many of his co-workers from the plant who had also been arrested. The confluence of race and class in black autoworkers' consciousness was not a new development, but it was intensified in the climate of the BPM and the expanding Vietnam War.

In this context, it was not lost on black workers that even as they suffered the racism of the shop floor, they were essential to the production of the most sought-after highly valued finished goods for the domestic and global market, American automobiles. The auto industry was the leading sector of U.S. production, and the United States was the most industrialized country in the world. The speedup of the assembly line, these workers knew implicitly, was driven not simply by the need for production for domestic consumption but increasingly for export to foreign markets. Both processes seemed to be driven by the greed of corporate owners in collusion with union bosses intent on extracting the maximum surplus value from their workers. Thus, in their everyday experience they appreciated, materially, the reach of domestic and international capitalism, which they associated with the exploitation of workers like themselves, at home and abroad, and the hub of this activity was the United States. Searching for a paradigm through which they could struggle, many of the workers who would form the League embraced the most prominent radical critique of capitalism: Marxism.

At the same time, League members recognized the special role of blacks in U.S. economic development. Eschewing reverse civilizationism or any *glorianna* approach to African or African American history, the League noted the unique position of African Americans as the only people who had been chattel (property) in the United States. Enslaved Africans had provided the essential unpaid labor and production to fuel both the Industrial Revolution and U.S. ascendance to superpower status. In addition, both slavery and post-slavery racial oppression had incubated a sense of national consciousness among black Americans that was distinctive from, but not unrelated to, a sense of class consciousness. In the 1960s, these former human chattel now occupied a position at one of the most important loci of industrial production in the United States: the automobile factories.

Like other BPM organizations, the League framed the condition of black Americans in terms of domestic colonialism. They acknowledged that blacks manifested a sense of national consciousness from their struggles as a racial out-caste, while their super-exploitation as workers, mirroring that of colonial laborers in Africa and Asia, bred a sense of class consciousness as well. This dual consciousness reflecting the racial and class dimensions of black oppression was exemplified in the African American domestic colonial worker. For the LRBW, these black proletarians constituted a critical element of the industrial working class, just as Haywood (1948) had argued. Now heavily concentrated in the cities where factories were located, positioned at the hub of industrial production in the most industrialized sector of the leading industrialized country in the world, blacks could leverage considerable power through coordinated action.

For example, through a coordinated series of strikes they could halt domestic production and bring U.S. automobile manufacturing to a halt, which had the potential to escalate to a general strike as it spread to other sectors, generating a "crisis of capitalism" by exposing a chink in the imperialist armor that revolutionaries could exploit. In some ways, the League's practice of establishing and coordinating the RUMs in industries and service sectors was analogous to the CRM's boycott strategy, but instead of simply withholding their patronage/consumption to create financial losses, by withholding their labor/production blacks could shut down production in important sectors of industry where their labor was critical. Therefore, although a demographic minority, blacks could leverage their disproportionate presence in important areas in industrial production to achieve their broader political-social-economic objectives. In the RUMs, the League had arrived at a practical and reproducible organizational tool for exercising black power. *No other major organization of the BPM had devised a more competent, focused, and deliberate strategy for a legitimate attack by black Americans on U.S. power.*

League members recognized the importance of a general strike strategy from the organization's inception. In his 1969 interview, John Watson (1969, p. 9) asserted that "[w]e have some definite conceptions of how the revolution is going to be accomplished in this country," and it involved "a protracted and intensive struggle," which "would inevitably lead to a general strike." He was explicit that "we have to think in terms of being able to have [a] national general strike" (ibid., p. 10). He was convinced that the strikers and their supporters would face massive retaliation and repression, which he thought would approximate what Detroiters had faced in their "unorganized general strike" of the rebellion of 1967. He expected that the agents of the ruling class "would probably try to garrison off the community and starve us out" (ibid.). Facing starvation, the revolutionary organization "would have no choice but to call for the workers to go back into the factories and assume control of the means of production and distribution" in order to feed the community and the workers, and in "[a]ssuming control of the means of production," they would achieve "the first stage of assuming state power" (ibid.). "[F]rom the escalation of this type of struggle and from the reaction of the ruling class to it" would develop "an overall revolutionary movement which will forever overthrow capitalism and imperialism and racism" (ibid.).

While there were elements of this strategy that required further development and coordination, from its inception the League had in mind a strategy grounded in that of the only successful black revolution in the United States: the General Strike of the U.S. Civil War that Du Bois had historicized in *Black Reconstruction*. Such a proposal by black workers in the hub of automotive manufacturing in the United States was bound to have popular appeal, as well. Part of the appeal of the League's program derived from the fact that it fused two tendencies evident in revolutionary politics in Detroit at the time. Detroit had long been a bastion of both black nationalist and black labor organizing since well before the CRM, and the League drew from and synthesized these two orientations (Boyd 2017). The younger cohort of League activists were workers, students, artists, intellectuals, and unemployed, who were politicized by the conditions of black Detroit, which was a haven of activism, and particularly by the preachments and programs of international and national leaders ranging from Fidel Castro (members of UHURU had participated in a trip to Cuba in 1961) to Malcolm X (who had been the assistant minister of Detroit's NOI Mosque #1) and Robert Williams, as well as prominent Detroit-based activists Rosa Parks (who had moved to Detroit in 1957 and continued her activism),[7] James and Grace Lee Boggs, Albert Cleage, Milton and Richard Henry, labor organizer and reparations activist Chris Alston, and for a short period, Harry Haywood, who lived in Detroit briefly during the 1960s.

As committed as they were to black liberation, the youthful cohort, which would ultimately form the core of the League, were eclectic in their theoretical orientations, drawing from Detroit's rich radical traditions in black nationalist struggles and the labor movement. Black activism in Detroit often focused on critiques of white racism both in the city government—especially in the police department, the public schools, and in public housing—and throughout the private sector in real estate, retail trade, public accommodations, and employment, and with respect to the latter, especially racism among management and unions in the automotive industry. Thus, Detroit's black revolutionists often appreciated race and class dynamics in ways that were not as contradictory as in regions that lacked a concentrated black industrial working class. The LRBW drew from the Motor City's industrial traditions to ground itself in a specific form of radicalism that addressed the factors highlighted by Cruse, the Boggses, and Haywood in novel ways, and in so doing, it formed the most potent revolutionary black American labor initiative of the postwar era. The League's nationalist and class orientation encouraged a dual strategy to free the black domestic colony through a black worker–led socialist revolution in the United States, in concert with a more extensive socialist revolution to eradicate Western imperialism abroad, which would free oppressed peoples globally.

The institutional elements of what would become the LRBW emerged from a varied and concerted, though initially uncoordinated, set of protest actions inside and outside the auto plants in and around Detroit, which eventuated in the establishment of the first and most influential of the RUMs, DRUM. The immediate impetus for these initiatives was the Detroit rebellion of 1967, which was the deadliest and most destructive of the urban insurrections that comprised the "Long Hot Summers" that swept major cities of the United States from Watts in 1965 to Washington, D.C., in 1968. The rebellion followed less than a week after a similar insurrection in Newark, which, prior to Detroit's, had been the most destructive of the rebellions of the BPM. The Detroit rebellion was the apex of a crescendo in the magnitude of urban civil disturbances throughout the United States; and the scale of the uprising was surpassed among standard lists of "riots" only by the New York City draft riots during the U.S. Civil War, some of the worst riots of Red Summer following World War I (and later by the 1992 Los Angeles rebellion).[8] As in previous rebellions of the era, the intense repression by the local and state police forces, including elements of the state's National Guard in Detroit, augmented by a task force of the U.S. Army's XVIII Airborne Corps with brigades from the 82nd and 101st Airborne Divisions, was epitomized in the police murder of three unarmed black teenagers (Fred Temple, Carl Cooper, and Aubrey Pollard) at the Algiers Motel and the National Guard killing by .50 caliber machine gun fire of four-year-old Tanya Blanding as she huddled in her home, led many Detroiters, especially many black youths, to rally to join various protest organizations in the city.[9] Many future members of the League participated in the Detroit rebellion and among those were several who developed a radical community newspaper, the *Inner City Voice* (*ICV*). The *ICV* was a key locus of the organizing that would lead to the creation of the League. Georgakas and Surkin (1975, p. 17) note that "[v]irtually all the individuals who later emerged as the leadership of the League of Revolutionary Black Workers worked on ICV." Thus, while the rebellion was both an expression of and a motivation for radical organization among black youths in Detroit, the institutional apparatus that merged the initiatives among black youths inside the plants and outside of them was the *ICV*.

Finally Got the News 'Bout How Our Dues Are Being Used: Our Thing Is DRUM!

The first issue of *ICV* was published in October 1967, just three months after the rebellion. In its first year, *ICV* had a monthly press run of ten thousand copies (Georgakas & Surkin, 1975, p. 17). The editors insisted that "[o]nly a people who are strong, unified, armed, and know the enemy can carry on the struggles which lay ahead of us. . . . The Revolution must continue" (ibid., p. 16). The *ICV*'s stated purpose was to serve as a "vehicle for political organization, education, and change" by providing "a positive response to The Great Rebellion, elaborating, clarifying, and articulating what was already in the streets." Its masthead read "Detroit's Black Community Newspaper" and "The Voice of the Revolution." Moreover, "*ICV* was not like the alternate-culture newspapers of that period," that is, "[i]ts editors did not see its function simply as one of a principled opposition to the dominant culture," but as "a vehicle for political organization, education, and change" (ibid.). One of its first editorials asserted:

In the July Rebellion we administered a beating to the behind of the white power structure, but apparently our message didn't get over. . . . We are still working, still working too hard, getting paid too little, living in bad housing, sending our kids to substandard schools, paying too much for groceries, and treated like dogs by the police. We still don't own anything and don't control anything. . . . In other words, we are still being systematically exploited by the system and still have the responsibility to break the back of that system. (ibid.)

Activists of a variety of ideological tendencies gravitated toward *ICV*. As a result, *ICV* challenged the major political, economic, and social institutions of white oppression in black communities in Detroit and beyond. Georgakas and Surkin (1975, p. 17) note that "[t]he people who put out *ICV* were not newcomers to struggle," nor were they "underground journalists of the type which produced hundreds of periodicals during the late sixties. Their collective experience included every major black revolutionary movement of the previous decade," including SNCC, the FNP, UHURU, and RAM. "Some of them had been part of a group which defied the State Department ban on travel to Cuba in 1964, and some of them had had personal conversations with Ernesto 'Che' Guevara." Thus, the articles, essays, and editorials showed the influence of Malcolm and Che; it reproduced articles from Robert Williams's *The Crusader*; it reprinted speeches by C. L. R. James; and it included a regular column by James Boggs. The "unifying ingredient" in the *ICV* "was the sharp emphasis on defining the strategy and tactics of the ongoing black liberation struggle and how it might prefigure and trigger a second American revolution" (ibid., pp. 18–19).

Of the core group of black activists who contributed to *ICV*, one of the most respected was the aforementioned General Baker, who was a member of UHURU. The core of what would become the LRBW emerged from UHURU. According to former RAM leader Muhammad Ahmad (2007, p. 242), UHURU was a "revolutionary black nationalist/socialist action cadre" whose youthful members had close relations with older activists of a range of ideologies such as the black nationalists Milton and Richard Henry and Rev. Cleage, former Trotskyists James and Grace Lee Boggs, and Marxists Chris Alston and Harry Haywood, among others. UHURU members studied Malcolm X and Robert Williams, but also Marx, Lenin, Mao, Fanon, and Che. They considered themselves black Marxist-Leninists who were inspired by the liberation struggle in Africa as well as the Cuban and Chinese revolutions. UHURU members Luke Tripp, John Williams, John Watson, Gwen Kemp, Charles Johnson, and General Baker had gained attention in 1963 during the protest regarding the use of public funds in Detroit's attempt to host a future summer Olympics, and Baker gained national attention after his draft refusal.

Future LRBW executive board member Mike Hamlin notes that Baker "began to pull together a group of workers who began to meet in the offices of the *Inner City Voice*" (Georgakas & Surkin, 1975, pp. 23–24). Members of *ICV* united with Baker and other workers who had initiated a wildcat strike on May 2, 1968, at the Dodge Main plant in response to a speedup of the assembly lines. At Dodge Main, more than 80 percent of the workers were black, but only 2 percent of the foremen and shop stewards, which was indicative of the long-standing racist promotion policies of Chrysler management as well as the UAW, bearing truth to DRUM's chant: "UAW means U Ain't White." Approximately three thousand workers were involved in this wildcat strike, and although it had been initiated by a multiracial coalition of workers, including men and women, punishment was meted out disproportionately to black workers.[10] In fact, all the fired strikers were rehired except General Baker and Bennie Tate. At *ICV*, Baker and other black workers met to discuss politically organizing the black autoworkers, which he and others had been attempting since the early 1960s. Baker was among several attendees who sensed that the Detroit rebellion had rejuvenated a sense of labor activism among blacks in the plants and inspired them toward guiding the broader black liberation struggle in Detroit and throughout the United States. As a result, Baker, Tate, and seven other workers from Dodge Main, along with the editors of the *ICV*, formed DRUM.

In the preamble to its constitution, DRUM proclaimed:

> We the super-exploited black workers at Chrysler's Hamtramck Assembly Plant recognize the historic role that we must play and the grave responsibility that is ours in the struggle for the liberation of black people in racist U.S.A. and people of color around the world from the yoke of oppression that holds all of us in the chains of slavery to this country's racist exploitative system.... Throughout our history, black workers, first slaves and later as pseudo-freedmen, have been in the vanguard of potentially successful revolutionary struggles both in all black movements as well as in integrated efforts. These movements failed because they were betrayed from within or ... by the white leadership exploiting the racist nature of the white workers they led.... [W]e have learned our lesson from history and we shall not fail.... [W]e who are the hope of black people and oppressed people everywhere dedicate ourselves to the cause of

liberation to build the world anew, realizing that only a struggle
led by black workers can triumph over our powerful reactionary
enemy. (LRBW, 1970, pp. 551–552)

DRUM argued that "[o]ur sole objective is to break the bonds of white racist control over the lives and destiny of black workers," understanding that "when we successfully carry out this mammoth task, relief will be brought to people all over the world oppressed by our common enemy," although "[w]ith stakes so high the enemy will undoubtedly resist with great ferocity" (ibid., pp. 553, 552). Thus, they challenged that

> [w]e must gear ourselves in the days ahead toward getting rid of the racist, tyrannical, and unrepresentative UAW as representation for black workers, so that with this enemy out of the way we can deal directly with our main adversary, the white racist management of Chrysler Corporation. (ibid., p. 552)

DRUM distributed an eponymous weekly newsletter in the plant, which addressed the main concerns of workers, including the deplorable, extremely hazardous, and often inhumane work conditions in the plant, as well as the racism of both the plant supervisors and administrators with respect to hiring, job placement, and especially discipline. *DRUM* challenged the racism of the leadership of the UAW, and was intent on developing the political consciousness of the black workers. In its first issue, *DRUM* "reviewed the wildcat strike," which it argued was caused by "a speedup in production," and it "described the harshness of the penalties meted out to Black strikers; accused the company of racist hiring practices, and included a memorial tribute to Malcolm X" (Geschwender & Jeffries, 2006, p. 139). The second issue assailed black union officials for failing to represent the rank and file and to stand up to white union officials and management. One black worker lamented: "It seems as though every time the white power structure is shaken another grinning and shuffling Uncle Tom will come running to their rescue" (ibid., p. 140). The issue posed the following nine questions under the heading "Have you ever wondered why?":

> (1) 95% of all foremen in the plants are whites; (2) 99% of all the general foremen are white; (3) 100% of all plant superintendents are white; (4) 90% of all skilled tradesmen are white; (5) 90% of all apprentices are white; (6) that systematically all of the easier jobs are held by whites; (7) whenever whites are on harder jobs, they have helpers; (8) when Black workers miss a

day from work they are required to bring 2 doctors' excuses as to why they missed work; (9) that seniority is also a racist concept, since black workers were systematically denied employment for years at this plant. (ibid.)

DRUM proposed remedies to address these conditions, including the immediate promotion of roughly sixty blacks to positions of foreman, general foreman, and plant superintendent, and called for the recruitment of all security guards, plant physicians, and half of the nursing staff from the black community and the appointment of a black person as the head of Chrysler's board of directors. It also proposed a separate organization of black workers apart from the UAW and argued that black workers had as much right as skilled workers to a separate contract negotiated directly with management. The third issue of *DRUM* raised the contradiction of black workers' union dues being used to support the UAW's endorsement of the annual Detroit police field day. The Detroit police was viewed largely as an occupying armed force in the black community. For example, in 1963 alone, among "nearly five hundred cases of police-inflicted injuries," well over half "were in the five predominantly Black precinct areas" in a city with barely 30 percent black population at the time (Geschwender & Jeffries, 2006, p. 143). The issue of police brutality had only heightened after the rebellion, and "The UAW endorsement of the field day was therefore seen as further evidence of an alliance between the UAW leadership and a 'racist' police department" (ibid., p. 140).

DRUM organized various actions in the plants, and one of the largest and most important was the wildcat strike of July 7, 1968, which occurred almost exactly a year after the Detroit rebellion. The strike focused on the often atrocious working conditions in the plant and the unwillingness and inability of the UAW to respond to and represent the interests and needs of black auto workers from whom they took union dues. The wildcat strike and rally brought black workers and community members together—including blacks of various ideological stripes and white radicals as well. DRUM viewed it as a success and, building on it, organized several other successful actions and events directed against both Detroit's auto industry and the UAW.

DRUM and *ICV* attracted radical activists who would make strong contributions to the LRBW. For example, while working at the West Central Organization (WCO), Marian Kramer was recruited to help type articles for *ICV*. A prominent Detroit activist, she had worked with SNCC in the South and was associated with Detroit's Black Panther Party—as were several League members. Kramer had organized tenants' unions, worked with the Westside Mothers, a welfare rights group, and organized against police brutality and urban renewal/removal. Kramer notes that when "[t]he printers in the city refused to print the ICV" they decided "to take over *The South End*, Wayne State [University]'s student newspaper, and continue to get the word out concerning the situation at the plants, the communities, and the students in the inner city of Detroit. Some of our people enrolled at school and became staff of the paper" (Mast, 1994, p. 93). One *ICV* staffer and DRUM supporter, John Watson, used his position as a Wayne State University (WSU) student to gain the editorship of *The South End*, which was not only WSU's student newspaper but the third-largest daily publication in Michigan. During the academic year, 1968–69, under Watson's leadership, *The South End* was refocused to reflect the interests of DRUM, black student activists, and Detroit's black community. Two *ICV* staffers and future leaders of the League, Luke Tripp and Mike Hamlin, joined the paper as paid staff. The efforts at the *The South End* were especially facilitated by the work of Kramer, Cassandra Smith, Edna Watson, Dorothy Duberry, Diane Bernard, and Gracie Wooten who "played tremendous roles in the paper" (ibid.). Indicative of the paper's new focus, Watson placed two black panthers on the masthead of the collegiate daily, below which it read: "One conscious worker is worth a 100 students." Luke Tripp's lead story in *The South End* of January 23, 1969, read: "D.R.U.M.—VANGUARD OF THE BLACK REVOLUTION."

DRUM's wildcat strike and rally at Dodge Main of the previous July had led to the development of other "revolutionary union movements" (RUMs) both within and outside of the auto industry. For example, the Ford Revolutionary Union Movement (FRUM) organized in Ford's gigantic Rouge plant in Dearborn, and the Eldon Avenue Revolutionary Union Movement (ELRUM) was organized in Chrysler's Eldon Avenue Gear and Axle plant. Both FRUM and ELRUM carried out militant and often successful strike actions at their respective plants, and both began their own newsletters.[11] JARUM was organized at the Jefferson Avenue Assembly plant, MARUM was organized at the Mack Avenue plant, CADRUM was organized at the Cadillac Fleetwood plant, DRUM II was organized at Dodge Truck plant, and MERUM at the Mound Road Engine plant. RUMs also spread beyond the auto industry to include workers at the United Parcel Service (UPRUM), health workers (HRUM), workers at Detroit's Lafayette Clinic (LARUM), and workers at Detroit's major evening daily, *The Detroit News* (NEWRUM).

As these initiatives spread, the League was formed in June 1969 as a central organization to provide leadership and coordination for the RUMs, as well as the community-based efforts of the *ICV* and campus-based activists at *The South End*,[12] and to integrate their efforts into a more concerted and broader struggle for a black worker–led revolution. The League consisted of from sixty to eighty central members, which "functioned as an integrative body coordinating general policy, political education, and strategies for its various components" (Geschwender & Jeffries, 2006, p. 142). It was headed by an executive board (EB) that included General Baker, Ken Cockrel, Mike Hamlin, Luke Tripp, John Watson, John Williams, and Chuck Wooten. As will become clearer below, only two of them were active autoworkers (Baker and Wooten) and notably absent were any of the women leaders such as Marian Kramer, Edna Watson, Gracie Wooten, Dorothy Duberry, Diane Bernard, and Cassandra Smith, who conducted and coordinated much of the work inside and outside of the plants.

The League's Dual Strategy

Marian Kramer notes that in early discussions on the focus of League organizing, "[o]ne faction said that the focus should be in the plants, at the point of production. I said, 'Yes, but all those men got to come back into the community; they live somewhere. We've got to be organizing in both places" (Mast, 1994, p. 104). Kramer's perspective was adopted and the League pursued a dual strategy of organizing in the plants and in the community. Thus, although League members would initially emphasize organizing inside the plants at the point of production, as EB member Mike Hamlin asserts, the League was compelled to "broaden our contacts within the community" because "[w]e needed support to continue the struggle" (Georgakas & Surkin, 1975, p. 87). Hamlin thought the League "should build several kinds of resources to serve the struggle," including "a printing operation, a legal apparatus, and stepped up political education." Pursuant to those objectives, "[t]he League began to recruit large numbers of students and professionals," but, Hamlin lamented, "I think that our understanding of proletarian consciousness at that time was very low, and we did not do a good job of transforming the understanding of our new members. We were held together by personal loyalties rather than ideology" (ibid.). Hamlin viewed "[c]ommunity organizing and industrial organizing a[s] linked up"—"[t]hey go together"—and he was convinced that the "working class should lead the community effort" (ibid.).

The emphasis that the League's leadership put on such community-based efforts is evident in its acquisition of the editorship of *The South End*; its leadership in community control initiatives associated with the WCO and its offshoot, the Parents and Students for Community Control (PASCC), which was centered on the city's planned decentralization of its public schools; its assistance and coordination with the black student unions in several Detroit high schools through the Black Student United Front (BSUF); its coalition with white radicals, progressives, and liberals in the Motor City Labor League (MCLL) and its associated bookstore; and, probably most fatefully, its involvement with the Black Economic Development Conference (BEDC). BEDC was an initiative of the Inter-Religious Foundation for Community Organizations (IFCO), and at its meeting in April 1969 in Detroit, attendees proposed that it become an initiative to create a national organization. The organization, among other things, would provide a source of funding for the League, but tied its leadership to James Forman, the former leader of SNCC, who had played an important role in establishing links between the BEDC and members of the League's executive board. Forman was fresh from a short-lived association with the Panthers and seized upon the initiative of the League as a new organizational base. Through the BEDC, Forman proposed a "Black Manifesto," which he famously read while disrupting religious services at New York's Riverside Church and demanding a half-billion dollars from white religious institutions for reparations for black Americans. Most religious organizations ignored these "demands," but IFCO provided nominal funding for some BEDC initiatives, which still were "considerably more than most radical groups had to work with" (Georgakas & Surkin, 1975, p. 96).

The resources made available to the League through BEDC raised concerns among leaders such as General Baker about both the influence of the ideology of those who provided the money as well as their commitment to the organization of industrial workers in the plants. Where the community efforts clearly complemented the in-plant organizing there was less controversy. For example, the League leadership supported the International Black Appeal (IBA), which was a national tax-exempt charity that union members could support through tax-deductible donations directly from their paychecks, utilizing a check-off system similar to the annual Torch Drive or the United Jewish Appeal. When approached, the UAW was less hostile to this plan than League members had initially expected, which may have reflected the union's view that the IBA was a first step at incorporating the League under its aegis. For the League, the IBA represented a potentially major source of financial support to provide for a strike fund for picketing and/or fired workers and their families, especially "if it was funneled to friendly charitable agencies that could hire fired workers and support strikers" (ibid., p. 97); "If each of the 250,000 black members of the UAW gave only $1 a month," then the League would have a monthly income of $250,000 (ibid.). Other initiatives facilitated by BEDC funding, such as that which gave rise to Black Star Publishing, were also broadly supported when focused mainly on helping to publish the newsletters and periodicals of the RUMs and other League components and to train League members in these skills. However, when Black Star moved into films, fissures began to emerge among the leadership and rank and file about the usefulness of the League's limited resources for out-of-plant activities.

The first production of Black Star, the influential film about the League titled *Finally Got the News*, was skilled, insightful, and a testament to the League's organizational efforts and programmatic focus; its practical and theoretical farsightedness and its appeals to workers and broader community members demonstrated the League's ability to utilize popular media to articulate and promote its political and organizational message to increase its appeal and extend its influence. *Finally Got the News* may have been the only professional-quality documentary film produced by a BPM revolutionary organization featuring the members themselves presenting its programs and objectives, with images, sounds, and commentary unadulterated by the control or censoring of mainstream media. In effect, it was one of the most effective propaganda vehicles produced in the BPM. It was the equivalent of *The Battle of Algiers* of the BPM. No other major BPM organization produced an educational and recruitment tool of this quality utilizing film on its own terms. In essence, *Finally Got the News* was a nascent attempt by the League to extend their challenge at the "point of industrial production" in the workplace to one at the "point of cultural production" in the community. In this sense, it represented one of the most sophisticated and effective attempts to adopt Cruse's approach of targeting the cultural system in the BPM.

Unfortunately, the League's success with *Finally Got the News* was not repeated in subsequent projects, which focused on tangential issues. For example, under Watson's direction, Black Star planned additional movies, such as one focusing on Rosa Luxemburg, for which Watson sought assistance from Jane Fonda, who suggested that funds might be better spent on a project with more direct relevance to the organizing of black industrial workers and their community supporters. Other projects led Watson to travel to Italy to seek additional support, which distanced him even farther from League activities in Detroit and drew greater attention to the fact that such efforts seemed irrelevant to the needs of the in-plant organization of black workers.

A more successful and enduring fusion of the League's in-plant and out-of-plant initiatives was evident in the court cases involving the League's lawyer, and executive board member, Ken Cockrel, including his successful defense of black auto worker James Johnson, who had killed a foreman and two co-workers (two whites and one black) at the Eldon Plant. In the trial, Cockrel successfully argued that the oppressive conditions of the auto plant and the virulent racism of its administrators had compelled Johnson's actions—essentially putting Chrysler on trial (encouraging the slogan of the trial: "Chrysler pulled the trigger"). Cockrel also successfully defended members of the RNA following a shootout with Detroit police who had attacked Rev. C. L. Franklin's (Aretha's father) New Bethel Baptist Church during the RNA's anniversary program. Although a Detroit policeman had been killed, Cockrel won the acquittal of RNA members Chaka Fuller, Rafael Viera, and Alfred 2X Hibbitt. Cockrel also defended Heyward Brown, who had joined revolutionaries Mark "Ibo" Bethune and John Percy Boyd to attack drug dealers in several of Detroit's crime-ridden neighborhoods and as a result had become involved in shootouts with Detroit's notorious STRESS (Stop The Robberies Enjoy Safe Streets) police decoy unit. STRESS was infamous for killing blacks and had a record of killing unarmed Detroiters that exceeded any other in the police department, which it achieved with impunity (Boyd 2003). Cockrel successfully put STRESS and the Detroit police on trial and held them accountable for their reign of terror among Detroit's black community, and Brown was acquitted.

Cockrel's successful legal strategies enhanced his stature in the city, and his association with the League and its larger projects increased the scope and relevance of the League in the eyes of many Detroiters, especially its auto workers, who appreciated the range of programs, policies, and practices within the plants and outside of them that the League promoted throughout the city. Moreover, the broader community came to embrace more of the League's efforts and to support its challenge(s) to the racist political, economic, and social structures that dominated the city from the offices of the mayor and police commissioner to the auto companies to whom they constantly deferred[13] and the UAW, which seemed more interested in doing the auto companies' bidding when it came to workers in general, and to black workers, in particular. The League also challenged Detroit's white supremacist media that supported and reinforced these glaringly racist interests.[14]

While there were clear positives associated with the League's broader community efforts, there were negatives, as well—the main one being that the energy and resources of the League were being spread thin by some of the out-of-plant organizing just as increasing demands were being made by workers across Detroit, the Midwest, and beyond for in-plant organizing. The League was initially successful in assisting the development of RUMs, but their number expanded rapidly. This was not simply a result of League efforts, but of the local and largely independent efforts of workers in their own facilities; however, the demonstration effect of DRUM, ELRUM, and FRUM inspired much of what occurred among the other RUMs, and the League's influence in those actions was pronounced. Just as apparent was the difficulty the League experienced in assisting the development of the other RUMs. The League assisted with quotidian tasks such as the production and distribution of the RUMs' newsletters, but it was less successful at the broader coordination of the RUMs' efforts, including several wildcat strikes. The latter exposed the League's lack of preparedness in response to the range of management and union actions aimed at destroying the League.

These difficulties both reflected and were exacerbated by the absence of a dues-paying structure among League affiliates that would have provided a strike fund to support fired workers. The League weighed whether to legitimize the union structure that it, rightfully, disparaged by running candidates for union office. When Ron March, the DRUM candidate, failed to win an election runoff after an impressive showing in the election itself, it was clear that his defeat resulted from the UAW's appeal to white and Polish American retirees regarding what they labeled the "black peril." The runoff election also witnessed, according to DRUM members, Hamtramck police acting in concert with white UAW members in seizing ballots and rigging the results in favor of the white UAW candidate. Beyond electioneering "dirty tricks," it was evident that the severity of the retributions both union and management directed toward RUM members necessitated an independent resource base within the League to financially support fired workers and provide them with legal assistance. If the League could not provide such support, then its efforts in the plants would be undermined by both the physical absence of fired League members from participation in in-plant organizing and the drain on its already limited financial resources as it attempted to provide support for fired members and their families in ad hoc fashion. An attrition strategy was just what management and the UAW were willing to employ against these black labor radicals, as they had for decades, and through its use they sought to either coopt or undermine the League's efforts.

The subsequent repression that its members endured was a major factor in the League's decline. The League contended that both management and the UAW employed methods that were legal, extralegal and at times blatantly illegal to undermine it, including selective firings, surveillance, electioneering, fraud, harassment, as well as physical assaults. The complicity of the UAW with management was captured in the spectacle of UAW's top executives, including Douglas Fraser (who would become UAW president in 1977), leading a forceful termination of a wildcat strike by workers at Mack stamping plant in 1969 and taking pride in siding with management against its own striking workers, in a clear indication to even the most jaded observers that black workers' closest liberal "allies" among organized labor could not be depended on for assistance, and demonstrating their open hostility to issues related to the interests of black workers. It didn't help that instances such as these occurred as the League was experiencing rapid growth, exacerbating strains on its resources and tensions within its executive board and between the board and the general membership.

White union members, management, and whites in general were given a ready-made opportunity for opposing the LRBW's challenge to their white supremacism, mismanagement, and exploitative practices that they exercised by red-baiting the avowedly Marxist organization. Actually, black workers—and an increasing number of whites—were aware that many of the LRBW's complaints about the automakers and the UAW had merit, regardless of their association with Marxism. In the event, the LRBW might have profited from a strategy, like Castro's (whom they studied) during and shortly after the Cuban Revolution, of concealing their Marxism until they had seized strategic objectives or accumulated more resources. The UAW collaborated with management to rid the plants of League workers and sympathizers, while providing superficial concessions to black representation by dispensing token union positions, which also had the effect of siphoning off some LRBW support in the plants. The upshot of these tactics of repression, collaboration, and cooptation was that LRBW members were often removed from the plants, which undermined the League's major function of organizing plant workers.

An even larger strategic failure was the League's apparent lack of appreciation for the declining influence of the black industrial proletariat during a period of deindustrialization, just as James Boggs (1963) had argued. But other problems associated with the League were internal and based in its need for an ideological compass to point its growing organization toward its revolutionary objectives. Executive board member Mike Hamlin admitted that the League "came to believe that the working class had to make the revolution, had to lead the revolution, and that we had to concentrate our energies on workers"; but, "[w]e didn't really understand what making a revolution entailed, what a proletarian revolution was, how, it took shape, and how it developed" (Georgakas & Surkin, 1975, pp. 86–87). Divergent viewpoints on the preferred course of revolutionary struggle were inevitable, and they would give rise to prominent divisions within the League. These external and internal factors threatened to implode the LRBW unless it found a way to synthesize its contradictions into a coherent theoretical thrust and program of action; but instead of synthesis, the divisions became even more fractious and the League began to crumble under its own weight.

Synthesizing Ideological Tensions within the League

Allen (1979, p. 84) notes that the divisions within the League were "two-fold": one was ideological, with one tendency "putting forward a general Marxist orientation" and "more amenable to working with white (mostly middle class) allies," and the other more inclined toward black nationalism, which "tended to oppose such alliances." He aligns Ken Cockrel, Mike Hamlin, Luke Tripp, John Watson, and John Williams with the first tendency and General Baker and Chuck Wooten with the second. Another division reflected a disagreement on strategy and tactics. According to Allen:

> Nominally, all Executive Board members agree that the principle [sic] political task of the League was the organizing of black workers.... A highly pragmatic section of the leadership advocated expanding League activities into many spheres at the same time.... Another group favored a more coordinated expansion but also concerned themselves with the consolidation of existing organizational ventures. Finally, there were more people who tended to resist involvement in any activities that were not immediately connected with the direct organization of black workers in Detroit. Hamlin, Cockrel and Watson were identified with the first tendency, Tripp and Williams with the second; and Wooten and Baker with the third. (1979, pp. 84–85)

Allen adds that this "two-fold political division on the EB was to produce curious alignments and realignments among its members, depending on the specific issues involved" (ibid., p. 85). Georgakas and Surkin (1975) observe three dominant tendencies among the executive board: One faction, including Baker and Wooten, focused on in-plant organizing of RUMs and less on out-of-plant activities; another, focused on out-of-plant organizing, stressed building networks of community support, and incuded Hamlin, Watson, and Cockrel, who also viewed media, such as films and newspapers, as vital to educating workers and supporters; and one, represented by Tripp and Williams, focused on the development of the political consciousness of both workers in the plants and supporters outside the plants, emphasizing strengthening the League in Detroit before expanding to other cities. The third tendency represented a middle road between the other two—Allen's "pragmatic section," reflecting a concern that neither of the other two tendencies should be permitted to skew the League's efforts too much in their preferred direction before a durable framework for a black revolutionary workers' movement with broad-based community support had been established.

Consistent with the argument in Geschwender (1977), which was the first monograph on the League, Geschwender and Jeffries (2006, pp. 153–157) emphasize a different axis of conflict among the League's leadership rooted in ideological strains, and note that the "failure to explicate a logically consistent model facilitating a cohesive direction for action was a constant source of strain within the organization" (ibid., p. 155). They argue that the League's ideology was rooted in two contradictory tendencies (ibid., pp. 153–157). The first, the "capitalist exploitation model," a Marxist framework, viewed blacks largely as super-exploited proletarians and posited the necessity for a socialist revolution to eradicate the capitalist oppression in the United States from which both racial and class oppression emanated. However, in the League's model, the socialist revolution would be led by black proletarians as the vanguard because white workers were inveterate racists, whose transformation was incumbent upon their recognition of the objective conditions compelling them to class consciousness and solidarity with their fellow black workers. In contrast, League members also subscribed to the "colonial model," which viewed blacks as a super-exploited domestic nationality whose liberation was incumbent upon waging a war of national liberation, such as those typified in the anticolonial wars of national liberation that dotted the Cold War landscape. It followed that "[a]cceptance of the colonial model logically entails cultural and revolutionary nationalism aimed at ultimate establishment of a separate Black political entity"; however, given that "[i]t is unlikely that Black workers could, by themselves, successfully bring about a socialist revolution," then, "[t]hey need white workers as allies"; "[y]et it is these very white workers that the colonial model entails defining as an enemy" (ibid., p. 155). Thus, the "combined model," which presumably was the one the League was operating under, was inherently contradictory because it "requires simultaneously working with and fighting against white workers" and "simultaneously working with and fighting against Black capitalists" (ibid.). The authors assert that "[i]t is undoubtedly possible to design a model that incorporates the desirable features of both models without requiring incompatible tactical lines of endeavor, but the [L]eague did not work this out" (ibid.). The authors also do not provide such a synthesis.

A related argument, first articulated by Geschwender (1977) and shared by Kadalie (2000), is Geschwender and Jeffries's (2006, p. 156) contention that inconsistencies in the League's competing ideologies were rooted in its "differentiated class composition," which presumably "explains its attraction toward apparently contradictory ideological currents" (ibid.). This argument tends to essentialize and ossify the categories of intellectuals and workers in ways that ignore their often common roots in the socialization of blacks in Detroit, from which the League drew the lion's share of its membership. For example, the authors assert that

> [i]ntellectuals and workers have different life experiences that lead them to view the world differently. Black intellectuals and workers will share the experience of being Black in a racist society but will not experience their Blackness in an identical manner. They

are likely to interpret the cause of Black oppression in terms of different conceptual and theoretical schemes. The conditions and organization of their work experiences also differ, and consequently they are likely to develop different orientations toward the need for, and value of, political education. (Geschwender & Jeffries, 2006, p. 156)

But in Detroit, this distinction was often more apparent than real. Workers and labor organizers were often intellectuals as well. Chris Alston and James Boggs are only two of the prominent Detroit black auto workers and labor organizers who were also noted Marxist intellectuals. Further, the practice of men and women workers providing intellectual guidance to movements by fusing work, social activism, and theory, focusing on the transformation of both work and society, was much more prevalent among blacks in Detroit's industries than a casual engagement with this history would suggest. This is not to say that each black worker was an intellectual—far from it; but it is to challenge the view that "the experience of their Blackness" was inherently different for black intellectuals and black workers in Detroit during the BPM. Often, black intellectuals and black workers were one and the same.

In addition, the common perception of workers as belonging to the "working class" and intellectuals the "middle class" was challenged in black power era Detroit. Given the relatively higher wages of auto workers as compared to other employment sectors open to blacks, the "working class" in Detroit was often "middle class" economically, or at least lower-middle class; they were less likely to remain among the city's poorest residents, such as those in Detroit's public housing projects. Similarly, the "intellectuals" often had some college education but rarely college degrees or advanced graduate training. Many had left college to devote themselves to the CRM and BPM, or simply to support their families through work while attending college part-time. The confluence of these practices made WSU a hub of students and workers in the heart of Detroit, quite unlike what was occurring at the University of Michigan in Ann Arbor or Michigan State University in East Lansing, or even at the private Jesuit University of Detroit on the northwest side of the city. As a result, the income of the "intellectuals" among Detroit's activists often derived less from employment within an academic environment, as is implied by Geschwender and Jeffries's dichotomy, and, to a lesser degree, Kadalie's, but typically from the same kind of employment in the public sector related to local government (i.e., city, state, or federal jobs), teaching or support jobs in the Detroit Public Schools, general service sector jobs, retail trade, or work in the associated businesses of the auto industry. Thus, the distinction between black workers and black intellectuals rarely suggested an economic class stratification as commonly understood.[15]

The authors' assumption rested on another dubious dichotomy separating auto workers from the black middle class in Detroit. Even those auto workers in the worst jobs in the paint shop, the foundry, and on the line earned wages that placed them firmly above the poverty line, and most with steady work were firmly situated in the black middle class. The impact of the auto industry on class differentiation in Detroit was such that by 1948 Detroit had among the highest per capita single-family home ownership in the United States, although these home owners were overwhelmingly white. Though in reality, the lives of black Detroiters were powerfully circumscribed by white racism, Detroit's black population was itself similarly stratified by class as a function of the industrial wages of its auto workers. Importantly, even blacks without high school diplomas had access to the relatively higher wages in the factory than similarly situated blacks outside of the auto plants who were often compelled to the welfare rolls and AFDC (Aid to Families with Dependent Children) and the city's housing projects. As a result, black auto workers were a diverse lot in terms of economic class—if not social class. Economically, even poorer auto workers could ascend to the middle class—if home ownership, or at least occupancy in a single-family dwelling were the measure. In fact, for members of Detroit's predominantly black housing projects, securing full-time work in the auto plant was typically a "ticket out" of the projects and its poverty.[16]

Further, instead of accepting the authors' assertion that "Black workers will not readily be attracted into political education programs" because "[m]ost Black workers, especially in the auto industry, work long hours at demanding jobs" and thus, "do not have a great deal of time and energy to spend on political education classes," one might consider that decades of Socialist and Communist Party organizing and their concomitant political education in black communities had demonstrated that black workers were as likely to respond to political education—even when associated with socialism and communism—as any other group of workers. This is not to disagree with the point that "auto workers work long hours" but to point out that effective political education speaks to the workers in ways that are not simply didactic but inspirational, uplifting, and reassuring as individual workers begin to associate themselves with a broader community of support and activism. In fact, a great deal of political education was occurring in the pews of churches every Sunday in black communities across the United States.

Another, more basic problem might have been the League's political education teachers' insufficient grounding in Marxist theory, especially that which addressed the historical development and contemporary conditions of the U.S. proletariat, coupled with the limited pedagogical skills of some League instructors. With respect to the latter, Geschwender and Jeffries (2006), following Georgakas and Surkin (1975) and Geschwender (1977), seem to lay the blame for the problems of political education at the feet of "black nationalists" in the League instead of the teachers of the Marxism-oriented political education classes, who typically were not associated with the black nationalist tendency among League leadership. This argument, like many of the suppositions from these analysts, should be weighed against the fact that influential DRUM and League members such as General Baker and Chuck Wooten, the two auto workers and in-plant members of the executive board who were most often associated with the "black nationalist" tendency, were not among the sources whom the authors drew on to develop their studies and inform their analyses, or at least not in direct interviews, while board members such as Watson, Hamlin, and Cockrel are heavily cited by them. Not surprisingly, when we examine Baker's views on the political education classes, we see that he does not associate their shortcomings with any "tendency" but simply with the absence of an understanding of Marxism among the League's founders, and the ineffectiveness of the teachers of the classes.[17]

For example, in his analysis of the LRBW drawn on his personal experience and interviews with Baker and Wooten, Muhammad Ahmad (2007, p. 270) notes that the League "was racked with a serious problem of uneven political development among its members." He points out that "Luke Tripp first taught the classes on the basics of Marxism-Leninism," and "not knowing how to break theory down into everyday language, would bore the workers, who often went to sleep in class." Tripp was not associated with the black nationalist tendency. Executive board members seemed to have hoped that Forman would provide a quality Marxist theoretician among their teaching cadre, but they were disappointed. Reflecting on those years, in 2014 General Baker was more ecumenical in his critique of the League founders, including himself, who, he argued, had insufficient understanding of Marxism-Leninism at the time, which was both reflected in and exacerbated by the absence of competent instruction of the ideology in the political education classes.[18] It was ironic that given the salience of Marxism in labor organizing in Detroit, the League did not have among their cadre, a pool of good teachers of Marxism.[19] Reflecting on his experience as an LRBW central staff member, Ernest Allen notes that the problem with political education courses was their overreliance on materials taught from the experience of the Chinese and Vietnamese, when

> what you needed and what we didn't have at the time in [sic] which we still don't really have adequately, was a literature that reflected the experience of black workers. That would bring the theory in but at the same time the historical examples would be

that of black workers themselves so they could see themselves in it as well as learn about their own historical experiences. (Ahmad, 2007, p. 271)

Ahmad (ibid., pp. 270–271) adds that Allen "was brought in to teach the political education courses," and "he broke it down plain and the workers enjoyed going to political education." While League members seemed more receptive to Allen's instruction, by the time of his instructing the political education classes the reticence of many members toward Marxist political education had become active resistance. Further, overwhelmed by the need to support the rapidly proliferating RUMs and to create support networks for fired strikers and their families, the time spent on Marxism seemed misplaced.

Analysts of the League do not suggest how their major contending perspectives on its ideology could be fused. This is what Du Bois and Haywood had undertaken in the 1930s, what Cruse and Boggs had attempted near the outset of the CRM, and what Malcolm had begun to struggle with on the cusp of the BPM. Harry Haywood had proposed such a fusion of black nationalism and Marxism rooted in a Marxist teleology and Haywood had lived for a time with John Watson in Detroit during DRUM's tenure. In fact, there were two such prominent fusions, one emphasizing a Marxist dimension and the other a black nationalist dimension but both attempting to ground its theoretical synthesis in African American political, economic, and social development. Both focused on addressing the racial oppression of blacks and the class oppression of the proletariat. Given that blacks are exploited by both race and class, and in the most powerful country in the world, then, in that context, they face not only the hostility of the white capitalist class but of white workers as well. Black proletarians might play a leading role in ending the super-exploitation of black people consistent with the conception of blacks as a black nation but also consistent with a Marxist conception of the proletariat of the nation liberating itself from its bourgeoisie, thereby characterizing more of a comprador class in a dependency relationship with metropolitan capital, represented by the white ruling class of the United States. Just as Marx encouraged an alliance of English workers with their fellow Irish proletarians, whom they often disparaged in ethnocentric if not "racialist" terms, whites should be encouraged to ally with revolutionary black proletarians; yet, in the United States, as the Slave Revolution implied, this alliance need not be with white proletarians, who, during the BPM, not only were not revolutionary as a class but were vicious racists and opponents of black union members, black workers, and black people in general.

The League's practice raised the issue of who constituted the relevant sector of the black community beyond the proletariat that would serve as a complementary revolutionary force and who occupied the respective revolutionary sector in the white community, if any. The BPP's white "mother country radicals" were poorly fitted into their professed Marxist formulation, and similarly, whites were integrated rather uncomfortably within the League's "black Marxism." For example, while the League's community work included alliances and coalitions with white groups such as the Motor City Labor League, in-plant organizing focused specifically on black workers. The latter, racially focused strategy was anathema to the emerging ideological purists among the League's executive board, who increasingly viewed themselves as Marxists rather than black Marxists and embraced alliances with whites—often including petit bourgeois, liberal, and radical whites—while eschewing similar cross-class alliances with black petit bourgeois and liberals. At the same time, alliances with whites, both petit bourgeois and proletarian, were opposed by those favoring race-based alliances. Kadalie (2000, p. 212) argues that the contention regarding the relative salience of race and class was not irreconcilable, but when their implications for alliances and coalitions created tactical contradictions, the executive board did not adequately address them. For him, this was less an ideological problem than one of organizational leadership and structure, since it was clear to him that the issue was not whether the League should have done organizational work with the black petite bourgeoisie at the expense of working with the black proletariat, given the reality "that some work needed to be done within the petit-bourgeoisie [*sic*]" (ibid., pp. 212–213). Kadalie (ibid.) implicates the cumbersome institutional structure of the League, which did not facilitate the amelioration of the dispute largely because the executive board was undemocratic, unwieldy, unresponsive, and unwilling to seriously consider legitimate critiques or calls for reforms of its internal decision-making practices.

As noted in chapter 4, Du Bois had resolved the most contentious aspects of the race/class tension in black American liberation struggles by demonstrating that black class stratification did not generate the class antagonisms that Marxism anticipates because the black proletariat (and peasantariat) were not exploited by a black bourgeoisie or black petite bourgeoisie; rather, they were mainly employed, and super-exploited, by a white bourgeoisie and petite bourgeoisie. Thus, interclass race-based organizations were more salient than interracial class-based ones because the principal axis of exploitation for black Americans was race and not class. He pointed out that the black bourgeoisie did not function as a national bourgeoisie in a Marxist sense since it possessed little capital and was not the primary exploiter of black labor. The black bourgeoisie had hardly ever employed even a miniscule percentage of black workers, and likely even less so by the BPM era. The black bourgeoisie had not even developed as a managerial class, much less a class of owners of capital, until the benefits began to accrue to middle-class blacks from the CRM. Even this incipient managerial class consisted less of private business owners—i.e., a petite bourgeoisie—than salaried workers in the public sphere, mainly in local, state, and federal government agencies. Without a black bourgeoisie in a Marxist sense, it followed that the class differences between it and the black working class did not manifest the class antagonisms that Marxism anticipates, and therefore organization for black liberation would correspondingly proceed along race lines more than class lines. There were class differences in black communities, and even more so by the BPM; however, they still didn't generate the class contradictions that Marxism predicts, mainly because neither the black bourgeoisie nor the petite bourgeoisie were the primary exploiters of black labor, which was the class position of white capitalists, and as Du Bois insisted, white organized labor as well. It followed that the League should take as its primary emphasis organizing intraracially across classes in black communities, and secondarily concern itself with organizing interracially as the situation presented itself (e.g., in the historic case with the white Union Army). What Du Bois had observed during the Great Depression was no less apparent in the BPM; thus, his analysis was no less accurate.

Beyond Du Bois's arguments, the League might have addressed its ideological tensions using Haywood's Black Belt thesis before they became so disputatious. That the executive board didn't attempt such an approach is surprising given that Haywood resided in Detroit briefly during the League era, staying with executive board member John Watson, and he could have provided intellectual guidance to orient the parties before they became estranged. However, it appears that the board had not considered Haywood's thesis as a synthesis of their contrasting ideological views because, surprisingly, they hadn't examined Haywood's works sufficiently. As a result, there was little synthesis of the League's practice with the "third trend" that Haywood had promoted in RAM's *Soul Book* in 1967 and had specifically associated with the initiatives of DRUM even prior to the formal establishment of the League. One result of the failure to achieve a theoretical synthesis was that the League did not privilege organizing RUMs among black workers in the Black Belt, which should have been a locus of revolutionary organizing, according to Haywood. Such organizing was likely to have been both more contentious and, potentially, more auspicious given the rising political efficacy of black Southern communities in light of the CRM and the likelihood that any appeal for assistance to these same communities would translate the political gains of the CRM into economic benefits in one of the most hostile labor climates in the United States. Such an orientation was much more promising than the RNA's program. Moreover, it might appeal to the interests of not only the agricultural workers but the black petite bourgeoisie in the region, and thereby encourage the further expansion of the successful civil rights efforts of SNCC, SCLC and CORE into the economic domain by using the tool of labor, which was a prominent part of the liberal coalition that had rallied to it during the CRM. The contradictions that the League raised with regard to industrial labor were even greater when applied to black agricultural workers in the South, as well as the black industrial and service workers in Southern cities, and the prospects for League success were promising in the South given the shifting focus of key civil rights organizers in the region. It's important to remember that Martin L. King's assassination in Memphis had occurred during his visit to the city at the behest of striking sanitation workers.

In fact, it was the use of the boycott, a type of strike, that ushered in the CRM in the first place. By building on the infrastructural latticework as well as the methods used to build the movement for voting rights in the rural areas of the South, and applying them to its urban centers, then, in conjunction with student activists, black labor leaders could organize sharecroppers as well as industrial workers in targeted labor actions throughout the Black Belt. In this way, the predominantly Northern-based League, having expanded into the South, offered the possibility, through its RUMs, of concerted strike actions across industries in both the North and the South simultaneously. In the event, the League did not develop a "Southern strategy," as the Black Belt thesis implied, nor did it extend its organizational efforts to the South. It is ironic that of the two Detroit-based black power organizations, the League and the RNA, the former, with its focus on organizing black workers, thus complementing the political program of the CRM with an economic thrust grounded in the region's earlier, albeit limited, unionization (e.g., the Alabama Sharecroppers Union, the Southern Tenant Farmers' Union), would choose not to go South to organize its poor disfranchised fellow black workers, while the RNA, which required blacks to consider themselves as New Africans, with a program that was largely detached from the everyday reality of poor disfranchised black Southern workers, chose to go South and present themselves as dashiki-clad, revolutionary polygamists.[20]

The League's focus on organizing in plants and companies in and around predominantly Northern cities where the black presence was pronounced was more in accord with Boggs's thesis of the "City as the Black Man's Land" than Haywood's. But Boggs's broader thesis regarding the impact of automation and cybernation on the U.S. politico-economy suggested that the League's in-plant organizing would yield diminishing returns as the plants became increasingly desensitized to strikes and shutdowns because they grew less reliant on large numbers of workers—especially unskilled black workers—to operate them. Instead, the strikes at the plants needed to be carried out not simply to shut down production, but in concert with targeted actions in black and nonblack communities utilizing the out-of-plant initiatives the League had developed to shut down the major operations of the cities. Although Boggs didn't seem to appreciate this, to its credit the League's program was amenable to a general strike strategy, such as was being carried out in Paris in 1968.

Clearly, the United States was not going to be revolutionized by a direct attack on its military forces by black insurgents utilizing a guerrilla strategy, or by any other military strategy that was being considered at the time for that matter, regardless of the fantastic claims made by black and white militants who not only were unprepared to engage U.S. military forces, but were being waylaid by local police and sheriffs in armed confrontations (e.g., the NOI, RAM, Us, the BPP, the RNA) that often placed more of a burden on black communities by creating the need to organize and fund "Free _____" campaigns to secure the release of those imprisoned (e.g., "Free Huey," "Free Angela"). Both Cruse and the League were correct that the key to black liberation was to target a critical point in U.S. society. For Cruse, that was the "weakest point," which he saw as the cultural front, and for the League it was the "point of production." In fact, these two worked hand in hand, and the League was better prepared than any other organization of the BPM to effect a strategy that fused the two in its focus on both in-plant and out-of-plant organizing. That is, the LRBW's strategy implied the necessity of simultaneously targeting both the point of industrial production as well as the point of cultural production, and this was a replication of the strategy of the Slave Revolution of the Civil War, which the League's predecessors had waged a century before.

For example, one can imagine a League plan targeting a specific automotive plant such as Eldon Gear and Axle in Detroit, which was crucial to Chrysler auto production throughout the United States because it was the company's sole provider of axles for all of its cars. Eldon employed more than four thousand workers, of whom 70 percent were black, and it had been cited for more than 150 safety violations and was the site of the Johnson shooting discussed above. ELRUM was a strong presence in the plant. A strike at Eldon would generate a strong media response. but the Detroit news media were largely racist and did the Big Four's bidding in much of their reporting, so key to the plan were the other RUMs in the various other, non-automotive industries, including the city's major daily *The Detroit News*, the more conservative of the city's two major daily newspapers.

NEWRUM would have to strike to shut down the production of *The Detroit News* and in this way provide a greater exposure for *The South End*, under the editorship of executive board member John Watson, and sympathetic coverage of the Eldon strike. At the same time, other selected RUMs would strike in both automotive and associated industries throughout the city and surrounding areas. Support would be provided by the community assets the League had developed in its out-of-plant organizing, including screenings of *Finally Got the News* by sympathetic churches, student organizations, unions, lodges, and other voluntary organizations to provide political education and garner popular support. Then, the Association of Black Students at Wayne State University would strike in coordination with a walkout of students from Northwestern and Northern high schools, both of which had staged walkout protests before and were sites of the League's organizing students in the BSUF. The students at other major universities in the area, including the University of Michigan, where black student protest was high, SDS had been founded and the Port Huron Statement written, and the first "teach-in" against the Vietnam War had been held, and Michigan State University, also a site of black student protest and Weather Underground organizing, would be part of this coordinated effort, as a result attracting white allies in support of a "creeping" general strike in the Detroit metropolitan area. The initial demands of the industrial workers (and those in other sectors) could be focused on redress of their immediate concerns with white racist practices and policies related to working conditions, as well as tied into enduring, unresolved issues of racist discrimination and exploitation tracing back to the previous century. Sympathetic media would highlight these connections in their reporting, reinforcing the continuity that bound present conditions to their historic roots.

The pattern might be repeated in other selected cities of the North, coordinated by the League's executive board. Concurrently, in the South, the "creeping general strike" would be initiated by either tenant farmers or industrial or service workers—RUMs having been organized among each group—and would extend to the campuses of the historically black colleges and universities. Then, as in the North, key opposition media would be targeted for strike action, so that the League's and more sympathetic media's depiction of the strikes could be projected. The introduction of high school students and white college students would be pivotal, as well. Even more than in the North, sympathetic churches in the South would serve as sites of coordinating networks of community-based initiatives. With such extensive coordination, the United States would face a "creeping general strike" throughout the main sectors—industrial, agricultural, and service—of its economy, whose demands would address not only the rights of workers in those sectors, but the duties and obligations of the public and private institutions to the black communities that they were sworn to serve. The demands raised would include not only the recognition of workers' and students' rights but the distribution of resources. Just as important would be reconciling contemporary and historic claims to damages. The creeping general strikes emerging simultaneously in the North and South would converge into one national general strike and culminate in the ultimate demand of these striking black workers and their community supporters for reparations for slavery and Jim Crow.

Both the Northern and Southern actions would generate responses from local police forces and the mobilization of the National Guard, especially to restore activity in key production sectors. The most critical issues would be based on the level of repression that these forces would wield in order to end the general strike and the extent to which the RUMs were prepared to hold the line on the strikes and the occupation of the strike sites, the latter a function of their operational preparedness and the nature of any white (or black) worker opposition, the degree and extent of support from non-RUM-affiliated industries, the resoluteness of the support from within black communities, and the degree of division in white communities (especially within the armed forces). In the event, the United States would face a situation similar to France in 1968, although involving a much larger territory and, given the already existing sociopolitical cleavages in the populace regarding the Vietnam War, possibly a more volatile domestic situation, with no DeGaulle on the horizon for the U.S. government to call in to resolve the crisis.[21] The League's general strike would have to be well planned, meticulously coordinated, and prolonged across months, if not years. It could not be a single event. As difficult as it would be to plan and organize, it was still more feasible and promising than what other BPM revolutionists were proposing.

Following our argument on the relationship between cultural and political revolution, the Du Bois-Locke synthesis, and the example of the Slave Revolution, a general strike of this orientation and magnitude would entail not only a focus on the black urban proletarians of the North and the black agrarians of the South, but on the cultural integument that wedded the political objectives of black national self-determination to black labor's class-based demands for economic resources. The glue binding these two into a coherent whole was the cultural claim that blacks could unify behind, but it also raised the potential issue of the "crisis of industrial capitalism" in the United States. That is, what was required was a cultural claim that had major political and economic implications, one, following Locke's thesis, which would be rooted in demands for cultural democracy but would implicate political and economic democracy as well. The ramifications of these interactions would create the desired revolutionary outcome: racial democracy, which would transform the United States into a multiracial democracy in political, economic, and social terms. As noted above, the major cultural claim of blacks that had the potential to ramify in this way was/is reparations for the black descendants of U.S. slavery and Jim Crow. Although myriad factors might generate local initiatives and result in mass strikes coordinated by the separate RUMs situated in various industries and institutions, the culmination and coordination of these in a general strike would have as its major objective securing black reparations.

Full and judicious reparations for blacks would entail not simply a redistribution of the resources of the U.S. economy; it would first require a reconsideration of the basis of equality among black and white Americans though the elevation of the rights of blacks, as a people, to the fruits of their own labor and the obligation of the U.S. government to recognize these rights based on their equality as "cultural" equals in a collective sense, rather than simply the political, economic, and social rights of individual blacks. That is, the "legal standing" of the descendants of blacks made chattel by slavery and oppressed by Jim Crow requires recognition of their cultural equality as a people, not simply as individuals. Such recognition necessitates not simply making them whole as individual citizens but, given that these individuals comprise a specifically targeted group, a nation, whose human rights were violated collectively as a racially distinct people and the crimes against them committed by the United States and its agents, then the United States and its agents were required to provide reparations for the political, economic, and social harm they inflicted.

Herein lies the importance of a reparations strategy, in light of Locke's thesis: reparation would have to be manifest across cultural as well as political, economic, and social spheres, because part of what was denied African Americans was their cultural practices, preferences, and often their cultural products. Understanding the depths of that would require an educational process not only for black Americans, but even more so for nonblack, specifically white, Americans. This cultural education would be required to force the U.S. populace to appreciate the impact of the depredations suffered by black Americans at the hands of white racists and their institutions. In that process, white Americans and their racism would be challenged. That is, this cultural education would necessitate a type of cultural revolution among white Americans to bring them to appreciate the need to redress the "crimes against humanity" of white supremacism in the United States and therefore lead them to reject ongoing and future white racist criminality and prevent the need for future reparations. Thus, reparations, as an issue, would ramify not only as a claim for political rights and economic resources, but as a cultural claim whose provision would also transform the major educational institutions of U.S. society. An approach focused on democratizing the cultural apparatus is subsumed in such a reparations strategy, and so is one focused on generating "the crisis of U.S. capitalism" insofar as the economic redistribution of resources to blacks would not only include the land claims from Reconstruction and the "ex-slave bounties and pensions," but also the socio-politico-economic damages wrought by Jim Crow. Whatever form the latter might take, it would involve a massive redistribution of wealth—including the transfer of land in the United States to its largest racial minority and, as a result, would have, at minimum, the impact on the U.S. economy of permanently lifting the poorest black Americans out of poverty.

Importantly, the demands would not simply be focused on providing blacks a "bigger piece of the pie," but of transforming the pie itself. Thus, politically, reparations would not call for blacks to enjoy political "rights" under the present political system but, recognizing that blacks would not be effectively enfranchised under the existing majority rule systems (ranging from seniority systems to redistricting and gerrymandering of black populated districts), systems would have to be devised to provide weighted or plural voting such that black representation would be secured against white electoral tyranny (e.g., through gerrymandering). This would involve a reconsideration of the democratic ideal that has underwritten, through "majority rule," white racial majority tyranny. The establishment of the political rights of blacks raises the question of the nature of "representative" democracy in the United States and, as a result, suggests challenges to the ways voting rights are extended to citizens, as well as the notion of one person, one vote, the privileging of the two-party system (or even political parties themselves) in elections, and institutions that do not reflect actual "representative" democracy, such as the U.S. Senate and the Electoral College. The establishment of the social rights of blacks is even more extensive.

I emphasize these points to be clear that the reparations strategy suggested by black cultural revolution is one that focuses on reparations as a claim that would require drastic transformations of the U.S. political, economic and social systems. The revolutionists in the League coordinating the RUMs that controlled the diverse industries, institutions, and organizations of society through their strike actions and supported by those who remain as support elements within community-based institutions, would not relent until these changes were enacted. One tactic to utilize the leverage of the workers at their work sites—be they industrial plants, farms, transportation facilities, or schools—would be to open up production, distribution, or administration to limited sectors or areas in which their demands were met, in order to extend the range of their support, and also to increase the cleavage between their real and potential adversaries.

Most importantly, however, the success of the general strike would turn on the strikers' ability to organize RUMs, sympathizers, or factions in the U.S. armed forces, intelligence agencies, and law enforcement bodies.

Among the important distinctions between a League strategy for reparations, as outlined, and the poorly conceived and executed *Black Manifesto* of Forman, or even the much better conceived legal arguments of the RNA, is that in the context of a nationwide general strike the League's demands for reparations would not only raise this fundamental unresolved issue of social justice in the U.S. body politic, but also as an organization of black workers, its standing to make such a claim would be unassailable. More importantly, during a general strike, black workers would be demanding reparations in a context in which automotive production in the United States was stymied. Thus, unlike Forman and the BEDC, which had a weak legal argument for reparations and little if any leverage over the U.S. government to obtain them, or the RNA, which had a strong legal argument for reparations but very little leverage over the government to obtain them, the League, during a general strike, would represent a powerful historical and legal claim for reparations, reinforced by tremendous leverage to obtain them.

As noted above, the key to the issue of reparations was not only its historical and legal basis, but that it was/is a culturally based political issue that had important economic implications. Importantly, such a culture-based claim of black Americans would call the question of the commitment of prospective white American (and other minority) allies to the issues of social justice that they ostensibly supported. In fact, a reasonable assumption was that the success of a black cultural revolution, as developed here, was likely either to stimulate or be contingent on a concurrent white cultural revolution, as well. The latter would transform, by seriously weakening, if not overthrowing the cultural system of white supremacism in the context of expanding protests and related discussions of the case for black reparations, while establishing and institutionalizing processes legitimizing among whites the political, economic, and social demands that blacks were making. The spearhead of such a transformation would be white revolutionist allies themselves. Just as important was the prospective role these white allies might play in demobilizing the rightist and racist elements in their communities, especially but not exclusively among the military and police forces. During the Vietnam War, a general strike with the objective of challenging if not wholly overturning white supremacism, coupled with a demand for reparations, in a context where whites were undergoing a cultural revolution of their own had the potential to divide white America in ways that would only further accentuate the League's leverage. Seen in this light, the general strike of the BPM would parallel the General Strike of the Civil War, although it was less clear whether it might generate a political revolution that could be resolved violently, nonviolently, or through a combination of both—or whether it could be resolved at all.

Clearly, no BPM organization advanced along this theoretical and programmatic path—and I am not suggesting that such a program would have reached fruition if it had been pursued—but with its strategy of organizing black workers and targeting strikes at the "point of production" initially in the automotive plants, establishing RUMs throughout a variety of other industries, organizing students and intellectuals, developing independent media, and building community-based institutional supports, the short-lived LRBW came the closest of any organization to succeeding along this path to black liberation in the Black Power era. This becomes evident when we strip the League's strategy of its lexical veneer and it is revealed as focused on achieving a mass strike to shut down production in the automotive industry and, through its impact on related industries, bring the U.S. economy to a halt. Sugrue (2018, p. 2) estimates that "[b]y the midtwentieth century, one in every six working Americans was employed directly or indirectly by the automobile industry, and Detroit was its epicenter." Such a strike would lead to massive losses of wealth within the U.S. economy, losses that would ripple throughout the heavily integrated political economies of the West. Corresponding strikes in other unionized industries, service sectors, among agricultural and domestic workers, and among students on both high school and college campuses would generate a general strike. The general strike would allow the League to exert leverage on the government to accede to the demands in its six-point general program, and at the point of its maximum leverage the general strike would demand reparations for blacks, with all the political, economic, and social implications that such a demand would generate.

The League's political education classes would have benefited from drawing on Du Bois's thesis rooted in the history of African Americans rather than poorly fitting paradigms from nineteenth-century Europe or contemporary Africa, Asia, and Latin America. Du Bois's analysis from *Black Reconstruction* demonstrated how black laborers had successfully prosecuted a revolution that transformed the United States, so the issue of whether as a class they could be revolutionary was moot. Further, it indicated that the League's organization of workers at the point of production was historically grounded and logistically promising in light of African American history. It would also have been obvious that the League's revolutionary forebears drew on transformed slave religion to provide ideological motivation for their insurgency. Thus, religion was not necessarily the "opiate of the people," but rather the "adrenaline of the slave," stimulating them to initiate the General Strike, to join the Union forces, and to fight for their freedom in the Slave Revolution of the Civil War.

Du Bois's thesis also demonstrated that organization outside the workplace, that is, in the community, was also essential inasmuch as elements of the black petite bourgeoisie (intellectuals, students, church members) had shown themselves willing to pursue revolutionary objectives, historically in the General Strike and contemporaneously in the BPM, and might be considered as analogous to those Northern blacks who joined the U.S. Colored Troops (USCT), free blacks in the South, slaves who abandoned the plantations or just stopped working. In light of the latter, Du Bois's thesis converged with the League's focus on out-of-plant organizing through media and inuniversities and high schools. Thus, drawing from Du Bois might have revealed and reinforced the importance of the League's dual strategy and demonstrated its convergence with previous strategies pursued for black liberation, as epitomized in the General Strike. Moreover, it would have shown that there was no contradiction in following a dual strategy; in fact, that was the pattern undertaken in the only successful revolution that paralleled what was being attempted in the BPM.

A divergence between Du Bois's and the League's perspectives was the institutional locus of revolutionary change each proposed. For the former, it would center on the most powerful cultural institution in the black community, the Black Church, and for the League it was the industrial workplace. Actually, Du Bois's exposition in *Black Reconstruction* demonstrates that it was changes in slave religion that motivated enslaved and free black labor to pursue the General Strike, and that in this way the revolutionary initiative emerged from both the community, represented by slave religion, and the workplace, through slave hiring. Thus, what Du Bois's analysis showed was what the League practiced: a focus on organizing in the workplace and in important community institutions. A synthesis of both implied that the locus of revolutionary change for blacks would need to be both localized in the workplace and, concurrently, grounded in black cultural institutions, utilizing media to keep the networks in each well connected and coordinated. Stated differently, the League's focus on the "point of industrial production" in the workplace should have been balanced by a focus on the "point of cultural production" in the community. Their bold challenge to a sector of industrial production in the United States, where among the most highly valued finished goods were produced, should have been complemented by a "challenge [to] free enterprise at its weakest link in the production chain, where no tangible commodities are produced" (Cruse, 1968, pp. 112–113), namely, the cultural system, beginning with black communities. In practice, the League's *Finally Got the News* was emblematic of attempts at the latter. Such a theoretical synthesis was absent from the League's program because the executive board and other important elements of leadership failed to appreciate the cultural aspects of black revolution, which they might have garnered by drawing on African American revolutionary antecedents.

Relatedly, because of its Marxist orientation the League did not seriously develop the religion-based aspect of Du Bois's thesis in *Black Reconstruction* or the related role of slave hiring in the slave revolts and like most BPM revolutionists, they were altogether unaware of Locke's thesis. Although the League's focus on community organization was exceptional, it failed to provide the social networks that black churches could supply from both within and across local black communities. Most importantly, black churches would have been essential for the League's Southern strategy, for without their participation the League's attempt at black unionization in the South would likely go the way of the CIO's abortive Operation Dixie.[22] In the event, the League's reliance on analyses that were inattentive to black revolutionary processes in the United States contributed to unnecessary tensions between two perspectives that were, in fact, complementary (i.e., the in-plant and out-of-plant initiatives), whose synthesis might have made moot the larger dispute between those who privileged organizing among an interracial proletariat that hardly existed in Detroit (or, arguably, anywhere else in the United States) and was antagonistic to mobilizing black workers and communities where it did exist, and those who focused on a black proletariat that was mobilizing inside industrial plants and across classes in black communities.

The League's organizing of the RUMs was the core activity preliminary to the anticipated general strike, and its efforts in media and community work were incipient attempts at a cultural transformation that would focus not on some esoteric "traditional African" or "spontaneously revolutionary" blackness but on the concrete conditions and reality of black workers and the modern, predominantly urban culture they practiced and drew upon for their strength, insights, and day-to-day interactions. The League failed to appreciate that it was not at the forefront of a Marxian revolution in the United States, of the sort presaged in the Bolshevik Revolution; rather, it stood on the cusp of a black revolution in the United States that had been presaged in the actions of its enslaved ancestors and the cultural revolution they undertook, which had generated the successful political revolution they had fought in the U.S. Civil War, a century earlier.

Conclusion

In this chapter, we have examined two major organizations of the BPM that promulgated in one form or another a thesis of black cultural revolution. First, the RNA proffered a thesis self-consciously wedded to Malcolm's arguments regarding land as the basis of independence and the importance of revolution to establish a black sovereign nation. An important implication of Malcolm's thesis was that blacks had the right to make claims on the states that comprised the historic Black Belt and to demand reparations in order to establish and sustain a sovereign New African nation in the U.S. South. The RNA focused its attention on the liberation of the five contiguous states of Louisiana, Mississippi, Alabama, Georgia, and South Carolina, where blacks had long settled. They made a salient historical, political, legal, and moral argument that reparations were owed to the black descendants of enslaved Africans, who constituted the New African population. In the event that reparations were not forthcoming, they advocated a "people's war" against the United States in order to liberate New Africa. Unlike many of the national groups that advocated armed struggle in the BPM, the RNA, which began in the North, moved South in order to press its claims. The RNA appointed several ministers of culture and incorporated the concept of cultural revolution into their doctrine. Although it drew on Haywood's Black Belt thesis, its program was not Marxist. Moreover, without a more expansive cultural program rooted in the major cultural institution of the black community, namely, the Black Church, the RNA's initiatives in Mississippi, for example, foundered before they were able to develop the social networks that might have strengthened their ties to the political machinery of the local communities, and their intellectual distancing from analyses such as Haywood's, which focused on organizing the rural peasantariat of the Black Belt, may have contributed to their lack of coordination and failure to develop the political interests of the black sharecroppers and other rural constituents who were central to their plans not only for the revolutionary transformation of the counties of the Black Belt but for the development of armed resistance in the South.

Contemporaneous to the development of the RNA in Detroit was the emergence of the League of Revolutionary Black Workers. What the League created is probably as important as it is ignored in any discussion of black power theory in the United States, but most important for the analysis here is that it proposed a theory and plan for black revolution, which included a general strike strategy. The League concentrated on organizing workers, and in many ways it was the most prominent black power organization that reflected Haywood's thesis. Unlike the BPP, the League insisted that the black working class, the proletariat, was the vanguard of the black revolution because alone as a class it held this position of power at "the point of production." The League sought to leverage this power into concessions from the auto companies to address the immediate demands of black workers and also to realize the broader objective of revolutionary change in the United States. The League focused mainly on developing independent black industrial unions, beginning in the automobile industry in Detroit, but it also incorporated a focus on community-based organizations, ranging from student-led initiatives in high schools and universities (including appropriating the editorship of the third-largest daily newspaper in the state of Michigan), and popular media (including publication of a radical newspaper), to the creation of anti-police-brutality organizations, parent-based school-decentralization organizations, welfare rights groups, and tenants' rights groups. Their dual strategy focused on in-plant organizing and out-of-plant organizing designed to culminate in a general strike that would shut down strategic sites of industrial production in the United States, and compel the government's concessions to the League's demands.

The League embraced the call for black reparations and the liberation of the Black Belt; however, where Haywood had focused on black sharecroppers in the South as the key to liberating the Black Belt, the League's focus was on the North, and it had great difficulty penetrating the South. The League failed to fuse its class and race-based analyses into a coherent theory to guide its strategy and orient its members and supporters around a consistent program and plan of action, and as a result, it devolved into sectarianism. Nevertheless, of the organizations within the BPM, it was the League that probably came closest to progressing towards a black cultural revolution as it had been historicized by Du Bois, theorized by Locke, and proposed by Cruse; unfortunately, it could not be fitted into the Marxist frame the League attempted to construct for it and, ultimately, the organization imploded under the weight of its varied and increasingly fissiparous ideological and organizational components.

Although neither the RNA nor the League explicitly developed theses on black cultural revolution, their individual programs were clearly informed by—and would've benefited by further development of—such theses. However, other black nationalists of the era focused more directly on the necessity for black cultural revolution in their theses as well as their programs, and two in particular, which we examine in the next chapter, grew to become among the most influential black nationalist revolutionist organizations of the era: the Congress of African People (CAP) and the Shrine of the Black Madonna (PAOCC).

Chapter 8

CAP, Shrine of the Black Madonna/ Pan-African Orthodox Christian Church

In this chapter, we focus on two of the most influential BPM organizations that espoused black cultural revolution: the Congress of African Peoples (CAP) and the Shrine of the Black Madonna, also known as the Pan-African Orthodox Christian Church (PAOCC). CAP's Newark chapter was led by Amiri Baraka and its Midwest chapter in Chicago by Haki Madhubuti. The former harnessed black cultural revolutionary theses to urban electoral mobilization and independent political party organizing before abandoning his kawaida-based black nationalism and adopting Haywood's Marxist political thrust. Baraka's organization initially integrated the emergent black elected officials (BEOs) under black nationalist leadership and institutions; however, in time, Baraka was outflanked by those same BEOs for a variety of reasons, including the fact that his analysis of black cultural revolution failed to appreciate sufficiently the dynamic processes of black political and economic development taking place in the cities during a period of deindustrialization. Chicago CAP remained committed to black nationalism, especially the development of independent black institutions, in particular black schools and black publishing, while explicitly rejecting Marxism. Madhubuti's CAP created the Institute of Positive Education and its network of independent black schools in Chicago, which were prototypes for other such schools around the country. The development of Third World Press in 1967 helped Madhubuti, more than any other activist/theorist of the BPM, lay the basis for popular conceptions of Afrocentrism. Madhubuti's CAP also embraced aspects of reverse civilizationism through its acceptance of kawaida, and, the Afrocentrism that emerged from it tended to privilege kawaida-based misperceptions of rural African cultures that it construed as "traditional," rather than the urban-based American industrial working-class culture of black Americans. However, Madhubuti was not simply a communicant of kawaida; he transformed aspects of it, significantly at times, at least on a theoretical level, to comport with the broader requirements of the development of the educational institutions and publishing enterprises he had established in Chicago. As a result, even after the implosion of CAP, the institutions associated with Madhubuti's efforts in Chicago became among the most enduring of the BPM.

Although the Newark and Chicago CAP chapters disagreed on the salience of Marxism in the BPM, both distanced themselves from the Black Church. In contrast, the PAOCC, also known as the Shrine of the Black Madonna, was led by Albert Cleage (aka Jaramogi Agyeman) and was the most prominent BPM organization centered on the Black Church. The Shrine has been an enduring BPM organization espousing black cultural revolution and, along with Madhubuti's institutions in Chicago, is the major BPM organization to have sustained uninterrupted operations since the beginnings of the BPM. The Shrine fused political, economic, and cultural aspects of the BPM into a coherent thesis of black cultural revolution. While Cleage/Jaramogi emphasized the primacy of the Black Church in cultural revolution, he did not specify which institutions should be subsequently transformed or in what order. Thus, after the church, it wasn't clear where activists should focus, for example, on a black political party, black trade unions, black schools, or black community cooperatives. Yet, Cleage's focus on the Black Church and counterinstitutions was one of the most influential theses of black cultural revolution in the United States and in many ways the Shrine was a culmination of the institutional expression of black cultural revolution in the BPM. In practice, however, it reflected a return to cultural *evolution* rather than cultural *revolution*. Ironically, in supporting the BEOs, the PAOCC, like CAP, helped bring to power the group that would supplant the BPM organizations of the era and help end their movement.

The Congress of African Peoples

One of the most influential theses of cultural revolution, and the most successful application of kawaida, was not in Los Angeles with Karenga's Us, but in Newark, New Jersey, under the auspices of Amiri Baraka's CAP. Although less prominent than Us with respect to its theoretical contributions to cultural revolution, CAP had much to offer, given that Baraka was probably the most popular literary figure within the Black Arts Movement. By his own admission, Baraka (1984, p. 232) "wanted to create a revolutionary art and a revolutionary institution to bring that art to the black masses." By the mid-1960s he was already a noted playwright, poet, and cultural critic and the leader of Spirit House in Newark. Prior to founding Spirit House, he had organized the short-lived, though influential, Black Arts Repertory Theater and School (BARTS) in Harlem (in which Harold Cruse had been an instructor).[1] Baraka viewed black culture as having its own aesthetic, as expressed in a range of forms exemplified in black music, especially jazz and the blues. He saw these traditions as given to radical, and potentially revolutionary, expression, and in the 1960s he attempted to develop black theatre and black literature in such revolutionary directions.

Like most leaders of the Black Arts Movement (BAM), Baraka advocated the propagandistic role of black art in a manner consistent with Du Bois's argument in "Criteria of Negro Art," but he didn't seem to appreciate the broader philosophical significance of the Harlem Renaissance and the nuanced arguments that it had generated regarding black culture, black aesthetics, and black cultural transformation. Although Baraka (1984, p. 204) viewed both periods as emanating from "[a] rise in black national consciousness among the people," he (1963, pp. 133–137) viewed the Harlem Renaissance primarily in class terms, with the upper-class intelligentsia projecting the "New Negro" concept, the middle class projecting a "milder form of nationalism" through the NAACP, and the lower class promoting Garveyism. This depiction ignored the variations within and across the strata evident in the organizations and institutions associated with the diverse tendencies explored during the Harlem Renaissance. Such an oversimplification of the interests and perspectives operative in the Harlem Renaissance undermined the usefulness of the era as a historical referent or an analytical point of departure by which to discern the trajectory of later attempts at cultural transformation. For the most part, Baraka, like Karenga, Neal, and many others in BAM seemed to have viewed the Harlem Renaissance largely as a localized episode of black cultural "flowering" that was overly beholden to the aesthetic ideals and aspirations of its white patrons. Instead of a "renaissance," they proffered a "reformation," which through its aesthetic expressions of "blackness" would facilitate the birth of the "black nation" for which they would serve as midwives. Ironically, the most divisive cultural issue for BAM advocates was one that Du Bois and Locke—and many other "New Negro" aesthetes—had already agreed upon, that is, the architecture of African American culture. Both of the Harlem Renaissance men of letters agreed that Aframerican culture was typified in black folk culture, which found expression in the "sorrow songs," the Spirituals. Both thought that the African contribution was only tributary, while the mainstream of Aframerican culture was derived from "slave culture." Both asserted the importance of the "migrating peasant" relocating to the cities during the Great Migration as a harbinger of a heightened expression of black culture in the urban environs of the North, such as Harlem. Both the trajectory of black social development and its cultural expression were increasingly urban and working class. However, by the 1960s, this orientation had become reversed. Under the aegis of Malcolm X's reverse civilizationism, BAM advocates such as Karenga were focusing more on black African cultural referents than on black American ones.

Reverse civilizationists in BAM were convinced that black Africans possessed culture but that black Americans had been stripped of theirs. It followed for them that *black African* culture possessed greater revolutionary potential than any putative *black American* culture. The political objective of BAM superseded and, in major ways, circumscribed its aesthetic one. BAM members took African names, draped themselves in African garb, and projected a revolutionary pose to merge their politico-cultural project with that of their African contemporaries. Ironically, of all the major BAM advocates, Baraka was uniquely positioned to challenge the reverse civilizationism of BAM theorists, and he did as much in his critique of Karenga's denigration of blues music. As noted in chapter 6, Baraka, like Neal, rejected Karenga's arguments that the blues were "counterrevolutionary" and Baraka penned a learned treatise on the musical form in his 1963 *Blues People*. But whereas Karenga's disdain for the blues could be associated with his maginalization of contemporary black urban working-class cultural expressions, Baraka's analyses of black culture were not limited in this way.

Baraka celebrated aspects of the urban proletarian culture of the black industrial working class, which was evident by the onset of the Harlem Renaissance. Although the revolutionary aspect of black music often is typified in the jazz of John Coltrane, Abbey Lincoln, Max Roach, and Nina Simone, some of its most influential popular expressions were found in soul music or rhythm and blues (R&B). Baraka (1993, p. 168) had argued in *Blues People* that R&B was "a kind of blues that developed around the cities in the late thirties" and emanated from "profound changes in the cultural consciousness of Negroes" (ibid., p. 171). It was characterized by "a kind of frenzy and extra-local vulgarity . . . that had never been present in older blues forms" (ibid.). Appreciative of the role of urbanization and migration in the transformation of black culture in the United States, Baraka posed a conception of black working-class culture, as expressed in music, that informed his appreciation of black aesthetics and black cultural transformation.

Reflecting on kawaida in his autobiography, Baraka (1984, pp. 244–245) relates that Karenga's appeal was largely in his emphasis on cultural revolution, which "as a cultural artist," Baraka notes, "appealed to my biases." Baraka was convinced that "[c]ulture and the arts can be used to help bring the people to revolutionary positions"; however, he was just as emphatic that "the culture of the black masses in the US is an African American working class culture" (ibid., p. 255). Therefore,

> [t]he "revolutionary culture" we must bring to the masses is not the pre-capitalist customs and social practices of Africa, but heightened expression of the lives and history, art and sociopolitical patterns of the masses of the African American people stripped of their dependence on the white racist society and focused on revolution. (ibid.)

But Baraka was so intent on preventing a repetition of the failures of BARTS, which he largely associated with poor organizational discipline and the lack of a cohesive politico-cultural message, that he accepted not only the organizational example of Us but also kawaida and its reverse civilizationism. Although Baraka seemed to recognize the shortcomings of Karenga's conception of African culture, nonetheless he adopted Karenga's kawaida for his own use in order to acquire several of its concomitants, namely, the ostensibly traditional but, more importantly, patrimonial structures that facilitated Baraka's greater control of his organization and its members, in order to prevent a replication of the breakdown of BARTS.[2] The result was that, just as the political objective of BAM superseded its aesthetic objective, Baraka's political objective of creating a centralized black nationalist institution led him to embrace kawaida and its cultural atavism. Later, Baraka (1984, p. 353) lamented the "idealism" and "subjectivism" of "[t]he idea that somehow we had to go back to pre-capitalist Africa and extract some 'unchanging' black values from historical feudalist Africa, and impose them on a 20th century black proletariat in the most advanced industrial country in the world."

Heavily influenced by Karenga and Us—and originally the BPP, as well—Baraka transformed his Newark group into one of the most influential black nationalist organizations of the 1960s and early 1970s. Spirit House became a central component of Baraka's CFUN (Committee For a Unified Newark), which took shape following the Newark revolt of 1967. CFUN included United Brothers and another organization, BCD (Black Community Development), which more closely resembled Us's organizational structure. Baraka took Malcolm X's "ballot or the bullet" perspective seriously and applied it to the political struggle in Newark. Like Us, CFUN eschewed the militant posturing of self-proclaimed revolutionaries, and instead set out to gain municipal power for blacks in Newark. In so doing, Baraka implemented several of the programs and policies that Malcolm had called for in the OAAU. Three in particular were decisive in the success of CFUN, and later CAP.³ First, he took seriously Malcolm's argument on the importance of pursuing an electoral strategy that sought material gains for black people reeling in the desperation and devastation of the urban ghettoes. Second, Baraka took seriously Malcolm's thesis on third world solidarity and sought alliances with other national minorities in the United States, in particular members of the Puerto Rican community of Newark. Third, largely through Amina Baraka's (Amiri's wife) and Malaika Akiba's initiatives, he challenged his organization's sexism, facilitating the politico-cultural transformation of his organization that women's liberation necessitated. This was important to address the sexism not only in kawaida but throughout the BPM and CRM, because given the challenge of cultural revolution to transform society, the eradication of sexism is a paramount concern.

Challenging sexism is often viewed as a matter of simple morality, and clearly it is a major moral issue; however, it is an issue of power as well. Simply put, many of the community-based initiatives that nationalists developed that centered on the development of parallel institutions to perform the tasks that local, state, and federal government agencies and institutions did not provide were staffed mainly by women. The greater role of women in these community development—as opposed to paramilitary—initiatives, reflected traditionally sexist role designations whereby men assigned women to staff community service programs, alternative education facilities, and the administrative and clerical tasks that were directly related to the functioning of an organization and the recruitment of its new members. These tasks were among those that most directly engaged and administered to community folk, and thus were actually transformative. In contrast, women were relatively absent from the leadership positions of most of these organizations. Thus, the transformative aspects of the movement, as found in community-based programs, were largely reflected in and articulated through the engagement of black women; however, with the women's voices silenced by sexist structures, BPM organizations could hardly benefit from the informed input drawn from their direct experiences with the community they serviced. As a result, the organizations were unlikely to transform along lines that reflected the learning experiences garnered from the women's engagements with the community because the women with those experiences rarely occupied the executive positions where the policies for the governance of the organization, which might have drawn on their transformative experiences, were formulated.

One result was that BPM organizations often were ill-equipped to create the relevant cultural transformations within their own institutions, much less to propose, promote, and achieve the transformations necessary to facilitate a cultural revolution in black society. By relegating women to subordinate roles in an organization that placed them in direct, frequently intimate contact with the larger community through grassroots programs, the group's leaders inadvertently ensured that the seeds of revolutionary change would be both found in and bound by the experiences of the organization's women. At the same time, since its sexist practices and policies denied women leadership positions, the organization was not able to profit from any insights born of women's experiences in these transformative processes, and was thus precluded not only from achieving its own cultural transformation but from promoting policies that might transform black society. In short, sexism was not only morally odious, it undermined the capacity of BPM organizations to realize their potential for revolutionary transformation, and in this way it neutralized them.

Seemingly in recognition of these relationships, Baraka transformed CFUN by challenging sexism within its structure, through a process largely absent from other major BPM organizations we've examined. This was mainly a result of the actions of women in the organization, especially following the departure of BCD, which was oriented toward Karenga's feudal—and futile—conception of women and their sexist subjugation in Us. It was a problem of most of the CRM organizations, as well as those of the White Left and BPM organizations that professed allegiance to Malcolm X. Woodard (1999, p. 123) notes that "while Black Revolution farsightedly envisioned self-emancipation for men, it shortsightedly imagined submission for women" (ibid., pp. 123–124). In contrast, "The women in CFUN began first to experiment with their own ideas and practices about the roles of women in Black Revolution," and "they were determined to become their own liberators." With this in mind, "the Women's Division began fashioning the institutional arrangements necessary for their own political development," including, "new arrangements for the collective organization of housework, meals, and child care, so that women could be fully mobilized for black liberation" (ibid., p. 124). Amina Baraka, for example, was the founder of the African Free School and leader of the study circle, United Sisters, which, after the break with BCD

> established itself as the leadership of the new women's division of the CFUN. These women felt that CFUN should have been better organized, especially in the administration of its headquarters. . . . They introduced a number of organizational innovations, including standard operating procedures for many of the regular functions. The women's division became the largest section of CFUN; that branch included the most original and enthusiastic activists within the organization. (Woodard, 1999, pp. 122–123)

Similarly, Muminina Salimu, a dancer and playwright, "had been involved in Newark's black arts and jazz circles prior to the development of Spirit House" and directed work at CFUN's central office, which developed "into the headquarters for several local, regional, and national structures" including "the Newark Black Leadership Council, Congress of African People, National Black Assembly, African Liberation Support Committee, and Black Women's United Front." Moreover, she trained the central staff of CFUN as it expanded, following "the new procedures developed by the women's division" such that "[w]hen observers praised the organizational expertise of CFUN, they were commenting on the work of the women's division" (ibid., p. 124). In fact, what CFUN had undertaken that made it so different from other BPM organizations was its concerted attack on its sexism, which unleashed the organization's immense potential. The significance of these feminist initiatives was so great that they propelled CFUN into the most powerful BPM organization.

Woodard observed the development of "a marked difference" between CFUN and Us, largely because "there was very little parallel" in Us to the "political role of the women's division in CFUN" (Woodard, 1999, p. 137). It was only after challenging sexism that CFUN rebounded from its previous failed attempt at electoral politics in Newark to accomplish an unprecedented feat: electing the first black mayor of a major Eastern Seaboard city. The strategy informing this project was the hallmark of black nationalist approaches in the BPM, which is often marginalized in the academic and popular literature because it is associated with "cultural nationalist" programs, as opposed to "revolutionary nationalist" undertakings such as the BPP's survival programs, which were, typically, simply extensions of the programmatic initiatives that "cultural nationalists," among others, had been undertaking throughout the era. As Woodard (1999, p. 115) notes:

> cultural nationalism proposed a strategy of black liberation involving struggles for regional autonomy in urban centers, in alliance with oppressed people of color in the United States, particularly Puerto Ricans and Mexican Americans. Tactically, this stratagem involved mass social mobilization for black self-government at the municipal level and for proportional representation at higher levels of government. From these semi-autonomous urban enclaves, the African American cultural nationalists sought to accelerate the process of black nationality formation through the rapid spread of independent black economic, institutional, cultural, social, and political development.

Woodard suggests two major "driving forces" behind these black nationalist initiatives. The first "was the increasing degree of conflict between the black community on the one hand and both the welfare and police bureaucracies on the other"; and "the highest expression of that conflict were the intrusion of urban renewal plans that threatened the physical existence of many black communities, followed by hundreds of mass urban uprisings" (ibid., p. 115). The second "was the collapse of basic government and commercial services in the second ghettos," and in light of that,

> The cultural nationalist strategy . . . was to develop parallel black institutions in that void left by the urban crisis, thereby emphasizing the failure of the American government and mainstream economy in providing basic services and offering black nationalism and cooperative economics as rational alternatives. Considerations of strategic allies revolved around other communities that experienced similar urban dynamics. (ibid.)

Importantly, Woodard points out that "[t]his black awakening was not a diversion from revolutionary nationalism; it reflected the rising political consciousness of a people mobilized in a life-and-death struggle against white racism and internal colonialism." Moreover, it "expressed a global consciousness that led its proponents not only to identify with the independence movements of Africa, Asia, and Latin America but also to see Newark's Puerto Rican community as a strategic ally against internal colonialism" (Woodard, 1999, p. 116).

The success of CFUN allowed the organization to heavily influence the National Black Political Assembly (NBPA) at the 1972 Gary Convention. The NBPA emerged from the Black Power Conferences of the late 1960s, and specifically from the efforts of CAP, which was established at the Black Power Conference in Atlanta, Georgia, in 1970, which was attended by three thousand blacks from across the country practicing "operational unity" in an effort to create a national framework to forge a common strategy for black liberation. CFUN was prominent in the conference and because of its superior organization and recent electoral success, its members staffed much of the administrative apparatus of CAP, and CFUN became CAP-Newark. The conference marked the split between Baraka and Karenga, who opposed the convening of the conference and advised Baraka to cancel it (Baraka, 1984, p. 404). When Baraka refused, Karenga sent Us members to Atlanta, in what Baraka (ibid., pp. 404–416) viewed as an attempt to disrupt the conference. This was averted by Baraka's nonconfrontational approach to Us members, who were treated as "emissaries of Maulana Karenga" and conference guests (ibid., p. 406). A major outcome of the Atlanta conference was the promotion of the NBPA, which was initially intended to develop a unified political strategy for black Americans for the presidential elections of 1972 and beyond. In pursuit of that objective, it became the largest and most serious attempt to create an independent black political party in U.S history.

The NBPA convention was attended by African Americans of diverse political persuasions, from avowed revolutionaries to mainstream elected officials, from Marxist radicals to liberal centrists, from grassroots organizers to elite politicians, from CRM and BPM activists to Democratic Party apparatchiks. The steering committee of the NBPA consisted of Mayor Richard Hatcher of Gary, Indiana, the convention's host, Detroit Congressman Charles Diggs, and Baraka. The three represented the two most prominent political tendencies of the time, with Hatcher and Diggs representing the BEOs and Baraka the black nationalists of the BPM, a particularly effective ascendant strain who were demonstrating their ability to compete in the electoral arena as well as mobilizing the grassroots "in the streets." Baraka had demonstrated the latter in the success of CFUN in Newark's municipal elections, which brought Kenneth Gibson to the mayor's office in 1970. Hatcher served as a moderating medium between the two tendencies, but the fact that another black elected official assumed this role was due not only to the fact that he was the host of the convention; it foreshadowed the pivotal role that BEOs intended to play at the Gary Convention and in its aftermath.

Although the relatively small in number but increasingly influential BEOs largely reflected the CRM's integrationist orientation, it was Baraka who headed the day to day proceedings of the conference, and who most directly influenced the agenda. Baraka's leadership reflected the fact that he was among the few political leaders who had been successful in achieving the major objectives sought by the two most prominent political tendencies among black Americans, black nationalism and black integrationism, namely, building independent black institutions associated with grassroots political power and successfully executing an electoral strategy to win major elective office.

From the perspective of black nationalists, the NBPA provided a framework for the creation of an independent black national political party, although this was opposed by many black elected officials at the convention. The creation of such a party would have serious implications for the Democratic Party, given that blacks were a major constituency, whose influence would certainly be challenged by an independent black political party but at the same time the viability of a black political party would itself be challenged by the relationship between BEOs and the Democratic Party. The creation of such a party for black Americans was a fulfillment of Malcolm

X's desire for an independent black political party (as well as the efforts of Cruse, Boggs, and Cleage, among others, in the FNP). Although there was a dispute as to its creation, the threat to the Democratic Party—at least in national elections—was real, since for many activists Democrats were no less responsible than Republicans for the disastrous ongoing Vietnam War, they were still reeling from internecine struggles related to their failed presidential election campaign in 1968, and they faced an impending defeat in the 1972 presidential election, which had already been made obvious by the convening of the NBPA. In this context, a defection of blacks from the Democrats, or the enervation of black support, was an outcome that party leaders were intent on preventing. Critically, the small but increasing cohort of BEOs represented an important constituency for Democratic Party presidential contenders vying for the black vote to buttress their probability of winning the party's nomination and possibly turning the tide in the national election as well.

Faced with the potential threat of a third party arising largely from within its ranks, it was unlikely that the Democratic Party would stand idly by and allow such an important constituency to leave and form an independent and potentially rival "third force" in national, or even local, elections.[4] Thus, the NBPA was faced with not only the diverse ideological perspectives among its members, from which it sought to articulate a "united front," but also the machinations of the Democratic Party intent to keep, through cooptation, coercion, and a variety of other methods, one of its most reliable constituencies in the fold. Whether or not blacks, or black elected officials as their representatives, held the "balance of power" (Moon, 1948) in national elections was less clear, but what was unmistakable was that the BEOs would be critical in determining the victor of the resultant power struggle between the nascent NBPA and the Democratic Party and in recognition of their potential power, BEOs in Congress had formed the Congressional Black Caucus (CBC) in 1971.[5]

The NBPA was attended by eight thousand black Americans, including 3,300 delegates representing forty-two states. BEOs were automatically granted delegate status and major civil rights organizations were each granted ten delegates, while other delegates were nominated in statewide caucuses and represented a variety of community-based institutions, civil rights groups, and black power organizations. The all-black delegates and observers ranged from nationalists such as Betty Shabazz, Queen Mother Moore, and Louis Farrakhan to integrationists such as Coretta Scott King, Julian Bond, and Jesse Jackson, and from revolutionists such as Imari Obadele and Bobby Seale to BEOs such as Barbara Jordan and Carl Stokes, as well as artists and entertainers such as Nikki Giovanni, Isaac Hayes, and Richard Roundtree.

Given its successes in mobilizing voters in Newark, Newark-CAP provided much of the administrative support for the NBPA. The substance of the policies emanating from the NBPA was an eclectic representation of the varying political perspectives of the attendees.

The policy recommendations of the resultant "Black Agenda" reflected this ideological mix and ranged from liberal reforms consistent with New Deal/Great Society initiatives such as national health insurance, welfare reform, jobs programs, and D.C. home rule, to support for proportional representation, reparations, and recognition of the RNA's right to hold a plebiscite. Two contentious proposals focused on opposing court-ordered busing in support of black community control of black neighborhood schools and supporting Palestinian self-determination and an end to Israel's occupation of Arab territories it captured in the Six Day War of 1967, in the name of third world solidarity. The latter included language referring to the Zionist state as "fascist" and "imperialistic."[6] These two issues contributed to the walkout of most of the Michigan delegation led by future Detroit mayor, State Senator Coleman Young. Significantly, the walkout signaled what the tripartite leadership of the convention had only superficially concealed: the BEOs would not be beholden to the black nationalists and their pursuit of an independent black politics, nor would they risk associations that put them too far afield of the Democratic Party's liberal constituency.

Instead of demonstrating the viability of independent black politics oriented by black power, to a greater extent the Gary Convention signaled the apex of the BPM, and from there it would decline precipitously as BEOs assumed the dominant role in black politics. In fact, the CBC largely rejected the NBPA's "Black Agenda" and a few months after Gary issued its own "Black Declaration of Independence," which included a "Black Bill of Rights." The latter eschewed the more black nationalist demands of the "Black Agenda" and instead mainly asserted liberal demands such as guaranteed full employment, a guaranteed national income, and a federal contract set-aside program for black businesses. Nevertheless, its more progressive elements and those focused on blacks were largely ignored by the Democratic Party and given no more than lip service by its presidential candidate, George McGovern, who would lose in a landslide to Republican Richard Nixon anyway.

It was not only in the NBPA, but even in Newark, which was the springboard for the ascendance of Baraka and CAP, that black nationalists were superseded by Democratic Party politicians in their appeal to the increasingly politically efficacious black masses. In fact, in an example of the proverbial "biting the hand that fed him," Kenneth Gibson won reelection in 1974 after repudiating Baraka and many of the nationalist programs he sought to implement; moreover, Gibson was reelected well into the mid-1980s and other BEOs who were among Baraka's detractors at the NBPA, such as Coleman Young, became stalwarts in the Democratic Party, and were reelected into the 1990s. Confronted with these setbacks, particularly the actions of BEOs such as Gibson, Baraka framed the problem less in his tactics or the broader national patterns of deindustrialization of the cities in which blacks were ensconced, further undermining their ability to deliver on the promise of patronage politics through their control of city budgets, and the rising conservative "backlash" in U.S. national politics that would lead national unions such as the Teamsters to support Nixon in 1972, and more in the limitations of black nationalism. Baraka rationalized *his* failures as *the* failure of black nationalism; thusly: "internal colonialism, when faced with the challenge of Black Power, had changed to neocolonialism" (Woodard, 1999, p. 254). At a point where he might have redirected his initiatives more closely with those of potentially progressive institutions in Newark's black communities or employed different tactics toward developing such institutions, as he had with CFUN, Baraka viewed his organization's defeat as a failure of black nationalism itself, thereby turning a tactical loss in Newark politics into a strategic defeat for his ideology. As early as 1972, he had begun to study Marxism in meetings with the African Liberation Support Committee (ALSC) in order to incorporate socialist analyses into a "revolutionary kawaida," and by 1974, Baraka repudiated black nationalism for Marxism.

Baraka's rejection of black nationalism for Marxism split CAP irreparably. Upon his announcement at the Midwest CAP conference in 1974 that CAP was encouraging its members to study Marx, Lenin, and Mao Zedong, both Jitu Weusi of The East and CAP's Midwest chair Haki Madhubuti (Don L. Lee) of the IPE and TWP in Chicago resigned their positions in CAP. The loss of these two chapters was immense given what each represented as institution in its own regard. The East was born of Uhuru Sasa, a seminal organization in the independent black school movement, in Brooklyn, which was probably the largest CAP contingent. The IPE was an influential independent black school in Chicago, and TWP was the prominent independent black press headed by one of the most influential artists of BAM. The resignations of Weusi and Madhubuti from CAP's leadership and the loss of their institutional support signaled the demise of CAP as a locus of the BPM. The ensuing debate between Baraka and his supporters, on one side, and Madhubuti and his supporters on the other was dramatically played out in the pages of *The Black Scholar* and *Unity & Struggle*, and it largely replayed debates that had ushered in the BPM, as captured in Cruse's "Revolutionary Nationalism and the Afro-American." Madhubuti's critique of Baraka's embrace of Marxism, and his grounding CAP in it, was an uabashed endorsement of black nationalism, a denial of the applicability of Marxism to black liberation in the United States, and an insistence on independent black institution building focused on schools and businesses to serve and support revolutionary initiatives.

Madhubuti's critique was especially impactful given that unlike many other prominent black nationalists of the era, he could rival Baraka as a member of the upper echelon of BAM. Madhubuti was one of the most popular poets and essayists of BAM and, as Don L. Lee—along with Johari Amini (Jewel C. Latimore) and Carolyn Rodgers and acting on the inspiration of Dudley Randall's Detroit-based Broadside Press (Boyd 2003)—he founded TWP in 1967, which published some of the leading artists of BAM including Baraka, Sonia Sanchez, Mari Evans, Margaret Walker, Kalamu ya Salaam, Keorapetse Kgositsile, and Dudley Randall, as well as prominent black authors whose reputations had been made well before BAM, such as Ruby Dee, Sterling Plumpp, and Lee's literary mentor and Pulitzer Prize–winning author, Gwendolyn Brooks, and important authors and essayists of black history such as Chancellor Williams and John Henrik Clarke.

Putting into effect one of the key tenets of kawaida, *ujamaa* (cooperative economics), Lee intended that TWP would publish the bourgeoning literature of the BPM without the editorial censorship of mainstream publishing houses while creating an institution that was black owned and politically oriented to the cultural transformation of black American society. The press generated funds that could be used to support other black institutions; and key to this institutional development was the creation of independent black schools that would teach students using a pedagogical perspective that Du Bois had labeled by no later than 1961 as Afrocentric. For Lee, who by the early 1970s had taken the Swahili name Haki Madhubuti, this would become the Institute of Positive Education (IPE) which opened in 1969 on Chicago's south side, and eventually, TWP served as the publishing branch of the IPE, which, more than just an independent black school, was a community resource and research center specializing in education and communications.

Given Lee's grounding in BAM and his organizational and institutional work in Chicago, it is not surprising that he became a ranking member of the executive committee of CAP and that Chicago was the Midwest headquarters of the organization. But unlike Baraka's CFUN, which was wedded from its inception to kawaida and programmatically influenced by Us, Lee's Chicago organization exercised relative autonomy from Karenga even as it embraced important elements of kawaida, mainly the *nguzo saba*, but, importantly not its sexist orientation, especially under the influence of Lee's wife Carol (Safisha), who was an educator in her own right, and of Lee's emerging feminism. Like Baraka, Lee was a military veteran as well as a veteran of the BPM. Born in Little Rock, raised on the east side of

Detroit, and coming to the south side of Chicago as a teen, he resonated with the incipient BAM and produced and helped develop its signature style and some of its seminal poetry, but his activist roots had been planted in CORE and SNCC, especially during their black power phases, as well as Chicago's Organization of Black American Culture (OBAC), which was one of the important BAM organizations (Smethurst, 2005). His aesthetics and activism led him to realize the importance of independent black institutions and the central role that black art could play in their development. In this way, Lee's participation in the black liberation struggle emerged prior to his massive contributions to BAM. Thus, by the time that Lee penned his response to Baraka's unilateral imposition of Marxism on CAP to *The Black Scholar* in his essay "The Latest Purge," his was among the most prominent voices of black nationalism in the United States and his essay would solidify the major fissure initiated by Baraka's breach, from which the movement would not recover.

Lee, now Madhubuti, voiced his opposition to both the new direction of CAP, and to Marxism as an ideological guidepost to the previously black nationalist–oriented CAP. Baraka's response, at its best, pointed to the embrace of Marxism as a necessary evolutionary development of his and his organization's intellectual growth, but also as a strategic shift necessary to confront what he viewed as the reconstitution of domestic colonialism as neocolonialism. The debate on both sides would too often descend into the ad hominem and crude sectarianism that typified the era. In many ways, it was a repetition of the Cruse-Boggs tension that had implicitly or explicitly provided the theoretical axes of the BPM since the founding of RAM. As discussed in chapter 1, these perspectives were not irreconcilable, but in the event adherents of each so scorched the discourse and inflamed the rhetoric of BPM revolutionaries that the substantive basis for either their theoretical amalgamation or transcendence was lost, as was the attention of many of those blacks and nonblacks at whom these programs were ostensibly directed.

One aspect of that resolution—or at least a perspective that might have moved the protagonists toward synthesis—was Haywood's Black Belt thesis, which recognized both the importance of black workers and the revolutionary elements within the black petit bourgeoisie, as well as the self-determination rights of blacks as a subjugated nation under U.S imperialism and black culture as an important aspect of black nationhood. Haywood affirmed the potentially revolutionary aspects of black nationalism that emanated from the cultural assertions of the black nation for self-determination. Such claims in the context of the Black Belt thesis would have to be expansive and unifying, galvanizing blacks across classes. The workers would provide the spearhead of the struggle by asserting their leverage against the system and in that way compel it to address and resolve the political, economic, and cultural demands of the black nation. However, Haywood's synthesis privileged political activity in the U.S South rather than the North and it's not clear that such an approach would have resulted in a much different outcome than what Baraka experienced in Newark.

The Du Bois-Locke thesis also recognized class differences in black communities but rejected the class antagonism presumed by Marxism. It also suggested the expansive and unifying cultural claim that could galvanize blacks across classes: reparations. What was implicit in Haywood's framework was explicit in the Du Bois-Locke thesis, that the cultural claim needed to be wedded to economic and political objectives that both appealed to the masses of blacks and also spoke to the major unresolved issues of social justice that would motivate continued political mobilization and that contained the prospect of radically transforming the systems of governance in the United States, namely, the political oligarchy, the economic oligopoly, and the white supremacist cultural system. Failing that, the issues could be readily co-opted by the array of institutions of civil society in the United States and, in the case of black American political mobilization, into the extant framework of the local political machinery and/or the national Democratic Party, with only lip service paid to the actual enduring issues of black liberation, as had been accomplished in Newark by the local Democratic Party, in the aftermath of the NBPA by the national Democratic Party, and by the Carter administration with respect to the Humphrey-Hawkins full employment bill by the end of the 1970s (Smith, 1996).

By the early 1970s it was apparent that as the victories of the CRM and BPM provided political and economic resources to black communities, mobilized elements within these communities were realigning themselves to take advantage of these resources to advance their own interests and claims. The sectarian and often abstract ideological disputes of black nationalists and black Marxists decreased their relevance to these struggles for material gains in both the political and, increasingly, the economic spheres, and BEOs and their patrons in the Democratic Party, often aligned with prominent church leaders, appeared to be much more able to deliver resources to their black constituents; as a result, they outmaneuvered black nationalists of whatever political stripe, and black Marxists as well, in their struggle for relevance among—and support from—African Americans. This intervention by the Democrats was made easier by black revolutionists of the BPM who were drawn to the siren song of the need for "unity" and the desire for a "national" organization to both mobilize and channel grassroots black political interests, namely, a national black political party.

Even with the qualification "unity without uniformity," the notion that unity should be an objective of black nationalist mobilization was chimerical. The appeal of the united front was that it would unify black protest efforts under a solid overarching operational, if not organizational, rubric; but the diversity of black political interests in the aftermath of the successful overthrow of de jure Jim Crow made unity, even with respect to the main political objectives of black Americans, extremely difficult to obtain. That is, while blacks shared a common interest across regions to oppose the apartheid system of the Jim Crow South, the absence of such a uniformly regarded object of opprobrium in the post–Jim Crow era severely diminished the prospects of a unified political orientation among them. Clearly, there were national concerns about poverty, unemployment, health care, police brutality, and political representation, but even prominent national issues such as opposition to the Vietnam War found sizable numbers of blacks on both sides of the dispute.[7] As long as an appeal to unity was necessary there would be sizable fractures in the organizational framework of the resulting political formation, and these divisions would be obvious and relatively easy targets for attempts by both adversaries and potential allies, such as the Democratic Party, to exploit them in pursuit of their own ends. Also, the attempt to build a single, ostensibly unified party at the outset, rather than disaggregated and more locally focused parties in selected cities such as Newark, Detroit, Atlanta, and Oakland, which had already demonstrated their ability to elect black nationalist–oriented candidates, seemed a less propitious focus of black nationalist electoral efforts. Instead of concentrating their limited resources on a few select cities, however, they sought—prematurely, as it happened— a *national* party organization, which was immensely difficult to build. One result was that opposition to an independent national black political entity could focus its disruptive efforts on a single organization rather than several, concentrating its resources and increasing its likelihood of successfully undermining that organization.

In addition, the desire to form a national organization should have been balanced by the realization that no single black nationalist organization had a national appeal that was grounded in both grassroots organizing and electoral success. In fact, only Baraka's CAP had been able to succeed in a major city. A black nationalist party open to a united front orientation could not sustain itself as a national organization unless it took on those non-nationalist tendencies that had a national presence, as represented in entities such as the NAACP, the Democratic Party, and selected national labor unions; however, these types of organizations would support neither a black nationalist ideological orientation nor a separate black political party.

Thus, while unity was chimerical, an attempt at creating a nationwide black nationalist political party could not survive the very constituents it would have to appeal to in order to create itself. The NBPA was saddled with both of these problems simultaneously and it failed largely because it attempted to create in a single entity a viable third party focused on electoral politics and a sustainable nationwide black organization committed to mobilizing grassroots interests around the diverse concerns of black communities. It could not deliver on the promise of electoral success because only in exceptionally rare cases had black nationalists demonstrated skills at electoral activism—many dismissing the need for it altogether—and where they did they were no match for local Democratic Party organizations. Neither could it deliver on a national party because of the need to appeal to a broad spectrum of interests, which a national party required, which reduced its ability to generate an actual black nationalist political organization that would be national in scope. As a result, the NBPA imploded under the weight of its own expectations.[8]

For Baraka, in particular, his turn from black nationalism to Marxism was based on his rationalization that while black nationalism may have been useful in confronting U.S domestic colonialism, it was ineffective in challenging its domestic *neo*colonialism. Marxism, according to this view, was a more potent ideological weapon in this context; therefore, a shift to Marxism could be viewed as progressive. This argument reflects a rhetorical turn intended to rationalize a tactical shortcoming, Baraka's failure to compel the Gibson administration to fulfill its obligations to the program of CFUN/CAP in Newark. Baraka, however, magnified this tactical failure into a strategic one by jettisoning the ideology that was the fulcrum upon which his local and national organizations rested. Accepting, for the moment, that Baraka was correct that black nationalism had been outflanked by neocolonialism, and because of it had outlived its usefulness as an ideology for black liberation, it made little sense to replace it with Marxism/Maoism, which not only most of his membership and important allies rejected wholesale but was even more out of touch with U.S. society.

For example, Mao's widely lauded endorsement of the CRM was attuned to black initiatives against Jim Crow but totally out of touch with the reality of white workers' racism. This is evident in his "Statement Supporting the Afro-Americans in Their Just Struggle Against Racial Discrimination by U.S. Imperialism" of August 8, 1963, in which Mao included his observation that

> [i]n the United States, it is only the reactionary ruling clique among the whites which is oppressing the Negro people. They can in no way represent the workers, farmers, revolutionary

intellectuals, and other enlightened persons who comprise the overwhelming majority of the white people.

This displays an utter ignorance of the endemic nature of white racism throughout all classes of white Americans, which was no less pronounced among "white workers and farmers" in the South and the North (the latter exemplified in the Boston Busing Crisis and the "Hard Hat Riot" of the early 1970s). Mao's 1968 statement in response to King's assassination was similarly myopic with respect to the orientation of white workers in its conflation of the issue of black national self-determination with that of class struggle, the same rationalization that Haywood had opposed in the 1920s.[9] In fact, previously, Baraka himself had argued that Marxism/Maoism was largely irrelevant to African American urban communities and the United States in general. For example, he had asserted, in a manner consistent with Cruse, the uniqueness of the black American context, which called for a unique social theory and political program:

> The United States is not China nor nineteenth-century Russia, nor even Cuba or Vietnam. It is the most highly industrialized nation ever to exist, a place where the slaves ride in Cadillacs and worship their slave master's image, as God. American power over Africans around the world must be broken before the other colonial powers are completely broken. Also, it should never be forgotten that we are a different people, want a different nation, than our slavemasters. (Baraka, 1974, p. 118)

It made even less sense to adopt Mao's concomitant notion of cultural revolution, which was ravaging China at the time and theoretically was applicable to an immediately postrevolutionary context, which the United States during the BPM was clearly not experiencing, at least, not according to Baraka. In fact, most BPM leaders would maintain that it was experiencing, at best, a prerevolutionary or reformist context, in a Marxist sense. Baraka (1992, pp. 117–118) seemed to have recognized this earlier, as well, in his admonition that what was necessary for black liberation was the pursuit of black cultural revolution—not a purging of Party ranks such as was occurring in the Great Proletarian Cultural Revolution in Mao's China—that was focused on capturing the hearts and minds of black Americans to wage a conscious struggle for black liberation. It also made little sense for Baraka to adopt Maoism at the same time that local, regional, and federal authorities in the United States had demonstrated their ability to thoroughly undermine black Maoist groups such as RAM and the BPP. Moreover, Maoism was hardly a coherent ideology in the 1970s, even in China; it was "an amalgam of perspectives associated with different factions within the Chinese Communist Party." Its dominant framework was associated with Marxist-Leninist orthodoxy; another, trumpeted by Lin Biao, was populist, focusing on the people more than the working class and emphasizing support for third world nationalism; while another, "Cultural Revolution Maoism," bordered on anarchism (Elbaum, 2002, pp. 139–140). The contending perspectives within Maoism made it difficult for those who attempted to apply its precepts uniformly in the United States. Not surprisingly, the major explicitly Maoist group in the United States, the Revolutionary Union, formally disbanded in 1975.[10] Finally, the irony could not have been lost on Baraka that even as he turned to Maoism as a more effective ideology to address Nixon-era domestic neocolonialism in the United States, Mao himself had turned to Nixon, with whom he sought and achieved a rapprochement with the United States, having received Nixon in Beijing in February 1972.[11]

In fact, Baraka was half right: the successes born of black nationalist initiatives were important in promoting the political assertiveness of blacks and therefore increased their electoral power, resulting in the ascendancy of BEOs as a counterweight to nationalist organizations, even those that had catapulted them into political leadership, such as CFUN. The logical extension of this work would have been the creation of an independent black political party; however, the national Democratic Party, through its local affiliates, provided a competitive option for mobilized black political interests by providing them access to local patronage and more extensive financial resources distributed through networks and clients honeycombed throughout Democratic Party–dominated city and county governments, congressional districts, and voting precincts. As a result, many black activists channeled their protests into electoral politics under the aegis of the Democratic Party. A more accurate characterization might be that the Democrats incorporated, coopted, channeled, or cajoled prominent political tendencies toward independent black political party organizing. The ascendancy of the BEOs and the threat posed by the Democratic Party and its resources to anyone seeking to organize an independent black political party required a revised black nationalist strategy. Such a revised strategy would have needed to center on political mobilization by utilizing some powerful indigenous institution in the black community that could rival the local Democratic Party, such as a black political party or labor union, had such an entity existed. Among the few viable candidates, the one that was not only politically efficacious but culturally grounded in the black community, was the Black Church. This was the direction undertaken by Albert Cleage, an early ally of CAP, and his Shrine of the Black Madonna, in Detroit. Cleage's focus was not only propitious as a strategy, for the reasons just given, but it provided an opportunity to further entrench the cultural focus of the transformation that Baraka sought, rather than abandoning it; however, Baraka did not pursue this option.

Although in applying it, Baraka had taken kawaida "theory" farther than even its founding organization, Us, had been able to in L.A., he was forced to face up to the limitations of his kawaida approach to addressing the challenges of patronage politics and the hegemony of the Democratic Party in a major postindustrial U.S city by appealing to the emerging sector of BEOs who had thrown their support to the Democrats rather than the black nationalists. Baraka's *practical* difficulty was a function of his inability to provide sustained pressure on BEOs through his grassroots mobilization of the black and brown vote in Newark and elsewhere. Baraka was not alone among black nationalists who failed to appreciate that the strength of their appeal to increasingly politically efficacious blacks and their increasing number of elected representatives was in their ability to exert leverage in the form of votes. It was not rhetoric about revolution and "taking it to the streets" that was most salient to this expanding "political class," but the ability to produce desirable—or undesirable—election outcomes. The decline of Baraka's and Newark-CAP's influence in this regard was rapid, such that by 1974, just four years after delivering Kenneth Gibson's victory as the first black mayor of Newark against a white incumbent, Baraka's forces

> could be safely ignored by the mayor in his reelection campaign because [Gibson] was confident that Baraka and his organization could not deliver sufficient votes to affect the outcome of the election. This is all the more telling since Baraka at the time had probably the best local organization of any nationalist leader. (Smith, 1996, p. 306)[12]

This development had implications far beyond Newark. For example, commenting on the failure of most black elected officials to even attend the 1974 Little Rock NBPA, which was the followup to the Gary Convention (only three of the sixteen members of the CBC at the time attended), black St. Louis congressman William Clay (D-MO), a founding member of the CBC and delegate to the Gary Convention, remarked: "My district is 49 percent black and 51 percent white and I get elected every two years. Baraka's district is 65 percent black and they send Peter Rodino, a white man, to Congress. Now tell me, what business do I have letting him tell me about political power and political organization?" (Smith, 1996, pp. 63–64).

Baraka's *theoretical* difficulty was rooted in a broader problem evident in the prominent theses on black cultural revolution in the 1960s, namely, their rootedness in a version of black nationalism that theorized the black American as a colonial subject in a domestic colonial structure. What was necessary, in this view, was to reorient this colonial subject to his/her indigenous identity and in the light of their reoriented perspective proceed toward the revolutionary objective, that is, freedom for the colonial subjects. This perspective borrowed heavily from the anticolonial struggles that were ongoing throughout Africa and Asia during the 1960s, but, as noted in chapter 1, this conception of black nationalism misunderstands the "American-ness" of white racist oppression, black American identity, and black American political development.

The availability of the colonial analogy decreased the motivation of bright black leaders to articulate a theoretical argument rooted in the peculiarities of black America, as opposed to colonial Africa. The colonial analogy offered a ready-made theoretical framework to graft onto the very different U.S. political economy and society and thus lent itself too readily to already-dated theses regarding the city and ethnic succession. No one seemed to understand this better than James Boggs, who articulated as much in his critique of RAM's advocacy of separate statehood, which had motivated the dispute that led to his resignation from RAM's board in 1966; nevertheless, it did not prevent him from articulating an urban-based corollary to the ethnic succession thesis in his essay "The City Is the Black Man's Land" of that same year. The RNA's "free the land" orientation displayed a similar myopia born of a misapplication of the colonial analogy, and although not rooted in a cultural revolution thesis, the BPP's myriad ideological bents all seem to turn on acceptance of variants of domestic colonialism.

The colonial analogy did not fit the African American "domestic colony," as discussed in chapter 1, insofar as it suggested a relationship between a powerful, rich Western country and a much weaker, poor non-Western country, notwithstanding that the black domestic colony was not a third world backwater, but a technologically advanced, industrialized, relatively well-educated, and politically developed nation within the borders of the most powerful country in the world. Black nationalists in search of an analogy were so preoccupied with third world revolutionaries that they ignored the greater structural similarities between the putative domestic colonialism in the United States and that found in other advanced industrialized nations, such as Great Britain with respect to Ireland—suggesting that Michael Collins may have been a more useful referent than Che Guevara. But even these were insufficient analogies, because American blacks were a minority nation in diaspora away from their ancestral homeland, which meant that they didn't have the prior land claims that existed in every African colonial scenario and were attempting a revolution against a majority racial regime, which also didn't apply in African colonial contexts. Actually, there was no precedent in the contemporary colonial world, or in the twentieth century, especially considering that BPM revolutionists were attempting it in the most powerful country in the world. Analogues were not to be found in the contemporary colonial world but in the prior experience of black Americans, specifically in the Slave Revolution. But BPM revolutionists did not study this black American revolution as a reference for the black American revolution they envisioned.

Further, the problems contained in the domestic colonial analogy that are evident with respect to political revolution are even more germane to cultural revolution. For example, black cultural revolution theses failed to specify the culture that was being overthrown or that which was replacing it. The most prominent theses relied too much on the analogy to third world colonialism, which largely ignored how the differences in cultural development that colonialism had impacted might affect the way cultures might develop in the aftermath of cultural revolution. That is, unlike in Africa, African American cultural development would entail much more than simply continuing extant cultural practices that had been restricted or undermined during colonialism. Instead, black cultural revolution would entail a process of cultural education, and cultural institutionalization, far more extensively in the United States than in Africa.

What is more, most black Americans were not likely to accept a vision of themselves as African, New African, or any other imposed designation given the historic fight for their rights as American citizens; therefore, approaches that were dependent on such cultural adoption or appropriation by large swaths of black Americans were unlikely to succeed. In the U.S. context, blacks were unlikely to begin learning KiSwahili or to become Muslim en masse, or even in a sufficient number of critical communities of black activists, any more than they were going to stop speaking English or attending church. In fact, many black Americans had come to even more strongly embrace their cultural roots in their churches, which were increasingly demonstrating their political salience during the apogee of the CRM. If nothing else, the CRM under Martin L. King's influence had given new political life to the Black Church as a key to black political mobilization, including black electoral mobilization, especially following the Voting Rights Act of 1965. The contradictions facing black nationalists were based on the fact that whereas historically the Black Church stood on a black nationalist base, its programmatic and political thrust during the CRM and BPM had been integrationist. The contradictions didn't run one way, because integrationist organizations relied on the Black Church, which even if no longer nationalist was an independent black institution, and one that blacks were hardly intent on integrating out of existence. This inconsistency provided an opening for black nationalists if they cared to engage the Black Church as it was and not as so many of them imagined it: an institution whose time had passed. But many black nationalists failed to appreciate this opportunity, as Larry Neal pointed out, until they had lost the church to the BEOs and the Democratic Party, which basically ended the BPM.

Many nationalists failed to resolve the contradictions between their domestic colonial arguments and the interest group politics that confronted them in the United States particularly with the rise of BEOs, something they anticipated but poorly incorporated into their broader strategy. Cleage was alone among prominent black nationalist proponents of cultural revolution to appreciate these contradictions in such a way as to see the necessity of centering cultural transformation on the major cultural institution in the black community, the Black Church, and to more thoroughly integrate the church's role in the transforming urban communities in which black Americans were situated.

Black nationalists needed to wed their revolutionary theory to the level of political, economic, and social development of the society they were attempting to transform. This was especially evident given the changes underway in many of the major U.S cities in which blacks were concentrated. Kawaida approaches were ill-equipped to account for these transitioning urban contexts and, as a result, kawaida advocates such as Baraka, and many of the black nationalists in Newark, largely

> underestimated the extent to which the problems of Black America are a component part of the dynamics of the political economy of the United States. As blacks and Puerto Ricans migrated to urban industrial centers like Newark, the metropolis was in the midst of a postindustrial transformation. Once they sought streets paved with promise for those who labored hard in factories; now many of them languish unemployed in the shadow of opulent corporate centers, still haunted by the horror of poverty and the violence of despair. (Woodard, 1999, p. 262)

Essentially, Baraka oriented his program of cultural revolution to a thesis rooted in the second ghetto, even as Newark and much of the rest of black urban America were being transformed into the third ghetto (Nightingale, 2003). Baraka's organization initially integrated the BEOs under black nationalist leadership and institutions; however, he was outflanked by those officials for a variety of reasons, not least of which was their appeal to local representatives in the Democratic Party and many church leaders among them, and partly because his analysis of black cultural revolution failed to appreciate the dynamic processes of deindustrialization. Finally, circumvented by the BEOs that his organization had helped promote, Baraka abandoned black nationalism for Maoism and, as a result, ensured that the NBPA—now an avowedly communist-led organization—would be irrelevant in local, state, or national electoral politics. In this way, Baraka conceded the electoral field to the Democratic Party and their affiliated BEOs by associating the most viable major organization for independent black political party organizing with the one ideology that was anathema to most black Americans, and Americans in general: communism—and doctrinaire communism at that. With this concession, BEOs of various stripes gave their allegiance to the Democratic Party and by the time of its Little Rock convention in 1974, the NBPA was reduced to a shell. The convention was poorly attended, and was largely ignored by most BEOs, who realized that it was irrelevant to their electoral success (Smith, 1996), and in 1975 Baraka was ousted from his position as secretary general of the NBPA.[13]

At the same time, Madhubuti's black nationalism remained wedded to the "revolutionary kawaida" that Baraka abandoned, although it distanced itself from its reverse civilizationism. For example, Madhubuti (1978, p. 206) did not argue that blacks had been stripped completely of their culture, but instead that "the slave-making process, in part, belittled and erased from our consciousness those positive aspects of our Afrikan [sic] selves except that which we were able to retain in our dance, music, art, religion, and family structure"; but "in our mere acts of survival we have developed a new culture that combines the Afrikan with the Euro-American." Distancing himself from kawaida as social theory, he admonished that "[w]e Black people, at this late date, must come up with a self-conscious theory of Black Nationalism," one that "takes into account our 'Americanness' and its positives, its negatives. . . . We do not need reactionary theory: we need affirmative theory" (ibid., p. 26). Purusant to this, Madhubuti called for research into Cruse's works, among others (ibid., p. 214).

Although it continued to play an important role in the development of independent black institutions, especially black schools, the remnant of Midwest-CAP often became embroiled in competition for resources, with which they were consistently underfunded. Competitors to black nationalist institution building in black communities, such as churches linked to the Democratic Party, were often offered resources by government agencies and corporate interests to provide services to black communities sans the political education and orientation that a black nationalist framework would have demanded. These developments contributed to the officially encouraged view that the United States had already been transformed in meaningful ways sufficient to address the demands of the CRM and BPM, thereby making further changes unnecessary, gratuitous, intolerable (or all of the above), or at least of a sort that no longer necessitated a social movement "in the streets" to achieve them.

In a theoretical advancement, Madhubuti expanded the conceptual repertoire of kawaida by incorporating what would become known as Afrocentrism into its theoretical core, and ushered in the more recent phase of Afrocentric black nationalism in the broader African American discourse, namely, policy activism, especially regarding K-12 instruction, independent black schools, and university curricula, along with campus activism and black institution building, more generally. This was initiated, for example, in his introduction of the works and arguments of one of the most important modern Afrocentrists, Cheikh Anta Diop, into movement discourse, both in "The Latest Purge" (1974) and in an article and interview with Diop in one of his publications, *Black Books Bulletin*, in 1976, four years before the 1980 publication of Molefi Asante's more popular, albeit atheoretical and solipsistic, articulation of "Afrocentricity" (see Henderson, 1995). Well before Karenga would turn his kawaida thesis to focus on Ancient Egypt, Madhubuti emphasized the salience of Diop's arguments on the African origins of civilization, the cultural unity of African people, and the classical anteriority of Ancient Egypt to Classical Greece—the latter the common reference point for Western classicists—which were convergent with earlier arguments by Afrocentric historians such as Yosef Ben-Jochannan, Drusilla Houston, and Chancellor Williams. A decade before the founding of the major organization of Afrocentric scholars and activists, the Association for the Study of Classical African Civilizations (ASCAC), in 1984, Madhubuti instilled Diop's Afrocentric arguments into the educational programs of the independent schools that he directed.

Although kawaidaists developed mainly short-lived, independent institutions, Madhubuti's TWP and IPE have been exceptional in that they both continue to this day. These BPM instituions occupied a niche in the broad landscape of black political mobilization by the mid-1970s as the *nguzo saba* and Kwanzaa became more widely supported even among integrationists. By the end of the 1970s, kawaidaists conceded a fair portion of that niche among black nationalists, in popular discourse at least, to the retrograde theses of a resurgent NOI under Louis Farrakhan, who reinstituted Elijah Muhammad's black supremacist teachings, which his successor and son, W. D. Muhammad, had abandoned after his father's death in 1975 (as Malcolm X had a decade before). Madhubuti and other black nationalists in Chicago helped Farrakhan reestablish the NOI after his defection from W. D. Muhammad and his reassurance that he was not involved in Malcolm's assasination; by the mid-1980s Farrakhan had become one of the most recognizable and prominent black nationalists in the United States, and once his prominence was established he wasted little time before renewing his slanders against Malcolm X. In fact, in 1993 in NOI Mosque #2 in Chicago he referred to Malcolm as "our traitor" and implied that the NOI "dealt with him like a nation deals with a traitor." The irony, which eluded the flamboyant now-millionaire Muslim preacher, was that this same accusation could have been directed at him with respect to his defection from Wallace Muhammad's NOI. Elijah Muhammad had appointed his son Wallace, not Louis Farrakhan, as his successor and leader of the NOI. Farrakhan's defection and elevation of himself as leader of the NOI was in direct violation of Elijah Muhammad's stated intention. Therefore, following his own logic from his 1993 speech, Farrakhan was as much—if not more—a "traitor" to the original NOI, which Wallace Muhammad renamed the World Community of Islam in the West (WCIW). If so, and again following Farrakhan's own logic, did members of the original NOI have the "right" to "deal with Farrakhan like a nation deals with a traitor"? Tellingly, just as Baraka's Newark-CAP inadvertently gave rise to the markedly less than revolutionary, and in some cases not even progressive, BEOs that would supplant them, Madhubuti's Chicago-CAP contributed to the rise of the conservative, largely apolitical NOI, the very organization whose stifling millenarianism and cult of personality Malcolm had castigated and abandoned, which became among the most popular representations of black nationalism in the post-BPM era.

In practice, as the BPM waned, kawaida advocates increasingly turned their focus toward independent black institution building, especially independent black schools. But without the BPM to support it, momentum slowed precipitously, although many BPM tenets persisted in popular conceptions of Afrocentrism. Ironically, both the Marxist CAP in Newark and the kawaidist CAP in Chicago would see many of their political mobilization initiatives superseded by the efforts of the Black Church in conjunction with the Democratic Party, especially after the implosion of the NBPA. This church/party nexus gave rise to an emerging class of BEOs who would become prominent political actors in the post-BPM. One of the major BPM organizations that advocated black cultural revolution anticipated the increased importance of focusing on the Black Church as the key institution for the change BPM revolutionists sought: the Shrine of the Black Madonna, which we'll examine in the next section.

The Shrine of the Black Madonna/Pan-African Orthodox Christian Church

By the mid-1960s, Rev. Albert Cleage of the Central Congregational Church was both a prominent black nationalist and a veteran of the black liberation struggle. He had organized with Harold Cruse, James and Grace Lee Boggs, Milton and Richard Henry (Gaidi and Imari of the RNA), William Worthy, and Conrad Lynn in groups such as GOAL and the FNP and with prominent ministers such as C. L. Franklin (Aretha Franklin's father, friend of Martin L. King, and pastor of Detroit's New Bethel Baptist Church), U.S. congressmen Charles Diggs and John Conyers, as well as state senator and future Detroit mayor Coleman Young, in whose election as Detroit's first black mayor Cleage's organization of the *Black Slate* played a prominent role. With respect to the latter, Cleage was successfully implementing the strategy employed by his ally Amiri Baraka; however, his electoral work drew less from kawaida than from his previous experience with the FNP, including his own run for governor on the FNP slate in 1964. Cleage saw himself, his church, and black institutions such as the FNP as applying Malcolm X's thesis of the "ballot or the bullet" to Detroit politics. Successful precinct work enabled the FNP to get on the ballot in Michigan, and Cleage directed the party's effort, which fielded thirty-nine candidates for local and statewide offices. Although FNP candidates did not win any of their races, they received tens of thousands of votes in Detroit and across the state, and while Cleage received only slightly more than four thousand votes, this was the most of any of the FNP candidates on the ballot (Ali, 2008).

Cleage had been a confidante of Malcolm X, who referenced him in his "Message to the Grass Roots" speech delivered in Detroit in 1963, and Cleage shared a podium at the historic Great March for Freedom in Detroit with King, where the civil rights leader first made his historic "I Have A Dream" speech to a Detroit crowd that some estimate as larger than the gathering at the March on Washington the following year. Cleage's theology was oriented to black liberation and he was one of the few ministers of the black power era who wedded his theology, and not simply the rhetoric of the church or its pastor, to black liberation. There is an important distinction to make between the message of the church and the theology of the church. For example, the liberation theology of pastors such as King called on congregants to dedicate themselves to their God-inspired, and God-sanctioned duty of becoming involved in not only social welfare but social justice issues pertaining to black Americans and especially to the "least of these" in the United States and beyond. In fact, King famously called for a "revolution of values" among Americans, and especially Christians, to oppose what he saw as the triple evils of racism, militarism, and consumerism; however, after his death King's mature message, as influential as it was, could not necessarily sustain the impact it wielded while he was alive because it was tied so closely to his personal style, his personal narrative, his personal advocacy, and the sway of an ongoing CRM. Thus, after his death, "the faithful" could be deferential to his "message" focusing on social justice and social welfare, and even the "revolution in values," without devoting much if any effort to emulating, much less institutionalizing, King's practice among themselves and within their individual churches. Simply put, after his death, congregants could walk away from King's activist social justice program using a variety of rationalizations. King transformed *the message* of the Black Church toward social activism, but once he died, his "message" could be (and was) reframed, refocused, and recast in myriad ways to rationalize the new status quo.

By contrast, Cleage not only transformed the message of the Black Church, he transformed its *theology*. He was emphatic that "[t]he Black church must face the simple fact that its basic problem is a theological one" (1972, p. 183). By grounding the liberatory message within the theology of the church itself, Cleage was institutionalizing the changes that he sought in black theology. In this case, the obligations regarding social justice and social activism were not simply a matter of the personal spiritual and organizational appeal of a pastor such as King, or the prominence of the individual church, but were central to the theology of the religion; these beliefs and practices were a requirement for membership in the church. Thus, even after the death of the pastor these messages are no less influential because they constitute the theoretical core of the institution. Unlike King's message, which, while powerful, was ultimately personal and faded with his passing, Cleage's message was institutional and, as such, potentially timeless.

Cleage argued that the Black Church must promote a gospel of liberation rather than a gospel of salvation. A gospel of liberation insists that black liberation is the barometer of what is morally good and righteous, as Cleage stated: "That which supports the Struggle is good. That which advances the Struggle of Black people is moral" (Cleage, 1972, p. 188). Therefore, "[t]he Black church must find its new direction in the acceptance of a new theology which holds that nothing is more sacred than the liberation of Black people" (ibid.). He was convinced that "[t]he theological basis for the gospel of liberation can be found in the life and teachings of Jesus. Not in his death, but in his life and in his willingness to die for the Black Nation" (ibid.). Eschewing the Pauline Gospels as an adulteration of Jesus's original revolutionary message to the black nation of Israel, Cleage (1972, p. 3) argued that the "New Testament reflects the primitive pagan distortions that the Apostle Paul foisted upon the early church as a self-appointed apostle to the white gentile world"; but, he emphasized, "Jesus was a revolutionary Black religious leader fighting for the liberation of Israel." He added that

> [w]e can understand Jesus more fully by looking at Moses and the Maccabees than by looking at the Apostle Paul with his pagan

concept of blood redemption. The teachings of Jesus and of Israel reflect the deep spirituality of Black people. The religious ideas of Israel that shaped the ministry of Jesus can only be understood in the light of the history and culture of Africa. . . . Black Christian Nationalism finds a pattern for today's Black Liberation Struggle in the efforts of Moses to create a Black Nation . . . to move Black men from oppression and powerlessness to a Promised Land here on earth where Black people could live together with dignity. (Cleage, 1972, pp. 3–4)

Expanding on the insights of historic black religious leaders such as AME Bishop Henry McNeal Turner and AOC Bishop McGuire, Cleage argued that God was black and Jesus was a black man; moreover, he argued, Jesus was a "revolutionary black Messiah." Cleage was not interested in simply painting Christianity black. He insisted that "[y]ou can take anything and paint it Black, but that does not make it Black if it is still serving white interests and if it still comes out of the white experience" (1972, p. 14). For Cleage, "[a] thing is not Black because it is painted Black. If it is not building a Black institution it is not Black" (ibid.). This maxim was no less applicable to religion; thus, he was emphatic that "Black people cannot worship a white God and a white Jesus and fight white people for Black liberation" (ibid., p. 15). The fact that they did was a reflection of their acceptance of what Cleage called the white man's *declaration of black inferiority*, which was embedded and reinforced in the major political, economic, and social institutions of the United States. Cleage (ibid., p. xxv) argued that black Americans "have been programmed for inferiority" through "[t]he white man's *declaration of Black inferiority*," which "is basic to all American life." He emphasized that "[t]here is no institution in America, no aspect of American life that does not basically reflect the declared inferiority of all Black people"; moreover, it is "[n]ot poor Black people, not ignorant Black people, not uncouth Black people, but all Black people" that "have been declared inferior." In his view, the "*declaration of Black inferiority* is the foundation on which American history has been built," which since slavery has been "the framework within which the Black man was forced to build his existence"; and, importantly, "the Black man was not only 'declared' inferior but everything possible was done to make that 'declaration' a statement of fact."

Blacks were compelled to maintain a separate and subordinate existence politically and socially apart from whites and to reaffirm their inferiority through supplications to whites. Both of these factors "precluded the possibility of the white man's feeling any genuine guilt about the logical contradiction inherent in the actual treatment of Black people, as opposed to the American

Dream of equality, justice, and opportunity for all men" (Cleage, 1972, p. 154). Since "Black people are deliberately excluded from participation in the American Dream by the white man's *declaration of Black inferiority*," they are outside the system as they should be; therefore, "[w]hen [blacks] demand that American institutions be restructured to include [them], or that they be destroyed as the instruments of [their] oppression, [blacks] are challenging the American way of life and ought to expect violence and conflict until the question of [their] position in American life is resolved" (ibid.). Cleage insists that "[t]he Black man is permitted to exist only if he will constantly reaffirm his inferiority by approaching the white man as a supplicant, with hat in hand" (ibid.). As it stands,

> [t]he white man can withdraw his *declaration of Black inferiority*, thereby permitting a restructuring of his institutions, or Black people can withdraw their challenge to the *status quo* and accept inferiority as a way of life. Unless one group is willing to alter its position, continuing conflict is inevitable. The Black man cannot naively assume that the white man is going to give up his privileged position without conflict. The Black man must therefore mobilize the total Black community in an attack upon repressive white institutional power. This is the emerging nature of the Black Liberation Struggle to which Black Christian Nationalism calls all Black people everywhere. (ibid.)

Cleage implores black Americans that "[w]e must escape from powerlessness through the building of Black counterinstitutions and attacking the white institutional power establishment upon every front" (Cleage, 1972, ibid.). Like other BPM revolutionists, Cleage targeted the multiple fronts of white racist institutional power, but unlike the LRBW, he did not focus on attacking the point of production, instead, as Cruse suggested, he focused on a key institution of the cultural apparatus, arguably one more important than Cruse's thesis recognized since it was the central cultural institution in the black community: the Black Church. Convinced that "[a] people cannot seriously engage in a Liberation Struggle until they have developed a revolutionary theology" (ibid., p. 15), Cleage began in earnest to transform the Black Church. He was the first major organizational leader and theorist of the BPM to focus his cultural revolution program on the major cultural institution in the black community. This should have been obvious, but it wasn't, and the absence of focus on the church as the central change agent in a proposed black cultural revolution was one of the primary failures of theorists of the BPM.

On Easter 1967, at Central Congregational Church in Detroit, Cleage unveiled a towering painting of the Black Madonna and child in the church sanctuary. As Angela Dillard (2007, p. 288) describes it:

> In this striking painting, which is eighteen feet high by nine feet wide, an imposing and very dark woman in a white headdress or veil and a white robe with a blue shawl cradles an equally dark infant swaddled in saffron cloth. The pair is posed before a blue sky standing defiantly on gray and rocky ground with a town barely visible along the horizon.

This remarkable painting is the work of Glanton Dowdell, a member of RAM, who honed his artistic talent in a Michigan prison while serving a murder sentence that began in 1949, before being paroled in 1962. Dowdell had helped to organize the 1966 Black Arts Conference in Detroit, which held sessions in Cleage's church. Assisting Dowdell in the portrait was future LRBW leader General Baker. Cleage's church drew many of the young Detroit activists who were organizing with the League, RAM, the RNA, and the BPP around what would become his newly renamed black nationalist church, the Shrine of the Black Madonna. This reflected the fact that it was to these increasingly radical young workers, student organizers, and community activists, many of them representative of the lower classes who Cleage was convinced maintained a "critical perspective and cultural authenticity" that "had been abandoned by their middle class peers," that Cleage wanted the Black Church in general, and his church in particular, to be relevant (Cleage, 1972, pp. 252–253). In March 1968 Cleage had argued that "the Negro church has prospered poorly in the North because it has been unable to relate the gospel of Jesus Christ meaningfully to the everyday problems of an underprivileged people in urban industrial communities" (ibid., p. 251). His "Black Christian nationalism" was intended to change this situation and it attracted many young black nationalists, although it also led many of his congregants to leave his church.

Cleage's (1972, p. 173) black Christian nationalism began "with the basic premise that the Black church is essential to the Liberation Struggle, because it is controlled by Black people and is capable of being restructured to serve the Black Revolution." Cleage assumed that "a Black Revolution is impossible unless Black people are able to build an entire system of counterinstitutions, created and designed to serve the interests of Black people as all American institutions now serve the white-supremacy interests of white people" (ibid.). This was Cleage's extension of the prominent practice among black nationalists of the 1960s to build parallel institutions to provide services and resources to black people and in so doing expose the contradiction between what was provided by government institutions and social service agencies to white communities and what was provided to blacks. For Cleage, these "counterinstitutions" were available for cooptation by government and private interests of the white establishment; therefore, it was important to ensure that the counterinstitutions not only serve the material, mental, and even martial interests of blacks, but that they provide an independent base of political, economic, and social organization for black communities, as well. These institutions were not to be created in an ad hoc manner, nor were they simply to emerge in response to the quotidian though important issues that arise in the course of the interaction of blacks with white supremacist institutions and individuals.

Cleage had learned from his earlier involvement with independent black electoral politics through the FNP that it was more advantageous for a political party to be grounded in a powerful black counterinstitution rather than have the party itself serve as the core counterinstitution from which black political organization would proceed.[14] The latter may have informed Cleage's relationship with the NBPA, given that he didn't attend the Gary Convention, but, whether or not that was the reason, clearly subsequent developments regarding the NBPA seemed to validate his argument. Cleage insisted that in order "[t]o build a system of counterinstitutions we must first build one basic Black institution which has the acceptance of the masses of Black people, facilities and economic stability not directly dependent on the hostile white world and the capacity to spin off all the other institutions needed for the establishment of a Black Nation within a nation" (Cleage, 1972, pp. 173–174). The obvious choice for Cleage was the Black Church, specifically, a revolutionary Black Church. Nevertheless, Cleage realized that during the height of the black power era that

> [t]hese basic concepts are a source of general confusion to many young Black revolutionaries who have rejected religion in general and the Christian religion in particular—because it is a white man's religion, is counterrevolutionary, and serves to perpetuate the Black man's enslavement by teaching otherworldly escapism and distracting his attention from his powerlessness, exploitation, and oppression. The Christian Church has served the Black man poorly, and certainly a white Christ sitting in heaven at the right hand of a white Father God could not be expected to champion the Black man's cause against the cause of his own people, who owe their present white supremacy at least in some measure to the inspiration of his divine whiteness. White Christianity is a bastard

religion without a Messiah and without a God. Jesus was not white and God is not white. Jesus was a Black Messiah, the son of a Black woman, a son of the Black Nation, Israel. (ibid., p. 174)

Cleage asserted that

> [w]e have now reclaimed our covenant as God's Chosen People and our revolutionary Black Messiah, Jesus. Slave Christianity which we learned from our white masters is counterrevolutionary and has served to perpetuate our enslavement. The revolutionary teachings of the Black Messiah commit us to revolution and Nation building. Today our task is clear. We must free the Black church from slave Christianity and call it back to the original teachings of Jesus, and we must liberate the Black church as an institution and restructure it so that it can become the center of the Black Liberation Struggle. Young Black revolutionaries who cannot put aside their ideological hang-ups (largely inherited from white people) and be about this very serious business must stand accused of frivolity and of playing games with liberation. (ibid., p. 175)

For Cleage, any other starting point to black liberation that he foresaw was either unrealistic (e.g., separate black statehood in the United States or abroad), untenable (e.g., interracial proletarian-led Marxist revolution) utopic (integrationism), or liable to be easily undermined by white supremacist forces aligned against it (ad hoc nationalist formations). He was insistent that

> [w]e are trying to build Black institutions and our only possible point of beginning is the Black church. As wrong as it is, as biased as it is, as weak as it is, as corrupt as it is, as counterrevolutionary as it is, as Uncle Tom as it is, it is the only starting point we have. We have churches on every corner housed in buildings of every size, shape, and description. We have nominal control over it, but because of our confusion and psychological sickness it does not serve our interests. We have billions of dollars tied up in church buildings. If we are seriously interested in Black liberation we cannot realistically afford just to turn and walk away and leave this huge capital investment in the hands of the enemy. We must devise a way to co-opt it, restructure it, and make it the heart and center of the Black Revolution. The Black church must be programmed for Black liberation. (Cleage, 1972, p. 200)

He added,

> That is why. . . . We are seriously attempting to restructure a Black church upon the basis of a Black theology. Upon this restructured institutional base we can build anything else we need. We can spin off economic, educational, political, and cultural institutions as rapidly as we can train the necessary specialists. The Black church restructured as a power base can guarantee the success of any organized undertaking designed to serve the interests of Black people. . . . The Black church must program for power. . . . Only the Black church has the potential capacity to mobilize the total Black community. (ibid., pp. 200–201)

Cleage was taking the battle for black power to the pulpit and the pews; he was taking the black revolution to church. Finally, one of the major theorists of the BPM was conjoining Malcolm X's cultural revolution to the major cultural institution in black America. Cleage was arguing that the black cultural revolution was to begin with something akin to a Protestant Reformation. His was not going to be a "Letter from a Birmingham Jail"; it was going to be the "Ninety-Five Thesis on the Door of the All Saints Church at Wittenburg." In fact, he characterized his movement at one point as a "Black Protestant Reformation" (Cleage, 1972, p. 184). The Black Church, in Cleage's vision, would be the foundation for the development of parallel institutions in the black community. But not only that, its Savior, Jesus, would be a "black revolutionary Messiah." Its Gospel would be black liberation. It would assert the religious duty to pursue revolutionary change. It would provide religious sanction for black power. In this conception, the Black Church was the central cultural institution to transform black society, and subsequently, U.S. society, as a whole.

Grounded in a black revolutionary theology, in Cleage's view black churches would be transformed and spin-off counterinstitutions that would reflect, reinforce, and reinvigorate black power. They would assert the political, economic, and social rights of black Americans, for instance, such as reparations, among other black revolutionists' organizations, as well. Thus, during the BPM, the Shrine was supportive of many of the major BPM organizations such as RAM, Us, the BPP, RNA, LRBW, and CAP. It had the capacity to organize community relief for striking black workers and their families; it could organize sanctuary for black revolutionists associated with the major militant groups; it could provide programmatic and curricular guides for educational and cultural centers, and the administrative and infrastructural support for subsequent counterinstitutions, including a black political party. The Shrine would participate in activities such as these and it would expand beyond Detroit, establishing Shrines in two major Southern cities, Atlanta and Houston.

Although his objective was revolutionary, Cleage averred that his religious project was oriented by "pragmatic realism," grounded in part in an appreciation of Reinhold Niebuhr's argument that even if individuals attempt to behave morally, the control and dominance of an immoral society often make doing the "right thing" appear morally wrong. Cleage acknowledged the centrality of the "will to power" in order to realize the objectives of his moral vision and insisted that "there is nothing immoral about our quest for power"; instead, "Immorality lies in weakness and in the fear of power. Immorality lies in the acceptance of powerlessness and the indignities which [it] forces upon a people who are created in the image of God and are expected to maintain dignity" (Cleage, 1972, p. 140). For Cleage, social relations in the United States approximated a domestic balance of power system, which blacks were compelled to acknowledge, operate within, and manipulate successfully. In this framework

> Black institutions must be prepared to seek power, which means that they must inevitably face confrontation and conflict with the white power structure, because no one gives up power easily, quietly, or happily. The only way that power is transferred is through confrontation and conflict. The church is no exception. The Black church exists in a world in which the conditions of Black people will not be changed until Black people are willing to confront and accept the inescapability of conflict. (ibid., p. 181)

Implicitly, Cleage was rejecting the supposition of many black power advocates who were attempting to derive lessons for black American struggles from third world national liberation strategies such as the "war of the flea" or foco theory that emphasizes the leverage of militarily weaker guerrilla bands upon stronger conventional forces and/or advocate the spontaneous generation of revolutions even in the absence of the concrete conditions assumed to give rise to them. Instead, Cleage's logic of struggle sought to employ the same approach that white nations had used to achieve their hegemonic positions, namely, balance of power theory, in order to bring about their downfall. Importantly, "[p]ower for Black people," according to Cleage, "will not come from the barrel of a gun but from liberated minds willing to accept the theology of here and now expressed in the Black Christian Nationalist Creed" (Cleage, 1972, p. 188). Further, although he denounced the needless militarization of activism and didn't articulate his approach to black revolution in military terms, he also did not eschew the militant pursuit of one's objectives, in principle, and he maintained a paramilitary security force, the Maccabees, to provide security for the Shrine and its members.

Cleage's emphasis was on the central role of the church in black liberation, which for some BPM activists was a peculiar focus, but one that indicated his recognition of what Du Bois and others had viewed as the peculiar situation of blacks in America and the resultant requirement of a theoretical orientation that recognized and was responsive to it. Relatedly, Cleage's characterization of the black community in terms of its institutional underdevelopment was not beholden to the domestic colonialism thesis, nor to neoMarxist arguments suggesting the need to eradicate this perceived domestic colonialism through guerrilla warfare that was more applicable to third world contexts. Cleage's thesis on the development of counterinstitutions was more germane to black America.

Cleage asserted the uniqueness of the black American's situation and, particularly, what it suggested for revolutionary struggle. For example, he argued that Malcolm's thesis, which viewed land as the basis of independence and the objective of revolution, "must be re-evaluated." Insisting that the "concept of revolution must be developed by a people out of their particular situation" (Cleage, 1972, p. 119), in the case of Malcolm's thesis he noted that "[i]n Africa every liberation struggle involved a racial majority fighting against a racial minority to control its own land" but that in "America conditions are different" (ibid., pp. 118–119). For Cleage, the "unique condition" of blacks in the United States makes it "foolish to talk about the struggle for land as the basis for revolution without an analysis of [that] unique condition." Specifically, "We are a minority and we are struggling against a majority"; therefore, "Past revolutions do not furnish guidelines for our struggle" (ibid., p. 119). Further, the uniqueness of the black American context also undermines the relevance of Marxist revolution to the United States. He acknowledged that "[i]n any country where Black people are a majority and there are just a few white people trying to keep power, communism or socialism can become a philosophy of liberation. But in America there is a totally different situation." He insisted that "[t]here will never be a communist revolution in America" because "Marxism does not suit the American condition."

For Cleage, the "pattern of relationships between white people in a country with a large racial minority which has been structured out of the system is entirely different from the way it would otherwise be. For this reason no place in the world is like the United States" (1972, p. 158). Again, the complications born of the intersection of race, class, and demography are such that the class conflict between white elites and poor whites is mitigated by their racial alliance. Specifically, white elites are willing to make concessions to poor whites in return for the maintenance of a racial fissure between poor whites and blacks, provided and reinforced by a white supremacist system that poor whites support because it rewards them materially, psychologically, and socially in comparison to blacks of all classes. In such a context, white elites "feel compelled to make some kind of reconciliation with the poor, realizing that if they don't Black people are going to attack all of them while they are fighting each other" (ibid.). Clearly, white elites are not expected to participate in a revolution that might overthrow white supremacy, which fundamentally benefits them, but Cleage is also convinced that poor whites, or white workers, will not either. He insists that "[p]oor whites will not revolt against a system which perpetuates their racial superiority unless driven to the wall, and intelligent whites who control the system are ever conscious of the point of no return" (ibid., p. 159). In light of this, Cleage argues that "[a]ll white institutions come together to fight against any kind of an attack on the white establishment." Therefore,

> The existence of thirty million more or less alienated Black people in America means that a framework for revolution with built in protection for white supremacy is an essential prerequisite for any serious American revolution. The fact that the very nature of revolution makes this kind of built-in protection for white supremacy impossible serves to make the existence of the Black man the most important stabilizing force in American society. (ibid., pp. 158–159)

Thus, the major reason that there will "never be a communist revolution in America," according to Cleage, is because blacks are a safety valve against it.

Convinced of the uniqueness of the liberation struggle in the United States, and of blacks within it, his strategy eschewed Marxism while simultaneously embracing Malcolm's focus on black cultural revolution. In fact, Cleage's plan of action was oriented more to the logic of black cultural revolution in the United States than many of his predecessors and contemporaries may have realized. For example, he articulated the necessity for the psychological transformation of blacks to bring them to appreciate the depth of their oppression and miseducation, in a manner that acknowledges Malcolm X's, RAM's, Us's, the RNA's, and CAP's arguments in favor of cultural revolution. In light of this, he was a chief sponsor of the Detroit Black Arts Movement, who in 1962 hosted a forum in his church that discussed the relationship between jazz and black nationalism and featured Abbey Lincoln and Max Roach, following the release of their influential *Freedom Now Suite*, which many blacks celebrated at the same time that some notable whites criticized it—ridiculously—for "politicizing jazz." Dillard (2007, p. 254) correctly points out that this forum "highlighted [Cleage's] early interest in cultural struggles"; and Suzanne Smith (1999, p. 173) argued that the forum, along with the cultural revolution plank in the FNP draft platform and Cleage's promotion of the June 1966 Black Arts Convention in Detroit, showed that "Black activists in the city were exploring the role of art in black life several years before international festivals were organized on the topic," and even before the origination of BARTS, which most herald as the beginning of BAM. Importantly, Cleage did not share other cultural revolutionists' dismissal of the role of the Black Church in this process—just the opposite: Cleage was taking Malcolm X to church! This is evident in his approach to the role of the Black Church in cultural revolution. He asserts that

> [t]he first task of the Black Church is to liberate the Black man's mind. It must be willing to deal with truth and stop telling fairy tales to men and women. If the Black church is to move in new directions it must learn the nature of reality and become committed to truth. The Black church must become a teaching church. It cannot be a church that says what people want to hear. It must help Black people begin to think realistically about everyday problems. This is the process by which we will move from a gospel of salvation to a gospel of liberation. We must define liberation, define struggle, analyze tactics, and develop methods for the struggle. We must look at history to find out what works and what does not work. The Black church must define liberation in terms of reality. Then we must put together the organization and structure to make it effective. (Cleage, 1972, p. 189)

He saw the black nation as "a group working, thinking, and planning together," although he realized that "[o]ne of our basic problems is the development of a process which will make this possible" (ibid., p. 190). He eschewed the notion of pursuing unity for unity's sake or even in the face of "valid reasons for uniting," such as a commonality of oppression based in black racial identity or the fear of genocide, because most rationales for black unity did not suggest how unity would "make a Black Nation come into being" (ibid.); in this way, Cleage appreciated the collective action problems that kawaida, for example, ignores. He argued that "[w]e must deliberately reject the values and thought patterns of the white Western world. We must consciously create a new Black mentality and value system which recognizes the equal worth of every Black brother and sister" (ibid.). Like Jesus, who "preached to multitudes" but "did not count on the great crowds, but on the small cadres with whom he worked," Cleage maintained that "[t]he Black Nation will be built around small well-trained cadres" who "organize and train black people everywhere" (1972, pp. 222–223). These cadres would be organized through "rigid discipline during training, highly centralized controls, and carefully standardized organization structures." He fashioned the Shrine of the Black Madonna "to use the methods of the Essene order to train cadres capable of going out and organizing Shrines, Information Centers, and cultural centers in the Black urban ghettos and rural areas of America and throughout the world" (ibid., p. 222). Prospective members received a twelve-month catechism with advanced leadership training recommended. Cleage noted that other than the NOI, "[e]very other Black group tries to program with Black people the way they are (which is obviously an impossibility) or to readjust prejudices and misconceptions (which is equally impossible)" (ibid., pp. 212–213).

Although membership in the PAOCC focused on the theology of black Christian nationalism, the educational component of the catechism emphasized politics, history, and religion. An additionally important aspect of this training was devoted to the development of program specialists who could institutionalize the essential elements of black culture across specific program areas. Unlike theorists such as Boggs and Newton, he did not imagine that a revolutionary culture would emerge from the political revolution itself, but neither did he separate the struggle for cultural self-determination from that of political (or economic) self-determination (Cleage, 1972, pp. 222–223). Cleage argued that "[c]ulture grows out of struggle," yet he admonished his contemporaries that "[w]e have made an artificial separation between cultural revolution and the power struggle" (Dillard, 2007, p. 254). He saw that too many of his contemporaries "are more excited about culture than they are excited about the struggle for power, because it is easier to put on African clothes than it is to struggle and sacrifice" (ibid.). Cleage was criticizing those activists who ignored the massive educational and institutional undertaking that "capturing the hearts and minds" of black people entailed. It required more than a sartorial exercise in African dress, but models of social change rooted in African American processes and not expropriated from contexts that did not apply to black America. In this way, Cleage recognized the importance of Africa, but asserted the necessity of centering on the United States, and, to this extent, rejected reverse civilizationism; however, the latter was more apparent than real.

That is, while the logic of Cleage's approach challenged reverse civilizationism by privileging the black experience in the United States, especially noting how this experience challenged both Malcolm's focus on land as the basis of revolution and the relevance of Marxist revolution, practically, Cleage embraced reverse civilizationism, as is evident in the training program he devised for the Shrine's program specialists. This training utilized the *nguzo saba* as the representative element of black American culture, which it sought to instill across the specific program areas. In adopting the *nguzo saba* as a fundamental reference for black culture, and placing them at the heart of the training for the program specialists of the Shrine, Cleage was centering the cultural atavism of kawaida into his modern black nationalism. On its face, the adoption of the *nguzo saba* seems consistent with the Shrine's mission to "reject the white man's values, the values of the Western world," to "reject American values" (Cleage, 1972, p. 241), to "develop a new value system" (ibid., p. 242), and "to create a new Black mentality and value system which recognizes the equal worth of every Black brother and sister" (ibid., p. 190). On closer inspection, it is difficult to reconcile the Shrine's adoption of the *nguzo saba* as a centerpiece of its training with Cleage's trenchant argument that "[o]ur values as Black people must be derived from the Black experience as that experience has been shaped by our continuing struggle for liberation and survival" (ibid., p. 242). Although Cleage recognized that black Americans "are not Americans in the sense that white people are Americans," and that blacks are "an African people who against our will were brought to America," nevertheless, he also acknowledged that black Americans "are a people because here in America common experiences have welded us together" (ibid., p. xxx). He added that "[w]e share a common background and a common cultural heritage. Our cultural heritage has been confused and modified by our experience in America, but it binds us together even when we would break apart" (ibid., pp. xxx–xxxi). The experience that Cleage is referring to in these passages is that which characterizes the African American saga in the United States, not in Africa.

The experiences of black Americans, even at their lowest, were not only a symptom to be decried but a source of inspiration, as articulated in Stuckey's "slave culture" or the "Aframerican culture" of Du Bois, Locke, and Cruse. To facilitate black cultural revolution, it was essential, in Cleage's view, to bring those varied experiences into the Black Church, which too often seemed to ignore important aspects of black culture, especially that which was associated with the black ghetto. In contrast, Cleage extols the cultural practices and expressions emanating from the ghetto as much as he deplores the privations suffered by its people. For Cleage,

> The music, the laughter, the anger of the ghetto, the frustration—even with the horrors of white exploitation the ghetto has a beauty that white America does not have. There is the sense of people being together, the sense of fellowship, and even the

> bond of common misery. It is a beautiful thing. . . . The Black ghetto must come into the church and the church must build in terms of the Black experience. (1972, p. 247)

The "ghetto" that Cleage describes is not African, much less the "traditional" and "communal" Africa that kawaida invents, imagines, and promotes; it is a distinctly African American, modern, and urban condition and context. Further, the cultural characteristics he ascribes to it, its sights, sounds, smells, moods, intensity, fellowship, beauty, reflect distinctly African American experiences. This is not to argue that the substance of the ghetto is monolithic or unique; it takes many forms that are found, unfortunately, throughout both rich and poor countries, but the ghetto that Cleage describes emerged from and reflects a unique set of historical developments in the United States, with respect to African Americans, which are not reducible to, nor synonymous with, prominent historical processes in the colonial world, or Africa, in particular.

Moreover, the "beauty" that Cleage observes in the ghetto, and its values that he lauds, are not rooted in kawaida nor do they derive from the *nguzo saba*; instead, they are associated with the traditions of values of blacks in America—not Africa. Blacks predominantly in the South—both urban and rural—where most resided until the last half-century, created and cultivated value systems drawn from "slave culture" that generated their collective identities, practices, customs, and institutions in the United States. These were epitomized in the "invisible institution" of the black Christian religious tradition, an activist religious tradition, as well as those central elements of black culture—freedom, family, and education—that Franklin (1984) acknowledges. In fact, Cleage had already made the point regarding the distinctiveness of African American social development in his arguments regarding the inapplicability of Marxist formulations to African Americans, and his critique of Malcolm's thesis that land is the basis of revolutionary struggle. Appreciating this uniqueness, his choice to embrace the *nguzo saba* and kawaida is theoretically inconsistent, at best.

The impact of Cleage's decision to incorporate kawaida as a centerpiece of the program training of the Shrine is not simply an academic matter; it has practical implications for the program that the Shrine created, distilled, and promoted. It detached a central component of the training from the relevant history of black American cultural practices, especially those associated with revolutionary initiatives; thus, ironically, the black church, which promoted Jesus as a revolutionary black Messiah, had separated its catechism from the religiously inspired proletarians who had authored the only lasting tradition of black revolt and black revolution in the United States. Any serious examination of this history would lead inexorably to Gabriel, Denmark

Vesey, Nat Turner, and a host of black Christian revolutionaries epitomized in those who transformed the U.S. Civil War into a revolution. The values they practiced and promoted were those of the invisible institution and the consciousness of an emergent black working class, utterly unrelated to the *nguzo saba*. Kawaida and its centerpiece, the *nguzo saba*, suggested that these revolutionaries had no culture, that they left no cultural remnant greater than that which could be concocted from an African "tradition" that existed largely and exclusively in the imaginations of many BPM activists.

This ahistorical and anthropologically confused view of both African cultures and African American national development allowed Cleage to make the claim that "[t]he more highly developed, African, communal conception of man's relationship with God had been lost when the Black man was uprooted and his history and culture stripped from him" (1972, p. 46). This conception led Cleage to declare that "we will build a Black Liberation movement which derives its basic religious insights from African spirituality, its character from African communalism, and its revolutionary direction from Jesus, the Black Messiah" (p. 16). The notion of a black God or a black Jesus was not novel but Cleage's insistence on wedding this to African "communalism" rather than African American urbanism or cosmopolitanism (or even African urbanism/cosmopolitanism), and his focus on "African spirituality" instead of African American spirituality were unnecessary addenda that took both his theology and his program away from the actual sources of its revolutionary potential, namely, African American history, and especially the role of slave culture and the slave church in black revolutionary struggle in the United States. Ironically, reverse civilizationism, in one sense, converged with one of the most glaring aspects of white supremacism, that which denied that black Americans possessed a culture worthy of the name. Just as Moses (1978) had noted the contradictory aspect of classical black nationalism in its embrace of civilizationism, the black nationalism of the BPM created its own contradictions in its embrace of reverse civilizationism. Where Cleage could have asserted the centrality of the Black Church and its historical and contemporary values as the centerpiece of the only successful black revolution in the United States, the Slave Revolution of the U.S. Civil War, he eschewed the very basis for this contention by deferring to a feudal and futile conception of black culture, kawaida and the *nguzo saba*, and inserting it into the heart of the Shrine's catechism.

The evidence of the distorted orientation away from relevant revolutionary African American history and towards much less relevant African history is evident in the "BCN [Black Christian Nationalism] Orientation Reading List," which provided required readings for Shrine members across three general categories: political, historical, and religious. This academic training reflects Cleage's view that "emotional involvement" is insufficient to maintain a liberation struggle; instead, "[s]erious commitment to the Black Struggle involves an intellectual understanding" (Cleage, 1972, pp. 191–192). However, a majority (thirteen out of twenty-five) of the political works on the BCN list were authored by Africans or focused on African politics rather than African American subjects. Similarly, nine out of sixteen of the historical works were authored by Africans or focused on African history. Finally, only two of the six religious references, both authored by Cleage, could be said to focus on African American religion. There is no reference to any of Du Bois's major political or historical works, although Cruse's two major works of the time are included, and even the Africanist studies are dominated by Nkrumah and Fanon, with one reference to Cabral. Mine is a critique less of the substance of these works, although this is a serious limitation, as well, than of their focus, in that BCN training was focused less on the actual cultural practice and institutions of African Americans and more on replicating "African" forms. In the first place, these were hardly representative of the great diversity of African cultures and often projected a singularly myopic, predominantly "communalist," picture of a presumably monolithic "African" traditional culture; and in the second place, they were hardly representative of, or applicable to, the African American context in which the BCN members operated. One result was that in the heart of Detroit, the Motor City, the industrial core of the most advanced industrialized society in the world and the fifth-largest city in the United States at the time, in whose economic, political, social, and cultural development black Americans had played a key role, the leading black power organization promoted a conception of black people that treated them as if they were participants in a communal harvest festival from a feudal era and assumed that this was the basis for the revolutionary transformation of its people and their society.[15] The incongruity was as profound as it was debilitating.

As a result, when Cleage turned his focus to revolutionary developments among blacks in the United States, he was compelled to resort to self-contradiction. For example, he lauded the slave revolts, and Nat Turner in particular, but at the same time he disparaged the "slave-church," which was the basis of each of the major slave revolts (1972, p. 16). Cleage acknowledged the significance of slave revolts as a challenge to white power in the United States and asserted that "[t]he only time white people have really felt that their basic power institution was actually endangered was when the slave insurrections swept the South," and that these "[s]lave insurrections could come out of no place and shake America to its foundations." Instead of developing their significance with respect to the role of Christianity in these challenges to white power, he turned instead to the white response to them: "White people recognized the danger." Therefore, "Slave attacks on basic white institutions," in his view, "only served to increase the stability of the white structure" (ibid., p. 161).[16] That is, "The result was not the freeing of Black people (because the insurrections failed) but the solidification of the white dominant group" (ibid.). In fact, he insisted that "[f]rom the time of the insurrections the white group said that they could never permit Black people to have the slightest possibility of launching a real attack upon the white power structure," and that "[t]he development of the Klan following the Civil War reinstitutionalized the separation and oppression of Black people and was condoned by white people and their governmental units all over America" (ibid.). Such an interpretation ignores the role of the revolts as revolutionary expressions of black Christianity; and specifically, the Slave Revolution and the central role of the "slave church" in it. Thus, the reverse civilizationism implicit in Cleage's thesis generates a historical myopia that undermines his ability to perceive, much less build on, previous black revolutionary engagements in the antebellum era. As a result, the black revolution during the Civil War that was Du Bois's focus and should have served as the point of departure for black revolutionists during the BPM was hidden in plain sight for Cleage.

Cleage's thesis suffers from additional limitations, as well. For example, although the PAOCC ordained several women bishops and promoted gender equality in its major programs and prominent practices, the church leadership remained predominantly male, as have Cleage's successors. The issue of sexism in the PAOCC is not unrelated to its persistence in the Black Church as a whole. Cleage's major pronouncements of his religious doctrine are largely silent on issues of gender discrimination, and he does not specifically focus on it in either his depiction of the declaration of black inferiority or his discussion of counterinstitutions. He utilizes the masculinist language prominent among Christian theologians and religious leaders, which suggests that his new direction for the Black Church did not include a challenge to its God-ordained and sanctioned patriarchy.

In addition, while emphasizing the primacy of the Black Church in the black cultural revolution that he envisioned, Cleage did not specify which institutions should be subsequently transformed, or in what order. For example, after the church had been transformed, it wasn't clear whether it was necessary to focus on a political institution, such as an independent black political party like the NBPA, economic organizations such as consumer/producer cooperatives, as Du Bois had proposed, labor unions, such as those the LRBW pursued, or educational institutions, like the ones Weusi and Madhubuti created. It also was not clear what constituted a critical mass of counterinstitutions that would generate the revolution that Cleage envisioned. These issues were not only important because of the need for coordination, but because it was not clear how the values associated with the Church should transfer to secular political, economic, and social institutions. Consumed by the effort demanded in overhauling the church, Cleage did not delineate the order by which subsequent counterinstitutions should be developed to effectuate the changes that he sought.

There also are limitations in centering cultural revolutionary struggles on the Church. That is, if one is proposing black cultural revolution from a Lockean cultural perspective, then the Church might initiate and participate in black cultural revolution but it probably cannot lead it, given its tendency to impose restrictions on cultural expression, including revolutionary expression. The church's limitations are a function of its inability to project a perspective and practice of black culture apart from its own theological dictates. This forces an arbitrary imposition on cultural expression, which a Lockean approach does not countenance because it restricts the inherent dynamism of culture that Locke insisted upon. Further, in Locke's view, culture reaches its full cosmopolitan expression in democratic frameworks, and churches are fundamentally nondemocratic, and often openly autocratic.

Thus, unlike black culture, which is inherently dynamic according to Locke, the church, by comparison, is relatively static, changing at a tectonic pace but not *inherently* revolutionary. So, from a Lockean cultural perspective, the inability of the Church to lead a cultural revolution does not dictate that the Black Church can serve as Moses but not Joshua; it's more like the Black Church cannot be both Jesus and Charlie Parker (who was not only a jazz saxophone virtuoso but an atheist). The point is that the Black Church may conceive of, but probably would have great difficulty projecting, a black culture, or those aspects of black culture that do not converge with the teachings of the Church. Black culture encompasses much more than the Gospel of Jesus, even a revolutionary black Jesus, because black cultural expression is potentially boundless; therefore, the cultural revolution that it inspires may reflect, require, and recommend what might appear to be some very un-Christian initiatives. Cleage's pragmatic realism recognizes this insofar as it makes a reasoned argument as to why the church should be engaged with essential worldly issues such as the "will to power." The appropriation of Jesus as a revolutionary black Messiah represents a similar convergence between the Gospel and the exigencies of black power. Cleage's thesis is less engaged in asserting gender equality by challenging sexism within Christian theology, the church as an institution, and black power as a social movement.

Nevertheless, among prominent proponents of black cultural revolution in the BPM, Cleage was alone in centering his thesis on the major cultural institution in the black community. For instance, Malcolm X's adoption of

Sunni Islam, which led to a major "re-identification" by many African Americans of their religious identity, was more likely to have limited his influence on the black masses given their ingrained Christian religious identification. Moreover, while King changed the narrative associated with the Black Church by his espousal of black liberation theology, Cleage/Jaramogi changed the catechism of Scripture itself. In proposing that Jesus was a revolutionary black Messiah, he, unlike King, created a new doctrinal identity for blacks within Christianity, in light of which the religion did not simply encourage participation in black liberation struggle but required it. Given this, it is unlikely that the Shrine can be easily transformed to promote a theological framework such as "prosperity gospel" that some black clerics have begun to endorse even as they rhetorically embrace King's theology.[17]

Yet, at the helm of a dominant cultural institution in the African American community, Cleage's proposed black cultural revolution was wedded to a conceptualization of black culture distant from African American cultural practice. As an expression of reverse civilizationism, it privileged African over African American culture, history, and revolutionary praxis. Even with these theoretical limitations, however, Cleage's application of his model of cultural change had a powerful impact on the culture and politics of Detroit. This was evident in the prominent role the Shrine played in the election of Coleman Young as Detroit's first black mayor in 1973, before the city had a majority black population. Likewise, the prominence of its *Black Slate* figured in the election of Atlanta's first black mayor, Maynard Jackson, as well as in electoral politics in Houston (the third of the three major cities where Shrines are located today). Moreover, the *Black Slate* has been influential in elections of local candidates since its founding.[18] Similarly, Cleage/Jaramogi's arguments on cultural revolution have remained influential in the years since his death. Ironically, by helping support the ascendancy of the BEOs, the PAOCC helped bring to power the leadership group that would supplant the black power organizations of the era and ultimately signal the end of the Black Power Movement.

Conclusion

In this chapter, I've expanded on the examination of the historical and theoretical development of the concept of black cultural revolution in black politics through an analysis of CAP and the PAOCC, aka the Shrine of the Black Madonna. CAP's Newark chapter was led by Amiri Baraka, and its Midwest (Chicago) chapter by Haki Madhubuti. The former harnessed black cultural revolutionary theses to urban electoral mobilization and independent political party organizing before abandoning black nationalism and adopting Haywood's Marxist political thrust. The latter rose from similar origins but remained committed to independent black community institutions, focusing on two important counterinstitutions, black independent schools and black publishing, while explicitly rejecting Marxism. Baraka's organization initially gathered the emergent black elected officials (BEOs) under the aegis of black nationalist leadership and institutions; however, Baraka was outflanked by those same officials for a variety of reasons, partly because his analysis of black cultural revolution failed to appreciate the dynamic processes of black political and economic development in the cities during a period of deindustrialization. Circumvented and then repudiated by the very BEOs that his organization had helped promote, Baraka abandoned black nationalism for Maoism.

In contrast, Chicago CAP, like Brooklyn CAP, maintained its black nationalist orientation and developed a critical response to Baraka's neo-Marxism that contributed to the demise of CAP and the broader ideological sectarianism of the BPM. Haki Madhubuti established Third World Press in 1967, and the Institute of Positive Education and its network of independent black schools in Chicago, which became a blueprint for other such schools around the country. More than any other theorist of the BPM, he laid the basis for the Afrocentrism that would become prominent after the BPM. However, Madhubuti embraced aspects of reverse civilizationism, as well, and the Afrocentrism that emerged from his organizations followed two tracks: an activist course that focused on independent black organizations and a reverse civilizationist thrust that led to an overindulgence in ancient African societies instead of focusing on the largely urban-based industrial working-class culture of African Americans living in the most powerful country in the world. The former course continued on the trajectory of building independent black institutions and advocating black liberation, even as the latter course departed from the spirit and praxis of cultural revolution that Malcolm espoused.

The Shrine of the Black Madonna/PAOCC was led by Albert Cleage (Jaramogi Agyeman) and has been one of the most consistent and enduring BPM organizations espousing black cultural revolution. The Shrine fused political, economic, and cultural aspects of the BPM and, most importantly, was the most prominent BPM organization that centered on—instead of dismissed—the Black Church. The PAOCC utilized the methods of the Essene order to train cadres capable of organizing churches as well as informational and cultural centers throughout the United States and abroad. Cleage's model of cultural change had a powerful impact on the culture and politics of Detroit, playing a prominent role in the election of Coleman Young as Detroit's first black mayor in 1973. More successfully than the RNA, the PAOCC expanded into the South and established itself in Atlanta and Houston (as well as in South Carolina). While Jaramogi emphasized the primacy of the Black Church in black cultural revolution, he did not specify which institutions should be subsequently transformed or in what order, and it was unclear what would constitute a critical mass of counterinstitutions that might effectuate the cultural revolution that he envisioned. Thus, apart from the church, it wasn't clear where activists should focus, for example, on an independent black political party, black trade unions, black schools, or black economic cooperatives. Although Cleage's focus on the Black Church and the development of counterinstitutions remains one of the most influential theses for black cultural revolution in the United States, in practice it reflected a return to Du Bois's thesis on cultural *evolution* rather than cultural *revolution* insofar as it privileged the incremental building of counterinstitutions of black civil society. Further, and ironically, in helping support the BEOs, the PAOCC helped bring to power the leadership group that would supplant the BPM organizations of the era, which ultimately signaled the end of their movement.

Conclusion

Black Revolutionary Theory in the BPM

Throughout this work I have maintained that prominent Black Power Movement (BPM) activists were often theorists of black revolution, as well. Most took Malcolm X's thesis on black revolution, which was the most influential revolutionary framework emanating from the Civil Rights Movement (CRM), as their theoretical and programmatic point of departure. Malcolm's thesis evolved from a static, unidimensional, religious-based conceptualization into a dynamic, multidimensional, secular framework. Among the most important aspects of it was his thesis on black cultural revolution. Malcolm associated a cultural revolution among black Americans with a broader political revolution to radically transform the United States and culminate in a worldwide revolution; yet BPM revolutionists who built on Malcolm's legacy rarely captured the fullness of his thesis, often minimized contradictions in his arguments, and generally failed to address major shortcomings in Malcolm's analyses, particularly its reverse civilizationism.

An examination of the major BPM organizations reveals that they had difficulty overcoming the contradictions inherent in reverse civilizationism to create a coherent theory reconciling black cultural and political revolution in the United States. Such a thesis was available to them in the historical arguments of W. E. B. Du Bois and the theoretical arguments of Alain Locke, but these alternatives were predicated on the assumption that African Americans possessed a culture, which reverse civilizationism denied. Reverse civilizationism assumed that black Americans had been stripped of their culture and that revolutionary developments were more advanced in Africa than in the United States. Under its influence, Malcolm's thesis and those of BPM revolutionists who followed suit became preoccupied with African rather than African American cultural institutions and practices, while inadequately appreciating the urbanized, Christian-identified, working-class culture of the African American communities that they sought to revolutionize. Their approaches focused on African (or "third world") anticolonial movements, assuming that they offered the most relevant models for a black liberation movement in the United States. As a result, BPM revolutionists were attempting to fashion a movement across the terrain of the most powerful country in the world using a theoretical compass better suited to an African or third world country.

The Problem of Reverse Civilizationism in Malcolm X's Revolutionary Theory

Reverse civilizationism led to the failure to recognize the historical antecedents of black revolution in the United States, epitomized in the prominent slave revolts and ultimately the Slave Revolution of the Civil War. In privileging contemporary African anticolonial struggles, Malcolm's thesis neglected black American revolutionary precedents that could more readily have served as referents. Seemingly oblivious to this history, BPM revolutionists didn't realize the extent to which the Slave Revolution served as a referent more than anticolonial struggles abroad that they sought to emulate. The Slave Revolution suggested the salience of a general strike strategy in future black liberation struggles and demonstrated the revolutionary potential of black culture, specifically, black religion merged with an incipient working-class consciousness, to encourage black liberation in the antebellum era. BPM revolutionists, under the influence of reverse civilizationism, did not recognize the significance of African American culture, nor the religiously inspired incipient working-class culture that helped generate it. That is, not only did they fail to recognize the salience of the Slave Revolution as a historic case of black American revolutionary activity, they also did not appreciate the centrality of black culture in generating it, even as they called for a cultural revolution. Relatedly, they missed a major implication of the aftermath of the Slave Revolution, which was that future black revolutionists would need to adopt strategies that utilized their independent institutions, primarily their cultural institutions, to target the cultural system that bound Northern and Southern whites in a shared white supremacism that fused their political and economic agendas. A similar fusion of white interests, nationally, in the early postbellum era, was the basis for Northern whites' betrayal of their former black allies, transforming the black military victory of the Slave Revolution into politico-economic defeat in the post-Reconstruction era.

A century later, the cultural system of white supremacism still provided the sinews binding and reinforcing politico-military and socioeconomic power in the United States, suggesting the continued salience of a cultural revolutionary focus. As before, with comparatively little political and economic resources as compared to federal, state, and municipal agencies, as well as the major institutions of civil society, which were all dominated by white racists, black revolutionists were forced to organize within their own community-based institutions, primarily their cultural institutions, to target the white supremacist cultural system of U.S. society in ways that ramified into the political, economic, and social systems. Simply put, they required a program of action guided by a theory of black cultural revolution in the United States.

Yet as essential as it was, BPM revolutionists had great difficulty developing such a theory, or at least one that would transcend Malcolm X's flawed formulation. At the root of the problem was the reverse civilizationism that they often adopted, which influenced their understanding of black culture, black nationalism, and black revolution. It contributed to a range of inconsistencies in their conceptualization of black cultural revolution, the manner in which such a revolution would be prosecuted, and the relationship between it and political revolution. This problem was evident among the major BPM organizations that we examined in the previous chapters, leading some of them to adopt dubious "traditional African" forms (e.g., Us, RNA, [kawaida-phase] CAP, PAOCC); and/or replicate "third world" models of revolution that were inapplicable to U.S. society (e.g., RAM, BPP, RNA, LRBW, and [Marxism-phase] CAP). As a result, major BPM revolutionists failed to construct a revolutionary theory that drew on the peculiar context of African American history to guide their initiatives and provide meaningful strategies to achieve their objectives. Devoid of adequate grounding in the cultural history of black America, many did not fully appreciate the role of black culture in the social transformation of black Americans, including their revolutionary initiatives as epitomized by the Slave Revolution during the U.S. Civil War. Even when they made references to a "Second Civil War" or a "Second Reconstruction," these were mainly rhetorical rather than analytical expressions.

A corollary was that not only did the Civil War and the General Strike provide a guide for the revolutionary organization and mobilization of black Americans, they suggested them for white Americans as well. How different in their orientation toward black liberation—in some ways even in their spatial locus—from abolitionists, Readjusters, Copperheads, and Redeemers were white civil rights supporters, white liberals, white Democratic and Republican segregationists, and white rightists from the KKK and Citizen's Councils to the John Birch Society, respectively? A white cultural revolution might have been considered to be as central to the success of a black cultural revolution as the Union Army was to the success of the Slave Revolution. This is not simply an argument from analogy; it's supported by the enduring relevance of the factors and objectives that compelled the former which are still evident in the latter, namely, the fact that conditions the BPM confronted were largely the result of the unfulfilled and unresolved issues of black liberation that persisted after the Civil War, and especially after the white counterrevolution that overthrew Reconstruction.

In effect, BPM revolutionists failed to adequately historicize their own movement. The most deleterious results of that failure were that instead of (1) developing a theoretical focus recognizing the importance of religiously inspired proletarians in the previous black revolution (the Slave Revolution), which was the same social group that was most prominent in the ongoing CRM and BPM, and (2) concentrating on the revolutionary propensities of the Black Church, in which many of them were institutionally grounded, resource dependent, and emotionally attached, BPM revolutionists often dismissed, denigrated, or denied the salience of the Black Church in the revolution they sought. In fact, with notable exceptions (e.g., the PAOCC), they failed to link their *cultural* revolutionary theses to the prominent *cultural* institution in black communities, the Black Church, which was also the institutional hub of political mobilization in black communities throughout the United States at the time, much as it is today. The prospect of mobilizing black communities on a national scale for revolution—or almost any major political objective—without a strategy that utilized, neutralized, or mobilized the Black Church was doomed to failure. Moreover, the vacuum left by the distancing of BPM activists from the Black Church was filled by black elected officials (BEOs), who often grounded themselves in, or emerged from, the revitalized and politicized black urban churches. Although predominantly integrationist in political orientation, nonetheless, both prospective and successful BEOs often drew heavily on black nationalist rhetoric, practices, and initiatives to gain political power, not through an independent black political party, as nationalists preferred, but by linking their programs to the Democratic Party, an alignment that Malcolm X decried, disparaged, and proscribed. In this way, the BEOs outflanked the BPM organizations and turned the political trajectory of black communities toward reform rather than revolution.

The Crusian Influence on Revolutionary Theory in the BPM

A prominent exception to the historical myopia of major BPM revolutionists was Harold Cruse's influential thesis on cultural revolution, which was not hamstrung by Malcolm's reverse civilizationism. According to Cruse, since cultural institutions in the United States are embedded in white supremacism, the revolutionary transformation of U.S. society would have to address the cultural as well as political and economic dimensions of black oppression. Cruse's thesis was only superficially adopted by the major BPM organizations in practice, and, no less importantly, it suffered from its own inconsistencies. For example, while Cruse's thesis targeted the cultural apparatus—primarily the mass communications media—of the United States, it focused inadequately on the cultural apparatus of the black community itself as a precursor to, or concomitant of, the cultural revolution. That is, it insufficiently addressed the role of cultural agents and institutions within black communities as instruments of the cultural change he sought. For example, he failed to integrate the major black cultural institution, the Black Church, into his thesis, which both reflected and reinforced the propensity of BPM revolutionists to dismiss the political, much less the revolutionary, efficacy of the Black Church in their revolutionary theses. In addition, he did not address the major cultural contradiction in black communities, sexism, as a key aspect of the cultural revolution he envisioned. He also did not attend sufficiently to the substantive cultural demands of black America, such as reparations, which would ramify into the political and economic sphere, and, in this way, augur cultural revolution. These shortcomings would resonate among BPM revolutionists and, likewise, hamstring their theses and the programs derived from them.

Although the major BPM organizations did not develop an explicit theory of black cultural revolution that transcended Cruse's formulation, they devised programs and practices oriented toward and involving factors suggestive of such a revolutionary formulation, both in terms of adopting the sine qua non of the Slave Revolution, the general strike (e.g., RAM, the LRBW) as well as focusing on the importance of black religion as a change agent (e.g., the Shrine). Among these organizations, the League of Revolutionary Black Workers (LRBW) came closest to developing programs and practices that reflected the importance of black cultural revolution—even if they didn't refer to them in this way. For example, the League's approach reflected an understanding of the general strike strategy, the importance of the black working class, the centrality of coordinating the major social institutions of black society, and the salience of proposing cultural claims that ramify into the political and economic spheres. In its focus on organizing the black working class, the League sought to leverage its power as an organization of both black workers inside the auto plants and community members outside the plants to garner concessions from the auto companies that would address the immediate demands of black workers as well as to realize the broader objective of revolutionary change in their communities. This dual strategy, focusing on both in-plant and out-of-plant coordination, sought to organize strikes to disable the auto industry, which would culminate in a general strike shutting down core sectors of industrial production in the United States and compelling companies and ultimately the government to concede to the League's demands.

Besides political repression and internal dissent, structural factors such as deindustrialization spelled the death knell of the League's focus on industrial union organizing, as did the hostility of major unions to civil rights, ranging from white workers' protests epitomized in the Hard Hat Riot to the Teamsters' endorsement of Nixon, as well as teachers' unions' rejection of black and brown community control, as exemplified in the New York City/Ocean Hill-Brownsville Strike. Such developments not only undermined the League, but suggested the need for black labor organizers in the future to focus on more clearly exploitable and critical sectors in the changed politico-economic context of the third ghetto and beyond. By comparison, other major BPM organizations, such as the Congress of African Peoples (CAP) and the Pan-African Orthodox Christian Church (PAOCC), proceeded on important but what turned out to be less auspicious paths toward the black cultural revolution that they sought, focusing less on black union workers as change agents and instead on black political parties or black churches, respectively.

Although BPM revolutionists left behind an influential set of insights, practices, and programs that continued to inform black American activism, nevertheless, during the BPM itself they were unable to integrate them into a coherent theory of black cultural revolution. At the outset of the BPM, the revolutionists' program focused on the need to develop parallel institutions staffed by black revolutionists, which would highlight the contradictions illustrated by the provision of services to blacks, especially poor blacks, by these dedicated activists in contrast to the absence of the same from the government agencies mandated to provide them; and the additional contradictions embodied in the exceptionally poor quality of both the provision and the delivery by government institutions and social service agencies of services and resources to black people and black communities as compared to those delivered to whites and white communities. The struggle waged to generate and secure resources for these parallel institutions would result in conflict between the black community and the agencies and representatives of municipal governments, as well as the white homeowners' associations and civic groups, etc., intent on maintaining white resource supremacy in the cities and towns (McRae, 2018). The intracity conflicts ultimately would generate a large-scale politico-economic struggle centered on the delivery of resources, in which blacks would play a central role.

However, with the ascendancy of BEOs, much of the energy of the CRM focused on gaining and maintaining control of the major agencies of city government and promoting the political, economic, and social development of black communities using the resources these institutions commanded. When these resources were parceled out as patronage directed at privileged elements of an emerging black elite and middle class but not at the masses of black residents, the BPM's appeal was less effective at targeting black political leadership for these failures than it had been in targeting the previous white leadership. As a result, the anticipated intracity conflict did not materialize, and the failed strategy employed by BPM revolutionists reflected the decreased relevance of the BPM's programs, plans, and priorities, and especially its call for revolution.

The nominal distribution of resources to some elements in black communities undermined BPM claims of the inability and unwillingness of the central governments to deliver resources to blacks, including those in the ghetto. Just as importantly, as blacks exercised their newfound access to electoral politics by electing black candidates in historic numbers across the country, they viewed the accession of this black electoral leadership, as an opportunity to take their place in the ethnic succession that the melting pot myth promised. Even in the face of the grave inequalities in the country's inner cities, especially the presence of black elected officials at different levels of, mainly, local government seemed to undermine the claim that blacks could not achieve an electoral form of black power. It appeared that for the most part the black masses aspired to the middle class, where they might reap the benefits of a reformed if inadequately transformed U.S. society. Black electoral success was viewed less as one component of a broader revolutionary strategy, but in a kind of crass and politically expedient version of Malcolm's "ballot or the bullet" rationale, the apparent success of blacks' use of the ballot was viewed more as an end in itself (i.e., the attainment of black elective office), and thus a repudiation of the call for the bullet. In the event, calls for revolution seemed passé.

If Malcolm had difficulty conceptualizing black revolution in the United States at the outset of the BPM, a different set of challenges beset revolutionists as the BPM waned. As Cruse might have had it, this was largely a problem of black intellectuals and activists once again failing to adequately interpret and orient their struggle in the ongoing phase of U.S. national development, even as black power played an important role in the transformation the country was experiencing. That is, the challenges facing black power were partly a result of the movement's successes in challenging white power, as well as the ongoing responses of the white supremacist system to those challenges. A key response of the U.S. political economy was the transformation of the second ghetto into the third ghetto, which resulted from a combination of factors, including deindustrialization, advanced suburbanization, the decline of unionism, economic decline (exacerbated by the first oil crisis and the inflation resulting from spending for the Vietnam War), white flight from black jurisdictions (both cities and school districts), declining support of civil rights gains, black middle class movement from inner cities, the end of the Vietnam War, emergence of national and local "law and order" regimes, prominent media depictions of black cultural deficiency, the promotion of culture of poverty discourse, and general white racist revanchism. These factors expanded the second ghetto, manifested in enclaves of black underdevelopment within the cities, into the third ghetto, represented by the underdevelopment of whole cities, particularly those under black political leadership (Nightingale, 2003). Facing the intellectual—and, of course, the practical and programmatic—requirement of theorizing these developments in their particular and often peculiar American context, BPM revolutionists simply, and simplistically, grafted the colonial analogy onto it. Thus, instead of recognizing the proclivity of the U.S. politico-economic system to channel ethnic/racial/class demands into resource competition among ethnic interest groups in the context of the richest and most powerful country in the world with its highly institutionalized civil society, most leading BPM revolutionists, following Baraka, explained that the decline of the BPM was simply a matter of the transformation of black domestic colonialism into black domestic *neo*colonialism.

The domestic neocolonial analogy was as myopic as the domestic colonial analogy from which it derived. In particular, it obscured the fact that the United States could deliver on any of the resource requirements that black Americans demanded but simply lacked the political will to do so until the protests of the CRM and the BPM pressured it to begin to do so. The demands of black power that were channeled through the electoral system could be accommodated with even fewer resources. Thus, the challenge faced by BPM revolutionists was to devise a theory centered on a program focused on resources that arose from the legitimate but unfulfilled claims of black Americans that were not easily accommodated by the faux interest group politics paradigm. The main unfulfilled claim was reparations, and it could not be accommodated as simply another interest group claim, just as the claim of African Americans for freedom a century earlier was not reconcilable with a war aimed simply to preserve the union. Reparations implicated both the economic and the political systems of the United States. In fact, if fulfilled, it would have necessitated a major redistribution of resources on a scale unseen since Reconstruction. To be sure, reparations was a specific cultural claim for which blacks had exclusive standing as an "interest group," but one that addressed such a major unresolved issue of socio-economic-political injustice that it not only foretold a systemic crisis given the expansive resource redistribution demands it required but it called into question the ability of the extant system to serve as an arbiter of the competing interests implicated in it. That is, a white supremacist system could not be expected to fairly arbitrate a case against its white supremacist practices, institutions and personages. Either an international institution would have to serve this function, or the national system would have to be transformed prior to or along with the consideration of the reparations demands.

When BPM revolutionists and their allies asserted the necessity for black reparations in the 1970s, they put themselves in a position to shift the agenda claimed by the BEOs in meaningful ways, and at the same time to appeal to the revitalized and politicized black churches, on whom both the elected officials and, increasingly, the Democratic Party relied.[1] A push for representative change within the electoral system took place, as blacks asserted themselves as the most recent entrant among those ethnic/racial/cultural groups able to practice interest group politics following the passage of the Voting Rights Act. Coupled with systemic change occurring within the economic system as they asserted their reparations claims, as a political demand the reparations issue presented an opportunity to keep black protest relevant as a continuation of the movement to eradicate Jim Crow in the economic realm. Of all the major demands made by the BPM, the reparations demand seemed to be the one whose chief impact would actually be systemic. Not surprisingly, then, this was the major demand that was never seriously addressed by any government entity at any level, and the absence of any serious engagement with the issue makes it obvious that the politico-economic-social system of the United States was never seriously challenged by the BPM. Thus, "domestic colonialism" was never compelled to shift to "neocolonialism," because it had not been sufficiently threatened at the system level. It was not as if African Americans had achieved "independence" on par with the independence gained by former African colonies, which included at least nominal sovereignty for African states and full citizenship rights for African people. In the CRM and BPM, the change had not been as dramatic as the eradication of chattel slavery a century earlier, although it was hugely transformative of the sociopolitical and, to a more modest extent, economic opportunity structure afforded Southern blacks, insofar as it ended de jure Jim Crow. Thus, the actual change that resulted did not require a major redistribution of resources. The Vietnam War and the Great Society programs probably exerted greater pressure on government agencies for the delivery of goods, services, and resources than either the CRM or the BPM. The U.S. government's power was not effectively challenged by its "domestic colony," because it modulated the movement's demands to suit the interest-group orientation of its polity and the commodity production and (re)distribution of its economy, and utilized its powerful media and cultural institutions to maintain its white supremacist society. The change wrought from the CRM and BPM was incremental and evolutionary, not revolutionary. The revolution had not been adequately theorized.

Nonetheless, the BPM, by building on the reforms of the CRM, was important in promoting the political assertiveness of blacks and increasing their electoral participation, which resulted in greater black political efficacy, and promoted the ascendancy of BEOs. Ironically, in helping develop this new political constituency of BEOs, BPM revolutionists simultaneously created a potential counterweight to their own nationalist organizations, including those that had catapulted the BEOs into political leadership, such as CAP in Newark, the *Black Slate* in Detroit, and the BPP in Oakland. The logical extension of this electoral work was the creation of an independent black political party, which was key to the original mission of the NBPA; however, the Democratic Party provided a powerful alternative for these mobilized black political interests, including access to well-funded sponsorship and patronage and extensive financial resources distributed through established networks and clients honeycombed throughout the elected offices, agencies, institutions, and political organizations within Democratic Party–dominated city and county governments, congressional districts, and voting precincts. Thus, for many black activists, the protests and pleadings of their black constituents increasingly were channeled through the Democratic Party and its representative BEOs. In this way, the Democrats counterbalanced, coopted, or coerced tendencies in black communities toward independent political party organizing. The CRM and BPM had been effectively channeled into the institutions of the U.S. politico-economic system and its extensive civil society institutions and organizations through the conduit of the BEOs and a reinvigorated, integrationist, and reformist-oriented Black Church.

The ascendancy of the BEOs and the threat of the Democratic Party to those seeking to organize an independent black political party required a revised black nationalist strategy to address these specific challenges within the changed context created by the "black urban regimes" whose leadership black nationalists had played no small role in creating. Such a revised strategy would need to center on political mobilization utilizing a powerful indigenous institution in the black community that could not only rival local Democratic Party formations, such as an independent black political party or black labor unions such as the LRBW, but would not be easily counterbalanced, coopted, or coerced. Among the viable alternatives would be one that was not only politically efficacious but culturally grounded in the black community, which was also the main one that BPM revolutionists dismissed, the Black Church.

This left the Black Church largely in the hands of integrationists and reformers under the influence of Martin L. King following the CRM. The CRM institutions and organizations were not passive or undeserving recipients of this increased support; it was earned from activist and often heroic struggle, yet many black church leaders and congregants accommodated their political concerns in the electoral sphere to those of the Democratic Party and more mainstream interest group politics.

BPM revolutionists competed with CRM reformists in black communities not only in supporting prospective BEOs, or over the direction of the Black Church, but even on the terrain of revolutionary transformation. With respect to the latter, they faced challenges from King's call for a "revolution of values," which seemed reconcilable with the call for a progressive, if not necessarily revolutionary, black culture, one that many, black and nonblack, associated with the victories of the CRM, especially the overthrow of de jure Jim Crow and the passage of the Voting Rights Act. CRM leaders such as King had appropriated aspects of the cultural revolutionary theses of BPM activists while remaining situated in a reformist context. In fact, King even evoked the sine qua non of the BPM, domestic colonialism, to contextualize the black ghetto. The salience of King's revolution of values approach went to the heart of the BPM's claims regarding the necessity of cultural transformation, mainly because King had centered his appeal on the Black Church while also focusing on other major established black institutions, ranging from historically black colleges and universities (HBCUs) to black-owned media. The significance of the breadth of King's appeal was evident in his largest initiative during the last years of his life, the Poor Peoples Campaign. Notably, King was killed as his organization participated in a strike of black sanitation workers in Memphis. Thus, it was King's Southern Christian Leadership Conference (SCLC), not black Marxists or white leftists, that played a key role in mobilizing protesting black workers in the South.

While King's assassination quashed the momentum of the CRM and motivated the BPM, the former had succeeded in creating an institutional power base in black communities that would endure for decades, rooted in alliances among black churches allied with the Democratic Party and selected labor unions, which the BPM would challenge but never supercede. Among major BPM organizations, it was the Shrine that came closest to developing a social theory grounded in the changed reality that suggested the increased salience of the Black Church in association with but not deferential to these other elements; but the PAOCC was hampered by its commitment to reverse civilizationism and atrophied by its kawaida-associated catechism of political education. The LRBW came closest to developing a black cultural revolution as historicized by Du Bois in *Black Reconstruction*, theorized by Locke, and proposed by Cruse, but the revolution they sought could not be fitted into the Marxist conceptual frame the League constructed for it.

The stultifying reality for black revolutionists was that no Western power of that time that even approximated the vast and entrenched institutions of the civil society of the United States had ever been overthrown or was likely to be, and in those that came close, such as France in 1968, it happened when revolutionists coordinated with labor unions, major political parties, major universities, and the military. The BPM had little influence within any of these, so that it would require the actions of only one institutional force (local police, for instance), whether or not it was augmented by any of the others (e.g., the Democratic Party, major labor unions) to undermine and redirect their attacks on the state. To break through the structures of civil society would require a black cultural revolution, and presumably a white cultural revolution as well. Failing that, claims on the polity, economy, and society would have to be channeled through the expansive moderating institutions of U.S. civil society, which would more likely only serve to reinforce their powers. In the event, however seriously they were considered in mainstream black politics, BPM claims were reconceptualized as ethnic interest group claims when applied in a broader plural context. Black protest was redefined as black transactional politics and black revolutionary discourse distanced itself from much of what was viewed as black politics in the post-BPM era. Even though they became marginalized, black revolutionary theses, and the BPM organizations that propounded them, were not irrelevant in the post-BPM era, but without a social movement to buttress them, and from which they might derive inspiration and resources, they receded into the background throughout black communities in the United States.

Conclusion

As the Long Hot Summers and massive demonstrations that characterized the height of the CRM receded into the background, by the mid-1970s the BPM, which in important ways was motivated by and reflected in these events, also began to wane. Like the CRM, the BPM declined, in part as a result of its successes, which seemed to make it no longer necessary, but also from the effects of systemic government repression and the overwhelming but still poorly documented white civilian opponents of both movements (McRae, 2018). Among the important failures of the BPM itself were those that fell short on an intellectual level, one of the most glaring of which was the inability of the BPM to successfully theorize the revolution it envisioned. Specifically, the BPM ended as it had begun, lacking a theory of black cultural revolution to guide its program and practices. Ironically, given the persistence of many of the political, economic, and social justice issues that BPM revolutionists confronted and attempted to resolve—from de facto white supremacism in general to black poverty and police brutality—an assessment of the theoretical arguments of the major revolutionists of the BPM and their precursors that we've discussed in this volume may inform another generation of activists and inspire them to revisit their work and apply its lessons.

The prospects for a Crusian-style strategy remain auspicious in the present era of social media–accentuated activism (i.e., hashtag [#] activism), and to some extent they are being demonstrated in the major African American political activism of the day. For example, the #BlackLivesMatter (BLM) movement, founded by three black women, Alicia Garza, Opal Tometi, and Patrice Cullors, emerged mainly in response to extrajudicial police killings of unarmed or otherwise law-abiding blacks, which evokes the BPM's mobilization against police brutality, racism and classism in the criminal (in)justice system, and political repression and imprisonment.[2] Remember that Cruse had argued that a major impediment to black cultural revolution during the black power era was that "Negro radicals" at the time were "severely hampered in their tasks of educating the black masses on political issues because Negroes do not own any of the necessary means of propaganda and communications" (1968, p. 239), an issue that may be largely moot in an era of social media. That is, given the accessibility and mobilizing potential of social media and the fact that a sizeable number of Americans walk around daily with a computer on their person (i.e., a cell phone), the likelihood of utilizing this powerful element of the cultural apparatus for social transformation is markedly enhanced in twenty-first-century America.

BLM has influenced an array of associated hashtag activism, including the most recent protests during the playing of the national anthem at National Football League (NFL) games (and other professional sports events), inspired by the actions of former San Francisco 49ers quarterback Colin Kaepernick who initiated his protest in response to the police killings of unarmed blacks.[3] Kaepernick's protest is more than nominally related to an earlier "revolt of the black athlete" (Edwards, 1969) inasmuch as the lead organizer of the Olympics Protest of 1968, Harry Edwards (who has also served as a staff consultant to the San Francisco 49ers), had studied Cruse's *Crisis of the Negro Intellectual* as a sociology graduate student and intended to use the mechanism of a boycott and the medium of sport as a catalyst to a larger transformative objective oriented around human rights (ibid.). Edwards's association with the Kaepernick protests links them to these previous efforts and is indicative of the ramifying of the political protests associated with BLM to aspects of the popular cultural apparatus—in the case of the NFL protests, to sports and entertainment—such as the music (especially hip hop), television, and the motion picture industry; but also including challenges to the white supremacism in so much of the U.S. cultural milieu, such as in protests seeking the removal of Confederate and other white supremacist statuary and symbols in public spaces and the renaming of public institutions, especially schools, parks, and streets.

The potency of social media as a propaganda tool for activists in the United States was made starkly evident by the Russian misinformation campaign, conducted primarily through social media, during the 2016 U.S. presidential campaign, which successfully targeted Democratic Party candidates Hillary Clinton and Bernie Sanders in order to promote Republican Donald Trump's long-shot electoral victory. The decentralized BLM has been effective in mobilizing large numbers of protesters using social media and a largely nonhierarchical network-based organizational framework toward its social movement goals. In reply to Robert Smith's (1996) critique that post-BPM black America was hindered politically because black Americans "ha[d] no leaders," one might contend that one of the reasons that BLM has been effective is largely *because* "they have no leaders," but a potential hindrance to BLM's achieving its objectives may be that "they have no theory" either. BLM's inclusive focus on cultural—as well as political and economic—aspects of African American liberation reflects its attempt to effectuate the "wholesale culture shift" its founding members advocate (Khan-Cullors & bandele, 2018, p. 197). Interestingly, although the use of social media and black popular culture as conduits of activism are convergent with Cruse's cultural revolution thesis, often BLM activists, leadership, and analysts seem largely indifferent or resistant to situating their movement in such an African American *theoretical* context. On the latter point, although it is difficult to pinpoint any ideological consensus in the confluence of interests that comprise BLM and related initiatives invoking its hashtag (#), and although it frames its movement, historically, in fundamental aspects of the CRM and BPM while foregrounding its critical intersectionality with respect to gender, sexuality, age, ableness, and criminal status (Clark et al., 2018), an engagement with Du Boisean-Lockean (or Crusian) black cultural revolution is distant from its theoretical discourse. To the extent that BLM's direct action and hashtag activism is interpreted through BPM revolutionary frameworks it is rarely attentive to the critiques outlined in previous chapters. Where it encourages a search for a theory of social change to explain its motive force and suggest its strategy and objectives it is more likely to draw from either liberal or radical egalitarianism/integrationism (e.g., Khan-Cullors & bandele, 2018), neither of which is revolutionary and both of which are devoid of an appreciation of black revolutionary antecedents in the United States and/or the role of black culture in them. To the extent that participants and analysts explicate BLM through a neo-Marxist lens (e.g., Taylor, 2014), it weds the "movement for *black* lives" to a regime of theory poorly fitted to black America and a ham-fisted analysis of black revolution in the United States that reduces its relevance almost exclusively to academic audiences. To the extent that BLM's objective is an American revolution, the lack of a theory of black cultural revolution is a deficiency for which having no leaders will not compensate.

Not surprisingly, in the changed context of the 1980s the issues related to black cultural revolution reemerged on the national stage, as many majority black cities failed to realize the promise of ethnic succession and the benefits that a black electoral strategy seemed to promise. Moreover, deindustrialization, urban decay, depreciation of city services, and increased violence in these communities generated new organizational attempts at black cultural revolution to respond to the new challenges facing urban black communities. In particular, in the 1980s a renewed focus emerged directed at the cultural imperatives of black sociopolitical change as black Americans challenged their continued oppression during the Reagan Era, which was the name given to the rightist turn in U.S. national politics, the political centrism of the Democratic Party in response to Jesse Jackson's attempt to fashion a "Rainbow Coalition" in a domestic context of entrenched politico-economic inequality, and an international context of a reheated Cold War.

Two of the major differences among various organizational attempts to fashion, formulate, and in some cases foment black cultural revolution in the 1980s was that they were much more committed to internal transformation in black communities and they were led by black working-class women, which may also explain why they have been largely ignored in the academic and popular literature. These women raised a claim that U.S. civil society seemed ineffective at channeling: ensuring the physical survival of black youth who were increasingly falling victim to homicide. That U.S. society was not providing for the physical survival of so many black youths raised such fundamental contradictions that it generated a new movement centered on the human rights of black Americans: the Urban Peace and Justice Movement (UPJM), whose most important organizations were led by mothers of slain black children.[4] Among the most influential of them were Save Our Sons and Daughters (SOSAD), led by Clementine Barfield in Detroit, Mothers of Murdered Sons (MOMS), led by Brenda Muhammad in Atlanta, and Mothers Reclaiming Our Children (Mothers-ROC), led by Barbara Meredith in Los Angeles. These women and their organizations provided a paradigm to promote peace in black communities besieged by the killing of black youths, and in so doing raised fundamental issues of cultural transformation in black communities and the broader U.S. society.[5] Among the ironies of #BlackLivesMatter is that although the founding members are all black women, two of whom self-identify as queer and one as Nigerian American (Tometi et al., 2015), they (and most major analysts of BLM) also have largely ignored the example of—and rarely if ever refer to—these black women predecessors who led the UPJM in the 1980s and '90s, even as they invoke similar—at times, derivative—arguments regarding the value of black lives, challenging police brutality, and the fundamental contradiction of the most powerful country in the world being unable and/or unwilling to provide for the physical survival/security of black children and adults (e.g., Khan-Cullors & bandele, 2018; Taylor, 2014). Interestingly, each of these organizations of the UPJM included BPM revolutionists in prominent positions. For example, SOSAD, probably the most influential of these post-BPM organizations, included James Boggs as a member of its executive board, Grace Boggs as its newspaper editor, Ron Scott, one of the co-founders of Detroit's Black Panther Party, as one of its chief organizers of its peace programs, and General Baker, formerly of the LRBW, as one of its many community volunteers. This "ignored cultural revolution" will be the focus of the next volume.

Notes

Introduction

1. For an excellent review of this literature, see Taylor (2011).

2. The exception is the voluminous literature on the Black Arts Movement (e.g., Smethurst, 2005); but this is also mainly historical and rarely linked to African American revolutionary theory.

3. What might appear a glaring omission from this list, for some, is the Student Non-violent Coordinating Committee (SNCC) during its black power phase. Actually, SNCC's black power concept as articulated originally by Carmichael and Hamilton was a pluralist modification of King's integrationism rather than Malcolm's black nationalist revolutionism. In the original *Black Power* (1967) there is no reference to Malcolm X or black nationalism (Taylor, 2011). Others might view the absence of the NOI as an omission; however, the NOI may have been "objectively revolutionary" as Baraka (2012) once claimed—and much more so than its Marxist critics were at the time; but other than Malcolm X and his supporters, as an organization, the NOI, did not advocate political revolution in the sense that it is considered herein.

Chapter 1. Malcolm X and the Revolutionary Turn in the Civil Rights Movement

1. Former RNA 2nd vice president Chokwe Lumumba won the mayor's office in Jackson, Mississippi, in 2014 on a platform reflecting aspects of a modified RNA strategy.

2. Malcolm X (1970, p. 123) proffered this logic on reparations: "If you are the son of a man . . . and you inherit your father's estate, you have to pay off the debts that your father incurred before he died. The only reason that the present generation of white Americans are in a position of economic strength . . . is because their fathers worked our fathers for over 400 years with no pay. . . . Your father isn't here to pay. My father isn't here to collect. But I'm here to collect and you're here to pay."

3. In a recording of MTTG, the voice of future LRBW leader General Baker, is heard responding from the audience, "We'll bleed!" to Malcolm's rhetorical challenge, generating Malcolm's repetition of the charge.

4. Moses refers to a prior "proto-nationalist" era as well.

5. Woodard (1999, p. 123) notes that after leaving the NOI, "Malcolm X eventually abandoned notions of gender exclusion"; in fact, Malcolm argued that "the Black Revolution pivoted on the political consciousness and social development of women." In the OAAU, he "encouraged the leadership of Lynn Shifflet and Sarah Mitchell" and "sought to recruit Maya Angelou from Ghana."

6. Following defeat of the segregationist Republican Barry Goldwater by the Democrat Lyndon Johnson in the 1964 presidential election, the Dixiecrats began a shift to the Republican Party, which was completed by the Reagan Era, creating a new home for segregationists and their apologists in the Republican Party—the party of Lincoln—which remains today.

7. The BPP advocated a similar UN petition strategy, as did the RNA.

8. Malcolm's allusion to support from "800 million" Chinese "waiting to throw their weight on our side" in the UN ignores that Mao's People's Republic of China was not a member of the UN at the time. China's seat was held at the time by U.S. ally, Taiwan, led by Chang Kai-shek.

9. Where the South openly oppressed Negroes attempting to vote, Malcolm noted that the North was simply shrewder in suppressing the black vote; and the key to the latter was gerrymandering.

10. In TBR of April 1964 in Detroit, he stated: "America is in a unique position. She is the only country in history in a position actually to become involved in a *bloodless* revolution" (original emphasis).

11. Malcolm implied as much in MTTG in reference to the dispute between Khrushchev and Mao, which he implied was instigated by the persistence of Russia's "white nationalism" in the USSR.

12. Malcolm asserted that "we need new ideas, new methods, new approaches. We will call upon young students of political science throughout the nation to help us. We will encourage these young students to launch their own independent study and give us their analysis and their suggestions."

13. While federal and local police forces were responsible for fomenting dissent in the NOI, the NOI leadership and its members carried out the assassination, introducing internal terrorism to the BPM.

14. I've referred to this previously as one of the "unintended consequences" of Malcolm's cosmopolitanism (Henderson, 2018a).

15. Notably, Hechter (1975) applied the concept of internal colonialism to Ireland.

16. It would not be ignored by important black feminists, such as Audre Lorde.

Chapter 2. Black Nationalism

1. On black feminists and emigrationism, Ida B. Wells-Barnett (1892b, p. 40) argued that "the right of those who wish to go to Africa should be as inviolate as that of those who wish to stay."

2. Another misrepresentation of black nationalism by prominent scholars is Dawson's (2001, p. 21) claim that "Black nationalism is the second oldest (after radical egalitarianism) ideological tendency within black political thought." Such an ahistorical view of black nationalism is so pervasive that he privileges "radical egalitarianism" as the earliest black American political ideology against the evidence that black nationalism is the original black American ideology—its roots tracing back to the 1700s; it is not derivative of other nationalisms, but is contemporaneous with French and American nationalism. Such ahistorical views more accurately gauge the difficulty of antinationalists such as Dawson in reconciling that historical reality with their own ideological preferences (see Taylor, 2011).

3. Moses (1989, p. 239) insists that "[t]here were no black nineteenth-century leaders who spent much time discussing the positive aspects of slavery, and many years would pass before it would become fashionable to promote the mythology of a healthy slave community." To be fair to Stuckey's perspective, an acknowledgment of "slave culture" is not an assertion that slave communities were "healthy" or that they were not sites of inhumane oppression.

4. While acknowledging that the view that black religion is foundational to the black nation is "reasonable enough," Moses (1990, p. 28) asserts that "there has never been any systematic demonstration of ties between black religion and black nationalism."

5. See Taylor (2011, pp. 195–202) for critiques of this strain of anti–black nationalist scholarship.

6. Moses (1998) notes that Du Bois appears to have first employed the term *Afrocentric* in 1961.

7. While these notions seem congruent with Garvey's, Du Bois viewed much of Garvey's program as retrogressive and escapist.

8. The quote from Fanon (1963, pp. 312, 315) is: "We today can do everything, so long as we do not imitate Europe, so long as we are not obsessed by the desire to catch up with Europe. . . . So comrades, let us not pay tribute to Europe by creating states, institutions, and societies which draw upon inspiration from her. Humanity is waiting for something from us other than such an imitation, which would be almost an obscene caricature."

9. It also borrowed from Paul Robeson's emphasis on African culture.

10. Arguably, there were some elements of civilizationism in Du Bois's (1897, p. 10) "Conservation of Races" in which he suggested the vanguard role of "the 8,000,000 people of Negro blood" in the United States, whom he characterizes as "*the advance guard* of the Negro people" (emphasis added).

Chapter 3. The General Strike and the Slave Revolution of the U.S. Civil War

1. Among the most prominent exceptions are Robinson (1983) and Roediger (2014).

2. He added: "Yet one would search current American histories almost in vain to find a clear statement or even faint recognition of these perfectly well-authenticated facts" (p. 717).

3. Among the most notable were Powhatan Beaty, a former slave, who took command of his company at the Battle of Chaffin's Farm after its officers had been killed and/or wounded and led a charge against Confederate lines, driving the Confederates from their fortified positions.

4. The point is as much stylistic as substantive given the actual context of Marx's oft-cited, though poorly contextualized quote, which is less dismissive of religious motivations than is often assumed: "The wretchedness of religion is at once an expression of and a protest against real wretchedness. Religion is the sigh of the oppressed creature, the heart of a heartless world, and the soul of soulless conditions. It is the opium of the people" (Marx, 1982, p. 131). The interpretation of the metaphor in its context has received much less attention.

5. Genovese (1981, pp. 4–5) notes that "[b]y the end of the eighteenth century the historical content of the slave revolts shifted decisively from attempts to secure freedom from slavery to attempts to overthrow slavery as a social system," with the Haitian Revolution "mark[ing] the turning point," and "[t]he nineteenth century revolts in the Old South formed part of this epoch-making transformation." Specifically, "the black demand for the abolition of slavery as a social system was something new and epoch-making" (p. xx).

6. McPherson (1991, p. 35) argues that the "enlistment of black soldiers to fight and kill their former masters" impelled Lincoln to change his initial war aims to "the revolutionary goal of a new Union without slavery" (p. 34).

7. Jackson (2019) provides indirect support for Du Bois' claim in her analysis of the positive uses of force and violence among black abolitionists. In Franklin's (1992, pp. 30–31) view, "For Du Bois, the value of freedom, like self-determination, reached the Afro-American masses through a 'trickle-down process' from the free blacks."

8. Du Bois's ambivalence is evident in *Black Reconstruction* when after evoking slaves' agency in the General Strike, near the end of the book he emphasizes black religion's otherworldliness and resignation: "a religion which taught meekness, sacrifice and humility" (pp. 692–693), similar to his portrayal of astonished bewildered slaves in *Souls*.

9. Du Bois was aware of these connections, but at the time of his writing *Black Reconstruction* he was much less positively inclined toward black religion as a change agent.

10. Starobin (1970, p. 89) notes several revolts and conspiracies involving industrial slaves after 1831, and while some may have been exaggerated by whites, actual cases such as the slave conspiracy in 1856 was "especially significant, since it involved industrial slaves almost exclusively."

11. Sidbury (1997, p. 88) rejects the claims that the revolt was rooted in "artisanal republicanism."

12. On whether Gabriel was hired out, contrast Egerton (1993, pp. 24–25) and Sidbury (1997, p. 83).

13. After escaping from Richmond, Gabriel was helped by a white boat captain and betrayed by a hired-out slave artisan. Gabriel and more than thirty conspirators

were hanged. In the aftermath, the legislature restricted slave hiring and limited the residency and movement of free blacks.

14. Several authors—most prominently Johnson (2001)—have argued that the Vesey conspiracy was a fabrication of white politicians; but this claim has been challenged, most convincingly, by Spady (2011).

15. A similar argument is made by Raboteau (1980, p. 163).

16. Ironically, the key informant, George Wilson, was a blacksmith, a class leader in the AME church, and a founding member of the church (Pearson, 1999; Robertson, 1999).

17. Oates (1975, p. 161) argues that "[t]hose who describe Nat as a skilled slave are wrong. In 1822, Nat was valued at $400—the price of a good field hand. During his trial for insurrection, he was valued at only $375. By contrast a slave blacksmith also tried for the rebellion was valued at $675. . . . Nat mentions nothing in the *Confessions* about ever being a skilled slave; rather, he refers to himself as a field hand at work behind his plow" (p. 38).

18. Similar laws were enacted across slaveholding states, contributing to vast illiteracy among slaves, such that most slaves freed by the Civil War were illiterate.

19. Among the hired-out slave artisans in the interstices between slavery and industrial society, were also those who would become members of the postbellum black petit bourgeoisie. Along with Southern free blacks, this contingent of slave artisans was no less compelled by an ideology rooted in slave religion, and had chosen revolution as well. Thus, there was likely a dual movement within incipient black working-class consciousness compelling proletarianization as well as petit bourgeosification, with both groups, during the Civil War, centered on pursuing black revolution to secure their freedom.

20. One might conjecture that if the temporal span of Du Bois's *Black Reconstruction* were broader, beginning in 1830, the year prior to the Turner Rebellion, instead of 1860, he might have made these connections more prominently, especially if he were able to draw from the research in his planned biography of Turner for *Black Reconstruction*, which might have led him to integrate at least a more militant form of "slave religion" into his broader thesis of black political revolution in the Civil War.

21. On networks, skilled labor, slave hiring, and religion, see Schermerhorn (2011).

22. For a useful synthesis of discussions on enslaved artisan workers and networks of communication, see Buchanan (2004).

23. The more formal clandestine networks, such as Webb describes, culminated in the Underground Railroad, which by the 1850s "had developed into a diverse, flexible, and interlocking system with thousands of activists residing from the upper South to Canada" (Bordewich, 2005, p. 5).

24. Although the commitment of the Founders to slavery and white supremacy is apparent (Hunt, 1987), the secessionists of the CSA also found inspiration in the commentary of Madison and especially Jefferson on the Kentucky and Virginia Resolutions of 1798 and 1799 with regard to their supportive implications for interposition and nullification (Moses 2019).

25. Conceived more broadly, the processes that compelled the incipient proletarianism of hired-out slaves, for example, the worker's degree of independence coupled with a radical formulation of religion, might also have contributed to the development of an incipient—and progressive—petite bourgeoisie as well (see footnote 19).

26. This was mainly an option of white ethnic groups and among racial minority communities, mainly available to LatinX, Asian Americans, and Amerindians/Native Americans.

27. Many of the major BPM organizations either rejected Christianity, conceptually, or the Black Church as an organizational or mobilizational focus, with the major exception of the PAOCC.

Chapter 4. Cultural Revolution and Cultural Evolution

1. To Du Bois's thesis I added the role of slave hiring, inducing an incipient working-class consciousness.

2. On the pendulum shifts of nationalism and integrationism, see Cruse (1967); and a test of Cruse's thesis in Henderson (2000).

3. Marx's is among the most popular conceptions of economic revolution, as are Weber's *The Protestant Ethic and the Rise of Capitalism* and Polanyi's *The Great Transformation*.

4. An ironic aftermath of the GPCR's persecution of "capitalist roaders" was Mao's rapprochement with the world's leading capitalist power, the United States, and his meeting with Richard Nixon in Beijing in 1972.

5. Deng incorporated market reforms that stimulated economic growth, reformed the educational system to promote skill sectors to develop the country's technological capacity, and provided a modicum of liberalization in domestic politics, which did not preclude centralized repression. Liu died in 1969 under house arrest and was subsequently rehabilitated by Deng and accorded a state funeral in 1980.

6. For further discussion of *prolekult*, see Mally (1990).

7. Prominent filmmaker Sergei Eisenstein was associated with the Prolecult Theatre.

8. Victor Serge, who witnessed the Russian Revolution, noted that young Soviet writers appeared to be "obstructed rather than assisted by doctrine" and "permanently tormented by a concern for orthodoxy" (Birchall, 2000, p. 83). He argued that proletarian literature often was simply not good, and he contrasted the rigid mechanistic *prolekult* literature with French proletarian literature (p. 85).

9. Unless otherwise noted, references from Lenin are accessed through the Lenin Internet Archive (1999, 2000, 2002).

10. For a Gramscian analysis of cultural revolution in the post-1960s United States, see Epstein (1991).

11. Simms (2000, p. 188) argues that "the Black church of South Africa . . . has a great potential for contributing to a cultural revolution," thus broadening Gramscianism to accommodate a progressive role for the black church in cultural revolution. For a contrasting view, see Billings (1990).

12. Wells Barnett's survey research on lynching may be viewed as laying the basis for modern sociological analyses that rest on fieldwork, interviewing techniques, and interpretive analysis that she utilized, even prior to Du Bois's (1899) seminal work, which established modern systematic sociology including use of quantitative methods.

13. Parsons likely was born enslaved (see Jones, 2017).

14. For example, Wells Barnett could not secure support of her own or any other black church in Chicago for a public meeting place for her efforts to respond to a lynching in Illinois in 1908.

15. For example, see his "Crusader Without Violence" (1959). Du Bois was prescient in recognizing the weakness of the CRM in its failure to provide a parallel economic program to address the needs of blacks, although he was unremitting in his praise of the courage of King and his followers.

16. Some of his feminist works include "The Burden of Black Womanhood," "The Black Mother," "Hail Columbia," "Woman Suffrage," and "The Damnation of Women."

17. On the latter point, see Du Bois's (1935, pp. 698–700) discussion of the use of crime as a source of income for Southern states through the convict lease system. Also see Blackmon (2008). On the role of terrorism in the reimposition of the slavocracy, see Wade (1987), especially pp. 9–116.

18. There is some dispute as to whether Wells Barnett was to be a member of the NAACP's governing board, the Committee of Forty. She was convinced of the connivance of Mary White Ovington in her exclusion (Giddings, 2008, pp. 477–480; Wells Barnett, 1970, pp. 321–329); and her name was eventually appended to the list (also see Lewis, 1993, pp. 394–399).

19. For an assessment of the elitism in the black feminism of the NACW, see Moses (1978).

20. Although *The Negro and Social Reconstruction* was published posthumously—a decade after the BPM, its main arguments were popularly known during the 1930s and 1940s because Du Bois had published them in two articles in the January and March 1934 volumes of *Crisis*: "Segregation" and "Separation and Self-Respect," respectively. He expanded on them in his 1940 autobiography *Dusk of Dawn*, which had sections lifted from *The Negro and Social Reconstruction*, and his *Current History* article, "A Negro Nation Within a Nation."

21. Du Bois (1991, p. 197) argued that his program could "easily be mistaken for a program of complete racial segregation and even nationalism among Negroes," but, "[t]his is a misapprehension." A few pages later, he uses the same language that he had disparaged: "Instead of letting this segregation remain largely a matter of chance and unplanned development . . . it would make the segregation a matter of careful thought and intelligent planning on the part of Negroes" (pp. 199–200).

22. Moses (1998) reports that Du Bois first used the term *Afrocentric* in 1961—almost two decades prior to Asante's (1980) more popular usage. Incredibly, and without evidence, Asante (1988, p. 16) insisted that Du Bois was not Afrocentric, but given the range of logical, historical, and empirical errors in Asante's work, such a mischaracterization is not surprising (see Henderson, 1995, pp. 85–90).

23. Although Du Bois (1915) was published prior to Lenin's more famous pamphlet, it is rarely anthologized in contemporary International Relations textbooks or readers (see Henderson, 2013b).

24. It is not clear that the increased salience of the Black Church in the CRM led him to reconsider his view of it as a change agent. It was during the CRM that he joined the Communist Party.

25. He observed a special role for youth in this process (pp. 510, 514); and presciently noted: "Just as soon as true art emerges, just as soon as the black artist appears, someone touches the race on the shoulder and says, 'He did that because he was an American, not because he was a Negro'" (p. 515).

26. Du Bois had declared himself "a socialist of the path" as early as 1907.

Chapter 5. Theorizing Cultural Revolution in the Black Power Era

1. Cruse lamented that the "long awaited" and "long overdue" book of Locke's writings by Butcher (1956) "greatly disappointed because it did not answer the question [whether Negroes should develop and uphold an Afro-American or an Anglo-American culture] at all" (Cruse, 1968, p. 49).

2. Cruse's thesis is similar to the Situationist perspective emerging contemporaneously in France, such as Guy Debord's (1967) *The Society of the Spectacle*, which was influential in the general strike in Paris of 1968.

3. That Cruse theorized the centrality of democratizing the cultural apparatus well before the blaxploitation film era and the creation of hip-hop is testament to his grounding in black cultural politics. It is ironic that in the hip-hop era, many of the same critics of Cruse's thesis admonish rap artists for not helping to develop an independent base for black politics and culture.

4. Black millionaire C. J. Walker's support for the Garvey Movement, and black banker A. C. Gaston's support for the CRM are noted examples of black petit bourgeois support of black activism.

5. In 1982, in *Manifesto for an American Revolutionary Party*, Boggs asserted that "no one race, no one class, no one sex" in the United States "is automatically revolutionary," and "individuals in all these groups have the potential for being counter-revolutionary as well as revolutionary" (pp. 40–41).

6. Pol Pot's Khmer Rouge demonstrated horrifically that revolutionary activity does not necessarily generate a revolutionary culture in a progressive sense; instead, it might create reactionary and genocidal culture, as evident in the killing fields of Cambodia or the Reign of Terror of the French Revolution.

7. In the subsequent decades, the Boggses clung to the view that a vanguard was necessary for revolution in the United States and alternated privileging "outsiders" and school-aged dropouts they called "opt-outs." A teleological rigidity bound them to nondialectical rationales enjoining a continual search for a vanguard to lead a revolution they prophesized and awaited with millenarian earnest. View-

ing revolution as both means and end—instrument and objective—what was lost in their analyses is that revolution is not the objective of political struggle but simply a means to social justice.

8. Although Boggs was clearly familiar with and encouraged the study of Du Bois's works and often traced black labor history to the slave revolts and invoked the General Strike, he had difficulty integrating the cultural aspects of these phenomena into his broader thesis. As a result, unlike Du Bois's exposition of the role of black cultural transformation in the slaves' prosecution of the General Strike, Boggs's (1963) analysis of the Civil War in *The American Revolution* is bereft of a sense of black cultural agency in the war, conflating issues of race and nation under a single rubric of class struggle (pp. 75–77).

9. Only shortly before her death a half century later—often in conversation with this author—did Grace Boggs begin to suggest the utility of cultural revolution in the United States both as an analytical device and sociopolitical objective; but one she still tethered to a neo-Marxist teleology embracing autonomist theorists such as Castoriadis rather than Du Bois, Locke, or Cruse.

10. Critics even two decades apart, such as Perkins (1977) and Smith (1999), and up to the present, continue to ignore Cruse's engagement of the issue of privileging Harlem in the follow-on essays of 1971 (Cruse, 1971abc). Many otherwise substantive crtiques of Cruse's thesis typically redounded to the oft-repeated neo-Marxist claim that cultural and racial factors were epiphenomena of class, while ignoring that Cruse's original thesis of black cultural revolution was intended to revolutionize an existing movement, the CRM, and not to pose a universal thesis of revolutionary change.

11. On the Nadir, see Logan (1954). For a review of "renaissances" outside of Harlem, see Moses (1990, pp. 201–222) on the renaissance in Washington, D.C., beginning in the 1890s, decades before Harlem's of the 1920s; Clark Hine and McCluskey (2012) on Chicago's a decade later; Whitaker's (2018) focus on Pittsburgh; and Glasrud and Wintz's (2012) discussion of black renaissances from Kansas City to the Bay Area.

12. Cruse disparaged what he viewed as ill-conceived "internationalist" and pan-Africanist rhetoric of the NBPA that detracted from domestic issues and led to needless internecine disputes that undermined the NBPA and contributed to its collapse.

13. Frances Beal of SNCC and the Third World Women's Alliance provided important discussions of black womens' agency in the CRM and BPM as well as incisive critiques of sexism such as her seminal 1969 pamphlet "Double Jeopardy: To be Black and Female." Grace Lee also contributed an essay to the important work *The Black Woman*, which also published a revised version of Beal's (1970) essay, and was edited by Toni Cade Bambara. The Boggses (1974) provided a trenchant critique of sexism and the necessity of overturning it as an essential element of revolution in the United States.

14. Cruse discusses BARTS in *Crisis*; also, see Goose's (2004), especially his discussion of Yuri Kochiyama's notes from Cruse's course in "Cultural Philosophy" at the school.

Chapter 6. Revolutionary Action Movement, Us, the Black Panther Party

1. RAM was more a "low profile"—to use Ernest Allen's term—than an underground organization.

2. Vitalis (2013) provides a critical assessment of this rather common but misleading association of Bandung with the nonaligned movement and a broader fusion of antiracism in a kind of Third Worldism/or third world internationalism. Also see Kahin (1956).

3. This was owed to RAM's favoring Mao in the "Sino-Soviet Split"; and RAM's rejection of the USSR's "peaceful coexistence" with the capitalist West (see *World Black Revolution*, pp. 12–13).

4. RAM's twelve-point program would be modified somewhat from its original 1964 version through the 1969 decimation of the organization, but mainly as a reflection of changing emphasis rather than broader theoretic and programmatic orientations.

5. Ahmad (2007, 112) and conversations with Muhammad Ahmad. This is also evident from the reading lists in the earliest editions of RAM's *Black America* and *Revolutionary Nationalist*.

6. Vesey's revolt sought coordination with President Boyer of Haiti, not Toussaint L'Ouverture.

7. The Turner revolt did not involve hundreds of slaves (see Greenberg, 2003; Henderson, 2015, pp. 205–207).

8. Stanford argued that "[a]ll AfroAmericans must begin to think like guerilla fighters" (p. 1).

9. Following the BPM, Stanford (1986, p. 199) noted a "major flaw" in RAM's "inability to perceive, until 1968, that the nature of the black liberation struggle in the United States would be protracted. Had the leadership of RAM understood protracted warfare, it would never had projected the theory of a '90-day' war of liberation." By no later than 1967, Williams (1967, p. 15) situated the "90 days" in a protracted framework, arguing that only after "[a] *few years* of violent, sporadic and highly destructive uprisings" would the stage be "properly set, through protracted struggle" and "America could be brought to her knees in 90 days of highly organized fierce fighting, sabotage and a massive firestorm."

10. The persistence of such misunderstandings well after the end of the BPM is apparent in Stanford's (1986, p. 72) reporting of Williams's praise of Giap's prosecution of Tet, citing this as support for a similar strategy in the BPM. While Tet was a propaganda victory for the North Vietnamese Army (NVA) it was a military defeat—a strategic and tactical miscalculation of the NVA, which Giap may have opposed (Pribbenow, 2008). It failed because it violated the principle of mass, underestimated U.S. ability to deploy forces across an extended front, and failed to generate the uprisings in the South that it sought. Tet decimated the NLF's fighting capacity in the South that it had spent decades building, yet BPM revolutionists perpetuate a view of Tet as a military rather than a political victory.

11. Williams's argument—adopted by RAM—that the proximity of blacks to whites in the United States was an impediment to whites employing their most destructive weapons against black revolutionaries is as accurate as it is irrelevant. Blacks, as a racial minority, are easily differentiated from whites and isolated, and their concentration in the Black Belt made this even less difficult.

12. RAM made specific pleas to black troops in Vietnam, such as in its 1965 "Message from RAM (Revolutionary Action Movement) the Black Liberation Front of the U.S.A. to Afro-Americans in the United States Racist Imperialist Army" (Stanford, 1986, 212).

13. Brown (2003) capitalizes "Us," as "US."

14. In the SNCC newspaper *The Movement*, Terence Cannon (1966, p. 2) reports from an evening patrolling with the CAP on July 1, 1966, in South Central Los Angeles that the lead car had affixed to its bumper "a black panther with the slogan 'We're the Greatest.'" This was almost a year after the CAP began, yet still before the BPP was founded in Oakland in October 1966.

15. While admonishing "protest" art, Neal (1989, 64) viewed "the motive behind the black aesthetic" as "destruction of the white thing . . . white ideas, and white ways of looking at the world."

16. There are other contradictions between Fanon's and Karenga's arguments. I'm focusing on examples from Karenga's early formulations of kawaida and Fanon's *The Wretched of the Earth*.

17. Mazrui (1986, p. 14) notes that the colonial period was so brief that "[w]hen Jomo Kenyatta was born, Kenya was not yet a crown colony"; yet he "lived right through the period of British rule and outlasted British rule by fifteen years." He asks, "[i]f the entire period of colonialism could be compressed into the life span of a single individual, how deep was the impact?" (p. 14). In contrast, slavery was hardly episodic—it was clearly epic, in Mazrui's terms—its impact was not only enduring but defining. The presence of conflicting views on the impact of African colonialism as compared to American slavery suggests another divergence of the African and American contexts.

18. For Bunche (1941, p. 63), the importance of *irua* to Gikuyu is not only circumcision, "but the entire process of initiation and teaching" that is the basis of "important age-groups." They view "any effort to modify [*irua*] as a vital attack upon the foundations of their society" that "would bring about the collapse of the age-group structure and hence of the social stability of the tribe."

19. Kenyan Luo, the group from which Barack Obama is descended, do not practice circumcision.

20. Malinowski, who wrote the introduction to *Facing Mount Kenya*, "was as scathing of Nordic supremacist theories as he was of ideas of race equality," and his 1931 "A Plea for an Effective Colour Bar" rationalized support for the "colour bar" (Furedi, 1998, p. 93).

21. Ranger subsequently modified some of these claims, but others, such as Berman and Mamdani, would make arguments consistent with Ranger's earlier insights.

22. Probably the best brief treatment of the UCLA shootout is in Brown (2002, pp. 91–99).

23. Given that the internal calendar of Us projected 1971 as the *Year of the Guerrillas* (Brown, 2003, p. 90) and suggested major uprisings throughout the United States in that year, it is unlikely Karenga appreciated the time and effort needed to organize the uprisings the BPM revolutionists envisioned.

24. On *The Lumpen*, see Vincent (2013); also, Elaine Brown recorded a musical album with Motown entitled *Elaine Brown: Until We're Free*.

25. The final point (# 10) of the original BPP platform of 1966 advocates, "*as our major political objective, a United Nations-supervised plebiscite to be held throughout the black colony.*"

26. See Huey Newton's "To the Republic of New Africa: September 13, 1969," in Newton (1995).

27. Brown (2003, p. 114) adds that this view permeated the party and is reflected in the BPP's "most elaborate statement on the subject by Linda Harrison entitled 'On Cultural Nationalism.'"

28. According to Kathleen Cleaver (2001, p. 125), Matilaba (aka Tarika Lewis), one of the earliest women members of the BPP, also published drawings in the BPP newspaper along with Douglas. Teemer (aka Akinsanya Kambon) was another prominent BPP artist.

29. Bukhari (2010, p. 56) concludes: "Thus, there were three basic evils that had to be confronted: male chauvinism, female passivity, and ultrafemininity (the 'I'm only a woman' syndrome)."

30. These changes were motivated not only by Brown's superficial and often selective feminism but by the Party's turn to local electoral politics and the decorum that participation in such a forum necessitates.

31. In this practice, the BPP was not unlike other leftist organizations such as the major white leftist organization, SDS (see Barber, 2008).

32. Alkebulan (2007, 123) notes that the Son of Man Temple was the BPP's "church in Oakland," "a place of worship" intended to show "how a church should be involved in the community." It sponsored survival programs and was a forum for community organizers and speakers (p. 123).

33. Huey Newton (1995, pp. 105–106) stated that "[w]e now see the Black capitalist as having a similar relationship to the Black community as the national (native) bourgeoisie have to the people in national wars of decolonization," which is similar to the claims of both Cruse and Haywood (among others).

34. Unlike that in the BPP, SDS' lumpenism was motivated by its white revolutionists' privileged view of their "role" in the movements of the 1960s, which led the group to bestow leadership on itself and vanguardism on its preferred black group(s) (declaring that it was the BPP), its advocacy of wanton and fruitless violence by its white members, which often led to brutal recriminations by police on blacks such as resulted from the "Days of Rage" in Chicago, which led to police reprisals against Chicago's black communities after the white radicals left town, scorching the

political climate prior to the police murder of Illinois BPP leaders Fred Hampton and Mark Clark. SDS' internecine conflicts on the issue of its use of violence resulted in its members blowing themselves up in the detonation of their "bomb factory" in New York, which killed Diane Oughtton, Terry Robbins, and Ted Gold. Upon transforming into the Weathermen/Weather Underground, Bernadine Dohrn endorsed Charles Manson's white racist-inspired attack of "pigs" in the infamous Tate-LaBianca murders. Sexism, epitomized in the policies and statements of leaders such as Mark Rudd, was rampant in the group as well (see Barber, 2008).

35. Notwithstanding prominent individual examples such as Bob Zellner and Marilyn Buck.

36. Assata Shakur (1987, p. 267) asserts that "without a truly internationalist component nationalism was reactionary," but this is ahistorical with respect to the development of black nationalism in the United States since it has had an "international" component from its inception, as outlined in chapter 2.

37. Fila-Bakabadio (2018) demonstrates that Cleaver's understanding of Congolese politics was grossly uninformed and his thesis on the convergence of Congolese Marxism and the BPP's revolutionism largely incorrect.

38. On the typology of gangs, see Henderson & Leng (1999) and Taylor (1990, 1993).

39. For a discussion of the impact of violence in the BPP, see Curtis Austin (2006).

40. Forbes (2006) admitted to attempted murder of the witness to Newton's killing of Smith. Elaine Brown characterized Forbes's book containing his admission as "unadulterated truth" (p. xi).

41. In a recent popular culture example, if we compare the invective directed at the gangsta rap group NWA's release of "Fuck Tha Police" in 1988—even by activists—to the much greater receptivity for the song among activists in the context of #BLM decades later, one can appreciate Locke's contention regarding transvaluation and transposition of values.

42. This analysis focuses on activist black nationalist groups of the BPM, so it doesn't include non-activist groups of the era such as the NOI.

Chapter 7. Republic of New Africa, League of Revolutionary Black Workers

1. Karenga suggested the name "Imadi" to Richard, who confused the "d" sound in Swahili with an "r." He preferred "Imari" to "Imadi," and retained it as his name for the rest of his life.

2. New Africans emphasize collectives over individuals; so they capitalize the "w" in "We" and use a lowercase "i" for the personal pronoun, I.

3. Obadele notes that "Section Five says: The Congress shall have power to enforce, by appropriate legislation, the provisions of this article" (p. 28).

4. This policy was not a result of Karenga's influence directly, since he had been removed from his post as Minister of Culture in the aftermath of the UCLA shootout, and probably didn't result from Baraka either since CAP had rejected many of the sexist "traditions" associated with kawaida.

5. His son, Chokwe Antar Lumumba, eventually succeeded him as mayor of Jackson.

6. For a recent example, Tarana Burke, founder of the #MeToo movement, reportedly was associated with the MXGM.

7. In Detroit, Rosa Parks aligned with black nationalists. She praised Malcolm X, supported the FNP, and, following the Detroit Rebellion, worked with the RNA and the LRBW on issues of police brutality, serving on the people's tribunal investigating the police murders at the Algiers Motel (see Hersey, 1968). She worked to free political prisoners Joan Little and Gary Tyler well after the BPM.

8. The Detroit Rebellion resulted in forty-three dead, more than one thousand injured, over seven thousand arrests, and over two thousand buildings destroyed (Sugrue, 1996).

9. None of the white Detroit policemen (Ronald August, Robert Paille, David Senak) or the white Michigan National Guardsmen (Mortimer J. LeBlanc) were convicted of these killings—even those who admitted killing their black victim(s).

10. Georgakas (2002) notes that "[w]ith one exception, the first Dodge wildcat strike was not reported nationally. The exception was the *Wall Street Journal*."

11. Some LRBW members maintain that if the ELRUM strike had lasted another day that it would have shut down Chrysler's car production, since Eldon was its only axle plant in the United States.

12. The League initially published a newsletter, *The Spear*, but *ICV* became its official newspaper.

13. Cockrel remained widely popular after the League folded; he was elected to the city council and was the heir apparent to Mayor Coleman Young before his untimely death in 1989.

14. For example, after CBS reporter Joe Weaver refused to leave Watson's office after being denied an interview, he claimed he'd been accosted. His bogus charges were thrown out of court (Georgakas & Surkin, 1975).

15. One might argue that intellectuals are more likely to be petite bourgeoisie and workers proletarian, but this is still a procrustean fit to the reality of black Detroiters during the BPM.

16. The key is *full-time* work because managers colluded with the white unions to schedule the hiring and firing of black workers so that they would not secure the benefits of full-time employment.

17. Conversations with the author.

18. Conversations with the author.

19. James and Grace Lee Boggs's (1974) analysis of twentieth-century revolutions provided the kind of accessible intellectual presentation and synthesis that was often missing from BPM discourse.

20. The LRBW would need to suppress the atheism of Marxism to organize Southern blacks.

21. Since the Vietnam War had undermined popular support for the U.S. military, even the aging Eisenhower might not have been able to play such a role; regardless, he died in March 1969.

22. Operation Dixie was the failed CIO campaign to unionize the South from 1946 to 1953, which targeted twelve Southern states, focusing mainly on the textile industry; but after outlays of one million dollars and the deployment of more than two hundred organizers, it could not overcome the racism of Southern white workers, even though unionization promised to increase their wages, or that of white business owners and law enforcement, who were committed to the maintenance of Jim Crow and the cheap labor supply that it ensured. The passage of the Taft-Hartley Act, competition from the AFL, red baiting, and the rise of the Dixiecrats also contributed to its defeat (see Griffith, 1988).

Chapter 8. CAP, Shrine of the Black Madonna/Pan-African Orthodox Christian Church

1. Cruse discusses BARTS in *Crisis*. For another perspective, see Goose (2004), especially his discussion of Yuri Kochiyama's notes from Cruse's course in "Cultural Philosophy" at the school.

2. Baraka (1984, 255) drew on Cabral to explain: "Cabral . . . said that the African petty bourgeoisie, because they were too often exposed only to the master's culture and history, when they become radicalized want to identify with things African as much as possible. This was . . . my problem and Karenga's US was a perfect vehicle for working out the guilt of the overintegrated" (p. 255).

3. Woodard (1999) suggests that in addressing these issues that Baraka "modernized" black nationalism, but this is misleading. Baraka was institutionalizing aspects of Malcolm's Charter of the OAAU.

4. The presidential election of 1964 was a realigning election which saw a majority of blacks vote Democratic, following Johnson's support of civil rights legislation, while more Southern whites voted Republican, following the white supremacist Goldwater, who opposed major civil rights legislation. Nixon would successfully appeal to the latter in his Southern strategy of 1968—made difficult by Wallace's third party candidacy—and even more so in 1972.

5. These represented the Congressional BEOs—except Senator Edward Brooke (R-Mass.), who did not join the CBC—the number of BEOs at the state, county, and municipal levels was about 1,500 at the CBC's founding. No less influential were black mayors of major cities, such as Cleveland's Carl Stokes, Detroit's Coleman Young, Atlanta's Maynard Jackson, and Los Angeles's Tom Bradley.

6. The language of both proposals would be changed by the steering committee, but the "compromise language" received less press attention than the initial language (Smith, 1996, pp. 49–50).

7. Even issues such as women's reproductive rights found splits among blacks who viewed it not only in terms of women's rights but as promoting reductions in black births. During the NBPA, Smith (1996, p. 302) notes that "Yvonne Day, Chair

of Gary's Committee on the Status of Women sought to have the convention go on record in favor of legalization of abortion. It never came to [a] vote" because "the male leadership (including Jesse Jackson)" "roundly condemned" it "as genocide."

8. Smith (1996: pp. 70–71) casts greater blame on Baraka for the failure of the NBPA:

> To the extent that this project had any chance to beat the historical odds and endure it was destroyed by the leadership role of Baraka. His authoritarian style of leadership, his taste for rhetorical excess and bombast and his proclivity for ideological oscillation doomed the project from the outset. How could it survive the adoption, by the principal proponent of unity without uniformity, a rigidly exclusive and dogmatic ideology such as scientific socialism. . . . This thoroughly utopian ideology predictably would foreclose any possibility of unity with the black establishment but also with large parts of the nationalist community as well. And the very abruptness of this ideological flip-flop suggests a utopian mind-set manifestly unsuited for leadership of all but the most sectarian groups.

9. In 1968, Mao stated that "[t]he Black masses and the masses of white working people in the United States have common interests and common objectives to struggle for"; and that "[r]acial discrimination in the United States is a product of the colonialist and imperialist system. The contradiction between the Black masses in the United States and the U.S. ruling circles is a class contradiction."

10. Given its controversial positions on the issue of black self-determination in the aftermath of black urbanization, as well as its rightist position on the busing crisis in Boston (RU argued that the issue in the crisis was busing not racism), the radical group had been charged with varying degrees of "white chauvinism" and racism by other leftists (see Elbaum, 2002, pp. 186–189). The group became the Revolutionary Communist Party, which split in 1978, and its leader, Bob Avakian, went into exile.

11. If black power could be labeled conservative given Nixon's advocacy or cooptation of black power as black capitalism, as some Marxists argued, then what did it say about Maoism that Mao sought and achieved an accommodation with Nixon? Just as troubling was Mao's relationship with Zairean dictator Mobutu Sese Seko who was not only a puppet of the United States, France, and Belgium, but was complicit in the assassination of Lumumba and friendly with the apartheid regime of South Africa. Mao supported the FNLA, which was supported by Mobutu, and UNITA, which was supported by apartheid South Africa and the United States.

12. In poetic irony, forty years later, after winning the Newark mayor's race in 2014, Baraka's son mayor-elect Ras Baraka appointed former mayor Kenneth Gibson to his transition team.

13. In a broadside to Oklahoma State Representative Hanna Atkins, who resigned her post as treasurer in the NBPA citing the undesirability of serving in a

leadership position with a "scientific socialist," Baraka replied: "I ask why Hanna Atkins can be in the Democratic Party with [Alabama] Governor Wallace and she can't be here with me" (Smith, 1996, p. 306). Baraka contended that his turn to Marxism did not preclude the feasibility of the united front approach of the NBPA, insisting that

> [o]nly ignorant persons, tools or representatives of imperialism would seek to limit that front or try to put people out of the Assembly for the reason that they were communists or socialists as some petit bourgeois black elected officials had tried to do (to me). The absurdity of this, of course, was that these questionable patriots belong to political parties that feature George Wallace and James Eastland on one hand or Ronald Reagan and Nelson Rockefeller on the other. . . . Black elected officials are not resigning from these parties because of those fascists. (pp. 69–70)

14. Cleage's approach had matured since the time he advocated "an organized and deliberate strategy of chaos," which was "a deliberately conceived plan to tear up those things from which we are excluded in these United States—it either accepts us in it, or we'll do everything possible to tear it up" (Dillard, 2007, p. 279).

15. Arguably the most widely celebrated holiday in the United States, Thanksgiving, is a harvest festival.

16. This is similar to Du Bois's (1969, p. 12) discussion of slave revolts in *Black Reconstruction*.

17. That King's children held their mother Coretta Scott King's funeral in such a church—even as their daughter and pastor Rev. Bernice King heaped praised on the church's pastor as one in her father's tradition—demonstrates how a personal narrative, even one as profound as King's can be manipulated in a way that is antithetical to the original intent of the narrative's author.

18. Cleage's *Black Slate* was influential in the election of Detroit city council members, two U.S. Congresswomen, and a subsequent, albeit disgraced, Detroit mayor, Kwame Kilpatrick, who was forced to resign amid scandal and is serving a lengthy prison sentence for federal corruption charges.

Conclusion

1. Among black elected officials, this discourse became subsumed and redirected into a call for full employment, as in the Humphrey-Hawkins Act. The essential aspects of the act were substantially watered down when passed by the Carter administration (Smith, 1996).

2. #BlackLivesMatter is the most famous of the hashtag (#) activism prevalent in the era of social media; and although focused mainly on police killings of unarmed blacks, was created by three African American women, Alicia Garza, Opal Tometi, and Patrice Cullors, in the aftermath of the acquittal of a white Latino civilian, George Zimmerman, in his fatal shooting of unarmed black teenager Trayvon Martin.

3. Beyond the NFL protests, two of the most prominent examples of hashtag activism are #MeToo begun by African American activist Tarana Burke, and #SayHerName initiated after the controversial alleged suicide of black motorist Sandra Bland in police custody. The former emerged to mobilize against rapists, sexual assaulters, and sexual harassers and to support survivors; and the latter is a response to the privileging of male victims of police terrorism on social media and among protest organizations, and focused on the women and girls killed by racist, classist, homophobic and/or transphobic police forces, "hate groups," and individual civilians. Both are also aimed at supporting survivors and their families and "self-care" for activists themselves.

4. On the UPJM, see Upchurch (1996); also see Henderson & Leng, 1999; Taylor, 1990.

References

Ahmad, M. (2007). *We will return in the whirlwind: Black radical organizations, 1960–1975*. Chicago: Charles Kerr.
Ali, O. (2008). *In the balance of power: Independent black politics and third-party movements in the United States*. Athens: Ohio University Press.
Alkebulan, P. (2007). *Surviving pending revolution: The history of the Black Panther Party*. Tuscaloosa: University of Alabama Press.
Allen, E. (1979). Dying from the inside: The decline of the League of Revolutionary Black Workers. In D. Cluster (Ed.), *They should have served that cup of coffee* (pp. 71–109). Boston: South End Press.
Anderson, C. (2003). *Eyes off the prize*. Princeton: Princeton University Press.
Aptheker, H. (1966). *Nat Turner's slave revolt*. New York: Humanities Press.
Arnold, M. (1869). *Culture and anarchy*. London: Smith, Elder.
Asante, M. (1980). *Afrocentricity: The theory of social change*. Buffalo: Amulefi.
Ashbaugh, C. (1976). *Lucy Parsons: American revolutionary*. Chicago: Charles H. Kerr.
Austin, C. (2006). *Up against the wall: Violence in the making and unmaking of the Black Panther Party*. Fayetteville: University of Arkansas Press.
Baker, G. (1970). My fight is for freedom: Uhuru, libertad, halauga, and harambee! In J. Bracey, A. Meier, & E. Rudwick (Eds.), *Black nationalism in America* (pp. 506–508). New York: Bobbs-Merrill.
Baraka, A. (1984). *The autobiography of Leroi Jones/Amiri Baraka*. New York: Freundlich Books.
———. (1963). *Blues people: Negro music in white America*. New York: William Morrow.
———. (2012). Manning Marable's Malcolm X book. In Herb Boyd et al. (Eds.), *By any means necessary: Responses to Marable's biography of Malcolm X* (pp. 68–75). Chicago: Third World Press.
———, ed. (1972). *African congress: A documentary of the first modern Pan-African Congress*. New York: William Morrow.
Barber, D. (2008). *A hard rain fell: SDS and why it failed*. Jackson: University Press of Mississippi.
Beal, F. (1970). Double jeopardy: To be black and female. In Toni Cade Bambara (Ed.), *The black woman: An anthology* (pp. 109–122). New York: New American Library.

Bellah, R. (1967). Civil religion in America. *Daedalus* 96 (Winter), 1–21.
Bennett, L. (2000). *Forced into glory: Abraham Lincoln's white dream*. Chicago: Johnson.
Berlin, I., Reidy, J., & Rowland, L., eds. (1983). *The black military experience: A documentary history of emancipation, 1861–1867*. New York: Cambridge University Press.
Berman, B. (1998). Ethnicity, patronage, and the African state: The politics of uncivil nationalism. *African Affairs* 97 (388), 305–341.
Berry, M. F. (2005). *My face is black is true: Callie House and the struggle for ex-slave reparations*. New York: Alfred A. Knopf.
Biggart, J. (1987). Bukharin and the origins of the "proletarian culture" debate. *Soviet Studies* 39 (2) (April), 229–246.
Billings, D. (1990). Religion as opposition: A Gramscian analysis. *American Journal of Sociology* 96 (1) (July), 1–31.
Blackmon, D. (2008). *Slavery by another name: The re-enslavement of black Americans from the Civil War to World War II*. New York: Doubleday.
Blum, E. (2007). *W. E. B. Du Bois, American prophet*. Philadelphia: University of Pennsylvania Press.
Boas, F. (1911). *The mind of primitive man*. New York: Macmillan.
Bodley, J. (1994). *Cultural anthropology: Tribes, states, and the global system*. Mountain View: Mayfield.
Boggs, G. L. (1998). *Living for change: An autobiography*. Minneapolis: University of Minnesota Press.
Boggs, J. (1963). *The American revolution: Pages from a Negro worker's notebook*. New York: Monthly Review Press.
———. (1969). *Manifesto for a black revolutionary party*. Philadelphia: Pacesetter's.
———. (1970). *Racism and the class struggle: Further pages from a black worker's notebook*. New York: New York University Press.
———. (1976). Introduction to the fifth printing. In James Boggs, *Manifesto for a black revolutionary party* (pp. ii–viii). Philadelphia: Pacesetter's.
Boggs, J., & Boggs, G. L. (1974). *Revolution and evolution in the twentieth century*. New York: Monthly Review Press.
———. (1982). *Manifesto for an American revolutionary party*. Philadelphia: National Organization for an American Revolution.
Boyd, H. (2017). *Black Detroit: A people's history of self-determination*. New York: Amistad.
Boyd, M. (2003). *Wrestling with the muse: Dudley Randall and the Broadside Press*. New York: Columbia University Press.
Bracey, J., Meier, A., & Rudwick, E., eds. (1970). *Black nationalism in America*. New York: Bobbs-Merrill.
Breen, P. (2003). A prophet in his own land. Support for Nat Turner and his rebellion within Southampton's black community. In Kenneth Greenberg (Ed.), *Nat Turner: A slave rebellion in history and memory* (pp. 103–118). New York: Oxford University Press.
Breitman, G., ed. (1965). *Malcolm X speaks*. New York: Grove Press.

Brotz, H., ed. (1992). *Negro social and political thought, 1850–1920: Representative texts*. New York: Basic Books.
Brown, E. (1992). *A taste of power: A black woman's story*. New York: Pantheon.
Brown, S. (2003). *Fighting for US: Maulana Karenga, the US organization, and black cultural nationalism*. New York: New York University Press.
Buck, C. (2005). *Alain Locke: Faith & philosophy*. Los Angeles: Kalimat Press.
Bukhari, S. (1993). On the question of sexism within the Black Panther Party. *The Black Panther 1*, 2 (Fall/Winter), 4.
———. 2010. *The war before: The true life story of becoming a Black Panther, keeping the faith in prison, and fighting for those left behind*. New York: The Feminist Press at City University of New York.
Bunche R. (1941). The Irua ceremony among the Kikuyu of Kiambu District, Kenya. *Journal of Negro History 26*, 46–65.
Butcher, M. J. (1956). *The Negro in American culture*. New York: Alfred A. Knopf.
Cabral, A. (1972). *Revolution in Guinea: Selected texts by Amilcar Cabral*. New York: Monthly Review.
———. (1973). *Return to the source*. New York: African Information Service.
Cannon, T. (1966). A night with the Watts Community Alert Patrol. *The Movement 2*, 7: 1, 3.
Carlisle, R. (1975). *The roots of black nationalism*. Port Washington, NY: Kennikat Press.
Carson, C. (1981). *In struggle: SNCC and the black awakening of the 1960s*. Cambridge: Harvard University Press.
Clark, A., Dantzler, P., & Nickels, A. (2018). Black lives matter: (Re)Framing the next wave of black liberation. In Patrick Coy (Ed.), *Research in social movements, conflicts and change, Volume 42* (pp. 145–172). Bingley, UK: Emerald Publishing.
Clark Hine, D., & McCluskey, J. Jr., eds. (2012). *The black Chicago renaissance*. Champaign: University of Illinois Press.
Cleage, A. B. (1972). *Black Christian nationalism: New directions for the black church*. New York: Morrow.
Cleaver, E. (1974). Culture and revolution: Their synthesis in Africa. In R. Chrisman & N. Hare (Eds.), *Pan Africanism* (pp. 75–79). Indianapolis: Bobbs-Merrill.
Cleaver, K. (2001). Women, power, and revolution. In K. Cleaver & G. Katsiaficas (Eds.), *Liberation, imagination, and the Black Panther Party* (pp. 123–127). New York: Routledge.
Cobb, J., ed. (2002). *The essential Harold Cruse: A reader*. New York: Palgrave.
Cooper, A. J. (1892). *A voice from the South by a black woman of the South*. Xenia: Aldine.
Creel, M. W. (1988). *A peculiar people: Slave religion and community-culture among the Gullahs*. New York: New York University Press.
Crenshaw, K. (1989). Demarginalizing the intersection of race and sex: A black feminist critique of antidiscrimination doctrine, feminist theory, and antiracist politics. *University of Chicago Legal Forum*, 139–167.
Crummell, A. (1898). *Civilization: The primal need of the race*. Washington, DC: American Negro Academy.

Cruse, H. (1967). *The crisis of the Negro intellectual.* New York: William Morrow.
———. (1968). *Rebellion or revolution?* New York: William Morrow.
———. (1971a). Black and white: Outlines of the next stage (part one). *Black World* (January), 19–71.
———. (1971b). Black and white: Outlines of the next stage (part two). *Black World* (January), 4–31.
———. (1971c). Black and white: Outlines of the next stage (part three). *Black World* (January), 9–40.
———. (1974a). The Little Rock National Black Political Convention. *Black World* 23 (October), 10–17, 82–88.
———. (1974b). The National Black Political Convention. *Black World* (November), 4–21.
Cuffee, P. (1970 [1817]). Letter to Robert Finley. In B. John, A. Meier, & E. Rudwick (Eds.), *Black nationalism in America* (pp. 44–45). New York: Bobbs-Merrill.
Davidson, B. (1971). *The liberation of Guinea: Aspects of an African revolution.* New York: Penguin.
Dawson, M. (2001). *Black visions: The roots of contemporary African-American political ideologies.* Chicago: University of Chicago Press.
Dillard, A. (2007). *Faith in the city: Preaching radical social change in Detroit.* Ann Arbor: University of Michigan Press.
Doss, E. (2001). Women, power, and revolution. In K. Cleaver & G. Katsiaficas (Eds.), *Liberation, imagination, and the Black Panther Party* (pp. 175–187). New York: Routledge.
Douglass, F. (1855). *My bondage, my freedom.* New York: Miller, Orton, & Mulligan.
Drake, S. C., & Cayton, H. Jr. (1945). *Black metropolis: A study of Negro life in a Northern city.* New York: Harcourt, Brace and Company.
Draper, T. (1970). *The rediscovery of black nationalism.* New York: Viking.
Du Bois (1899). *The Philadelphia Negro.* Philadelphia: University of Pennslyvania Press.
———. (1903). *The Negro church.* Atlanta: Atlanta University Press.
———. (1915). The African roots of war. *Atlantic Monthly 115,* 707–714.
———. (1920). *Darkwater: Voices from within the veil.* New York: Harcourt, Brace and Howe.
———. (1933). Karl Marx and the Negro. *The Crisis 40* (3) (March), 55–56.
———. (1961 [1903]). *The souls of Black folk.* New York: Fawcett.
———. (1969 [1935]). *Black reconstruction in the United States, 1860–1880.* New York: Atheneum.
———. (1985 [1936]). The Negro and social reconstruction. In H. Aptheker (Ed.), *Against racism: Unpublished essays, papers, addresses, 1887–1961 (pp. 103–159).* Amherst: University of Massachusetts Press.
———. (1991 [1940]). *Dusk of dawn: An essay toward an autobiography of a race concept.* New Brunswick, NJ: Transaction.
——— (1995 [1959]). Crusader without violence. In D. Lewis (Ed.), *W. E. B. Du Bois: A reader* (pp. 361–362). New York: Henry Holt.

———. (1995a [1933]). Marxism and the Negro problem. In D. Lewis (Ed.), *W. E. B. Du Bois: A reader* (pp. 538–544). New York: Henry Holt.
———. (1995b [1933]). The Negro college. In D. Lewis (Ed.), *W. E. B. Du Bois: A reader* (pp. 68–75). New York: Henry Holt.
———. (1995c [1931]). The Negro and communism. In D. Lewis (Ed.), *W. E. B. Du Bois: A reader* (pp. 583–593). New York: Henry Holt.
———. (1995d [1933]). Criteria of Negro art. In D. Lewis (Ed.), *W. E. B. Du Bois: A reader* (pp. 509–515). New York: Henry Holt.
———. (1996 [1897]). The conservation of races. In W. Moses (Ed.), *Classical black nationalism: From the American revolution to Marcus Garvey* (pp. 228–240). New York: New York University Press.
Dudziak, M. (2000). *Cold war civil rights*. Princeton: Princeton University Press.
Egerton, D. (1993). *Gabriel's rebellion*. Chapel Hill: University of North Carolina Press.
———. (2003). Nat Turner in a hemispheric context. In K. Greenberg (Ed.), *Nat Turner: A slave rebellion in history and memory* (pp. 134–147). New York: Oxford University Press.
———. (2004). *He shall go out free: The lives of Denmark Vesey*. New York: Rowman & Littlefield.
Edwards, H. (1969). *The revolt of the black athlete*. New York: Free Press.
Elbaum, M. (2002). *Revolution in the air: Sixties radicals turn to Lenin, Mao, and Che*. New York: Verso.
Epstein, B. (1991). *Political protest and cultural revolution: Nonviolent direct action in the 1970s and 1980s*. Berkeley: University of California Press.
Essien-Udom, E. (1964). *Black nationalism—A search for identity in America*. New York: Dell.
Esteban, J. & Ray, D. (2008). Polarization, fractionalization and conflict. *Journal of Peace Research* 45 (2), 163–182.
Evans, C. (2007). W. E. B. Du Bois: Interpreting religion and the problem of the Negro church. *Journal of the American Academy of Religion* 75 (2), 261–297.
Fanon, F. (1968). *The wretched of the earth*. New York: Grove Press.
Fenn, R. (1977). The relevance of Bellah's "civil religion" thesis to a theory of secularization. *Social Science History* 1 (4) (Summer), 502–517.
Fila-Bakabadio, S. (2018). Against the empire: The Black Panthers in Congo, insurgent cosmopolitanism and the fluidity of revolutions. *African Identities* 16 (2), 146–160.
Flournoy, H. W., ed. (1890). *Calendar of Virginia state papers and other manuscripts, Vol. 9*. Richmond, VA.
Foner, P., ed. (1970). *The Black Panthers speak*. New York: Grove.
Forbes, F. (2006). *Will you die with me? My life and the Black Panther Party*. New York: Washington Square Press.
Franklin, V. P. (1984). *Black self-determination: A cultural history of African-American resistance*. 1st Ed. New York: Lawrence Hill.
———. (1992). *Black self-determination: A cultural history of African-American resistance*. 2nd Ed. New York: Lawrence Hill.

Fraser, N. (1999). Another pragmatism: Alain Locke, critical "race" theory, and the politics of culture. In L. Harris (Ed.), *The critical pragmatism of Alain Locke* (pp. 3–20). Lanham, MD: Rowman & Littlefield.
Freeman, D. (1964). Nationalist student conference. *Liberator 4* (7) (July), 18.
Furedi, F. (1998). *The silent war: Imperialism and the changing perception of race.* New Brunswick, NJ: Rutgers University Press.
Garnet, H. H. (1992 [1848]). The past and the present condition, and the destiny of the colored race. In H. Brotz (Ed.), *African-American social and political thought 1850–1920* (pp. 199–202). New Brunswick, NJ: Transaction.
Gellner, E. (1983). *Nations and nationalism.* Ithaca: Cornell University Press.
Genovese, E. (1981). *From rebellion to revolution: Afro-American Slave Revolts in the making of the modern world.* New York: Vintage Books.
Georgakas, D. (2002). Revolutionary struggles of black workers in the 1960s. *International Socialist Review 22* (March–April). Online edition. http://isreview.org/issues/22/black_workers.shtml.
———, & Surkin, M. (1975). *Detroit: I do mind dying.* New York: St. Martin's Press.
Geschwender, J. (1977). *Class, race, and worker insurgency: The League of Revolutionary Black Workers.* New York: Cambridge University Press.
———, & Jeffries, J. (2006). The League of Revolutionary Black Workers. In J. Jeffries (Ed.), *Black power in the belly of the beast* (pp. 135–162). Urbana and Chicago: University of Illinois Press.
Giddings, P. (2008). *Ida, a sword among lions: Ida B. Wells and the campaign against lynching.* New York: HarperCollins.
Gill, A. (2011). Religion and violence: An economic approach. In A. R. Murphy (Ed.), *The Blackwell companion to religion and violence* (pp. 35–49). Malden, MA: Wiley-Blackwell.
Giovanni, N. (1969). Black poems, poseurs and power. *Negro Digest 18* (8) (June), 30–34.
Glattharr, J. (1992). Black glory: The African-American role in Union victory. In G. Boritt (Ed.), *Why the Confederacy lost* (pp. 133–162). New York: Oxford University Press.
Glaude, E., ed. (2002). *Is it nation time? Contemporary essays on black power and black nationalism.* Chicago: University of Chicago Press.
Goldstone, J. (2001). Towards a fourth generation of revolutionary theory. *Annual Review of Political Science 4*, 139–187.
Goose, V. (2004). More than just a politician: Notes on the life and times of Harold Cruse and the origins of black power. In J. Watts (Ed.), *Harold Cruse's The Crisis of the Negro Intellectual reconsidered* (pp. 17–40). New York: Routledge.
Green, D., & Driver, E. (1978). *W. E. B. Du Bois on sociology and the black community.* Chicago: University of Chicago Press.
Greene, H., & Hutchins, H. (2004). *Slave badges and the slave-hire system in Charleston, South Carolina, 1783–1865.* Jefferson, NC: McFarland.
Griffith, B. (1988). *The crisis of American labor: Operation Dixie and the defeat of the CIO.* Philadelphia: Temple University Press.

Guanier, L. (1994). *The tyranny of the majority: Fundamental fairness in representative democracy.* New York: Free Press.
Guevara, E. "Che." (1961). *Guerrilla warfare.* New York: Monthly Review Press.
Hahn, S. (2004). *A nation under their feet.* Cambridge: Harvard University Press.
———. (2009). *The political worlds of slavery and freedom.* Cambridge: Harvard University Press.
Halisi, C., & Mtume, J., eds. (1967). *The quotable Karenga.* Los Angeles: US Organization.
Harcave, S. (1970). *The Russian revolution.* London: Collier Books.
Harris, L. (2004). The great debate: Alain L. Locke vs. W. E. B. Du Bois. *Philosophia Africana* 7 (1) (March), 13–37.
———, ed. (1999). *The critical pragmatism of Alain Locke.* Lanham, MD: Rowman & Littlefield.
———, & Molesworth, C. (2008). *Alain L. Locke: The biography of a philosopher.* Chicago: University of Chicago Press.
Hayes, F., & Jeffries, J. (2006). "Us does not stand for United Slaves!" In J. L. Jeffries (Ed.), *Black power in the belly of the beast* (pp. 67–92). Chicago: University of Illinois Press.
Haywood, H. (1933). The struggle for the Leninist position on the Negro question in the U.S.A. *The Communist* 12 (9) (September), 888–901.
———. (1934a). The theoretical defenders of white chauvinism in the labor movement. In *The Communist Position on the Negro Question* (pp. 29–40). New York: International Publishers.
———. (1934b). *The road to Negro liberation.* New York: Workers' Library Publishers.
———. (1948). *Negro liberation.* New York: International Publishers.
———. (1958). *For a revolutionary position on the Negro question.* Encyclopedia of Anti-Revisionism On-Line. https://www.marxists.org/history/erol/1956-1960/haywood02.htm.
———. (1967). The nation of Islam: An estimate. *Soul Book* 6 (Winter–Spring), 137–144.
———. (1978). *Black Bolshevik: Autobiography of an Afro-American communist.* Chicago: Liberator.
———, & Hall, G. M. (1965/66). The two epochs of nation-development: Is black nationalism a form of classical nationalism? *Soul Book* 4 (Winter), 257–266.
———. (1966). Is the black bourgeoisie the leader of the black liberation movement? *Soul Book* 5 (Summer), 70–75.
Hechter, M. (1975). *Internal colonialism: The Celtic fringe in British national development.* Berkeley: University of California Press.
Henderson, E. (1995). *Afrocentrism and world politics.* Westport, CT: Greenwood.
———. (1996). Black nationalism and rap music. *Journal of Black Studies* 26 (3), 308–339.
———. (1997). The lumpenproletariat as vanguard? *Journal of Black Studies* 28 (2), 171–199.
———. (2000). War, political cycles, and the pendulum thesis: Explaining the rise of black nationalism, 1840–1996. In A. Alex-Assensoh & L. Hanks (Eds.),

Black politics in multiracial America (pp. 337–374). New York: New York University Press.

———. (2012). The toothless pursuit of a revolutionary's truth: Marable's *Malcolm X*. In H. Boyd et al. (Eds.), *By any means necessary: Responses to Marable's biography of Malcolm X* (pp. 163–177). Chicago: Third World Press.

———. (2013a). Body and soul: The Black Panther Party and the fight against medical discrimination (Book Review). *Mobilization 18* (1), 364–365.

———. (2013b). Hidden in plain sight: Racism and international relations theory. *Cambridge Review of International Affairs 26* (1), 71–92.

———. (2015). Slave religion, slave hiring, and the incipient proletarianization of enslaved black labor: Developing Du Bois' thesis on black participation in the Civil War as a revolution. *Journal of African American Studies 19* (2), 192–213.

———. (2017a). The revolution will not be theorised: The "Howard School"'s challenge to white supremacist IR theory. *Millennium 45* (3), 492–510.

———. (2017b). *African realism? International relations theory and Africa's wars in the postcolonial era.* Lanham, MD: Rowman & Littlefield.

———. (2018a). Unintended consequences of cosmopolitanism: Malcolm X, Africa, and revolutionary theorizing in the black power movement in the US. *African Identities 16* (2), 146–160.

———. (2018b). Set the world on fire: Black nationalist women and the global struggle for freedom (Book Review). *The Black Scholar 48* (4), 71–74.

———, & Leng, R. (1999). Reducing intergang conflict: Norms from the interstate system. *Peace & Change 24* (4), 527–555.

Hersey, J. (1968). *The Algiers Motel incident.* New York: Alfred A. Knopf.

Hill, L. (2004). *The Deacons for Defense: Armed resistance and the civil rights movement.* Chapel Hill: University of North Carolina Press.

Hilliard, D., with Cole, L. (1993). *This side of glory: The autobiography of David Hilliard and the story of the Black Panther Party.* Boston: Little, Brown.

Hunt, M. (2009). *Ideology and U.S. foreign policy.* New Haven: Yale University Press.

Hutchinson, J. (1987). *The dynamics of cultural nationalism.* London: Allen and Unwin.

Jackson, K. C. (2019). *Force and freedom: Black abolitionists and the politics of violence.* Pennsylvania: University of Pennsylvaia Press.

Johnson, M. (2001). Denmark Vesey and his co-conspirators. *William and Mary Quarterly 58* (4) (October), 915–976.

Johnston, I. (1995). *Cultural realism.* Princeton: Princeton University Press.

Jones, C. (2011). An end to the neglect of problems of negro women. In C. B. Davies (Ed.), *Claudia Jones, beyond containment: Autobiographical reflections, essays and poems* (pp. 74–85). Oxfordshire, UK: Ayebia Clarke.

Jones, J. (2017). *Goddess of anarchy: The life and times of Lucy Parsons, American radical.* New York: Basic Books.

Joseph, J. (2012). *Panther baby.* Chapel Hill, NC: Algonquin Books.

Kahin, G. (1956). *The Asian-African Conference: Bandung, Indonesia, April 1955* Ithaca: Cornell University Press.

Kadalie, M. (2000). *Internationalism, pan-Africanism, and the struggle of social classes: Raw writings from the notebook of an early 1970s African-American radical activist.* Savannah: One Quest Press.
Karenga, M. (1968). Black art: A rhythmic reality of revolution. *Negro Digest 17* (3) (January), 5–9.
———. (1980). *Kawaida theory: An introductory outline.* Inglewood, CA: Kawaida Publications.
———. (1982). *Introduction to black studies.* Los Angeles: University of Sankore Press.
———. (1988). Black studies and the problematic of paradigm: The philosophical dimension. *Journal of Black Studies 18* (1) (June), 395–414.
———. (1993). *Introduction to black studies*, 2nd Ed. Los Angeles: University of Sankore Press.
———. (2000). *Introduction to black studies*, 3rd Ed. Los Angeles: University of Sankore Press.
———. (2012). The meaning and measure of Malcolm X: Critical remembrance and rightful reading. In H. Boyd et al. (Eds.), *By any means necessary: Responses to Marable's biography of Malcolm X* (pp. 10–26). Chicago: Third World Press.
———. (2015). Kawaida and the current crisis: A philosophy of life, love, and struggle. *Los Angeles Sentinel*, July 30, 2015, p. A6.
Katznelson, I. (1981). *City trenches: Urban politics and the patterning of class in the United States.* New York: Pantheon.
Kaye, A. (2007a). *Joining places.* Chapel Hill: University of North Carolina Press.
———. (2007b). Neighborhoods and Nat Turner: The making of a slave rebel and the unmaking of a slave rebellion. *Journal of the Early Republic 27* (Winter), 705–720.
Kenyatta, J. (1965). *Facing Mount Kenya.* New York: Vintage Books.
Khan-Cullors, P., & bandele, a. (2018). *When they call you a terrorist: A Black Lives Matter memoir.* New York: St. Martin's.
King, M. L. (1986 [1967]). Where do we go from here. In J. Washington (Ed.), *A testament of hope, The essential writings and speeches of Martin Luther King.* San Francisco: HarperCollins.
Koubi, V., & Böhmelt, T. (2014). Grievances, economic wealth, and civil conflict. *Journal of Peace Research 51* (1), 19–33.
Kroeber, A. L., & Kluckhohn, C. (1952). *Culture: A critical review of concepts and definitions.* Cambridge, MA: Peabody Museum.
League of Revolutionary Black Workers. (1970). Constitution of the Dodge Revolutionary Union Movement. In B. John, A. Meier, & E. Rudwick (Eds.), *Black nationalism in America* (pp. 551–555). New York: Bobbs-Merrill.
———. (1997 [1970]). General program (Here's where we're coming from). In W. Van De Burg (Ed.), *Modern black nationalism: From Marcus Garvey to Louis Farrakhan* (pp. 189–190). New York: New York University Press.
Lenin, V. I. (1966a). "Preliminary draft theses on the national and the colonial questions." In *Lenin's collected works, Vol. 31* (April–December 1920), translated by by J. Katzer (pp. 144–151). Moscow: Progress Publishers.

———. (1966b). "On proletarian culture." In *Lenin's collected works, Vol. 31* (April–December 1920), translated by J. Katzer (pp. 316–317). Moscow: Progress Publishers.

———. (1973b). The role and functions of the trade unions under the new economic policy. In *Lenin's collected works, Vol. 33*, translated by D. Skvirsky & G. Hanna (pp. 184–196). Moscow: Progress Publishers.

———. (1973a). On cooperation. In *Lenin's collected works, Vol. 33*, translated by D. Skvirsky & G. Hanna (pp. 467–475). Moscow: Progress Publishers.

———. (1973c). Better fewer, but better. In *Lenin's collected works, Vol. 33*, translated by D. Skvirsky & G. Hanna (pp. 487–502). Moscow: Progress Publishers, 1965.

Lewis, D. (1993). *W. E. B. Du Bois, 1868–1919: Biography of a race*. New York: Henry Holt.

———. (1995). *W. E. B. Du Bois: A reader*. New York: Henry Holt.

———. (2000). *W. E. B. Du Bois, 1919–1963: The fight for equality and the American century*. New York: Henry Holt.

Levine, L. (1977). *Black culture and black consciousness*. New York: Oxford University Press.

Litwack, L. (1980). *Been in the storm so long*. New York: Vintage.

Locke, A. ([1992] 1916). *Race contacts and interracial relations: Lectures on the theory and practice of race*. Edited by J. Stewart. Washington, DC: Howard University Press.

———. (1924). A note on African art. *Opportunity 2* (May), 134–138.

———. (1925a). The new Negro. In A, Locke (Ed.), *The new Negro: Voices of the Harlem Renaissance* (pp. 3–16). New York: Albert & Charles Boni.

———. (1925b). The new spirituals. In A. Locke (Ed.), *The new Negro: Voices of the Harlem Renaissance* (pp. 199–210). New York: Albert & Charles Boni.

———. (1951[1927]). The high cost of prejudice. In H. Aptheker (Ed.), *A documentary history of the Negro people in the United States, Vol. 3, From the N.A.A.C.P. to the New Deal* (pp. 553–564). New York: Citadel.

———. (1928). Art or propaganda. *Harlem 1* (November), 12–13.

———. (1932). Unity through diversity: A Baha'i principle. *The Baha'i World: A Biennial International Record 4*, 372–374.

———. (1943). *World view on race and democracy: A study guide in human group relations*. Chicago: American Library Association.

———. (1989). The concept of race as applied to social culture. In L. Harris (Ed.), *The philosophy of Alain Locke: Harlem Renaissance and beyond* (pp. 187–200). Philadelphia: Temple University Press.

———. (1992). *Race contacts and interracial relations*. Edited by J. Stewart. Washington, DC: Howard University Press.

Logan, R. (1954). *The Negro in American life and thought: The Nadir, 1877–1901*. New York: Dial Press.

Madhubuti, H. (1973). *From plan to planet: The need for Afrikan minds and institutions*. Chicago: Third World Press.

———. (1974). The latest purge: The attack on black nationalism and pan-Afrikanism by the New Left, the sons and daughters of the Old Left. *The Black Scholar 6* (1), 43–56.

———. (1978). *Enemies: The clash of races*. Chicago:Third World Press.
Mally, L. (1990). *Culture of the future: The proletkult movement in revolutionary Russia*. Berkeley: University of California Press.
Mamdani, M. (1996). *Citizen and subject: Contemporary Africa and the legacy of late colonialism*. Princeton: Princeton University Press.
Maoz, Z., & Henderson, E. (in press). *Scriptures, shrines, saints, and scapegoats: Religious sources of conflict and cooperation in world politics*. Ann Arbor: University of Michigan Press.
Marable, M. (2011). *Malcolm X: A life of reinvention*. New York: Viking.
Martin, J. (2004). *Divided mastery: Slave hiring in the American South*. Cambridge: Harvard University Press.
Marx, K. (1969 [1852]). *The eighteenth brumaire of Louis Bonaparte*. New York: International Publishers.
———. (1982 [1843]). *Critique of Hegel's "Philosophy of Right."* Translated by A. Jolin & J. O'Malley. New York: Cambridge University Press.
Mast, R. (1994). *Detroit lives*. Philadelphia: Temple University Press.
Mazrui, A. (1986). The African state as a political refugee: Institutional collapse and human development. *Journal of Refugee Law* (Special Issue) 7, 21–36.
McCurry, S. (2010). *Confederate reckoning*. Cambridge: Harvard University Press.
McFadden, R. (1973). 4 Panthers admit guilt in slaying. *New York Times*, May 22, p. 1.
McPherson, J. (1991). *Abraham Lincoln and the second American revolution*. New York: Oxford University Press.
———. (1993). *The Negro's Civil War*. New York: Vintage.
McRae, E. Gillespie. (2018). *Mothers of massive resistance: White women and the politics of white supremacy*. New York: Oxford University Press.
Meier, A., ed. (1973). *The transformation of activism*. New Brunswick, NJ: Transaction.
———. (1991). *Negro thought in America, 1880–1915*. Ann Arbor: University of Michigan Press.
———, Rudwick, E., & Broderick, F., eds. (1971). *Black protest thought in the twentieth century*, 2nd Ed. New York: Macmillan.
Miller, F. (1975). *The search for a black nationality: Black emigration and colonization 1787–1863*. Urbana: University of Illinois Press.
Moon, H. (1948). *Balance of power: The Negro vote*. Garden City, NY: Doubleday.
Moses, W. (1978). *The golden age of black nationalism, 1850–1925*. Hamden, CT: Archon Books.
———. (1989). *Alexander Crummell: A study of civilization and discontent*. New York: Oxford University Press.
———. (1990). *The wings of Ethiopia*. Ames: Iowa State University Press.
———. (1993). *Black messiahs and Uncle Toms*. University Park: Pennsylvania State University Press.
———. (1996). *Classical black nationalism: From the American Revolution to Marcus Garvey*. New York: New York University Press.
———. (1998). *Afrotopia: The roots of African American popular history*. New York: Cambridge University Press.

———. (2019). *Jefferson: A modern Prometheus.* Cambridge: Cambridge University Press.

Mullin, G. (1972). *Flight and rebellion: Slave resistance in eighteenth century Virginia.* New York: Oxford University Press.

Murphy, R. (1986). *Culture and social anthropology: An overture*, 2nd Ed. Englewood Cliffs, NJ: Prentice-Hall.

Neal, L. (1989). *Visions of a liberated future: Black Arts Movement writings.* New York: Thunder's Mouth Press.

Nelson, H. (2006). The Defenders. In J. Jeffries (Ed.), *Black power in the belly of the beast* (pp. 163–184). Urbana: University of Illinois Press.

Newton, H. (1970). An interview with Huey P. Newton. In J. Bracey, A. Meier, & E. Rudwick (Eds.), *Black nationalism in America* (pp. 534–551). New York: Bobbs-Merrill.

———. (1971). Black capitalism reanalyzed. *Black Panther*, Saturday, June 5, p. 9.

———. (1973). *Revolutionary suicide.* New York: Harcourt Brace Jovanovich.

———. (1980). War against the Panthers: A study of repression in America. Unpublished PhD dissertation, University of California, Santa Cruz.

———. (1995). *To die for the people.* New York: Writers and Readers Publishing.

Nightingale, C. (2003). A tale of three global ghettos: How Arnold Hirsch helps us internationalize U.S. urban history. *Journal of Urban History 29* (3) (March), 257–271.

Njeri, A. (1991). *My life with the Black Panther Party.* Oakland: Burning Spear.

Nyerere, J. (1974). *Freedom and development.* New York: Oxford University Press.

Nzongola-Ntalaja, G. (1984). Amilcar Cabral and the theory of the national liberation struggle. *Latin American Perspectives 11* (2) (Spring), 43–54.

Oates, S. (1975). *The fires of jubilee.* New York: Harper & Row.

Obadele, I. (1968). *War in America: The Malcolm X doctrine.* Detroit: The Malcolm X Society.

———. (1970). *Revolution and nation-building: Strategy for building the black nation in America.* Detroit: The House of Songhay.

———. (1972). The struggle is for land. *The Black Scholar 3* (6) (February), 24–36.

———. (1975). *Foundations of the black nation.* Detroit: The House of Songhay.

———. (1986). *A macro level theory of human organization.* Washington, DC: The House of Songhay.

———. (1989). *America the nation-state.* Washington, DC: The House of Songhay.

O'Donovan, S. (2011). William Webb's world. *New York Times* http://opinionator.blogs.nytimes.com/2011/02/18/william-webbs-world/.

Parramore, T. (2003). Covenant in Jerusalem. In K. Greenberg (Ed.), *Nat Turner: A slave rebellion in history and memory* (pp. 58–76). New York: Oxford University Press.

Parsons, L. (1896). On variety. *The Firebrand*, September 27, Free Society.

———. (1884). To tramps, October 4.

Pearson, H. (1994). *The shadow of the Panther: Huey Newton and the price of black power in America.* Reading, MA: Addison-Wesley.

Perkins, W. (1977). Harold Cruse: On the problem of culture and revolution. *Journal of Ethnic Studies* 5 (2) (Summer), 3–25.
Perry, B., ed. (1989). *Malcolm X: The last speeches*. New York: Pathfinder.
Pinkney, A. (1976). *Red, black, and green: Black nationalism in the United States*. Cambridge: Cambridge University Press.
Price, M. (2012). *Dreaming blackness: Black nationalism and African American public opinion*. New York: New York University Press.
Pye, L. (1986). Reassessing the cultural revolution. *China Quarterly* 108 (December), 597–612.
Quarles, B. (1964). *The Negro in the making of America*. New York: Collier Books.
Raboteau, A. (1980). *Slave religion*. Oxford: Oxford University Press.
Rahman, A. (2009). Marching blind: The rise and fall of the Black Panther Party in Detroit. In Y, Williams & J. Lazerow, *Liberated territory: Untold local perspectives on the Black Panther Party* (pp. 181–231). Durham: Duke University Press.
Ranger, T. (1983). The invention of tradition in colonial Africa. In E. Hobsbawm & T. Ranger (Eds.), *The invention of tradition* (pp. 211–262). Cambridge: Cambridge University Press.
Rhodes, J. (1999). *Mary Ann Shadd Cary: The black press and protest in the nineteenth century*. Bloomington: Indiana University Press.
Rice, J. F. (1983). *Up on Madison, down on 75th Street: Part 1: A history of the Illinois Black Panther Party, Part 1*. Evanston, IL: The Committee.
Robertson, D. (1999). *Denmark Vesey*. New York: Alfred A. Knopf.
Robinson, C. (1983). *Black Marxism*. London: Zed Books.
Robinson, D. (2001). *Black nationalism in American politics and thought*. Cambridge: Cambridge University Press.
Robinson, P. (2008). Ralph Bunche and African studies: Reflections on the politics of knowledge. *African Studies Review* 51, 1–16.
Rochon, T. (1998). *Culture moves: Ideas, activism, and changing values*. Princeton: Princeton University Press.
Rodney, W. (1974). *How Europe underdeveloped Africa*. Washington, DC: Howard University Press.
Roediger, D. (2014). *Seizing freedom: Slave emancipation and liberty for all*. London: Zed.
Rothstein, R. (2017). *The color of law: A forgotten history of how our government segregated America*. New York: W. W. Norton.
Sales, W. (1994). *From civil rights to black liberation: Malcolm X and the Organization of Afro-American Unity*. Boston: South End Press.
Schermerhorn, C. (2011). *Money over mastery, family over freedom: Slavery in the antebellum Upper South*. Baltimore: Johns Hopkins University Press.
Semmes, C. (1992). *Cultural hegemony and African American development*. Westport, CT: Greenwood.
Seale, B. (1970). *Seize the time: The story of the Black Panther Party and Huey P. Newton*. New York: Random House.

Shafer, B. (1955). *Nationalism: Myth or reality*. New York: Harcourt, Brace.
Shakur, A. (1987). *Assata: An autobiography*. Chicago: Lawrence-Hill Books.
Sidbury, J. (1997). *Ploughshares into swords: Race, rebellion, and identity in Gabriel's Virginia, 1730–1810*. Cambridge: Cambridge University Press.
———. (2003). Reading, revelation, and rebellion: The textual communities of Gabriel, Denmark Vesey, and Nat Turner. In K. Greenberg (Ed.), *Nat Turner: A slave rebellion in history and memory* (pp. 119–133). New York: Oxford University Press.
Silverman, J. (1988). Mary Ann Shadd and the search for equality. In A. Meier & L. Litwack (Eds.), *Black leaders of the nineteenth century* (pp. 87–100). Urbana: University of Illinois Press.
Simms, R. (2000). Black theology, a weapon in the struggle for freedom: A Gramscian analysis. *Race and Society 2* (2) (February), 165–193.
Smethurst, J. (2005). *The Black Arts Movement*. Chapel Hill: University of North Carolina Press.
Smith, A. (1991). *National identity*. Reno: University of Nevada Press.
Smith, R. (1996). *We have no leaders*. Albany: State University of New York Press.
Smith, S. (1999). *Dancing in the street: Motown and the cultural politics of Detroit*. Cambridge: Harvard University Press.
Snyder, J. (2000). *From voting to violence: Democratization and nationalist conflict*. New York: W. W. Norton.
Sobhe, K. (1982). Education in revolution: Is Iran duplicating the Chinese Cultural Revolution? *Comparative Education 18* (3), 271–280.
Spady, J. (2011). Power and confession: On the credibility of the earliest reports of the Denmark Vesey slave conspiracy. *William and Mary Quarterly 68* (2), 287–304.
Stalin, J. (1913). Marxism and the national question. *Prosveshcheniye*, Nos. 3–5, March–May.
Stanford, M. (1964). We can win. *Black America* (Fall), 1–3, 22.
———. (1966). *The world black revolution*. RAM.
———. (1970). Black guerrilla warfare: Strategy and tactics. *The Black Scholar 2* (3) (November), 30–38.
———. (1971). Black nationalism and the Afro-American student. *The Black Scholar 2* (10) (June), 27–31.
———. (1972). The roots of the pan-African revolution. *The Black Scholar 3* (9) (May), 48–55.
———. (1986). Revolutionary Action Movement: A case study of an urban revolutionary movement in Western capitalist society. MA thesis, Atlanta University.
Starobin, R. (1970). *Industrial slavery in the Old South*. New York: Oxford University Press.
———, ed. (1988). *Blacks in bondage: Letters of American slaves*. New York: Markus Weiner.
Stewart, J. (1992). Introduction. In J. Stewart (Ed.), *Race contacts and interracial relations: Lectures on the theory and practice of race* (pp. xix–lix). Washington, DC: Howard University Press.

Stuckey, S. (1972). Introduction. In S. Stuckey (Ed.), *The ideological origins of black nationalism* (pp. 1–30). Boston: Beacon Press.
———. (1987). *Slave culture*. New York: Oxford University Press.
Sugrue, T. (1996). *The origins of the urban crisis: Race and inequality in postwar Detroit*. Princeton: Princeton University Press.
———. (2018). Motor City: The story of Detroit. The Gilder Lehrman Institute of American History. Retrieved March 2, 2018.
Taylor, C. (1990). *Dangerous society*. East Lansing: Michigan State University Press.
———. (1993). *Girls, gangs, women, and Drugs*. East Lansing: Michigan State University Press.
Taylor, J. (2011). *Black nationalism in the United States: From Malcolm X to Barack Obama*. Boulder: Lynne Reinner.
Taylor, K. (2014). *From #BlackLivesMatter to black liberation*. Chicago: Haymarket.
Thurston, A. (1985). Victims of China's Cultural Revolution: The invisible wounds. *Pacific Affairs 57*, 599–620.
Tometi, O., Garza, A., & Cullors-Brignac, P. (2015). Celebrating MLK Day: Reclaiming our movement legacy. *The Huffington Post*, Updated Mar 20, 2015. https://www.huffingtonpost.com/opal-tometi/reclaiming-our-movement-l_b_6498400.html.
Touré, S. (1974). A dialectical approach to culture. In R. Chrisman & N. Hare, *Pan Africanism* (pp. 52–73). Indianapolis: Bobbs-Merrill.
Tripp, L. 1969. DRUM—Vanguard of the black revolution. *The South End* (Wayne State University Student Newspaper), *27* (62) (January 23, 1969).
Tsang, C-S. (1967). The Red Guards and the Great Proletarian Cultural Revolution. *Comparative Education 3* (3) (June), 195–205.
Tylor, E. (1920 [1871]). *Primitive culture*. New York: J. P. Putnam's Sons.
Upchurch, C. (1996). *Convicted in the womb*. New York: Bantam Books.
Van Deburg, W. (1992). *New day in Babylon, the black power movement and American culture, 1965–1975*, Chicago: University of Chicago Press.
———, ed. (1997). *Modern black nationalism: From Marcus Garvey to Louis Farrakhan*. New York: New York University Press.
Vincent, R. (2013). *Party music: The inside story of the Black Panthers' band and how black power transformed soul music*. Chicago: Lawrence Hill.
Vincent, T. (1971). *Black power and the Garvey movement*. San Francisco: Ramparts.
Vitalis, R. (2013). The midnight ride of Kwame Nkrumah and other fables of Bandung (Ban-doong). *Humanity 4* (2) (Summer), 261–288.
Wade, W. (1987). *The fiery cross: The Ku Klux Klan in America*. New York: Simon & Schuster.
Walker, D. (1830). *An appeal in four articles; Together with a preamble to the colored citizens of the world, but in particular, and very expressly, to those of the United States of America*. 3rd Ed. Boston: David Walker.
Walton, H. (1985). *Invisible politics*. Albany: State University of New York Press.
Washington, B. T. (1995 [1901]). *Up from slavery: An autobiography*. New York: Dover.

Watson, J. (1969). *To the point of production, an interview with John Watson.* Detroit: The Fifth Estate.
Webb, W. (1873). *The history of William Webb, composed by himself.* Detroit: Egbert Heokstra. Reprinted by Academic Affairs Library, University of North Carolina, Chapel Hill.
Wells Barnett, I. B. (1892). *Southern horrors: Lynch law in all its phases.* New York: New York Age.
———. (1895). *The red record: Tabulated statistics and alleged causes of lynching in the United States.*
Whitaker, M. (2018). *Smoketown: The untold story of the other great black renaissance.* New York: Simon & Schuster.
Williams, J. (2013). *From the bullet to the ballot: The Illinois chapter of the Black Panther Party and racial coalition politics in Chicago.* Chapel Hill: University of North Carolina Press.
Williams, R. F. (1964). USA: The potential of a minority revolution. *The Crusader* 5 (4) (May–June), 1–7.
Wilmore, G. (1983). *Black religion and black radicalism.* Maryknoll, NY: Orbis.
Wilson, J. (1979). *Public religion in American culture.* Philadelphia: Temple University Press.
Wintz, C., & Glasrud, B., eds. (2012). *The Harlem Renaissance in the American West.* New York: Routledge.
Woodard, K. (1999). *A nation within a nation: Amiri Baraka (Leroi Jones) and black power politics.* Chapel Hill: University of North Carolina Press.
Wright, R. (1956). *Color curtain: A report on the Bandung Conference.* New York: World.
X, M. (1970 [1964]). The Organization of Afro-American Unity: "For human rights and dignity" [Statement of basic aims of the Organization of Afro-American Unity]. In J. Bracey, A. Meier, & E. Rudwick (Eds.), *Black nationalism in America* (pp. 421–427). New York: Bobbs-Merrill.
———. (1971 [1963]). The black revolution. In B. Karim (Ed.), *The end of white world supremacy: Four speeches by Malcolm X* (pp. 67–80). New York: Arcade.
———. (2018 [1965]). Program of the Organization of Afro-American Unity. https://www.malcolm-x.org/docs/gen_oaau.htm; accessed February 2, 2018.
———, with Haley, A. (1964). *The autobiography of Malcolm X.* New York: Grove Press.

Index

Abiodun, Nehanda, 304
abolitionism, 57, 92, 96, 99, 120, 133, 425; ACS and, 59; Du Bois and, 101–102
Abubakari, Dara, 46, 328
Abu Jamal, Mumia, 304
Acoli, Sundiata, 304
Adefunmi, Nana Oserjiman, 312–313, 321–323
Aeyitoro, Adjoa, 315
Africa: black nationalists on, 70; Cruse on, 45, 178–179, 199; Malcolm X on, 5, 9, 22–25, 30–31, 33–34, 41, 44, 265. *See also* African cultures
African Blood Brotherhood, 77–78
African Communities League (ACL), 6, 13, 77
African Civilization Society, 62
African cultures, xi, xiii, xviii, xx–xxi, 30, 35–36, 45, 66, 130–131; BAM and, 376; Boggs on, 218–219; BPP's disinterest in, 289; circumcision in, 278–279, 449nn18–19; Cleage on, 415–416; Diop on, 398; diversity of, 131, 268, 274–275, 278–279; Du Bois and, xiv, 14, 44; names and clothes adopted from, 39–40, 44–45, 260, 264, 283, 300, 321, 376, 412, 425; RAM on, 251–252; RNA and, 321, 323; slave culture and, 65; Us and, 261–265, 268, 273–275, 278, 280, 322

African Free School, 379
African Liberation Support Committee, 380, 385
African Methodist Episcopalian (AME) Church, 65, 108, 136, 149; Du Bois on, 153
Afro-American Association (AAA), 234, 259–260, 283
Afro-American Institute, 234
Afro-American Student Conference on Black Nationalism, 237–238, 240, 251
Afro-American Student Movement, 239
Afrocentrism, xx, 45, 63–65, 71–72, 271–272, 399; Du Bois and, 72, 441n6, 445n22; Third World Press and, 373, 386, 398
Achad Ha'am, 51
Ahmad, Muhammad, 27, 235, 260, 312, 341, 356–357, 448n5. *See also* Stanford, Max
Aiyetoro, Adjoa, 46
Akiba, Malaika, 378
Algeria, 1, 9, 26, 248, 274, 288
Alkebulan, Paul, 39, 296, 450n32
Allen, Ernie Mkalimoto, 332, 351–352, 356–357
Allen, Richard, 53
Alston, Chris, 339, 341, 354
American Colonization Society (ACS), 59
American Negro Academy, 62
Amini, Johari (Jewel C. Latimore), 386

473

Angelou, Maya, 440n5
Anglophilia, 13–14, 44, 64–66, 73, 76
anticolonial struggles, influence on BPM of, xi–xiii, 1, 3, 7, 22–25, 35–36, 40, 130, 178–179, 236, 242, 284, 286, 295, 353, 394, 424
Aptheker, Herbert, 110, 185
armed resistance advocacy, xviii, xxii, 1–2; Malcolm X and, 2, 9, 15, 18, 20; RAM and, 235, 238–242, 247; RNA and, 314–315, 323, 326–327
Arnold, Matthew, 137
art as propaganda, 130, 266; BAM and, 375; Baraka and, 375; BPM and, 173; China and, 139, 141; Douglas and, 291; Du Bois and, 136, 139, 171–173, 265, 375, 446n25; Us and, 265–267
Asante, Molefi, 398, 445n22
Ashbaugh, Carolyn, 150
Ashwood, Amy, 46
Association for the Study of Classical African Civilizations, 398
Atkins, Hanna, 454n13
Aurobindo, Sri, 51
Awolo, Obaboa, 312
Axelrod, Beverly, 290–291
Ayers, Bill, 304

Back to Africa movements, 49, 77. *See* emigrationism
Baker, General, 234, 335–336, 341–342, 346–347, 352, 356, 439n3; *Black Madonna* painting and, 404; SOSAD and, 438
Bandung Conference, 24, 236, 242, 258, 448n2
Bandung Humanism, 236
Baraka, Amina, 46, 378–379
Baraka, Amiri: background of, 374–377; BAM/BARTS and, 210, 266–267,

290, 374–375, 377; *Blues People*, 267, 376; CAP and, xx, 177–178, 373–374, 384–394; CFUN and, 230, 264, 272, 282, 377–379, 381–382; critiques of, 454n8; Marxist/Maoist turn of, 385–387, 390–392, 397, 455n13; NBPA and, 454n8, 454n13; RNA and, 312, 321–322
Baraka, Ras, 454n12
Battle of Algiers, The (film), 348
Baynham, Michael, 303
Beal, Frances, 5, 46, 92, 148, 447n13
Beaty, Powhatan, 442
Bellah, Robert N., 67–69
Ben Bella, Ahmed, 1
Benjamin, Playthell, 234
Ben-Jochannan, Yosef, 398
Bennett, Fred, 303
Berman, Bruce J., 280
Bernard, Diane, 345–346
Bethune, Mark "Ibo," 349
Bibb, Henry, 61
Bibb, Mary, 46
Black Arts Movement (BAM), xvii, xx, 2, 27, 34, 139, 173, 178, 209–210, 222, 233, 265–266, 375–377; Cleage and, 410–411; Madhubuti/Third World Press and, 386–387
Black Arts Repertory Theater and School (BARTS), 178, 210, 229, 266, 375, 377, 411
black athletes, protests by, 435–436, 456n3
Black Belt. *See under* Haywood, Harry
Black Church, xii, xv–xvii, xix, xxi–xxii, 39–40, 44, 75, 113, 132, 145, 157–158, 250, 310, 392, 395–396, 414, 426, 432–433; BPM and, 132, 270, 432; BPP and, 296; CAP and, 374; Cleage/PAOCC and, 374, 401, 403–408, 411–415, 417–418, 426; Cooper and, 148–149; Cruse and, 229, 427; Democratic Party and, 399;

Du Bois and, xvi, 132, 153–160, 171; King and, 401, 419, 433; RAM and, 242, 258; RNA and, 327–328; sexism in, 417–418; critiques of, 46, 154, 157, 418; of South Africa, 444n11; Us and, 270, 277–278
Black Community Development (BCD), 377, 379
Black Congress, 263, 291
black cultural evolution, xvi, 131, 136, 146–175; Cruse on, 178–179; Du Bois and, 136, 152–174, 272; Karenga and, 272; PAOCC, 374. *See also* slave culture
black cultural revolution, x–xi, xvi–xviii, 39–41, 47–48, 136, 139, 144–146, 224; Baraka on, 376–377, 391; Boggs and, 211–221, 262; BPP's disdain for, 259, 289; CAP and, xx, 393–395; Civil War and, 117–118; Cleage and, 407, 410–411, 418–419; Cruse and, xvi–xvii, 177–210; Du Bois and, xi, xv–xvi, 25–26, 34, 47–48, 72–74, 121, 129, 136, 153, 199, 267–268; LRBW and, xix, 329–330, 371, 433; Malcolm X and, x–xi, xiii, xxii, 4, 15, 25, 27, 28–34, 40–41, 134, 175, 210, 219, 257, 264, 288, 309, 410, 423; in 1980s, 437; PAOCC and, xx–xxi; religion and, 75; RAM and, 240, 250–260; RNA and, xviii, 321–322, 324–325, 328; Us and, 261–282. *See also* cultural revolution theory
Black Economic Development Conference (BEDC), 347, 366
black elected officials (BEOs), xii, xx, xxii, 17, 373–374, 388, 392–393, 396–397, 399, 426, 431–433, 453n5, 455n13, 455n1; BPP and, 432; CAP and 432; CRM and, 428–429; NBPA and, 382–385; PAOCC and, 419
black feminism, 46–47, 57, 65–66, 92, 132–133, 136, 146–152, 447n13

black folk culture, 14, 44, 65–67, 72, 81, 121, 172, 178–179; 264, 267, 375. *See also* slave culture
Black Government Conference, 311–312, 316
Black Hebrew Israelites, 38
Black House (San Francisco), 290–291
black liberation, xiv, xvii, 2–4, 25, 35, 118; Haywood on, 87
Black Liberation Army, 2–3, 241
black liberation theology, 5, 14, 400–403, 407, 419
#BlackLivesMatter (BLM), 435–438, 451n41, 455n2
black nationalism, xiii–xiv, 11–15, 42–94, 287, 380–381; academic misrepresentations of, 47, 71, 187, 380, 441n2; CAP and, 373; classical vs. modern, 13, 43–44, 47, 49–51, 60, 66, 72; Cruse and, 178–180, 182–184, 190; cultural nationalism and, xiv, 4, 28, 44, 49, 72, 76, 93, 118, 259–260, 273, 283, 289–290, 296, 304, 306, 380, 450n6; definitions of, 48–53; Du Bois and, xiv, 14, 44, 47, 70, 72–78, 80, 93, 118, 177; economic autonomy and, 194–195; emigrationism and, 55–63; feminist contributors to, 46–47, 57; Haywood on, 79–80, 83, 183, 186, 191–192, 387; as an ideology, 60; LRBW and, 351–352, 356–357; Malcolm X and, 3–4, 11–12, 14–15, 17, 19, 33, 43–45, 47, 245–246; origin and development of, 12–14, 53–70; racist ventures and, 59–60; RAM and, 235; religion and, 66–69, 270–271, 444n27; "revolutionary nationalism," 4, 28–29, 180, 182, 186, 188, 191–192, 199, 234, 273, 289–290, 295, 353, 381, 385; sexism and, 14, 41, 45–46, 57, 146, 281; critiques of, xx, 33, 43–45, 385, 394

blackness, 3, 262, 353–354, 369, 375. See also *nguzo saba*
Black Panther Party (BPP), xi, 2, 4, 28–29, 41, 191, 216, 283–308; Boggs and, 220–221, 283; "brothers on the block" practices of, 130, 283; "cultural nationalism" disdain by, 259–260, 283–284, 288–290, 295–296, 304; fissures in, 259–260, 299–300; PAOCC and, 407; "pussy power" and 292, 294; RAM and, 283, 295, 300; sexism and "revolutionary misogyny" in, 46, 281, 291–294, 300, 450n29; critiques of, 300–304; Son of Man Temple of, 39, 277, 296, 450n32; "survival programs" of, 290, 295, 297–300, 380, 450n32; Us and, 259, 269, 273, 281–282, 290–291, 295, 302; violence by, 284, 287, 290, 302–303, 310. *See also* Oakland
black petit bourgeoisie, 165, 167, 192, 358–360, 387, 443n19, 444n25, 446n4; Cruse on, 184–185, 187–189, 192, 195, 207–208; BPP and, 298, 304; "lumpenbourgeoisie," 188, 207–208
black political party proposals, 132, 382, 388–390, 432; Malcolm X and, 3, 17, 20, 382–383; PAOCC and, 407–408
Black Power Conference (1970), 381–382
Black Power Movement (BPM): beginnings of, 2; Black Church and, 132, 269; the Boggs and, 211–213, 218, 220–221; Civil War implications for, 119–121, 128, 130; Cruse and, 198, 208, 224, 229, 233; culture disdain by, 259; decline of, 434–435; focus of, x, 121–122; Gary Convention and, 381–385; Maoism and, 259; militarization fetish of, 163, 247, 258, 281–282, 408–409; propagandistic uses of black art by, 173; RAM and, 240; sexism and, 378–379; critiques of, xii, xxi–xxii, 39–42, 130–132, 223, 248, 257–258, 378–379, 403, 425–429, 434–435
Black Slate (political action group), 400, 419, 432, 455n18
Black Star Line, 228
Black Star Publishing, 347; films by, 347–348
Black Student United Front (BSUF), 346, 362
Black Studies programs, 256, 272, 297, 300
black supremacism, 398
black unions, xix, 41, 132, 145, 329, 369, 428; RAM and, 238; sexism in, 90, 93
black voluntary organizations, 136, 146, 153, 171–172
Black Women's United Front, 380
Blackwood, Jesse, 109
Bland, Sandra, 456n3
Blanding, Tanya, 340
blues, 203, 208; argument over validity of the, 266–267, 376
Blum, Edward, 154–155
Blyden, Edward Wilmot, 54
Boas, Franz, 121, 152
Bodley, John H., 137
Boggs, Grace Lee, x, 5, 211–212, 216–218, 220, 234, 312, 339, 341, 438, 446n7, 447n9, 447n13, 452n19
Boggs, James, x, xvii–xviii, 5, 17, 210–221, 224, 231–232, 234, 283, 312, 339, 341, 351, 354, 446n5, 446–447n7–8, 452n19; on automation and cybernation, 211–212, 285, 360–361; on Chinese culture, 220–221; dialectical humanism thesis of, 211–221, 236; Malcolm X and, 219; RAM and, 235–236, 253, 394; critiques of, 218–221, 446n7; SOSAD and, 438

Bogdanov, Alexander, 141
Bond, Julian, 383
Boston Busing Crisis, 391
Boudin, Kathy, 304
Boyd, John Percy, 349
Boyer, Jean-Pierre, 110, 448n6
Bracey, John H., 68, 234; et al., 50, 53
Bradley, Tom, 453n5
Briggs, Cyril, 77–78, 196
Brooks, Gwendolyn, 386
Brotz, Howard, 53
Brown, Elaine, 284–285, 292–294, 298–299, 302–303, 450n24, 450n30
Brown, H. Rap, 312
Brown, Heyward, 349
Brown, John, 99
Brown, Scot, 260, 263, 268, 281–282, 290
Buck, Christopher, 127
Bukhari, Safiya, 293–294
Bullins, Ed, 290
Bunche, Ralph, 278–279, 449n18
Burke, Tarana, 452n6, 456n3

Cabral, Amílcar, 255–256, 271–272, 273–274, 281, 295–296, 453n2
Calverton, V. F., 175, 209
Canada, 54, 57, 60–61, 146
capitalism, 87; Boggs on, 211, 213–217; Cruse on, 197–199, 201, 204, 206–207, 226; Du Bois on, 158; Haywood on, 86–87; Lenin on, 205
Carlisle, Rodney P., 50, 53, 58
Carmichael, Stokely, 5, 46, 214, 439n3
Carr, James, 303
Casely-Hayford, J. E., 13
Castoriadis, Cornelius, 447n9
Castro, Fidel, 1, 236, 339, 351
Catt, Carrie Chapman, 60
China, 8, 26, 29, 139–141, 391–392; Boggs and, 220–221; Great Proletarian Cultural Revolution (GPCR) in, 140–141, 253, 259, 283, 391, 444n4; Malcolm X on, 16, 440n8
"civilizationism," xiv, 13–14, 43–45, 56–57, 64, 66, 87, 92, 441n10. *See also* "reverse civilizationism"
Civil Rights Movement (CRM), xxii, 1–3, 15–17, 19, 26, 28, 119, 128, 129, 193, 195–196, 205, 223, 310, 324, 359–360, 388, 426, 430–432; the Boggs and, 211–213, 220; boycott strategy of, 120, 155, 213, 338, 360; Communist Party and, 78, 88; Cruse and, 177–180, 187, 197, 199–200, 208, 224–226; integration and, 3, 6, 8, 11, 39, 178, 182, 195, 199, 208, 210, 235, 256, 327, 382; King and, 400, 433; as "Negro revolution," 6, 8, 9–11; North/South fissure in, 36–37, 234; religion and, 39, 155, 229, 242, 446n24; sexism in, 300, 378–379
Civil War, xi, xv, xxii, 12, 25–26, 34, 37–38, 48, 66, 87, 94–105, 109–110, 112–120, 127, 129–130, 132–135, 144, 152, 164, 227–228, 231–232, 242–246, 250, 274, 297, 305–306, 314, 338, 340, 361, 369, 415, 417, 425–426, 443n18–n20, 447n8; black troop numbers in, 97, 117; draft riots during, 340; Du Bois and, xi, xv, 25–26, 94, 96–98, 100–105, 113, 116, 119, 128, 135, 224, 241, 417; influence of, 119–120; RAM and, 241–246; LRBW and, 338, 361, 369; religion and, 97, 100–102, 104–105, 118, 135, 368, 416–417
Clarke, John Henrik, 386
Clay, Henry, 59
Clay, William, 393
Cleage, Albert (Jaramogi A. Agyeman): background and beliefs of, 5, 399–404, 455n14; on counterinstitutions, 171, 374, 403, 405, 407, 409,

Cleage, Albert *(continued)*
  417–418; on communism, 409–410;
  Detroit activism of, xxi, 339, 341,
  400; FNP and, 5, 17, 229, 383,
  400, 404; GOAL and, 5, 312, 400;
  Malcolm X and, 10, 400, 409;
  NBPA and, 405; PAOCC and,
  xxi, 311, 374, 392, 396, 404–421;
  theology of, 400–408, 415
Cleaver, Eldridge, 46, 260, 285, 289,
  290–292, 296; on Congolese politics,
  302, 451n37; split with Newton, 283,
  302
Cleaver, Kathleen, 293–294, 450n28
Cockrel, Kenneth, 334, 346, 348–349,
  352, 356, 452n13
COINTELPRO (Counter Intelligence
  Program), 257, 281, 295, 327
Collins, Michael, 37, 394
colonialism, 5, 193–195, 236, 279–
  280, 311; Marx on, 87. *See also*
  anticolonial struggles; domestic
  colonialism
Coltrane, John, 376
Committee for a Unified Newark
  (CFUN), xx, 230, 263–264, 272,
  278, 282, 377, 379–382, 386, 392;
  sexism and, 378–380; women's
  division of, 379–380
communism, 4, 29, 143, 162, 168–169,
  183, 186, 189, 193, 355, 397, 409
Communist Party, 46, 78, 83, 87–88,
  142, 145, 163, 170, 180, 186, 191–
  193, 195, 355; Du Bois and, 165,
  168–169, 180, 446n24; Haywood
  and, 183, 193; Scottsboro Boys case
  and, 228; sexism in, 90, 92
community alert patrol, 264
Confederate States of America (CSA),
  xv, 34, 96, 99, 117, 120, 128, 133,
  227, 245, 316, 326
Congress of African Peoples (CAP), xi,
  xx, 2, 4, 41, 130, 175, 177–178, 191,
  263, 278, 309, 373–374, 378, 380,
  381, 384–399, 428, 449n14; Chicago/
  Midwest chapter of, xx, 373–374,
  385–387, 399; East chapter of,
  385; PAOCC and, 407. *See also*
  CFUN
Congress of Racial Equality (CORE),
  22, 208, 360, 387
Congressional Black Caucus (CBC),
  383–384, 393
consumerism: Du Bois on, 158–159,
  170; King on, 400; Malcolm X on,
  400
Conyers, John, 314, 400
Cooper, Anna Julia, 147–149, 156
Cooper, Carl, 340
Cornish, Samuel, 53
Creel, Margaret Washington, 108
Crenshaw, Kimberlé, 148
Crockett, George, 328
Crummell, Alexander, 13–14, 44, 55,
  57, 59, 61–67, 73
Cruse, Harold, x, xvi–xviii, 17, 26,
  32–33, 35–36, 127, 131, 174–175,
  177–210, 212, 218–219, 221–226,
  267, 295, 298, 429, 435; on African
  heritage, 45, 178–179, 199; BARTS
  and, 178, 229, 375; on cities,
  221–223; cultural revolution thesis
  of, 197–210, 212, 218, 220, 224–226,
  228–231, 233, 257, 264, 268, 283,
  309, 323, 426–427, 436, 447n10;
  on Delany, 60; on Locke, 446n1;
  LRBW and, 348, 361; Madhubuti
  and, 397; Malcolm X and, 177;
  Marxism and, 177–187, 189–190,
  192–193, 195, 197–198, 205, 210,
  219; PAOCC and, 416; critiques
  of, 232. *See also* cultural apparatus;
  domestic colonialism
  WRITINGS BY: "An Afro-
  American's Cultural Views," 178,
  202; "Black and White: Outlines of

the Next Stage," 222; *The Crisis of the Negro Intellectual*, 222, 229, 435; "Rebellion or Revolution," 196, 199, 202; "Revolutionary Nationalism and the Afro-American," 180–192, 199, 234, 385
Cuban Revolution, 1, 26, 29, 180–181, 194, 351
Cuffee, Paul, 13, 52, 54, 56, 58, 313
Cullors, Patrice Khan, 435, 438, 455n2
cultural apparatus, control of, 144, 179, 199, 201, 204, 208, 210, 218, 225–226, 229, 231, 257, 271, 321–322, 427; LRBW and, 348, 365; contemporary inroads into, 435–436, 446n3
cultural assimilation, 13–14, 44, 62, 66, 136. *See also* "civilizationism"
cultural democracy, 26, 118, 127–128, 135, 200–201, 210
cultural revolution theory, xv–xvi, 27–30, 35; definitions of, 136–139; development of, 139–152, 174–175; Locke and, xi–xii, xv, 97, 121–129, 131–132, 134–135; Marxist, 135. *See also* black cultural revolution; Cruse, Harold; white cultural revolution

Damu, Ngao (Samuel Carr), 248, 260, 282
Daniels, Stan, 234
Davis, Angela, 304
Davis, Henrietta Vinton, 46
Davis, Miles, 270
Davis, Ossie, 220
Dawson, Michael, 282, 441n2
Day, Yvonne, 453n7
Deacons for Defense, 1–2
Debord, Guy, 446
Dee, Ruby, 220, 386
Defenders, the, 2
deindustrialization, xx, 214, 351, 373, 385, 397, 420, 428–429, 437

Delany, Martin, 13–14, 44, 54, 59–60, 61–62, 64
Democratic Party (and Dixiecrats), xii, xxii, 15–17, 20–21, 60, 133, 230, 388–389, 392–393, 397, 431, 432–433, 440n6; BEOs and, 426, 432; Black Church and, 399; NBPA and, 382–384, 388; in 1964, 453n4; in 1980s, 437; North hegemony of, 230
Deng Xiaopeng, 140–141, 444n5
Detroit: activists/theorists in, 5, 220, 222, 228, 234, 311–312, 336, 338–339, 354, 404; auto industry in, xix, 196, 329, 330–331, 333–337, 342–345, 348–349, 354–355, 361–362, 367; BPP chapter in, 294, 299–300, 312, 344; Central Congregational Church in, 311, 399, 404, 419; class differentiation in, 354–355; Kercheval Riot in, 336; New Bethel Baptist Church shootout in, 327–328, 349; news media in, 361–362, 452n14; police brutality and corruption in, 332, 335, 344–345, 349–350, 452n9; 1967 rebellion in, 315, 336, 338–341, 452n8; "Paradise Valley" in, 81; school system in, 346. *See also* Cleage, Albert; *Inner City Voice*; League of Revolutionary Black Workers
Diggs, Charles, 382, 400
Dillard, Angela, 404, 411
Diop, Cheikh Anta, 398
Dodge Revolutionary Union Movement (DRUM), 196, 257, 329, 333, 339, 342–344, 349–350, 356, 359
Dohrn, Bernadine, 304, 451n34
domestic colonialism, 14, 24, 35–39, 78, 130–131, 177, 179, 182–183, 199, 206, 394–395, 430–431; Baraka on, 387, 390, 430; BPP and, 283, 286–289, 394; King and, 433; LRBW and, 337; RAM and, 234–235, 237–238

Double V campaign, 228
Douglas, Emory, 283, 291, 450n28
Douglass, Frederick, 56, 60–61, 103
Dowdell, Glanton, 336; *Black Madonna* painting by, 404
Drake, St. Clair, and Horace R. Cayton, 81
Drew, Timothy (Noble Drew Ali), 6
Duberry, Dorothy, 345–346
Du Bois, W. E. B., x, xii, xvi, 13, 32–35, 82, 87, 120–121, 145, 152–174, 179, 409, 423, 442nn7–9; African culture and, xiv, 14, 386; Black Church and, xvi, 75, 101–102, 132, 153, 160, 170–171, 174; on black colleges, 160–162; black cultural evolution and, 136, 152–174, 272; black cultural revolution and, xi, xv–xvi, 25–26, 34, 47–48, 72–74, 97, 101–102, 118–119, 121, 129, 136, 153, 199, 267–268; on black culture as propaganda, 136, 139, 171–173; black nationalism and, xiv, 14, 44, 55, 64, 70, 72–78, 80, 93, 118; Civil War and, xi, xv, 25–26, 94, 96–98, 100–105, 113, 116, 119, 128, 135, 224, 241, 417; on class differences, 155, 164–165, 167, 358–359; *Crisis* editorship of, 158; critique of communism, 165–169; double consciousness concept of, 74, 148; on economic issues, 158–159, 163–170, 181, 445n15; on joining Communist Party, 180, 446 fn24; on King, 445n15; NNC and, 15; PAOCC and, 416; "self-segregation" thesis of, 158–159, 170–171; talented tenth concept of, 62, 147, 172–173, 271, 276; on Turner, 110; Washington and, 165, 184–186; on women, 155–156, 445n16; on World War I, 76–77, 86
WRITINGS BY: "The African Roots of War," 76–77, 165, 204, 446n23; *Black Folk Then and Now*, 73; *Black Reconstruction*, xi, xv–xvi, 25–26, 34, 42, 95–96, 101–102, 105, 121, 126, 131, 135, 152, 154–156, 171, 173, 231, 241, 247, 250–251, 338, 367–369, 434, 442n8–9, 443n20; "The Conservation of Races," 72–73, 75, 153, 441n10; "Criteria of Negro Art," 172, 375; "Crusader Without Violence," 445n15; *Darkwater*, 155; *Dusk of Dawn*, 163, 445n20; *The Gift of Black Folk*, 154; *The Negro*, 73; "The Negro and Communism," 165–168; *The Negro and Social Reconstruction*, 96, 136, 152, 158–160, 163–164, 445n20; *The Negro Church*, 153; "The Negro College," 160–161; "A Negro Nation within a Nation," 78–79, 196; *The Philadelphia Negro*, 153, 445n12; *The Souls of Black Folk*, 72, 74, 101–102, 153–154; "The Talented Tenth: Memorial Address," 155; "Will the Great Gandhi Live Again," 155; *The World and Africa*, 73
Duvalier, François (Papa Doc), 295

Edwards, Harry, 435
Egerton, Douglas R., 107–108, 111
Egypt, ancient, 269, 398
Eldon Revolutionary Union Movement (ELRUM), 333, 345, 349, 361, 452n11
emigrationism, xiv, 6, 7, 43–45, 47, 49, 55–63, 66; early African emigration proposals, 13, 52–55, 58, 64; emancipation and, 58; Garvey and, 77, 157, 193; Shadd Cary on, 57, 60–61, 146–147; Wells on, 440n1
Essene order, xxi, 412, 420
Essien-Udom, E. U., 48
Eurocentrism, xiv, 45, 47, 63–64, 71–72, 77. *See also* Anglophilia
Evans, Mari, 386

Fanon, Frantz, 73, 216, 273–274, 341; BPP and, 284–286, 288, 296
Farmer, James, 10
Farrakhan, Louis, 383, 398–399
Fenn, Richard K., 69
Ferguson, Herman, 260, 283, 312
Finally Got the News (film), 348, 362, 369
Forbes, Florestan, 303, 451n40
Ford Revolutionary Union Movement (FRUM), 333, 345, 349
Forman, James, 347, 356, 366
Forrestor, Lot, 109
Franklin, C. L., 327, 349, 400
Franklin, Joan, 312
Franklin, V. P., 65, 68–69, 72
Fraser, Douglas, 350
Fraser, Nancy, 122–123
Frazier, E. Franklin, 187
Freedom Now Party (FNP), 5, 17, 210, 212, 219–220, 229–230, 233, 312, 383, 411
Freeman, Donald, 234, 237, 240, 251
Freeman, Kenny, 283
French, Lynn, 299
Fugitive Slave Act, 60
Fuller, Chaka, 349

Gabriel's Rebellion, 32, 98, 100, 102, 105–107, 109, 414, 442n13
Gandhi, Mahatma, 1, 155
Gardner, Newport, 53
Garner, William, 109
Garnet, Henry Highland, 54, 58–60, 64, 66, 70
Garvey, Amy Jacques, 46
Garvey, Marcus (and Garveyism), 6, 13, 39, 55, 60, 64–66, 77, 83–84, 165, 170, 184, 193, 228, 300, 375; Du Bois on, 441n7; Moore and, 313; NAACP and, 186
Garza, Alicia, 435, 438, 455n2
Gaston, A. C., 446n4
Gell, Monday, 108–109

Gellner, Ernest, 51
general strike (strategy), xviii, xix, 119–120, 126, 130, 151, 241–242, 247, 250, 256–257, 329–330, 337–338, 361–367, 369–371, 424, 427–428, 446n2, 447n8
General Strike (during Civil War), 11, 15, 25–26, 95–98, 102, 104–105, 113, 119–120, 129–130, 132, 135, 153, 174, 238–239, 241, 244, 246–247, 256, 338, 367–368, 425, 442n8
Genovese, Eugene D., 442n5
Georgakas, Dan, 452n10
Georgakas, Dan, and Marvin Surkin, 334–336, 340–342, 346–347, 351–352, 355, 452n14
Geschwender, James, and Judson Jeffries, 334, 343–344, 346, 352–355
Giap, Vo Nguyen, 448n10
Gibson, Kenneth, 382, 384–385, 390, 393, 454n12
Gill, Anthony, 277
Giovanni, Nikki, 266, 383
Glaude, Eddie S., Jr., 71
Goldman, Emma, 150
Goldwater, Barry, 440n6, 453n4
Gramsci, Antonio, 144–145, 272, 444n11
Grant, William, 312
Great Depression, 158, 167
Great Migration, 44, 77, 86, 157–158, 184, 223, 375; Detroit and, 331; Second, 88, 223
Great Society programs, 216, 384, 431
Griffin, Rufus, 336
Group on Advanced Leadership (GOAL), 5, 311–312
guerilla warfare, xviii, 18, 27, 239–240, 242, 244–245, 247, 249, 282, 311, 408
Guevara, Ernesto "Che," 1, 37, 282, 341, 394

Hahn, Steven, 98–99, 100, 115–116

Haiti: emigration to, 54, 60; revolution in, 32, 98–100, 108, 243, 442n5
Halisi, Clyde, 261, 265–266, 269, 273, 301
Hall, Gwendolyn, 191–195
Hall, Otto, 83
Hall, Prince, 54; Prince Hall Masons, 136
Hamilton, Charles V., 439n3
Hamlin, Mike, 342, 345–346, 351–352, 356
Hampton, Fred, 299, 451n34
Harcave, Sidney, 119
Hard Hat Riot, 391, 428
Harlem, 228, 303, 375; Cruse and, 222, 447n10
Harlem Renaissance, xvi, 25, 41, 82, 157, 171–173, 265, 267, 376; Baraka on, 375; Cruse on, 197–198, 222; exoticism and, 171; other renaissances, 447n11
Harper, Frances Ellen Watkins, 146
Harris, Leonard, and Charles Molesworth, 125
hashtag activism. *See* social media activism
Hatcher, Richard, 382
Hayes, Floyd W, III, and Judson L. Jeffries, 282
Hayes, Isaac, 383
Hayes-Tilden Compromise, 84, 315
Hayford, Adelaide Casely, 46
Haywood, Harry, x, xvii–xviii, 298, 337; background of, 78; Black Belt thesis of, xvi, xviii–xix, 35, 78–89, 93, 145, 170, 177, 183–184, 193–196, 221, 313, 359, 387–388; on black nationalism, 79–80, 83, 183, 186, 191–192, 194; Communist Party and, 183, 193; on Cruse, 191–196; Detroit and, 339, 341, 357, 359; Marxism and, xx, 327, 357, 373, 391; on race, 212; on Reconstruction, 118–119; RNA and, 313
Hegel, Georg Wilhelm Friedrich, 118

Henry, Milton. *See* Obadele, Gaidi
Henry, Richard. *See* Obadele, Imari
Herder, Johann Gottfried, 51
Herzl, Theodor, 53
Hewitt, Masai, 297
Hibbitt, Alfred 2X, 349
Higgenbottom, Thomas, 234
Hilliard, David, 294–295, 297, 303
hipsters, 252
Hitler, Adolf, 9, 60
Hobsbawm, Eric, 51
Ho Chi Minh, 78, 296
Holly, Theodore, 54, 60
House, Callie, 228
Houston, Drusilla, 398
Huggins, Ericka, 303
Huggins, John, 303
Hughes, Langston, 286
human rights, x, 127, 151, 227, 437; Du Bois on, 76; Malcolm X on, 15–19, 311
Humphrey-Hawkins Full Employment Act, 388, 455n1
Hunt, Michael H., 69
Hutchinson, John, 51
Hyson, Brenda, 293

Idili-Davis, Gail, 281
Industrial Workers of the World (IWW), 150–151
Inner City Voice (newspaper), 340–342, 344–345, 452n12
Institute of Positive Education (IPE), xx, 373, 385–386, 398
integrationism, 8, 39, 46, 62, 137, 182; CRM and, 3, 6, 8, 11, 39, 178, 182, 195, 199, 208, 210, 235, 256, 327, 382; Cruse on, 178, 189; Douglass and, 60–61; Haywood and Hall on, 191; Malcolm X's opposition to, 2–3, 7, 18–19; sexism of, 46
internationalism, 13, 46–47, 54, 234, 236, 448n2, 451n36
International Black Appeal, 347

Inter-Religious Foundation for Community Organizations, 347
Irish Republican Army, 37
Islam and Black Muslims, 27, 38, 189, 193–194; Sunni Islam, 14, 28, 419
Israel–Palestine conflict, 384

Jackson, George, 304
Jackson, Jesse, 383, 437, 454n7
Jackson, Maynard, 419, 453n5
Jacquette, Tommy (Halifu), 260, 264, 269
Jamal, Dorothy, 260, 278
Jamal, Hakim, 260–261
James, C. L. R., 211, 341
jazz, 33, 202, 410–411; and other music genres, 203, 205, 208, 375, 376. *See also* blues; "sorrow songs"
Jeffries, Judson L., 282
Jesus as revolutionary black Messiah, 401–402, 406–407, 414–415, 418–419
Jim Crow, xiii, 1, 2, 36–37, 39, 82, 84, 128, 155, 166–167, 199, 226, 389, 431
John Birch Society, 425
Johnson, Andrew, 226
Johnson, Charles (Mao), 234, 335, 341
Johnson, Ethel, 234
Johnson, James, 348, 361
Johnson, Lyndon B., 216, 440n6, 453n4
Johnston, Alastair Iain, 138
Jones, Audrea, 293
Jones, Claudia, x, 89–93, 145, 148, 151
Jordan, Barbara, 383
Joseph, Jamal, 303

Kadalie, Modibo M., 353–354, 358
Kaepernick, Colin, 435
Karenga, Brenda Haiba, 260, 278, 281
Karenga, Maulana, 5, 234, 259–283, 285–286, 288, 301–303, 398; on the blues, 266–267, 376; CFUN and, 379, 381–382, Cleaver and, 291; RNA and, 312, 321–322
Karenga, Tiamoyo (Luz Maria Tiamoyo), 281
kawaida, xx, 5, 261–263, 265, 268–274, 277, 282, 286, 288, 302, 396, 398; Baraka and, 373–374, 386, 393, 396, 397; PAOCC and, 413–414; RNA and, 323, 326; sexism in, 272, 275, 278, 280–281, 378–379, 386, 452n4; Temple of Kawaida, 39. *See also nguzo saba*; Us
Kedourie, Elie, 51
Kemp, Gwen, 234, 335, 341
Kenyatta, Jomo, 273, 278–280, 286, 449n17
Key, Karl (Hekima), 260
Kgositsile, Keorapetse, 386
Kicheko, Joann, 280
Kilpatrick, Kwame, 455n18
Kimbro, Warren, 303
King, Coretta Scott, 383, 455n17
King, Martin Luther, Jr., 2, 10, 39, 307, 360, 395, 400–401, 419, 433, 455n17; Du Bois on, 445n15; "Letter from a Birmingham Jail," 407; Mao Zedong on, 391
King, Yvonne, 299
korenizatsiya (Soviet policy), 78–79
Kramer, Marian, 344–346
Kroeber, Alfred L., and Clyde Kluckhorn, 137
Ku Klux Klan, 84, 168, 185, 417, 425
Kush District, 316, 325, 327
Kwanzaa, 262, 264–265, 398

League of Revolutionary Black Workers (LRBW), xi, xix–xx, 2, 4, 29, 41, 130, 191, 221, 234, 309, 312, 329–371, 417, 427–428, 432, 433–434; beginnings and objectives of, 330–333, 339–340, 345–346; divisions within, 351–357, 369; PAOCC and, 407; RAM and, 238,

League of Revolutionary Black Workers (LRBW) *(continued)*
  257; critiques of, xix–xx, 349–351, 358, 369
Lee, Robert E., 97
Lenin, Vladimir, 51, 77, 83, 86, 141–144, 193, 205–206, 385
Levine, Lawrence W., 105
Lewis, David L., 154–155, 161–162
Lewis, John, 10
Lewis, Tarika "Matilaba," 450n28
Liberia, 57, 60–61
Lin Biao, 392
Lincoln, Abbey, 376, 410
Lincoln, Abraham, 26, 97, 105, 117, 135, 442n6
Litwack, Leon, 115
Liu Shaoqi, 140, 444n5
Locke, Alain, x, xi, xxii, xv, xix, 25–26, 32, 35, 82, 179, 418, 423; background of, 121–122; on cultural revolution, xi–xii, xv, 97, 121–129, 131–132, 134–135, 152, 173, 199, 242, 267–268, 304–305, 363, 364, 369; on stages of democracy, 127; on transvaluation and transposition of values, xv, 126, 451n41. *See also* cultural democracy
Lorde, Audre, 440n16
Los Angeles, 81, 263; Free Huey Rally in, 291; 1992 rebellion, 340; Us and, 210, 234, 259–260, 264, 269, 277. *See also* Watts rebellion
Lumpen, the (band), 283–284
lumpenproletariat (and lumpenism), xviii, xix, 27–28, 120, 208, 216, 219–220; BPP and, 284–292, 294, 299, 300, 302, 304, 330, 331; LRBW and, 330, 331; SDS and, 450n34
Lumumba, Chokwe, 315, 328, 439n1
Lumumba, Chokwe Antar, 452n5
Lumumba, Patrice, 1, 454n11
Luxemburg, Rosa, 51, 348
lynching, 91–92, 147, 154, 156

Lynn, Conrad, 400

Madhubuti, Haki (Don L. Lee), xx, 373–374, 385–387, 397–399, 417
Madhubuti, Safisha (Carol D. Lee), 386
Magee, Ruchel, 304
Makeba, Miriam, 40
Malcolm X, x–xiv, 2–42, 309–311, 339; African American culture dismissed by, 2, 5, 14, 44, 77; assassination of, 33, 398, 440n13; Baraka and, 377–378, 453n3; on black music, 33; black nationalism and, 3–4, 11–12, 14–15, 17, 19, 33, 43–45, 47, 245, 246; black revolution thesis of, xi, xii–xiii, xviii, 2–33, 41–43, 282; cultural revolution thesis of 4, 14–15, 25–42, 134, 175, 177, 210, 219, 232–233, 257, 261–262, 264, 283–284, 288, 307, 309–310, 329, 407, 410, 420, 423; Farrakhan and, 398–399; on field vs. house Negroes, 10, 13–14, 27, 329; on gender inclusion, 14, 440n5; on gerrymandering, 440n9; land focus of, 2, 7–10, 21, 41, 221, 235, 311, 409, 412; LRBW and, 329; personal transformation of, 27, 261; RAM and, 234–236, 240, 242, 251, 257; "reverse civilizationism" thesis of, xi, xiii, xv, 30–34, 41–42, 44, 77, 93, 95, 129, 130, 251, 257, 265, 376, 423–425; on reparations, 439n2; on "revolution" term, 8; RNA and, 311–313, 328; critiques of, 5–6, 27, 33, 41, 45, 93, 247, 419; "worldwide revolution" vision of, xiii, 3–4, 22–28, 32, 41, 236
SPEECHES AND WRITINGS: "The Ballot or the Bullet," 3, 15, 16–18, 230, 238, 311, 377, 429; "The Black Revolution," 3, 7, 18–20, 22, 440n10; "Last Message," 311; "Message to the Grassroots," 2–3, 7–10, 15, 17, 20, 311, 400,

439n3, 440n11; "Statement of the Basic Aims and Objectives of the Organization of Afro-American Unity," 25, 30, 323
Malcolm X Grassroots Movement, 328, 452n6
Malcolm X Society, 311–312, 314
Malinowski, Bronisław, 279, 449n20
Mamdani, Mahmood, 280, 449 n21
Mandela, Nelson, 1
Mao Zedong (and Maoism), 1, 138, 139–141, 194, 220–221, 249, 259, 341, 385, 390–392, 440n11, 454n11; on black liberation, 253, 390–391, 454n9; BPP and, 283, 296, 300, 391; Nixon and, 60, 220, 392, 444n4, 454n11
Marable, Manning, 11–12, 33
March on Washington, 10–11, 16, 400
Marshall, Wanda, 234
Martin, Trayvon, 455n2
Marx, Karl, 87, 98, 103, 144, 197, 199, 217, 284, 341, 357, 385, 444n3; on lumpenproletariat, 27, 285, 287–288, 302; on religion, 97, 226, 323, 368, 442n4
Marxism, xvi, xviii, xx, 32–33, 60, 66, 76, 78, 83–84, 86–89, 93, 139, 142, 144, 151, 163–165, 167, 197, 210, 285; Baraka and, 385–387, 390–392, 397, 455n13; black organizations, 77–78; Boggs and, 211–213, 219; BPP and, 295, 300–301, 329; CAP and, 373, 385–386; Civil War and, 97–98; class antagonism in, 208, 306, 388; Cleage on, 409–410; Cruse and, 177–187, 189–190, 192–193, 195, 197–198, 205, 210, 219; LRBW and, 329–331, 337, 351, 353, 355–358, 369, 434, 452n20; RNA and, 327; sexism in, 46–47. *See also* communism
Masekela, Hugh, 40

mass media, xvii, 144, 197–199, 210, 224, 226; LRBW and, 347–348, 352; RNA and, 321–324
Mazrui, Ali A., 73, 449n17
Mbulu, Letta, 263, 280–281
McCarthyism, 78, 88, 193
McCurry, Stephanie, 99–100, 115–116
McGovern, George, 384
McGuire, George Alexander, 402
McLucas, Lonnie, 303
McPherson, James M., 100, 442n6
Meier, August, 53
Miller, Floyd John, 53, 58
Miller, Kelly, 155, 157
Mills, C. Wright, xvii, 175, 197, 199, 201
Missouri Compromise, 108
Mitchell, Sarah, 440n5
Mobutu Sese Seko, 454n11
Montgomery Bus Boycott, 120, 155
Moore, Audley ("Queen Mother"), x, 46, 228–229, 313–315; Malcolm X and, 229; NBPA and, 383; RAM and, 234, 241, 258; RNA and, 312–313
Moorish Science Temple (MST), 6, 38
Moses, Wilson Jeremiah, 49, 52–54, 59, 64, 65, 112, 441nn3–4; on "Afrotopia," 73; on classical black nationalism, 13–14, 43–44, 48–49, 55–56, 60, 66–72, 415; on Crummell, 62–63, 67; on Du Bois and Black Church, 154; on Gabriel's Rebellion, 105–106; on Walker, 55–56
Mothers of Murdered Sons, 437
Mothers Reclaiming Our Children, 437
Motor City Labor League, 347, 358
Mtume, James, 261, 263, 265–266, 269–270, 273, 301
Muhammad, Elijah, 6–7, 398–399
Muhammad, W. D., 398
Muhammad, Wallace Fard, 6, 399
multiculturalism, 76, 125
Muntaquin, Jalil, 304
Murphy, Robert F., 137

Muslim Mosque Inc. (MMI), xiii, 28, 38
NAACP (National Association for the Advancement of Colored People), 1, 15, 22, 145–146, 157, 172, 375, 389; "Appeal to the World," 80; Cruse on, 186–187; Garvey and, 186; Legal Defense Fund of, 208, 227; Wells and, 445n18
Nadir (of black history), the, 222
Napier, Sam, 303
National Afro-American Organization, 234
National Association of Colored Women (NACW), 146, 157
National Black Political Assembly (NBPA), 226, 229, 263, 380, 399, 417; Baraka and, 454n8, 454n13; Cruse on, 447n12; Gary Convention of, 381–385, 390, 405, 453n7; Little Rock Convention of, 393, 397
National Coalition of Blacks for Reparations in America, 328
nationalism (general), 51–52. *See also* black nationalism
National Lawyers' Guild, 208
National Negro Congress (NNC), 15
Nation of Islam (NOI), xi, xiii, 2–3, 6–8, 15, 27–28, 41, 193–194, 234, 398–399, 439n3; "Asiatic" culture and, 130; Malcolm X's assassins from, 33, 440n14; Cruse on, 178, 209; under Farrakhan, 398–399; Fruit of Islam, 28; millenarianism of, 3, 6, 8, 11, 33, 43, 399; mosques of, 2, 38, 229, 399; racism and, 60, 398; sexism in, 46
Neal, Larry, 139, 267, 270–271, 375, 376, 396; on protest art, 266, 449n15
Negritude, 267
New Africa (concept). *See* Republic of New Africa
New African Peoples Organization, 328

Newark: 1967 rebellion in, 315, 339, 377; Puerto Rican community in, 378, 381, 396. *See also* Committee for a Unified Newark
Newark Black Leadership Council, 380
New Negro (concept), 82, 157, 375
Newton, Huey, 5, 234, 259–260, 283–287, 296, 302, 322, 450n33; Free Huey Rally, 291; on *The Godfather*, 294; mismanagement of BPP by, 299, 302–303; on revolutionary nationalism, 289–291; RNA and, 316; on survival programs, 297–298, 300
New York City/Ocean Hill-Brownsville Strike, 428
nguzo saba (seven principles of blackness), 262, 264, 274, 282, 398; CAP–Chicago and, 386; Cleage and 413–415; RNA and, 323
Niebuhr, Reinhold, 408
Nixon, Richard, 60, 220, 384–385, 392, 428, 444n4, 453n4, 454n11
Njeri, Akua (Deborah Johnson), 299
Nkrumah, Kwame, 1, 13, 273–274
nonviolence, 2–4, 6, 8, 15, 22, 155, 324
Northern Ireland, 37, 394
NWA (rap group), 451n41
Nyerere, Julius, 273–274, 313, 323, 325
Nyeusi, Sanamu, 260, 278

Oakland: BPP and, 222, 259–260, 264, 284, 292, 295, 298–299; elections in, 298–299; RAM and, 283
Obadele, Gaidi (Milton Henry), 229, 248, 311–312, 314–315, 317–322, 325–326, 328, 339, 341
Obadele, Imari (Richard Henry), 5, 311–312, 315, 339, 341, 383, 451n1
Obama, Barack, 449n19
O'Donovan, Susan, 116
Operation Dixie, 369, 453n22

Organization of African Unity, 28
Organization of Afro-American Unity (OAAU), x, xiii, 3–4, 12, 14, 28, 30–31, 34, 177, 233, 235; Baraka and, 377, 453n3; BPP and, 297; Us and, 264, 272
Organization of Black American Culture, 387

Palmares, 54
pan-Africanism, 3, 13, 28, 49–50, 54–56, 76, 77, 156, 258, 274; BPP and, 296; "pan-Negroism," 73; RAM and, 235, 238
Pan-African Orthodox Christian Church (PAOCC, aka Shrine of the Black Madonna), xi, xii, xx, xxi, 2, 5, 39, 41, 130, 177, 261, 310, 374, 392, 404–421, 428, 433; "BCN Orientation Reading List," 415–416; Maccabees (security force), 409; sexism in, 417; critiques of, 416–418
pan-Islamism, 6
Parents and Students for Community Control, 346
Paris, May 1968 events in, 361, 363, 434
Parker, Charlie, 418
Parks, Rosa, 339, 452n7
Parsons, Lucy, 92, 150–151
Paul, 401
Peaches (Renee Moore), 293
Pinkney, Alphonso, 49–50, 53
Plumpp, Sterling, 386
police brutality, xix, 327, 332, 335, 344–345, 349, 389, 435, 455n2
political prisoners, 150, 304, 328, 452n7
Pollard, Aubrey, 340
Pol Pot, 138, 141, 294, 446n6
Poor Peoples Campaign, 433
Pratt, Geronimo, 248, 293
Pritchard, "Gullah Jack," 108–109
prolekult (Russian proletarian culture), 141–142, 444nn7–8

race theory, 121–125, 152, 212
racism, 37, 54, 62–63, 69, 71, 76, 85–87, 117, 121–122, 126, 146, 151, 154, 169, 177, 180, 194, 212, 223, 225, 274, 330, 332, 335–336, 338–339, 343, 348, 355, 364, 381, 390–391, 400, 435, 448, 453–454, 458, 460, 464
Rackley, Alex, 303
Rainbow Coalition, 437
Randall, Dudley, 386
Randolph, A. Philip, 10
Ranger, Terence, 279–280, 449n21
Ransom, Reverdy, 157
Raskin, Eleanor, 304
Reconstruction, 62, 80, 84, 87, 104, 113, 115, 118–120, 128, 156, 164–165, 226–227, 315, 365, 426
Red Summer, 76–77, 86, 340
religion: civil, 67–68; BPM rejection of, 444n27; Civil War and, 97, 100–102, 104–105, 118, 135, 368, 416–417; CRM and, 39; Cruse's neglect of, 229; Marx on, 97, 226, 323; messianism, 67–68, 101; mobilization abilities, 277; RNA and, 325–326; slave religion, xv, 25–26, 67–69, 72, 75, 100–102, 105–112, 114, 118, 126, 129, 171, 367. *See also* African Methodist Episcopalian (AME) church; Black Church; black nationalism: religion and; Cleage, Albert
reparations, xvii–xix, 6–7, 117, 128, 132, 226–229, 257, 311, 363–366, 384, 430–431; Forman and, 347, 366; Malcolm X on, 439n2; Moore and, 313–314; RNA and, 313–316, 324, 326–327, 366
Republican Party, 133, 440n6
Republic of New Africa (RNA), xi, xviii–xix, 2, 4–5, 29, 41, 130, 175, 191, 221, 278, 311–329, 349, 360, 384; Black Legion of, 314–315;

Republic of New Africa (RNA) *(continued)*
  "Malcolm X Doctrine" of, 311–313; police and FBI raids on, 327–328; sexism and polygamy in, 325; critiques of, xix, 323–328
Revels, Hiram, 325
"reverse civilizationism," xi, xiii, xv, xviii, xx, 33, 39–40, 63, 129, 306, 423–426; assumptions behind, xiii, 44, 423; BAM and, 376; CAP and, 373; Cleage and, 412–413, 417, 419; Cruse and, 45, 178–179, 199; Malcolm X and, xi, xiii, xv, 30–34, 41–42, 44, 77, 93, 95, 129, 130, 251, 257, 265, 376, 423–425; RNA and, 322, 325–326; Us and, 262–264, 267, 269, 273; white supremacism and, 415
revolution, definition of, 138; types of, 138–139
Revolutionary Action Movement (RAM), xi, xvii–xviii, 2, 29, 32, 41, 210, 233–260, 283, 309, 312, 448n1; Boggs and, 212, 218, 394; BPP and, 283, 295, 300; Cruse and, 175, 177, 182, 191, 196, 230, 233–235, 238; journals of (*Black America, Soul Book*), 191, 234, 235, 240, 359; Northern strategy of, 234–235, 310; PAOCC and, 407; sexism and, 258–259; critiques of, 242–244, 247–249, 257–259, 448n9; twelve-point program of, 238–240, 448n4; "World Black Revolution" essay, 236–237
Revolutionary Union, 392, 454n10
revolutionary union movements (RUMs), 332–333, 337–338, 345, 347, 349–350, 352, 357, 359–366, 369
Rhodes, Jane, 61
Roach, Max, 376, 410
Robeson, Paul, 64, 219, 267, 441
Robinson, Cedric, 87, 97, 441n1

Robinson, Dean E., 71
Robinson, Pearl, 279
Rodgers, Carolyn, 386
Rodino, Peter, 393
Rodney, Walter, 87
Roediger, David, 119
Roosevelt, Eleanor, 15
Rosenberg, Susan, 304
Ross, Wanda, 299
Roundtree, Richard, 383
Rousseau, Jean-Jacques, 51
Rudd, Mark, 304, 451n34
Rudwick, Elliott, 53
Russian Revolution, 8, 29, 97, 119, 141, 369

Salaam, Kalamu ya, 386
Sales, William W., 32
Salimu, Muminina, 380
Sams, George, 303
Sanchez, Sonia, 290, 386
Satchell, Ronald "Doc," 299
Save Our Sons and Daughters (SOSAD), 437–438
Schoatz, Russell "Maroon," 304
Scott, Cynthia, 335
Scott, Ron, 438
Scottsboro Boys case, 168, 228
Seale, Bobby, 234, 259, 283–284, 291–292, 298–299, 383
Seaton, Ken (Msemaji), 260
"second ghettos," 223, 381, 396, 429–430; transformation into third ghettos, 223, 396, 429–430
Sefu-Glover, Fred, 281
segregation, 2, 8, 15, 20, 36; Du Bois on, 158–159, 170–171, 445n21. *See also* separatism
self-determination, x, 78, 180, 186, 190, 227, 235, 313, 315, 454n10; economic, 194–195; GOAL and, 312; PAOCC and, 412; Us and, 262
Senghor, Léopold Sédar, 286

separatism, 2–3, 6–7, 18–19, 49–50, 52, 56, 64, 66, 189
sexism, xvii, 41, 45–47, 151, 229, 278–279, 378–379; the Boggs on, 447n13; Cleaver and, 290–292. *See also specific organizations*
Shabazz, Betty, 312, 383
Shadd Cary, Mary Ann, 13, 46, 54, 57, 60–61, 146–147
Shafer, Boyd C., 50
Shakur, Assata, 300–301, 304, 451n36
Shakur, Mutulu, 304
Shakur, Tupac, 304, 328
Shifflet, Lynn, 440n5
Shrine of the Black Madonna. *See* Pan-African Orthodox Christian Church
Sidbury, James, 105–106
Sidney (black nationalist), 64
Sigidi, Charles, 263
Silverman, Jonathan, 61
Simms, Rupe, 444n11
Simone, Nina, 376
Situationist International, 446m 2
slave culture, 31, 64–67, 71, 252, 263, 375, 413, 441n3
slave religion. *See under* religion
slave revolts, 32, 98–99, 102, 103–113, 132, 277, 297, 414–15, 442n5, 442n10; Cleage on, 416–417; RAM and, 241–246. *See also* Civil War
Slave Revolution, xi, xv, xix, xxii, 26, 34, 48, 95–102, 105, 113, 117, 119, 121, 126, 128–129, 132–135, 144, 152, 173, 224, 228, 231, 241–242, 244–245, 250, 277, 306, 329, 357, 361, 363, 368, 395, 415, 417, 424–427
slavery, 25–26, 64–65, 80, 102–103, 226, 242–243, 275, 324, 364, 397; amendments ending, 315, 317–319; black nationalism and, 12–13, 43, 52, 56–59, 66–70; communication networks under, 113–117; Cruse on, 183; Founding Fathers and, 117, 443n24; hired-out slaves, 103–104, 106–110, 112–113, 117–118, 126, 129, 369, 442n13, 443n19; LRBW on, 337; Malcolm X on, xi, xiii, 5, 7, 30–32. *See also* reparations
Smith, Anthony D., 51
Smith, Cassandra, 345–346
Smith, Kathleen, 303
Smith, Louis-Sedu, 281
Smith, Robert, 436, 454n8
Smith, Suzanne, 411
Snyder, Jack, 51–52
social democracy, 33, 127, 205
Socialist Workers' Party, 195
social media activism, 132, 435–436, 455–456nn2–3
Soledad Brothers, 304
"sorrow songs," 33, 72, 121, 264
Soul Students Advisory Council, 259, 283
Soul Train, 269–270
South End (student newspaper), 345–346, 362
Southern Christian Leadership Conference (SCLC), 10, 360, 433
Spirit House (Newark), 375, 377, 380
Stalin, Josef, 51, 60, 78, 193, 195
Stanford, Max (aka Muhammad Ahmad), 234–236, 240, 243–246, 251–257, 260, 448nn8–10
Starobin, Robert S., 103, 108
Stewart, Maria, 49, 54, 146
Stokes, Carl, 383, 453n5
"street force," 218–220, 253
strike and boycott strategies, 119–120, 130, 151, 210; CRC and, 120, 155, 213, 338, 360; LRBW and, 329, 337–338, 342, 344, 345, 347, 350, 361–363; RAM and, 239–242, 246–247, 256–257; in sports, 435–436
Stuckey, Sterling, 31–32, 53–55, 62–66, 69–72, 234, 441n3

Student Non-violent Coordinating Committee (SNCC), 2–3, 22, 46, 191, 194, 208, 234, 281, 310, 312, 360, 387, 439n3
Students for a Democratic Society (SDS), 46, 191, 234, 301, 304, 362, 450n31; critiques of, 450n34
Subira, George, 263
Sugrue, Thomas J., 223, 367, 452n8
Sunni Ali, Bilal, 328

Taft–Hartley Act, 453n22
Taifa, Nkechi, 315
Taifa Dance Troupe, 263, 269
talented tenth concept, 62, 147, 172, 173, 271, 276
Tate, Bennie, 342
Teemer (aka Akinsanya Kambon), 450n28
Temple, Fred, 340
Third World Press, xx, 373, 385–386, 398
third world revolutions. *See* anticolonial struggles
Thomas, Norman, 168
Tometi, Opal, 435, 438, 455n2
Toure, Askia, 290
Touré, Sékou, 1, 273–275
Tripp, Luke, 234, 335, 341, 345–346, 352, 356
Trotsky, Leon (and Trotskyism), 142, 195, 211
Trump, Donald, 436
Truth, Sojourner, 146–147
Tubman, Harriet, 146, 300, 325
Turner, Henry McNeal, 14, 44, 55, 60, 402
Turner, Nat, 32, 100, 102, 110–112, 241, 243–245, 300, 325, 415–416, 443n17, 448n7
Tylor, Edward, 137

UHURU, 234, 300, 312, 335–336, 339, 341–342

Uhuru Sasa, 385
ujamaa, 313, 323, 325, 386
Umkhonto we Sizwe, 40
Underground Railroad, 57, 242, 247, 250, 443n23
United Automobile Workers (UAW), 335, 342–344, 347, 349–351
United Nations, 15–16; BPP and, 311, 450n25; Malcolm X and, 5–6, 16, 41, 238, 311, 316; Moore's appeals to, 229, 234, 313; RNA and, 33; Universal Declaration of Human Rights, 227
Universal Association of Ethiopian Women, 228, 313
Universal Negro Improvement Association (UNIA), 6, 13, 77, 145, 157, 193–194
uplift: racial, 57, 62, 66, 74–75, 77, 149–150; social, 146, 157; of women, 156
Urban League, 157
Urban Peace and Justice Movement, 437–438
Us, x, xi, xvii–xviii, xx, 2, 5, 29, 32, 41, 130, 175, 177, 191, 210, 230, 260–282, 309–311, 380; Baraka and, 377, 381–382, 386; BPP feud with, 259, 269, 273, 281–282, 291, 295, 302, 322; militarization of, 281–282; name of, xvii, 260, 282; PAOCC and, 407; critiques of, 263, 267, 272–273, 277–278, 450n24. *See also* kawaida

Van Deburg, William L., 50–51
Vesey, Denmark, 32, 100, 102, 108–110, 243, 414–415, 443n14, 448n6
Viera, Rafael, 349
Vietnam War, 1, 26, 29, 34, 133, 227, 247–249, 253, 296, 336, 362, 363, 366, 383, 389, 430–431, 453n21; RAM and, 449n12; Tet Offensive, 247, 448n10

Voting Rights Act, 34, 228, 395, 431, 433

Walker, C. J., 446n4
Walker, David, 49, 54–56, 64, 66, 70
Walker, Margaret, 386
Walton, Hanes, 47
Ward, Samuel Ringgold, 54, 60
Warden, Donald, 234, 260
Washington, Booker T., 114; Du Bois and, 165, 184–186
Watson, Edna, 345–346
Watson, John, 333–335, 338, 341, 345–346, 348, 352, 356, 362; Haywood and, 357, 359
Watts rebellion, 2, 33–34, 254, 260, 269, 339
Watts Summer Festival, 269
Wattstax (film and record), 269
Weather Underground, 221, 304, 362, 451n34
Weaver, Joe, 452n14
Webb, Robert, 303
Webb, William, 116
Wells Barnett, Ida B., 146–147, 154, 440n1, 445n12, 445n14, 445n18
West Central Organization (WCO), 344, 346
Western imperialism, xiii–xiv, 3, 8, 13, 23, 25, 44, 87, 171, 181; RAM on, 236–237; World War I and, 76–77, 86, 165
Weusi, Jitu, xx, 385, 417
Whipper, William, 62–63, 136
White, Walter, 15
white cultural revolution, 133–134, 227, 366, 425–426, 434
White Leftists, 46, 93, 221, 259, 300–301, 327, 379; BPP and, 296–297, 301; crimes and violence by, 303–304, 451n34; RNA and, 327; sexism by, 46, 300, 379, 450n31
white supremacism, xiii, 1–2, 4, 8, 20–21, 25, 29, 31, 36–37, 56, 60, 63, 76–77, 90, 119–120, 127, 129–130, 133–134, 136, 172, 181, 210, 227, 287, 316, 364, 410, 424–425, 427, 431; Boas on, 121; in Detroit, 349, 351; music challenges to, 203, 209; in postbellum era, xv, 117–118, 128, 324; RAM and, 242, 258; reverse civilizationism and, 415
Wilkins, Roy, 10
Williams, Chancellor, 386, 398
Williams, John, 234, 335, 346, 352
Williams, Raymond, 137
Williams, Robert, xviii, 27, 234, 238–239, 242, 245–246, 339, 341, 448–449nn9–11; military tactics of, 248–249, 315; RNA and, 312–313, 326
Willis, Raymond, 312
Wilson, George, 443n16
Wilson, Lionel, 298
Wilson, Woodrow, 51
women's rights, 4, 14, 41, 46, 61, 89–93, 119, 132, 145–152, 453n7; Du Bois on, 156–157; Claudia Jones on, 89–93. *See also specific organizations*
Woodard, Komozi, 5, 379, 380–381
Woodson, Carter G., 53, 56, 154, 157, 321
Woodson, Lewis, 64
Wooten, Chuck, 346, 352, 356
Wooten, Gracie, 345–346
Worthy, William, 17, 400
Wright, R. R., Jr., 157
Wright, Richard, 286

X, Malcolm. *See* Malcolm X
X, Marvin, 290

Young, Coleman, xxi, 384–385, 400, 419, 452n13, 453n5
Young, Robert, 64
Young, Whitney, 10

Zionism, 53, 384

www.ingramcontent.com/pod-product-compliance
Lightning Source LLC
Chambersburg PA
CBHW022006300426
44117CB00005B/49